READING

토익마법
2주의 기적
990

이교희 지음

BM (주)도서출판 **성안당**

머리말

독자 여러분께

'토익 마법 – 2주의 기적'에 이어 **'토익 마법 – 2주의 기적 990'**을 내놓았습니다. 전작은 토익 문법 문제 중 거의 매회 출제되는 유형들을 주로 소개했고, 700점 정도를 달성하기에 알맞은 어휘력을 목표로 연습 문제를 제공했습니다. 이번에는 토익 시험에 출제되는 문법 문제의 모든 유형을 빠짐없이 다루었습니다. 이 책에 없는 유형은 시험에 나오지 않는다고 볼 수 있으며, 어떤 문제든 가장 정확하고 빠른 풀이 방식을 제시합니다. 고득점을 원하는 독자들을 위해 고난도 어휘 문제도 대거 포함시켰습니다. Part 7에서도 길고 복잡한 문장, 고급 어휘, 고난도 문제를 많이 다루어서 독자 여러분의 독해력 완성을 꾀했습니다.

공부를 시작하기 전에 '필독 서론'과 '이 책의 학습법'을 반드시 읽고 숙지하기 바랍니다. 유형에 대한 설명과 예제 풀이를 꼼꼼히 읽고, 연습 문제를 풀 때는 되도록 주어진 시간 내에 해결하도록 노력하기 바랍니다. Actual Test를 풀 때는 Today's Vocabulary를 반드시 먼저 암기하고, 마찬가지로 주어진 시간을 넘기지 않도록 연습해야 합니다. 정답을 맞힌 문제를 포함하여 모든 문제의 해설을 자세히 읽어 보고, 몰랐던 단어는 따로 정리해서 외우기 바랍니다.

토익 공부에 쓸 시간이 충분히 있다면 책 제목대로 2주, 주말 빼고 열흘 만에 공부를 끝내 보세요. 시간이 충분하지 않다면, 하루치로 제시되어 있는 양을 2, 3일에 나누어 공부해서 20일이나 한 달 만에 끝내는 것도 괜찮습니다. 열흘이든 한 달이든, 성실한 자세로 책에서 제시하는 문제 풀이 방식을 그대로 따라하면, 반드시 목표를 달성하게 될 것이라고 약속합니다.

엄마가 젖을 빠는 아기를 보며 기뻐서 산고(産苦)를 잊는 것처럼, 고생해서 쓴 이 책으로 토익을 정복해 나아갈 독자 여러분을 생각하니 참 행복합니다. 저에게 이런 행복을 주신 하나님께서 여러분의 앞날을 더 큰 행복으로 채워 주실 것을 진심으로 기도합니다.

저자 이교희 올림

추신 이번에도 책이 출간될 수 있게 힘을 모아 주신 성안당과 이재명 부장님, 김은주 부장님, 과정에 참여하신 모든 직원 여러분, 안산이지어학원 김창로 원장님, 남편과 아빠를 학원과 책에 양보해 준 사랑하는 나의 가족, 고맙습니다.

목차

이 책의 구성과 특징

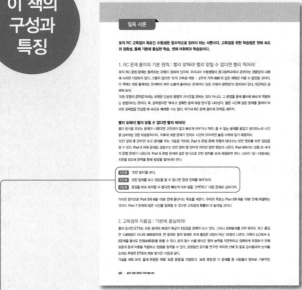

1 시험에 출제되는 모든 유형의 가장 빠르고 정확한 풀이 기술!

토익 10회 만점, 강의 경력 15년의 전문가가 40년간 출제된 모든 문제를 철저히 분석하여 가장 빠르고 정확한 풀이 방식을 알려드립니다.

2 전무후무, 매일 모든 파트 학습

다른 토익 교재에서는 볼 수 없는 방식. 매일 모든 파트를 공부함으로써 균형 잡힌 학습이 가능해집니다.

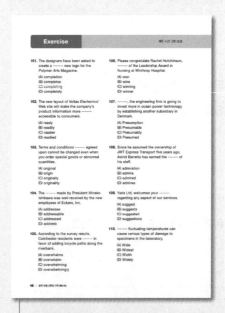

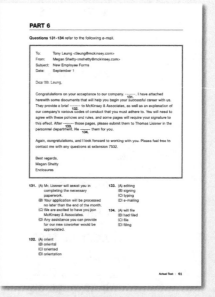

3 풍부한 실전 문제

문제 풀이 기술을 배웠다면 실전 문제에 적용하기 위해 끊임없는 반복 훈련이 필요합니다. 매일 충분한 연습 문제와 Actual Test를 풀며 실전 감각을 기를 수 있습니다.

4 상세한 해설과 실전에 유용한 팁

모든 문제에 정답과 오답에 대해 자세하게 설명합니다. 저자의 풍부한 응시 경험과 오랜 연구를 통해 얻은 실전에 유용한 팁도 함께 제공합니다.

5 고득점의 열쇠는 어휘력

점수 상승이 정체되는 가장 큰 원인은 어휘력입니다. 문항별 단어뿐 아니라 Today's Vocabulary의 짝을 이루어 출제되는 단어도 암기해 보세요. 문제를 쉽게 풀 수 있는 자신감을 얻게 됩니다.

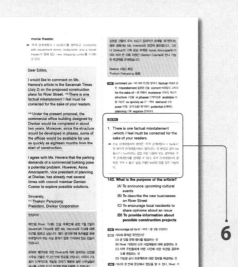

6 전무후무 Part 6, 7 문장 분석

Part 6, 7 지문의 해석뿐 아니라 문장 구조를 분석하는 방법까지 강의식으로 알려줍니다. 고난도 문제의 해결책은 수준 높은 독해력입니다.

TOEIC이란?

▶ TOEIC

Test Of English for International Communication(국제적 의사소통을 위한 영어 시험)의 약자로, 영어가 모국어가 아닌 사람들이 비즈니스 현장 또는 일상생활에서 원활한 의사소통에 필요한 실용영어 능력을 갖추었는가를 평가하는 시험이다.

▶ TOEIC 시험 구성

구성	PART	유형		문항 수	지문	번호	시간	배점
L/C	1	사진 묘사		6		1~6	45분	495점
	2	질의 응답		25		7~31		
	3	짧은 대화		39	지문 13 x 3	32~70		
	4	짧은 담화		30	지문 10 x 3	71~100		
R/C	5	단문 빈칸 채우기 (문법/어휘)		30		101~130	75분	495점
	6	장문 빈칸 채우기 (문법/어휘/문장 고르기)		16	지문 4 x 4	131~146		
	7	지문 독해	단일 지문	29	지문 10	147~175		
			이중 지문	10	이중 지문 2 x 5	176~185		
			삼중 지문	15	삼중 지문 3 x 5	186~200		
Total	7 PARTS			200 문항			120분	990점

▶ TOEIC 평가 항목

Listening Comprehension	Reading Comprehension
단문을 듣고 이해하는 능력	읽은 글을 통해 추론해 생각할 수 있는 능력
짧은 대화문을 듣고 이해하는 능력	장문에서 특정한 정보를 찾을 수 있는 능력
비교적 긴 대화문에서 주고받은 내용을 파악할 수 있는 능력	글의 목적, 주제, 의도 등을 파악하는 능력
장문에서 핵심이 되는 정보를 파악할 수 있는 능력	뜻이 유사한 단어들의 정확한 용례를 파악하는 능력
구나 문장에서 화자의 목적이나 함축된 의미를 이해하는 능력	문장 구조를 제대로 파악하는지, 문장에서 필요한 품사, 어구 등을 찾는 능력

▶ TOEIC 접수 방법

1. 한국 토익 위원회 사이트(www.toeic.co.kr)에서 시험일 약 2개월 전부터 온라인으로 24시간 언제든지 접수할 수 있다.
2. 추가 시험은 2월과 8월에 있으며 이외에도 연중 상시로 시행된다.
3. JPG 형식의 본인의 사진 파일이 필요하다.

▶ 시험장 준비물

1. 신분증: 규정 신분증(주민등록증, 운전면허증, 기간 만료 전의 여권, 공무원증, 장애인 복지 카드 등)
2. 필기구: 연필과 지우개(볼펜이나 사인펜은 사용 금지)
3. 아날로그 손목시계(전자식 시계는 불가)

▶ TOEIC 시험 진행 시간

9:20	입실 (09:50 이후 입실 불가)
09:30 ~ 09:45	답안지 작성에 관한 오리엔테이션
09:45 ~ 09:50	휴식
09:50 ~ 10:05	신분증 확인
10:05 ~ 10:10	문제지 배부 및 파본 확인
10:10 ~ 10:55	듣기 평가 (LISTENING TEST)
10:55 ~ 12:10	읽기 평가 (READING TEST)

▶ TOEIC 성적 확인

시험일로부터 약 10~12일 후 인터넷 홈페이지 및 어플리케이션을 통한 성적 확인이 가능하다. 최초 성적표는 우편이나 온라인으로 발급받을 수 있다. 우편으로는 발급받기까지 성적 발표 후 약 7~10일이 소요되며, 온라인 발급을 선택하면 즉시 발급되며, 유효기간 내에 홈페이지에서 본인이 직접 1회에 한해 무료로 출력할 수 있다. TOEIC 성적은 시험일로부터 2년간 유효하다.

▶ TOEIC 점수

TOEIC 점수는 듣기 영역(LC)과 읽기 영역(RC)을 합계한 점수로 5점 단위로 구성되며 총점은 990점이다. TOEIC 성적은 각 문제 유형의 난이도에 따른 점수 환산표에 의해 결정된다. 성적표에는 전체 수험자의 평균과 해당 수험자가 받은 성적이 백분율로 표기되어 있다.

토익 RC 고득점이 목표인 수험생은 필수적으로 읽어야 하는 서론이다. 고득점을 위한 학습법은 첫째 속도와 정확성, 둘째 기본에 충실한 학습, 셋째 어휘력과 학습량이다.

1. RC 문제 풀이의 기본 원칙 : 빨리 맞혀라! 빨리 맞힐 수 없다면 빨리 찍어라!

토익 RC 문법 문제는 출제되는 유형이 정해져 있으며, 우리나라 수험생들이 중고등학교에서 공부하는 영문법의 내용에 비하면 다양하지 않다. 그렇지 않다면 '토익 고득점 마법 – 2주의 기적 990'과 같은 제목은 지을 수 없었을 것이다. 이 책에는 매회 출제되는 문제부터 매우 드물게 출제되는 문제까지 '모든 유형의 공략법'이 정리되어 있다. 차근차근 공부해 보자.

'모든 유형의 공략법'이라는 표현은 단순히 문법적 지식만을 뜻하는 것이 아니고, 그 문법을 문제 풀이에 빠르게 적용하는 방법이라는 뜻이다. 즉, 공략법이란 '빠르고 정확한 문제 해결 방식'을 나타낸다. 짧은 시간에 많은 문제를 풀어야 하므로 공략법을 언급할 때 속도도 배제할 수는 없다. 여기서 RC 문제 풀이의 원칙을 세우자.

빨리 맞혀라! 빨리 맞힐 수 없다면 빨리 찍어라!

풀이 방식을 모르는 문제가 나왔다면 고민하지 말고 빠르게 아무거나 찍자. 풀 수 없는 문제를 붙잡고 생각하느라 시간을 낭비하는 것은 비효율적이다. 이후에 쉬운 문제가 있어도 시간이 모자라면 놓칠 수밖에 없기 때문이다.

'빈칸 앞뒤 몇 단어'만 보고 문제를 푸는 기술을 익히자. Part 5 문법 문제 유형의 대다수는 빈칸 앞뒤를 보면 정답을 알 수 있다. Part 5 어휘 문제도 상당수는 빈칸 앞뒤 몇 단어의 의미만 알면 정답이 나온다. Part 6에서는 보통 3~4개의 문법 문제가 나오는데, Part 5 문법 문제와 같은 방식으로 빈칸 앞뒤를 보며 해결하면 된다. 나머지 12~13문제는 지문을 읽으며 문맥을 통해 정답을 알아내야 한다.

1단계	'빈칸 앞뒤'를 본다.
2단계	빈칸 앞뒤를 보고 정답을 알 수 없다면 '문장 전체를 해석'하자.
3단계	문장을 바로 해석할 수 없다면 빠르게 아무 답을 '선택'하고' 다음 문제로 넘어가자.

이러한 방식으로 Part 5와 6을 15분 만에 끝낸다는 목표를 세운다. 우리의 목표는 Part 5와 6을 15분 안에 해결하는 것이다. Part 7 문제에 많은 시간을 할애할 수 있다면 고득점의 확률이 더 높아질 것이다.

2. 고득점의 지름길 : 기본에 충실하라!

출제 당사인 ETS는 모든 문제의 배점이 똑같이 5점임을 명확히 하고 있다. 그러나 200문제를 모두 맞혀도 최고 총점은 1,000점이 아니라 990점이며, 한 문제도 풀지 못해도 최저 총점은 0점이 아닌 10점이 나온다. 더욱이 LC에서 4, 5문제를 틀려도 만점(495점)을 받을 수 있다. 토익 점수 산출 방식은 영어 능력을 객관적이고 정확하게 측정하기 위해 모종의 통계 이론을 적용하고 있음을 짐작할 수 있다. 오랫동안 토익을 연구한 저자와 선배 및 동료 강사들과의 논의를 토대로 추정한 ETS의 채점 방식은 다음과 같다.

가설을 세워 보자. 출제 위원은 매회 '표준 문항'을 지정한다. '표준 문항'은 이 문제를 푼 사람들이 영어로 기본적인 의사소통을 할 수 있는 능력이 있다고 인정해 주는 문제이며, 매 시험 출제된다. 예를 들어, 품사 문제 중 '(관사) + ─────── + 명사' 형태에서 빈칸에 들어갈 품사는 형용사이다. 이러한 문제는 거의 항상 시험에 등장하는 표준 문항으로 지정된다. 따라서 표준 문항은 일종의 쉬운 문제로도 볼 수 있다.

이제 어떤 수험자가 표준 문항 하나를 맞히고 고난도 문제 하나를 틀렸다고 가정해 보자. 이는 흔하게 발생하는 상황이며, 이 경우 5점이 감점된다. 최고난도 문제를 틀리는 경우 점수가 감점되지 않는 경우도 있지만, 대부분 한 문제를 틀리면 5점이 감점된다고 이해해야 한다. 반대로 어떤 수험자가 표준 문항 하나를 틀렸지만 고난도 문제 하나를 맞혔다고 가정해 보자. 그런데 이 사람이 고난도 문제를 어떻게 맞힐 수 있었을까? 아마도 운이 좋아서 맞힌 것으로 보인다. 출제위원도 틀린 문제는 표준 문항 하나라도, 점수는 두 문제를 모두 틀린 것으로 간주하여 점수를 감점한다. 운이 좋지 않으면, 다른 RC 문제를 모두 맞히고 표준 문항 하나만 틀린 경우에도 최대 30점까지 감점될 수도 있다.

표준 문항	고난도 문제	감점
O	X	5
X	O	10 ~ 30

표준 문항 가설은 ETS에서 공식적으로 확인되지는 않았지만, 실제 사례를 통해 신빙성이 높다고 여겨진다.

고득점을 원하는가? 그렇다면 여러분이 집중적으로 학습해야 하는 부분은 잘 출제되지 않는 고난도 문제들이 아니다. 높은 점수를 받기 위해서는 표준 문항, 즉 거의 매회 출제되는 쉬운 문제들을 틀리지 않는 것이다. 이 책에는 전반부에 시험마다 출제되는 문제들이 포함되어 있다. 만약 이 유형의 문제를 틀린다면, 고득점은 다음 기회로 미루어야 한다는 사실을 기억하자. 기본에 충실한 학습에 최선을 다하기를 바란다.

3. 나의 생명, 어휘력과 학습량!

단어를 외우는 것은 밥을 먹는 것과 같다. 밥을 먹지 않으면 굶어 죽는다. 힘든 일을 하려면 더 많은 에너지를 내기 위해 밥을 더 많이 먹어야 하는 것과 마찬가지로, 토익 고득점을 원한다면 당연히 남들보다 더 많은 어휘력이 필요하다. 2주 동안 주말을 제외하고 열흘이면, 매우 많은 단어를 암기할 수 있다. 하루에 50개씩 암기하면 열흘 후에는 500개, 100개씩 1,000개의 단어를 암기할 수 있다. 어휘력이 풍부할수록 학습의 효과도 더 크게 나타날 것이다.

거의 모든 수험생이 어휘력의 중요성을 인식하며 실제로 많은 노력을 기울이고 있다. 그러나 많은 수험생이 인식하지 못하는 부분이 바로 학습량이다. 단어를 많이 알고 있어도 Part 5, 6 문제를 빨리 풀지 못하거나 단어를 거의 알고 있어도 지문 독해에 여전히 시간이 걸린다면, 궁극적인 해결책은 학습량을 늘리는 것이다. 인내심을 가지고 잘될 때까지 많이 풀어 보고 독해 연습을 멈추지 말자.

Day 01부터 Day 10까지 열흘 동안 RC Part 5, 6, 7을 매일 공부하자. 일일 학습 진행 순서는 다음과 같다.

1	Part 5, 6 문법 설명 및 예제
2	문법 연습 문제
3	Part 7 독해 설명 및 예제
4	Today's Vocabulary
5	Actual Test

파트별 학습 강조점은 다음과 같다.

▶ PART 5, 6 문법

문제 유형별로 빈칸 앞뒤를 보며 빠르고 정확하게 문제를 해결하는 방법을 소개할 것이다. 출제 빈도순으로 공부할 수 있도록 '거의 매회 출제되는 문제(★★★★로 표시)'와 '자주 출제되는 문제(3, 4개월에 한 번 정도, ★★★로 표시)', '가끔 출제되는 문제(매년 3, 4회 정도, ★★로 표시)', '드물게 출제되는 문제(매년 1, 2회 이하, ★로 표시)'로 분류하였다. '거의 매회 출제되는 문제'를 틀리면 고득점은 물 건너간 것이라는 점을 명심하고 열심히 공부하자. 모든 세부 유형은 이해하기 쉽게 예제와 함께 소개하고, 파트별로 그날의 학습 분량을 마친 후에는 연습 문제와 실전 문제를 풀며 연습할 기회를 제공한다. 문제를 풀 때는 권장 시간을 지키며 도전해 보자.

▶ PART 5 어휘

정기 토익 시험에서 Part 5는 2단으로 배열되어 있다. 각 문장의 길이는 두 줄에서 네 줄이다. 그러나 최근 시험에서 네 줄 분량의 문장은 잘 나오지 않는다. Part 5에서 두 줄 분량의 어휘 문제는 문장이 짧으니 모두 읽고 풀자. 세 줄이나 네 줄 분량의 문제는 빈칸 앞뒤에 있는 단어들의 의미를 고려하여 풀자. 빈칸 앞뒤를 보고 정답을 알 수 없을 때는 문장 전체를 해석한다. 단, 접속사 어휘 문제는 빈칸 앞뒤에서 정답을 알 수 없으므로 처음부터 문장을 읽으며 풀어야 한다.

단어의 의미를 모르면서 빈칸 앞뒤만을 보고 문제를 풀 수는 없다. 단어의 뜻을 모르면 문장을 모두 읽어도 문제 푸는 것이 어려울 수 있다. 풍부한 어휘력을 갖추기 위한 노력은 매우 중요하다. 어휘 교재 한 권을 선택해서 매일 암기하고, 동시에 원활한 학습을 위해 실전 문제를 풀기 전 Today's Vocabulary를 반드시 암기하자. 실전 문제를 풀어본 후에는 맞은 문제의 해설도 꼼꼼히 읽어 보자. 해설에 매우 유용한 정보가 많이 들어 있다.

▶ PART 6

Part 6에는 매회 서너 개의 문법 문제가 있고, 이는 Part 5와 동일한 방식으로 풀면 된다. 나머지 12~13문제 즉 어휘 문제와 문장 삽입 문제는 모두 문맥을 이해하여 정답을 찾아내야 한다. 매일 제공하는 실전 문제를 풀면서 성실히 연습해 보자.

▶ PART 7

Part 7 문제를 푸는 시간을 단축하려면 항상 문제를 먼저 읽은 후에 지문을 읽어야 한다. 문제를 읽을 때 질문과 보기 네 개를 모두 읽자. 여러 문제를 한꺼번에 읽지 말고, 한 문제만 읽고 위로 올라가서 정답을 찾고, 다시 내려와서 다음 문제를 읽는 방식으로 하자. 지문의 위아래에서도 정답의 단서를 발견할 수 있다. 예를 들어 이메일의 발신자, 수신자, 날짜, 제목, 기사의 제목, 편지지 윗부분의 회사 로고나 주소, 편지지 아랫부분 발신자의 직함 등이다. 이 부분에서도 정답을 찾을 수 있으므로 꼼꼼히 읽어 두는 것이 좋다.

Part 7의 문제 유형은 다음 7가지로 분류할 수 있다.

1	주제, 목적 문제
2	세부사항 문제
3	Not / True 문제
4	추론 문제
5	동의어 문제
6	의도 파악 문제
7	문장 삽입 문제

매일 실전 문제를 풀어본 후 모든 문제의 해설을 꼼꼼히 읽어서 유형별 공략법을 익히도록 하자.

또한 길고 복잡한 문장의 구조를 파악하는 훈련, 지문과 문제 사이의 패러프레이즈 관계를 알아차리는 연습, 이런 일들을 빠르게 하는 훈련도 중요하다. 이 책의 특징은 고득점을 원하는 독자들을 위해 다른 유형보다 난이도가 높은 기사(article) 지문 위주로 실전 문제를 구성했다는 점이다. 해설에 정답의 근거뿐만 아니라 문장의 구조까지 자세히 설명했다는 점도 고득점을 위해 신경 쓴 부분이다. 맞힌 문제의 해설까지도 꼼꼼히 읽으면서 독해력을 키워보자.

학습 플랜

10-Day Plan
하루에 많은 시간을 투자할 수 있다면 **Day별로 하루씩**, 열흘 안에 공부를 끝내자.

1	2	3	4	5
☐ Day 1 / PART 5, 6, 7 ☐ Actual Test	☐ Day 2 / PART 5, 6, 7 ☐ Actual Test	☐ Day 3 / PART 5, 6, 7 ☐ Actual Test	☐ Day 4 / PART 5, 6, 7 ☐ Actual Test	☐ Day 5 / PART 5, 6, 7 ☐ Actual Test
6	**7**	**8**	**9**	**10**
☐ Day 6 / PART 5, 6, 7 ☐ Actual Test	☐ Day 7 / PART 5, 6, 7 ☐ Actual Test	☐ Day 8 / PART 5, 6, 7 ☐ Actual Test	☐ Day 9 / PART 5, 6, 7 ☐ Actual Test	☐ Day 10 / PART 5, 6, 7 ☐ Actual Test

20-Day Plan
시간이 부족하거나 많은 양의 학습이 부담스러우면, '파트별 학습'과 Actual Test를 나눠서
Day 별로 이틀 동안 공부하자.

1	2	3	4	5
☐ Day 1 / PART 5 ☐ PART 6, 7	☐ Actual Test	☐ Day 2 / PART 5 ☐ PART 6, 7	☐ Actual Test	☐ Day 3 / PART 5 ☐ PART 6, 7
6	**7**	**8**	**9**	**10**
☐ Actual Test	☐ Day 4 / PART 5 ☐ PART 6, 7	☐ Actual Test	☐ Day 5 / PART 5 ☐ PART 6, 7	☐ Actual Test
11	**12**	**13**	**14**	**15**
☐ Day 6 / PART 5 ☐ PART 6, 7	☐ Actual Test	☐ Day 7 / PART 5 ☐ PART 6, 7	☐ Actual Test	☐ Day 8 / PART 5 ☐ PART 6, 7
16	**17**	**18**	**19**	**20**
☐ Actual Test	☐ Day 9 / PART 5 ☐ PART 6, 7	☐ Actual Test	☐ Day 10 / PART 5 ☐ PART 6, 7	☐ Actual Test

30-Day Plan
하루에 많은 시간을 내기 힘들면 '파트별 학습 ➡ 복습, Today's Vocabulary ➡ Actual Test로 나누어서
Day 별로 사흘 동안 공부하자.

1	2	3	4	5
☐ Day 1 / PART 5, 6, 7	☐ PART 5, 6, 7 복습 ☐ Today's Vocabulary	☐ Actual Test	☐ Day 2 / PART 5, 6, 7	☐ PART 5, 6, 7 복습 ☐ Today's Vocabulary
6	**7**	**8**	**9**	**10**
☐ Actual Test	☐ Day 3 / PART 5, 6, 7	☐ PART 5, 6, 7 복습 ☐ Today's Vocabulary	☐ Actual Test	☐ Day 4 / PART 5, 6, 7
11	**12**	**13**	**14**	**15**
☐ PART 5, 6, 7 복습 ☐ Today's Vocabulary	☐ Actual Test	☐ Day 5 / PART 5, 6, 7	☐ PART 5, 6, 7 복습 ☐ Today's Vocabulary	☐ Actual Test
16	**17**	**18**	**19**	**20**
☐ Day 6 / PART 5, 6, 7	☐ PART 5, 6, 7 복습 ☐ Today's Vocabulary	☐ Actual Test	☐ Day 7 / PART 5, 6, 7	☐ PART 5, 6, 7 복습 ☐ Today's Vocabulary
21	**22**	**23**	**24**	**25**
☐ Actual Test	☐ Day 8 / PART 5, 6, 7	☐ PART 5, 6, 7 복습 ☐ Today's Vocabulary	☐ Actual Test	☐ Day 9 / PART 5, 6, 7
26	**27**	**28**	**29**	**30**
☐ PART 5, 6, 7 복습 ☐ Today's Vocabulary	☐ Actual Test	☐ Day 10 / PART 5, 6, 7	☐ PART 5, 6, 7 복습 ☐ Today's Vocabulary	☐ Actual Test

Day 01

1. 형용사 ★★★★

> ## 유형 1 ─────── + 명사
>
> 명사 앞 빈칸에는 형용사가 정답이다. 보기에 형용사가 없을 때는 분사를 선택한다. 만약 형용사와 분사가 모두 있다면 대부분 형용사가 정답이므로 '형용사 우선' 원칙을 세운다. 분사가 답이 되는 문제는 이후에 다룰 예정이다.

Ex 1. Castala Catering requests the ------- number of banquet attendees in order to issue a cost estimate.

    (A) approximate
    (B) approximating
    (C) approximation
    (D) approximates

문제를 풀 때는 언제나 보기를 먼저 살펴보면서 유형을 파악하자. 이 문제와 같은 품사 문제는 대부분 빈칸 앞뒤를 보면 정답을 알 수 있다. 빈칸 앞뒤가 the ------- number로서 명사 앞에 빈칸이 있으므로 형용사가 정답이다. 보기 중 형용사가 없을 때는 분사를 선택하고, 둘 다 있을 때는 우선 형용사를 고르는 원칙에 따라 (A)가 정답이다.

어휘 catering 출장 요리, 요식 조달업 approximate 대략의, 대체적인; 근사치를 내다[계산하다] approximation 근사치 banquet 연회, 만찬 issue 발행하다 cost estimate 비용 견적서

해석 Castala 출장 뷔페는 비용 견적서를 발행하기 위해 대략적인 연회 참석자 수를 요청합니다.

Ex 2. Two investigations of a comparable nature completed at Mr. Eames' laboratory yielded ------- results.

    (A) conflict
    (B) conflicts
    (C) conflicting
    (D) to conflict

빈칸 앞뒤 yielded ------- results만 보고 정답을 알아내자. 명사 앞에 빈칸이 있으므로 형용사 역할을 하는 분사 (C)가 정답이다.

어휘 investigation 조사, 연구 comparable 비슷한 nature 종류, 유형 yield (결과를) 내다 conflict 대립; 상충하다 conflicting 모순된, 상반된

해석 Mr. Eames 실험실에서 완료된 비슷한 유형의 두 건의 연구가 상반된 결과를 내놓았다.

유형 2 be[become/remain/stay/seem/appear/prove] + -------

be동사 뒤에 빈칸이 있을 때는 형용사가 정답이다. 2형식 문장이며 빈칸은 주격 보어 자리이므로 명사도 가능하지만 **항상 형용사만 정답으로 출제된다.**

2형식 문장에서는 대부분 be동사를 사용하지만, become, remain, stay, seem, appear, prove와 같은 동사도 be동사와 같은 용법이므로 뒤에 형용사를 써야 한다.

My assistant is -------.

(A) competent   (B) competence   (C) competition   (D) compete

이 문제의 정답은 (A) 형용사 competent이고 보기를 위와 같이 파생어로 구성할 수 있다. 그러나 정답을 명사(예: a man, a woman)로 하려면 파생어로 보기를 구성하기 어렵다. 이러한 이유로 주격 보어 자리에는 항상 형용사가 정답으로 출제된다. 여기서도 보기 중 형용사가 없을 때는 분사를 선택하고, 형용사와 분사가 모두 있다면 일단 형용사를 고른다.

Ex 3. Authorities say they are quite ------- that the signs of a recovery in the economy will emerge by the end of the year.

(A) optimism
(B) optimistically
(C) optimize
(D) optimistic

빈칸 앞뒤 they are quite ------- that만 보면 해결할 수 있다. 빈칸 바로 앞에 있는 quite는 부사인 수식어이므로 없는 것으로 생각하자. be동사 뒤에 빈칸이 있으므로 형용사 (C)가 정답이다.

어휘 authorities 당국 quite 상당히, 꽤 optimism 낙관론, 낙관[낙천]주의 optimize 최적화하다 optimistic 낙관적인, 낙관하는 sign 징후, 조짐 emerge 나타나다, 출현하다

해석 당국은 연말까지는 경기 회복의 징후가 나타날 것이라고 상당히 낙관하고 있다고 말한다.

Ex 4. The company has become ------- enough to hold its own against foreign firms.

(A) competitive
(B) compete
(C) competition
(D) competitively

빈칸 앞뒤 has become ------- enough를 보고 정답을 알아내자. 빈칸 앞에 become이 있으면 형용사가 들어가야 하므로 (A)가 정답이다.

어휘 competitive 경쟁력 있는 compete 경쟁하다 competition 경쟁, 대회 hold one's own against ~에 뒤지지 않고 맞서다

해석 그 회사는 외국 기업들과 맞붙어 뒤지지 않을 만큼 충분히 경쟁력을 가지게 되었다.

유형 3 **make / keep / find / consider + 목적어 + -------**

5형식 문장을 만드는 동사들을 기억하자. 이 동사들이 보일 때 목적격 보어 자리에는 형용사가 정답이다. 보기에 형용사가 없다면 분사를, 둘 다 있다면 형용사를 정답으로 선택하면 된다.

$$\begin{bmatrix} \textbf{make}, \text{get, turn, } \textbf{keep}, \text{leave, drive,} \\ \text{think, believe, } \textbf{find}, \textbf{consider}, \text{suppose,} \\ \text{deem, call, describe} \end{bmatrix} + \text{목적어} + \text{-------}$$

Ex 5. The manager of the New Delhi Railway Station considered it ------- to suspend all the scheduled trains until the inspection of the railways is completed.

(A) necessity
(B) necessary
(C) necessitate
(D) necessarily

빈칸 앞뒤 considered it ------- to suspend에서 정답을 알아내자. 빈칸 앞에 있는 동사 considered를 보면서 빈칸이 목적격 보어 자리라는 것을 파악한 후, 정답으로 형용사 (B)를 선택하면 된다.

어휘 necessity 필요(성) necessitate ~을 필요로 하다 necessarily 어쩔 수 없이, 필연적으로 suspend 중단하다 scheduled (교통편이) 정기적으로 운행되는, 예정된

해석 New Delhi 철도역장은 선로 점검이 완료될 때까지 예정된 모든 열차를 중단시키는 것이 필요하다고 생각했다.

2. 부사 1 ★★★★

부사는 수식어이므로 부사가 빠져도 문장은 완전한 상태이다. 그 반대로 완전한 문장에 빈칸이 있다면 정답은 부사이다.

완전한 문장 + -------

"완전한 문장에 빈칸이 있으면 부사가 정답이다."가 문제 풀이의 기본 원리이다. 그렇다면 빈칸 앞뒤를 보고 이 문장이 완전한 문장인지 어떻게 알 수 있을까?

유형 1 **주어 + ------- + 동사**

주어 뒤에는 동사가 오며, 주어와 동사 사이에는 어떤 문장 성분도 필요하지 않다. 따라서 '주어 + -------+ 동사'가 있는 구조는 완전한 문장이며 부사 문제로는 이 유형이 가장 많이 출제된다.

Ex 1. Mr. Brambs ------ responds to incoming telephone calls with cheerful greetings.

　(A) habit
　(B) habitually
　(C) habits
　(D) habitual

빈칸 앞뒤를 보고 빠르게 정답을 선택하자. Mr. Brambs ------ responds가 '주어 + ------ + 동사' 구조이므로 부사 (B)가 정답이다.

어휘 habitual 습관적인 incoming 들어오는, 걸려 오는 cheerful 발랄한, 쾌활한 greeting 인사

해석 Mr. Brambs은 습관적으로 쾌활한 인사말로 걸려 오는 전화에 응답한다.

유형 2　조동사 + ------ + 동사원형

조동사는 바로 뒤에 주로 동사원형이 오는데 그 사이에 빈칸이 있다면 완전한 문장이므로 빈칸에 부사가 들어가야 한다.

Ex 2. The research team headed by Ms. Suh is developing a kitchen faucet that can ------ respond to a voice command.

　(A) reliably
　(B) rely
　(C) reliability
　(D) reliable

빈칸 앞뒤 can ------ respond만 보고 정답을 선택하자. '조동사 + ------ + 동사원형'이므로 부사 (A)가 정답이다.

어휘 head 이끌다 faucet 수도꼭지 reliably 확실하게, 안정적으로 reliability 신뢰성 reliable 믿을 만한 respond to ~에 반응하다, 대응하다 command 명령

해석 Ms. Suh가 이끄는 연구팀은 음성 명령에 안정적으로 대응하는 주방 수도꼭지를 개발 중이다.

유형 3　1형식 자동사 + ------

빈칸 앞에 1형식 자동사가 있다면 완전한 문장이므로 부사가 정답이다. 시험에 가장 많이 나오는 1형식 자동사 work 뒤에 빈칸이 있으면 부사가 정답이라고 기억해 두자.

Ex 3. Training will allow employees to respond ------ to customer care concerns.

　(A) appropriate
　(B) more appropriate
　(C) appropriately
　(D) appropriateness

빈칸 앞뒤 respond ------ to를 보며 정답을 알아내야 한다. 동사 respond는 항상 전치사 to와 함께 사용하는 1형식 자동사이다. 1형식 문장이 완성되어 있으므로 부사 (C)가 정답이다.

어휘 allow ~을 가능하게 하다 employee 직원 appropriate 적절한 customer care 고객 관리 concern 관심사

해석 교육은 직원들이 고객 관리 문제에 적절히 대응할 수 있게 해 줄 것이다.

유형 4 **타동사 + 목적어 + ̶ ̶ ̶ ̶ ̶ ̶ ̶**

'타동사 + 목적어' 구조는 완전한 3형식 문장임을 뜻하므로 빈칸에 부사가 들어가야 한다.

Ex 4. When the fire alarms sound, all occupants of the building are expected to vacate the premises as ̶ ̶ ̶ ̶ ̶ ̶ ̶ as possible.

(A) rapidly
(B) rapidity
(C) rapid
(D) rapidness

as ̶ ̶ ̶ ̶ ̶ ̶ ̶ as는 원급 비교 구문이므로 형용사 원급 (C)와 부사 원급 (A) 중 정답을 선택해야 한다. 바로 앞에 vacate the premises라는 '타동사 + 목적어' 구조가 완성되어 있으므로 부사 (A)를 정답으로 고르자.

어휘 fire alarm 화재 경보 occupant 거주자, 입주자 be expected to-V ~해야 한다 vacate 비우다 premises 건물 rapid 빠른, 신속한 rapidity 신속, 급속 rapidness 빠르기

해석 화재 경보가 울리면 건물의 모든 거주자는 가능한 한 빨리 건물을 비워야 합니다.

유형 5 **be + p.p. + ̶ ̶ ̶ ̶ ̶ ̶ ̶**

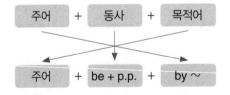

3형식 문장에서 목적어를 주어 자리로 옮기면 동사는 수동태가 된다. 전치사구 'by ~'는 어차피 수식어구이므로 없는 것이나 다름없다. 그렇다면 수동태 문장은 be + p.p.에서 마무리된다. 여기서 **수동태 문장은 완전한 문장**이라는 결론을 얻게 된다. 이것은 앞으로 문법에서 매우 중요한 개념이므로 반드시 기억하고 있어야 한다. 'be + p.p. + ̶ ̶ ̶ ̶ ̶ ̶ ̶'의 구조가 보이면 완전한 문장이므로 부사가 정답이다.

Ex 5. The operator of a crane must ensure that all the moving parts of the machine are fastened ̶ ̶ ̶ ̶ ̶ ̶ ̶ before use.

(A) security
(B) securely
(C) secures
(D) securing

빈칸 앞뒤 are fastened ̶ ̶ ̶ ̶ ̶ ̶ ̶ before use에서 정답을 알아내자. 수동태 동사 뒤에 있는 빈칸에는 부사가 들어가야 하므로 (B)가 정답이다.

operator (기계 · 장치의) 조작자, 기사 crane 기중기, 크레인 ensure 반드시 ~하게[이게] 하다 fasten 고정시키다 secure 안전한, 확실한 securely 확실히, 단단히

크레인 기사는 사용 전에 기계의 모든 움직이는 부품이 단단히 고정되었는지 확인해야 한다.

유형 6 be + ------- + p.p.

빈칸 앞뒤의 be와 p.p.로 수동태 동사가 만들어지므로 이 형태를 보고 문장이 완전하다는 것을 파악할 수 있다.

Ex 6. You are ------- invited to participate in this informative workshop which will help you sharpen your competitive edge.

(A) cordial
(B) cordialness
(C) cordially
(D) cordiality

빈칸 앞뒤 are ------- invited를 보는 순간 바로 정답을 알아야 한다. 'be + ------- + p.p.' 구조이므로 부사 (C)가 정답이다.

be invited to V ~할 것을 권유받다 cordial 진심에서 우러나는 cordiality(=cordialness) 진심, 친절한 태도 informative 유용한 정보를 주는, 유익한 sharpen 연마하다, 강화하다 competitive edge 경쟁 우위

당신의 경쟁 우위를 강화하는데 도움이 될 이 유익한 워크숍에 참가할 것을 진심으로 권합니다.

유형 7 be + ------- + V-ing

빈칸 앞뒤의 be와 V-ing로 진행형 동사가 만들어지므로 여기서 이 문장이 완전하다는 것을 파악할 수 있다.

Ex 7. Ouko Realty is ------- seeking new rental properties to add to its portfolio.

(A) actively
(B) activate
(C) activity
(D) active

빈칸 앞뒤 is ------- seeking을 보고 바로 정답을 선택하자. 'be + ------- + V-ing' 구조이므로 부사 (A)가 정답이다.

realty 부동산 actively 적극적으로 activate 활성화하다 seek 찾다 rental 임대의 property 부동산; 건물 add A to B A를 B에 추가하다 portfolio (회사 · 기관의) 상품[서비스] 목록

Ouko 부동산은 포트폴리오에 추가할 새 임대용 건물을 적극적으로 찾고 있다.

have + ------- + p.p.

빈칸 앞뒤의 have와 p.p.로 완료형 동사가 만들어지므로 여기서 이 문장이 완전하다는 것을 파악할 수 있다.

Ex 8. Ms. Parker has ------- impressed her supervisors by successfully completing the projects despite tight budgets.

(A) consistently
(B) consist
(C) consistent
(D) consistency

빈칸 앞뒤 has ------- impressed를 보고 정답을 선택하자. 'have + ------- + p.p.' 구조이므로 부사 (A)가 정답이다.

어휘 consist (of) ~로 구성되다 consistent 한결같은, 일관된 consistency 한결같음, 일관성; 농도, 밀도 impress 깊은 인상을 주다 complete 완료하다 despite ~에도 불구하고 budget 예산

해석 Ms. Parker는 빠듯한 예산에도 불구하고 성공적으로 프로젝트를 완료함으로써 지속적으로 상사들에게 깊은 인상을 남겼다.

---

be + ------- + 형용사

빈칸 앞에 동사가 있고, 빈칸 뒤에 주격 보어가 있는 구조이다. 완성된 2형식 문장이므로 빈칸에는 부사가 들어가야 한다.

Ex 9. While the first season of the television series was ------- slow, the pace picked up in later seasons.

(A) admit
(B) admission
(C) admittedly
(D) admitting

빈칸 앞뒤 was ------- slow를 보면 'be + ------- + 형용사'의 구조로 2형식 문장이 완성되어 있다. 그러므로 부사 (C)를 정답으로 선택해야 한다.

어휘 admit 인정[시인]하다 admission 가입, 입장; 시인[인정] admittedly 인정하건대 pace 속도 pick up 호전되다, 개선되다

해석 그 텔레비전 시리즈의 첫 시즌은 느린 것을 인정하지만, 이후 시즌들에서는 속도가 개선되었다.

101. Mr. Kovách, Director of Marketing, will determine the ------- time to announce the launch date of Forari's new model of laptop computers.

(A) optimal
(B) optimize
(C) optimally
(D) optimist

102. Applicants for the position must be capable of typing at least 50 words per minute -------.

(A) accuracy
(B) accurately
(C) accurate
(D) accurateness

103. All the issues addressed by members of the board of trustees remain ------- as a matter of organizational policy.

(A) confidence
(B) confidentially
(C) confidentiality
(D) confidential

104. The latest novel by Byron Hayes is ------- based on the events that took place in Glasgow several decades ago.

(A) loosely
(B) loosened
(C) loose
(D) loosening

105. Zat Industries wants to make the partnership between the Personnel and Planning teams -------.

(A) stronger
(B) strongly
(C) strength
(D) strengths

106. Regular mailing list updates have ------- supported TVS Company's efforts to find the right target markets.

(A) succeed
(B) succeeded
(C) successful
(D) successfully

107. Valery Lisov is the ------- choice for the position of board chairperson.

(A) expects
(B) expectantly
(C) expected
(D) expectation

108. Royalty payments will be divided ------- between the two writers of the coauthored book.

(A) equals
(B) equally
(C) equal
(D) equality

109. Although analysts deemed it -------, Kintetsu Corporation succeeded in generating large profits in their first fiscal year.

(A) impossible
(B) impossibility
(C) impossibly
(D) impossibleness

110. Some of the members of the product development, marketing, and art departments worked ------- to design this year's packaging.

(A) collaborate
(B) collaborative
(C) collaboration
(D) collaboratively

111. Floor supervisors have complained that the unscheduled maintenance work has been ------- to their vehicle production.

(A) disruptive
(B) disruptions
(C) disrupt
(D) disrupted

112. Sales at Fairfield International's La Jolla office have been ------- lower than those at Hillcrest branch.

(A) notices
(B) noticing
(C) noticeably
(D) notice

113. Mr. Sasaki's eloquent speech ------- convinced the members of the city council of the necessity for more public parks.

(A) easiest
(B) easy
(C) easier
(D) easily

114. Keira Convention Center is ------- reopening after a year of renovation.

(A) final
(B) finality
(C) finals
(D) finally

115. President of Nichiro Industries is confident that the recent sluggish retail sales will not ------- affect its stock price.

(A) adversely
(B) adversarial
(C) adversary
(D) adversity

정답 및 해설 p.2

1. 주제 / 목적 문제

What is the main topic of the memo?

What is the purpose of the e-mail?

What does the article mainly discuss?

What is the online chat discussion about?

Why was the letter written?

What is described in the notice?

· 문제 풀이 전략

지문의 주제나 목적을 묻는 문제는 첫 번째로 등장한다. 정답의 단서는 주로 지문의 도입부, 즉 첫 서너 줄 이내에 들어 있다. 난이도가 높은 기사(article) 지문에서는 지문 중반에 있거나 끝까지 모두 읽어야 정답을 알 수 있을 때도 있다.

Examples 1-2 refer to the following notice.

Shoreline Community College, in conjunction with the Shoreline Department of Labor (SDL), is offering a discounted Plumbing and Heating Apprenticeship Program for apprentices who seek to be certified plumbing design technicians.

This is a 4-year program, in which an apprentice will learn to plan, select, install, service, commission, and maintain all aspects of plumbing and heating systems. It is now being offered at a 30% discount to those employers who register their apprentices before July.

Commencing in September for the fall semester, this course is only open to apprentices working for an employer accredited by the SDL. To enroll workers in the course, employers should visit www.shorelinecommunitycollege.org, click on the Apprenticeship Program tab, and follow the instructions carefully. You may also call 555-4156 for further information. Please prepare to provide your SDL membership number, along with the personal information and employment history of your apprentices.

Ex 1. What is described in the notice?

    (A) An upcoming career fair
    (B) A newly established company
    (C) A workplace safety workshop
    (D) A career development opportunity

Ex 2. What is indicated about the program?

    (A) It will run from July through September.
    (B) It is only open to employees of specific companies.
    (C) It will be taught by government officials.
    (D) It is only available to apprentices with 4 years of experience.

Examples 1-2 refer to the following notice.

1–2번 예제는 다음 안내문에 관한 것입니다.

Ex1.Shoreline Community College, in conjunction with the Shoreline Department of Labor(SDL), is offering a discounted Plumbing and Heating Apprenticeship Program for apprentices who seek to be certified plumbing design technicians.

This is a 4-year program, in which an apprentice will learn to plan, select, install, service, commission and maintain all aspects of plumbing and heating systems. It is now being offered at a 30% discount to those employers who register their apprentices before July.

Commencing in September for the fall semester, Ex2.this course is only open to apprentices working for an employer accredited by the SDL. To enroll workers in the course, employers should visit www.shorelinecommunitycollege.org, click on the Apprenticeship Program tab, and follow the instructions carefully. You may also call 555-4156 for further information. Please prepare to provide your SDL membership number, along with the personal information and employment history of your apprentices.

Shoreline 전문대학은 Shoreline 노동부(SDL)와 함께 공인 배관 설계 기술자가 되고자 하는 수습생들을 위한 할인된 배관 및 난방 수습 프로그램을 제공합니다.

이것은 4년짜리 프로그램이며, 여기서 수습생은 배관 및 난방 시스템의 모든 면을 계획하고, 선택하고, 설치하고, 점검하고, 위임하고, 유지보수하기를 배웁니다. 수습생을 7월 전에 등록시키는 고용주에게는 현재 30% 할인하여 제공되고 있습니다.

9월에 가을 학기가 시작되는데, 이 코스는 SDL의 인가를 받은 고용주 아래에서 근무하는 수습생에게만 개방됩니다. 직원들을 코스에 등록시키려면 고용주는 www.shorelinecommunitycollege.org를 방문해서 수습 프로그램 탭을 클릭하고 지시 사항을 세심히 따라야 합니다. 또한 추가 정보를 위해 555–4156으로 전화하셔도 좋습니다. 수습생들의 개인 정보와 근무 경력과 함께 본인의 SDL 회원 번호를 제시할 수 있도록 준비하시기 바랍니다.

어휘 community college 지역 전문대학 in conjunction with ~와 함께 Department of Labor 노동부 plumbing 배관 heating 난방 apprenticeship 수습 기간 apprentice 수습생 seek to-V ~하려고 노력하다, 시도하다 certified 공인의 install 설치하다 service 점검[정비]하다 commission 위임하다 maintain 유지 관리하다 aspect 측면 register 등록하다 commence 시작되다 semester 학기 accredit 승인하다, 인가하다 enroll 등록시키다 instruction (주로 복수로) 지시 사항 further information 추가 정보 employment history 근무 경력

Ex 1. What is described in the notice?

(A) An upcoming career fair
(B) A newly established company
(C) A workplace safety workshop
(D) A career development opportunity

안내문에 무엇이 서술되어 있는가?

(A) 다가오는 취업 박람회
(B) 신규 설립 회사
(C) 작업장 안전 워크숍
(D) 경력 개발의 기회

어휘 upcoming 다가오는, 곧 있을 career fair 취업 박람회 career development 경력 개발

해설 주제를 묻는 문제는 대부분 지문의 도입부에서 정답을 알 수 있다. 첫 번째 문단에서 배관 기술자가 되기를 원하는 사람들을 위한 직업 교육이 제공되고 있다고 안내하고 있다.

Ex 2. What is indicated about the program?

(A) It will run from July through September.
(B) It is only open to employees of specific companies.
(C) It will be taught by government officials.
(D) It is only available to apprentices with 4 years of experience.

프로그램에 대해 무엇이 나타나 있는가?

(A) 7월부터 9월까지 진행될 것이다.
(B) 특정 회사의 직원들에게만 개방된다.
(C) 정부 공무원들이 가르칠 것이다.
(D) 4년 경력이 있는 수습생들만 이용할 수 있다.

어휘 run (특정 시기에) 진행되다 specific 특정한 official (고위) 공무원 available to ~가 이용 가능한

해설 마지막 문단의 this course is only open to apprentices working for an employer accredited by the SDL.에서 정답을 알 수 있다. "SDL의 인가를 받은 고용주 아래에서 근무하는 수습생에게만 개방됩니다."라고 했으므로 이 문장이 패러프레이즈된 (B)가 정답이다.

Today's
Vocabulary

▶Actual Test를 풀기 전에 이 단어들을 암기하자.

짝을 이루어 출제되는 단어

· a limited number of 한정된 수의

· a [large / great / good / significant] number of 많은 수의

· a [growing / increasing] number of 점점 더 많은 수의

· be responsible for
 ~을 담당하다, ~의 원인이 되다

· complimentary [meal / breakfast / lunch / coupon]
무료 [식사/아침 식사/점심 식사/쿠폰]

· a [considerable / substantial / significant] amount of [effort / time / money]
상당량의 [노력/시간/돈]

· limited amount of [effort / time / money]
제한된 [노력/시간/돈]

· [creative / innovative] [design / solution / marketing strategy]
[독창적인/혁신적인] [디자인/해결책/마케팅 전략]

adverse 부정적인, 불리한
extended 장기간에 걸친
publish 게재하다, 싣다
journal 학술지, 정기 간행물
regionally 지역 내에서
deposit 침전물
subject (다뤄지고 있는) 문제[사안]
show up 나타내다, 드러내다
bring up (화제를) 꺼내다
use up ~을 다 쓰다
(new) recruit 신입 사원
initially 처음에
shortly 곧, 얼마 안 되어

diversify 다양화하다
readership 독자층
dynamic 정력적인, 역동적인
distracting 산만하게 하는
succinct 간단명료한, 간결한
accommodate (요구 등을) 수용하다
agenda 의제, 안건
boundary 경계(선), 한계
overview 개요, 개관
formula 공식, 방식
feature 특징, 특색
capability 성능; 능력
differ in (~에서) 다르다

alike 둘 다, 똑같이

just 정말; 완전히

present 발표하다, 공개하다; 진열하다

adequate 충분한, 적절한

perpetual (오랫동안) 끊임없이 계속되는

impulsive 충동적인

deficient in ~이 부족한, 결핍된

proofreading 교정, 교열

document 기록하다

delegation 대표단

precision 정확(성), 정밀(성)

intention 의도; 목적

reimbursable 환급할 수 있는

detergent 세제

optimistic 낙관적인

mutual 상호간의

inspired 영감을 받은

supportive 지원하는, 도와주는

quarterly 분기별의

projection 예상, 추정

along with ~와 함께

co-presenter 공동 발표자

authenticate 증명하다, 인증하다

institute (규칙·관례를) 제정하다

likewise 마찬가지로, 또한

hours of operation 영업시간

patron (특정 상점·식당의) 고객

check in with ~와 연락하다

occasional 가끔의

vendor (특정한 제품) 판매 회사

close a deal with ~와 거래를 체결하다

sponsorship 후원, 협찬

acknowledgment (공식적인) 감사의 말

program 프로그램 책자

monitor (추적) 관찰하다, 감시하다

negotiate 협상하다

pricing 가격 책정

particularly(=in particular) 특히, 특별히

impressed 깊은 인상을 받은, 감명받은

sell 팔리다

shortly thereafter 직후에

compensation 보상(금)

modification 수정, 변경

botanical garden(s) 식물원

greet 맞다, 환영하다

bouquet 꽃다발

acknowledge 인정하다

superb 대단히 훌륭한

flourish 번창하다

imprint 찍다, 새기다, 인쇄하다

post 게시하다

solicit 요청하다, 얻으려고[구하려고] 하다

existing 기존의, 현재 사용되는

emerge 부상하다, 부각되다

contender 경쟁자

ambitious 야심 찬, 어마어마한

tenant 세입자, 임차인

privilege 특전, 특혜

district 지구, 지역

challenging 힘든, 어려운

at present 현재는

inaccurate 부정확한, 오류가 있는

timetable 일정표

be involved with[in] ~에 관여하다, ~와 관계가 있다

Actual Test

PART 5

1. 빈칸 앞뒤를 보며 문제를 푼다.
2. 빈칸 앞뒤를 보고 정답을 알 수 없다면 문장을 해석한다.
3. 두 줄 분량의 어휘 문제는 문장 전체를 해석해서 푼다.
4. 접속사 어휘 문제는 빈칸 앞뒤만을 보고 풀 수 없다. 문장 전체를 해석해 보자.

PART 6

1. 문법 문제라면 Part 5와 같은 방식으로 빈칸 앞뒤를 보며 푼다.
2. 다른 유형의 문제는 문맥을 통해 정답을 파악한다.

PART 7

1. 문제와 보기 (A), (B), (C), (D)를 먼저 읽은 후에 지문을 읽는다.
2. 지문 위아래의 모든 부분을 자세히 읽어 본다.
3. 문제의 해설을 꼼꼼히 읽고, 문장 구조를 분석하며 복습한다.

101. Speedflow Communications offers a ------- range of social media services as well as Web site development and maintenance.

(A) wide
(B) widen
(C) widely
(D) widest

102. A ------ on the adverse effects of sitting for extended periods was recently published in the *New England Journal of Medicine*.

(A) research
(B) participant
(C) study
(D) request

103. In November, Premier Shoes will expand ------- by opening two additional stores.

(A) region
(B) regional
(C) regionally
(D) regionalize

104. The accounting figures from all the branch offices must be ------- verified for accuracy.

(A) regularity
(B) regular
(C) regularize
(D) regularly

105. A limited ------- of time has been allotted for questions following Mr. Molinsky's speech.

(A) value
(B) record
(C) amount
(D) setting

106. Bano Cleaner removes mineral deposits from hard floors -------, so polishing is not required.

(A) chemical
(B) chemicals
(C) chemically
(D) chemist

107. At the latest city council meeting, the subject of transportation was ------ by Ms. Pinter.

(A) shown up
(B) gotten up
(C) brought up
(D) used up

108. Laboratory conditions should be monitored ------- to ensure temperature and humidity stability.

(A) frequent
(B) frequents
(C) frequently
(D) frequency

109. Valdez City ------- reduced its electricity usage by replacing the old lampposts with the energy-efficient models.

(A) considerable
(B) consideration
(C) considerably
(D) considerate

110. New recruits at Balally are ------- offered two weeks of vacation in a standard contract.

(A) initially
(B) shortly
(C) particularly
(D) completely

111. The online course focuses on how to expand and diversify your blog's -------.

(A) read
(B) reading
(C) reader
(D) readership

112. Nairobi Move has a ------- team to accommodate all your travel requirements.

(A) dynamic
(B) surprised
(C) distracting
(D) succinct

113. Using Dataretrieve software program, Mr. Wong recovered most files that he had ------- deleted from his computer's hard drive.

(A) accidentally
(B) accidental
(C) accidents
(D) accident

114. The user guide provides a clear ------- of the features and capabilities of your device.

(A) agenda
(B) boundary
(C) overview
(D) formula

115. Mr. Reynold's study shows that types of hay differ ------- in their nutritional content.

(A) significant
(B) signify
(C) significance
(D) significantly

116. The testimonials from satisfied customers show ------- how powerful and easy it is to use our product.

(A) near
(B) alike
(C) just
(D) along

117. Nervousness notwithstanding, Ms. Kim ------- presented her report to the Board of Directors.

(A) confide
(B) confidence
(C) confident
(D) confidently

118. Articles should be submitted at least two weeks prior to the date of publication to leave ------- time for proofreading.

(A) adequate
(B) perpetual
(C) impulsive
(D) deficient

119. Mature perennial plants should be planted in your garden ------- six weeks before your first fall frost date.

(A) even if
(B) at least
(C) in case of
(D) away from

120. How ------- a company receives, documents, and reacts to complaints has an impact on customer satisfaction.

(A) efficient
(B) efficiently
(C) efficiency
(D) efficiencies

121. When members of the Hanoi ------- arrive on Thursday, Ms. Goldingay will give them a tour of the factory.

(A) delegation
(B) precision
(C) intention
(D) translation

122. Associates of LPN auto company are provided with ------- breakfast and lunch at Bain Hall cafeteria.

(A) complimentary
(B) accountable
(C) replaced
(D) secured

123. Ms. Trinacria referred to the corporate travel policy to assert that her expenses are ------- reimbursable.

(A) definitive
(B) define
(C) definite
(D) definitely

124. This ------- allows for the easy and convenient laundering of any garment without the use of harmful chemicals.

(A) management
(B) failure
(C) detergent
(D) satisfaction

125. Autroprime Inc., posted some quite ------- quarterly projections in its interim financial report.

(A) optimistic
(B) mutual
(C) inspired
(D) supportive

126. Ms. Choi, ------- her co-presenter, will be asked to remain at the front of the conference room to speak with individual participants.

(A) as soon as
(B) in order to
(C) along with
(D) in case of

127. Shaloub Copies produces brochures on high-grade, glossy paper that was ------- chosen for its quality and sturdiness.

(A) caring
(B) careful
(C) carefully
(D) cares

128. All users of this software program are required to ------- their e-mail addresses when security updates are performed.

(A) authenticate
(B) determine
(C) discover
(D) institute

129. ------- expanding its hours of operation at some locations, the restaurant began offering new menu items for patrons.

(A) Despite
(B) Likewise
(C) In comparison to
(D) In addition to

130. Of the 645 executives questioned for the survey, 62 percent plan to check in with their offices ------- while on vacation.

(A) occasionally
(B) occasional
(C) occasion
(D) occasions

GO ON TO THE NEXT PAGE

PART 6

Questions 131-134 refer to the following letter.

Mr. Anurag Khan
Bharat Heavy Electricals Ltd.
613 G.I.D.C. Industrial Estate
Gujarat 391350

Dear Mr. Khan:

We would like to extend an invitation to you to participate in the India Electrical Engineering Association (IEEA) trade fair this year. As always, this annual event will provide you with ------- opportunities for networking.
131.
A number of vendors have already reserved their booth spaces. However, there are other ways to ------- your business. Those who close a sponsorship deal with us
132.
receive a special acknowledgment in the program.

Enclosed please find the brochure for the trade fair. The information contains pricing ------- for reserving a booth space, posting advertisements, and sponsoring an
133.
event, as well as a list of past participants.

-------. If you have questions, feel free to contact me by e-mail at any time.
134.

Sincerely,

Additi Gupta

IEEA Vendor Coordinator
agupta@elecengineer.org.in
Enclosure

---

131. (A) extend
     (B) extends
     (C) extensively
     (D) extensive

132. (A) promote
     (B) monitor
     (C) construct
     (D) negotiate

133. (A) markets
     (B) details
     (C) labels
     (D) receipts

134. (A) We would be delighted if you decide to join us this year.
     (B) We will have placed your advertisement in the brochure by then.
     (C) Your participation in the event will be free of charge.
     (D) Your presentation on the novel material is scheduled for the second day.

Questions 135-138 refer to the following e-mail.

To: Montserrat Caballé
From: Yeon-kyeong Kim
Date: June 2
Re: Yong-in Showcase Request

Dear Ms. Caballé,

Mr. Sunwoo, the owner of The Sunwoo Gallery of Seoul, was happy to display your work as part of the Contemporary Art Festival last month. He was ------- impressed
135.
with your beautiful collection of abstract paintings, and so was the audience. He now would like to ask for your permission to present these same pieces at his other gallery in Yong-in in September. Will they be available for ------- and sale? -------.
                                                                                              136.   **137.**
Please let us know if you are interested and, -------, we can set up a meeting to
                                                                    138.
discuss compensation and further details.

Sincerely yours,

Yeon-kyeong Kim

Administrative Assistant
The Sunwoo Gallery

---

135. (A) particular
(B) particularity
(C) particularize
(D) particularly

136. (A) repair
(B) analysis
(C) exhibition
(D) treatment

137. (A) Any piece that does not sell would be returned to you shortly thereafter.
(B) We are committed to restoring the art to its original condition.
(C) The gallery's permanent collection includes sculptures of all kinds.
(D) You will receive a considerable discount on any piece you decide to buy.

138. (A) even if
(B) if so
(C) so long as
(D) in case

GO ON TO THE NEXT PAGE

PART 7

News from Kew Botanical Gardens

KEW (October 16)—Visitors to Royal Botanical Gardens, Kew are now greeted by a bright new logo displayed on the welcome sign at the entry gate. Most people say they are pleased with the new logo, which features a colorful bouquet of wildflowers. —[1]—.

The management of the botanical gardens decided to replace the old logo on the basis of public input. "We collected opinion cards deposited in boxes at the gardens and reviewed responses to an online questionnaire. —[2]—. We discovered that receptivity to the original logo had become negative," said Jacob Kunchai, the director of the gardens, when he was interviewed by the Kew Evening Courier. The old logo spelled out the name of the gardens above a drawing of an elaborate Tudor greenhouse.

New designs were submitted by Nonpareil Graphics. —[3]—. Members were invited to choose which one would be the attractive logo. The board acknowledged that the members' decision was superb.

Jamie Lee, the manager of the Botanical Gardens on-site visitors' shop, is one of those happy with the new logo selected by members. —[4]—. The new logo now appears on clothing and other merchandise, and she is sure it will help increase sales. "Previously, I have often been disappointed. Even though a large number of visitors entered the store, many left without making any purchase. They weren't impressed by our imprinted items."

139. What does the article discuss?

(A) A prospective business partnership

(B) A modification made to a graphic design

(C) Promotion of an upcoming exhibit

(D) New signs identifying plants in the gardens

140. Who made the final decision about the logo?

(A) Employees of Nonpareil Graphics

(B) The director of Kew Botanical Gardens

(C) The manager of the visitors' shop

(D) Members of Kew Botanical Gardens

141. What did Ms. Lee imply about the visitors' shop?

(A) It was not visited by enough people.

(B) Its aesthetics had to be improved.

(C) It was not easy to locate the spot.

(D) The business was not flourishing.

142. In which of the positions marked [1], [2], [3], and [4] does the following sentence best belong?

"Three of them were posted on the Botanical Gardens Web site."

(A) [1]

(B) [2]

(C) [3]

(D) [4]

TRANSFORMING THE LOOK OF RIVER STREET AREA

SAVANNAH CITY — Following the announcement of the relocation of the city's art museum across town into a larger building on East Bay Street, the mayor's office has been soliciting proposals for a new use of the museum's existing space on River Street. Numerous proposals from both local and national developers have been presented. Two proposals in particular are emerging as strong contenders.

Among the bids, the one submitted by Diwikar Corporation to put up a high-rise office building on the site was fairly promising. This project would attract a number of new businesses and generate jobs in the local area over the next five years. Nevertheless, this is an ambitious plan that would require almost three years to realize. In addition, since business tenants normally require full-day parking privileges for their employees, the parking situation in the district could become even more challenging than at present. Diwikar, a ten-year-old firm headquartered in Portland, is currently completing similar construction projects in Vancouver and Seattle.

Another proposal has come from PXY Enterprises, a developer of commercial buildings in the city. The company has put forward an elaborate plan for a new shopping center, complete with department stores, restaurants, and a movie theater. This is an attractive option for the city because it would provide residents with a much sought-after shopping and entertainment area. PXY Enterprises is best known for its renovation of the city's Lake District.

In a recent poll, Savannah City residents were asked which plan they prefer. Results showed a somewhat higher level of support for the PXY Enterprises proposal, although the general feeling among residents is that both plans would be beneficial to the city's economy. One group of citizens, however, is strongly opposed to the development of the area for commercial interests and is petitioning the city to reserve the space for a community park.

— Dina Herrera

Dear Editor,

I would like to comment on Ms. Herrera's article in the *Savannah Times* (July 2) on the proposed construction plans for River Street. There is one factual misstatement I feel must be corrected for the sake of your readers.

Under the present proposal, the commercial office building designed by Diwikar would be completed in about two years. Moreover, since the structure would be developed in phases, some of the offices would be available for use as quickly as eighteen months from the start of construction.

I agree with Ms. Herrera that the parking demands of a commercial building pose a potential problem. However, Asina Amorapanth, vice president of planning at Diwikar, has already met several times with council member Damien Cosme to explore possible solutions.

Sincerely,

Thaksin Panupong
President, Diwikar Corporation

143. What is the purpose of the article?

(A) To announce upcoming cultural events

(B) To describe the new businesses on River Street

(C) To encourage local residents to share opinions about an issue

(D) To provide information about possible construction projects

144. What is NOT mentioned as a possible new use for the River Street area?

(A) A public park

(B) An art museum

(C) A shopping center

(D) An office building

145. What is implied about Savannah City?

(A) Its Lake District is in need of renovation.

(B) The city has used Diwikar Corporation before.

(C) It is known for its downtown shopping district.

(D) Parking is considered a problem in the city.

146. What is Mr. Panupong's main complaint about the article?

(A) It provided an inaccurate timetable.

(B) It misquoted Asina Amorapanth.

(C) It did not report the results of a poll.

(D) It did not mention any benefits of his company's proposal.

147. What is suggested about Mr. Panupong?

(A) He has an office in Savannah City.

(B) He recently built a shopping complex.

(C) He is involved with a project in Vancouver.

(D) He previously collaborated with Dina Herrera.

Day

02

1. 부사 2 ★★★★

문제 풀이의 기본 원리는 "완전한 문장에 빈칸이 들어 있으면 부사가 정답이다."이다. 여기에 원리 한 가지를 추가하자. **"명사를 제외한 모든 것은 부사가 수식한다."**

유형 10 **------- + 형용사 + 명사**

명사는 형용사가 수식하고, 형용사는 부사가 수식한다.

Ex 10. We are likely to be having this issue because some of the ------- insignificant details were overlooked.

(A) seem
(B) seems
(C) seemingly
(D) seemed

빈칸 앞뒤 the ------- insignificant details 에서 정답을 알아내자. '------- + 형용사 + 명사'에서 형용사를 수식할 부사가 필요하므로 (C)가 정답이다.

어휘 be likely to-V ~할 것 같다 seemingly 겉보기에는 insignificant 하찮은, 중요하지 않은 overlook 간과하다, 무시하다
해석 우리는 겉으로는 중요하지 않아 보이는 세부사항 중 일부가 간과되었기 때문에 이 문제를 겪게 될 것 같다.

유형 11 **------- + 준동사 (동명사, to부정사, 분사)**

명사를 제외하고 무엇이든 부사가 수식한다. 준동사를 수식하는 자리도 자주 빈칸으로 출제된다.

Ex 11. Summit Chemicals has become one of the leading companies in the industry by ------- developing technological innovations.

(A) constant
(B) constancy
(C) constancies
(D) constantly

빈칸 앞뒤 by ------- developing만 보고 정답을 파악하자. 전치사 by의 목적어로 동명사가 사용되었다. 준동사를 수식하기 위해 부사 (D)가 빈칸에 들어가야 한다.

어휘 leading 중요한, 선도하는 constant 끊임없는, 지속적인 constancy 불변성

해석 Summit 화학은 끊임없이 기술 혁신을 진전시킴으로써 업계에서 선도 기업 중 하나가 되었다.

유형 12 ------- + 전치사 + 명사

전치사구를 수식하는 것도 부사이다.

Ex 12. The international seminar on the protection of the marine environment is supposed to begin ------- at 10 A.M. on Friday at Dupont Convention Center.

(A) preciseness
(B) precisely
(C) precise
(D) precision

빈칸 앞뒤 begin ------- at 10 A.M.을 보면 정답을 알 수 있다. 빈칸 뒤 전치사구를 수식하도록 부사 (B)를 정답으로 선택해야 한다.

어휘 protection 보호 marine 바다의, 해양의 precision(=preciseness) 정확성, 정밀성 be supposed to-V ~하기로 되어 있다

해석 해양 환경 보호에 관한 국제 세미나는 Dupont 컨벤션 센터에서 금요일 오전 정각 10시에 시작하기로 되어 있다.

유형 13 ------- + 부사

부사를 수식하는 것도 부사이다.

Ex 13. Those who shop with us ------- frequently are rewarded with "Platinum Member" status.

(A) except
(B) exception
(C) exceptional
(D) exceptionally

빈칸 앞뒤 shop with us ------- frequently를 보면서 생각하자. 빈칸 뒤에 있는 부사 frequently를 수식하도록 부사 (D)를 정답으로 선택해야 한다.

어휘 exceptional 특출한, 이례적인 exceptionally 유난히, 특별히 frequently 자주, 흔히 reward A with B A에게 B로 보상하다, 보답하다 status 신분, 자격

해석 특별히 자주 저희와 쇼핑하시는 분들께 '플래티넘 회원' 등급으로 보답해 드립니다.

유형 14 ------- + 한정사 + 명사

이 유형은 오답률이 높으므로 부사가 들어갈 자리로 잘 기억해 두자. '한정사'는 명사 앞에 쓰이지만 형용사가 아니다. 관사와 소유격 (대)명사가 대표적인 한정사이며, 한정사 앞에서 의미를 추가하는 기능을 하는 것은 부사이다.

Ex 14. Industry analysts believe that the economic recovery this quarter is most ------- the result of an unexpected boost in local tourism.

(A) probable
(B) probability
(C) probably
(D) probabilities

most는 형용사나 부사 앞에서 최상급을 만들므로 형용사 (A)나 부사 (C) 중에서 정답을 선택하면 된다. that절은 2형식인 완전한 문장이고, 관사 the 앞에 빈칸이 있으므로 부사인 (C)가 정답이다.

어휘 analyst 분석가 recovery 회복 quarter 분기 probability 가능성 unexpected 예상치 못한 boost 증가 tourism 관광
해석 업계 분석가들은 이번 분기의 경기 회복이 예상치 못한 지역 관광 증가의 결과일 가능성이 높다고 보고 있다.

유형 15 -------, 주어 + 동사

'-------, 주어 + 동사' 구조에서도 부사가 정답이다. 이때 부사는 문장 전체를 수식한다.

Ex 15. -------, we are forced to cancel the order we placed last month due to financial difficulties.

(A) Regret
(B) Regrettable
(C) Regretted
(D) Regrettably

-------, we are forced만 보고 정답을 선택하자. '-------, 주어 + 동사' 구조이므로 부사 (D)가 정답이다.

어휘 regrettable 유감스러운 be forced to-V 하는 수 없이 ~하다 place an order 주문하다 financial 재정의
해석 유감스럽게도 저희는 재정적인 어려움 때문에 지난달에 한 주문을 취소할 수밖에 없습니다.

2. 명사 ★★★★

유형 1   ------- + 동사

빈칸 뒤에 동사가 있으면 빈칸은 주어 자리이다. 주어 자리에는 명사를 써야 한다.

Ex 1. The database is now accessible again, after significant ------- was carried out on our Internet server over the weekend.

  (A) maintenance
  (B) maintained
  (C) maintains
  (D) maintain

빈칸 앞뒤 after significant ------- was carried out을 보고 정답을 찾아야 한다. 빈칸 뒤에 동사 was carried out이 있으므로 빈칸은 주어 자리이다. 그러므로 명사인 (A)가 정답이다.

어휘 accessible 접근[입장/이용] 가능한 significant 중요한, 중대한 maintenance 유지보수 carry out ~을 수행하다
해석 주말 동안 우리 인터넷 서버에 대한 중요한 유지보수 작업이 수행된 후 이제 다시 데이터베이스에 접근할 수 있습니다.

유형 2   타동사 / 전치사 + -------

타동사나 전치사 뒤에는 목적어가 필요하다. 목적어 자리에도 명사가 정답이다.

Ex 2. In her blog, investment consultant Sonia Zheng discusses ------- to prepare for a comfortable retirement.

  (A) strategies
  (B) strategize
  (C) strategic
  (D) strategically

빈칸 앞뒤 discusses ------- to prepare를 보면서 정답을 알아내자. 타동사 discusses의 목적어가 필요하므로 명사 (A)가 정답이다.

어휘 investment 투자 strategize 전략[작전]을 짜다 retirement 은퇴 생활
해석 투자 컨설턴트 Sonia Zheng은 자신의 블로그에서 편안한 은퇴 생활을 준비하기 위한 전략을 논의한다.

Ex 3. In ------- to your request, your account password has been sent to the e-mail address we have on our file.

(A) respond
(B) responded
(C) response
(D) responsive

빈칸 앞뒤 In ------- to만 보면 된다. 전치사 in의 목적어가 필요하므로 명사 (C)가 정답이다.

어휘 in response to ~에 응하여[답하여] responsive to 즉각 반응[대응]하는 account (거래, 서비스의) 계정

해석 요청에 응하여 당신의 계정 비밀번호가 저희 파일에 있는 이메일 주소로 발송되었습니다.

Ex 4. Harvey West Plumbing Company is seeking apprentices with strong interest in ------- plumbing techniques.

(A) to learn
(B) will learn
(C) learning
(D) learns

빈칸 앞뒤 in ------- plumbing techniques를 보고 정답을 알아내야 한다. 전치사 in의 목적어가 필요하므로 명사가 들어갈 자리인데, 보기 중에는 명사가 없다. to부정사 (A)와 동명사 (C)가 명사를 대신할 수 있는데, to부정사는 전치사의 목적어로 쓰이지 않으므로 (C)가 정답이다. 명사 자리에 동명사도 정답으로 출제될 수 있다.

어휘 plumbing 배관 공사[업] apprentice 수습생

해석 Harvey West 배관회사는 배관 기술을 배우는 데 관심이 많은 수습생을 찾고 있습니다.

유형 3 ## 관사 + ------- + 전치사

관사와 전치사 사이는 명사가 들어가는 자리로 가장 많이 출제되고 있다. 이 자리에는 명사를 대신해서 동명사가 들어갈 수 없다는 점에 주의하자.

Ex 5. At the next staff meeting, Mr. Reynolds will share his research on the ------- for markets in Asia.

(A) competitive
(B) competitively
(C) competed
(D) competitors

빈칸 앞뒤 the ------- for만 보고 정답을 선택하자. 관사와 전치사 사이에는 명사가 들어가야 하므로 (D)가 정답이다.

어휘 staff 직원, 사원 competitive 경쟁하는, 경쟁력 있는 competitor 경쟁자, 경쟁 상대

해석 다음 직원회의에서 Mr. Reynolds는 아시아 시장의 경쟁업체들에 대한 조사를 공유할 것이다.

(관사) + 형용사 + -------

명사 앞에 빈칸이 있으면 형용사가 정답이므로, 거꾸로 형용사 뒤에 빈칸이 있으면 명사가 정답이다.

Ex 6. At Wednesday's meeting, it was mentioned that there is a slight ------- the Glynn County Science Center will be closed.

(A) possible
(B) possibility
(C) possibly
(D) possibilities

빈칸 앞에 있는 형용사 slight의 수식을 받을 명사가 필요하다. (B)와 (D)가 모두 명사이지만 앞에 관사 a가 있으므로 단수 명사 (B)가 정답 이다.

어휘 mention 언급[거론]하다 slight 약간의

해석 수요일 회의에서 Glynn County 과학 센터가 폐쇄될 가능성이 약간 있다고 언급되었다.

유형 5 **소유격 (대)명사 + -------**

소유격 (대)명사 뒤에는 항상 명사가 있어야 한다.

Ex 7. During yesterday's staff meeting, Ms. Ellis offered her ------- to the sales team for their excellent results this quarter.

(A) congratulations
(B) congratulate
(C) congratulating
(D) congratulatory

빈칸 앞뒤 offered her ------- to the sales team을 보면서 정답을 알아내자. 빈칸은 타동 사 offered의 목적어 자리인데, 소유격 대명사 her의 수식을 받고 있으므로 명사 (A)가 정답 이다.

어휘 offer (생각, 감정을 나타내다, 표하다 congratulatory 축하의 results 결과, 실적

해석 어제 직원회의에서 Ms. Ellis는 영업팀에게 이번 분기의 우수한 실적에 대해 축하 인사를 전했다.

유형 6 **명사 + -------**

자주 출제되는 유형이므로 절대 잊지 말자. 명사 뒤에 빈칸이 있으면 또 다른 명사를 넣어서 복합 명사를 만들 어야 정답이 된다.

Ex 8. Croydon Dental Clinic has been meeting the oral health care ------- of the greater Reidsville area for almost thirty years.

(A) to need
(B) has needed
(C) needs
(D) needing

빈칸 앞뒤 the oral health care ------- of 만 보고 정답을 선택하자. 명사 뒤 빈칸에는 명사를 넣어야 한다는 사실을 잊지 말고 (C)를 골라야 한다.

> **어휘** meet 충족시키다 oral 입의, 구강의 health care 의료 서비스, 건강 관리 greater ~를 포함한 (주변 지역)
>
> **해석** Croydon 치과는 거의 30년 동안 Reidsville과 주변 지역의 구강 건강 관리 요구를 충족시켜 왔다.

유형 7 **명사와 동명사의 구별**

명사 자리 빈칸의 보기로 명사와 동명사가 모두 나오기도 한다. 동명사는 명사의 자리에서 동사의 용법으로 쓰이며, 특히 타동사인 경우 목적어를 취한다. 명사와 동명사를 구분해 보자.

① 빈칸 뒤에 목적어가 있으면 동명사, 목적어가 없으면 명사가 정답이다.
② 형용사 뒤에 빈칸이 있으면 명사가 정답이다. 준동사인 동명사는 부사가 수식한다.
③ 관사는 명사 앞에만 써야 한다. 동명사 앞에는 관사를 쓸 수 없다.

Ex 9. Actor Nguyen Luong is credited with ------- the latest style of sportswear to flood the over-fifty market.

(A) popularized
(B) popularizing
(C) popularize
(D) popularization

빈칸 앞뒤 with ------- the latest style of sportswear를 보면서 정답을 찾아야 한다. 전치사 with의 목적어가 필요하므로 명사 (D)와 동명사 (B) 중에서 정답을 골라야 한다. 빈칸 뒤의 the latest style of sportswear를 목적어로 취할 수 있는 동명사 (B)가 정답이다.

> **어휘** be credited with ~의 공로를 인정받다 popularize 대중화하다 latest (가장) 최근의[최신의] sportswear 스포츠웨어, 운동복 flood ~에 넘쳐나게 하다
>
> **해석** 배우 Nguyen Luong은 최신 스타일의 스포츠 의류를 대중화해서 50세 이상 시장에 널리 퍼지게 한 것에 대한 공로를 인정받았다.

Ex 10. Visa applicants who are under the age of 18 must submit a letter of ------- signed by both parents.

(A) consented
(B) consenting
(C) consentaneous
(D) consent

빈칸 앞뒤 of ------- signed by both parents에서 정답을 알 수 있다. 전치사 of의 목적어로 명사 (D)와 동명사 (B) 중에서 골라야 한다. 빈칸 뒤에 목적어를 취하고 있지 않으므로 명사 (D)가 정답이다.

> **어휘** applicant 신청자 submit 제출하다 consentaneous 일치한, 합치된 consent 동의[허락]; 동의[허락]하다
>
> **해석** 18세 미만의 비자 신청자는 부모 모두가 서명한 동의서를 제출해야 한다.

101. The designers have been asked to create a ------- new logo for the *Polymer Arts* Magazine.

(A) completion
(B) completes
(C) completing
(D) completely

102. The new layout of Voltas Electronics' Web site will make the company's product information more ------- accessible to consumers.

(A) ready
(B) readily
(C) readier
(D) readied

103. Terms and conditions ------- agreed upon cannot be changed even when you order special goods or abnormal quantities.

(A) original
(B) origin
(C) originally
(D) originality

104. The ------- made by President Minako Ishikawa was well-received by the new employees of Eckero, Inc.

(A) addresses
(B) addressable
(C) addressed
(D) address

105. According to the survey results, Corchester residents were ------- in favor of adding bicycle paths along the riverbank.

(A) overwhelms
(B) overwhelm
(C) overwhelming
(D) overwhelmingly

106. Please congratulate Rachel Hutchinson, ------- of the Leadership Award in Nursing at Winthrop Hospital.

(A) won
(B) wins
(C) winning
(D) winner

107. -------, the engineering firm is going to invest more in ocean power technology by establishing another subsidiary in Denmark.

(A) Presumption
(B) Presumable
(C) Presumably
(D) Presumed

108. Since he assumed the ownership of JWT Express Transport five years ago, Astrid Barretto has earned the ------- of his staff.

(A) admiration
(B) admire
(C) admired
(D) admires

109. Yaris Ltd. welcomes your ------- regarding any aspect of our services.

(A) suggest
(B) suggests
(C) suggested
(D) suggestions

110. ------- fluctuating temperatures can cause various types of damage to specimens in the laboratory.

(A) Wide
(B) Widest
(C) Width
(D) Widely

111. Judging from the ability to close deals he has shown in his previous job, Mr. Park is ------- a very skilled negotiator.

(A) clearest
(B) clear
(C) clarity
(D) clearly

112. Li Mines, Inc., a global ------- of copper, gold, and other metals, is trying to attract new clients in Europe.

(A) supplier
(B) supplying
(C) supplied
(D) supplies

113. Alamitos West Health Care Center requests that all employees attending the international medical conference next month make travel ------- by the end of the week.

(A) arranged
(B) arranges
(C) arranging
(D) arrangements

114. President Yamada plans on ------- the company's expansion at the press conference, which will be held at Smith Convention Center tomorrow morning.

(A) outline
(B) outlined
(C) outlining
(D) outliner

115. The maintenance department has submitted an initial budget ------- for upgrading our security system.

(A) estimate
(B) estimates
(C) estimating
(D) estimations

2. 세부사항 문제

빈출 질문 유형

What is scheduled to take place on Thursday?

Where will the free event be held?

Who is Mr. Tanaka?

How will the group travel from Macapa to Porto Grande?

According to the article, why has the sale of the Josée Group been considered controversial?

What is Leafman Capital's announced plan for the Hôtel Jean-Claude?

• 문제 풀이 전략

밑줄 친 부분은 주요 단어 즉 키워드이다. 문제의 키워드에 밑줄 또는 동그라미 표시를 해 두면, 지문을 읽을 때 표시한 키워드를 찾는 데 도움이 된다. 키워드는 지문 안에 원문 그대로 나오기도 하지만, 패러프레이즈된 형태로 나오는 경우가 더 많다. 정답도 지문에서 자주 패러프레이즈되므로, 고득점을 원한다면 어휘력을 끊임없이 향상시켜야 한다.

Examples 1-3 refer to the following article.

THE GROVELAND TRIBUNE

Local News
May 25

Colin Cavanaugh, who for the past 15 years has been a flutist with the Groveland Symphony Orchestra, has many fond memories of the Ironwood Theatre. He attended a lot of performances there, initially with his parents, then with his friends as a young adult, and finally with his own children. But a decade has passed since the last performance at the Ironwood was staged; in fact, until recently, the city council was considering tearing down the 95-year-old structure to make way for a shopping center.

That is when Mr. Cavanaugh decided to buy the property. He began to gather the funds necessary to achieve his goal, requesting donations from several businesses in the area. He also organized various fundraising events, the highlight of which was an open-air concert at South Groveland Park featuring local musicians, including himself.

In the end, Mr. Cavanaugh managed to realize his goal and over the past year he has lovingly overseen every aspect of the detailed renovation. He sought out volunteers to do carpentry work and painting; shortly thereafter a number of craftspeople from the area were offering their services free of charge for this worthwhile cause.

On Saturday, June 4, the Ironwood Theatre will once again open its doors to the public with the screening of the documentary film titled "The Rise, Fall, and Rebirth of the Ironwood Theatre." As the title implies, the film captures the history of the Ironwood Theatre, featuring prominently the efforts of Mr. Cavanaugh to preserve the building. The event will be held at 6:30 P.M., with Mr. Cavanaugh having the honor of being the projectionist for the evening. After the screening, a reception will take place from 7:30 P.M. to 9:30 P.M.

Ex 1. Who is Mr. Cavanaugh?

(A) A painter
(B) A carpenter
(C) A film director
(D) A musician

Ex 2. What is indicated about the Ironwood Theatre?

(A) It was the main performance stage of the Groveland Symphony Orchestra.
(B) It was acquired with monetary assistance from the local community.
(C) It is located in the area of South Groveland Park.
(D) It has been featured in a documentary film before.

Ex 3. According to the article, what will Mr. Cavanaugh do on June 4?

(A) Show a movie
(B) Attend a city council meeting
(C) Go to a concert
(D) Resume work on a project

Examples 1-3 refer to the following article.

1–3번 예제는 다음 기사에 관한 것입니다.

THE GROVELAND TRIBUNE

Local News
May 25

Ex1.Colin Cavanaugh, who for the past 15 years has been a flutist with the Groveland Symphony Orchestra, has many fond memories of the Ironwood Theatre. He attended a lot of performances there, initially with his parents, then with his friends as a young adult, and finally with his own children. But a decade has passed since the last performance at the Ironwood was staged; in fact, until recently, the city council was considering tearing down the 95-year-old structure to make way for a shopping center.

Ex2.That is when Mr. Cavanaugh decided to buy the property. He began to gather the funds necessary to achieve his goal, requesting donations from several businesses in the area. He also organized various fundraising events, the highlight of which was an open-air concert at South Groveland Park featuring local musicians, including himself.

In the end, Mr. Cavanaugh managed to realize his goal and over the past year he has lovingly overseen every aspect of the detailed renovation. He sought out volunteers to do carpentry work and painting; shortly thereafter a number of craftspeople from the area were offering their services free of charge for this worthwhile cause.

On Saturday, Ex3.June 4, The Ironwood Theatre will once again open its doors to the public with the screening of the documentary film titled "The Rise, Fall, and Rebirth of the Ironwood Theatre." As the title implies, the film captures the history of the Ironwood Theatre, featuring prominently the efforts of Mr. Cavanaugh to preserve the building. Ex3.The event will be held at 6:30 P.M., with Mr. Cavanaugh having the honor of being the projectionist for the evening. After the screening, a reception will take place from 7:30 P.M. to 9:30 P.M.

THE GROVELAND 신문

지역 소식
5월 25일

Colin Cavanaugh는 지난 15년 동안 Groveland 심포니 오케스트라의 플루티스트로 활동해 왔는데, Ironwood 극장에 대한 좋은 추억이 많다. 그는 처음에는 부모님과 함께, 그 후 젊은 시절에는 친구들과 함께, 그리고 마지막으로 자신의 아이들과 함께 많은 공연을 관람했다. 그러나 Ironwood에서 마지막 공연이 무대에 올려진 지 10년이 지났다. 사실 최근까지만 해도 시의회는 이 95년 된 건축물을 철거하고 쇼핑센터에 자리를 내주는 것을 고려하고 있었다.

그때 Mr. Cavanaugh는 그 부동산을 사기로 결심했다. 그는 지역의 몇몇 사업체에 기부를 요청하면서 목표를 달성하는 데 필요한 자금을 모으기 시작했다. 그는 또한 다양한 기금 마련 행사를 조직했는데, 그중 하이라이트는 자신을 포함한 지역의 음악가들이 특별히 출연한 South Groveland 공원에서 열린 야외 음악회였다.

마침내 Mr. Cavanaugh는 목표를 달성해 냈으며, 지난 한 해 동안은 세세한 보수 공사의 모든 측면을 애정을 담아 감독했다. 그는 목공 작업과 페인트칠을 해 줄 자원봉사자들을 구했다. 얼마 지나지 않아 지역 출신의 많은 장인이 이 가치 있는 운동을 위해 무료로 봉사해 주었다.

6월 4일 토요일 Ironwood 극장은 'Ironwood 극장의 흥망과 재탄생'이라는 제목의 다큐멘터리 영화를 상영하면서 다시 한 번 대중에게 개방된다. 제목이 시사하다시피 이 영화는 아이언우드 극장의 역사를 담고 있으며, 건물을 보존하기 위한 Mr. Cavanaugh의 노력이 눈에 띄게 드러난다. 행사는 Mr. Cavanaugh가 그날 저녁의 영사 기사가 되는 명예를 가지는 가운데 저녁 6시 30분에 열릴 것이다. 상영 후에는 7시 30분부터 9시 30분까지 축하연이 있다.

어휘 fond 애정 어린 attend 보러 가다 initially 처음에 young adult 청년 decade 10년 stage ~을 무대에 올리다 city council 시의 회 tear down 허물다, 철거하다 structure 건축물 make way for ~에 자리를 내주다, ~로 교체하다 property 부동산, 건물 organize 조직하다 fundraising 기금 모금 highlight 압권, 하이라이트 open-air 옥외[야외]의 feature ~를 출연시키다, 보여주다 prominently 특별히, 현저히 in the end 마침내 manage to-V ~을 잘 해내다 realize 실현하다, 달성하다 lovingly 애정을 담아 oversee 감독하다 aspect 측면 renovation 보수 seek out(sought-sought) (노력을 기울여) ~을 찾아내다 carpentry 목수일 shortly thereafter 얼마 지나지 않아 craftspeople 장인들 worthwhile 가치[보람] 있는 service 근무; 봉사 free of charge 무료로 cause 대의명분; (가치 있는) 사업 screening 상영, 방영 title 제목을 붙이다 rise and fall 흥망성쇠 rebirth 부활, 재탄생 imply 암시하다 capture 포착하다, 담아내다 preserve 보존하다 have the honor of -ing ~라는 명예를 누리다 projectionist 영사 기사 take place (행사, 회의가) 열리다

[문장 분석]

1. He began to gather the funds (which are) necessary to achieve his goal, requesting donations from several businesses in the area.

➡ funds와 necessary 사이에 '주격 관계대명사 + be동사(which are)'가 생략된 형태로 necessary to achieve his goal이 앞의 the funds를 수식하고 있다.

2. He also organized various fundraising events, the highlight of which was an open-air concert (at South Groveland Park) (featuring local musicians, including himself).

➡ the highlight of which를 whose highlight로 바꿔 쓸 수 있다.

➡ at South Groveland Park와 featuring local musicians, including himself 모두 앞의 an open-air concert를 꾸며 준다.

3. The event will be held at 6:30 P.M., with Mr. Cavanaugh having the honor of being the projectionist for the evening.

➡ with Mr. Cavanaugh having the honor는 'Mr. Cavanaugh가 명예를 누린 채'라는 뜻으로, 'with + 명사 + 형용사[분사/전치사구/to-V]' 구문은 '~가 ~인 채로[~하면서]'라는 뜻으로 쓰인다. 모든 파트에서 매우 자주 사용되는 표현으로 절대 잊어버리지 말자.

Ex 1. Who is Mr. Cavanaugh?

   (A) A painter
   (B) A carpenter
   (C) A film director
   (D) A musician

Mr. Cavanaugh는 누구인가?

   (A) 도장공
   (B) 목수
   (C) 영화감독
   (D) 음악가

해석 첫 문장에서 지난 15년 동안 Groveland 심포니 오케스트라에서 플루티스트로 활동했다고 말하고 있다.

Ex 2. What is indicated about the Ironwood Theatre?

   (A) It was the main performance stage of the Groveland Symphony Orchestra.
   (B) It was acquired with monetary assistance from the local community.
   (C) It is located in the area of South Groveland Park.
   (D) It has been featured in a documentary film before.

Ironwood 극장에 대해 무엇이 나타나 있는가?

   (A) Groveland 심포니 오케스트라의 주 공연 무대였다.
   (B) 지역 사회의 재정적 도움으로 매입되었다.
   (C) South Groveland 공원 구역 내에 위치해 있다.
   (D) 전에 다큐멘터리 영화에 등장한 적이 있다.

어휘 acquire (사거나 받아서) 획득하다 monetary 금전의, 재정의 be featured in ~에 출연하다, 실리다

해설 첫 문단에 나오는 "Ironwood 극장에서 많은 공연을 관람했다(He attended a lot of performances there)."에서 attend를 '참석하다'라는 뜻으로 생각하고, 오케스트라 단원으로써 극장에서 연주했다는 의미로 해석해서는 안 된다. 잘못된 이해를 근거로 (A)를 정답으로 선택하지 않도록 주의하자. 둘째 문단에 Mr. Cavanaugh가 극장 건물을 사기로 결심한 후 목표를 달성하기까지의 과정이 나와 있다. 지역 사업체들에 기부를 요청하고, 야외 콘서트 같은 기금 마련 활동을 한 것이었다. 그 후 목표를 달성했다는 내용이 있으므로 그가 건물을 매입한 것은 지역 사회의 재정적 뒷받침이 있었기 때문에 가능한 일이었다는 것을 알 수 있다.

Ex 3. According to the article, what will Mr. Cavanaugh do on June 4?

(A) Show a movie
(B) Attend a city council meeting
(C) Go to a concert
(D) Resume work on a project

기사에 따르면 Mr. Cavanaugh는 6월 4일에 무엇을 할 것인가?

(A) 영화를 보여준다
(B) 시의회 회의에 참석한다
(C) 음악회에 간다
(D) 프로젝트 작업을 재개한다

어휘 resume 재개하다

해설 June 4가 키워드이다. 마지막 문단에서 6월 4일에는 극장이 다큐멘터리 영화를 상영하면서 다시 문을 열고 Mr. Cavanaugh가 영화의 영사 기사 역할을 맡을 것이라고 했으므로 여기서 정답을 알 수 있다.

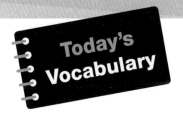

Today's Vocabulary

▶Actual Test를 풀기 전에 이 단어들을 암기하자.

짝을 이루어 출제되는 단어

- in / for / over + the past / the last / the next / the following + 기간 — 지난 ~ 동안 / 향후 ~ 동안

- mounting / increasing + pressure — 증가하는 압력

- affordable / reasonable + price / rate — 저렴한 가격[요금]

- potential / prospective / probable + client / customer — 잠재 고객, buyer / investor — 잠재 구매자, 잠재 투자자

- potential / prospective / probable + employer — 지원 회사, employee — 입사 지원자

- qualified / successful + candidate / applicant — 자격을 갖춘 지원자, 합격자

---

affix 부착하다, 붙이다
adhesive 접착제
ornament 장식품
evidently 분명히, 눈에 띄게
elsewhere 다른 곳에(서), 다른 곳으로
thoroughly 철저하게, 꼼꼼하게
beyond 건너편에, 그 너머에
reflect upon 되돌아보다, 반추하다
occasion 때, 경우
along with ~와 마찬가지로
surgical 외과의, 수술의
gala 경축 행사
contemporary 동시대의; 현대의, 당대의
frugal 절약하는
immature 미숙한
make an assessment of ~를 평가하다
take precautions 예방 조치를 취하다
enroll in ~에 등록하다
enrollment 등록; 등록자 수
accounts 회계 기록, 장부
productivity 생산성

driving 강력한, 영향력이 큰
thermal 보온성이 좋은
disposable 일회용의
gardening 원예
abandon 버리다; 포기하다
classify 분류하다, 구분하다
withdraw 물러나다, 그만두다
absorb 흡수하다
receipt 받기, 수령, 인수, 접수
workplace 직장, 업무 현장
publishing house 출판사
book deal 출판 계약
founding 설립, 수립, 창립
distribution 배부, 배급; 유통
treatment 취급
assign 배치하다
recruit 모집하다; 신입 사원
file (문서 등을) 보관하다, 철하다
offering 제공된 것, 내놓은 것
effort 노력, 성과
seek to-V ~하려고 노력하다

comprehend 알다, 파악하다

varietal 변종, 품종

address (문제 · 사안 등을) 다루다, 해결하려 하다

nursery 묘목장, 원예 시장

turn out (대량으로) ~을 생산하다

drought-tolerant 가뭄을 잘 견디는, 내건성의

breed 품종

streamline 간소화하다, 능률화하다

track 추적하다

archaeological 고고학적인

find 발견물

artifact 인공 유물

excavate 발굴하다, 출토하다

concerning ~에 관한

adequately 충분하게, 적합하게

document (문서에) 기록하다

readily 쉽게, 손쉽게

establish 확립하다

field (실험실 · 연구실 등이 아닌) 현장

focus group 포커스 그룹(시장 조사나 여론 조사의 대상으로 뽑힌 소수 집단)

moderator (토론회 등의) 사회자

capacity 자격, 역할

align with ~와 나란히 하다

area (활동) 분야, 영역

on a positive note 긍정적으로 말하면

apprentice 수습생

reach out to (정보, 기회, 요청을 위해) ~에게 연락해 보다

explore 탐구하다, 알아보다

Actual Test

PART 5

1. 빈칸 앞뒤를 보며 문제를 푼다.
2. 빈칸 앞뒤를 보고 정답을 알 수 없다면 문장을 해석한다.
3. 두 줄 분량의 어휘 문제는 문장 전체를 해석해서 푼다.
4. 접속사 어휘 문제는 빈칸 앞뒤만을 보고 풀 수 없다. 문장 전체를 해석해 보자.

PART 6

1. 문법 문제라면 Part 5와 같은 방식으로 빈칸 앞뒤를 보며 푼다.
2. 다른 유형의 문제는 문맥을 통해 정답을 파악한다.

PART 7

1. 문제와 보기 (A), (B), (C), (D)를 먼저 읽은 후에 지문을 읽는다.
2. 지문 위아래의 모든 부분을 자세히 읽어 본다.
3. 문제의 해설을 꼼꼼히 읽고, 문장 구조를 분석하며 복습한다.

101. When applying a transparent screen protector to an Etin smartphone, affix the side with adhesive ------- to the display screen.

(A) direction
(B) directing
(C) directly
(D) directs

102. Sales representatives are instructed to investigate the businesses of ------- customers before contacting them for the first time.

(A) total
(B) potential
(C) equal
(D) factual

103. The Mount Martha Briars Craft Market offers one-of-a-kind handcrafted ornaments that are not available -------.

(A) evidently
(B) elsewhere
(C) thoroughly
(D) beyond

104. The Oceanic Preservation Society relies on generous donations from the local community for ------- its variety of research facilities.

(A) maintenance
(B) maintains
(C) maintaining
(D) maintain

105. During exit interview surveys for employees leaving the company prematurely, you will be asked to reflect upon your ------- at this company.

(A) permission
(B) amount
(C) occasion
(D) experience

106. ------- Dr. Carreras, who will be in Barcelona, all the members of the surgical team will attend the appreciation gala dinner in Winnipeg.

(A) Except for
(B) Along with
(C) Whereas
(D) Likewise

107. The chapter on traveling in Southeast Asia was ------- the best part of the book.

(A) definite
(B) definitive
(C) defined
(D) definitely

108. The investment manager will have extensive authority on asset selection and make a ------- assessment of the funds' profitability.

(A) regular
(B) contemporary
(C) frugal
(D) immature

109. The entire medical staff of CPC Hospital must take ------- while caring for patients to keep themselves safe and healthy.

(A) element
(B) precautions
(C) advantage
(D) conditions

110. ------- in the evening management classes has nearly tripled thanks to Professor Bradely's easy and efficient lecture.

(A) Enroll
(B) Enrollment
(C) Enrolls
(D) Enrolling

111. In spite of ------- pressure by other countries to open its automobiles market, the government refuses to discuss this sensitive issue.

(A) mounting
(B) approachable
(C) respective
(D) deceptive

112. ------- are the accounts that Sales Director asked Mike Thompson to update by the end of the day.

(A) These
(B) Something
(C) Another
(D) More

113. In an effort to improve -------, Moon Microprocessors is offering financial incentives for enhanced job performance.

(A) produces
(B) producer
(C) productive
(D) productivity

114. Entering the European market was the best decision we made over the ------- ten years.

(A) past
(B) next
(C) following
(D) ultimate

115. Starting next month, ------- umbrella covers will no longer be available for visitors at the entrances of government buildings.

(A) driving
(B) thermal
(C) disposable
(D) gardening

116. Leafman Capital has made successful ------- in two emerging data companies.

(A) investments
(B) invested
(C) invest
(D) investor

117. The steel maker said that its fast rise in overseas sales was attributable to its flexibility in meeting market changes and providing high quality material at ------- prices.

(A) affordable
(B) allowable
(C) accountable
(D) compatible

118. Despite the ringing endorsement from the former chairperson, Mr. Ishihara has decided to ------- from consideration for the position.

(A) abandon
(B) classify
(C) withdraw
(D) absorb

119. The Texas Department of Public Safety has not yet given its ------- to Dhital Petroleum's request for building permits.

(A) approved
(B) approvingly
(C) approves
(D) approval

120. Many ------- buyers have expressed intentions to take over the bankrupt company, but there has been no firm offer yet.

(A) prospective
(B) appreciable
(C) portable
(D) inevitable

121. The ------- of Saitama factory has had a significant impact on Lasner Technology's employee productivity.

(A) expanding
(B) expanded
(C) expansion
(D) expand

122. At Exraterram, all types of correspondence must be treated equally and responded to within three days ------- receipt.

(A) of
(B) throughout
(C) about
(D) by

123. ------- Ms. Lee's blog dealing with workplace satisfaction is so popular, a major publishing house has offered her a book deal.

(A) In case
(B) Because
(C) Whenever
(D) Even if

124. Mr. Bac's letter is in response to the fax and e-mail dated 20 and 23, March, -------.

(A) respects
(B) respecting
(C) respective
(D) respectively

125. The department is looking for a ------- candidate with experience in both the Singapore and Malaysia markets.

(A) retained
(B) numerous
(C) qualified
(D) definitive

126. The newly hired logistics consultant's outstanding performance has resulted in faster ------- of goods to our stores.

(A) founding
(B) distribution
(C) treatment
(D) revision

127. -------, the college professor did not know that classes had been suspended in all levels because of an incoming typhoon.

(A) Apparent
(B) Apparently
(C) Appear
(D) Appearance

128. The average precipitation in the contiguous U.S. ------- the past three years has been 26.57 inches.

(A) on
(B) for
(C) to
(D) under

129. To provide quality feedback on the projects done by new employees, Ms. Vuong will be assigning individual mentors to ------- this year.

(A) recruited
(B) recruiter
(C) recruiting
(D) recruits

130. Although ------- planned for a warehouse, the facility was converted into another quality control laboratory by the management.

(A) original
(B) originality
(C) originally
(D) originate

GO ON TO THE NEXT PAGE

PART 6

Questions 131-134 refer to the following e-mail.

To: Tony Leung <tleung@mckinsey.com>

From: Megan Shetty<mshetty@mckinsey.com>

Subject: New Employee Forms

Date: September 1

Dear Mr. Leung,

Congratulations on your acceptance to our company. -------. I have attached
131.
herewith some documents that will help you begin your successful career with us.
They provide a brief ------- to McKinsey & Associates, as well as an explanation of
132.
our company's various codes of conduct that you must adhere to. You will need to
agree with these policies and rules, and some pages will require your signature to
this effect. After ------- those pages, please submit them to Thomas Lissner in the
133.
personnel department. He ------- them for you.
134.

Again, congratulations, and I look forward to working with you. Please feel free to
contact me with any questions at extension 7532.

Best regards,

Megan Shetty

Enclosures

---

131. (A) Mr. Lissner will assist you in
completing the necessary
paperwork.
(B) Your application will be processed
no later than the end of the month.
(C) We are excited to have you join
McKinsey & Associates.
(D) Any assistance you can provide
for our new coworker would be
appreciated.

132. (A) orient
(B) oriental
(C) oriented
(D) orientation

133. (A) editing
(B) signing
(C) typing
(D) e-mailing

134. (A) will file
(B) had filed
(C) file
(D) filing

Questions 135-138 refer to the following article

TORONTO (13 August) — Simonte unveiled its annual Plant Showcase today. According to Simonte spokesman Toru Okamoto, this ------- offering highlights
135.
the company's latest efforts in botanical research. Many of these efforts result from customer surveys that sought to comprehend the most typical difficulties.

-------. This year, the company's specialized nurseries have turned out drought-
136.
tolerant breeds, such as the Dovyalis Apple Tree. These varietals can withstand prolonged dry conditions without sustaining damage. "Gardeners in desert

------- will be especially fond of the Dovyalis," noted Okamoto. "And -------
137.   138.
might be interested in our new R-7 rose bushes as well, which flourish in a similar climate."

---

135. (A) daily
(B) weekly
(C) monthly
(D) yearly

136. (A) The company occupies one of the most profitable sectors in agriculture.
(B) The company recruits researchers from across the world.
(C) Afterward, the research and development team works to develop varietals that address these challenges.
(D) Their comprehensive research produces some of the most flavorful plants on the market.

137. (A) region
(B) regions
(C) regional
(D) regionally

138. (A) he
(B) she
(C) we
(D) they

GO ON TO THE NEXT PAGE

PART 7

Questions 139-140 refer to the following press release.

New Database to Streamline Tracking of Archaeological Finds

Barr Associates is proud to announce that it will soon partner with museums and archaeological societies from all around the world to construct a broad database of artifacts excavated from archaeological sites. Says Christopher Barr, CEO of Barr Associates, "A significant portion of the information concerning treasures of the ancient world is not adequately documented and is not readily available. Our goal is to establish an electronic database that will enable museums and professionals working in the field to obtain complete descriptions of artifacts." The initial database will store information on 500,000 objects, and will be updated periodically.

139. What product will Barr Associates offer?

(A) Supplies for archaeological excavations
(B) Theft prevention systems for museums
(C) Software containing information about artifacts
(D) Devices for detecting fake artifacts

140. According to the press release, who will use the product?

(A) Dealers who buy and sell antiques
(B) Security guards in museums
(C) Publishers that deal with books on archaeology
(D) Museum employees and archaeologists

Questions 141-145 refer to the following two letters.

Marissa James
Unadilla Advertising Group
3220 Avenue A
Unadilla, NY 13849

February 22

Dear Ms. James,

I spoke with your assistant on the telephone last week, and he suggested that I write directly to you to express my interest in an internship at your firm.

I will graduate soon and I am seeking hands-on experience in the field of market research. I am specifically interested in an internship where I will be trained as a focus group discussion moderator. I believe that my business degree and my interpersonal skills qualify me for an internship in this area.

As indicated in the enclosed résumé, I was employed in a part-time capacity as assistant to the moderator of focus groups at Mindspot Research for one academic year. Additionally, I have gained further experience through executing opinion polls for my university newspaper and monitoring focus groups for an advertising class at the university. I am very eager to work at Unadilla Advertising Group and would appreciate an opportunity to have a conversation with you about the internships you have on offer.

Sincerely yours,
Lynnette Leathers

Lynnette Leathers
305 Carver Avenue
Brooklyn, NY 11201

March 19

Dear Ms. Leathers,

Thank you for your letter and the accompanying résumé. Our organization is always interested in extending opportunities to recent graduates whose credentials and background match yours. Regrettably, we do not have any current internships that align with your particular area of focus. On a more positive note, however, we are currently in search of an apprentice to assist in the process of market research opinion polls. This is a twelve-month internship program that may culminate in an offer for permanent employment. If this line of work intrigues you, I advise that you reach out to Ayesha Chandran, the head of our human resources department, to explore the duties of the internship.

Yours truly,
Marissa James
Marissa James
Unadilla Advertising Group

141. What does Ms. Leathers hope to do?

   (A) Launch an advertising campaign
   (B) Contribute to a newspaper
   (C) Obtain training from a company
   (D) Supervise a human resources department

142. What previous experience does Ms. Leathers mention?

   (A) She served as an assistant at an advertising agency.
   (B) She was the instructor of a marketing course.
   (C) She sold newspaper advertisements.
   (D) She worked as a telephone marketer.

143. What news does Ms. James give Ms. Leathers?

   (A) Ms. Leathers lacks the requisite work experience.
   (B) The organization has no open positions for work with focus groups.
   (C) Ms. Leathers needs more education to become eligible for a job.
   (D) The organization is not currently offering internships.

144. Why should Ms. Leathers contact Ayesha Chandran?

   (A) To arrange for a training session
   (B) To secure work documents
   (C) To participate in an opinion poll
   (D) To acquire further information about an opportunity

145. In the second letter, the word "positive" in line 4 is closest in meaning to

   (A) convinced
   (B) plausible
   (C) optimistic
   (D) absolute

Day

03

1. 접속사와 전치사

| 유형 1 | **부사절 접속사 vs. 전치사** ★★★★ |

부사절 접속사와 전치사 중에서 빈칸에 들어갈 정답을 고르는 문제이다. 종속접속사는 절(주어 + 동사)을 이끌고, 전치사는 명사(구)나 동명사를 목적어로 가진다. 그러므로 빈칸 뒤에 '주어 + 동사' 구조가 있는지 확인하고, 보기의 단어가 접속사인지 전치사인지도 구별해야 한다. 아래 표에 있는 단어의 의미나 품사를 꼭 기억하자!

의미	접속사 (+절)	전치사 (+목적어)
양보	although, even though, though, even if	despite, in spite of, notwithstanding (~에도 불구하고)
시간	while, when, as soon as, by the time, as, since, before, after, until, every time, whenever, at the time(~한 때에)	during, over, throughout(~ 내내), amid(~의 한창 때에), prior to(~ 전에), following(~ 후에), as of (~일자로), effective(~ 현재), beginning/starting(~부(附)로), since, before, after, until
이유	because, since, as, now (that)	because of, due to, owing to(~ 때문에), on account of(~ 때문에), according to(~에 따르면)
조건	if, in case (that)(~할 경우에 대비해서), in the event (that), as long as, as far as, insofar as[inasmuch as](~하는 한), once, unless, provided (that)(~라면), considering[given] (that) (~을 고려[감안]하면)	in case of, in the event of, with, without, but for(~이 없다면, ~이 없었더라면), except (for), barring(~가 없다면), excluding(~을 제외하고), apart from[aside from/besides](~ 외에도) considering[given](~을 고려하면)
양태	as if[though](마치 ~인 것처럼)	like, unlike, such as
기타	while(~인 반면), whereas(~인 반면), whether[if]	about[on/over/concerning/regarding](~에 대해), as(~로서)

★접속사로 착각하면 안 되는 부사 therefore, nevertheless(그럼에도 불구하고), however, moreover, furthermore, instead, otherwise(그렇지 않으면), regardless(개의치 않고), in the meantime[meanwhile](그 동안에), afterward(그 후에), accordingly(그에 따라), then, thus, rather, as well

– 위 단어들을 접속사로 착각하는 경우가 많은데, 모두 부사이다. '부사절 접속사 vs. 전치사' 유형의 문제에서 선택지 한두 개는 부사가 나오므로 확실히 암기하고, 부사는 항상 오답이므로 제외하고 시작하자!

Ex 1. ------- the researchers all employed special instruments for the experiment, they were not able to obtain any satisfactory outcomes.

(A) Despite
(B) Regarding
(C) Although
(D) In spite

(A) 전치사, (B) 전치사, (C) 접속사이다. 빈칸 뒤 the researchers all employed만 보면 된다. '주어 + 동사'로 앞에 접속사가 들어가야 하므로 (C)가 정답이다. (D)는 in spite of 형태로만 사용되며, 이런 보기는 수험자를 헷갈리게 하는 것이므로 주의해야 한다.

어휘 employ 쓰다, 사용하다 instrument 기구, 도구 obtain 얻다 satisfactory 만족할 만한 outcome 결과
해석 연구원들이 모두 실험을 위해 특별한 기구를 사용했음에도 불구하고 만족할 만한 결과는 전혀 얻을 수 없었다.

Ex 2. ------- the two-day conference, the heads of state were able to come to an accord to advance closer economic and social integration.

(A) During
(B) While
(C) Unless
(D) Furthermore

(A) 전치사 (B) 접속사 (C) 접속사 (D) 부사이다. 부사는 일단 제외하고 시작한다. 빈칸 뒤에 명사구인 the two-day conference가 있으므로 전치사 (A)가 정답이다.

어휘 head of state 국가수반[원수] come to an accord 합의에 이르다 advance 진전시키다 close 긴밀한, 밀접한 integration 통합
해석 이틀간의 회의에서 국가수반들은 더 긴밀한 경제, 사회적 통합을 진전시키자는 합의에 도달할 수 있었다.

유형 2 분사 구문을 활용한 문제 ★

이 유형은 오답률이 높다. 예문을 통해 부사절을 분사 구문으로 변환하는 과정을 이해하고 잘 기억해 두자.

❶   ❷
Before you use the equipment, you have to read the manual carefully.

❶ 접속사 빼기
❷ 부사절의 주어(you)와 주절의 주어(you)가 동일하면, 부사절의 주어 빼기
❸ 부사절의 동사를 현재분사로 바꾸기

= **Using** the equipment, you have to read the manual carefully. (1)

하나 더 해보자.

❶   ❷
Children are free of charge when they are accompanied by an adult.

❶ 접속사 빼기
❷ 부사절의 주어(they)가 주절의 주어(Children)와 동일하면, 부사절의 주어(they) 빼기
❸ 부사절의 동사를 현재분사로 바꾸기

= Children are free of charge, **being accompanied** by an adult.

＊분사 구문이 being으로 시작하는 경우 대부분 being도 생략한다.

= Children are free of charge, **accompanied** by an adult. (2)

(1)과 (2)는 완성된 분사 구문이다. 문맥에 따라 생략된 접속사를 추측해야 한다. 아래 (1)′이나 (2)′처럼 명확한 의미를 위해 분사 구문 앞에 접속사를 넣기도 한다. 분사 구문 앞에 시간 접속사(when, after, before)나 양보 접속사(though, although)가 있는 경우가 많고, 이유 접속사(because, since, as)나 that을 포함하는 접속사(provided that, considering that), as if, as though는 잘 사용하지 않는다.

(1)′ Before **using** the equipment, you have to read the manual carefully.

(2)′ Children are free of charge when **accompanied** by an adult.

시험에서는 분사 구문 앞 접속사 자리에 빈칸을 주는데, 이때 빈칸 뒤에 '주어 + 동사'의 구조가 없다고 해서 전치사를 선택하면 안 된다. 빈칸에는 접속사가 정답이다.

Ex 3. Sopot Tech's latest running shoes earned enthusiastic responses ------- tested by a group of professional athletes.

(A) when
(B) are
(C) this
(D) from

빈칸에 (B)를 넣으면 are tested라는 수동태 동사가 생기지만 앞에 동사 earned가 있어서 또 쓸 수는 없다. (C)는 문법이나 의미상으로 설명이 불가능하다. 따라서 접속사 (A)나 전치사 (D) 중 정답을 골라야 하는데, 빈칸 뒤에 분사 구문 tested by a group of professional athletes가 있으므로 접속사 (A)가 정답이다.

어휘 latest 최신의 earn 얻다 enthusiastic 열렬한, 열광적인 athlete 운동선수

해석 Sopot Tech의 최신 운동화는 프로 운동선수 한 그룹이 테스트했을 때 열광적인 반응을 얻었다.

Ex 4. Anton Silva was recognized with the Employee of the Month award after ------- twelve cars in just one month.

(A) was selling
(B) to have sold
(C) had sold
(D) having sold

빈칸 앞의 after는 접속사와 전치사로 모두 사용할 수 있다. after가 전치사라면 전치사의 목적어가 되는 동명사 (D)가 정답이다. after가 접속사라면 뒤에 '주어 + 동사'가 와야 하는데, 보기를 보면 주어가 없다. 이때 이 문장은 분사 구문으로 빈칸에 분사가 들어간다는 것을 떠올리자. after의 두 가지 용법을 모두 설명할 수 있는 현재분사 (D)가 정답이다.

어휘 be recognized with (공로를 인정받아) ～를 받다

해석 Anton Silva는 한 달 만에 12대의 자동차를 판매한 후 '이달의 직원' 상을 받았다.

유형 3 **상관접속사** ★★

상관접속사 문제는 함께 쓰는 단어만 찾아내면 된다. 문제를 보자마자 정답을 선택할 수 있도록 짝을 지어 암기하고 문제 풀이도 충분히 연습해 두자.

either A or B	**no sooner A than B** A 하자마자 B 하다
neither A nor B	**so + 형용사/부사 + that절**
both A and B	**such + (a/an) + (형용사) + 명사 + that절**
between A and B	**so (that) + S + can[may/will] + V**
not only A but also B	
whether A or B[or not]	＊빈칸 뒤에 'S + can[may/will] + V'가 있으면 언제나
would rather A than B	so (that)가 정답이다.

Ex 5. We must devise strategies either to cut costs
------- to increase employee productivity
promptly.

(A) nor
(B) and
(C) or
(D) than

보기를 보자마자 상관접속사 문제라는 것을 알 수 있다. 빈칸 앞을 보고 짝을 이루어 함께 쓰는 표현을 찾아내자. either가 있으므로 (C)가 정답이다.

어휘 devise 고안하다, 창안하다 strategy 전략, 계획 employee productivity 직원 생산성 promptly 바로, 즉시

해석 우리는 비용을 절감하거나 직원 생산성을 향상하기 위한 전략을 즉시 고안해야 한다.

Ex 6. The motor companies neither criticized -------
endorsed the amended regulations of carbon
dioxide emissions.

(A) or
(B) and
(C) nor
(D) but

보기를 보자마자 상관접속사 문제라는 것을 알 수 있다. 빈칸 앞에 neither가 있으므로 짝이 되는 (C)가 정답이다.

어휘 criticize 비판하다 endorse (공개적으로) 지지하다 amend 개정하다, 수정하다 regulation 규정, 규제 carbon dioxide 이산화탄소
emission (빛·열·가스 등의) 배출

해석 자동차 회사들은 개정된 이산화탄소 배출 규제를 비판하지도 지지하지도 않았다.

Ex 7. Ms. Chen must decide ------- or not to submit
the proposal to the manager of the Buenos
Aires office.

(A) whether
(B) neither
(C) either
(D) unless

보기를 살펴보면 상관접속사 문제라는 것을 알 수 있다. 빈칸 바로 뒤에 있는 or not과 짝이 되는 (A)를 정답으로 선택해야 한다.

어휘 submit 제출하다 proposal 기획안

해석 Ms. Chen은 Buenos Aires 지사장에게 기획안을 제출할지 말지 결정해야 한다.

Ex 8. The trade balance, which measures the difference ------- a nation's imports and exports of goods, reported a marginal surplus of $1.03 billion in June.

(A) not only
(B) either
(C) between
(D) among

빈칸 앞뒤 the difference ------- a nation's imports and exports of goods를 보면서 정답을 알아내야 한다. imports and exports에 주목하고 and와 짝이 되는 (C)를 선택하자.

어휘 trade balance 무역 수지 measure 측정하다 report 기록하다 marginal 미미한, 주변부의 surplus 흑자, 잉여

해석 국가의 상품 수입과 수출의 차이를 측정하는 무역 수지가 6월에 10억 3천만 달러의 소폭 흑자를 기록했다.

Ex 9. The doctors in some hospitals are ------- pressed for time that their treatment of patients is rushed and of poor quality.

(A) such
(B) both
(C) so
(D) whether

빈칸 앞뒤 are ------- pressed for time that을 보면 'so + 형용사/부사 +that절' 구조임을 알 수 있다. 짝을 지어 함께 쓰는 표현을 기억하고 (C)를 정답으로 선택하자.

어휘 pressed for ~이 부족한, ~에 쫓기는 treatment 치료 rushed 서두른, 성급히 한 of poor quality 질이 나쁜

해석 일부 병원의 의사들은 시간에 너무 쫓겨서 환자 치료가 성급히 이루어지고 질이 나쁘다.

Ex 10. Navona Industries introduced the latest scheduling software ------- employees could record their work hours more easily and quickly.

(A) so that
(B) if
(C) which
(D) due to

빈칸 뒤 employees could record를 보고 정답을 알아내자. '------- + S + can[may/will] + V'가 있으면 항상 so (that)이 정답이다.

어휘 introduce 도입하다 due to ~ 때문에

해석 Navona Industries는 직원들이 더 쉽고 빠르게 근무 시간을 기록할 수 있도록 최신 일정 관리 소프트웨어를 도입했다.

Ex 11. The CEO would rather spend his vacation taking a walking tour of the historic city ------- stay at a comfortable hotel.

(A) when
(B) than
(C) both
(D) so

빈칸 앞부분에 would rather가 있는 것을 보고 짝이 되는 (B)를 선택해야 한다.

어휘 take a tour 둘러보다, 견학하다 historic 역사적인, 역사가 깊은

해석 CEO는 편안한 호텔에 머무르기보다는 역사적인 도시를 도보로 둘러보며 휴가를 보내고 싶어 한다.

2. 대명사 1

대명사 문제는 (1) 인칭대명사의 격, (2) 인칭대명사의 수와 성, (3) 지시대명사 those와 anyone, (4) 지시대명사 that 과 those에 대한 문제가 출제된다. 먼저 '인칭대명사의 격'에 대해 살펴본 후, 다음 장에서 나머지 부분을 공부해 보자.

(1) 인칭대명사의 격 ★★★★

> **유형 1** ──────── + 명사
>
> 명사 앞 빈칸에는 소유격 대명사가 정답이다. 대명사 문제로는 이 유형이 가장 많이 출제된다.

Ex 1. Employees are expected to provide ------- direct supervisor with 24 hours' notice of any planned absences.

(A) theirs
(B) their
(C) them
(D) they

빈칸 앞뒤 to provide ------- direct supervisor에서 정답을 알아내자. 명사 앞에 빈칸이 있으므로 소유격인 (B)가 정답이다.

어휘 be expected to-V ~할 것으로 기대되다, ~해야 한다 direct supervisor 직속 상사 24 hours' notice 24시간 전 통보 absence 결근

해석 직원은 예정된 어떤 결근이든 24시간 전에 직속 상사에게 통보해야 한다.

> **유형 2** ──────── + 동사
>
> 동사 앞 빈칸은 주어 자리이므로 대부분 주격 대명사가 정답이다. 그러나 매우 드물게 소유대명사가 정답인 경우도 있다. 빈칸 앞부분에 '소유격 + 명사'가 있을 때 소유대명사가 정답이다.

Ex 2. Not only is Edwin Hughes the producer of many best-selling recordings, but ------- is also an acclaimed guitarist.

(A) he
(B) his
(C) him
(D) himself

빈칸 뒤에 동사 is가 있으므로 빈칸은 주어 자리이고, 주격 (A)와 소유대명사 (B) 중에서 고르면 된다. 빈칸의 앞부분에 소유대명사가 대신할 수 있는 '소유격 + 명사'가 없으므로 주격 (A)가 정답이다.

어휘 producer 제작자 recording 녹음된[녹화된] 것 acclaimed 호평받는

해석 Edwin Hughes는 많은 베스트셀러 음반의 제작자일 뿐만 아니라 호평받는 기타리스트이기도 하다.

Ex 3. Whereas Ms. Jackson's study dealt with consumer spending generally, ------- focuses more specifically on purchasing trends among 18- to 23-year-olds.

(A) I
(B) my
(C) me
(D) mine

빈칸이 주어 자리이므로 주격 (A)나 소유대명사 (D)에서 선택하면 된다. "Ms. Jackson의 연구는 ~인 반면 나의 연구는 ~이다"라는 의미의 문장이므로 my study에서 명사 study가 중복되지 않도록 소유대명사 (D)를 사용해야 한다. 이처럼 대부분 문장 앞부분에 '소유격 + 명사(Ms. Jackson's study)'가 있으면 소유대명사가 정답이 된다.

어휘 deal with ~을 다루다 consumer spending 소비자 지출 specifically 구체적으로 purchasing trend 구매 경향

해석 Ms. Jackson의 연구는 소비자 지출을 일반적으로 다루었지만, 나의 연구는 더 구체적으로 18세에서 23세 사이의 구매 경향에 초점을 맞춘다.

유형 3 타동사 / 전치사 + -------

타동사와 전치사 뒤에는 목적어가 필요하므로 빈칸에는 목적격 대명사가 대부분 정답이지만, 소유대명사와 재귀대명사도 정답이 될 수 있다. 목적어 자리가 빈칸인 경우 목적격 대명사, 소유대명사, 재귀대명사가 모두 보기에 나올 수 있으므로, 문장 앞부분을 잘 읽어 보고 선택해야 한다.

3-1 빈칸 앞부분에서 '소유격 + 명사'가 있으면 보이면 대부분 소유대명사가 정답이다.

Ex 4. His approach to work is like -------, apart from the fact that he uses his own program to process data.

(A) me
(B) myself
(C) mine
(D) my

빈칸에 전치사 like의 목적어가 들어가야 하므로 목적격 (A)와 소유대명사 (C), 재귀대명사 (B)가 모두 들어갈 수 있다. 그러나 문장 앞부분에 His approach to work(소유격 + 명사)가 있으므로 소유대명사 (C)를 정답으로 선택하자. 빈칸에 들어갈 말은 my approach to work이지만 명사(구)의 중복을 피하기 위해 소유대명사를 사용한다.

어휘 approach to ~에 대한 접근법 apart from ~외에는, ~을 제외하고

해석 업무에 대한 그의 접근법은 자신이 만든 프로그램을 사용해서 데이터를 처리한다는 사실을 제외하면 나와 같다.

3-2 '행위의 주체'와 목적어가 동일한 대상인 경우 목적어 자리에는 재귀대명사를 사용한다. '행위의 주체'는 대부분 문장의 주어이지만, 항상 그렇지는 않으므로 문장의 의미를 정확하게 이해해야 한다.

Ex 5. Following the budget cuts, we found ------- struggling to get all the paperwork done without any assistants.

(A) we
(B) ourselves
(C) us
(D) our

동사 found의 목적어가 필요하므로 빈칸에는 목적격 (C)와 재귀대명사 (B)가 모두 들어갈 수 있다. 그러나 보기가 모두 we의 변화형인 것을 보면, 동사 found의 목적어가 행위의 주체인 we와 같은 사람임을 알 수 있다. 그러므로 재귀대명사인 (B)가 정답이다.

어휘 following ~후에, ~에 따라 budget cut 예산 삭감 struggle to-V ~하느라 애쓰다 get ~ done ~를 끝내다 assistant 조수, 보조

해석 예산 삭감 이후 우리는 보조 직원도 없이 모든 서류 작업을 끝내느라 애를 먹었다.

Ex 6. Medical experts advise that double coats of sunscreen, headgear, and long-sleeved clothes will not completely protect ------- from the scorching sun.

(A) you
(B) your
(C) yours
(D) yourself

빈칸에 동사 protect의 목적어가 있어야 하므로 목적격인 (A)와 소유대명사 (C), 재귀대명사 (D)가 모두 들어갈 수 있다. 그런데 문장 앞부분에 '소유격 + 명사' 표현이 없으므로 소유대명사인 (C)는 제외하자. 행위 protect의 주체는 double coats of sunscreen, headgear and long-sleeved clothes이고, 보기를 보면 행위의 주체가 목적어와 같은 사람이 아니다. 그러므로 목적격 (A)를 정답으로 선택한다.

어휘 coat 칠, 층 sunscreen 자외선 차단제 headgear 쓸 것, 모자 long-sleeved 긴 소매의 scorching 타는 듯한, 몹시 더운

해석 의료 전문가들은 두 겹의 선크림, 모자, 긴팔 옷이 뙤약볕으로부터 당신을 완전히 보호하지는 못할 것이라고 조언한다.

유형 4 **by + -------**

by 뒤에 빈칸이 있으면 무조건 재귀대명사가 정답이다. 'by+재귀대명사'는 '혼자서, 자기 힘으로'라는 뜻으로 사용한다.

Ex 7. Ms. Chu had to finish this statistical analysis by -------, because her assistant was on sick leave.

(A) she
(B) hers
(C) herself
(D) her

전치사 by의 목적어가 될 대명사를 선택해야 하므로 목적격 (D)와 소유대명사 (B), 재귀대명사 (C)가 모두 빈칸에 들어갈 수 있다. 그런데 보기를 보면 동사(구)인 had to finish의 주체인 Ms. Chu가 by의 목적어와 같은 사람임을 알 수 있다. 따라서 재귀대명사 (C)가 정답이다. 시험에 by -------가 자주 출제되므로, by 다음에 빈칸이 오면 재귀대명사를 정답으로 선택하자.

어휘 statistical 통계의 analysis 분석 on sick leave 병가 중인

해석 Ms. Chu는 비서가 병가 중이었기 때문에 혼자 이 통계 분석을 마무리해야 했다.

유형 5 **완성된 문장 + -------**

완성된 구조의 문장에 빈칸이 있을 때, 즉 부사 자리에는 재귀대명사가 정답이다. 부사 문제로도 자주 출제되는 '타동사 + 목적어 + -------'나 '주어 + ------- + 동사'의 형태로 출제된다.

Ex 8. Mr. Song has not been able to examine the proposal -------, although it has been on his desk for the past three days.

    (A) him
    (B) himself
    (C) his
    (D) he

빈칸 앞 has not been able to examine the proposal을 보면서 정답을 알아내자. 3형식 문장이 완성되어 있으므로 재귀대명사 (B)가 정답이다.

어휘 examine 검토하다 proposal 기획안

해석 기획안이 지난 3일 동안 책상 위에 있었지만, Mr. Song은 직접 검토할 수 없었다.

Ex 9. The Restoration Society president Kathleen Crowther ------- greeted guests at the fundraising event.

    (A) she
    (B) her
    (C) herself
    (D) hers

빈칸 앞뒤 The Restoration Society president Kathleen Crowther ------- greeted에서 정답을 알아내자. 부사 자리가 빈칸인 '주어 + ------- + 동사'와 같은 완성된 문장이면 재귀대명사 (C)를 정답으로 선택해야 한다.

어휘 restoration 복구, 복원 society 협회, 학회 greet 맞이하다 fundraising 모금

해석 복원협회 회장 Kathleen Crowther가 직접 기금 마련 행사에서 손님들을 맞이했다.

유형 6　a(n) + 명사 + of + -------

'내 친구 한 명'이라는 표현은 a my friend가 아니라 a friend of mine을 사용한다. 관사나 소유격 대명사와 같은 한정사는 단독으로만 사용하고 두 개를 연달아 쓰지 않는다. 시험 문제는 'a friend of -------'와 같은 형태로 출제된다. 'a(n) + 명사 + of + -------'가 있으면 소유대명사를 정답으로 선택하자.

Ex 10. I have decided to participate in the workshop for team leaders at the recommendation of a longtime colleague of -------.

    (A) me
    (B) mine
    (C) myself
    (D) my

a longtime colleague of -------를 보면 'a(n) + 명사 + of + -------' 구조임을 알 수 있다. 그렇다면 소유대명사가 정답임을 기억하고 (B)를 정답으로 선택해야 한다.

어휘 at the recommendation of ~의 추천으로 longtime 오랜

해석 나는 오랜 동료 중 한 사람의 추천으로 팀장들을 위한 워크숍에 참석하기로 했다.

------- + 명사

명사 앞에 빈칸이 있으면 소유격이 정답이지만, 보기 중 소유격이 없을 때에는 one's own이 정답이다. own 은 소유격 one's를 강조하는 형용사이다.

Ex 11. Previously employed by Richard Allen Pharmaceuticals, Jennifer Johnson started ------- pharmaceutical company five years ago.

(A) she
(B) hers
(C) her own
(D) herself

빈칸 앞뒤 started ------- pharmaceutical company를 보고 정답을 알아내자. 명사 앞 빈칸에는 주로 소유격이 오지만, 이 문제에서 처럼 보기 중 소유격이 없을 때는 one's own 인 (C)가 정답이다.

어휘 previously 전에 employ 고용하다, 종사하다 pharmaceutical 제약; 제약의

해석 이전에 Richard Allen 제약에서 근무했던 Jennifer Johnson은 5년 전에 자신의 제약회사를 시작했다.

유형 8 **명사 + of + -------**

one's own은 of와 함께 사용하기도 하는데, 이때는 명사 뒤에서 소유의 의미를 강조한다. '명사 + of + -------'이 있다면 one's own을 정답으로 선택하자.

Ex 12. Instead of purchasing a new software program for record-keeping, the accountants decided to design one of -------.

(A) their
(B) they
(C) their own
(D) themselves

one of -------을 보면서 '명사 + of + -------'를 기억하면 항상 one's own이 정답임을 알 수 있으므로 (C)를 선택해야 한다.

어휘 record-keeping 기록 관리 accountant 회계사

해석 회계사들은 기록 관리를 위해 새 소프트웨어 프로그램을 구매하는 대신 자신들만의 프로그램을 설계하기로 했다.

앞에서 by 뒤에 빈칸이 있으면 항상 재귀대명사가 정답이라는 사실을 알았다. 이번에는 on 뒤에 빈칸이 있으면 항상 one's own이 정답이라는 것을 기억하자. by oneself와 on one's own의 의미는 '혼자서, 도움을 받지 않고'이다.

Ex 13. Addressing customer concerns is sometimes difficult to do on -------, so we have added a frequently asked questions page to our Web site.

(A) yours
(B) yourself
(C) your own
(D) you

on -------가 있으면 바로 one's own을 선택하자. 따라서 (C)가 정답이다.

어휘 address 다루다, 해결하려 하다 concern 관심사, 우려

해석 고객 우려 사항을 다루는 것이 때로는 혼자 하기 어려워서 우리는 '자주 묻는 질문' 페이지를 웹사이트에 추가했다.

101. Successful candidates for this position should have at least three years of working experience in a related field ------- strong academic credentials.

(A) otherwise
(B) in addition to
(C) meanwhile
(D) even though

102. Please notify Ms. Kobayashi that ------- visit to the Osaka office has been postponed until February 20.

(A) my
(B) me
(C) myself
(D) mine

103. The customers who are picking up the rental vehicle should be told that ------- is the white minivan.

(A) their
(B) theirs
(C) they
(D) themselves

104. Please e-mail Mr. Mori to let ------- know when he can expect you in Tokyo.

(A) he
(B) him
(C) himself
(D) his own

105. As ------- in the lease agreement, one of the maintenance team members will respond to every service request submitted online or by phone within 2 hours.

(A) notes
(B) note
(C) noted
(D) notation

106. Ms. Yang has requested the use of a company car from the airport to the new manufacturing plant for ------- and two clients this Thursday.

(A) her
(B) she
(C) herself
(D) hers

107. Moon Micro Systems has been a major client of ------- for over 15 years in the Asia-Pacific region.

(A) us
(B) our
(C) we
(D) ours

108. Mr. Kowalski will meet us for the initial consultation this afternoon, ------- his flight is not delayed.

(A) according to
(B) as well as
(C) as long as
(D) apart from

109. To meet the deadline for the presentation at Monday's executive meeting, Mr. Kim completed the market research report by ------- over the weekend.

(A) he
(B) him
(C) himself
(D) his own

110. Mr. Sarrafan has enrolled in a business management program to pursue the goal of establishing a venture of ------- in the long run.

(A) him
(B) himself
(C) his own
(D) his

111. The soccer tournament was -------
a popular event in the region that
the stadiums were always packed on
match days.

(A) so
(B) huge
(C) such
(D) too

112. Blue Heron Paper Company
encourages its staff members to
take responsibility for ------- training
schedules.

(A) they
(B) them
(C) themselves
(D) their own

113. Director Angela Lane will be
interviewing the final candidates for the
manager position -------.

(A) herself
(B) she
(C) hers
(D) her

114. The South America team has already
submitted its sales projection report,
but we haven't completed ------- yet.

(A) we
(B) us
(C) ours
(D) our

115. Mark Walker maintained that he
possessed the necessary expertise
to complete the translation of all the
documents on -------.

(A) him
(B) himself
(C) his own
(D) his

3. Not / True 문제

빈출 질문 유형

What is true about ~?

What is indicated about ~?

What does Mr. Dalton indicate in his e-mail?

What is NOT mentioned as ~?

What is NOT provided in ~?

• 문제 풀이 전략

질문에 NOT을 포함한 틀린 내용 찾기 문제는 오답률이 높다. 보기 네 개를 각각 지문과 대조해서 없는 내용을 파악해야 해서 시간이 오래 걸리며, 대부분의 보기가 지문 내용을 패러프레이즈한 것이기 때문에 풀이가 쉽지 않다. 토익 문제는 무조건 빨리 풀어야 하지만 이 유형은 시간을 길게 잡자. 서두르다 지문에서 보기의 내용을 확인하지 못하면 틀리기 쉽다.

Examples 1-3 refer to the following article.

Highfields Capital Purchases Barrière Group

Highfields Capital, a leading Canadian investment firm, announced today that it has completed its long-anticipated acquisition of Barrière Group, a Paris-based hotel company. According to Highfields Capital executives, the transaction has an estimated value of 500 million euros.

The French-owned Barrière Group's transition to Canadian ownership has been met with a great deal of controversy in France; Barrière Group owns 20 historic hotels in Paris and the surrounding areas, including the famous Hôtel Jules Cesar, which had hosted numerous prominent nineteenth-century French authors and political figures. Jonathon Jacobson, owner of Highfields Capital, announced that his firm would strive to retain the important historic heritage of the Hôtel Jules Cesar but would carry out the necessary renovations to modernize the heating and plumbing systems. In addition to the Hôtel Jules Cesar, Barrière Group owns smaller hotels across France, including La Citadelle Metz and the Hôtel Cabourg, both of which are considered to be among the finest examples of French architecture in the neoclassic style.

Mr. Jacobson said that his firm purchased the Barrière Group as a means of diversifying its portfolio. He intends to make further investments in Europe, with the potentiality of acquiring luxury accommodations in Germany, Luxembourg, and Austria. Highfields Capital has also recently added to their holdings with the procurement of multiple high-rise apartment and office blocks located in Singapore and Indonesia.

Ex 1. According to the article, why has the sale of the Barrière Group been considered controversial?

(A) It was disposed of for a lesser amount than predicted.
(B) Historic French properties were being acquired by a foreign enterprise.
(C) Employees of the Barrière Group are expected to laid off.
(D) The sale was not disclosed to the public until it had been settled.

Ex 2. What is Highfields Capital's announced plan for the Hôtel Jules Cesar?

(A) To operate it as a budget hotel
(B) To construct apartments on the property
(C) To make improvements to certain facilities
(D) To convert it into a historical museum

Ex 3. What kind of property is NOT mentioned as a recent acquisition of Highfields Capital?

(A) Apartments
(B) Office buildings
(C) Historic hotels
(D) Retail stores

해설

Examples 1-3 refer to the following article.

1-3번 예제는 다음 기사에 관한 것입니다.

Highfields Capital Purchases Barrière Group

Highfields Capital, a leading Canadian investment firm, announced today that it has completed its long-anticipated acquisition of Barrière Group, a Paris-based hotel company. According to Highfields Capital executives, the transaction has an estimated value of 500 million euros.

Ex1.Ex3.The French-owned Barrière Group's transition to Canadian ownership has been met with a great deal of controversy in France; Barrière Group owns 20 historic hotels in Paris and the surrounding areas, including the famous Hôtel Jules Cesar, which had hosted numerous prominent nineteenth-century French authors and political figures. Ex2.Jonathon Jacobson, owner of Highfields Capital, announced that his firm would strive to retain the important historic heritage of the Hôtel Jules Cesar

Highfields, Barrière 그룹을 사들이다

캐나다의 일류 투자 회사 Highfields 캐피탈은 오늘 오랫동안 고대하던 파리에 본사를 둔 호텔 기업인 Barrière 그룹의 인수를 마무리했다고 발표했다. Highfields 캐피탈 중역들의 말에 따르면 이 거래는 5억 유로의 가치로 추정된다.

프랑스 소유의 Barrière 그룹이 캐나다 소유로 전환되면서 프랑스에서 많은 논란에 직면해 있다. Barrière 그룹은 파리와 주변 지역에서 20개의 역사적인 호텔을 소유하고 있는데, 그중에는 유명한 Jules Cesar 호텔이 있으며, 수많은 19세기 프랑스의 저명한 작가들과 정치인들이 머물렀다. Highfields 캐피탈의 소유주 Jonathon Jacobson은 자신의 회사가 Jules Cesar 호텔의 중요한 역사 유산을 유지하기 위해 애쓰겠지만,

but would carry out the necessary renovations to modernize the heating and plumbing systems. In addition to the Hôtel Jules Cesar, Barrière Group owns smaller hotels across France, including La Citadelle Metz and the Hôtel Cabourg, both of which are considered to be among the finest examples of French architecture in the neoclassic style.

Mr. Jacobson said that his firm purchased the Barrière Group as a means of diversifying its portfolio. He intends to make further investments in Europe, with the potentiality of acquiring luxury accommodations in Germany, Luxembourg, and Austria. ^{Ex3.}Highfields Capital has also recently added to their holdings with the procurement of multiple high-rise apartment and office blocks located in Singapore and Indonesia.

필요한 보수 공사를 해서 난방 및 배관 장치를 현대화할 것이라고 발표했다. Jules Cesar 호텔 외에도 Barrière 그룹은 프랑스 전역에 걸쳐 더 작은 호텔들도 소유하고 있는데, 그중에는 La Citadelle Metz와 the Cabourg 호텔이 있으며, 두 곳 모두 신고전주의 프랑스 건축 양식의 가장 좋은 예로 여겨진다.

Mr. Jacobson은 자신의 회사가 포트폴리오를 다각화하는 수단으로 Barrière 그룹을 인수했다고 말했다. 그는 유럽 내에 추가로 투자할 생각인데, 독일과 룩셈부르크, 오스트리아의 호화 숙박 시설들을 인수할 가능성이 있다. Highfields 캐피탈은 또한 최근에 싱가포르와 인도네시아에 있는 고층 아파트와 사무실 건물들을 매입함으로써 자산을 늘리기도 했다.

어휘 leading 일류의 acquisition (기업) 인수 based ~에 본사를 둔 executive 임원, 이사, 중역 transaction 거래, 매매 estimated 추정되는 transition 이행, 전환, 변화 ownership 소유(권) be met with ~에 직면하다 a great deal of 많은 controversy 논란 surrounding 주변의 host 접대하다, 묵게 하다 prominent 저명한, 유력한 figure 인물, 저명인사 strive to-V 힘껏 노력하다, 애쓰다 retain 유지하다 heritage 유산, 전통 carry out ~을 수행하다 renovation 보수, 수리 plumbing 배관 architecture 건축 neoclassic 신고전주의의 as a means of ~의 수단으로 diversify 다각화하다 potentiality 가능성, 잠재력 accommodation 숙박 시설 add to ~을 늘리다 holding 보유 자산 procurement 획득, 입수 high-rise 고층의 block 건물, 빌딩

Ex 1. According to the article, why has the sale of the Barrière Group been considered controversial?

(A) It was disposed of for a lesser amount than predicted.
(B) Historic French properties were being acquired by a foreign enterprise.
(C) Employees of the Barrière Group are expected to be laid off.
(D) The sale was not disclosed to the public until it had been settled.

기사에 따르면, 왜 Barrière 그룹의 매각이 논란이 되고 있는가?

(A) 예상보다 더 적은 금액에 처분되었다.
(B) 역사적인 프랑스의 건물들이 외국 기업에 의해 매입되었다.
(C) Barrière 그룹의 직원들은 정리 해고될 것으로 예상된다.
(D) 매각은 마무리될 때까지 대중에게 공개되지 않았다.

어휘 dispose of ~을 처분하다, 매각하다 predict 예상하다 property 부동산, 재산 enterprise 기업, 회사 lay off ~를 (정리) 해고하다 disclose 밝히다, 공개하다 settle 결정하다, 정리하다

해설 둘째 문단에서 프랑스 소유의 Barrière 그룹이 캐나다 소유로의 전환은 프랑스 내에서 많은 논란에 직면해 있다는(The French-owned Barrière Group's transition to Canadian ownership has been met with a great deal of controversy in France) 내용 뒤에 부연 설명으로 Barrière 그룹이 역사적으로 큰 의의를 지니는 호텔들을 다수 소유하고 있다는 내용이 있다.(Barrière Group owns 20 historic hotels ... and political figures.)

Ex 2. What is Highfields Capital's announced plan for the Hôtel Jules Cesar?

(A) To operate it as a budget hotel
(B) To construct apartments on the property
(C) To make improvements to certain facilities
(D) To convert it into a historical museum

Highfields 캐피탈이 발표한 Jules Cesar 호텔에 대한 계획은 무엇인가?

(A) 저가 호텔로 운영하기
(B) 부지에 아파트 건설하기
(C) 일부 시설 개선하기
(D) 역사 박물관으로 전환하기

어휘 operate 운영하다 budget 저가의, 저렴한 construct 건설하다 facility 시설 convert A into B A를 B로 전환하다

해설 둘째 문단에 나오는 Jonathon Jacobson이 호텔의 역사적 유산은 유지될 것이지만, 개조 공사를 통해 난방 및 배관 시스템은 현대화될 것이라고(Jonathon Jacobson, owner of Highfields Capital, announced that ... to modernize the heating and plumbing systems) 말하는 내용이 있다.

Ex 3. What kind of property is NOT mentioned as a recent acquisition of Highfields Capital?

(A) Apartments
(B) Office buildings
(C) Historic hotels
(D) Retail stores

어떤 종류의 건물이 Highfields 캐피탈의 최근 매입물로 언급되지 않는가?

(A) 아파트
(B) 사무실 건물
(C) 역사적인 호텔
(D) 소매상점

해설 1번 예제를 풀었으므로 (C)를 제외하고 시작하자. 지문을 끝까지 읽으면 마지막 문장에서 Highfields Capital이 최근 아시아에서 고층 아파트와 사무실 건물들을 사들였다는(Highfields Capital has also recently added to their holdings with the procurement of multiple high-rise apartment and office blocks located in Singapore and Indonesia.) 사실을 알 수 있으므로 (A)와 (B)도 제외할 수 있다.

Today's Vocabulary

▶Actual Test를 풀기 전에 이 단어들을 암기하자.

짝을 이루어 출제되는 단어

- be [eligible / qualified] [to-V / for N]   ~할[의] 자격이 있다

- be [concerned / worried / anxious] about   ~에 대해 걱정하다

- [concerns / worries / anxiety] about   ~에 대한 걱정

- [handle / address] promptly   즉시 처리하다
- [deliver / answer / report] promptly   배달하다 / 대답하다 / 보고하다

- [promptly / exactly / precisely] at + 시각   정각 ~시에

- [promptly / shortly / immediately / rightly / soon / just] [after / afterward / thereafter]   직후에   before   직전에

regardless of ~에 상관없이
consequently 그 결과, 따라서
likewise 똑같이, 마찬가지로
subject matter 주제, 소재
consolidated (모회사와 자회사) 통합의
net profit 순(이)익
hi-tech 최첨단의
make sure that ~임을 확인하다
competitive 경쟁력 있는
comparable 비슷한, 비교할 만한
compatible 호환이 되는
existing 기존의, 현재 사용되는
factory floor (공장의) 작업 현장

alike 양쪽 모두, 둘 다 똑같이
cautiously 조심스럽게, 신중히
set sb/sth apart from ~를 ~과 차별화하다
budget surplus 재정 흑자
assembly 모임, 집회
compress 압축하다, 압축되다
prioritize 우선으로 처리하다
diminish 줄어들다; 약화되다
in advance 미리, 사전에
entry 출품작, 응모작
plan (건물 · 기계 등의) 도면
revise 수정하다
gift token 상품권

evaluate 평가하다, 감정하다

convene 소집하다

nominate (후보자로) 지명하다, 추천하다

redeem (상품권 등을) 현금[상품]으로 바꾸다

regarding ~에 관하여

tracking 추적

direct an inquiry to(ward) ~에게 문의하다

release 출시

compare with ~와 비교되다

coincide with 동시에 일어나다, 시기가 일치하다

virtual currency 가상 화폐

gain in popularity 인기가 많아지다

balance 잔고, 잔액

faulty 결함이 있는, 불완전한

sufficient 충분한

uneasy 불안한, 걱정되는

plumbing 배관 작업[공사]

welcome 반가운; 기쁜, 고마운

publicity 홍보, 광고

publicist 홍보 담당자

widely 널리, 폭넓게

recognized 인정된, 알려진

authority 권위자

authorization (공적인) 허가, 인가

quota (요구되거나 해야 할) 몫, 할당량

record 기록적인

initiative (특정 목적을 위한) 계획, 프로젝트

retreat 수련회, 캠프

interest (사업상의) 지분, 투자분

critical 결정적인, 중대한

component (구성) 요소

financing 자금 조달[공급]

erect 건립하다, 짓다, 세우다

subsequent 그 다음의, 차후의

phase 단계, 국면, 시기

set a precedent 전례를 세우다, 선례를 만들다

gratitude 고마움, 감사, 사의

coordinate 조정하다

effective 효과적인, 인상적인

graduate student 대학원생

faculty 교수진

commend 칭찬하다

polished (기교 등이) 세련된, 우아한

overview 개관, 개요

career opportunity 취업 전망

corporate Hong Kong 홍콩의 기업 환경

scrupulous 세심한, 꼼꼼한

launch 개시하다, 착수하다

keep -ing ~을 계속하다, 반복하다

beneficial 유익한, 이로운

generate 발생시키다, 만들어 내다

Actual Test

PART 5

1. 빈칸 앞뒤를 보며 문제를 푼다.
2. 빈칸 앞뒤를 보고 정답을 알 수 없다면 문장을 해석한다.
3. 두 줄 분량의 어휘 문제는 문장 전체를 해석해서 푼다.
4. 접속사 어휘 문제는 빈칸 앞뒤만을 보고 풀 수 없다. 문장 전체를 해석해 보자.

PART 6

1. 문법 문제라면 Part 5와 같은 방식으로 빈칸 앞뒤를 보며 푼다.
2. 다른 유형의 문제는 문맥을 통해 정답을 파악한다.

PART 7

1. 문제와 보기 (A), (B), (C), (D)를 먼저 읽은 후에 지문을 읽는다.
2. 지문 위아래의 모든 부분을 자세히 읽어 본다.
3. 문제의 해설을 꼼꼼히 읽고, 문장 구조를 분석하며 복습한다.

PART 5

101. Sandy Sawyer is so versatile a writer that his books are always among the best sellers ------- the subject matter.

(A) regardless of
(B) consequently
(C) in addition to
(D) likewise

102. Beximco Pharmaceuticals Ltd. reported a consolidated net profit of 106 million rupees last quarter, ------- it to fund its planned expansion.

(A) allowing
(B) allows
(C) allowance
(D) allowably

103. When he made his debut in the opera, Jose could hardly stand on his feet because of the anxiety ------- singing before the audience for the first time in his life.

(A) about
(B) at
(C) of
(D) with

104. Most computer engineering students at Saint Joseph College work as interns before getting ------- first professional job.

(A) them
(B) theirs
(C) their
(D) they

105. Before the new hi-tech devices are installed in the museum, the security team would first like to make sure that they are ------- with the existing security system.

(A) competitive
(B) comparable
(C) compatible
(D) comfortable

106. Mr. Frazier cannot attend today's board meeting but indicated that ------- would ask a colleague to take his place.

(A) him
(B) he
(C) his
(D) himself

107. New protective clothing will soon be available for use by factory floor workers and visitors -------.

(A) nearly
(B) quite
(C) alike
(D) cautiously

108. Sandra Contreras has set ------- apart from other candidates in the mayoral race by suggesting an amended version of the tax law to solve the city's financial crisis.

(A) herself
(B) her
(C) she
(D) hers

109. West Virginia ended the most recent fiscal year with an overall budget ------- of over 450 million dollars.

(A) surplus
(B) assembly
(C) launch
(D) committee

110. The newly released accounting software package will allow all our clients to perform regular payroll tasks by -------.

(A) they
(B) them
(C) theirs
(D) themselves

111. Mr. Park advises that the employees wait for the heavy snow to ------- before returning to the work site.

(A) compress
(B) anticipate
(C) prioritize
(D) diminish

112. Alice Steele was delighted to discover that a proposal of ------- was endorsed by the committee.

(A) she
(B) her
(C) hers
(D) herself

113. Kulula Airways advises passengers planning to travel during the peak tourist season to purchase tickets ------- in advance in order to ensure availability.

(A) very
(B) far
(C) so
(D) hardly

114. The marketing consultants have trained the service representatives of Kaltex Electronics, Inc., thoroughly to address any customer complaints -------.

(A) recently
(B) promptly
(C) convincingly
(D) steadily

115. Mr. Alvarado will return from vacation tomorrow, but the steering committee will not meet with ------- until next week.

(A) himself
(B) him
(C) his
(D) he

116. ------- all the entries for the Arcoda Times Photograph Contest have been received, they will be distributed among the judges for evaluation.

(A) Near
(B) Once
(C) How
(D) Yet

117. Mr. Vasquez developed the architectural plans for the Onishi Firm's office building ------- since the client required a complicated design.

(A) he
(B) his
(C) him
(D) himself

118. Please have ------- three tubes of revised posters delivered to our booth in the convention center by 8 A.M.

(A) many
(B) these
(C) other
(D) such

119. The supervisor notified them that all employees are ------- for seven days of sick leave per year after one full year of employment.

(A) approachable
(B) considerable
(C) eligible
(D) creditable

120. This gift token is valid at its full face value and can be ------- only by the recipient within domestic locations.

(A) evaluated
(B) convened
(C) nominated
(D) redeemed

121. Any inquiries regarding order tracking should be ------- to the New York office.

(A) directed
(B) recovered
(C) ensured
(D) allowed

122. The product release of Intrawest Company's new line of coats will ------- with the winter holidays.

(A) argue
(B) compare
(C) produce
(D) coincide

123. Technology experts predict that virtual currencies used for online commerce will continue to gain in -------.

(A) personality
(B) attitude
(C) balance
(D) popularity

124. Mr. Schmidt discovered that ------- plumbing was the cause of the clogged drain line.

(A) faulty
(B) patient
(C) sufficient
(D) uneasy

125. Mr. Rodriguez thinks that the article in *Cuanza Sul Times* will bring welcome ------- to the farm's greenhouse smart application project.

(A) publicize
(B) publicity
(C) publicist
(D) publicized

126. The panel discussion is set to begin ------- after the guest speaker wraps up his speech.

(A) promptly
(B) assertively
(C) especially
(D) cordially

127. Mira Lawson is a widely recognized ------- in the area of customer satisfaction and retention.

(A) authority
(B) authorized
(C) authorizing
(D) authorization

128. Mr. Wallace has already surpassed his sales quota, whereas Ms. Ellis has yet to reach -------.

(A) her
(B) herself
(C) she
(D) hers

129. Barner Corporation's record profits resulted from the recent ------- to identify operating efficiencies.

(A) initiative
(B) initiating
(C) initiation
(D) initiator

130. ------- the additional costs of maintaining the new PRX 3 printing press, the Voxel Printing Company has seen an overall decrease in its operating expenses.

(A) While
(B) Such
(C) Furthermore
(D) Despite

GO ON TO THE NEXT PAGE

PART 6

Questions 131-134 refer to the following invitation.

The San Bernardino Association of Photographic Artists invites you to the 5th

------- retreat at Rio Zadorra Conference Center from August 21 to August 24.
131.

This event is an opportunity for professional photographers to meet and share

------- work at a serene and beautiful location every year. This year's program
132.

has been expanded to include both morning and afternoon sessions. ------- are
133.

asked to bring several prints or digital files of their work to present at each of the

sessions. The registration fee is $700 and includes room, meals, and gratuities.

-------.
134.

---

131. (A) initial
(B) monthly
(C) early
(D) annual

132. (A) they
(B) their
(C) them
(D) themselves

133. (A) Participants
(B) Organizers
(C) Candidates
(D) Supervisors

134. (A) The conference center houses the Museum of Photography.
(B) Nonmembers are charged an extra program fee of $30.
(C) The association accepts photo submissions via e-mail only.
(D) Nowadays most photographers prefer to use lightweight digital cameras.

Questions 135-138 refer to the following press release.

FOR IMMEDIATE RELEASE

Contact: Jean Iau, 604-555-0273

Ulsan Gains Momentum

SINGAPORE (December 1) - Kim Heng Offshore & Marine(KHOM) ------- a 30 percent
  135.
interest in the Ulsan offshore wind farm project. This was a critical component in the
financing of Ulsan, which will be the largest offshore wind farm in Korea. During the
pilot period of the project, two turbines were erected. -------. The total number of
  136.
turbines in the Ulsan project will be enough to power a small urban area.

"We are delighted to offer assistance to the key players in a project of such
consequence," said Thomas Tan, the CEO of KHOM. "Not only is Ulsan on track to
become a major wind farm in Asia, ------- the involvement of international sponsors
  137.
will also set a new precedent for projects of this nature. We hope this will stimulate
future ------- in the region."
  138.

---

135. (A) was acquired
    (B) has acquired
    (C) is acquiring
    (D) will acquire

136. (A) KHOM funds turbines on wind
       farms in other countries, too.
    (B) The wind farms will encounter
       some challenges in the foreseeable
       future.
    (C) Fifty more units will be constructed
       in the subsequent phase of the
       project.
    (D) Multiple companies chose not to
       finance supplemental turbines.

137. (A) as
    (B) or
    (C) so
    (D) but

138. (A) travel
    (B) events
    (C) regulations
    (D) investment

GO ON TO THE NEXT PAGE

PART 7

Questions 139-142 refer to the following letter.

Department of International Business
Hong Kong Business University
4578 Pok Fu Lam, Hong Kong

September 30

Ms. J. Bian
Aramco Oil and Gas Corporation
Hong Kong

Dear Ms. Bian,

I am writing to express my gratitude for you allowing Mr. Pingyang Gao of your staff to coordinate a highly effective visit by twelve graduate students and faculty from the Hong Kong Business University to the Aramco Oil and Gas Corporation. Mr. Gao planned a very interesting round-table discussion in the morning with several of your senior executives responsible for the implementation of strategies, focusing in particular upon consumer behavior, cost dynamics, and corporate social responsibility — some of my students' particular areas of interest.

After having lunch with the group, Mr. Gao provided a highly polished overview of career opportunities in corporate Hong Kong, especially at Aramco Corporation. As a former executive of Aramco, I was pleased that he did such an outstanding job representing the company. His professional demeanor and the scrupulous attention he paid to numerous details of the visit made a profound impression on us.

Very truly yours,

Hongbin Cai
Hongbin Cai

139. What is the purpose of this letter?

(A) To commend a company employee
(B) To issue official permission for a tour
(C) To set up a seminar
(D) To explore potential partnerships

140. Where does Hongbin Cai work?

(A) At an accounting office
(B) At a travel agency
(C) At a university
(D) At an engineering firm

141. Which of the following did the visitors NOT do in the afternoon?

(A) Eat lunch with Mr. Gao
(B) Take a tour of Aramco Corporation
(C) Learn about corporate Hong Kong
(D) Hear about career opportunities

142. What does Hongbin Cai say about Mr. Gao?

(A) He is employed in the human resources department.
(B) He possesses an adept sense of humor.
(C) He is placed in a senior executive position.
(D) He is scrupulous in his attention to detail.

Taste de France

Dear Valued Customers,

On October 14, after three decades in operation, Taste de France will shut its doors for the last time. During the week of October 8-14, please join us to commemorate the store's history. All customers will receive a piece of our specialty croissant for free with the purchase of any fresh baked goods.

Please keep an eye out for Taste de France pastry chef Melissa Murphy. Within the next few months, she is going to launch her own bakery, where customers will be able to order custom pastries and cakes for parties and weddings.

It has been a privilege to cater to our fantastic Louisville City customers.

Sincerely,

Florian Bellanger, owner

---

http://www.louisvillerestaurants.com

Sweet Melissa Patisserie

HOME	MENUS	**REVIEW**	LOCATIONS

I was sad that Taste de France closed — I had wanted them to make my wedding cake. So, I was excited when their former pastry chef opened Sweet Melissa Patisserie in the Hollydell Shopping Center. She made our cake, and it was perfect! Our guests kept commenting on how much they liked the cake. I would recommend Sweet Melissa Patisserie to anyone.

– Claire Heitzler
★★★★★

The Evolution of a City

When the Hollydell Shopping Center opened on Cherry Hill Road in January of last year, Mayor Alfredo Rojas of Louisville City anticipated that it would be beneficial to the city by attracting shoppers from neighboring towns. Judging by the 20 percent growth in the city's sales tax revenues over the last six months, Mr. Rojas appears to have been correct.

However, less frequently mentioned was the potential effect of such commercial development on the city's downtown business district, which includes a number of small, family-owned stores and restaurants. In the past two months, three of these businesses — Wayland Books, Amy's Beauty Salon, and Taste de France — have either closed or announced plans to close, all citing a decline in customers since the Hollydell's opening.

Notwithstanding, the mayor is of the opinion that the overall effects of new developments such as the Hollydell outweigh any potential drawbacks. "It's certainly disappointing when a beloved business like Wayland Books closes," he said. "But new businesses bring new opportunities for all residents of Louisville City, including new jobs."

---

143. Why most likely is Mr. Bellanger closing his business?

(A) Because he wants to retire
(B) Because he lost business to a new shopping center
(C) Because he cannot afford to make necessary renovations
(D) Because he intends to launch a different type of business

144. What is indicated about Ms. Murphy's bakery?

(A) It opened on October 14.
(B) It was once owned by Mr. Bellanger.
(C) It is located on Cherry Hill Road.
(D) It is giving away free croissants.

145. In the review, the word "kept" on line 4 is closest in meaning to

(A) held
(B) continued
(C) saved
(D) gave

146. What is suggested about the Hollydell Shopping Center?

(A) It has generated a lot of income for Louisville City.
(B) It has brought in business for local family-owned stores.
(C) It was financed by Mayor Rojas.
(D) It was constructed in downtown Louisville City.

147. According to his statement, why does Mr. Rojas have a positive view of the Hollydell Shopping Center?

(A) Because it has a good beauty salon
(B) Because it was completed on schedule
(C) Because it offers discounts on expensive products
(D) Because it provides city residents with jobs

Day

04

1. 대명사 2

Day 03에서 인칭대명사의 격을 판단하는 유형 9가지를 공부했다. 다른 유형 몇 가지를 더 살펴보자.

(2) 인칭대명사의 수와 성 ★

유형 10 주어진 인칭대명사의 격이 모두 같은 경우

보기가 (A) his (B) her (C) its (D) their와 같이 모두 소유격이라면, 인칭대명사의 '격'이 아니라 '수'와 '성'을 판단해야 한다. '수'와 '성'을 판단해야 하는 문제에서는 빈칸 앞뒤만을 보고 답을 알 수 없다. 문장 전체를 해석한 후, 빈칸이 가리키는 명사가 무엇인지 알아야 한다.

Ex 14. When the sign we ordered for our new office is ready to be picked up, send Ms. Lee and Ms. Sugawara to pick ------- up.

(A) them
(B) her
(C) it
(D) one

빈칸에 pick up의 목적어가 들어가야 한다. 빈칸은 앞 절의 the sign을 가리키고 있으므로 (C)가 정답이다. one은 특정 대상을 가리키지 않는 부정대명사로써, (우리가 주문한 것이든 아니든) 아무 간판이나 하나 가져오라는 뜻이므로 알맞지 않다.

어휘 sign 간판 pick up ~을 찾다, 찾아오다

해석 새 사무실에 쓰려고 주문한 간판을 수령할 준비가 되면 Ms. Lee와 Ms. Sugawara를 보내 그것을 찾아오세요.

(3) 지시대명사 ★★

유형 11 ------- who ~ [분사 구문 / 형용사구 / 전치사구]

빈칸 뒤에 관계대명사 ① who로 시작하는 구문이나 ② 분사 구문, ③ 형용사구, ④ 전치사구가 있으면 항상 those가 정답이다. 만약 보기에 those가 없으면 anyone이 정답이다. those는 복수, anyone은 단수인 점만 다르고, 의미는 같다. '------- + who ~'나 '------- + 분사 구문'이 대부분 출제되며, 분사 구문을 이용할 때는 90% 이상 '------- + interested ~'로 출제된다.

❶ **Those who want to use the company vehicle** are required to make a reservation in advance.

회사 차량을 사용하고 싶은 사람들 (＊those who ～하는 사람들)

❷ **Those interested in the workshop** should notify their department manager.

= Those (who are) interested in the workshop　워크숍에 관심 있는 사람들

❸ **Those eager to take part in the multifunctional team** should see Mr. Newman or send him an e-mail before November 25.

= Those (who are) eager to take part in the multifunctional team

　　다기능팀에 간절히 참여하고 싶은 사람들

❹ At Big Pines Mountain Resort. special meals are available upon request for **those with dietary restrictions**.

= those (who are) with dietary restriction　식단 제한을 하는 사람들

Ex 15. Should the hiking trip not go ahead, ------- who prepaid the registration fee will receive a full refund.

(A) those
(B) which
(C) them
(D) whichever

빈칸 뒤 who prepaid the registration fee를 보면 정답을 알 수 있다. 관계대명사 who로 시작하는 구문 앞 빈칸에는 those가 들어가야 하므로 정답은 (A)이다.

어휘 go ahead 진행되다　prepay 선납하다　registration fee 등록비　refund 환불

해석 혹시 하이킹이 진행되지 않는다면, 등록비를 선납하신 분들은 전액 환불받으시게 됩니다.

＊Should the hiking trip not go ahead는 if가 생략되어 주어와 조동사가 도치된 가정법 절이다. (Day 08 참조)

Ex 16. The business consultant highlighted that long-term planning is an important consideration for ------- engaging in international business.

(A) anyone
(B) yourself
(C) who
(D) that

빈칸 앞에 전치사 for가 있으므로 ------- engaging in international business가 전치사의 목적어가 되어야 한다. 빈칸 뒤에 분사 구문이 있으면 '～하는 사람들'이라는 뜻이 되도록 those를, those가 보기에 없으면 anyone이 빈칸에 들어가야 하므로 정답은 (A)이다.

어휘 highlight 강조하다　consideration 고려 사항　engage in ～에 종사하다

해석 비즈니스 컨설턴트는 장기적인 계획이 국제 비즈니스에 종사하는 사람들에게 중요한 고려 사항이라고 강조했다.

Ex 17. Director Holt's position is that the ultimate responsibility for the hiring process should rest with ------- with expertise in the field.

(A) them
(B) those
(C) himself
(D) who

빈칸 앞에 should rest with가 있으므로 ------- with expertise in the field가 전치사 with의 목적어임을 알 수 있다. 전치사구 앞에 빈칸이 있으면 '~하는[~가 있는] 사람들'이라는 뜻이 되도록 those가 빈칸에 들어가야 하므로 정답은 (B)이다.

어휘 director 이사, 임원 position 입장, 견해 ultimate 최종의 responsibility 책임 hiring 채용 rest with (책임 등이) ~에게 있다 expertise 전문지식 field 분야, 영역

해석 Holt 이사의 입장은 채용 과정의 최종 책임은 그 분야의 전문 지식을 가진 사람들에게 있어야 한다는 것이다

유형 12 ------- + 전치사구 (of ~)

전치사구가 앞에 있는 빈칸을 수식하는 구조이면 정답은 that이나 those이다. 보기가 that, those를 모두 포함하고 있다면, 문장 앞부분을 읽어서 빈칸이 가리키는 명사가 단수인지 복수인지 확인 후 정답을 선택하자.

❶ The **size** of the new office building is smaller than **that** of the assembly plant.
새 사무실 건물의 규모는 조립 공장의 규모보다 작다.

❷ Our **kitchen appliances** are even more reliable than **those** of any of our competitors.
우리의 주방용품들은 어떤 경쟁업체들의 주방용품보다도 훨씬 더 신뢰할 만하다.

Ex 18. The company's new tablet computer has a design that looks somewhat similar to ------- of competing firms, but the technology it uses is much more advanced.

(A) those
(B) that
(C) them
(D) this

전치사구 of competing firms가 앞의 빈칸을 수식하고 있다. 이때 정답은 that과 those 중 하나이다. 앞부분을 보면, 빈칸이 단수 명사인 tablet computer를 가리키므로 (B) that이 정답이다.

어휘 somewhat 어느 정도, 다소 firm 회사 advanced 진보된, 발전한

해석 그 회사의 새 태블릿 컴퓨터는 디자인이 경쟁업체들의 태블릿 컴퓨터와 다소 유사해 보이지만, 그것이 사용하는 기술은 훨씬 더 발전했다.

2. 능동태와 수동태

유형 1 **능동태 vs. 수동태** ★★★★

능동태 문장의 목적어를 주어 자리로 옮기면 동사는 수동태로 변환된다. 이때 능동태 문장의 주어는 대부분 전치사구 'by ∼'가 되지만 수식어구이므로 없어도 무관하다. 그렇다면 수동태 문장은 동사 be + p.p.에서 완성된 것이라고 볼 수 있다. 수동태에서는 첫째, 능동태의 목적어를 주어 자리로 보내면 동사는 수동태가 되고, 둘째, 수동태 문장은 완성된 문장이라는 것을 기억하자.

시험에서는 동사 자리를 빈칸으로 하고 능동태와 수동태 중 정답을 선택할 것을 요구한다. 능동태 동사는 목적어가 있고, 수동태 동사는 뒤에 목적어가 없다. 그러므로 빈칸 뒤에 목적어가 있으면 능동태를, 목적어가 없으면 수동태를 정답으로 고르자.

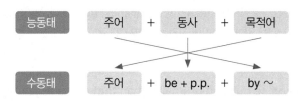

Ex 1. Barring any unforeseen problems, the new international airport is expected to ------- at the end of the year.

(A) complete
(B) completes
(C) completion
(D) be completed

> be expected to-V의 형태로 빈칸에는 동사원형이 와야 하므로 (A)와 (D) 중에서 정답을 골라야 한다. 빈칸 뒤에 목적어가 없기 때문에 수동태 (D)가 정답으로 알맞다.

어휘 barring ∼이 없다면 unforeseen 예측하지 못한, 뜻밖의

해석 예상치 못한 문제가 없다면, 새 국제공항은 연말에 완공될 것으로 예상된다.

Ex 2. The new business tax laws, although their effects may take years to be seen, are intended ------- local economic growth.

(A) facilitating
(B) facilitation
(C) to facilitate
(D) to be facilitated

> intend는 to부정사와 함께 사용하므로 (C)와 (D) 중에서 정답을 선택해야 한다. 빈칸 뒤에 목적어 local economic growth가 있으므로 능동태인 (C)가 정답이다.

어휘 business tax 사업 소득세 effect 효과 be intended to-V ∼하기 위한 것이다 facilitate 촉진하다 facilitation 촉진, 조장

해석 새로운 사업 소득세법은 효과를 보려면 수년이 걸릴 수 있지만 지역의 경제 성장을 촉진하기 위한 것이다.

유형 2 4형식 동사의 수동태 ★

4형식 동사는 목적어(간접목적어, 직접목적어)가 두 개이므로 목적어 유무에 따라 능동태와 수동태가 결정되지 않는다. 목적어가 두 개면 능동태 문장, 하나만 있으면 수동태 문장이다. 이런 유형의 4형식 동사로 give, send, award, offer, grant 등이 있다.

능동태 The coordinator gave Mr. Wilson the agenda for the meeting.
　　　　　　　　　　　S　　　　V　　　　　I·O　　　　　　　　D·O

목적어를 주어 자리로 옮기면 동사가 수동태로 변환되므로, 목적어가 두 개인 문장은 수동태를 두 가지로 만들 수 있다.

수동태 Mr. Wilson was given **the agenda for the meeting** by the coordinator.

was given이 빈칸이었을 때 뒤에 목적어 the agenda for the meeting이 있다고 능동태 동사를 정답으로 선택하면 안된다.

Ex 3. The inventors of Titan Tech and Gadgets ------- first prize in the 2023 Children and Family Game Design Contest for their creative idea.

　(A) awarded
　(B) were awarded
　(C) to award
　(D) having awarded

The inventors of Titan Tech and Gadgets는 주어이고, the first prize는 목적어이다. 그러므로 빈칸에는 동사가 될 수 있는 (A)나 (B)가 들어가야 한다. award는 4형식 동사로 목적어가 두 개 있으면 능동태, 하나 있으면 수동태이므로 (B)가 정답이다.

〈주의〉 4형식 동사를 3형식으로 사용한 경우 빈칸 뒤에 목적어가 있다면 능동태일 수 있다. 이를 구별하기 위해 빈칸 앞뒤의 구문 해석이 자연스러운지 확인해 보자. '개발자들이 1등상을 수여받았다'는 의미가 자연스러우므로 수동태 동사가 되어야 한다.

어휘 inventor 발명가, 개발자 award ~에게 ~을 주다, 수여하다

해석 Titan Tech and Gadgets의 개발자들이 2023 어린이 가족 게임 디자인 대회에서 창의적인 아이디어로 1등 상을 받았다.

name, appoint, call, make, consider 같은 동사는 목적어(O)와 목적격 보어(O·C)가 있는 5형식 구문으로 사용한다. 5형식 문장에서는, 빈칸 뒤에 **명사가 두 개 있으면** 각각 목적어와 목적격 보어이므로 **능동태**가 빈칸에 들어가야 한다. 빈칸 뒤에 **명사 하나만 있으면** 목적격 보어이고, 목적어가 없으므로 **수동태**가 정답이다. 5형식으로 쓰이는 동사를 반드시 기억하자.

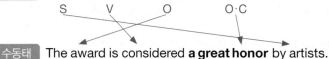

능동태 Artists consider the award a great honor.
　　　　　 S 　　　 V 　　　 O 　　　　 O·C

수동태 The award is considered **a great honor** by artists.

＊5형식 동사는 수동태 문장으로 바꿔 쓸 때, 목적어를 주어 자리로 옮겨야 하고 목적격 보어를 옮길 수는 없다. 밑줄 친 is considered를 빈칸으로 하는 문제가 출제되었을 때, a great honor를 목적어로 알고 능동태 동사를 선택하면 안 된다. a great honor는 목적어가 아니라 목적격 보어이다. 빈칸(is considered) 뒤에 목적어가 없으므로 수동태 동사를 정답으로 선택하자!

Ex 4. Pepito Bistro ------- "Best New Restaurant" by two local magazines.

(A) name
(B) has named
(C) was named
(D) naming

문장에 동사가 없으므로 빈칸에는 동사가 들어가야 하므로 준동사 (D)는 먼저 제외하자. 주어인 Pepito Bistro가 단수 명사이므로, 주어가 복수일 때 쓰는 (A)도 정답이 아니다. 따라서 능동태 (B)와 수동태 (C) 중에서 정답을 선택해야 한다. name이 5형식 동사이므로 빈칸 뒤에 명사 하나는 목적격 보어이다. 이 문장에서는 목적어가 없으므로 수동태 (C)가 정답이다.

어휘 **bistro** (작은) 식당, 술집　**name** 선정하다, 임명하다

해석 Pepito Bistro는 두 개의 지역 신문에서 '최우수 신규 식당'으로 선정되었다.

유형 4 **5형식 동사의 수동태 ②**

to부정사를 목적격 보어로 사용하는 5형식 동사는 아래와 같다.

enable	allow	permit	encourage
advise	persuade	expect	ask
request	require	invite	cause

능동태 A ramp allows wheelchairs to access the building entrance easily.
S   V   O   O·C

수동태 Wheelchairs are allowed **to access** the building entrance easily by a ramp.

＊수동태 문장에서 동사인 are allowed를 빈칸으로 출제한 문제에서, to부정사를 목적어로 착각하지 말자. allow는 to부정사를 목적격 보어로 사용하는 5형식 동사이고, 빈칸 뒤에 목적격 보어만 있고 목적어가 없는 문장이므로, 수동태 동사를 정답으로 선택해야 한다.

Ex 5. Consumers are ------- to use caution when applying this product to fabrics that have been dyed manually.

(A) advising
(B) advisory
(C) advised
(D) advise

advise는 to부정사를 목적격 보어로 사용하는 5형식 동사이다. 빈칸 뒤에 목적어가 없으므로 수동태 동사가 되도록 (C)를 정답으로 선택해야 한다.

어휘 advisory 자문의, 고문의 use caution 조심하다 apply A to B A를 B에 바르다 fabric 직물 dye 염색하다 manually 손으로, 수공으로

해석 소비자는 이 제품을 수공으로 염색된 직물에 바를 때 주의하시기를 바랍니다.

＊Day 01에서 공부한 바에 따르면 be동사 뒤에는 형용사가, 형용사가 없으면 분사가, 둘 다 있으면 형용사가 정답이 되어야 하는데, 이 문제에서는 주의가 필요하다. 형용사 advisory는 be동사 뒤에는 사용하지 않고, 항상 명사 앞에서만 쓰이기 때문이다. 토익에서는 advisory committee[office/board](자문 위원회[자문실/고문단])가 자주 등장하므로 기억해 두자.

101. Those who register in advance for the seminar will be ------- the privilege to interact with Dr. Suarez in person.

(A) offers
(B) offering
(C) offer
(D) offered

102. Ms. Gwok will prepare a marketing budget and present ------- during the client meeting.

(A) those
(B) its
(C) it
(D) her

103. ------- who have faith in the expansion of the solar power industry will likely put money into solar-panel-manufacturing business this year.

(A) Ours
(B) Them
(C) Those
(D) Their

104. Our company's shoes can be distinguished from ------- of other companies by the spiral pattern imprinted on the vamps.

(A) this
(B) them
(C) that
(D) those

105. Since online coding courses are increasingly popular, ------- interested in programming can easily enhance their skills at home.

(A) they
(B) those
(C) he
(C) who

106. After the levels of fine dust reached a record high, ------- with respiratory problems are being warned to stay indoors.

(A) those
(B) them
(C) whose
(D) which

107. When you buy a chicken, make sure to place it in a plastic bag to keep ------- juices from leaking onto other foods.

(A) they
(B) it
(C) their
(D) its

108. Orlingo Data International ------- a shuttle van service for all employees attending the digital marketing conference in Manchester next week.

(A) has arranged
(B) was arranged
(C) arranging
(D) arrangement

109. Any requests to obtain a leave of absence must be ------- to a department manager at least two weeks in advance.

(A) submitted
(B) submit
(C) submitting
(D) submission

110. As a former chief financial officer of Beneful Foods, Ms. Collins recently ------- chairperson of the International Chamber of Commerce.

(A) named
(B) is named
(C) was named
(D) has named

111. Since the information on performance appraisals is highly confidential, only the senior managers are ------- to access it.

(A) allowing
(B) allowed
(C) allowance
(D) allow

112. ------- eager to become part of the task force team may see Mr. North or send him an e-mail before July 25.

(A) Those
(B) They
(C) Them
(D) These

113. Kothari Gowns returned three boxes of lace to the supplier because the actual color differed from ------- in the catalog description.

(A) that
(B) including
(C) those
(D) only

114. Mr. Campbell ------- that only the senior loan officers should participate in the conference on recent trends in lending.

(A) specify
(B) to specify
(C) has specified
(D) is specified

115. Mr. Martinez was ------- a medal in recognition of his performance in the contest last weekend.

(A) given
(B) won
(C) received
(D) acquired

4. 추론 문제

- most likely, probably가 들어가는 질문
- What is suggested[implied] ~?
  무엇이 암시되어 있는가?
- What can be inferred ~?
  무엇을 추론할 수 있는가?
- 누구를 대상으로 쓴 글인가?

- 문제 풀이 전략

추론 문제에서는 지문 내용으로 미루어 짐작하여 사실일 가능성이 높은 보기를 선택하는 것이다. 깊은 사고를 요구하는 문제는 출제되지 않으며, 지문의 문장들을 정확히 해석할 수만 있으면 쉽게 해결할 수 있다. 다만 추론의 근거는 반드시 지문에 있는 내용이어야 한다는 점에 주의하자. 지문에 없으면 모두 오답이다.

Examples 1-4 refer to the following information.

Lago Grande Museum of Art
Meeting Minutes
17 October

Attendees

Byung Dae Yoon, managing director
Gerry Zimmerman, facilities director
Astrid Geensen, curator (ancient Egyptian art)
Keito Tanaka, curator (ancient Greek art)
Alexa Alves, curator (African art)
Colin Cavanaugh, curator (French art)
Agata Tomczyk, development director

- Mr. Cavanaugh proposed that the Ancient Greek Art exhibition be transferred from the second floor to the lower level of the museum so as to make room for the special exhibition of Expressionist paintings in March. Mr. Tanaka consented to his suggestion and will lead the effort.

- Mr. Yoon proposed to hold a fundraiser in January. Proceeds would be allocated to next year's construction of the new wing, which will house an exhibition of traditional Brazilian gemstone crafts and pottery. The third-floor banquet hall would be the venue for the event. Ms. Tomczyk consented to obtain cost estimates from three caterers.

- Mr. Zimmerman requested that an additional security guard be recruited for the fourth floor. He pointed out that the recent expansion of the ancient Egyptian art collection has resulted in the rise in the number of visitors to this area. He will discuss this with the budget officer.

- The focus of the upcoming meeting will be the loan of the Ngoy Collection of African Art to the Macapá Art Museum.

Ex 1. What most likely will happen in March?

    (A) A collection of Ancient Greek art will be sold.

    (B) A new exhibition will be on display.

    (C) An event will take place in the banquet hall.

    (D) Brazilian paintings will be moved.

Ex 2. What is implied about the construction project?

    (A) It will be supervised by Mr. Cavanaugh.

    (B) It is slated to commence in three months.

    (C) It has not yet been fully financed.

    (D) Its completion date has been extended.

Ex 3. Why does Mr. Zimmerman request additional security?

    (A) To protect an invaluable painting

    (B) To inspect visitors at the front entrance

    (C) To implement new safety regulations

    (D) To keep track of heightened visitor traffic

Ex 4. Who most likely will present at the next meeting?

    (A) Ms. Geensen

    (B) Ms. Tomczyk

    (C) Mr. Tanaka

    (D) Ms. Alves

> 해설

Examples 1-4 refer to the following information. 1–4번 예제는 다음 정보에 관한 것입니다.

Lago Grande Museum of Art **Meeting Minutes** **17 October** **Attendees** Byung Dae Yoon, managing director Gerry Zimmerman, facilities director Astrid Geensen, curator (ancient Egyptian art) Keito Tanaka, curator (ancient Greek art) Ex4.Alexa Alves, curator (African art) Colin Cavanaugh, curator (French art) Agata Tomczyk, development director • Ex1.Mr. Cavanaugh proposed that the Ancient Greek Art exhibition be transferred from the second floor to the lower level of the museum so as to make room for the special exhibition of Expressionist paintings in March. Mr. Tanaka consented to his suggestion and will lead the effort. • Ex2.Mr. Yoon proposed to hold a fundraiser in January. Proceeds would be allocated to next year's construction of the new wing, which will house an exhibition of traditional Brazilian gemstone crafts	**Lago Grande 미술관** **회의록** **10월 17일** **참석자** Byung Dae Yoon, 전무이사 Gerry Zimmerman, 시설 책임자 Astrid Geensen, 큐레이터 (고대 이집트 미술) Keito Tanaka, 큐레이터 (고대 그리스 미술) Alexa Alves, 큐레이터 (아프리카 미술) Colin Cavanaugh, 큐레이터 (프랑스 미술) Agata Tomczyk, 개발 책임자 • Mr. Cavanaugh가 3월에 있을 표현주의 회화 특별 전시회를 위한 공간을 만들기 위해 고대 그리스 미술 전시회를 미술관 2층에서 아래층으로 이전할 것을 제안했다. Mr. Tanaka가 제안에 동의했으며 이 일을 이끌 것이다. • Mr. Yoon이 1월에 기금 마련 행사를 열자고 제안했다. 수익금은 내년은 새 부속 건물 공사에 할당될 것이며, 이곳에는 브라질 전통 보석 공예 및 도자기 전시가 들어갈 것이다.

and pottery. The third-floor banquet hall would be the venue for the event. Ms. Tomczyk consented to obtain cost estimates from three caterers.

• ^{Ex3.}Mr. Zimmerman requested that an additional security guard be recruited for the fourth floor. He pointed out that the recent expansion of the ancient Egyptian art collection has resulted in the rise in the number of visitors to this area. He will discuss this with the budget officer.

• ^{Ex4.}The focus of the upcoming meeting will be the loan of the Ngoy Collection of African Art to the Macapá Art Museum.

3층 연회장이 행사 장소가 될 것이다. Ms. Tomczyk가 세 군데의 출장 뷔페 업체로부터 비용 견적을 받아보는 데 동의했다.

• Mr. Zimmerman이 4층에 경비원을 한 명 더 뽑아 달라고 요청했다. 그는 최근 고대 이집트 미술 소장품 증가로 이 구역 방문객 수가 증가하게 되었다고 지적했다. 그는 이것에 대해 예산 담당자와 논의할 것이다.

• 다가오는 회의의 중점 사항은 Ngoy 아프리카 미술 소장품을 Macapá 미술관에 대여해 주는 일이 될 것이다.

어휘 minutes 회의록 managing director 전무이사, 상무이사 facilities 시설 transfer from A to B A에서 B로 옮기다, 이전하다 level (건물의) 층 expressionist 표현주의의 consent to ~에 동의하다 effort 활동, 프로젝트 fundraiser 기금 마련 행사 proceeds 수익금 allocate 할당하다 wing (돌출되게 지은) 동(棟), 부속 건물 house 수용하다, 소장하다 gemstone 보석, 준보석 craft (수)공예 pottery 도자기 banquet hall 연회장 venue 장소 cost estimate 비용 견적 caterer 출장 뷔페 업체 recruit 모집하다, 뽑다 point out 지적하다, 언급하다 expansion 확대, 증가 result in ~를 초래하다 budget officer 예산 담당자

문장 분석

• Mr. Cavanaugh proposed that the Ancient Greek Art exhibition be transferred from the second floor to the lower level of the museum ~

• Mr. Zimmerman requested that an additional security guard be recruited for the fourth floor.

➡ 주절의 동사가 proposed와 requested이기 때문에 that절에 동사원형이 사용되었다. '요구, 주장, 권고/추천, 제안'을 나타내는 동사를 주절에 사용할 때 that절에는 동사원형이 들어가야 한다. Part 5에서 that절의 동사가 빈칸으로 출제되므로 다음 동사들을 암기해 두자.

요구 request. require. ask. demand	주장 insist
권고/추천 recommend. advise. urge	제안 suggest. propose

Ex 1. What most likely will happen in March?

(A) A collection of Ancient Greek art will be sold.
(B) A new exhibition will be on display.
(C) An event will take place in the banquet hall.
(D) Brazilian paintings will be moved.

3월에 무슨 일이 있을 가능성이 가장 큰가?

(A) 고대 그리스 미술 소장품이 판매될 것이다.
(B) 새 전시회가 열릴 것이다.
(C) 연회장에서 행사가 있을 것이다.
(D) 브라질 회화 작품들이 옮겨질 것이다.

어휘 collection 소장품 on display 전시된, 진열된 take place 일어나다, 열리다

해설 회의록 첫 항목으로 Mr. Cavanaugh가 고대 그리스 미술 전시회 장소를 옮기자고 제안했다는 내용이 나오는데(Mr. Cavanaugh proposed that the Ancient Greek Art exhibition be transferred from the second floor to the lower level of the museum), 이유는 3월에 있을 특별 전시회의 공간을 마련하기 위해서이다(so as to make room for the special exhibition of Expressionist paintings in March). 상설 전시회가 아니라 새로 추가된 것이므로 정답은 (B)이다.

Ex 2. What is implied about the construction project?

(A) It will be supervised by Mr. Cavanaugh.
(B) It is slated to commence in three months.
(C) It has not yet been fully financed.
(D) Its completion date has been extended.

건설 프로젝트에 관하여 무엇이 암시되어 있는가?

(A) Mr. Cavanaugh가 감독할 것이다.
(B) 3개월 후에 시작될 예정이다.
(C) 아직 재원이 충분히 마련되지 않았다.
(D) 완공 날짜가 연기되었다.

어휘 supervise 감독하다 be slated to-V ~할 예정이다 commence 시작되다 finance 재원을 대다 extend 연장하다

해설 회의록 두 번째 항목이 기금 마련 행사를 열자는 제안인데(Mr. Yoon proposed to hold a fundraiser in January), 여기서 나오는 수익금을 새 부속 건물의 공사에 할당하겠다는 것은(Proceeds would be allocated to next year's construction of the new wing) 아직 건설 재원이 충분히 마련되지 않았음을 시사하므로 정답은 (C)이다.

Ex 3. Why does Mr. Zimmerman request additional security?

(A) To protect an invaluable painting
(B) To inspect visitors at the front entrance
(C) To implement new safety regulations
(D) To keep track of heightened visitor traffic

Mr. Zimmerman은 왜 추가적인 보안을 요청하는가?

(A) 매우 귀중한 그림을 보호하기 위해
(B) 정문에서 방문객들을 검사하기 위해
(C) 새 안전 규정을 시행하기 위해
(D) 증가한 방문객 통행량을 계속 파악하기 위해

어휘 security 보안, 경비 invaluable 아주 귀중한 inspect 검사하다 implement 시행하다 safety regulation 안전 규정 keep track of ~을 계속 파악하다 heighten 증가시키다 traffic 통행(량)

해설 request additional security가 질문의 키워드로, 회의록 세 번째 항목이 경비원의 추가 채용에 관한 것이다(Mr. Zimmerman requested that an additional security guard be recruited for the fourth floor). Mr. Zimmerman은 최근에 이 구역의 방문객 수가 늘어났다는(the rise in the number of visitors to this area) 것을 지적하고 있으므로 (D)가 정답이다.

Ex 4. Who most likely will present at the next meeting?

(A) Ms. Geensen
(B) Ms. Tomczyk
(C) Mr. Tanaka
(D) Ms. Alves

다음 회의에서는 누가 발표할 가능성이 가장 높은가?

(A) Ms. Geensen
(B) Ms. Tomczyk
(C) Mr. Tanaka
(D) Ms. Alves

해설 회의록 마지막 항목에 '다음 회의에서 중점적으로 다룰 사안은 아프리카 미술 소장품의 대여'라고 나와 있다.(The focus of the upcoming meeting will be the loan of the Ngoy Collection of African Art to the Macapá Art Museum). 회의 참석자 명단을 보면 아프리카 미술 담당 큐레이터 Alexa Alves가 논의를 이끌 것이라고 추론할 수 있으므로 (D)가 정답이다.

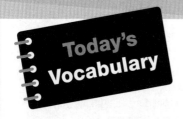
Today's Vocabulary

▶Actual Test를 풀기 전에 이 단어들을 암기하자.

짝을 이루어 출제되는 단어

- conveniently / perfectly / ideally ⎤ located / situated — 편리한 곳에 있는 / 딱 좋은 곳에 있는

- and ⎡ also 그리고 또한 / then 그다음에

- and ⎡ therefore / thus / so 그래서[따라서]

- have ⎡ always 항상 ~했다 / already 이미 ~했다 / recently 최근에 ~했다 / finally 마침내 ~했다 / consistently 지속해서 ~했다 ⎤ p.p.

- far too 너무
- far beyond ~을 훨씬 뛰어넘는

- be ⎡ ready 쉽게 / easily 쉽게 / always 항상 / generally 흔히 / usually 흔히 / freely 무료로 ⎤ available 이용할 수 있는

transform (모양 등이) 바뀌다, 변형되다
transparent 투명한
opaque 불투명한
plan (보험, 전화, 인터넷) 상품, 정책
deductive 연역적인
regard A as B A를 B로 여기다
means 수단, 방법
pay increase 임금 인상
refer to A as B A를 B라고 부르다
performance 성과, 실적
account for (부분·비율을) 차지하다
one-third 3분의 1
unoccupied (집, 건물이) 비어 있는

unopposed 반대도 받지 않고, 반대가 없는
defer 미루다, 연기하다
discontinue 중단하다, 단종하다
uphold 들어 올리다, 떠받치다
sustain 지속하다, 유지하다
content (문서·연설 등의) 내용
relieved 안도하는, 다행으로 여기는
defective 결함이 있는
perplexed 당혹한
confused 혼란스러워 하는, 혼란스러운
communication skill 의사소통 능력
pledge 기부금, 서약
press conference 기자 회견

fill in[out] (서식을) 작성하다

pass on 넘겨주다, 전달하다

break in 끼어들다, 방해하다

count on ~을 믿다, 기대하다

production schedule 생산 일정

shortly 얼마 안 되어

estimate 견적(서)

caterer 출장 뷔페 업체

category 범주

portion 부분; 몫

shortcoming 결점, 단점

adequate 적절한, 적당한

employee productivity 직원 생산성

rating 평점

overshadow 빛을 잃게[무색하게] 만들다

bundle plan 패키지 상품

strategic 전략적인

in force 시행 중인

in agreement 일치하는, 동의하는

commencement 시작, 개시

general 전체적인

overview 개관, 개요

in regard to ~과 관련하여, ~에 대하여

proposal 기획안

be met with approval 동의를 얻다

assume (권력·책임을) 맡다

distinct 뚜렷이 다른, 구별되는, 별개의

exert (힘·지식 따위를) 쓰다, 발휘하다

aspect 측면

volcanic 화산의

eruption (화산의) 폭발, 분화

feature (매체에서) 특집으로 다루다

issue (정기 간행물의) 호

activate 활성화시키다

readership (신문·잡지의) 독자 수, 독자층

dedicate (특정 역할을) 전담[전임]시키다

commemorate 기념하다

(up)on + 명사[V-ing] ~하자마자

succeed 잇따르다, 계속되다

encounter 접하다, 마주치다

portray 묘사하다, 그리다

present-day 현대의, 오늘날의

present 참석한, 출석한

set in ~을 배경으로 하는

available (사람들을 만날) 시간이 있는

arrange 계획하다, 준비하다

lodge 묵다, 숙박하다

explore 탐구하다, 분석하다

Actual Test

PART 5

1. 빈칸 앞뒤를 보며 문제를 푼다.
2. 빈칸 앞뒤를 보고 정답을 알 수 없다면 문장을 해석한다.
3. 두 줄 분량의 어휘 문제는 문장 전체를 해석해서 푼다.
4. 접속사 어휘 문제는 빈칸 앞뒤만을 보고 풀 수 없다. 문장 전체를 해석해 보자.

PART 6

1. 문법 문제라면 Part 5와 같은 방식으로 빈칸 앞뒤를 보며 푼다.
2. 다른 유형의 문제는 문맥을 통해 정답을 파악한다.

PART 7

1. 문제와 보기 (A), (B), (C), (D)를 먼저 읽은 후에 지문을 읽는다.
2. 지문 위아래의 모든 부분을 자세히 읽어 본다.
3. 문제의 해설을 꼼꼼히 읽고, 문장 구조를 분석하며 복습한다.

PART 5

101. To boost morale, employees who report best sales in their teams ------- a special bonus for their hard work.

(A) are offered
(B) was offered
(C) offering
(D) offers

102. Researchers at the University of Cambridge have developed a type of smart glass that transforms ------- transparent to opaque in less than a minute.

(A) from
(B) against
(C) between
(D) throughout

103. Greer Agency's travel insurance can be purchased over the phone, though most of ------- plans are bought online.

(A) whose
(B) his
(C) its
(D) this

104. The restaurant is ------- located in the middle of the entertainment district, so that diners can comfortably attend a movie or concert either before or after a meal.

(A) superficially
(B) unanimously
(C) prudently
(D) perfectly

105. ------- who would like to view the statistics featured in the presentation to the board of directors should contact Mr. Dominguez.

(A) Whichever
(B) Anyone
(C) Other
(D) Themselves

106. Each full-time permanent employee's travel expenses can be ------- from taxable income by a certain percentage.

(A) deduct
(B) deducted
(C) deductive
(D) deducting

107. Food prices rose nearly 15 percent overall, with the price of meat going up by 10 percent, and ------- of vegetables by 20 percent.

(A) this
(B) that
(C) these
(D) those

108. Eli Fry is ------- the most competent person working in the R&D Department.

(A) considered
(B) appeared
(C) regarded
(D) agreed

109. The delivery charge for your purchase ------- on the shipping method you choose at the checkout step on our Web site.

(A) have depended
(B) will depend
(C) depending
(D) are depended

110. The various means used to determine appropriate annual pay increases ------- to as the merit criteria.

(A) are referred
(B) referring
(C) have referred
(D) to refer

111. Each manager is required to evaluate their employees' job ------- at the end of every quarter and submit the results to the personnel department.

(A) confirmation
(B) medication
(C) performance
(D) emission

112. The annual profit of the Singapore branch ------- for one-third of the total annual profit of CNTC Enterprise.

(A) calculates
(B) takes
(C) accounts
(D) features

113. ------- wishing to join the task force team should notify Cynthia Holt by e-mail no later than April 24.

(A) Fewer
(B) Another
(C) Whoever
(D) Anyone

114. The building has been left ------- for almost three years, prompting the city to tear it down.

(A) revealed
(B) unoccupied
(C) unopposed
(D) disappointed

115. Mr. Nettles understands what needs to be done better than ------- originally in charge of the project.

(A) who
(B) them
(C) those who
(D) those

116. PX-001 printer model has been -------, but the contents of the instruction manual for PX-005 are almost the same.

(A) deferred
(B) discontinued
(C) upheld
(D) sustained

117. Any ------- product can be returned to our offices for an exchange, provided the customer brings the merchandise to our customer care center with a valid receipt.

(A) relieved
(B) defective
(C) perplexed
(D) confused

118. Ms. Anderson was appointed ------- for the outreach program.

(A) facilitate
(B) facilitated
(C) facilitating
(D) facilitator

119. Advanced ------- skills both in Spanish and English are required for the qualified applicants along with a strong business and accounting background.

(A) communication
(B) communicates
(C) communicate
(D) communicative

120. ------- donors substantially increase their pledges will Doctors Without Borders be able to meet its goals.

(A) In case
(B) Even
(C) Only if
(D) Except

121. The official spokesperson of the Orion Technologies announced at a press ------- held at the Hilton Hotel today that a merger negotiation with their rival H&D Electronics is in progress.

(A) conference
(B) committee
(C) maintenance
(D) participation

122. A diverse range of employee comments and suggestions are regularly ------- to the multifunctional review team.

(A) filled in
(B) passed on
(C) broken in
(D) counted on

123. Thanks to the newly installed equipment, we are currently well ahead of our initial ------- schedule for most of the important items.

(A) producing
(B) productive
(C) production
(D) produce

124. Mr. Mangal ------- obtained estimates from several companies before hiring a caterer.

(A) sharply
(B) shortly
(C) wisely
(D) purely

125. A major ------- of the convention center's design was the lack of adequate parking space.

(A) category
(B) portion
(C) shortcoming
(D) responsibility

126. Ms. Wagner is planning to conduct a training session on the new time tracking software since ------- people know how to use it.

(A) few
(B) more
(C) other
(D) all

127. In an effort to increase employee -------, the company has introduced an automated assembly line in their new processing plant.

(A) necessity
(B) possibility
(C) complexity
(D) productivity

128. The performance ratings of the veteran salesman were overshadowed by ------- of a newcomer who joined the sales department only a year ago.

(A) they
(B) that
(C) them
(D) those

129. The Aargenso Telecommunication's new TV, Internet, and phone bundle plan is a ------- move to attract more customers.

(A) strategic
(B) preventable
(C) distant
(D) previous

130. Ms. Aguilar and Mr. Liu are in ------- about the agenda for the next board meeting.

(A) submission
(B) fulfillment
(C) force
(D) agreement

GO ON TO THE NEXT PAGE

PART 6

Questions 131-134 refer to the following e-mail.

Dear Ms. Johnson,

We are pleased that you have accepted our invitation to join Aflac Financial.

We would like you to fill out three documents and ------- e-mail them to us or
131.
bring them with you for your first day of work next Monday. You must complete

the Personnel Information Form, the Confidentiality Agreement Form, and the

Method of Payment Form, which are ------- to this e-mail. -------. If you have any
132. **133.**
trouble accessing the forms, please let me know immediately. We look forward

to the commencement of your ------- at Aflac Financial.
134.

Sincerely,

Akari Ito

---

131. (A) if
(B) either
(C) as
(D) both

132. (A) attach
(B) attached
(C) attaching
(D) attachment

133. (A) Please fill them out completely and correctly so that your file can be processed.
(B) Your Personnel Information Form has been omitted from your personal file.
(C) Please submit all these forms six weeks before you leave the company.
(D) You can find the latest version of this employee handbook in your office.

134. (A) event
(B) presentation
(C) visit
(D) employment

Questions 135-138 refer to the following e-mail.

To: Kaylee Keane, Staff Writer
From: Lizanne Schwartz, Editor in Chief
Date: February 3
Re: Cover Story Assignment

Hi Kaylee,

Thank you for agreeing to work on the feature article about Valia Zulli's ------- **135.** role in her recent film as actress and director. By the end of next week, please submit a general overview explaining what your plans are in regard to the focus of the interview with her. Once your ------- **136.** has been met with approval by our editors, make sure to confirm the date and time of the interview with one of our staff photographers. It would be ideal if the article ------- the two roles Ms. Zulli **137.** assumed in the production of the film. -------. If you have any questions, I will be **138.** available throughout the week before going on vacation next week.

Liz

135. (A) double
(B) doubles
(C) doubling
(D) to double

136. (A) drawing
(B) hiring
(C) proposal
(D) edition

137. (A) comparing
(B) compared
(C) to compare
(D) were compared

138. (A) For instance, you might ask her about the upcoming project on her schedule.
(B) Furthermore, it should discuss the distinct skills she exerted in each aspect.
(C) In other words, your work should be completed in three weeks.
(D) In addition, the article will be published in the May issue.

GO ON TO THE NEXT PAGE

PART 7

To: Linas Pilypas <lpilypas@moto.net>
From: Jennifer Goodies <jgoodies@pdn_mag.com>
Date: 4 July
Subject: Your submission

We've got some great news for you. Your photograph *Volcanic Eruption in Reykjanes* has been selected as the third-place winner in the third Natural Landscape Photography Awards sponsored by *Photo District News Magazine*. Our judges felt that your scene of the orange lava cascading down the steep slope, with the ambient blue light on the background layers, conveys a feeling of radiating heat and that the impressionistic image you captured shows your skill as an artist.

Your photograph will be featured in the September issue of *Photo District News Magazine*, alongside the other winning photographs. In addition, your work will be featured in a special nature landscape photography exhibit in Milan at Luciana Matalon Art Museum from 18 November to 30 November.

You will receive a prize of €2,000 as well as a two-year subscription to *Photo District News Magazine*. A cheque for the amount of the prize will be sent to you in August, and your subscription will be activated with the issue featuring your photograph.

When you submitted your photograph, you stated that you used a Pillai DSLR 240 camera and a Summilux M ASPH lens. Kindly confirm if this is accurate by responding to this e-mail. This information will accompany your photograph in the magazine and in the museum exhibit.

Congratulations on your success! We are excited to be able to share your work with our international readership and look forward to seeing more of your work in the future.

Sincerely,

Jennifer Goodies
Editor

139. What is implied about Mr. Pilypas'
photograph?

    (A) It is in black and white.
    (B) It has previously been published.
    (C) It has been purchased by a
        collector.
    (D) It depicts a nature landscape
        scene.

140. When will Mr. Pilypas' subscription
begin?

    (A) In July
    (B) In August
    (C) In September
    (D) In November

141. What is Mr. Pilypas asked to do?

    (A) Provide some additional
        photographs
    (B) Verify that some information is
        correct
    (C) Sign a release form
    (D) Confirm a mailing address

142. What is mentioned about *Photo
District News Magazine*?

    (A) It is read in many places around the
        world.
    (B) It sponsors multiple competitions
        annually.
    (C) It is a newly released publication.
    (D) It is published quarterly.

The Museum of Contemporary Art Barcelona presents...

Time Travel

By Teresa Gancedo

11-25 October

Ms. Gancedo is a painter and sculptor who lives in Barcelona.

Teresa Gancedo's artwork will occupy our entire museum, with each museum hall dedicated to a different time period in Spanish history, particularly highlighting the city of Barcelona. Ms. Gancedo commemorates moments from Barcelona's history that are not widely known, sourced from literature and film.

Upon entering the museum, visitors will experience Barcelona as it was 2,200 years ago, at the beginning of Roman occupation. Each succeeding gallery that visitors encounter will portray younger versions of the city up to present-day Barcelona. Ms. Gancedo's creative output makes use of a broad range of media, including paint, video, and even recycled material. All pieces in this exhibition are Ms. Gancedo's original creations.

Tickets:

Museum entrance: €12 per person

Teresa Gancedo will discuss her exhibition at Meier Hall on Friday, 19 October, at 7:00 P.M. Tickets are €15 and half of all proceeds will be donated to the Institute of Historic Building Conservation. Please call (093) 481 3368 for further information.

From:	aragallj@libris.co.es
To:	tgancedo@likmail.com
Date:	30 October
Subject:	Book project

Dear Ms. Gancedo,

I was present at the recent event where you talked about your work, and I had the joy of visiting your exhibition afterwards.

I'm in the process of writing a novel set in 15th century Spain, mainly Barcelona, and I am seeking an illustrator for this work. My publisher, Moleiro and Co., is prepared to provide generous compensation and has granted me the discretion to select a collaborator. I am certain that you would make an ideal creative companion.

Are you interested in partnering with me on this endeavor? Your agent informed me that you are currently in Marseille. I will be there myself next week. Should you be available for a meeting, please feel free to reach out to me at aragallj@libris.co.es.

Jaume Aragall

From: tgancedo@likmail.com
To: aragallj@libris.co.es
Date: 1 November
Re: Book project

Dear Jaume,

I am greatly intrigued by your invitation and would be absolutely thrilled to discuss the project you have outlined. I am arranging to travel to Rome next Friday, so please let me know where you will be lodging and when, so that we will find the time to explore your proposal further.

Best wishes,

Teresa Gancedo

---

143. What does the notice suggest about the exhibition?

(A) It portrays a city from a unique perspective.
(B) It is made entirely of recycled materials.
(C) It contains historical artifacts.
(D) It is inspired by a well-known novel.

144. What is implied in the notice?

(A) The museum exhibition will commence with a lecture.
(B) Self-guided audio tours of the exhibition are available for an extra fee.
(C) Viewers of the exhibition are urged to experience it in a particular order.
(D) Ms. Gancedo is overseeing a building restoration project.

145. Where most likely did Mr. Aragall hear Ms. Gancedo speak?

(A) At a meeting of the Institute of Historic Building Conservation
(B) At the Museum of Contemporary Art
(C) At Moleiro and Co. headquarters
(D) At an event at Meier Hall

146. What is suggested about Ms. Gancedo?

(A) She has agreed to a contract with Mr. Aragall.
(B) She will meet with Mr. Aragall in Marseille.
(C) She is returning from Rome next week.
(D) She is selling some of her paintings.

147. In what field do Mr. Aragall and Ms. Gancedo share some expertise?

(A) Spanish history
(B) Fictional writing
(C) Contemporary art
(D) Museum administration

Day

05

1. 관계사 ★★★

관계사는 관계대명사, 관계부사, 복합관계대명사, 복합관계부사로 분류된다. 시험에서는 관계대명사가 정답인 문제가 자주 출제되며, 특히 주격 관계대명사가 정답인 경우가 가장 많다.

(1) 기본 문장 구조

선행사	+	관계대명사	+	불완전한 문장
선행사	+	관계부사	+	완성된 문장
No 선행사	+	복합관계대명사	+	불완전한 문장
No 선행사	+	복합관계부사	+	완성된 문장

(2) 예외 규칙

기본 문장 구조만 알아도 문제는 풀 수 있지만, 반대로 이 구조를 모르면 아무 문제도 풀 수 없다. 기본 문장 구조가 문제 풀이의 핵심이며 예외 규칙을 추가로 암기해서 문제 풀이에 적용해야 한다.

❶ 전치사 뒤나 쉼표 뒤에는 관계대명사 that을 사용할 수 없다.
❷ 관계대명사 what은 반드시 선행사 없이 사용한다.
❸ 소유격 관계대명사 whose는 뒤에 완성된 문장이 온다.
❹ 목적격 관계대명사와 '주격 관계대명사 + be동사'는 생략할 수 있다.
❺ 관계부사의 선행사를 생략할 수 있다. (the place) where, (the time) when, (the reason) why
❻ 관계부사 how는 반드시 선행사 없이 사용한다.
❼ 복합관계부사는 부사절을 이끈다.
❽ 복합관계부사 however(=no matter how) 뒤에는 형용사나 부사를 추가해서 사용하는 경우가 많다.
❾ 빈칸 뒤에 *sb* think[believe/guess/suppose]가 있으면 삽입 구문이므로 제외하고 문제를 풀자.
❿ 시험에서 보기 중 두 개 이상이 관계사이면, 관계사가 정답인 경우가 많다. 일단 관계사만 가지고 문제를 풀어 보자. 관계사가 정답이 아니면 다른 보기를 살펴보자.

유형 1 **선행사 + ------- + V**

빈칸 앞에 선행사가 있고, 빈칸 뒤에 동사가 있다면, 즉 주어가 없는 문장이 있으면, 주격 관계대명사가 정답이다. 관계사 중 주격 관계대명사가 정답인 경우가 가장 많다.

Ex 1. Most applicants ------- applied for the engineering position at Farber Systems were so qualified that the hiring committee had trouble selecting one.

(A) which
(B) whose
(C) who
(D) when

빈칸 앞의 선행사 applicants가 사람이므로 (A)와 (D)는 사용할 수 없다. 빈칸 뒤에 동사 applied가 있는 것을 보고 주격 관계대명사 (C)를 정답으로 선택하자.

어휘 applicant 지원자 apply for ~에 지원하다 qualified 자격을 갖춘 have trouble ~ing ~하기가 어렵다. ~하는데 애를 먹다

해석 Farber Systems의 엔지니어 자리에 지원한 지원자 대부분이 충분히 자격을 갖추고 있어서 채용 위원회는 한 명을 선택하는 데 애를 먹었다.

유형 2 선행사 + ------- + S + Vt. / 전치사

빈칸 앞에 선행사가 있고, 빈칸 뒤에 타동사나 전치사로 끝나는 문장이 있다면, 즉 목적어가 없는 문장이 있으면 목적격 관계대명사가 정답이다.

Ex 2. Enclosed please find the notes from yesterday's strategic planning and budgeting seminar ------- you requested.

(A) then
(B) that
(C) what
(D) when

관계사가 아닌 (A)는 제외하고, 관계사인 보기만으로 문제를 풀어 보자. 빈칸 앞 from yesterday's strategic planning and budgeting seminar는 전치사구이고, 그 앞에 있는 the notes가 선행사이다. 빈칸 뒤에는 동사 requested의 목적어가 없으므로 목적격 관계대명사 (B)가 정답이다. what은 선행사가 없을 때만 사용하고, 관계부사 when은 선행사가 시간 표현일 때 사용한다.

어휘 Enclosed please find ~을 동봉합니다 note 필기, 노트, 기록 strategic 전략적인

해석 요청하신 어제 전략 기획 및 예산안 작성 세미나에서 한 필기를 동봉합니다.

유형 3 선행사 + 전치사 + -------

'선행사 + 전치사 + -------'가 있으면 목적격 관계대명사가 정답이다.

Mr. Brantley will compile a list of readers (who / [whom] / whose) the subscription expiration notices should be sent **to**.

➡ 괄호 뒤 문장에서 전치사 to의 목적어가 없으므로 목적격 관계대명사 whom을 선택해야 한다.

이때 문장 끝에 있는 전치사는 관계대명사 앞으로 자리를 옮길 수 있다.

Mr. Brantley will compile a list of readers **to** (whom) the subscription expiration notices should be sent.

➡ whom을 빈칸으로 하는 문제가 출제된다. '선행사 + 전치사 + ------'가 있다면 목적격 관계대명사를 정답으로 선택하자. 이때 빈칸 뒤를 보지 말고, readers to ------만 보고 정답을 선택하자. 빈칸 뒤 문장(the subscription expiration notices should be sent.)이 완전한 문장이어서 관계대명사가 정답이 아니라고 생각할 수 있기 때문이다.

Ex 3. The dedication of Di Falco Hall was marked with a brief ceremony in ------ the Di Falco family was recognized for their outstanding contributions to the university.

(A) what
(B) which
(C) how
(D) where

빈칸 앞 a brief ceremony in ------만 보고 정답을 선택하자. '선행사 + 전치사 + ------' 구조이므로, 목적격 관계대명사 (B)가 정답이다. what이나 how는 선행사가 없을 때만 사용한다.

어휘 dedication 봉헌식, 헌정식 **mark** 기념하다, 축하하다 ceremony 기념식 **be recognized for** ~에 대한 공로를 인정받다 outstanding 뛰어난, 두드러진 contribution 기여, 공헌

해석 Di Falco 홀 헌정식은 Di Falco 가족이 대학교에 뛰어난 공헌을 한 것을 인정받는 간단한 행사로 진행되었다.

유형 4 **선행사 + ------ + 관계대명사**

'선행사 + 전치사 + 관계대명사' 구조에서 전치사를 빈칸으로 하는 문제이다.

Ex 4. One of the accomplishments ------ which Mr. Yang is best known is having started his own fabric design company at the age of 23.

(A) between
(B) from
(C) into
(D) for

빈칸 뒤에 목적격 관계대명사가 있으므로, 빈칸에 들어갈 전치사를 선택해야 한다.

① 선행사 the accomplishments를 수식하는 관계사절이 어디까지인지 확인한다.
   ➡ ------ which Mr. Yang is best known
② 빈칸을 원래 있던 자리인 관계사절 끝부분으로 옮기고 선행사를 그 뒤에 적어 본다.
   ➡ Mr. Yang is best known ------ the accomplishments
③ 관계사절을 해석하여 알맞은 전치사를 선택한다.
   ➡ be known은 전치사 for와 함께 사용해서 '~로 알려져 있다'라는 뜻이 되므로 (D)가 정답이다.

어휘 accomplishment 업적, 공적 fabric 직물, 천

해석 Mr. Yang이 가장 잘 알려진 업적 중 하나는 23세의 나이에 자신의 직물 디자인 회사를 시작한 것이다.

No 선행사 + -------

관계대명사 what과 관계부사 how, 복합관계대명사, 복합관계부사는 선행사가 없을 때만 정답이 될 수 있다. how를 제외한 다른 관계부사를 사용할 때도 선행사를 생략할 수 있다.

Ex 5. The employee handbook outlines -------
new recruits need to know concerning the
employee benefits package.

(A) which
(B) where
(C) how
(D) what

빈칸 앞에 '주어 + 동사(The employee handbook outlines)'만 있고 선행사가 없으므로 (A)는 정답이 아니다. 빈칸 뒤에는 동사 need to know의 목적어가 없는 불완전한 문장이 있으므로, 완전한 문장과 함께 사용하는 관계부사인 (B)와 (C)도 정답이 아니다. 불완전한 문장 앞에는 관계대명사가 있어야 하므로 (D)가 정답이다.

어휘 employee handbook 직원 안내서 outline 개요를 서술하다 recruit 신입 사원 employee benefits package 복리 후생 제도 concerning ~에 관하여

해석 직원 안내서는 신입 사원들이 복리 후생 제도에 관하여 알아야 하는 것을 약술(略述)하고 있다.

Ex 6. In an effort to improve energy efficiency,
lights throughout the building will turn off
automatically ------- the external doors are
locked.

(A) when
(B) which
(C) according to
(D) what

먼저 관계사가 아닌 (C)는 제외하고 생각하자. 빈칸 앞에 '자동사+부사(will turn off automatically)'만 있고, 선행사가 될 명사가 없으므로 (B)는 정답이 아니다. 남은 관계부사 (A)와 관계대명사 (D) 중에서 정답을 선택해야 한다. 빈칸 뒤에 수동태로 완성된 문장인 the external doors are locked가 있으므로, 관계부사 (A)가 정답이다.

어휘 in an effort to-V ~하려는 노력의 일환으로 efficiency 효율성 throughout 도처에 automatically 자동으로 external 외부의

해석 에너지 효율성을 개선하려는 노력의 일환으로 건물 곳곳의 조명이 바깥 출입문들이 잠길 때 자동으로 꺼진다.

Ex 7. Participants are allowed to bring -------
they like on the tour of the Tonopah Historic
Mining Park, provided it is not on the list of
prohibited items.

(A) wherever
(B) however
(C) whomever
(D) whatever

보기가 선행사가 필요 없는 복합관계사로만 구성되어 있으므로 빈칸 앞은 보지 않아도 된다. 빈칸 뒤에는 동사 like의 목적어가 없는 불완전한 문장이 있으므로, 복합관계대명사인 (C)나 (D)에서 정답을 고르면 된다. '그들이 좋아하는 것은 무엇이든(whatever)'이 의미가 자연스러우므로 (D)가 정답이다.

어휘 participant 참가자 be allowed to-V ~하도록 허용되다. ~할 수 있다 mining 광(산)업 provided (만약) ~라면 prohibited 금지된

해석 참가자들은 Tonopah 광산업 역사 공원 투어에서 금지 품목 목록에 없다면 좋아하는 것은 무엇이든 가지고 갈 수 있다.

Ex 8. It is Ms. Rettson's responsibility to notify all office personnel ------ a new software update is installed.

(A) whenever
(B) however
(C) whoever
(D) whichever

보기가 선행사가 필요 없는 복합관계사로만 구성되어 있으므로 빈칸 앞은 보지 않아도 된다. 빈칸 뒤에는 수동태로 완성된 문장인 a new software update is installed가 있으므로, 관계부사인 (A)나 (B)에서 정답을 고르면 된다. '새 소프트웨어가 설치될 때마다(whenever)'가 의미상 자연스러우므로 (A)가 정답이다.

어휘 responsibility 책임 notify 알리다. 통보하다 personnel 직원 install 설치하다
해석 새 소프트웨어 업데이트가 설치될 때마다 사무실 모든 직원에게 알리는 것은 Ms. Rettson의 책임이다.

유형 6 선행사 + all[most/half/some/one/숫자/none] of + ------ + V

'수량 표현 + of' 뒤에 빈칸이 있으면, 목적격 관계대명사가 정답이다. 빈칸 뒤에 동사가 있다고 주격 관계대명사를 선택하면 안 된다. 빈칸 뒤를 보지 말고 빈칸 앞에 있는 '수량 표현 + of'만 보고 정답을 고르자.

Ex 9. Purblu Beverages sold one billion dollars' worth of bottled water last year, most of ------ was consumed in Europe.

(A) many
(B) that
(C) which
(D) who

관계사가 아닌 (A)는 일단 제외하자. '수량 표현 + of' 뒤 빈칸에는 목적격 관계대명사가 정답이다. 전치사 뒤에는 관계대명사 that을 사용할 수 없으므로 (C)가 정답이다. 빈칸 뒤 동사 was consumed만 보고 주격 관계대명사 (D)를 정답으로 고르지 않도록 주의하자.

어휘 beverage (물 이외의) 음료 **[금액]**'s worth of [금액] 상당의 ~ bottled water 병에 담긴 생수 consume 소비하다
해석 Purblu 음료는 작년에 10억 달러 상당의 생수를 팔았는데, 그중 대부분은 유럽에서 소비되었다.

유형 7 선행사 + ------ + 완성된 문장

빈칸 앞에 선행사가 있고 빈칸 뒤에 완성된 문장이 있으면, 소유격 관계대명사인 whose나 관계부사가 정답이다.

Ex 10. Most customers surveyed were quite familiar with the organic products by Brosnan Foods, ------ advertisements often appear on TV and the Internet.

(A) what
(B) whose
(C) which
(D) who

빈칸 앞에 선행사 Brosnan Foods가 있으므로 (A)는 제외하고, 나머지 관계대명사 중 정답을 선택해야 한다. 빈칸 뒤에 1형식으로 완성된 문장이 있으므로, 소유격 관계대명사 (B)가 정답이다.

어휘 survey ~의 의견을 조사하다 be familiar with ~에 익숙하다 organic 유기농의 advertisement 광고 appear on ~에 나오다

해석 설문조사에 응한 소비자 대부분은 TV와 인터넷에 광고가 자주 나오는 Brosnan 식품의 유기농 제품에 상당히 익숙했다.

Ex 11. The hotel ------- the banquet is being held is located in the center of Hanoi.

(A) which
(B) where
(C) in that
(D) in it

관계사가 아닌 (D)는 제외하자. 관계대명사 that은 전치사 뒤에 사용할 수 없으므로 (C)도 제외하자. 관계대명사 (A)와 관계부사 (B) 중 정답을 선택해야 하는데, 빈칸 뒤에 수동태로 완성된 문장인 the banquet is being held가 있으므로 관계부사 (B)가 정답이다.

어휘 banquet 연회, 만찬 be located in ~에 위치하다

해석 연회가 열리고 있는 호텔은 Hanoi 중심부에 있다.

유형 8 **관계대명사 생략**

목적격 관계대명사의 생략은 문장에서 '목적어가 빠진 절'을 발견하면 어렵지 않게 파악할 수 있다. 반면 '주격 관계대명사 + be동사'의 생략은 쉽게 눈에 들어오지 않기 때문에 문장 구조 분석을 많이 연습해야 한다.

Ex 12. Intercommerce Bank of Canada customers are encouraged to update the passwords ------- use for online banking annually.

(A) they
(B) them
(C) their
(D) themselves

빈칸 뒤에 동사 use의 목적어가 없는 것을 알아야, 선행사 the passwords와 빈칸 사이에 목적격 관계대명사가 생략된 것을 알 수 있다. 빈칸은 관계대명사절의 주어 자리이므로 주격 대명사 (A)가 정답이다.

어휘 be encouraged to-V ~할 것을 권장받다 update 갱신하다 annually 매년

해석 Intercommerce Bank of Canada 고객 여러분은 온라인 은행 업무에 사용하는 비밀번호를 매년 업데이트하실 것을 권장합니다.

Ex 13. We regret to inform you that the jacket you ordered is currently unavailable in the color you -------, but the rest of your order will be sent out promptly.

(A) requests
(B) requested
(C) are requested
(D) requesting

in the color you -------서 보기에 있는 동사의 원형인 request를 빈칸에 넣어보면, 목적격 관계대명사가 생략된 절임을 알 수 있다. 그러므로 준동사 (D)와 수동태로 완성된 문장을 만들어 (C)는 정답이 아니다. (A)는 주어 you와 수가 일치하지 않으므로 과거형 동사 (B)가 정답이다.

어휘 regret to inform ~을 알리게 되어 유감이다 currently 현재 unavailable 이용[구입]할 수 없는 the rest 나머지 promptly 곧바로

해석 주문하신 재킷이 요청하신 색상으로는 현재 구입할 수 없음을 알려드리게 되어 유감입니다만, 나머지 주문품은 곧바로 발송될 것입니다.

Ex 14. As an accountant ------- in all areas of financial reporting and tax preparation, Ms. Nikolov has been an invaluable asset to our firm.

(A) competence
(B) competently
(C) competent
(D) competency

빈칸에 형용사 competent를 넣어 보자. 그러면 '주격 관계 대명사 + be동사'인 who is를 생략하여 competent in all areas of financial reporting and tax preparation이 앞의 an accountant를 수식하는 구문임을 알 수 있다. 그러므로 정답은 (C)이다.

어휘 accountant 회계사 competency(=competence) 능력, 실력 competent 유능한 financial 재무의 tax preparation 세무 준비 invaluable 매우 소중한 asset 자산, 재산 firm 회사

해석 Ms. Nikolov는 재무 보고와 세무 준비의 모든 영역에서 유능한 회계사로서, 우리 회사의 매우 소중한 자산이었다.

유형 9 **however[no matter how] + 형용사/부사 + S + V**

복합관계부사 however[no matter how]는 관계사 중 유일하게 바로 뒤에 형용사나 부사를 추가해서 사용할 수 있으며, 부사절을 이끈다.

Ex 15. ABM Industries guarantees on-time delivery of all replacement parts ------- remote the destination may be.

(A) no matter how
(B) insofar as
(C) wherever
(D) in order that

빈칸 뒤에 있는 형용사 remote에 주목하자. 보기 네 개 모두 부사절 맨 앞에 올 수 있지만, 바로 뒤에 형용사나 부사를 추가해서 사용할 수 있는 것은 no matter how이므로 정답은 (A)이다.

어휘 on-time 정시의 delivery 배송, 배달 replacement part 교체 부품 no matter how 아무리 ~해도 insofar as ~하는 한에 있어서는 in order that ~하기 위해 remote 먼, 멀리 떨어진 destination 목적지

해석 ABM Industries는 목적지가 아무리 멀리 떨어져 있더라도 모든 교체 부품의 정시 배송을 보장합니다.

2. 문장의 구조 1

문장의 구조를 파악하기 위해서는 두 가지 규칙을 기억해야 한다.
(1) 절에는 반드시 동사가 있어야 한다.
(2) 절 하나에는 반드시 동사가 '하나만' 있어야 한다.

유형 1 **동사 VS 준동사** ★★★★

절에는 반드시 동사가 있어야 하므로, 절 안에 동사가 없다면 빈칸에 동사를 넣자. 절 하나에는 반드시 동사가 한 개여야 하므로, 이미 동사가 있다면 준동사가 정답이다.

Ex 1. The turnout for yesterday's product demonstration ------- the director's expectations.

(A) surpassed
(B) surpassing
(C) to surpass
(D) having surpassed

[(A) 동사/준동사, (B) 준동사, (C) 준동사 (D) 준동사]이다. 문장에 동사가 없으므로, 빈칸에는 동사 (A)가 알맞다.

어휘 turnout 참가자 수 product demonstration 제품 시연회 surpass 넘어서다 expectation 기대
해석 어제 있었던 제품 시연회의 참석자 수는 책임자의 기대를 넘어섰다.

Ex 2. The chief technician ------- that Internet systems were operational once more following a brief service interruption.

(A) to announce
(B) announced
(C) announce
(D) announcing

[(A) 준동사 (B) 동사/준동사 (C) 동사 (D) 준동사]이다. The chief technician ------- 이 주절, that 이후는 종속절이다. 주절에 동사가 필요하므로, 빈칸에는 동사 (B)나 (C)가 들어갈 수 있다. 그런데 주어가 단수 명사이므로, 주어와 동사의 수가 일치하는 (B)가 정답이다.

어휘 technician 기술자 operational 작동 가능한 following ~ 후에 brief 짧은. 단시간의 interruption (일시적) 중단
해석 수석 기술자가 잠시 서비스가 중단된 후 인터넷 시스템이 다시 작동하고 있다고 발표했다.

Ex 3. The celebration will commence at 7 P.M. with a buffet-style dinner ------- by coffee, tea, and dessert.

(A) follows
(B) will follow
(C) was followed
(D) followed

[(A) 동사 (B) 동사 (C) 동사 (D) 동사 / 준동사]이다. 문장에 동사 will commence가 있으므로 빈칸에는 동사가 들어갈 수 없다. 그러므로 준동사인 (D)가 정답이다.

어휘 celebration 축하 (행사) commence 시작하다 be followed by ~이 이어지다

해석 축하 행사는 저녁 7시에 뷔페식 만찬으로 시작하며 커피와 차, 후식이 이어집니다.

Ex 4. ------- the lucrative manufacturing contract was a welcome accomplishment for the small design firm.

(A) Winning
(B) Wins
(C) Won
(D) Had won

[(A) 준동사 (B) 동사/명사 (C) 동사/준동사 (D) 동사]이다. was가 문장의 동사이므로 (D)는 먼저 제외하자. 빈칸 뒤에 목적어 the lucrative manufacturing contract가 있어서 명사 (B)와 과거분사 (C)는 정답이 아니다. 그러므로 목적어와 함께 올 수 있는 준동사 (A)가 정답이다.

어휘 lucrative 수익성이 좋은 welcome 반가운, 환영받는 accomplishment 성과, 업적 firm 회사

해석 수익성이 좋은 제조 계약을 획득한 것은 작은 디자인 회사에게는 반가운 성과였다.

유형 2 **------- + (주어) + 동사1 ~ + 동사2 ~** *

절에는 동사가 하나만 있어야 하므로 동사가 둘이라면 이는 각각 다른 절에 속해 있음을 나타낸다.

따라서 '------- + (주어) + 동사1 ~'은 종속절로 문장의 주어이고, 동사2가 문장 전체의 동사이다. 주어 자리의 종속절은 명사절이므로, 빈칸에는 명사절 접속사가 들어가야 한다.

명사절 접속사로 **that**이 90% 출제되고, **whether, 의문사, 복합관계대명사** 순서로 출제 빈도가 높다. **if**도 명사절 접속사로 빈칸에 들어갈 수 있지만, 구어체 문장에서 주로 사용하기 때문에 정답인 경우가 거의 없다.

명사절 접속사 – that, whether, 의문사, 복합관계대명사, if

Ex 5. ------- Hercules Computers constructs a new manufacturing plant in Vietnam depends on the amount of cost savings projected by its financial analysts.

(A) While
(B) Whether
(C) Although
(D) Despite

빈칸 뒤에 완성된 3형식 문장(Hercules Computers constructs a new manufacturing plant in Vietnam)이 있으며, 바로 다음에 동사 depends가 이어진다. depends는 문장 전체의 동사이며, 앞의 3형식 절은 주어이다. 따라서 주어가 되도록 빈칸에는 명사절 접속사를 써야 하므로 (B)가 정답이다.

어휘 construct 건설하다 manufacturing plant 제조 공장 depend on ~에 달려 있다 cost saving 원가 절감 project 예상하다, 추정하다 financial analyst 금융 분석가

해석 Hercules Computers가 베트남에 새로운 제조 공장을 지을 것인지는 금융 분석가들이 예상하는 원가 절감액에 달려 있다.

Ex 6. ------- wants to join the library's book club
should register by December 21.

(A) Which
(B) Other
(C) Someone
(D) Whoever

빈칸 뒤에는 '동사+목적어(wants to join the library's book club)'가 있고, 동사 should register가 바로 다음에 등장한다. should register는 문장 전체의 동사이고, 그 앞의 절은 주어이다. 따라서 해당 절은 명사절로서, 빈칸에 명사절 접속사인 의문사 (A) 혹은 복합관계사 (D)가 들어갈 수 있다. 이중 문장의 의미가 자연스러운 (D)가 정답이다.

어휘 join ~에 가입하다 register 등록하다

해석 도서관 독서 클럽에 가입하고자 하는 사람들은 누구나 12월 21일까지 등록해야 한다.

유형 3 **be동사/타동사/전치사 + ------- + (주어) + 동사 ~ ***

be동사 뒤에는 보어, 타동사나 전치사 뒤에는 목적어가 필요한데, 보어나 목적어가 있어야 할 자리에 절 (------- + (주어) + 동사 ~)이 있는 문장 구조이다. 따라서 보어나 목적어 역할을 하는 명사절이어야 하므로, 빈칸에는 명사절 접속사가 들어가야 한다. 유형 2에서 소개한 **that**, **whether**, **의문사**, **복합관계대명사**, **if** 중 하나를 정답으로 선택하자.

*부가 규칙도 함께 기억하자

❶ whether와 if는 명사절뿐 아니라 부사절을 이끌 수 있다.

❷ whether가 부사절 접속사인 경우 반드시 짝으로 or (not)이 함께 있어야 한다. 명사절 접속사인 경우 or (not)이 반드시 필요한 것은 아니다.

❸ whether와 의문사는 to부정사와 함께 'whether to-V'나 '의문사 + to-V'의 형태로 사용할 수 있다.

Ex 7. A key attribute of the Sorvine Hotel is
------- the guest rooms feature fully stocked
kitchenettes and workstations.

(A) to
(B) whether
(C) then
(D) that

------- the guest rooms feature fully stocked kitchenettes and workstations가 동사 is의 보어이므로 명사절이어야 한다. 명사절 접속사로는 (B) whether와 (D) that이 있는데, 문장의 의미를 자연스럽게 하는 (D)가 정답이다.

어휘 attribute 특징, 특성 feature ~을 특징으로 갖추다 fully stocked 물품이 완비된 kitchenette 간이 주방 workstation 업무 공간

해석 Sorvine 호텔의 주요 특징은 객실에 모든 것이 갖춰진 작은 주방과 사무 공간이 있다는 점이다.

*문장 해석이 어렵다면 명사절 접속사의 90%는 that이라는 점을 기억하자. 또한 유형2에 있는 that, whether, 의문사, 복합관계대명사, if가 출제 빈도순이라는 점을 기억해서 정답을 찍을 수밖에 없을 때는 순서가 앞서는 것을 고르도록 하자.

Ex 8. Make sure to indicate in your reply ------- you will be accompanied by a guest at the banquet.

(A) another
(B) in case
(C) whether
(D) in order that

------- you will be accompanied by a guest at the banquet이 동사 indicate의 목적어이므로 명사절이여야 한다. 그러므로 빈칸에는 명사절 접속사 (C)가 알맞다.

어휘 make sure to-V 반드시 ~하다 indicate ~라는 것을 밝히다, 알리다 be accompanied by ~와 동행하다 banquet 연회, 만찬

해석 연회에 손님을 동반할 것인지 답장에 반드시 알려주세요.

Ex 9. Helen Kang, president of Easthaven Glassworks, is considering ------- to renew the contract with Hartwick Trucking.

(A) whether
(B) if
(C) what
(D) so

------- to renew the contract with Hartwick Trucking이 동사 is considering의 목적어이므로 명사절이여야 한다. 이어서 to부정사를 써야 하므로 명사절 접속사 (A) whether와 (C) what 중에서 골라야 한다. 이 중 문장 해석이 자연스러운 (A)가 정답이다.

*동사 consider는 목적어로 동명사를 취하므로 빈칸 뒤 to renew를 목적어로 착각하지 말자.

어휘 renew 갱신하다

해석 Easthaven Glassworks의 회장 Helen Kang은 Hartwick Trucking과의 계약을 갱신해야 할지 고려하고 있다.

Ex 10. The user guide shows ------- the camera's lens should be cleaned.

(A) could
(B) not only
(C) either
(D) how

------- the camera's lens should be cleaned가 동사 shows의 목적어이므로 명사절이여야 한다. 보기 중 명사절을 이끄는 접속사는 의문사 how이므로 정답은 (D)이다.

어휘 user guide 사용 설명서

해석 사용 설명서가 카메라 렌즈를 어떻게 청소해야 하는지를 보여준다.

Ex 11. The contract for the Meadowlands Sports Complex project will be awarded to ------- construction firm presents the most energy-efficient design.

(A) any
(B) whichever
(C) each
(D) those

------- construction firm presents the most energy-efficient design이 전치사 to의 목적어이므로 명사절이여야 한다. 보기 중 복합관계대명사 whichever가 명사절을 이끌 수 있으므로 (B)가 정답이다.

어휘 complex 복합 건물, 단지 award the contract 계약을 체결하다 construction 건설 firm 회사 present 제시하다, 제출하다

해석 Meadowlands 스포츠 단지 프로젝트 계약은 어느 건설 회사든 에너지 효율성이 가장 높은 설계를 제시하는 곳과 체결될 것이다.

101. Ms. Perez, as chief information officer for Dayton Enterprises, ------- responsibilities for all technology training workshops.

(A) assume
(B) will assume
(C) to assume
(D) assuming

102. The discount coupon ------- customers receive with their initial order is redeemable within six months.

(A) that
(B) whom
(C) whose
(D) who

103. The school is seeking teachers ------- job will involve regularly caring for or being in charge of disabled children under 12.

(A) whom
(B) what
(C) whose
(D) when

104. Dr. Montaine is offering a four-hour workshop during ------- she will share some perspectives on effective time management.

(A) whose
(B) while
(C) whatever
(D) which

105. Four diamonds, two of ------- were over a carat in size, were unexpectedly discovered on the site.

(A) them
(B) what
(C) who
(D) which

106. All shipments are brought to the receiving dock, ------- a warehouse worker verifies their tracking labels.

(A) who
(B) which
(C) when
(D) where

107. The director has decided to hire a systems engineer ------- he thought would solve the software interface problems.

(A) who
(B) whose
(C) which
(D) what

108. The toaster ovens we compared ------- in terms of price, size, and durability.

(A) vary
(B) varying
(C) variety
(D) variously

109. Peake Ltd. is a company ------- for its comprehensive employee training and skill development programs.

(A) knowledge
(B) known
(C) knowing
(D) knows

110. Derek Levin from our shipping department will contact you on Friday ------- transportation and installation of your furniture at your office.

(A) will discuss
(B) to discuss
(C) discussion
(D) discusses

111. ------- interests many visitors about the city's downtown area is its rich array of historical buildings and varied architectural styles.

(A) This
(B) What
(C) While
(D) Besides

112. The city has decided to grant the land ------- which the company wants to construct its production facilities.

(A) on
(B) for
(C) from
(D) to

113. Whenever customers need some technical assistance, they may contact us by telephone or through our Web site, ------- they prefer.

(A) whoever
(B) however
(C) whichever
(D) where

114. Tourists are encouraged to participate in the tour of the Libbey–Owens Glassware factory to see ------- various glass products are made.

(A) during
(B) what
(C) how
(D) whom

115. The survey showed ------- almost all members of the focus group found Eucalyptus soap's floral scent appealing.

(A) that
(B) what
(C) these
(D) whose

정답 및 해설 p.70

5. 동의어 문제

Examples 1-4 refer to the following book review.

From Coins to Credit: A Look at the Evolution of Banking is a concise history of financial institutions and the banking industry from ancient times to the present. Miguel Hernández, who has built a career in covering financial news for multiple newspapers, has conducted a thorough investigation of the topic. Despite carefully presenting facts, Mr. Hernández has managed to make what could have been a dry book into a captivating and pleasurable read. Through his narratives of amusing anecdotes about historical figures, he makes them come alive. Even people who have no particular interest in the subject matter will find this book engrossing.

Ex 1. What most likely is Mr. Hernández's job?

(A) Banker
(B) Librarian
(C) Journalist
(D) Publisher

Ex 2. What does the reviewer NOT mention about the book?

(A) It is quite lengthy.
(B) It is entertaining.
(C) It gives an account of people from the past.
(D) It has been researched in depth.

Ex 3. The word "dry" in line 5 is closest in meaning to

(A) dull
(B) vacant
(C) droughty
(D) humorous

Ex 4. What does the reviewer suggest?

(A) The majority of people lack interest in history.
(B) The banking sector is in complete chaos.
(C) Mr. Hernández is a seasoned lecturer.
(D) The book will appeal to multiple demographics.

Examples 1-4 refer to the following book review. 1~4번 예제는 다음 서평에 관한 것입니다.

From Coins to Credit: A Look at the Evolution of Banking is a concise history of financial institutions and the banking industry from ancient times to the present. Ex1.Miguel Hernández, who has built a career in covering financial news for multiple newspapers, Ex2.(D)has conducted a thorough investigation of the topic. Despite carefully presenting facts, Ex2.(B)/Ex3.Mr. Hernández has managed to make what could have been a dry book into a captivating and pleasurable read. Ex2.(C)Through his narratives of amusing anecdotes about historical figures, he makes them come alive. Ex4.Even people who have no particular interest in the subject matter will find this book engrossing.

'동전부터 신용 거래까지: 은행업의 발전 살펴보기'는 고대부터 현대에 이르는 금융 기관들과 은행 산업의 간략한 역사이다. 다수의 신문사에서 금융 뉴스를 취재하며 경력을 쌓은 Miguel Hernández는 이 주제에 대해 철두철미한 조사를 시행했다. Mr. Hernández는 사실들을 꼼꼼하게 제시하지만, 지루한 책이 될 수 있었던 것을 마음을 사로잡는 즐거운 읽을거리로 만들어 냈다. 그는 역사적 인물들에 대해 재미있는 일화를 서술함으로써 그 사실들이 생생하게 살아나게 한다. 이 주제에 대해 특별한 관심이 없는 사람조차도 이 책에 눈을 떼지 못하게 한다는 것을 알게 될 것이다.

> **어휘** credit 신용 거래 a look at ~를 간략히 살펴보기 evolution 발전, 진전 concise 간결한 financial institution 금융 기관 build a career 경력을 쌓다 cover 취재하다, 보도하다 conduct 수행하다 thorough 철두철미한, 빈틈없는 investigation 조사 despite ~에도 불구하고 present 제시하다 manage to-V ~을 해내다 dry 건조한, 지루한, 재미없는 captivating 마음을 사로잡는 pleasurable 즐거운 read 읽을거리 narrative 묘사, 이야기 amusing 재미있는 anecdote 일화 figure (유명) 인물 come alive 생생하게 살아나다, 활기를 띠다 have interest in ~에 관심이 있다 particular 특별한 subject matter 주제 find ~라고 알게 되다 engrossing 주의를 사로잡는, 눈을 떼지 못하게 하는

Ex 1. What most likely is Mr. Hernández's job?

(A) Banker
(B) Librarian
(C) Journalist
(D) Publisher

Mr. Hernández의 직업은 무엇일 가능성이 가장 높은가?

(A) 은행가
(B) 도서관 사서
(C) 언론인
(D) 출판업자

> **어휘** librarian 도서관 사서 journalist 언론인 publisher 출판업자

> **해설** 두 번째 문장에서 다수의 신문사에서 금융 뉴스를 취재하며 경력을 쌓았다고(who has built a career in covering financial news for multiple newspapers) 소개하고 있으므로 Mr. Hernández의 직업은 언론인이다.

Ex 2. What does the reviewer NOT mention about the book?

(A) It is quite lengthy.
(B) It is entertaining.
(C) It gives an account of people from the past.
(D) It has been researched in depth.

서평가는 책에 관하여 무엇을 언급하지 않는가?

(A) 상당히 길다.
(B) 재미있다.
(C) 과거의 사람들에 대한 이야기를 한다.
(D) 심도 있게 연구되었다.

어휘 lengthy 너무 긴, 장황한 entertaining 재미있는, 즐거움을 주는 give an account of ~에 대해 이야기하다 in depth 깊이, 심도 있게

해설 지문을 읽으면서 신중하게 보기 하나하나 대조해야 한다. 두 번째 문장에서 주제에 대한 철두철미한 조사를 시행했다는(has conducted a thorough investigation of the topic) 내용을 읽으면서 (D)를 제외하자. 이어지는 두 문장에서는 책이 마음을 사로잡고(captivating), 즐겁고(pleasurable), 재미있고(amusing), 활기차다고(come alive) 묘사하고 있으므로 (B)를 제외하자. 동시에 역사적 인물들에 관한 일화를 서술한다는 설명도 있으므로(Through his narratives of amusing anecdotes about historical figures) (C)도 제외해야 한다.

Ex 3. The word "dry" in line 5 is closest in meaning to

(A) **dull**
(B) vacant
(C) droughty
(D) humorous

다섯째 줄의 단어 "dry"와 의미상 가장 가까운 것은

(A) 따분한, 재미없는
(B) 비어 있는
(C) 건조한, 가뭄이 계속되는
(D) 재미있는, 유머러스한

해설 동의어 문제에서 주어지는 단어는 항상 다의어이며, 보기에 여러 개의 동의어가 있다. dry가 사물의 상태를 나타낼 때는 '건조한'이라는 뜻이므로 사막의 기후를 표현할 때 사용하는 (C)와 동의어가 될 수 있다. 하지만 dry book에서의 dry는 '지루한, 재미없는'이라는 뜻이므로, 정답은 (A)이다.

Ex 4. What does the reviewer suggest?

(A) The majority of people lack interest in history.
(B) The banking sector is in complete chaos.
(C) Mr. Hernández is a seasoned lecturer.
(D) **The book will appeal to multiple demographics.**

서평가는 무엇을 시사하는가?

(A) 대다수 사람은 역사에 관심이 없다.
(B) 은행업 부문은 완전히 혼돈 상태에 있다.
(C) Mr. Hernández는 노련한 강연자이다.
(D) 책이 여러 인구 집단의 관심을 끌 것이다.

어휘 lack ~이 없다, 부족하다 the majority of 대부분의 sector 부문, 분야 chaos 혼돈, 혼란 seasoned 경험 많은, 노련한 appeal to ~의 관심을 끌다, ~에게 매력적이다 demographic 인구통계 (집단)

해설 마지막 문장에 책의 주제에 별다른 관심이 없는 사람도 몰두하여 읽게 될 것이라는 예상(Even people who have no particular interest in the subject matter will find this book engrossing.)은 책이 여러 부류의 사람들에게 매력적으로 느껴질 것이라는 점을 시사하고 있으므로 정답은 (D)이다.

Today's Vocabulary

▶Actual Test를 풀기 전에 이 단어들을 암기하자.

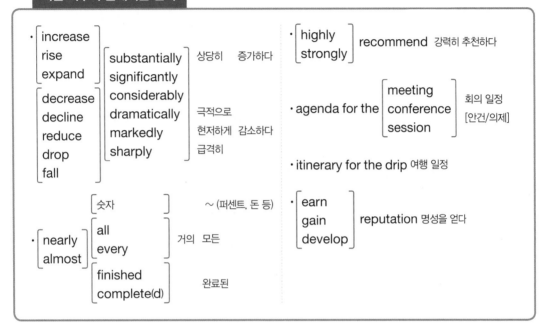

짝을 이루어 출제되는 단어

- [increase / rise / expand] [substantially / significantly / considerably / dramatically / markedly / sharply] 상당히 증가하다
- [decrease / decline / reduce / drop / fall] 극적으로 / 현저하게 감소하다 / 급격히
- [nearly / almost] [숫자] ~ (퍼센트, 돈 등) / [all / every] 거의 모든 / [finished / complete(d)] 완료된

- [highly / strongly] recommend 강력히 추천하다
- agenda for the [meeting / conference / session] 회의 일정 [안건/의제]
- itinerary for the drip 여행 일정
- [earn / gain / develop] reputation 명성을 얻다

unilaterally 일방적으로
perilously 위험하게
adequately 충분하게, 적절하게
presidency 회장직, 회장 임기
vacate 비우다
come with ~이 딸려 있다
capture (정보를) 캡쳐하다
name ~에 지명하다, 임명하다
immune 면역성이 있는
undisciplined 규율이 안 잡힌, 버릇없는
according 부합되는
unwavering 변함없는, 확고한
commitment to ~하겠다는 약속
suspend (일시적으로) 중지하다, 정지시키다
subsequent 그[이] 다음의, 차후의

subjective 주관적인
sustain 지속시키다
acquire 획득하다, 인수하다
property 부동산; 건물
be opposed to ~에 반대하다
interfere 방해하다(with); 간섭[개입/참견]하다(in)
lag behind ~에 뒤처지다
present 현재의; 참석한, 출석한
derive (본원·원천에서) ~을 얻다, 끌어내다
discard 버리다, 폐기하다
priceless 값을 매길 수 없는, 대단히 귀중한
container 그릇, 용기
forward 보내다, 전달하다
designate 지정하다
expiration date (식품의) 유통 기한

refrigerate 냉장하다, 냉장고에 보관하다

fragile 부서지기 쉬운, 손상되기 쉬운

perishable 잘 상하는

attest to ~을 증명하다, 입증하다

performance 실적, 성과

demonstrate (행동으로) 보여주다, 발휘하다

unparalleled 비할[견줄] 데 없는

work ethic 직업 정신

profound (지식 · 이해 등이) 깊은, 심오한

insight into ~에 대한 통찰력, 식견

business affairs 비즈니스 업무

query 문의

apprehension 우려, 불안

dismantle (기계 · 구조물을) 분해하다, 해체하다

dispose of ~을 없애다, 처리하다

erect (똑바로) 세우다

accountable for ~에 대해 책임이 있는

furnish 제공하다, 공급하다

sum 합계, 총계

deposit 착수금

reserve (권한 등을) 갖다, 보유하다

the right to-V ~할 (법적 · 도덕적) 권리, 권한

withdraw 취소하다, 철회하다

terms (지급 · 계약의) 조건, 조항

void 무효의, 법적 효력이 없는

up front 선불로

secure 획득하다, 확보하다

balance 지불 잔액, 잔금

hectic 정신없이 바쁜

prioritize 우선순위를 매기다

commitment 약속(한 일); 책무

periodic 주기적인

integral 필수적인, 필요불가결한

optimal 최고의, 최적의

medical practitioner 개업의(開業醫)

carry out ~을 수행하다, 이행하다

make a case for ~에 대한 옹호론을 펴다

argument 주장, 논거

make ~ known ~을 알리다, 발표하다

explore 탐구하다, 분석하다

applaud (박수)갈채를 보내다

Actual Test

PART 5

1. 빈칸 앞뒤를 보며 문제를 푼다.
2. 빈칸 앞뒤를 보고 정답을 알 수 없다면 문장을 해석한다.
3. 두 줄 분량의 어휘 문제는 문장 전체를 해석해서 푼다.
4. 접속사 어휘 문제는 빈칸 앞뒤만을 보고 풀 수 없다. 문장 전체를 해석해 보자.

PART 6

1. 문법 문제라면 Part 5와 같은 방식으로 빈칸 앞뒤를 보며 푼다.
2. 다른 유형의 문제는 문맥을 통해 정답을 파악한다.

PART 7

1. 문제와 보기 (A), (B), (C), (D)를 먼저 읽은 후에 지문을 읽는다.
2. 지문 위아래의 모든 부분을 자세히 읽어 본다.
3. 문제의 해설을 꼼꼼히 읽고, 문장 구조를 분석하며 복습한다.

101. All the fragile items should be ------- wrapped in foam plastic before being boxed for shipping.

(A) unilaterally
(B) steadily
(C) perilously
(D) adequately

102. The software has been ------- entirely designed in India, proving that Indian programmers are capable of original and creative work.

(A) almost
(B) most
(C) most of
(D) partly

103. The magazine article presents a list of precautions ------- delicate fabric such as silk usually requires.

(A) who
(B) whose
(C) which
(D) of which

104. The new radio talk show, ------- which listeners can phone in with their questions, will start broadcasting at 2 P.M. next Thursday.

(A) even
(B) while
(C) during
(D) between

105. At the upcoming Building Your Business workshop, attendees will gain insight into ------- small businesses can create a unique brand image.

(A) which
(B) how
(C) what
(D) who

106. The project manager cannot continue the work until she receives an explicit answer about the changes ------- proposed.

(A) she
(B) that
(C) were
(D) until

107. We have to choose a ------- who can lead our sessions during the seminar in order to create a positive work environment.

(A) preside
(B) presidential
(C) president
(D) presidency

108. New Heritage, an antique store ------- in unique home furnishings and garden decorations, opened in Belk Department Store yesterday.

(A) specializing
(B) will be specializing
(C) is to be specializing
(D) is specializing

109. Security personnel must ensure that all employees ------- the office building promptly after the fire alarm goes off.

(A) have vacated
(B) to vacate
(C) vacating
(D) vacancy

110. The board of directors has decided to acquire Arbus Autos, ------- will make Bikkel Motors the largest vehicle manufacturer in Asia.

(A) there
(B) which
(C) whose
(D) that

111. Cars from Tarnall Motors come with a warranty lasting 36 months or 60,000 kilometers, ------- is reached first.

(A) whichever
(B) whoever
(C) whenever
(D) however

112. Pacific Cargo was able to expand profits ------- by attracting new customers in China and Thailand.

(A) tightly
(B) substantially
(C) warmly
(D) subjectively

113. The repair shop is well known for its expertise in repairing old watches, some of ------- have been discontinued.

(A) their
(B) whose
(C) whom
(D) which

114. This year's Harbortown Poetry Prize will be awarded to Miranda Blethyn, ------- poem "Atlas" was selected from over 300 entries.

(A) which
(B) whom
(C) whose
(D) what

115. We're looking forward to our colleague's return from Canada, ------- he gave a presentation to the potential clients.

(A) while
(B) which
(C) where
(D) why

116. When you are to change a ------- reservation, there will be at least a 10 percent extra charge.

(A) confirmed
(B) determined
(C) decided
(D) suspended

117. ------- uncomfortable they may be, safety gear such as helmets, goggles, and gloves absolutely must be worn by anyone entering the construction site.

(A) Almost
(B) Nevertheless
(C) Seldom
(D) However

118. The Prodeliax Pro-6 software program captures ------- is visible on your computer screen and stores it in its archive.

(A) wherever
(B) everything
(C) whatever
(D) anyway

119. Promotions should not automatically be granted to ------- has the most seniority.

(A) nobody
(B) whoever
(C) anyone
(D) oneself

120. Ventralcom recently announced ------- Pamela Wang has been named senior vice president of mergers and acquisitions at the company.

(A) what
(B) because
(C) while
(D) that

121. The CEO has an ------- commitment to enhancing market value of the company in any manner possible.

(A) immune
(B) undisciplined
(C) according
(D) unwavering

122. Management ------- recommends that all employees familiarize themselves with the new software that will be installed in the office next week.

(A) intermittently
(B) superbly
(C) collaboratively
(D) strongly

123. The merger negotiation of Dexia International and Devon Ltd. is expected to be finalized ------- next month.

(A) amid
(B) already
(C) within
(D) until

124. ------- events showed that the company's decision to acquire the property adjacent to their main office had been a great one.

(A) Suspended
(B) Subsequent
(C) Subjective
(D) Sustaining

125. The managing director, Allen Schmidt, remains ------- to any changes to the company logo and motto.

(A) opposed
(B) anxious
(C) eager
(D) interfered

126. The company was lagging ------- its competitors in a number of important technological fields, which caused a continual reduction in market share.

(A) away
(B) behind
(C) ongoing
(D) afterwards

127. According to the most ------- inventory figures, Kakua brand denim jackets need to be reordered immediately.

(A) close
(B) near
(C) recent
(D) present

128. The Woodward City Council is requesting all households to collect ------- containers, which will be forwarded to a designated recycling center.

(A) derived
(B) discarded
(C) precious
(D) priceless

129. Please make sure you check the ------- date on the bottom of the milk carton before you purchase it.

(A) expiration
(B) expire
(C) expiring
(D) expired

130. We regret to inform you that we don't have any refrigerated trucks available right now, so we cannot transport these ------- items until tomorrow afternoon.

(A) durable
(B) fragile
(C) spoiled
(D) perishable

GO ON TO THE NEXT PAGE

PART 6

Questions 131-134 refer to the following letter.

February 18

Dear Mr. Welsh:

This letter serves to confirm that Natsume Sugahara ------- with Tommykaira
                                              131.

Motors. Ms. Sugahara has held the title of Business Technology Analyst for

five years and earns a salary at the top of the pay grade range for that post.

-------. I will also attest to ------- high level of performance. ------- working with
132.   **133.**   **134.**

Tommykaira Motors, Ms. Sugahara has demonstrated an unparalleled work ethic

and a profound insight into our business affairs.

Should you have any further inquiries, please do not hesitate to contact me at

04-2103-9485.

Sincerely,

Jasmine Keller

Director, Engineering Program Management

Tommykaira Motors

131. (A) had been employed
    (B) will be employed
    (C) is employed
    (D) has employed

132. (A) Our new entry-level vehicle is also
        scheduled to be released.
    (B) Additionally, she is paid an annual
        bonus that is higher than average.
    (C) Likewise, she is doing well despite
        the mounting pressure.
    (D) I will be happy to offer her a
        position in the upper management
        of our company.

133. (A) our
    (B) its
    (C) your
    (D) her

134. (A) While
    (B) Whether
    (C) Prior to
    (D) As long as

Questions 135-138 refer to the following e-mail.

To: Baey Yam Keng
From: Meiplus Dental Care
Date: 23 July
Subject: Your teeth

Dear Mr. Pon,

Your smile is ------- to us. It is time for you to schedule a checkup and cleaning
        135.
appointment. It has been over fifteen months since your last ------- with us.
                                                        136.
Meiplus Dental Care advises ------- you schedule a routine cleaning every six
                        137.
months and an examination each year.

We look forward to hearing from you and are prepared to take care of your

dental needs. -------.
            138.

Sincerely,

Jeanette Aw, Hygienist

Meiplus Dental Care
1 Tanjong Pagar Plaza
#02-24 Singapore
082001
Phone: 65 6538 1400

---

135. (A) important
        (B) polite
        (C) available
        (D) similar

136. (A) course
        (B) reunion
        (C) visit
        (D) stay

137. (A) what
        (B) each
        (C) most
        (D) that

138. (A) It has been a privilege doing
            business with your firm.
        (B) Feel free to contact us if you have
            any queries or apprehensions.
        (C) This is your last opportunity to alter
            your decision.
        (D) We look forward to welcoming new
            patients to our practice.

GO ON TO THE NEXT PAGE ➡

PART 7

Questions 139-142 refer to the following document.

Toledo Fence and Supply, Inc.
2525 Hill Ave., Toledo, OH 43607-3694
1-419-535-6833

Fabrication --- Sales --- Installation --- Repairs
Residential --- Commercial --- Industrial
Privacy --- Security --- Ornamental --- Guard Rail
Aluminum --- Vinyl --- Metal --- Wood

Proposal submitted to *Ganesha Mahajan*	Home Phone *607-555-1327*
Street *25 Anthony Wayne Trail*	Job Location *East on Stitt Road to River Road. Right after two*
City and State *Toledo, OH*	*miles to Dutch Road. Left onto Anthony Wayne Trail.*

We hereby tender specifications and estimates for the furnishing and installation of the following:

Dismantle and dispose of 18 sections of 4-rail fence with attached wire mesh. Erect approximately 210 feet of 4.5-foot-tall fence with standard posts. 25 fence sections, two 4.5-foot gates. Strive to make the top of the fence level.

Customer accountable for defining property lines and location of fence, clearing space for fence, and obtaining relevant permits.

We hereby propose to furnish labor and materials in accordance with the above specifications for the sum of *Four Thousand Three Hundred and Ninety dollars ($4,390)*. 50 percent deposit required. Outstanding balance due upon completion.

Toledo Fence and Supply, Inc., reserves the right to withdraw this proposal if not accepted within 30 days.

139. What type of document is this?

(A) An advertisement
(B) A proposal
(C) A work schedule
(D) An order form

140. What kind of work is being discussed?

(A) Replacement of a fence
(B) Construction of a patio
(C) Lawn maintenance
(D) Furniture restoration

141. What is NOT stated in the document?

(A) The terms will become void after 30 days.
(B) The total amount must be paid up front.
(C) The customer must secure permits for the work.
(D) The materials are included in the cost.

142. The word "balance" in paragraph 4, line 3 is closest in meaning to

(A) deficit
(B) remainder
(C) resource
(D) supply

Care Delivered to Your Doorstep

In our current hectic lifestyles, it is not uncommon to prioritize a work commitment or a social gathering over seeing a medical professional. Even with proper exercise and diet, though, periodic medical examinations are integral to maintaining optimal health. One medical practitioner in Melbourne devised a strategy to aid time-pressed people in obtaining the necessary attention. "If people don't have the time to come to me, I'll go to them instead," said Bradley Martin, M.D. Mondays and Thursdays are the days when Dr. Martin closes his clinic to carry out home visits to clients. "Making home visits to clients can now eliminate the need for clients to come to the clinic in the future," said Dr. Martin. "For this reason, preventive health care is the foundation of my approach to medicine. I believe this will play a part in making Melbourne a healthier environment."

— Greta Harrison for *Health Today*

Irish Author's Stellar Performance Continues

Mayanti Langer's newest book, *Ireland's Changing Waves*, is an exceptional chronicle of the evolution of the fishing industry in Ireland, from self-sustaining fishing villages to present-day fish farming. A Howth native, Ms. Langer was taught the trade by her fisherman father, so her book contains vivid firsthand accounts of the Irish fishing lifestyle as well as top-notch research. She makes her preference for traditional fishing practices over modernized seafood harvesting very clear. Along with that, she makes a good case for the ecological value of a less complicated way of life in rural communities. All in all, *Ireland's Changing Waves* is a worthy companion volume to Ms. Langer's preceding book on the history of agriculture, *Proliferating Prosperity*. Ms. Langer has already made known her plan to create a new book dealing with medical care, entitled *Mending the Crowd*. *Ireland's Changing Waves* and other titles written by Ms. Langer can be located on her publisher's Web site, www.mercierpress.ie.

1 September

Bradley Martin, M.D.
Healthjoy Distributors Clinic
537 George St.
Fitzroy North Victoria 3068
Australia

Dear Dr. Martin,

I recently came across an article in *Health Today* that highlighted your unique medical practice. I am currently writing a book that explores the history of medical care, and I think your story would be beneficial to my research. I'd very much like to interview you for the book when I visit Melbourne this winter. If this is possible, please contact my office at +353 (020) 918-2148.

On a personal note, I'd like to applaud your efforts to make your city healthier. I think your approach is brilliant, and I'm sending you my best wishes.

Most sincerely,

M. Langer

Mayanti Langer

143. What is the article mainly about?

(A) A clinic adjusting its hours
(B) A new type of patient visits
(C) Guidance for selecting a physician
(D) Health benefits of exercise

144. In the review, the word "case" in paragraph 1, line 7, is closest in meaning to

(A) argument
(B) container
(C) situation
(D) encounter

145. What does the review suggest about Ms. Langer?

(A) She is in favor of traditional fishing practices.
(B) She is currently authoring a book about farming.
(C) She spent her childhood in Australia.
(D) She recently set up her own Web site.

146. For what book does Ms. Langer want to interview Dr. Martin?

(A) *Ireland's Changing Waves*
(B) *Mending the Crowd*
(C) *Proliferating Prosperity*
(D) *Health Today*

147. What does Ms. Langer imply in her letter?

(A) She is convinced that eating fish is part of a healthy diet.
(B) She desires to present Dr. Martin with a copy of her book.
(C) She is eager to suggest a medical strategy to Dr. Martin.
(D) She believes that doctors visiting homes is a good idea.

정답 및 해설 p.73

MEMO

Day

06

1. 문장의 구조 2 ★★★

유형 4   완성된 문장 ------- + 주어 + 동사

Day 01을 공부했으므로, "완성된 문장!" 하면 '부사'가 떠오를 것이다. 즉, '------- + 주어 + 동사 ~' 전체
가 부사 자리에 있는 것이다.

$$ \boxed{완성된 \ 문장} \ + \ \boxed{\text{------- + 주어 + 동사} \sim} $$

주절   부사절

앞에 있는 완성된 문장은 주절, '------- + 주어 + 동사 ~'는 부사절이므로 빈칸에는 부사절 접속사가 들어
가야 한다. 부사절 접속사는 Day 03에 표로 정리되어 있다.

Ex 12. The judges may commence their review of
the entries ------- the deadline for submitting
slogans is over.

(A) how
(B) nor
(C) now that
(D) whether

빈칸 앞에 3형식 문장이 완성되어 있고, 빈칸
뒤에 '주어 + 동사'가 있으므로, 앞 문장이 주
절, 빈칸 뒤는 부사절이다. 빈칸에는 부사절 접
속사 (C)와 (D) 중에서 들어가면 된다. (D)를 부
사절에 사용하려면 or (not)이 필요하므로 (C)
가 정답이다.

어휘 judge 심사위원 commence 시작하다 review 검토 entry 출품작, 참가작 submit 제출하다 over 끝난, 지난
해석 구호 제출 마감 기한이 지났으므로 심사위원들은 응모작 검토를 시작해도 좋습니다.

유형 5   ------- 주어 + 동사 ~, 주어 + 동사 ~

Day 02에서 공부한 내용을 토대로, '-------, 주어 + 동사'에서 빈칸은 부사 자리이다.

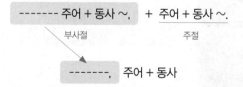

부사가 들어갈 자리에 '------- 주어 + 동사 ~'가 있으므로 빈칸에는 부사절 접속사가 필요하다. 빈칸 부분
이 부사절, 쉼표 뒤가 주절이 된다.

Ex 13. ------- the regional manager pays a visit to a local branch, she brings treats for the office staff.

(A) Whenever
(B) During
(C) Around
(D) How

'------- 주어 + 동사 ~, 주어 + 동사 ~'의 구조가 있다면 쉼표 앞이 부사절이므로 빈칸에 부사절 접속사가 들어가야 한다. 그러므로 (A)가 정답이다.

어휘 regional 지역의 pay a visit to ~를 방문하다 local branch 지사 treat (가끔 맛보는) 별미 (음식)

해석 지역 담당 매니저는 지사를 방문할 때마다 사무실 직원들을 위한 별미를 가져온다.

2. 수의 일치 ★★★★

수의 일치 문제는 능동태/수동태, 동사/준동사, 시제와 같은 다양한 문법 요소를 결합한 형태로 출제된다.

유형 1 주어와 동사의 수의 일치

가장 많이 출제되는 유형으로, 주어와 동사 사이에 있는 전치사구나 분사 구문, 관계대명사절 같은 수식어구를 잘 구분해야 함정에 빠지지 않고 정답을 알아낼 수 있다.

Ex 1. Scientists at the Wrigley Institute for Environmental Studies in Los Angeles ------- the impact of using fossil fuels on the environment.

(A) researches
(B) have researched
(C) researching
(D) had been researched

[(A) 능동태 동사 (B) 능동태 동사 (C) 준동사 (D) 수동태 동사] 문장에 동사가 필요하므로 준동사 (C)는 제외하자. 빈칸 뒤에 목적어 (the impact of using fossil fuels on the environment)가 있으므로 능동태 동사 (A)와 (B) 중 정답을 선택한다. 빈칸 앞에 있는 두 개의 전치사구 at the Wrigley Institute for Environmental Studies와 in Los Angeles를 제외하면 주어(Scientists)가 복수 명사임을 알 수 있다. 그러므로 주어와 동사의 수가 일치하도록 (B)를 정답으로 고르자.

어휘 institute 협회, 연구소 impact (up)on ~에 미치는 영향 fossil fuel 화석 연료

해석 Los Angeles에 있는 Wrigley 환경 연구소의 과학자들은 화석 연료 사용이 환경에 미치는 영향을 연구했다.

유형 2 one[each/either/neither] of + 복수 명사 + 단수 동사

전치사구 'of + 복수 명사' 앞에 단수 대명사 one[each/either/neither]가 있으므로 동사도 단수형으로 해야 한다. 밑줄로 표시한 세 부분이 모두 빈칸으로 출제된다.

Ex 2. ------- of the recruits was given an employee handbook that provides information about company policies and procedures.

　　(A) Each
　　(B) Most
　　(C) All
　　(D) Every

------- of the recruits was given을 보면 'Each of + 복수 명사 + 단수 동사' 구조이므로 (A)가 정답이다.

어휘 recruit 신입 사원 employee handbook 직원 편람 policy 정책 procedure 절차

해석 신입 직원 각자에게 회사의 정책과 절차에 대한 정보를 제공하는 직원 편람이 주어졌다.

유형 3 **부정수량형용사와 명사의 수의 일치**

❶ each(각각의), every(모든), another(또 다른, 또 하나의) + 셀 수 있는 단수 명사

❷ ┌ many/a lot of(많은), various/a variety of(다양한)
　 │ several/a number of(몇몇의), a few(몇 개의), few(거의 없는), fewer(더 적은) ┤ + 셀 수 있는 명사 복수형
　 └ both(둘 다의), one of(~ 중 하나)

❸ much(많은), a little(적은), little(거의 없는), less(더 적은) + 셀 수 없는 명사

❹ any(어떤 ~라도), some(일부의), most(대부분의), all(모든), other(다른) + ┌ 셀 수 있는 명사 복수형 ┐
　　　　　　　　　　　　　　　　　　　　　　　　　　　　　　　　　　　└ 셀 수 없는 명사 　　　┘

　* any 뒤에는 셀 수 있는 명사 단수형도 사용할 수 있다.

Ex 3. In order to enhance interaction with the local community, ------- workshop participant is encouraged to join a social work group.

　　(A) single
　　(B) several
　　(C) all
　　(D) each

빈칸 뒤에 셀 수 있는 명사 단수형(workshop participant)이 있으므로 (D)를 정답으로 선택해야 한다. (B)와 (C) 뒤에는 셀 수 있는 명사가 복수형으로 나와야 한다. (A)가 정답이 아닌 이유는 아래 〈참고〉에서 확인하자.

어휘 enhance 향상시키다 participant 참석자 be encouraged to-V ~하도록 권장받다 social work 사회 (복지) 사업

해석 지역 사회와의 소통을 향상하기 위해 각 워크숍 참가자에게 사회 복지 단체에 가입할 것을 권장합니다.

참고 single이 오답인 이유

(1) 한정사: 명사 앞에서 한정의 뜻을 나타내며, 관사, 명사의 소유격, 소유격 대명사, 부정수량형용사 등이 있다.

(2) 한정사와 보통명사의 규칙

　① 한정사는 반드시 하나만 사용한다. 예를 들어, 부정수량형용사와 관사를 함께 사용할 수 없다.

　② 보통명사는 반드시 관사와 함께 사용하거나 복수형으로 만들어야 문장에 사용할 수 있다.

➡ 두 가지 규칙에 따라 보통명사 workshop participant 앞에는 관사 a나 the가 있어야 하지만, 부정수량형용사 each가 올 경우 관사를 쓸 필요가 없다. 반면 일반 형용사 single은 보통명사의 규칙에 따라 a single workshop participant의 형태가 되어야 한다.

most[half/some/the rest/분수/percent] of + $\begin{bmatrix} \text{셀 수 있는 명사의 복수형} \\ \text{셀 수 없는 명사} \end{bmatrix}$ + 동사

most[half/some/the rest/분수/percent] 뒤에는 셀 수 있는 명사의 복수형과 셀 수 없는 명사가 모두 올 수 있다. 명사에 따라 뒤에 나오는 동사는 이 명사의 수와 일치해야 한다.

참고 분수 읽는 법: 분자(기수) → 분모(서수)

$\frac{1}{3}$ one third or a third $\frac{2}{3}$ two thirds $\frac{3}{5}$ three fifths

Ex 4. Most of the office ------- are stored in the supply cabinet of each department.

(A) supply
(B) supplier
(C) supplied
(D) supplies

빈칸 앞 Most of the office -------을 보면 빈칸에는 명사가 들어가야 하므로 동사 (C)는 제외하자. 또한 most of 뒤에는 단복수 명사 모두 가능하지만 동사와 수가 일치해야 하므로 복수 동사 are stored에 알맞은 복수 명사 (D)가 정답이다.

어휘 office supply 사무용품 supplier 공급자. 공급 회사 store 보관하다 supply cabinet 소모품 캐비닛

해석 사무용품은 대부분 각 부서 소모품 캐비닛에 보관된다.

유형 5 ------- + 주격 관계대명사 + -------

주격 관계대명사 앞에 있는 선행사와 그 뒤에 있는 동사는 수가 일치해야 한다.

Ex 5. Chinalco Mining will open new processing plants in ------- that are more convenient for transportation, currently under way in Blue Ridge Mountains.

(A) locate
(B) located
(C) location
(D) locations

전치사 in의 목적어가 필요하므로 명사 (C)나 (D) 중에서 정답을 골라야 한다. 빈칸에는 주격 관계대명사 that의 선행사가 들어가야 하므로 뒤에 있는 동사 are를 보고 복수 명사 (D)를 정답으로 선택하자.

어휘 mining 광(산)업 processing plant 가공 처리 공장 convenient 편리한 transportation 수송 currently 현재 under way 시작된, 진행 중인

해석 Chinalco Mining은 수송에 더 편리한 위치에 새 가공 처리 공장들을 개설하려고 하는데, 현재 Blue Ridge 산맥에서 진행 중이다.

101. Taking advantage of online banking, bills can be settled ------- it fits your schedule.

(A) whenever
(B) simply
(C) accordingly
(D) quite

102. ------- Mr. Villalobos has been employed at Atzeret Communications for ten years, he is still eager to learn new skills and take on additional responsibilities.

(A) Although
(B) But
(C) Neither
(D) Yet

103. A thorough review of staff recruitment procedures ------- in the annual report to First Commonwealth Bank's board of directors.

(A) includes
(B) including
(C) was included
(D) were included

104. Matt Yoon, president of Anyang Industries, ------- to disclose substantial profits at the end of the year.

(A) expect
(B) is expected
(C) expecting
(D) were expecting

105. At Romulus Ltd., there are ------- opportunities for career advancement.

(A) plenty
(B) each
(C) every
(D) many

106. Roughly a third of the employees at Bryer Accounting ------- to work by bus.

(A) commutes
(B) commute
(C) is commuting
(D) has commuted

107. We were surprised and pleased that our job posting for an assistant manager generated so much -------.

(A) interested
(B) interest
(C) interests
(D) interesting

108. Mr. and Mrs. Rodriguez ------- in charge of the development of the medicine since the company was merged with Miracle Pharmaceuticals.

(A) have been
(B) were
(C) to be
(D) has been

109. A price reduction in public transportation fares ------- people to drive less and decrease fuel usage.

(A) would encourage
(B) is encouraged
(C) encouraging
(D) encourage

110. Invitations to the annual charity reception were sent to all board members, but ------- will be able to attend.

(A) little
(B) few
(C) whoever
(D) so

111. Tassel Tower, one of the premium office ------- in Bogotá, has lowered its monthly rents by 10 percent, but many of its offices still remain unoccupied.

(A) location
(B) located
(C) locations
(D) locating

112. The Incheon Airport has an underground train system that ------- the international and domestic flight terminals.

(A) connects
(B) connecting
(C) connection
(D) connect

113. Employees who consistently finish their assignments ------- they are due may receive bonuses in accordance with the compensation guidelines.

(A) before
(B) how
(C) why
(D) either

114. ------- Vice President Jepsen's schedule alters, we will reschedule the strategy session for a different date.

(A) Ever
(B) If
(C) In order that
(D) So

115. One of the ------- of the researchers at Rangel-Moreno Laboratories is to keep materials in their work areas labeled accurately at all times.

(A) responsible
(B) responsibly
(C) responsibility
(D) responsibilities

6. 의도 파악 문제

* At 13:12 P.M., what does Mr. Ponce most likely mean when he writes, "No need"?

· 문제 풀이 전략

문자 메시지와 온라인 채팅 형식으로만 출제되는 유형이다. 대부분 주어진 대사의 바로 앞에 있는 한두 개의 대사에 정답의 단서가 있다. 지문과 함께 있는 문제 중 첫 문제가 이 유형이라면 지문을 처음부터 모두 읽지 말고 바로 앞 대사부터 읽어서 시간을 절약하자.

Examples 1-4 refer to the following text-message chain.

Mariano Ponce (1:10 P.M.)	Hi Adrian, can you e-mail me your notes from the conference call this morning?
Adrian Kuang (1:11 P.M.)	Do you mind if I send them tomorrow? I'd like to make some revisions to them first.
Mariano Ponce (1:12 P.M.)	No need. I'm sure I can make them out.
Adrian Kuang (1:13 P.M.)	OK. I'm finishing up at the cafeteria now, but I'll send them as soon as I get back to work.
Mariano Ponce (1:14 P.M.)	Terrific! When will that be?
Adrian Kuang (1:15 P.M.)	In about a quarter of an hour. What's the rush?
Mariano Ponce (1:16 P.M.)	I need to collect some more data for my quarterly report. It's due this afternoon.
Adrian Kuang (1:17 P.M.)	Oh, wow! I thought that wasn't due until next Tuesday.
Mariano Ponce (1:18 P.M.)	It was, but Michael Keogh moved up the deadline.
Adrian Kuang (1:19 P.M.)	OK, I'll get the notes to you as soon as possible. Let me know if you'd like me to proofread the report before you submit it
Mariano Ponce (1:20 P.M.)	Thank you very much! Will do.

Ex 1. Why does Mr. Ponce request Ms. Kuang's notes?

   (A) He misplaced the notes that he took himself.
   (B) He was not content with some data.
   (C) He needs them for a report he is writing.
   (D) He wants to know how many people attended the meeting.

Ex 2. At 1:12 P.M., what does Mr. Ponce most likely mean when he writes, "No need"?

   (A) He has changed his mind about acquiring the notes.
   (B) He doesn't need to pick up the notes in person.
   (C) He will utilize the notes that are unorganized.
   (D) He prefers to wait for the notes until next Tuesday.

Ex 3. What does Ms. Kuang offer to do?

   (A) Check a report for errors
   (B) Change a report's deadline
   (C) Get in touch with Mr. Keogh
   (D) Deliver some mail for Mr. Ponce

Ex 4. What is Ms. Kuang most likely doing while texting?

   (A) Eating lunch
   (B) Attending a conference call
   (C) Revising data
   (D) Reading a document

Examples 1-4 refer to the following text-message chain. 1~4번 예제는 다음 문자 메시지에 관한 것입니다.

Mariano Ponce (1:10 P.M.) Hi Adrian, Ex1·can you e-mail me your notes from the conference call this morning?

Adrian Kuang (1:11 P.M.) Ex2·Do you mind if I send them tomorrow? I'd like to make some revisions to them first.

Mariano Ponce (1:12 P.M.) Ex2·No need. I'm sure I can make them out.

Adrian Kuang (1:13 P.M.) OK. Ex3·I'm finishing up at the cafeteria now, but I'll send them as soon as I get back to work.

Mariano Ponce (1:14 P.M.) Terrific! When will that be?

Adrian Kuang (1:15 P.M.) In about a quarter of an hour. What's the rush?

Mariano Ponce (1:16 P.M.) Ex1·I need to collect some more data for my quarterly report. It's due this afternoon.

Adrian Kuang (1:17 P.M.) Oh, wow! I thought that wasn't due until next Tuesday.

Mariano Ponce (1:18 P.M.) It was, but Michael Keogh moved up the deadline.

Adrian Kuang (1:19 P.M.) OK, Ex3·I'll get the notes to you as soon as possible. Ex2·Let me know if you'd like me to proofread the report before you submit it.

Mariano Ponce (1:20 P.M.) Thank you very much! Will do.

Mariano Ponce (오후 1:10) 안녕 Adrian, 오늘 오전 전화 회의 기록을 이메일로 보내 줄 수 있겠어요?

Adrian Kuang (오후 1:11) 내일 보내 드리면 안 될까요? 먼저 수정을 좀 하고 싶어서요.

Mariano Ponce (오후 1:12) 그럴 필요 없어요. 분명히 이해할 수 있을 거예요.

Adrian Kuang (오후 1:13) 알겠습니다. 지금 구내식당에서 식사를 마치는 중이라서요. 자리로 돌아가자마자 보내 드릴게요.

Mariano Ponce (오후 1:14) 좋아요! 그게 언제일까요?

Adrian Kuang (오후 1:15) 한 15분 정도 후에요. 왜 그렇게 서두르세요?

Mariano Ponce (오후 1:16) 분기 보고서 때문에 데이터를 더 모아야 해요. 오늘 오후에 제출해야 하거든요.

Adrian Kuang (오후 1:17) 어머! 다음 주 화요일까지만 제출하면 되는 줄 알았어요.

Mariano Ponce (오후 1:18) 그랬었는데, Michael Keogh가 마감 기한을 앞당겼어요.

Adrian Kuang (오후 1:19) 알겠습니다. 되도록 빨리 기록을 드릴게요. 보고서 제출하시기 전에 제가 교정해 주길 원하시면 알려주세요.

Mariano Ponce (오후 1:20) 정말 고마워요! 그럴게요.

어휘 notes 필기, 메모, 기록 conference call 전화 회의 Do you mind if ~? ~해도 될까요? make revisions to ~를 수정하다 make out ~을 이해하다 finish up 다 먹다 cafeteria 구내식당 terrific 아주 좋은 a quarter 15분 rush 서두름 quarterly report 분기 보고서 due 기일이 되는 move up 앞당기다 proofread 교정을 보다

Ex 1. Why does Mr. Ponce request Ms. Kuang's notes?

(A) He misplaced the notes that he took himself.
(B) He was not content with some data.
(C) He needs them for a report he is writing.
(D) He wants to know how many people attended the meeting.

Mr. Ponce는 왜 Ms. Kuang의 기록을 요구하는가?

(A) 자신이 작성한 기록을 어딘가에 두고 잊어버렸다.
(B) 일부 데이터에 만족하지 못했다.
(C) 작성하고 있는 보고서에 필요하다.
(D) 회의에 몇 명이 참석했는지 알고 싶다.

어휘 misplace ~을 놓고 잊어버리다 take notes 필기하다, 기록하다 content with ~에 만족하는

해설 Mr. Ponce가 1시 10분에 오전에 있었던 전화 회의 기록을 요청한 후(can you e-mail me your notes from the conference call this morning?), 1시 16분에 오후에 제출해야 하는 분기 보고서에 들어갈 데이터가 필요하다고(I need to collect some more data for my quarterly report. It's due this afternoon.) 설명하고 있다.

Ex 2. At 1:12 P.M., what does Mr. Ponce most likely mean when he writes, "No need"?

  (A) He has changed his mind about acquiring the notes.

  (B) He doesn't need to pick up the notes in person.

  (C) He will utilize the notes that are unorganized.

  (D) He prefers to wait for the notes until next Tuesday.

오후 1시 12분에 "그럴 필요 없어요."라고 쓸 때 Mr. Ponce는 무엇을 의미할 가능성이 가장 높은가?

(A) 기록 입수에 대해 마음을 바꿨다.

(B) 직접 기록을 찾아올 필요는 없다.

(C) 정리되지 않은 기록을 활용할 것이다.

(D) 다음 주 화요일까지 기록을 기다리기를 선호한다.

어휘 acquire 손에 넣다, 얻다 notes 필기, 노트, 기록 pick up ~을 찾다, 찾아오다 in person 직접, 몸소 utilize 활용하다, 이용하다 unorganized 정리되지 않은

해설 주어진 대사의 바로 앞 대화를 보면 정답을 알 수 있다. 1시 11분에 Ms. Kuang의 "내일 보내드리면 안 될까요? 먼저 수정을 좀 하고 싶어서요(Do you mind if I send them tomorrow? I'd like to make some revisions to them first)."라는 대사에 대한 대답이므로, "그럴 필요 없어요."는 "수정되지 않은 자료를 사용할 테니 빨리 보내달라"는 뜻이다.

Ex 3. What does Ms. Kuang offer to do?

  (A) Check a report for errors

  (B) Change a report's deadline

  (C) Get in touch with Mr. Keogh

  (D) Deliver some mail for Mr. Ponce

Ms. Kuang은 무엇을 해 주겠다고 제안하는가?

(A) 보고서에 오류가 있는지 확인한다

(B) 보고서의 마감 기한을 변경한다

(C) Mr. Keogh와 연락한다

(D) Mr. Ponce에게 온 우편물을 전달한다

어휘 get in touch with ~와 연락하다 deliver 전달하다

해설 1시 19분에 보고서의 교정을 봐 줄 사람이 필요하면 얘기하라고(Let me know if you'd like me to proofread the report before you submit it.) 말하고 있다. 동사 proofread가 무슨 뜻인지 알면 정답을 쉽게 찾을 수 있다.

Ex 4. What is Ms. Kuang most likely doing while texting?

  (A) Eating lunch

  (B) Attending a conference call

  (C) Revising data

  (D) Reading a document

Ms. Kuang는 문자를 보내면서 무엇을 하고 있겠는가?

(A) 점심을 먹고 있다

(B) 전화 회의에 참석하고 있다

(C) 데이터를 수정하고 있다

(D) 문서를 읽고 있다

어휘 text 문자를 보내다 conference call 전화 회의 revise 개정하다, 수정하다

해설 1시 13분에 지금 식사를 거의 다 했고 자리로 돌아가는 대로 기록을 보내겠다고 말했는데(I'm finishing up at the cafeteria now, but I'll send them as soon as I get back to work.), 1시 19분에 되도록 빨리 기록을 전달하겠다는 말을 다시 하고 있다(I'll get the notes to you as soon as possible.). 그러므로 대화가 끝날 때까지도 Ms. Kuang은 여전히 구내식당에서 식사를 하고 있는 것을 알 수 있다.

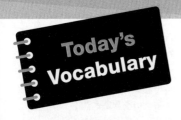

Today's Vocabulary

▶Actual Test를 풀기 전에 이 단어들을 암기하자.

짝을 이루어 출제되는 단어

· written ⌈ notice   ⌉ 서면 통지
         │ notification │
         └ consent   ┘ 서면 동의

· prior notice 사전 공지
· in writing 서면으로

· unless otherwise ⌈ noted   ⌉ 별다른
                    │ specified   │ 명시[지시]가
                    │ instructed │ 없는 한
                    └ directed   ┘

· until further notice 추후 공지가 있을 때까지

---

appreciative 안목이 있는
estimate 추정하다, 추산하다
likable 호감이 가는, 마음에 드는
determined 단단히 결심한
correspondence 서신, 편지
correspond to/with 일치하다, 부합하다
correspond to ~에 해당하다, 상응하다
correspond with ~와 편지를 주고받다
correspondent 통신원, 특파원
clarify 명확하게 하다, 분명히 말하다
familiarize (사람을) 익숙하게 하다;
            (사물을) 일반화하다, 보급시키다
employee handbook 직원 편람
cease 그만두다, 끝내다
retail 소매의, 소매상의
outlet 판매 대리점, 직판장
shift 이동하다, 옮기다
affix 부착하다, 붙이다
evolve (점진적으로) 발달하다, 진전하다
recognized 인정된, 알려진
the very (최상급을 강조하여) 그야말로, 실로, 단연
factor 요인, 요소
composition 구성
field 분야

portion 부분, 일부
designate 지정하다
be credited with ~한 공로를 인정받다
assure 장담하다, 확언하다
nomination 지명, 추천, 임명
vacant (일자리가) 비어 있는, 결원의
appealing 매력적인, 흥미로운
sapling 묘목, 어린나무
variety (식물·언어 등의) 품종, 종류
refer A to B A에게 B를 안내하다, 소개하다
nursery 묘목장
stock (상점의) 재고품, 재고
bulk 대량의, 대량으로 매매되는
pick (과일 등을) 따다
freshly 갓[막] ~한
make arrangements 준비하다, 마련하다
arrange for ~을 준비하다, 계획하다
initiate 시작하다, 개시하다
secure (특히 힘들게) 얻어 내다, 확보하다
rate 요금
exclusively 독점적으로; 오로지 (~만)
courtesy 무료의, 서비스의
established 확립하다, 마련하다

Actual Test

PART 5

1. 빈칸 앞뒤를 보며 문제를 푼다.
2. 빈칸 앞뒤를 보고 정답을 알 수 없다면 문장을 해석한다.
3. 두 줄 분량의 어휘 문제는 문장 전체를 해석해서 푼다.
4. 접속사 어휘 문제는 빈칸 앞뒤만을 보고 풀 수 없다. 문장 전체를 해석해 보자.

PART 6

1. 문법 문제라면 Part 5와 같은 방식으로 빈칸 앞뒤를 보며 푼다.
2. 다른 유형의 문제는 문맥을 통해 정답을 파악한다.

PART 7

1. 문제와 보기 (A), (B), (C), (D)를 먼저 읽은 후에 지문을 읽는다.
2. 지문 위아래의 모든 부분을 자세히 읽어 본다.
3. 문제의 해설을 꼼꼼히 읽고, 문장 구조를 분석하며 복습한다.

101. Through his vibrant oil paintings, Kyung-Ho Park, a Korean artist, presents innovative ways of ------- color and light.

    (A) appreciate
    (B) appreciative
    (C) appreciating
    (D) appreciation

102. The contractor ------- it would take five hours to replace the cracked tiles in the lobby.

    (A) designed
    (B) managed
    (C) estimated
    (D) installed

103. Ms. Yakut appears ------- to undertake more demanding administrative tasks.

    (A) friendly
    (B) likable
    (C) determined
    (D) separate

104. When sending ------- to customers, it is imperative to utilize the organization's revised letterhead.

    (A) correspondence
    (B) corresponded
    (C) corresponding
    (D) correspondent

105. Ms. Chen stated that the vacation policy will be ------- once the employee handbook has been updated.

    (A) connected
    (B) clarified
    (C) familiarized
    (D) participated

106. Anyone who ------- an oil change at Frank's Auto Care will be offered a complimentary car wash.

    (A) purchases
    (B) purchasing
    (C) purchasable
    (D) purchase

107. For safety reasons, warehouse employees who work at sites of construction projects must wear protective gear at ------- times.

    (A) every
    (B) all
    (C) full
    (D) each

108. Zarb Shoes will cease operations in all of its remaining retail outlets and shift ------- to online sales.

    (A) entirely
    (B) commonly
    (C) famously
    (D) equally

109. Employees must affix the mandatory warning labels ------- transferring products to the quality control department.

    (A) prior to
    (B) and
    (C) last
    (D) otherwise

110. We monitored the temperature at fifteen-minute ------- throughout the experiment.

    (A) divisions
    (B) priorities
    (C) intervals
    (D) intersections

111. Foreign financial firms have a number of ------- about regulations governing their business activities.

(A) complain
(B) complaint
(C) complaining
(D) complaints

112. Production of the second shift machine operators ------- significantly lower than that of the third shift workers.

(A) is
(B) to be
(C) are
(D) being

113. The goal of the customer service department ------- all customer complaints that they have in both a friendly and timely manner.

(A) resolve
(B) is resolved
(C) had resolved
(D) is to resolve

114. Employees who want to file for client entertainment reimbursement must submit a written ------- detailing their expenditure with valid receipts to the company.

(A) notification
(B) approach
(C) information
(D) introduction

115. All guests who ------- our services to book hotel rooms in Bangkok will be provided a free tour of the city and its temples.

(A) to use
(B) uses
(C) using
(D) use

116. Greenwood Printing has ------- from a local supplier to a widely recognized regional distributor.

(A) determined
(B) focused
(C) evolved
(D) permitted

117. Front Force Ltd. offers customized digital and print design ------- that meet the individual client's needs.

(A) to service
(B) service
(C) serviced
(D) services

118. Nature Hills Nursery utilizes the ------- latest agricultural techniques.

(A) so
(B) more
(C) very
(D) much

119. Computer science, especially High Performance Computing, has become a key ------- in the development of many research fields, establishing a new paradigm called computational science.

(A) factor
(B) position
(C) instructor
(D) composition

120. The burnt-out museum will be closed to the public until further -------.

(A) mark
(B) notice
(C) consent
(D) bill

121. ------- the Golden One Credit Union parking area is now available to the public, a portion of it has been designated for credit union personnel.

(A) While
(B) When
(C) For
(D) But

122. Please take note of the attached flowchart, which illustrates the ------- of responsibilities among the various leadership positions.

(A) support
(B) attention
(C) division
(D) statement

123. Mr. Tang is ------- with instituting a few modifications that have led to an increase in Bentler Stationery's business.

(A) credited
(B) scored
(C) agreed
(D) relied

124. The hospital regulations stipulates that the patient should be asked to sign a written ------- before an operation.

(A) consent
(B) condition
(C) contraction
(D) convergence

125. In the photograph, President Vieira is shown standing ------- Dr. Stanton.

(A) from
(B) reverse
(C) opposite
(D) distant

126. Municipal authorities have ------- McLeod Avenue businesses that street improvements will be completed within 48 hours.

(A) assured
(B) arranged
(C) disclosed
(D) committed

127. Friday is the deadline for nominations to the ------ seat on the Heirs Holdings Board of Trustees.

(A) approaching
(B) adjustable
(C) vacant
(D) united

128. ------- poorly the high-speed printer may be operating, it is still capable of making copies that are sufficient for our purposes.

(A) Rather
(B) Seldom
(C) However
(D) Thoroughly

129. By means of our vast national network, Supertech can send a technician to help ------- assistance is needed.

(A) wherever
(B) quickly
(C) each other
(D) out

130. ------- of Ardashir Ali's international performances was captured on camera for a documentary.

(A) All
(B) Others
(C) Their own
(D) Each one

GO ON TO THE NEXT PAGE

PART 6

Questions 131-134 refer to the following memo.

To: All staff
From: Vitale Renato, Vice President of Product Development
Date: February 17
Subject: Elegante game (Product #ET9103)

Considering the results from our trial customer testing, we have opted to postpone the release of the Elegante video game. Results from customer surveys suggested that the game was less ------- than anticipated. For the next
131.
few months, the game development team will implement several ------- to make
132.
the product more attractive. -------. If the changes prove to be successful, our
133.
hope is to release the game by July ------- August.
134.

131. (A) expensive
     (B) repetitive
     (C) appealing
     (D) surprising

132. (A) modification
     (B) modifies
     (C) modifying
     (D) modifications

133. (A) At that point, additional tests will
         be conducted.
     (B) The release will be our biggest of
         the year.
     (C) Nevertheless, the surveys are not
         reliable.
     (D) Each team member must sign the
         form.

134. (A) since
     (B) or
     (C) if
     (D) later

Questions 135-138 refer to the following e-mail.

From: cyoo@pomarius.com

To: erikjohansson@skansennursery.se

Subject: Sparreholm Yellow

Date: October 12

Dear Mr. Johansson,

I am writing on behalf of the Pomarius Garden Stores chain, which is currently

in the process of ------- its range of products to include newly developed types
        135.

of trees. We would like to carry Sparreholm Yellow apple saplings in our stores.

Given that this ------- originated in Sweden, we consulted the Association of
                136.

Swedish Fruit Exporters, which referred us to your apple nursery. It appears

from your Web site that you do ------- have the product in stock. Initially, we
                              137.

would be interested in procuring a small sample of saplings. -------. Do you offer
                                                           138.

discounts for bulk purchases?

I look forward to hearing from you.

Sincerely,

Carol Yoo

Pomarius Garden Stores

---

135. (A) expanding
   (B) expanded
   (C) expands
   (D) expand

136. (A) response
   (B) method
   (C) ability
   (D) variety

137. (A) indeed
   (B) alone
   (C) quite
   (D) ever

138. (A) Our nursery has been family-owned
      for more than a century.
   (B) I'm sorry to say that they are not in
      stock at the moment.
   (C) However, we plan to place a larger
      order in the foreseeable future.
   (D) Please visit our Web site to learn
      more about our offer.

GO ON TO THE NEXT PAGE

PART 7

Questions 139-142 refer to the following online chat discussion.

Venkatraju Blunt (1:30 P.M.)	Hello, Saira and Kristiono. Welcome to Venkat Spices! Thank you for joining me for this online meeting on a short notice. You are two of the many overseas farmers we collaborate with. Do you have any products ready to ship?
Saira Gupta (1:31 P.M.)	I have 150 kilos of fresh Tellicherry black peppercorns that were just picked yesterday here in India. They'll be ready for shipment within a few days.
Venkatraju Blunt (1:32 P.M.)	That's great to hear! I can't wait to try them. Kristiono, you will be our first supplier from Indonesia.
Kristiono Agus (1:33 P.M.)	I'm pleased to join the team. I have 200 kilos of beautiful, freshly picked black Lampong peppercorns that are ready to ship.
Venkatraju Blunt (1:34 P.M.)	Super! Have you both made shipping arrangements with Atlantic-Pacific Express?
Saira Gupta (1:35 P.M.)	Yes, I've already got in touch with them.
Kristiono Agus (1:35 P.M.)	Me too.
Venkatraju Blunt (1:36 P.M.)	I'll let our warehouse staff in Amsterdam know about your peppercorns. Upon arrival, I will transfer your payments. I look forward to having a long and productive relationship with both of you. Thank you very much!

139. Who most likely is Ms. Blunt?

(A) A farmer
(B) An event promoter
(C) A business owner
(D) A grocery store manager

140. What is indicated about Ms. Gupta's and Mr. Agus's peppercorns?

(A) They will be delivered within three business days.
(B) They all belong to the same variety.
(C) They were all grown in Indonesia.
(D) They were harvested recently

141. At 1:35 P.M., what does Mr. Agus most likely mean when he writes, "Me too"?

(A) He has arranged for shipping.
(B) He is excited about his new business.
(C) He wants to try Ms. Gupta's peppercorns.
(D) He is pleased to adopt new crop varieties.

142. What will Ms. Blunt most likely do next?

(A) Request recommendations of other vendors
(B) Sign an agreement with Atlantic-Pacific Express
(C) Inspect the items sent by Ms. Gupta and Mr. Agus
(D) Tell the warehouse staff to expect two shipments

Questions 143-147 refer to the following e-mail, letter, and calendar.

To: dsoto@abengineer.com
From: jcarroway@abengineer.com
Date: March 27
Subject: Corporate credit card

Dear Ms. Soto,

I have received your application for a corporate credit card. In order to issue a card to you, I require verification of one of the following.
- Anticipated business-related expenses of $400 or more
- Two or more scheduled international business trips for this year
- Signed documentation from a manager confirming your responsibility to entertain corporate patrons

As you await your card, kindly take time to look over our expense and travel policies in pages 46-62 of the employee handbook. Here are some highlights from those policies.
- All transportation (airline, train, etc.) and lodging arrangements must be made through the corporate travel department.
- Your supervisor's permission must be obtained before initiating a request for a car rental through the corporate travel department.
- Meals are covered by the company provided they do not exceed daily allowances (refer to section 10, page 51).

Thank you,
Jeff Carroway
Corporate Travel Department, Aucoin-Braud Engineering

The Institute of Science and Technology (IST)

Denise Soto   April 6
Aucoin-Braud Engineering
1820 Avenue B
New York, NY 10010

Dear Denise Soto,

You have successfully registered for the IST Conference in Rio de Janeiro, Brazil, and your payment of $450 has been processed. Thank you.

IST advises that you make travel and hotel arrangements as early as possible to ensure availability. We have secured discounted rates for conference participants at Hotel Miramar, which is the conference venue, and also at Hotel Prodigy; rooms at Hotel Miramar are exclusively available for booking by the IST members, however. Complimentary breakfast will be available from 6 to 10 A.M. and coffee and tea from 1 to 4 P.M. daily, both in the hotel lobby. Participants are responsible for all other meals.

For inquiries or recommendations, feel free to contact us at info@istconference.org.

Sincerely,

IST Conference Committee

Calendar for Denise Soto: Week of June 26

June 26	June 27	June 28	June 29	June 30
Depart 9:30 A.M., New York, NY (flight BW288) Arrive 8:25 P.M., Rio de Janeiro, Brazil Travel via Taxi Minuto to Hotel Miramar (late check-in confirmed by hotel manager)	9:30 A.M. - 4:00 P.M. conference sessions 5:00 P.M. Alexa Alves job interview, hotel lobby	9:30 A.M. - 3:30 P.M. conference sessions 3:40 P.M. Alexa Alves presentation	9:30 A.M. - 4:00 P.M. conference sessions 5:30 P.M. closing ceremony and reception, Salon C	7:45 A.M. Travel to airport via hotel courtesy bus Depart 10:00 A.M., Rio de Janeiro, Brazil (flight BW424) Arrive 7:00 P.M., New York, NY

143. What qualifies Ms. Soto to receive a corporate credit card?

(A) Her upcoming business trip is international.
(B) Her registration fee is over $400.
(C) She will be traveling for more than two days.
(D) She will be entertaining corporate clients.

144. What is a purpose of the letter?

(A) To share opinions about a hotel
(B) To advertise a dining establishment
(C) To confirm a successful registration
(D) To encourage participation in a conference

145. In the letter, the word "secured" in paragraph 2, line 2, is closest in meaning to

(A) guarded
(B) established
(C) paid
(D) enclosed

146. What is suggested about Ms. Soto?

(A) She is a member of the IST.
(B) She will give a presentation at the conference.
(C) She is leaving the conference before its conclusion.
(D) She works with Ms. Alves at Aucoin-Braud Engineering.

147. What expense policy does NOT apply to Ms. Soto's trip?

(A) The policy about food costs
(B) The policy about lodging arrangements
(C) The policy about flight bookings
(D) The policy about car rentals

Day

07

PART 5 & 6

1. 현재분사와 과거분사 ★★★★

빈칸에 현재분사와 과거분사 중 어느 것이 들어가야 하는지 선택하는 문제가 출제된다. 현재분사는 능동적으로 '～하다'라는 의미이고 과거분사는 수동적으로 '～되다/당하다'라는 의미이다. 또한 현재분사는 목적어를 취할 수 있지만, 과거분사는 목적어를 가질 수 없다.

현재분사 – 의미상 능동	과거분사 – 의미상 수동
현재분사 + 목적어 ○	과거분사 + 목적어 ×

유형 1 ------- + 명사

Day 01에서 공부한 대로 명사 앞에 빈칸이 있으면 형용사가 정답이다. 보기에 형용사가 없으면 분사를 선택하면 되는데, 현재분사와 과거분사가 모두 있다면 어느 것을 고를지 결정해야 한다. 이때 뒤에서 '수식받는 명사'와 앞에서 '수식하는 분사'의 관계가 의미상 능동인지 수동인지 생각해야 한다.

Ex 1. On June 23, a fashion show for buyers and other ------- guests will be hosted by Fiorucci Fashion Trends.

(A) invite
(B) inviting
(C) invitation
(D) invited

명사 guests 앞에 빈칸이 있으므로 형용사가 정답인데, 보기에는 형용사가 없으므로 현재분사 (B)와 과거분사 (D) 중 정답을 선택해야 한다. 수식받는 명사 guests(손님들)는 '초대하는' 것이 아니라 '초대받는' 것이므로, 수동의 의미가 있는 과거분사 (D)가 정답이다.

어휘 host 주최하다

해석 6월 23일에 구매자들과 그밖에 초대받은 내빈들을 위한 패션쇼가 Fiorucci Fashion Trends에 의해 주최될 것이다.

Ex 2. Due to the ------- typhoon, all morning flights are being redirected to Nagoya Airport.

(A) approached
(B) approach
(C) approaches
(D) approaching

명사 typhoon 앞에 빈칸이 있으므로 형용사가 정답이다. 보기에는 형용사가 없으므로 현재분사 (D)와 과거분사 (A) 중 정답을 선택해야 한다. 수식받는 명사 typhoon(태풍)이 '접근하는' 것이므로 능동의 의미가 있는 현재분사 (D)가 정답이다.

어휘 due to ～로 인해 typhoon 태풍 redirect ～의 방향을 바꾸다

해석 접근 중인 태풍으로 인해 모든 오전 비행편은 Nagoya 공항으로 방향이 바뀌고 있다.

유형 2   be + ------

Day 01에서 공부한 대로 be동사 뒤에 빈칸이 있으면 형용사가 정답이다. be동사 자리에 become, remain, stay, seem, appear, prove 같은 2형식 동사가 있으면 be동사와 같이 빈칸에 형용사가 들어가야 한다. 보기에 형용사가 없으면 분사를 선택하고, 현재분사와 과거분사가 모두 있으면 어느 것을 고를지 결정해야 한다. 빈칸은 주격보어 자리이므로 '주어'를 찾아보자. 주어인 명사와 주격보어인 분사의 관계가 의미상 능동인지 수동인지 생각해야 한다.

Ex 3. Although the reviews of the Coby Electronics itself have largely been positive, sales of their new line of smartphones have thus far been ------.

(A) disappoint
(B) disappointed
(C) disappointment
(D) disappointing

be동사 뒤에 빈칸이 있으므로 형용사가 정답이다. 보기에는 형용사가 없으므로 현재분사 (D)와 과거분사 (B) 중 정답을 선택해야 한다. 빈칸이 주격보어 자리이므로 주어를 보자. 전치사구 of the new line of smartphones를 제외하면 sales(판매량)가 주어임을 알 수 있다. sales가 실망하는 대상이 아니라 실망을 주는 주체이므로 현재분사 (D)가 정답이다.

어휘 review 논평, 비평 largely 대체로 positive 긍정적인 line 제품군 thus far 지금까지

해석 Coby 전자 자체에 대한 평가는 대체로 긍정적이지만, 새 스마트폰 제품군의 판매량은 지금까지는 실망스럽다.

Ex 4. Users are advised never to operate a toaster oven if its electrical cord appears ------.

(A) to damage
(B) damaged
(C) damaging
(D) damages

빈칸 앞에 appear가 있으면 be동사라고 생각하고 형용사를 정답으로 선택해야 한다. 보기에는 형용사가 없으므로 현재분사 (C)나 과거분사 (B)가 정답이다. 주어인 its electrical cord(전기 코드)가 '손상시키는' 것이 아니라 '손상되는' 것이므로 과거분사 (B)가 정답이다.

어휘 be advised to-V ~하는 것이 좋다, ~하기 바랍니다 operate (기계를) 작동하다, 조작하다 electrical 전기의 damage 손상시키다

해석 오븐 토스터의 전기 코드가 손상된 것으로 보인다면, 사용자는 절대 조작하지 마시기를 바랍니다.

유형 3   5형식 동사 + 목적어 + ------

Day 01에서 암기한 5형식 동사를 다시 외워 보자.

make, get, turn, **keep**, leave, drive, think, believe, **find**, **consider**, suppose, deem, call, describe

이 동사들 뒤의 목적격 보어 자리를 빈칸으로 하는 문제가 출제되면 형용사가 정답이다. 보기에 형용사가 없다면 분사를 선택해야 하는데, 현재분사와 과거분사가 모두 있다면, 둘 중 하나를 정답으로 정해야 한다. 이 유형에서 빈칸은 목적격 보어 자리이므로 '목적어'를 함께 봐야 한다. 목적어인 명사와 목적격 보어인 분사의 관계가 의미상 능동인지 수동인지 생각해야 한다.

Ex 5. Mr. Miller found the long waiting time for the connecting flight ------- and regretted not having brought something to read with him.

(A) exhausted
(B) exhaustingly
(C) exhaustion
(D) exhausting

빈칸 앞에 5형식 동사 found가 있고 빈칸이 목적격 보어 자리이므로 형용사가 정답이다. 보기에는 형용사가 없으므로 현재분사 (D)나 과거분사 (A)가 정답이다. 빈칸이 목적격 보어 자리이므로 목적어를 보자. 전치사구 for the connecting flight를 제외하면 the long waiting time(긴 대기 시간)이 목적어임을 알 수 있다. the long waiting time이 '기진맥진하게 하는' 것이므로 현재분사 (D)가 정답이다.

> **어휘** find ~라고 여기다, 생각하다 waiting time 대기 시간 connecting flight 연결 항공편 exhaust 기진맥진하게 하다 regret ~ing ~한 것을 후회하다

> **해석** Mr. Miller는 연결 항공편의 긴 대기 시간이 진 빠지게 한다고 생각하면서 읽을거리를 가져오지 않은 것을 후회했다.

Ex 6. A voyage around Rabbit Island will leave passengers quite ------- about its beauty.

(A) exciting
(B) excited
(C) excite
(D) excitement

빈칸 앞에 5형식 동사 leave가 있고 빈칸이 목적격 보어 자리이므로 형용사가 정답이다. 보기에는 형용사가 없으므로 현재분사 (A)나 과거분사 (B)가 정답이다. 목적어(passengers)와 함께 빈칸 뒤 about its beauty도 보자. passengers가 its beauty를 보고 '흥분하게 되는' 것이므로 과거분사 (B)가 정답이다.

> **어휘** voyage 여행, 항해 leave (계속) ~을 ~되게 하다 quite 아주, 정말

> **해석** Rabbit 섬 주변 항해는 승객들이 그 아름다움에 정말 흥분하게 만들 것이다.

유형 4 　 분사 구문

Day 03에서 공부한 분사 구문의 형성 과정을 기억하자. 부사절에서 접속사와 주어가 없으면 분사 구문이 된다. 분사 자리를 빈칸으로 하는 문제가 출제되는데, 분사의 원형이 되는 동사의 주어는 주절의 주어이다. 따라서 빈칸에 들어갈 분사를 선택할 때 '주절의 주어'를 함께 봐야 된다. 주절의 주어만 보고 판단하기 어려울 때도 있으므로 '목적어가 있는지 없는지'도 확인한 후 정답을 선택하자.

Ex 7. ------- with other companies in the industry, the company's growth rate is expected to be one of the top three highest.

(A) Comparing
(B) Comparative
(C) Comparisons
(D) Compared

쉼표 뒤에 주절이 있고 쉼표 앞에는 부사절이 있다. 부사절은 '접속사 + 주어 + 동사' 형태이지만, 보기를 통해 이 문장에서는 접속사와 주어가 없다는 것을 알 수 있다. 접속사와 주어가 없는 부사절은 분사 구문이므로 현재분사 (A)나 과거분사 (D) 중 정답을 선택해야 한다. 주절의 주어인 the company's growth rate(회사의 성장률)이 '비교하는' 것이 아니라 '비교당하는' 것이므로 수동의 의미인 과거분사 (D)가 정답이다.

어휘 compared with ~와 비교하면 comparative 비교의, 상대적인 growth rate 성장률 be expected to-V ~로 예상되다

해석 업계의 다른 회사들과 비교했을 때 그 회사의 성장률은 상위 세 곳 중 하나로 예상된다.

Ex 8. Ms. Tang will provide one week prior notice by e-mail when ------- your annual performance review meeting.

(A) scheduled
(B) schedules
(C) scheduling
(D) will schedule

빈칸 앞 접속사 when 뒤에는 '주어 + 동사'가 있어야 하는데, 보기를 보면 주어가 없음을 알 수 있다. 따라서 이 부사절은 분사 구문이므로 현재분사 (C)와 과거분사 (A) 중 정답을 선택해야 한다. 주절의 주어인 Ms. Tang이 일정을 '잡는' 것이므로 능동의 의미인 현재분사 (C)가 정답이다. 또한 빈칸 뒤 your annual performance review meeting도 목적어이므로 현재분사가 정답임을 나타내고 있다.

어휘 prior notice 사전 공지 performance review 고과 평가

해석 Ms. Tang이 연례 고과 평가 회의 일정을 잡을 때 이메일로 일주일 전에 미리 공지할 것입니다.

유형 5   **명사 + -------**

빈칸으로 시작하는 **분사 구문이 앞에 있는 명사를 수식하는 구조이면**, 빈칸 뒤에 목적어가 있는지 없는지 확인하고 알맞은 분사를 선택해야 한다.

Ex 9. Anyone ------- in attending the seminar should contact Mr. Wilkinson in the human resources department by the end of the week.

(A) interesting
(B) interest
(C) interested
(D) interests

should contact가 문장의 동사(구)이므로 빈칸에 동사인 (B)와 (D)는 들어갈 수 없다. 명사로 쓰인 interest라고 해도 anyone과 나란히 쓸 수 없다. 따라서 빈칸에는 현재분사 (A)나 과거분사 (C)가 들어갈 수 있다. ------- In attending the seminar가 명사 Anyone을 수식하는 구조이고 빈칸 뒤에 목적어가 없으므로 과거분사 (C)가 정답이다.

어휘 attend 참석하다 contact 연락하다 human resources department 인사부

해석 세미나 참석에 관심이 있는 사람은 누구든지 주말까지 인사부의 Mr. Wilkinson에게 연락해야 합니다.

유형 6   **자동사의 분사 선택**

자동사는 목적어가 없기 때문에 수동태를 만들 수 없으므로 과거분사형으로 쓰이지 않는다. 따라서 자동사의 분사 형태를 선택할 때는 반드시 현재분사만 정답이 된다.

※ 빈출 자동사

the **existing** regulation 기존의 규정

the **rising** cost 증가하는 비용

the **growing** number 증가하는 수

lasting effect 지속적인 효과

the **declining** economy 하강하는 경기

an **emerging** market 신흥 시장

an **impending** storm 임박한 폭풍우

remaining period 남은 기간

Ex 10. Though Brandon Snyder did not have a major role in the play, his stirring performance left a ------- impression on the audience.

(A) lasts
(B) lasting
(C) lasted
(D) lastly

빈칸 앞뒤 a ------- impression을 보자. 빈칸이 명사 impression 앞에 있으므로 형용사가 들어가야 하는데 보기에는 형용사가 없으므로 현재분사 (B)와 과거분사 (C) 중 정답을 선택해야 한다. last는 1형식 자동사이므로 현재분사인 (B)가 정답이다.

어휘 stirring 마음을 흔드는, 감동적인 impression 인상, 감동

해석 Brandon Snyder가 연극에서 중요한 역을 맡지 못했지만 마음을 흔드는 그의 연기는 관객들에게 오랜 감명을 남겼다.

유형 7 **분사의 관용적 사용**

관용적으로 현재분사와 과거분사 중 어느 한쪽으로만 쓰이는 타동사가 있다. 또한 'as + 과거분사'의 형태로만 쓰이는 관용 표현도 암기하자.

❶ 현재분사로만 쓰이는 경우

a **challenging** task 힘든 업무

a **demanding** customer 까다로운 고객

a **rewarding** job 보람 있는 일

missing luggage 분실된 짐

an **opposing** point of view 반대의 관점

an **outstanding** painter 뛰어난 화가

a **promising** candidate 유망한 후보자

a **verifying** document 입증 서류

misleading information 오해의 소지가 있는 정보

outstanding debts 미지불 채무

❷ 과거분사로만 쓰이는 경우

an **accomplished** chef 기량이 뛰어난 요리사

a **complicated** problem 복잡한 문제

a **crowded** street 붐비는 거리

a **dedicated** employee 헌신적인 직원

detailed information 자세한 정보

a **distinguished** scholar 유명한 학자

an **established** company 자리를 잡은 회사

experienced employee 경력 직원

The audience was **impressed**. 청중은 감동했다.

a critically **acclaimed** film 비평가들의 찬사를 받은 영화

an **informed** decision 잘 알고 하는 결정

an **involved** task 관련 업무

repeated delay 반복된 지연

a **skilled** engineer 숙련된 기술자

specialized skills 전문적인 기술

sophisticated technology 세련된 기술

a **valued** customer 소중한 고객

a **varied** selection of 다양한

an **expired** voucher 기한이 지난 상품권

an **authorized** dealership 공식 대리점

❸ as + p.p.

as discussed 논의한 대로   **as indicated** 나와 있는 것처럼

as noted 기록된 대로   **as printed** 인쇄된 대로

as mentioned 언급된 대로   **as advertised** 광고된 대로

as stated 명시된 대로   **as projected** 예상한 대로

as stipulated 명기된 대로

Ex 11. New employees of Limepower Software must attend a very ------- four-week training course upon being hired.

    (A) demands
    (B) demanded
    (C) demanding
    (D) demand

빈칸 앞뒤 a very ------- four-week training course를 보자. 명사 four-week training course 앞에 빈칸이 있으므로 형용사가 정답인데, 보기에는 형용사가 없으므로 분사를 선택해야 한다. 현재분사와 과거분사가 모두 있지만, demand는 항상 현재분사로만 사용한다는 사실을 기억하고 (C)를 선택하자.

어휘 demanding 부담이 큰, 힘든 (up)on + V-ing ~하자마자

해석 Limepower Software의 신입직원은 채용되자마자 4주간의 매우 힘든 교육 코스에 참석해야 한다.

Ex 12. The more we work with Mr. Hwang, the more ------- we are by his outstanding project management skills.

    (A) impressing
    (B) impressed
    (C) impress
    (D) impresses

이 문장은 'the + 비교급 ~, the + 비교급 ~ (~할수록 더 ~하다)' 구문이다. 비교급이 되려면 빈칸에는 형용사나 부사가 들어가야 하므로 형용사 역할을 하는 분사가 정답이다. 현재분사와 과거분사가 모두 있지만, impress는 관용적으로 과거분사로만 쓰이므로 (B)가 정답이다.

어휘 impress 깊은 인상을 주다, 감명을 주다 outstanding 뛰어난, 걸출한

해석 Mr. Hwang과 함께 일할수록 그의 뛰어난 프로젝트 관리 능력에 더 깊은 인상을 받게 된다.

Ex 13. As ------- in the company regulations, sales representatives are compensated for time spent traveling to visit clients.

    (A) state
    (B) stating
    (C) statement
    (D) stated

시험에 자주 나오는 표현 as stated를 기억하자. As ------- in the company regulations가 '회사 규정에 명시된 대로'라는 뜻이 되도록 (D)를 정답으로 선택해야 한다.

어휘 regulation 규정 sales representative 영업 사원 compensate A for B A에게 B를 보상하다 travel 이동하다

해석 영업 사원은 회사 규정에 명시된 바와 같이 고객 방문을 위한 이동에 소요된 시간을 보상받는다.

2. 비교 ★★★

원급과 비교급, 최상급을 만드는 간단한 규칙 몇 가지만 잘 기억하면, 비교 문제는 쉽게 풀 수 있다.

유형 1 as ------- as

as ------- as가 있으면 원급이 정답이다. 또한 twice, three times, four times 같은 배수 표현도 정답의 단서가 된다.

Ex 1. Scientists at Bakelite Synthetics are developing a new material that will be twice as ------- as ordinary concrete.

(A) durably
(B) durable
(C) more durable
(D) most durably

보기를 보면 비교 문제라는 것을 알 수 있다. 빈칸 앞뒤 twice as ------- as를 보면서 원급이 정답임을 파악하자. 형용사 원급 (B)와 부사 원급 (A) 중 정답을 선택해야 하는데, will be 뒤에 빈칸이 있으므로 형용사 (B)가 정답이다.

어휘 synthetics 합성 화학 (공업) durable 내구성이 있는, 오래가는

해석 Bakelite Synthetics의 과학자들은 일반 콘크리트보다 두 배 더 내구성 있는 신소재를 개발하고 있다.

유형 2 비교급 + than

빈칸 뒤에 than이 있으면 비교급이 정답이다. than을 빈칸으로 하는 문제도 출제될 수 있으니 앞에 비교급이 있으면 than을 정답으로 고르자.

Ex 2. Ms. Cho takes her job ------- than her predecessor did.

(A) serious
(B) seriously
(C) more seriously
(D) most seriously

보기를 보면 비교 문제라는 것을 알 수 있다. 빈칸 뒤에 than이 있으므로 비교급 (C)가 정답이다.

어휘 predecessor 전임자 take *sth* seriously ~를 진지하게 받아들이다, 생각하다

해석 Ms. Cho는 전임자보다 더 자기 업무를 진지하게 생각한다.

Ex 3. According to the research, there were about 10 percent more accidents on the roads this year ------- in the past few years.

(A) as
(B) over
(C) as well as
(D) than

빈칸 앞에 형용사 비교급 more가 있으므로 than이 빈칸에 들어가는 것이 알맞다. 그러므로 (D)가 정답이다.

해석 조사에 따르면 올해는 도로에서 발생한 사고가 지난 몇 년보다 10퍼센트 더 많았다.

Ex 4. Diseases diagnosed in the early stages can be addressed ------- easily than those found toward the end.

(A) right
(B) later
(C) very
(D) more

빈칸 뒤에 than이 있기 때문에 그 앞에 있는 부사 easily를 비교급이 되게 하는 (D)가 정답이다.

어휘 diagnose 진단하다 address 다루다. 해결하려 하다
해석 초기 단계에 진단되는 질병은 말기에 발견되는 것보다 더 쉽게 해결할 수 있다.

Ex 5. China's economy has been growing at a faster pace ------- surrounding country in the past decade.

(A) as that of others
(B) than that of other
(C) that of most other
(D) than that of any other

빈칸 앞에 형용사 비교급 faster가 있으므로 than이 필요하다. (B)와 (D) 중 정답을 선택해야 하는데, other 뒤에는 셀 수 있는 명사의 복수형이 있어야 하므로 (B)는 정답이 될 수 없다. any other 뒤에는 단수 명사를 사용한다는 사실을 기억하고 (D)를 선택하자.

어휘 pace 속도 surrounding country 주변 국가 decade 10년
해석 중국의 경제는 지난 10년 동안 다른 어떤 주변 나라보다 더 빠른 속도로 성장해 왔다.

유형 3 비교급 강조 부사

비교급을 강조하는 다음 부사들을 암기하자 : much, still, even, far, a lot, considerably, significantly, substantially, greatly, noticeably, remarkably
비교급 앞에 very, so, really, extremely, quite는 사용할 수 없다.

참고 출제 빈도가 높지 않지만, 원급과 최상급을 강조하는 부사도 몇 개 알아두자.

❶ 원급 강조

  not nearly as + 형용사[부사] + as : ∼보다 훨씬 덜 ∼한[하게]

❷ 최상급 강조

  simply, easily, by far 단연코 가장 ∼한

  the very 그야말로 가장 ∼한

Ex 6. Over the past year, it has been Crestron Paper's major objective to forge even ------- ties between domestic and international divisions.

  (A) strong
  (B) stronger
  (C) strengthen
  (D) strongest

> 빈칸이 동사(forge)와 목적어(ties) 사이에 있으므로 동사 (C)는 정답이 아니다. 빈칸 앞에 비교급을 강조하는 부사 even이 있으므로 (B)가 정답이다.

어휘 objective 목표, 목적 forge ties 관계를 맺다 division 분과[부/국]

해석 지난 한 해 동안 국내와 국제 사업부 간에 훨씬 더 강력한 연대를 구축하는 것이 Crestron 제지의 주요 목표였다.

유형 4 – or형 비교급

주로 비교급은 형용사나 부사에 – er을 붙여서 만들지만, 어떤 것들은 – or을 붙이기도 한다. –or형 비교급은 '∼보다'라는 뜻으로 than이 아니라 to를 사용한다.

prior to ∼보다 먼저

superior / inferior to ∼보다 우수한 / 열등한

senior / junior to ∼보다 손위의 / 손아래의, ∼보다 상급자인 / 하급자인

참고 prefer는 '선호하다'라는 뜻의 비교를 내포한 동사이다. '∼보다'라는 뜻으로 비교 대상을 나타낼 때는 전치사 to[over]를 사용한다.

  prefer A to[over] B B보다 A를 더 좋아하다

Ex 7. Exquisite craftsmanship and the world's finest materials have made Longzhu Furniture ------- to its competing brands.

  (A) better
  (B) advanced
  (C) superior
  (D) improve

> 빈칸 앞뒤 made Longzhu Furniture ------- to its competing brands를 보자. made는 5형식 동사로, 빈칸은 목적격 보어 자리이다. 그러므로 "Longzhu Furniture를 경쟁 브랜드들보다 더 우수하게 만들었다."라는 의미가 자연스러우므로, '∼보다'라는 뜻의 전치사 to와 함께 쓸 수 있는 (C)가 정답이다. (A)는 than과 함께 사용해야 하므로 정답이 아니다.

어휘 exquisite 매우 아름다운, 정교한 craftsmanship 장인정신, 솜씨 advanced 고급의, 상급의 competing 경쟁하는

해석 정교한 장인정신과 세계 최고 소재가 Longzhu 가구를 경쟁 브랜드들보다 더 우수하게 만들었다.

Ex 8. The extensive survey shows that the majority of consumers prefer Morrison Food's classic-style potato chips ------- its flavored varieties.

(A) toward
(B) over
(D) during
(D) along

빈칸 앞뒤 prefer Morrison Food's classic-style potato chips ------- its flavored varieties를 보면 비교 대상을 나타내는 '~보다'라는 뜻의 전치사가 필요하다는 것을 알 수 있다. prefer는 to나 over와 함께 사용하므로 (B)가 정답이다.

어휘 extensive 광범위한 the majority of 다수의 flavored 맛을 첨가한 variety 종류, 품종

해석 광범위한 조사가 대다수 소비자는 다양한 맛의 감자칩보다 Morrison 식품의 전통 스타일을 더 선호한다는 것을 보여준다.

유형 5 **The + 비교급 ~, the + 비교급 ~**

'The + 비교급 ~, the + 비교급 ~' 구문은 '더 ~ 할수록 더 ~ 하다[이다]'라는 뜻이다. 밑줄로 표시한 비교급 자리가 빈칸으로 출제된다.

Ex 9. The ------- we wait for interest rates to be lowered, the more difficult it could be to launch the project.

(A) long
(B) longest
(C) longer
(D) more longer

(D)는 비교급 longer 앞에 more가 있어 잘못된 표현이므로 제외한다. 문장 구조가 'The + 비교급 ~, the + 비교급 ~'이므로 빈칸에는 비교급 (C)가 들어가야 한다.

어휘 interest rate 금리 launch 시작하다, 착수하다

해석 금리가 낮아지기를 더 오래 기다릴수록 프로젝트를 시작하는 것은 더 어려워질 수 있다.

유형 6 **최상급**

최상급이 정답임을 알려주는 키워드를 암기하자. 빈출 유형으로는 빈칸 앞에 관사 the가 있으면 최상급이 정답인 경우이다. 그밖에 다음과 같은 키워드들이 있다.

(that) ~ ever, one of ~, of all, in + 기준명사 (예: in the world), 서수

Ex 10. Enclave Technologies has evaluated several offers from local landscaping firms, and it will select the ------- bid.

(A) most affordable
(B) more affordable
(C) affordably
(D) affordability

보기를 보면 비교 문제임을 알 수 있다. 빈칸 앞에 관사 the가 있으므로 최상급 (A)가 정답이다.

어휘 evaluate 평가하다 landscaping firm 조경 회사 affordable (가격이) 알맞은 bid 가격 제시, 호가, 응찰

해석 Enclave Technologies는 지역 조경업체들의 몇몇 제안을 평가했으며 응찰액이 가장 알맞은 것을 선택할 것이다.

Ex 11. Ms. Heo has reported that the new tablet computers are the lightest ------- to be bought by the company.

(A) ever
(B) before
(C) quite
(D) well

빈칸 앞뒤 the lightest ------- to be bought by the company를 보자. 최상급 the lightest를 보면 최상급과 짝을 이루는 키워드 ever를 기억해야 한다. ever는 '여태껏, 지금까지'라는 뜻으로 최상급을 강조할 때 사용된다.

해석 Ms. Heo는 새 태블릿 컴퓨터가 이제껏 회사에서 구매한 가장 가벼운 것이라고 보고했다.

Ex 12. *The City Overview* is the third ------- distributed newspaper in the southeastern region.

(A) wide
(B) widen
(C) most widely
(D) more widely

빈칸 앞에 관사 the와 서수, 빈칸 뒤에 범위를 나타내는 'in + 기준 명사(in the southeastern region)'이 있으므로 최상급 (C)가 정답이다.

어휘 distribute 배포하다, 유통하다

해석 *The City Overview*는 남동부 지역에서 세 번째로 널리 배포되고 있는 신문이다.

Ex 13. If Dowell Machines merges with the Hinkle Corporation, the resulting conglomerate will be ------- of the largest technology enterprises in the world.

(A) much
(B) some
(C) those
(D) one

빈칸 앞뒤 will be ------- of the largest technology enterprises를 보자. 빈칸 뒤에 최상급 the largest를 보면 one of가 최상급과 잘 어울리는 키워드이므로 (D)가 정답이다.

어휘 merge 합병하다, 합치다 conglomerate (거대) 복합 기업, 대기업

해석 만약 Dowell 기계와 Hinkle 사(社)가 합병한다면 그 결과로 생기는 대기업은 세계에서 가장 큰 기술 기업 중 하나가 될 것이다.

101. Online retailers are not as ------- as they used to be as prices remain generally the same across all stores.

(A) competitively
(B) competition
(C) more competitive
(D) competitive

102. Ericsson laptop computers are ------- than those of its competitors and features more powerful processors for faster computing.

(A) slim
(B) slimmer
(C) slimness
(D) sliming

103. The ratings received by Nancy Meyer's television news program were the ------- of all local news shows.

(A) high
(B) highest
(C) highly
(D) heightened

104. Most customers think that the new registration system is excessively -------.

(A) complicate
(B) complicating
(C) complicated
(D) complicatedly

105. The company has decided to liquidate some of its subsidiaries and increase investment in some areas of information technology that are obviously more -------.

(A) to promise
(B) promising
(C) promised
(D) promises

106. E-mail is the ------- means of communication for the transaction of business among colleagues.

(A) preferring
(B) preference
(C) preferably
(D) preferred

107. All employees are asked to turn off the lights when ------- their offices to reduce electricity costs.

(A) exit
(B) exits
(C) exited
(D) exiting

108. Accountants and other finance professionals are busy ------- to the filing due date for tax returns.

(A) suited
(B) conducive
(C) prior
(D) forward

109. Coffee is a good gift idea for almost everyone whether you want to show your appreciation to a client or keep your employees ------- every morning.

(A) energizing
(B) has energized
(C) energize
(D) energized

110. The National Organization for Rare Disorders, also ------- as NORD, publishes a quarterly medical journal.

(A) known
(B) knowing
(C) knew
(D) knows

111. When you step into the aisles of the supermarket, you may encounter a ------- array of products, making it difficult to decide what to buy.

(A) bewildered
(B) bewildering
(C) bewilderment
(D) bewilders

112. Since the regulations governing importation became too ------- to accommodate, the Importers Association asked them to be revised.

(A) frustrating
(B) frustrated
(C) frustrate
(D) frustration

113. Please visit our office in San Jose by noon on that day so that we can complete any ------- paperwork before you begin your tour.

(A) remaining
(B) remained
(C) remains
(D) remain

114. The latest software from Stripo Tek makes it much ------- for companies to create newsletters.

(A) easy
(B) easily
(C) easier
(D) ease

115. The analysis of the spreadsheet ------- data on retail sales during the last quarter will provide valuable insights for our marketing strategy.

(A) contains
(B) contained
(C) containing
(D) containable

정답 및 해설 p.106

7. 문장 삽입 문제

· 문제 풀이 전략

문장 삽입 유형은 문맥을 이해하기 어렵기 때문에 한 문제를 푸는 데 몇 분을 소모할 수 있다. 수월한 문맥 파악을 위해 주어진 문장에서 '앞뒤 문장과의 연결고리인 키워드'가 무엇인지 찾아야 한다.

Examples 1-4 refer to the following e-mail.

From: Helena Bregoli <hbregoli@echostartech.com>
To: Tech Support Staff <techsupport@echostartech.com>
Date: October 3
Re: Professional Development Workshops

To all tech support staff members,

Here at Echostar Technologies, we pride ourselves on our commitment to providing the best technical support to our customers. —[1]—. That is why we periodically organize a series of workshops to aid our staff in continuing professional development. Word has just been received that all technical support employees are to attend this four-week course of workshops and will be provided with overtime pay for doing so. Sessions will take place from 7 P.M. to 8:30 P.M. on Mondays and Thursdays, beginning on Monday, November 10. —[2]—. Anyone unable to attend due to previous engagements must inform Michael Austen, the head of human resources department, as soon as possible.

These development workshops will be conducted by Mr. Joshua Green, the previous vice president of customer service at Walton Electronics. Mr. Green has over thirty years of experience in the area of technical support and customer service. —[3]—. Since his retirement, he has authored several publications on the subject, and his highly acclaimed seminars have attracted numerous participants from around the country. We are truly fortunate to have him lead us on this occasion.

Study materials for each session will be provided in advance. —[4]—. If you have any questions, feel free to contact me at any time.

Regards,

Helena Bregoli
Director, Technical Support

Ex 1. What is the e-mail mainly about?

    (A) The promotion of a technical support director

    (B) An employee's participation in an upcoming conference

    (C) An improvement in customer service ratings

    (D) A series of professional development workshops

Ex 2. Who should employees notify if they have a conflict in their schedules?

    (A) Mr. Green

    (B) Ms. Bregoli

    (C) Mr. Austen

    (D) Mr. Walton

Ex 3. What is suggested about Mr. Green?

    (A) He is currently an executive at a company.

    (B) He is embarking on a nationwide lecture tour.

    (C) He was in charge of hiring Ms. Bregoli.

    (D) He is proficient in solving customer problems.

Ex 4. In which of the positions marked [1], [2], [3], and [4] does the following sentence best belong?

"One way to guarantee that we conform to our high standards is by constantly improving our employees' customer service skills."

    (A) [1]

    (B) [2]

    (C) [3]

    (D) [4]

해설

Examples 1-4 refer to the following e-mail.

1–4번 예제는 다음 이메일에 관한 것입니다.

From: Helena Bregoli
        <hbregoli@echostartech.com>
To: Tech Support Staff
        <techsupport@echostartech.com>
Date: October 3
Re: ᴱˣ¹·Professional Development Workshops

To all tech support staff members,

ᴱˣ⁴·Here at Echostar Technologies, we pride ourselves on our commitment to providing the best technical support to our customers. —[1]— ᴱˣ¹·ᴱˣ⁴·That is why we periodically organize a series of workshops to aid our staff in continuing professional development. Word has just been received that all technical support employees are to attend this four-week course of workshops and will be provided with overtime pay for doing so. Sessions will take place from 7 P.M. to 8:30 P.M. on Mondays and Thursdays, beginning on Monday,

발신: Helena Bregoli
        〈hbregoli@echostartech.com〉
수신: 기술 지원 직원
        〈techsupport@echostartech.com〉
날짜: 10월 3일
제목: 전문성 개발 워크숍

모든 기술 지원 직원들에게,

이곳 Echostar Technologies에서 우리는 고객에게 최고의 기술 지원을 제공하는 일에 대한 헌신을 자랑스럽게 여기고 있습니다. —[1]— 그것이 바로 우리가 정기적으로 워크숍 시리즈를 준비해서 직원들의 지속적인 전문성 개발을 돕는 이유입니다. 모든 기술 지원 직원은 4주 코스의 워크숍에 참석해야 하며 그것에 대해 초과 근무 수당을 제공받을 것이라는 소식이 지금 막 들어왔습니다. 수업은 11월 10일 월요일에 시작하여, 월요일부터 목요일 오후 7시부터 8시 30분까지 있습니다.

November 10. —[2]— Ex2.Anyone unable to attend due to previous engagements must inform Michael Austen, the head of human resources department, as soon as possible.

These development workshops will be conducted by Mr. Joshua Green, the previous vice president of customer service at Walton Electronics. Ex3.Mr. Green has over thirty years of experience in the area of technical support and customer service. —[3]— Since his retirement, he has authored several publications on the subject, and his highly acclaimed seminars have attracted numerous participants from around the country. We are truly fortunate to have him lead us on this occasion.

Study materials for each session will be provided in advance. —[4]— If you have any questions, feel free to contact me at any time.

Regards,

Helena Bregoli
Director, Technical Support

선약 때문에 참석할 수 없는 사람은 인사팀장 Michael Austen에게 가능한 빨리 알려 주어야 합니다.

이번 개발 워크숍은 Walton 전자의 전 고객 서비스 담당 부사장 Mr. Joshua Green이 진행할 것입니다. Mr. Green은 기술 지원과 고객 서비스 분야에서 30년 이상의 경력이 있습니다. 은퇴 이후에는 이 주제에 관한 몇몇 출판물을 저술했으며, 큰 호평을 받는 그의 세미나는 전국에서 수많은 참가자를 끌어모았습니다. 이번에 그분이 우리를 지도해 주시게 되었으니 우리는 정말 운이 좋습니다.

각 수업의 학습 자료는 미리 제공될 것입니다. 질문이 있다면 아무 때나 자유롭게 저에게 연락하셔도 좋습니다.

이만 줄입니다.

기술 지원 책임자
Helena Bregoli

어휘 Re: ~와 관련하여(regarding) professional development 전문성 개발 pride oneself on ~에 대해 자랑스럽게 여기다 commitment 헌신 periodically 주기적으로; 정기적으로 organize 준비하다, 조직하다 aid sb in V-ing ~가 ~하는 것을 돕다 word 소식, 전갈 be to-V ~해야 한다 overtime pay 초과 근무 수당 session 강의 시간 unable to-V ~할 수 없는 previous engagement 선약 inform 알리다 head of human resources department 인사팀장 conduct (수업을) 진행하다 vice president 부사장 retirement 은퇴 author 저술하다 publication 출판물 highly acclaimed 크게 칭송받는, 호평받는 on this occasion 이번에 material 자료 in advance 미리, 사전에 feel free to-V (~을) 마음 놓고 해도 괜찮다

Ex 1. What is the e-mail mainly about?

    (A) The promotion of a technical support director

    (B) An employee's participation in an upcoming conference

    (C) An improvement in customer service ratings

    (D) A series of professional development workshops

이메일은 주로 무엇에 관한 것인가?

(A) 기술 지원 책임자의 승진
(B) 한 직원의 다가오는 회의 참석
(C) 고객 서비스 평점의 향상
(D) 전문성 개발 워크숍 시리즈

어휘 promotion 승진 upcoming 다가오는, 곧 있을 conference 회의, 학회 improvement 향상 rating 평점, 등급

해설 이메일을 읽을 때는 보내는 사람이나 받는 사람, 제목, 날짜 등의 정보도 함께 읽어야 한다. 제목 Professional Development Workshops만 봐도 정답을 알 수 있다. 또한 주제나 목적은 지문의 도입부에서 확인할 수 있다. 회사에서 직원들의 지속적인 전문성 개발을 위해 정기적으로 워크숍 시리즈를 진행하며(That is why we periodically organize a series of workshops to aid our staff in continuing professional development.), 모든 기술 지원 직원이 이번 워크숍에 참석해야 한다고 했다 (all technical support employees are to attend this four-week course of workshops). 그러므로 (D)가 정답이다.

Ex 2. Who should employees notify if they have a conflict in their schedules?

(A) Mr. Green
(B) Ms. Bregoli
(C) Mr. Austen
(D) Mr. Walton

직원이 일정에 충돌이 있다면 누구에게 알려야 하는가?
(A) Mr. Green
(B) Ms. Bregoli
(C) Mr. Austen
(D) Mr. Walton

어휘 notify 알리다 conflict 충돌

해설 if they have a conflict in their schedules라는 키워드가 지문 첫째 문단 마지막 문장에서 Anyone unable to attend due to previous engagements(선약 때문에 참석할 수 없는 사람)로 패러프레이즈 되어 있다. Mr. Austen에게 연락해야 한다고 나와 있으므로 (C)가 정답이다.

Ex 3. What is suggested about Mr. Green?

(A) He is currently an executive at a company.
(B) He is embarking on a nationwide lecture tour.
(C) He was in charge of hiring Ms. Bregoli.
(D) He is proficient in solving customer problems.

Mr. Green에 대해 무엇이 암시되어 있는가?
(A) 현재 어떤 회사의 중역이다.
(B) 전국적인 강연 투어를 시작할 것이다.
(C) Ms. Bregoli를 채용하는 일을 담당했다.
(D) 고객의 문제를 해결하는 데 능하다.

어휘 currently 현재 executive 간부, 이사, 중역 embark on ~에 착수하다 nationwide 전국적인 in charge of ~을 담당하는 hire 채용하다 proficient 능숙한, 능한

해설 Mr. Green이라는 이름은 둘째 문단에 등장한다. 기술 지원과 고객 서비스 분야에서 30년 이상의 경력이 있다고 소개하고 있다(Mr. Green has over thirty years of experience in the area of technical support and customer service). 이 문장을 통해 Mr. Green은 고객의 문제를 해결하는 데 매우 능숙한 사람이라고 추론할 수 있다.

Ex 4. In which of the positions marked [1], [2], [3], and [4] does the following sentence best belong?

"One way to guarantee that we conform to our high standards is by constantly improving our employees' customer service skills."

(A) [1]
(B) [2]
(C) [3]
(D) [4]

다음 문장은 [1], [2], [3], [4]로 표시된 자리 중 어느 곳에 가장 적당한가?
"우리가 높은 기준에 부합하도록 보장하는 한 가지 방법은 끊임없이 우리 직원들의 고객 서비스 역량을 향상시키는 것입니다."
(A) [1]
(B) [2]
(C) [3]
(D) [4]

어휘 conform to ~에 따르다, 부합하다 constantly 끊임없이, 거듭

해설 밑줄로 표시한 부분은 앞뒤 문장과의 연결고리가 되는 키워드이다. 문맥이 자연스러우려면 '우리의 높은 기준(our high standards)'이 무엇인지 앞에서 나와야 하는데, 첫 문단 첫 문장에 '최고의 기술 지원 서비스를 제공하는 일에 대한 우리의 헌신(our commitment to providing the best technical support to our customers)'이라는 키워드가 있으므로, '최고에 대한 헌신'이 이 회사의 '높은 기준'이라고 할 수 있다. 또한 '끊임없이 직원들의 고객 서비스 역량을 향상시키는 것(constantly improving our employees' customer service skills)'에 대한 내용은 —[1]—에 이어지는 문장에 나와 있다(That is why we periodically organize a series of workshops to aid our staff in continuing professional development). 이렇게 키워드를 연결해서 생각하면 문맥을 정확히 파악할 수 있다.

Today's Vocabulary

▶Actual Test를 풀기 전에 이 단어들을 암기하자.

짝을 이루어 출제되는 단어

- go[come] into effect (=become effective)
  효력을 발생하다
- customer satisfaction 고객 만족
- customer service representative[desk]
  고객 서비스 직원[데스크]
- sales representative[associate]
  영업 사원, 판매 직원

- $\begin{bmatrix} \text{research} \\ \text{survey} \\ \text{study} \\ \text{test} \end{bmatrix}$ $\begin{bmatrix} \text{suggest} \\ \text{reveal} \\ \text{indicate} \\ \text{show} \end{bmatrix}$ that

  조사[(설문)조사/연구/실험]가 ~임을 시사하다[밝히다/나타내다/보여주다]

---

be accustomed to ~에 익숙하다
concise 간결한
classified section 광고면
mandated 법에 규정된
waterfront (도시의) 해안가
a wealth of 풍부한
personify 의인화하다
magnify 확대하다
specify 명시하다, (구체적으로) 지정하다
testify 증명하다, ~의 증거가 되다
banquet (공식) 연회, 만찬
startle 깜짝 놀라게 하다
haltingly 주저하며
intimately 친밀하게
permissibly 허용되어, 무방하게
markedly 명백하게, 현저하게
knowledgeable 아는 것이 많은, 많이 아는
typically 보통, 일반적으로
based (~에) 근거지[본사]를 둔
certify (특히 서면으로) 증명하다
associate 연관 짓다, 결부 짓다
ethical 윤리적인
meadowland 목초지

measurement 치수, 크기, 길이, 양
outline 개요를 서술하다
up front 미리, 사전에
assure 장담하다, 확언[확약]하다
superb 최고의, 최상의, 대단히 훌륭한
leading 주요한, 선도하는
wind turbine 풍력 발전용 터빈
allocate 할당하다
in excess of ~이상의
refurbish (방·건물 등을) 새로 꾸미다, 재단장하다
equip 장비를 갖추다
abandon (물건·장소를) 버리고 떠나다
employ (기술·방법 등을) 쓰다, 이용하다
association 협회
generate 발생시키다, 만들어 내다
administrative 관리의, 행정의
undertake (책임을 맡아서) 착수하다
transformation (완전한) 변화, 탈바꿈, 변신
supplementary 보충의, 추가의
tailor (특정한 목적·사람 등에) 맞추다, 조정하다
solely 오로지, 단지
craft (수)공예
put *sth* to use ~을 사용하다, 이용하다

Actual Test

PART 5

1. 빈칸 앞뒤를 보며 문제를 푼다.
2. 빈칸 앞뒤를 보고 정답을 알 수 없다면 문장을 해석한다.
3. 두 줄 분량의 어휘 문제는 문장 전체를 해석해서 푼다.
4. 접속사 어휘 문제는 빈칸 앞뒤만을 보고 풀 수 없다. 문장 전체를 해석해 보자.

PART 6

1. 문법 문제라면 Part 5와 같은 방식으로 빈칸 앞뒤를 보며 푼다.
2. 다른 유형의 문제는 문맥을 통해 정답을 파악한다.

PART 7

1. 문제와 보기 (A), (B), (C), (D)를 먼저 읽은 후에 지문을 읽는다.
2. 지문 위아래의 모든 부분을 자세히 읽어 본다.
3. 문제의 해설을 꼼꼼히 읽고, 문장 구조를 분석하며 복습한다.

101. New recruits should attend their
------- training workshops at 9 A.M.
with all necessary materials.

(A) assigned
(B) assign
(C) assigns
(D) assigning

102. ------- the effectiveness of Dominic
Campion's leadership on the city
council, he will likely win next month's
mayoral election.

(A) Since
(B) Given
(C) Among
(D) Upon

103. Customers are still accustomed
to placing concise notices in the
classified section ------- there is no
longer a mandated word limit.

(A) as if
(B) so that
(C) in case
(D) even though

104. Studies have ------- that positive
interactions with coworkers are
associated with high job satisfaction
levels.

(A) prepared
(B) shown
(C) outgrown
(D) funded

105. The Busan Visitor Centre offers boat
rides ------- the city's renowned
waterfront every day.

(A) between
(B) along
(C) below
(D) apart

106. Milngavie's Farmers Market sells the
------- fruit and vegetables in all of
Glasgow.

(A) freshest
(B) fresh
(C) freshly
(D) fresher

107. Industry experts predicted that Brent
crude oil price would rise to as -------
as 90.65 dollars per barrel this year, up
more than 5 dollars from the previous
year.

(A) more
(B) much
(C) most
(D) many

108. Fissel School has business mentors
who are retired executives with a
------- of expertise across a wide
range of industries.

(A) wealth
(B) height
(C) labor
(D) fame

109. Techmania Science Museum offers
the ------- collection of facts and
information ever to be made available.

(A) wide
(B) widely
(C) more widely
(D) widest

110. Last quarter Eximion Technology did
not sell ------- as many downloads as
it had hoped to.

(A) nearly
(B) nearest
(C) nearer
(D) nearing

111. In a press release ------- yesterday, Raleigh Convention Center announced plans to improve its facilities.

(A) issued
(B) issuing
(C) to issue
(D) was issued

112. The Chairman of the Board of Governors of the Federal Reserve System is one of the ------- influential figures in the world.

(A) most
(B) many
(C) more
(D) much

113. We are continually upgrading our surveillance systems, ------- you the highest level of security services available in the industry today.

(A) ensured
(B) ensuring
(C) be ensured
(D) will ensure

114. Pomodoro Bistro has requested that we ------- the number of banquet guests by Tuesday.

(A) personify
(B) magnify
(C) specify
(D) testify

115. Popovich Textiles, Inc., is well-known ------- the fashion industry as being a trendsetter for young men's clothing.

(A) toward
(B) throughout
(C) regarding
(D) aboard

116. After twenty years in business, Arai and Ramos Home Health Services remains dedicated to customer -------.

(A) satisfaction
(B) production
(C) energy
(D) opportunity

117. Please submit the ------- sales report by the end of the week for senior accountant Sugata Mitra's review.

(A) revise
(B) revised
(C) revising
(D) revision

118. Analysts were ------- by the increasing number of consumers who are planning to buy property this year.

(A) startle
(B) startling
(C) startled
(D) startles

119. For additional information regarding international flight fares, please consult the list ------- in the envelope.

(A) provide
(B) providing
(C) was provided
(D) provided

120. The software for tracking orders has been ------- successful as it has substantially reduced the amount of time spent on the task.

(A) haltingly
(B) intimately
(C) permissibly
(D) markedly

121. The next generation Airbus is expected to offer 20 percent more cabin space and twice ------- cargo capacity as the previous model.

(A) much more
(B) more than
(C) as much
(D) too much

122. Please use the attached questionnaire to inform us of how ------- your recent stay at the Sandy Shores Inn was.

(A) knowledgeable
(B) considerable
(C) enjoyable
(D) available

123. Although Ms. Eisner is absent today, she ------- attends all school board meetings.

(A) previously
(B) typically
(C) almost
(D) well

124. Present this postcard to a sales ------- at any of our stores to receive a £3.00 gift card.

(A) accessory
(B) associate
(C) faculty
(D) formula

125. Last night, Channel Fifteen News aired an exclusive interview with the ------- actress Paula Olivera.

(A) accomplish
(B) accomplishment
(C) accomplished
(D) accomplishing

126. The songs on Young Ho Woo's latest album are ------- the most innovative musical arrangements of his artistic journey.

(A) beside
(B) over
(C) among
(D) upon

127. Processes such as automated cutting and stitching will enable factory workers to complete their tasks much -------.

(A) more efficiently
(B) efficiently
(C) efficient
(D) most efficiently

128. Skystream Air, an airline ------- in Kuala Lumpur, is offering budget flights to Manila and Hong Kong.

(A) stored
(B) stayed
(C) based
(D) moved

129. Once quality control inspectors ------- that all specifications have been met, the product is able to be shipped.

(A) affect
(B) replace
(C) certify
(D) associate

130. The ------- meadowlands in the vicinity of the museum are designated as wildlife habitat.

(A) ethical
(B) vast
(C) absolute
(D) economic

GO ON TO THE NEXT PAGE

PART 6

Questions 131-134 refer to the following customer review.

I have been recently extended a last-minute invitation to a formal dinner.

I purchased a suit and had to have it tailored as ------- as possible. A friend
                                                      131.

recommended that I use Riccardo Tailoring in downtown Wellington. When

I met Riccardo, he gave me his entire attention ------- his shop was crowded. He
                                                  132.

listened to me patiently and diligently wrote down all my measurements. He then

outlined all the tailoring charges up front and assured me that he would have my

suit done in three days, but it was ready within two! -------.
                                                       133.

Riccardo has been running his shop for more than two decades, and his

experience really shows. He is a ------- tailor. I highly recommend him.
                                  134.

Ronald Grayson, Wellington

---

131. (A) quickly
(B) quicken
(C) quickest
(D) quickness

132. (A) as far as
(B) even though
(C) such as
(D) whether

133. (A) Saturday is always the busiest day
for the shop.
(B) The suit fits me perfectly as well.
(C) I made an additional purchase.
(D) He used to sell shirts.

134. (A) former
(B) temporary
(C) superb
(D) best

Questions 135-138 refer to the following information.

EBR Industries guarantees that its products will work as ------- for a minimum
                                                         135.
of one year from date of purchase. -------. This ------- is valid only for products
                                    136.   **137.**
purchased from EBR Industries stores and other licensed distributors. Products

that are found to be defective can be sent to our address for either repair or

replacement. When feasible, please make sure that products being returned due

to damage are shipped back to us in their ------- packaging.
                                         138.

135. (A) advertising
    (B) advertised
    (C) advertisement
    (D) advertises

136. (A) This period may be extended for
       certain products.
    (B) EBR Industries stores are located
       in four countries.
    (C) At that moment, an electronic
       receipt was generated.
    (D) Product samples are available in
       stores.

137. (A) agenda
    (B) sale
    (C) requirement
    (D) warranty

138. (A) originally
    (B) original
    (C) origin
    (D) originality

GO ON TO THE NEXT PAGE

PART 7

Questions 139-142 refer to the following article.

Positive Change for Charleroi

Lagerwey Wind, the leading developer of wind turbines and wind energy technology across Europe, has announced plans to open a manufacturing plant in Charleroi, Belgium. —[1]—. The Dutch firm is allocating in excess of €20 million to acquire, refurbish, and equip the abandoned C-Tech Telephone factory. It is anticipated that the venture will generate approximately two hundred manufacturing positions and fifty administrative positions over the following two years. This is a welcome announcement for Charleroi, an industrial area that has been adversely affected by the closure of numerous factories and the subsequent diminishment of employment opportunities in recent years. —[2]—.

Caddell Builders has already been contracted to undertake the plant's transformations. —[3]—.

The facility will primarily be utilized for the assembly and testing of gear drives to be incorporated in the company's wind turbines. —[4]—. Lagerwey Wind, in partnership with the Charleroi Business Development Association (CBDA), will furnish development grants to train its incoming workforce in green technology. Jomarie Fredericks, CBDA president, says "the city is proud to be part of an effort that is beneficial to energy conservation and to the economic prosperity of our region."

139. What does the article mainly discuss?

(A) The appointment of a new company president
(B) The consolidation of two firms
(C) The process of manufacturing wind turbines
(D) The opening of a facility

140. What will happen to the C-Tech Telephone factory?

(A) It will be preserved as a historic site.
(B) It will be employed by a different industry.
(C) It will be relocated to another location.
(D) It will be demolished to form an unoccupied space.

141. Who is Ms. Fredericks?

(A) A Lagerwey Wind executive
(B) A media correspondent
(C) The head of an organization
(D) The mayor of a city in Belgium

142. In which of the positions marked [1], [2], [3], and [4] does the following sentence best belong?

"It also anticipates hiring supplementary personnel to complete the construction project."

(A) [1]
(B) [2]
(C) [3]
(D) [4]

Questions 143-147 refer to the following notice, e-mail, and comment form.

 Waikiki Monarch Hotel

Scheduled activities for guests in August

Start time for all activities is 10:00 A.M. at the Guest Services desk in the lobby.

Activity and instructor/guide	Description
Every Tuesday Surfing lesson Conducted by Kalani Kealoha	Master the art of surfing in Waikiki. Should be an adept swimmer. $60 per person. All participants must be 12 years or older.
Every Wednesday Hawaiian flower crafts Conducted by Elina Aquino	Your instructor will provide you with guidance in creating a lei: an ornamental Hawaiian flower garland or necklace. All supplies included. $12 per person.
Every Thursday History tour Conducted by Leilani Ogawa	This 2-hour walking tour will provide participants with an insight into Waikiki's history. No charge.
Every Friday Hawaiian cookery class Conducted by head chef Jessica Chen	Learn how to prepare authentic Hawaiian cuisine. (Lessons can be tailored to focus solely on vegetarian recipes.) All participants must be 12 years or older. $25 per person.
Visit the Guest Services desk for more information and to sign up.	

To: Guest Services Staff <gsstaff@waikikimonarchhotel.com>
From: Soo-Min Lee <smlee@waikikimonarchhotel.com>
Date: August 17
Subject: Update

Hi all,

This month's program of guest activities needs to be revised. Elina Aquino and Jessica Chen will be away August 20-26. I will lead Elina's activities and Astrid Geensen will lead Jessica's. Everything will return to normal on August 27, when Elina and Jessica both return.

Sincerely,

Soo-Min Lee
Guest Services Director, Waikiki Monarch Hotel

https://www.waikikimonarchhotel.com/guest_comments

 Waikiki Monarch Hotel

Comments:

My family and I thoroughly enjoyed our stay at your hotel. We really appreciated the activities that were planned and I would like to give all the instructors my compliments. I had to skip the activity guided by Ms. Ogawa, but my family told me they learned a lot from her. My daughter and I found it very entertaining to learn how to make flower garlands, and my husband has already cooked some of the dishes he was taught in Ms. Geensen's class. Finally, my son and daughter both had a wonderful time with Mr. Kealoha. They are looking forward to putting his lessons to use when we travel on holiday to Costa Rica next year.

Name: Sarah Virtanen   **Today's date:** 13 September

Number of guests: 4   **Date of stay:** 20-26 August

Submit

143. What activity can be customized?

(A) Tuesday's activity
(B) Wednesday's activity
(C) Thursday's activity
(D) Friday's activity

144. What is the purpose of the e-mail?

(A) To welcome two new employees
(B) To address a guest inquiry
(C) To make changes to a schedule
(D) To arrange training sessions for staff

145. In the comment form, the word "skip" in paragraph 1, line 3, is closest in meaning to

(A) jump
(B) miss
(C) pay for
(D) look over

146. Who taught the course enjoyed by Ms. Virtanen and her daughter?

(A) Ms. Aquino
(B) Ms. Lee
(C) Ms. Ogawa
(D) Ms. Chen

147. What are Ms. Virtanen's children planning to do in Costa Rica?

(A) Go surfing
(B) Learn traditional crafts
(C) Take a walking tour
(D) Try local food

Day
08

1. 시제 ★★★

시제 문제는 다른 유형과 달리 빈칸 앞뒤에서 정답의 단서를 찾을 수 있는 경우가 거의 없다. 시제 문제에서는 문장을 처음부터 읽으면서 시제를 나타내는 키워드를 찾아야 한다.

유형 1 **현재완료 시제**

문장 안에 'since + 시점'이나 'for[over/in] the last[past] + 기간'이 있으면 현재완료 시제가 정답이다.

Ex 1. Dr. Amit Sharma, who ------- a tireless advocate of economic policy reform since the 1990s, is the keynote speaker at the conference.

(A) will be
(B) is
(C) was
(D) has been

보기를 보면 시제 문제임을 알 수 있다. 빈칸 앞뒤를 보지 말고 문장을 처음부터 읽어 보자. 키워드 since가 있으면 현재완료 시제 (D)가 정답이다.

어휘 tireless 지칠 줄 모르는, 한결같은 advocate 옹호자, 지지자 reform 개혁, 개선 keynote speaker 기조연설자

해석 Amit Sharma 박사는 1990년대 이후 경제 정책 개혁의 한결같은 옹호자로 학회의 기조 연설자이다.

Ex 2. For the last three years, Kavya Robinson ------- to be the leading salesperson at Eicher Motors.

(A) aspiring
(B) aspire
(C) has aspired
(D) is aspiring

문장에 동사가 없으므로 빈칸에 동사가 들어가야 한다. 따라서 준동사 (A)는 제외하고, 나머지 보기에서 정답을 선택하자. For the last three years를 보면 현재완료 시제인 (C)가 정답임을 알 수 있다.

어휘 aspire to-V ~하기를 열망하다 salesperson 영업 사원

해석 지난 3년 동안 Kavya Robinson은 Eicher 자동차에서 최고의 영업 사원이 되기를 열망해 왔다.

유형 2 **since / for**

보기가 전치사나 접속사로 구성되어 있고, 그중 since나 for가 있다면 주절의 시제가 현재완료인지 확인해 보자. 현재완료 시제 문장의 빈칸에는 since나 for가 정답이다. 둘 다 보기에 있다면 다음과 같이 구분하면 된다.

since + 시점 (명사구 또는 '주어+동사' 절 모두 가능)
for + 기간 (명사구만 가능)

Ex 3. The number of visitors to the Hamburg Maritime Museum has grown twofold ------- the opening of the Antarctic Expedition Exhibit.

(A) for
(B) except
(C) among
(D) since

보기에 since와 for가 있고 문장의 동사가 현재완료 시제 has grown이다. 빈칸 뒤에 the opening of the Antarctic Expedition Exhibit(남극 탐험 전시회의 시작)이라는 '시점'이 나오므로 (D)가 정답이다.

어휘 maritime 바다의, 해양의 twofold 2배로, 2중으로 Antarctic 남극의 expedition 탐험, 원정
해석 남극 탐험 전시회의 시작 이후 Hamburg 해양 박물관의 방문객 수는 두 배로 증가했다.

Ex 4. The automobile company has enjoyed growing sales in Europe, with its hybrid vehicles staying on best-seller positions ------- years.

(A) since
(B) on
(C) with
(D) for

보기에 since와 for가 있고 문장의 동사가 현재완료 시제 has enjoyed이다. 빈칸 뒤에 years(수년)라는 '기간'이 나오므로 (D)가 정답이다.

어휘 automobile 자동차 vehicle 차량 with + 명사 + 형용사[분사/전치사구/to-V] ~가 ~하는 채로
해석 그 자동차 회사는 하이브리드 자동차가 수년간 인기 상품 자리를 유지하면서 유럽에서 판매량이 증가하는 것을 누려 왔다.

과거 시제

과거 시제의 키워드로 last, ago, yesterday가 가장 많다. 그밖에 'in + 과거 연도[세기]', once, at one time, recently와 같이 명확한 과거의 시점을 나타내는 키워드가 있으면 과거 시제를 정답으로 고르자.

Ex 5. Cassandra Veras ------- her training at Riverside County Animal Hospital last week and is ready to start her career as a veterinary technician.

    (A) will conclude
    (B) to conclude
    (C) concludes
    (D) concluded

빈칸 앞 Cassandra Veras가 주어, 빈칸 뒤 her training이 목적어로 빈칸에는 동사가 들어가야 한다. and 앞 첫 번째 절 끝에 키워드 last week이 있으므로 과거 시제 (D)가 정답이다.

어휘 conclude 끝내다, 마치다 veterinary technician 수의학 조무사, 동물보건사

해석 Cassandra Veras는 지난주에 Riverside County 동물병원에서 수련을 마쳤으며 수의학 조무사로서의 경력을 시작할 준비가 되어 있다.

현재 시제

usually, often, sometimes 같은 빈도 부사가 있으면 현재 시제가 정답이다. 키워드 없이 출제되는 경우도 있기 때문에, '반복되는 동작'이나 '지속하거나 유지되는 상태'는 현재 시제로 나타낸다는 규칙을 기억하자.

Ex 6. Low interest rates usually ------- to increased spending, which in turn stimulates economic activities, but such conditions may also fuel inflation at the same time.

    (A) lead
    (B) led
    (C) had led
    (D) will lead

빈도 부사 usually가 있으므로 현재 시제 (A)가 정답이다.

어휘 interest rate 금리, 이율 lead to ~로 이어지다 spending 지출 in turn 그 결과로, 곧이어 stimulate 자극하다, 촉진하다 fuel 부채질하다 at the same time 동시에

해석 낮은 금리는 보통 지출 증가로 이어져, 그 결과로 경제 활동을 촉진하지만, 그런 상태는 동시에 인플레이션을 부채질할 수도 있다.

Ex 7. Mr. Vieri ------- office supplies from the warehouse every Thursday, so please make sure he is aware of what you need by Wednesday.

(A) orders
(B) ordered
(C) order
(D) to order

빈칸 앞뒤의 Mr. Vieri와 office supplies가 각각 주어와 목적어이므로 빈칸에는 동사가 들어가야 한다. 준동사인 (D)는 제외하고, 단수 명사인 주어의 수와 일치하지 않는 (C)도 정답이 아니다. 문장에서 '매주 목요일에 사무용품을 주문한다'는 반복, 지속하여 일어나는 일을 말하고 있으므로 현재 시제인 (A)가 알맞다.

어휘 office supplies 사무용품 warehouse 도매점; 큰 상점 make sure 반드시 ~하도록) 하다 be aware of ~을 알다

해석 Mr. Vieri가 매주 목요일에 도매상으로부터 사무용품을 주문하니 반드시 수요일까지는 필요한 것을 그가 알도록 해주세요.

유형 5 **미래 시제**

미래 시제의 키워드로 next week, next month 같이 'next + 시간'을 가장 많이 사용한다. in the future, someday, sometime, 'in + 시간', tomorrow, later, today 등이 있어도 미래 시제가 정답이다.

Ex 8. Following the team meeting next week, Ms. Valspar ------- whether the project deadline needs to be adjusted.

(A) to decide
(B) deciding
(C) will decide
(D) has decided

빈칸 앞 Ms. Valspar가 주어, 빈칸 뒤의 whether로 시작하는 명사절이 목적어이다. 빈칸에는 동사가 있어야 하므로 준동사인 (A)와 (B)는 제외하자. (C)와 (D) 중 next week이 있으므로 미래 시제인 (C)가 정답이다.

어휘 following ~후에 deadline 기한, 마감일 adjust 조정하다, 조절하다

해석 다음 주 팀 회의 후에 Ms. Valspar가 프로젝트 마감일을 조정할 필요가 있을지 결정할 것입니다.

Ex 9. Podell Automotive is in the process of introducing a new Web site that ------- its customers to access invoices.

(A) has allowed
(B) allow
(C) will allow
(D) allowed

주격 관계대명사 that 뒤의 동사 자리가 빈칸이므로 선행사 a new Web site의 수와 일치해야 한다. 선행사가 단수 명사이므로 복수 동사인 (B)는 제외하자. 개발 중인 새 웹사이트에서 고객이 송장을 볼 수 있는 것은 미래의 일이므로 미래 시제 (C)가 정답이다.

어휘 automotive 자동차의 in the process of ~하는 중인 introduce 도입하다, 선보이다 access 접속하다, 이용하다 invoice 송장(送狀)

해석 Podell 자동차는 고객이 송장에 접속하게 해주는 새 웹사이트를 도입하는 과정 중에 있다.

미래완료 시제

미래완료 시제의 키워드로 'by + 미래 시점', 'as of + 미래 시점(~부(附), ~를 기(期)하여)', 'by the time + S + 현재 시제 동사'를 기억하자.

Ex 10. By the time Ms. Li retires as CEO of Datafine Technologies, she ------- a substantial surge in the company's market share.

(A) sees
(B) will have seen
(C) saw
(D) has been seeing

'by the time + 주어(Ms. Li) + 현재 시제 동사 (retires)'가 있으므로 미래완료 시제 (B)가 정답이다.

어휘 retire 물러나다, 은퇴하다 see 경험하다, 목격하다 substantial 상당한 surge 급증, 급등 market share 시장 점유율

해석 Ms. Li는 Datafine Technologies의 CEO 자리에서 물러날 때쯤이면 회사의 시장 점유율의 상당한 급등을 경험했을 것이다.

Ex 11. ------- this time next year, AFT Technology will have acquired two new subsidiaries in Europe.

(A) To
(B) By
(C) Quite
(D) Begin

문장의 동사는 will have acquired로 미래완료 시제이다. ------- this time next year를 보면서 'by + 미래 시점'이 미래완료 시제의 키워드임을 기억하여 (B)를 정답으로 선택하자.

어휘 acquire 획득하다, 인수하다 subsidiary 자회사

해석 내년 이맘때쯤이면 AFT Technology는 유럽에서 두 개의 새 자회사를 인수하게 될 것이다.

유형 7 **과거완료 시제**

'by the time + S + 과거 시제 동사'가 있으면 과거완료 시제가 정답이다. 또한 특정한 시제를 나타내는 키워드가 없는 문장이라면, 과거의 어떤 사건보다 더 앞선 일을 말할 때 과거완료 시제를 사용한다는 규칙을 기억하자.

Ex 12. By the time the merger of the two companies was announced, Daiwon Co. ------- operating under its new name, CM-Daiwon, Inc.

(A) begins
(B) will begin
(C) had begun
(D) having begun

빈칸에는 주절의 동사가 들어가야 하므로 준동사인 (D)는 제외하자. 'by the time + 주어 + 과거 시제 동사'가 있으므로 과거완료 시제인 (C)가 정답이다.

어휘 merger 합병 announce 발표하다 operate 영업하다
해석 두 회사의 합병이 발표되었을 때 Daiwon 사(社)는 이미 새 이름 CM-Daiwon으로 영업하기 시작했다.

Ex 13. Dr. Nakagawa arrived for the awards ceremony on time even though her train ------- twenty minutes behind schedule.

(A) is leaving
(B) will leave
(C) to leave
(D) had left

부사절 빈칸에 동사가 들어가야 하므로 준동사인 (C)는 제외하자. Nakagawa 박사가 시상식에 도착한 것은 과거 사건인데, 기차가 출발한 것은 그전에 있었던 일이므로 과거완료 시제 동사인 (D)가 정답으로 알맞다.

어휘 awards ceremony 시상식 on time 정시에, 제시간에 behind schedule 예정보다 늦게
해석 Nakagawa 박사는 기차가 예정보다 20분 늦게 출발했음에도 불구하고 제시간에 시상식에 도착했다.

유형 8 **시제의 일치**

직접 화법 문장을 간접 화법 문장으로 전환할 때 주절의 시제에 맞게 종속절의 시제를 바꿔 써야 한다.

Mayor James A. Garner said at yesterday's interview. "The stores near the new shopping center are benefiting from the increased traffic."

➡ Mayor James A. Garner said at yesterday's interview that the stores near the new shopping center [are / were] benefiting from the increased traffic.

직접 화법 문장의 are는 간접 화법 문장에서 were가 되어야 한다. 직접 화법 문장에서 따옴표 안의 인용문은 간접 화법 문장에서 명사절 접속사 that이 이끄는 종속절이 된다. 종속절의 시제는 주절의 시제에 영향을 받게 된다. 주절의 동사(said)가 과거이므로, 직접 화법에서 현재 시제인 동사(are)는 간접 화법에서 종속절에 있으므로 과거형(were)으로 바뀌어야 한다.

Ex 14. Ms. Ahmed decided that she ------- the conference next month.

(A) would not be attending
(B) will not have been attending
(C) would not have been attended
(D) will not be attended

빈칸 뒤에 목적어 the conference가 있으므로 능동태 동사인 (A)와 (B) 중 정답을 선택해야 한다. next month만을 보고 (B)를 고르지 말자. 주절의 동사(decided)가 과거 시제이므로 종속절에서도 조동사 will 대신 과거형 would를 사용해야 한다. 따라서 정답은 (A)이다.

어휘 conference 회의, 학회 attend 참석하다
해석 Ms. Ahmed는 내년에는 학회에 참석하지 않기로 했다.

유형 9 | 시간, 조건의 부사절

시간, 조건의 부사절에서는 미래에 있을 일을 미래 시제 대신 현재 시제나 현재완료 시제로 써야 한다.

The manager **will call** us **when** she **arrives** at the construction site **tomorrow**.

➡ 내일 도착하지만 시간 부사절이므로 현재 시제를 사용해야 한다.

The summary of the revised company procedures **will be distributed as soon as** it **is available**.

➡ 앞으로 이용할 수 있게 될 것이지만 시간 부사절이므로 현재 시제를 사용해야 한다.

The factory tour **will start next week if** ten more people **sign up** for it.

➡ 앞으로 등록할 것이지만 조건 부사절이므로 현재 시제를 사용해야 한다.

Once the two companies **agree** to merge with each other. the soon-to-be created conglomerate **will be** a potential threat to us.

➡ 앞으로 합의할 것이지만 시간 부사절이므로 현재 시제를 사용해야 한다.

Ex 15. Lorenzo Raspallo will bring up the topic of the advertising budget to the board of directors when they ------- formally next week.

(A) will meet
(B) meet
(C) be meeting
(D) meeting

when 부사절의 빈칸에 동사가 들어가야 하므로 준동사인 (D)는 제외하자. 나머지 보기 중 next week이 있다고 (A)를 고르면 안 된다. when으로 시작하는 시간 부사절은 미래 시제 대신 현재나 현재완료 시제를 사용해야 하므로 (B)가 정답이다.

어휘 bring up (화제를) 꺼내다 **board of directors** 이사회 **formally** 정식으로, 공식적으로

해석 Lorenzo Raspallo는 다음 주에 이사회와 공식적으로 만나면 광고 예산 문제를 화제로 꺼낼 것이다.

Ex 16. Construction on a new wing at the Izmit Museum ------- as soon as additional funds have been secured.

(A) has been resumed
(B) will resume
(C) was resumed
(D) to be resuming

주절에 동사가 없으므로 빈칸에는 동사가 들어가야 한다. 준동사인 (D)는 제외하고 나머지 동사 중 알맞은 시제를 선택해야 한다. as soon as로 시작하는 시간 부사절의 시제가 현재완료 (have been secured)인 것은 이 문장이 미래 사건을 말하고 있다는 것을 나타내므로 (B)가 정답이다. (A)나 (C)가 정답이 되려면, 주절보다 앞선 일을 말하고 있는 부사절의 시제가 과거완료여야 한다.

어휘 wing (돌출된) 동(棟), 부속 건물 **resume** 재개되다 **additional** 추가의 **fund** 자금 **secure** 얻어 내다, 확보하다

해석 Izmit 미술관의 새 부속 건물 공사는 추가적인 자금이 확보되는 대로 재개될 것이다.

208 | 토익 마법 2주의 기적 990 RC

Ex 17. If you ------- in any business courses during the upcoming week, the institute will give you a ten percent discount.

(A) enrolls
(B) enrolled
(C) enroll
(D) will enroll

if절의 주어가 you이므로 수가 일치하지 않는 동사 (A)는 제외하자. 나머지 보기 중 during the upcoming week가 있다고 (D)를 고르지 않도록 주의하자. 조건 부사절이므로 미래 시제 대신 현재 시제나 현재완료 시제를 사용해야 하므로 (C)가 정답이다.

[어휘] enroll in ~에 등록하다 upcoming 다가오는 institute 기관, 협회
[해석] 다음 주 동안 아무 비즈니스 과정에 등록하면 기관에서 10퍼센트를 할인해준다.

2. 가정법 ★

가정법 문장은 세 가지 시제를 주로 사용한다. 각 시제에 따라 정해진 문장의 형태에 맞게 빈칸을 채우면 된다. 가정법 문제는 모양 맞추기 게임이다.

유형 1   가정법 과거

If + S + [과거 시제 동사 / were] ~, S + [would / could / should / might] + V ~.

---

* 가정법 문장에서는 if절의 be동사로 were만 사용하고 was는 쓰지 않는다.

If we **had** more time, we **would do** the work better.
If she **were** here, she **would be** happy to hear this news.

대부분 굵은 글씨 부분을 빈칸으로 한 문제가 출제된다.
또한 if절의 동사가 were일 때는 if를 생략하고 주어와 동사를 도치한 형태도 있다.

If I **were** a bird, I **would fly** to her.
= **Were I** a bird, I **would fly** to her.

Ex 1. If fares ------- any further, the bus system would not be able to retain financial sustainability.

(A) are lowered
(B) will lower
(C) have lowered
(D) were lowered

주절의 동사가 would not be이므로 가정법 과거 시제 문장임을 알 수 있다. 형식에 맞게 과거 시제 동사 (D)를 정답으로 선택해야 한다.

어휘 fare 요금 lower 내리다, 낮추다 retain 유지하다, 보유하다 sustainability 지속 가능성
해석 요금이 더 내려가면 버스 시스템은 재정적 지속 가능성을 유지할 수 없을 것이다.

유형 2 가정법 과거완료

$$\text{If} + \text{S} + \textbf{had p.p.} \sim, \text{S} + \begin{bmatrix} \textbf{would} \\ \textbf{could} \\ \textbf{should} \\ \textbf{might} \end{bmatrix} + \text{have p.p.} \sim.$$

If I **had known** your address. I **would have sent** you a letter.
If she **had worked** hard. she **could have passed** the exam.

대부분 굵은 글씨 부분을 빈칸으로 한 문제가 출제된다.
또한 부사절에서 if를 생략하고 주어와 동사를 도치할 수도 있다.

Had I **known** your address. I **would have sent** you a letter.
Had she **worked** hard. she **could have passed** the exam.

Ex 2. If we had ordered the office furniture last week, we ------- a substantial discount.

(A) have received
(B) be receiving
(C) will receive
(D) would have received

> if절의 동사가 had ordered이므로 이 문장이 가정법 과거완료 시제 문장인 것을 알 수 있다. 주절의 빈칸에는 정해진 형식에 맞게 (D)가 들어가야 한다.

어휘 furniture 가구

해석 우리가 지난주에 사무실 가구를 주문했더라면 상당한 할인을 받았을 것이다.

Ex 3. ------- he listened to the advice from the analysts on the deal, he would not have gone through with it.

(A) Have
(B) Had
(C) Has
(D) Would have

> 주절의 동사 would not have gone을 보면 이 문장이 가정법 과거완료 시제 문장인 것을 알 수 있다. 부사절에서 if가 생략되면 주어와 동사를 도치해야 하므로 (B)가 정답이다.

어휘 analyst 분석가 go through with (계속) 이행하다, 추진하다

해석 그가 거래에 대한 분석가들의 조언을 들었더라면 그것을 추진하지 않았을 것이다.

유형 3   가정법 미래

> If + S + **should** + **V** ~, S + V ~.

if절에서 'should + 동사 원형'을 사용하며, 주절은 정해진 형태 없이 미래에 대한 내용이면 된다.

If it **should rain** tomorrow, we will not go fishing.
If anyone **should call** me, take the message.

또한 부사절에서 if를 생략하고 주어와 should를 도치한 형태도 있다. 가정법 미래 시제 문장은 거의 도치된 형태로 출제된다.

Should it **rain** tomorrow, we will not go fishing.
Should anyone **call** me, take the message.

Ex 4. Mr. Lee's sales team may be assigned to our exhibit booth at the weekend trade show ------- additional staffing be necessary during the event.

(A) while
(B) should
(C) during
(D) in addition

보기가 [(A) 접속사 (B) 조동사 (C) 전치사 (D) 부사]로 구성되어 있으므로 이 문제가 '접속사 vs 전치사' 유형이라는 생각을 해야 한다. 따라서 부사 (D)는 제외하고 시작하자. 빈칸 뒤에 '주어 + 동사(additional staffing be)'가 있어 전치사 (C)는 오답이지만, 바로 접속사 (A)를 정답으로 선택하면 안 된다. 동사원형(be)과 보기의 조동사(should)가 눈에 들어와야 한다. 가정법 미래 시제 문장으로 if가 생략되고 주어와 should를 도치한 형태임을 알고 (B)를 정답으로 골라야 한다.

어휘 assign 배치하다 trade show 무역 박람회 staffing 직원 제공[채용]

해석 주말 무역 박람회에서 추가적인 직원 배치가 필요하게 된다면 Mr. Lee의 영업팀이 우리 전시 부스에 배치될 것입니다.

101. ------- Mr. Wilkinson not out of town on a business trip, he would be the one to lead today's training session for the new interns.

(A) In fact
(B) Whereas
(C) Only
(D) Were

102. Management was notified yesterday that the arrival of the shipment sent to the London office ------- due to a customs issue.

(A) being delayed
(B) would be delayed
(C) has been delayed
(D) have delayed

103. Golota Remodeling may charge more than the initial estimate ------- additional time be required to install the shelves and cabinets.

(A) in fact
(B) when
(C) through
(D) should

104. If we had not received approval for the additional funding so quickly, we ------- in establishing our presence in Asia in only 12 months.

(A) have to succeed
(B) would not have succeeded
(C) had not succeeded
(D) have not succeeded

105. Ms. Han ------- employed by the same company in many different positions over the last 20 years.

(A) is
(B) has
(C) has been
(D) could be

106. ------- receiving notice that the conductor of the Cape Philharmonic Orchestra will retire, the operations committee has been searching for a replacement.

(A) Since
(B) While
(C) Once
(D) For

107. ------- the region's tallest skyscraper was completed, Pace and Brown Architects had already begun designing a taller one.

(A) By the time
(B) Whenever
(C) Unless
(D) Due to

108. Starting next Monday, Lehman's Hardware ------- its hours of operation until 9:00 P.M. daily.

(A) had extended
(B) was extending
(C) will be extended
(D) will be extending

109. Amanda Lee ------- the suit designs by the time she meets the president of Klim Clothing next week.

(A) will have completed
(B) is completing
(C) completed
(D) completes

110. ------- the recruiting team received a greater number of responses to the online job posting, the candidate selection process would have taken more time.

(A) Had
(B) Instead of
(C) Except
(D) Whether

111. I eagerly anticipate hearing from you as soon as you ------- from your vacation.

(A) return
(B) will return
(C) would return
(D) had returned

112. Bank employees will forward the loan application to the appropriate department as soon as the form ------- submitted.

(A) was
(B) will be
(C) has been
(D) to be

113. Mr. Lehrman ------- at this school three years ago and may return this fall.

(A) teaches
(B) is teaching
(C) taught
(D) has taught

114. On Saturday, the train service from Kingston Station to Waterloo Station ------- from 8:00 P.M. to midnight while the railroad is closed for maintenance.

(A) will be suspended
(B) was suspended
(C) is suspended
(D) to suspend

115. We plan to visit Rosie's Cantina after work because it ------- authentic Mexican cuisine.

(A) offered
(B) offer
(C) offers
(D) offering

정답 및 해설 p.123

8. 기사 지문

• 문제 풀이 전략

토익 시험에는 여러 종류의 실용문이 등장하지만, 익숙하지 않은 단어와 길고 복잡한 문장이 많은 기사 지문으로 공부하는 것이 독해 실력 향상에 가장 좋다. 기사 지문의 주제나 목적을 묻는 문제에서는 도입부에서 정답을 알 수 없고 지문을 중간 혹은 끝까지 읽어야 하는 경우가 종종 있다. 이 책에서는 고득점을 목표로 하는 독자들을 위해 기사 지문을 많이 사용했다(Day 01~07에 8개의 기사 지문 포함). Day 08에서는 기사 지문만을 읽으며 고난도 문제를 풀어 보자.

Examples 1-3 to the following article.

Rice Crop Projected to Achieve Near-Record Levels

The Ministry of Agriculture, Food and Rural Affairs(MAFRA) has declared that the farms across the country are on pace to produce their second-largest annual rice crop and fourth-largest annual soybean crop ever. Consequently, grain prices are projected to decrease nationally in the upcoming months, according to the government's economic advisory office.

The forecast is derived from the actual on-site inspections and farmer surveys conducted by MAFRA. Owing to the higher-than-average precipitation during the early summer planting season, initial estimates had been far lower than normal. But the cooler and ideal weather that has followed has been beneficial to many farmers across the country, aiding in their recovery from the heavy rains experienced in June. MAFRA forecasts that farmers will harvest 4.3 million metric tons of rice, up more than 780 thousand metric tons from last month's estimate of 3.5 million. The new estimate is only 4 percent lower than last year's record crop of 4.5 million metric tons.

It is expected that the recovery will lead to lower prices for rice and soybeans, two of the nation's most important agricultural exports. This could be a boon for meat producers who depend on rice and soybeans for feed, as well as for regular citizens who had been expecting to pay higher prices for rice and rice products in grocery stores. MAFRA has lowered its estimate for soybeans slightly, to 2.51 million metric tons from 2.73 million last month.

The new estimate is welcome news for numerous other businesses as well. High rice prices had cut deeply into profits for restaurant chains, for instance, since they allocate a substantial portion of their budget to purchasing rice and rice products.

Ex 1. What is expected for rice production this year?

    (A) It will be of higher quality than last year's crop.

    (B) It will decrease by 4 percent because of flooding.

    (C) It will be higher than previous forecasts.

    (D) It will break records for the fourth consecutive year.

Ex 2. Who is NOT mentioned as being affected by grain prices?

    (A) Meat producers

    (B) Supermarket shoppers

    (C) Soybean packagers

    (D) Restaurant owners

Ex 3. When was rice production the highest?

    (A) This year

    (B) Last year

    (C) Two years ago

    (D) Four years ago

해설

Examples 1-3 refer to the following article.

1–3번 예제는 다음 기사에 관한 것입니다.

Rice Crop Projected to Achieve Near-Record Levels

The Ministry of Agriculture, Food and Rural Affairs(MAFRA) has declared that the farms across the country are on pace to produce their second-largest annual rice crop and fourth-largest annual soybean crop ever. Consequently, grain prices are projected to decrease nationally in the upcoming months, according to the government's economic advisory office.

The forecast is derived from the actual on-site inspections and farmer surveys conducted by MAFRA. Owing to the higher-than-average precipitation during the early summer planting season, ^{Ex1.}initial estimates had been far lower than normal. But the cooler and ideal weather that has followed has been beneficial to many farmers across the country, aiding in their recovery from the heavy rains experienced in June. ^{Ex1.}MAFRA forecasts that farmers will harvest 4.3 million metric tons of rice, up more than 780 thousand metric tons from last month's estimate of 3.5 million. ^{Ex3.}The new estimate is only 4 percent lower than last year's record crop of 4.5 million metric tons.

^{Ex2.}It is expected that the recovery will lead to lower prices for rice and soybeans, two of the nation's most important agricultural exports. ^{Ex2.(A)}This could

쌀 수확량, 사상 최고 수준에 근접할 것으로 예상

농림축산식품부(MAFRA)는 현재 속도라면 전국의 농장들이 역대 두 번째로 많은 쌀 수확량과 네 번째로 많은 콩 수확량을 생산할 것이라고 발표했다. 정부 경제자문실에 따르면 그 결과 곡물 가격이 향후 몇 달 내에 전국적으로 하락할 것으로 예상된다.

이러한 예측은 MAFRA가 실시한 현장 실사와 농장주 설문 조사로부터 도출된 것이다. 초여름 모내기 철 평균 이상의 강수량 때문에 초기 추산치는 평균보다 훨씬 낮았다. 그러나 뒤이은 상쾌하고 이상적인 날씨가 전국의 많은 농장주에게 유익하여 6월에 겪은 폭우로부터 회복하는 데 도움이 되었다. MAFRA는 농장주들이 430만 미터 톤의 쌀을 수확할 것으로 예상하는데, 이것은 지난달의 추산치 350만 미터 톤에서 78만 톤 이상 오른 것이다. 새 추산치는 작년의 기록적인 수확량 450만 미터 톤보다 단 4퍼센트 낮은 것이다.

이러한 회복은 국가의 가장 중요한 농업 수출품 중 두 가지인 쌀과 콩의 가격 하락으로 이어질 것으로 예상된다. 이것은 식료품점에서 쌀

be a boon for meat producers who depend on rice and soybeans for feed, Ex2.(B)as well as for regular citizens who had been expecting to pay higher prices for rice and rice products in grocery stores. MAFRA has lowered its estimate for soybeans slightly, to 2.51 million metric tons from 2.73 million last month.

Ex2.(D)The new estimate is welcome news for numerous other businesses as well. High rice prices had cut deeply into profits for restaurant chains, for instance, since they allocate a substantial portion of their budget to purchasing rice and rice products.

과 쌀 제품을 사기 위해 더 높은 가격을 내게 될 줄 알았던 일반 시민들뿐 아니라 사료를 마련하기 위해 쌀과 콩에 의존하는 육류 생산업자들에게도 혜택이 될 수 있다. MAFRA는 콩에 대한 추산치를 지난달의 273만 미터 톤에서 251만으로 약간 낮추었다.

새로 나온 추정치는 많은 다른 사업체들에도 반가운 소식이다. 예를 들어 높은 쌀 가격으로 인해 식당 가맹업체들의 이윤이 많이 줄어들었는데, 이것은 그들이 예산 상당 부분을 쌀과 쌀 제품을 사는데 할당하기 때문이다.

어휘 projected to-V ~할 것으로 예상되는 crop 수확량 near-record 기록에 가까운 ministry (정부의) 부처 rural 시골의, 지방의 affair 일, 문제 declare 발표하다 pace 속도 annual 연간의 soybean 콩, 대두 consequently 그 결과, 따라서 grain 곡물 nationally 전국적으로 upcoming 다가오는, 곧 있을 advisory 자문의, 고문의 forecast 예측 be derived from ~에서 유래하다, 파생되다 actual 실제의 on-site 현장의 inspection 검사, 조사 conduct 실시하다 precipitation 강수, 강수량 planting season 파종기, 모내기 철 initial 처음의, 초기의 estimate 추정(치), 추산 beneficial 유익한, 이로운 aid in ~을 돕다 recovery 회복 harvest 수확하다 metric ton 미터 톤(1,000 킬로그램) record 기록적인 it is expected that ~할 것으로 예상되다 lead to ~로 이어지다 agricultural export 농업 수출품 boon 요긴한 것, 호재 depend on ~에 의존하다 feed 먹이, 사료 as well as ~뿐 아니라 regular 일반적인 lower ~을 낮추다 slightly 약간 numerous 다수의 cut into ~를 줄이다 allocate 할당하다 substantial 상당한 portion 부분, 일부 budget 예산

참고 Rice Crop Projected to Achieve Near-Record Levels
➡ 영자신문은 통상적으로 제목에서 be동사와 관사를 생략한다. 원래 문장은 Rice crop is projected to achieve near-record levels.이다.

metric ton(미터 톤)
➡ metric ton은 미터법에 따라 정확히 1,000㎏을 의미한다. 국제 무역에서 통용되는 long ton은 약 1,016㎏, short ton은 약 907㎏이다. 토익 시험에서 질량 단위에 이런 것들이 있다는 정도만 알아두자.

Ex 1. What is expected for rice production this year?

    (A) It will be of higher quality than last year's crop.
    (B) It will decrease by 4 percent because of flooding.
    (C) It will be higher than previous forecasts.
    (D) It will break records for the fourth consecutive year.

올해 쌀 생산량에 대해 무엇이 예상되는가?
(A) 작년 작물보다 품질이 더 좋을 것이다.
(B) 홍수로 인해 4퍼센트 감소할 것이다.
(C) 이전 예상치보다 더 높을 것이다.
(D) 4년 연속으로 기록을 경신할 것이다.

어휘 quality 품질 crop 작물 decrease 감소하다 flooding 홍수 previous 이전의 consecutive 연이은 break records 기록을 경신하다

해설 둘째 문단에서 모내기 철의 강수량이 평균 이상이었고(Owing to the higher-than-average precipitation during the early summer planting season), 이로 인해 예상 수확량은 평소보다 낮았지만(initial estimates had been far lower than normal) 초여름 이후의 이상적인 날씨가 쌀농사를 도왔고(But the cooler and ideal weather that has followed has been beneficial to many farmers across the country, aiding in their recovery from the heavy rains experienced in June.), 쌀 수확량의 예상치는 이전보다 높아졌다(MAFRA forecasts that farmers will harvest 4.3 million metric tons of rice, up more than 780 thousand metric tons from last month's estimate of 3.5 million.)고 했다.

Ex 2. Who is NOT mentioned as being affected by grain prices?

(A) Meat producers
(B) Supermarket shoppers
(C) Soybean packagers
(D) Restaurant owners

곡물 가격의 영향을 받는 것으로 언급되지 않는 것은 누구인가?

(A) 육류 생산업자
(B) 슈퍼마켓 쇼핑객
(C) 콩 포장업자
(D) 식당 소유주

어휘 affect 영향을 미치다 packager 포장업자 owner 소유주

해설 셋째 문단에 쌀 수확량 추정치의 회복이 쌀 가격 인하로 이어질 것이라는 예상이 나오는데(It is expected that the recovery will lead to lower prices for rice and soybeans), 이것은 육류 생산업자(meat producers)와 일반 시민들(regular citizens)에게 호재라고 말하고 있으므로 (A)와 (B)는 정답이 아니다. 또한 마지막 문단에서 다른 사업체들에게 새로운 추정치가 반가운 소식일 수 있다고(The new estimate is welcome news for numerous other businesses as well.) 식당 가맹업체들(restaurant chains)을 언급하고 있으므로 (D)도 정답이 아니다.

Ex 3. When was rice production the highest?

(A) This year
(B) Last year
(C) Two years ago
(D) Four years ago

언제 쌀 생산량이 가장 높았는가?

(A) 올해
(B) 작년
(C) 2년 전
(D) 4년 전

해설 둘째 문단의 마지막 문장에 '작년의 기록적인 수확량(last year's record crop)'이라는 키워드가 있다.

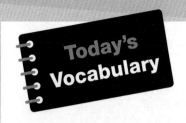

Today's Vocabulary

▶Actual Test를 풀기 전에 이 단어들을 암기하자.

짝을 이루어 출제되는 단어

· comply with ~을 준수하다, ~에 부합되다
· compliance with ~에 대한 부합
· deal with ~을 다루다

· notify / inform / advise / remind *sb of sth* ~에게 ~에 대해 알려주다
  remind — 상기시키다
· brief *sb of sth* 간략하게 알려주다

· attribute[ascribe] A to B
  A를 B의 덕분으로[탓으로] 돌리다

· hold a press conference — 기자 회견을
  meeting — 회의를
  conference — 회의를
  seminar — 세미나를
  session — 모임을
  party — 파티를   열다

---

conspicuously 눈에 잘 띄게, 두드러지게
marginally 아주 조금, 미미하게
regrettably 유감스럽게(도), 애석하게(도)
intriguingly 흥미를 자아내어, 호기심을 자극하여
income tax return 소득세 신고
file 제출하다, (소송을) 제기하다
give[make/deliver] a speech 연설하다
acknowledge receipt of (편지·소포 등을) 받았음을 알리다
compel 강요하다; (필요에 따라) ~하게 만들다
appeal to ~에게 호소하다, 매력이 있다
detect 발견하다, 알아내다, 감지하다
attract 끌어들이다, 끌어 모으다
account for (부분·비율을) 차지하다
lengthy (시간·치수가) 너무 긴, 장황한, 지루한
sizable 꽤 큰[많은], 상당한
offering (사용하거나 즐기도록) 제공된[내놓은] 것
coordinate 조직화하다, 편성하다
focus group 포커스 그룹(시장 조사나 여론 조사의 대상으로 뽑힌 소수 집단)
conflict 갈등, 충돌
proliferation 급증, 확산

individual 개인의, 1인용의
furnace 용광로
glassblowing 유리 불기(녹인 유리를 파이프 끝에서 불어서 형태를 만드는 것)
accessible 접근[이용] 가능한
sought-after 많은 사람들이 찾는, 인기가 많은
medium (화가·작가·음악가의) 표현 수단
last-minute 마지막 순간의, 막바지의
negotiation 협상, 교섭, 절충, 협의
specialize in ~을 전공하다, 전문으로 다루다
establish (법률·제도를) 설립하다, 신설하다
garner headlines 헤드라인을 장식하다
drastically 급격하게, 대폭
deliberate 고의의, 의도적인
adequate 적합한, 충분한
arguably (문장 수식) 이론의 여지는 있지만; (최상급 앞에서) 거의 틀림없이
reportedly (문장 수식) 전하는 바에 따르면, 소문에 의하면
incrementally 점진적으로
reimburse 환불하다, 환급하다
in its[their] entirety 통째로, 전부
apply to ~에 적용되다, 해당되다

typical 전형적인, 일반적인

endeavor (새롭거나 힘든 일을 하려는) 노력, 시도

headquarters 본사, 본부

be slated ~할 예정이다

subsidiary 재(子)회사

plant 공장

heavily (양·정도가) 심하게, 많이

venue 장소

presence 입지

add to ~을 늘리다, 증가시키다

take off (옷을) 벗다; 할인하다; 급격히 인기를 얻다; 갑자기 떠나다

boardwalk (해변이나 물가의) 판자 길, 판자 산책로

take out a lease on 빌리다, 임차하다

at the moment 지금, 현재

ponder 숙고하다, 곰곰이 생각하다

overlook (건물 등이) 바라보다, 내려다보이다

Actual Test

PART 5

1. 빈칸 앞뒤를 보며 문제를 푼다.
2. 빈칸 앞뒤를 보고 정답을 알 수 없다면 문장을 해석한다.
3. 두 줄 분량의 어휘 문제는 문장 전체를 해석해서 푼다.
4. 접속사 어휘 문제는 빈칸 앞뒤만을 보고 풀 수 없다. 문장 전체를 해석해 보자.

PART 6

1. 문법 문제라면 Part 5와 같은 방식으로 빈칸 앞뒤를 보며 푼다.
2. 다른 유형의 문제는 문맥을 통해 정답을 파악한다.

PART 7

1. 문제와 보기 (A), (B), (C), (D)를 먼저 읽은 후에 지문을 읽는다.
2. 지문 위아래의 모든 부분을 자세히 읽어 본다.
3. 문제의 해설을 꼼꼼히 읽고, 문장 구조를 분석하며 복습한다.

101. Based on recent data, Mesmio Trucking's plan to expand its business into Eastern Europe would be only ------- successful.

(A) conspicuously
(B) marginally
(C) regrettably
(D) intriguingly

102. Had Blue Veil Production not signed the contract with the young film director, another production company ------- so.

(A) should do
(B) will be doing
(C) has done
(D) would have done

103. Neatly Apparel has seen an increase in sales ------- the introduction of their new outerwear line last quarter.

(A) over
(B) for
(C) besides
(D) since

104. Mr. Dixon could successfully complete the project by the end of the week ------- the necessary materials arrived today.

(A) if
(B) or
(C) even
(D) both

105. It is essential that all components of the production line ------- with every quality standard listed on the form.

(A) associate
(B) comply
(C) compare
(D) bring

106. If the board of directors ------- about the situation prior to the takeover, some measures could have been taken.

(A) have known
(B) has known
(C) had known
(D) knew

107. Some 120 engineers and 10 organizations ------- collaboratively to develop a new superconductor since 2019 with an investment of 3.5 billion dollars.

(A) worked
(B) have worked
(C) work
(D) has worked

108. Income tax returns should be ------- with relevant receipts and documents by the end of May.

(A) brought
(B) filed
(C) done
(D) declared

109. Nowadays, electronic manufacturers are ------- with high precision instruments to build complex electronic and industrial components.

(A) taking
(B) evacuating
(C) dealing
(D) describing

110. A professor from Worley University will ------- a speech on the future of the global biotech sector.

(A) talk
(B) open
(C) deliver
(D) take

111. I am sending this e-mail to ------- receipt of your formal letter of complaint to our customer service center.

(A) suggest
(B) connect
(C) acknowledge
(D) pronounce

112. The spokesperson of Sparrow International Airlines ------- a press conference once a decision has been made regarding a potential merger with Malmo Aviations.

(A) is held
(B) holds
(C) will hold
(D) has been held

113. The new hotel built near the beach is expected to ------- more tourists to St. Corbino's Island, because of the fantastic view of the water that it provides.

(A) compel
(B) appeal
(C) detect
(D) attract

114. The annual profit of the Singapore branch ------- for one-third of the total annual profit of CNTC Enterprise.

(A) calculates
(B) takes
(C) accounts
(D) features

115. The impending construction of several new office buildings in Berkshire has necessitated a ------- demand for highly skilled workers.

(A) lengthy
(B) plenty
(C) sizable
(D) durable

116. It is the ------- of the marketing assistant to coordinate focus groups and write detailed reports.

(A) promotion
(B) offering
(C) production
(D) responsibility

117. Our team ------- in the policy meeting last Tuesday, but we had a scheduling conflict.

(A) can participate
(B) must have participated
(C) should participate
(D) would have participated

118. ------- the proliferation of small, individual furnaces, glassblowing has become a more accessible and sought-after art medium.

(A) Because of
(B) Instead of
(C) Rather than
(D) Such as

119. Renewable energies are regarded as a key ------- in tackling global climate changes and energy shortage crisis.

(A) factor
(B) role
(C) basis
(D) agency

120. The Chief of Staff of Dalytown Hospital meets with the staff on a regular basis to ensure that procedures ------- correctly.

(A) to be performed
(B) would have performed
(C) had been performed
(D) are being performed

121. ------- the city implemented parking restrictions in the downtown area, the number of people using public transportation has risen.

(A) If
(B) Why
(C) Yet
(D) Since

122. The attorneys have reported that the merger was successfully concluded ------- last-minute negotiations.

(A) as well as
(B) overall
(C) thanks to
(D) even if

123. In 2023, Pack-Pro Company ------- an internship program for trade school students, providing valuable experience in the field of electrical engineering.

(A) expressed
(B) specialized
(C) signaled
(D) established

124. ------- in the news, the Honorable Evelyn Chu is now garnering headlines with her proposal to drastically lower local taxes.

(A) Less
(B) Enough
(C) Apart
(D) Seldom

125. After assessing the G-P Meridian payroll management system, we concluded that it was the only one ------- for our needs.

(A) cooperative
(B) deliberate
(C) extensive
(D) adequate

126. Ms. Hong has correctly forecast that sales would increase ------- as the company's radio commercial keeps being aired.

(A) arguably
(B) reportedly
(C) productively
(D) incrementally

127. We will have already begun work on a new building in Surabaya ------- we end the construction in Abu Dhabi.

(A) by the time
(B) as soon as
(C) except when
(D) in the same way

128. Ms. Xu's responsibilities as Mr. Al-Omani's assistant includes ------- him on the latest financial news.

(A) discussing
(B) briefing
(C) resuming
(D) narrating

129. By this time next year, Komplet Industries ------- two new plants in East Java.

(A) launches
(B) will have launched
(C) is launching
(D) had launched

130. C.F. Martin & Co. ------- high-quality acoustic guitars for almost two centuries.

(A) to be designed
(B) has been designing
(C) was designed
(D) is designing

GO ON TO THE NEXT PAGE

PART 6

The Stadni Inn: Reservations

We suggest making reservations because hotel accommodations in Stadni are
very ------- Accommodations will be secured upon receipt of a one-night deposit
    131.
or 50 percent of total room charges for stays exceeding one night. Reservations
canceled seven days or more before the planned arrival date ------- in their
    132.
entirety. Should a reservation need to be cancelled within seven days of your
scheduled arrival date, you will be charged for the entire ------- of your stay.
    133.
-------.
134.

---

131. (A) limitation
(B) limit
(C) limits
(D) limited

132. (A) will be reimbursed
(B) were reimbursed
(C) are reimbursing
(D) had been reimbursing

133. (A) area
(B) degree
(C) length
(D) week

134. (A) Hotel guests are granted access to our fitness center.
(B) This policy applies to those who depart earlier than expected as well.
(C) Furthermore, we are soon to launch another hotel in the region.
(D) We hope that your experience with us has been satisfactory.

December 8 — Today the Hagersville City Council approved an agreement with Eurosan Enterprises. In accordance with the agreement, Eurosan ------- the 22-

135.

acre lot on State Street. The proposal calls for the construction of both offices and retail stores on the site. Hagersville's Mayor, Eun Sung Han, expresses his welcome for the ------- opportunities this project will afford the area. "We expect

136.

the project to create 500 permanent full-time jobs," he said. "I'm delighted that it was finally approved after so many postponements." -------. Aishah Noor, a

137.

Eurosan spokesperson, has said that it is expected to take five years to complete the project, yet cautions that setbacks may still occur. "We've given the council our best -------, but it's not possible to foresee all complications that may arise,"

138.

Noor said.

135. (A) to develop
(B) will develop
(C) has developed
(D) could have developed

136. (A) economic
(B) unforeseen
(C) volunteer
(D) frequent

137. (A) While the city is anxious for work to get underway, delays are typical for major commercial endeavors such as this.
(B) Nearby tenants, however, have raised some valid worries about the construction noise.
(C) In spite of the assurance of city officials to grant the company a long-term agreement, they now may have to reconsider.
(D) Council members will vote on four different proposals submitted by the architects.

138. (A) argument
(B) background
(C) estimate
(D) combination

GO ON TO THE NEXT PAGE

PART 7

Questions 139-141 refer to the following article.

Engineering Company to Expand

August 25 — Rosette, a well-known French engineering company recognized for its energy-efficient power generators, unveiled today its plans for expansion.

Speaking at a press conference in Nantes, Christian Frémont, the President of Rosette, announced plans to build a new global headquarters in the city.

Construction projects are also slated for the company's foreign subsidiaries, Astaldi, in Rome, Italy, and Belgatech, Inc., in Brussels, Belgium. Construction of extra production plants and expansion of personnel will occur at both companies.

In order to prioritize ocean power and other alternative energy sources, Rosette will establish an additional subsidiary in another international market. When pressed by reporters to provide more details, Frémont chose not to disclose the specific location, but instead mentioned that "Northern Europe has great potential in this regard and is crucial for our long-term objectives."

For industry analyst Marc Fiero, this comes as no surprise. "Rosette has invested heavily in ocean power technology, making Northern European natlons like Denmark or Norway ideal venues for the company's expansion."

Frémont's final comment at the press conference is certain to fuel speculation on this point. When asked what his short-term goals were, he replied that he is "currently planning a vacation by the seaside in Denmark."

139. How does Rosette plan to expand?

(A) By increasing funding for research and development

(B) By enlarging its international presence

(C) By generating greater sales in regions beyond Northern Europe

(D) By consolidating with another company

140. What is stated as one of Rosette's goals?

(A) To recruit additional staff in Norway

(B) To develop a new line of generators

(C) To focus exclusively on ocean power

(D) To add to its facilities in Rome

141. What does Mr. Fiero suggest about Denmark?

(A) It is gaining in popularity among tourists.

(B) It possesses resources for alternative energy.

(C) Fuel costs are lower there than elsewhere.

(D) Rosette might relocate its headquarters there.

Gulf Coast Business Review – April

The grand opening of the Ocean City Mall in Sarasota is scheduled for October, and the available spaces are filling up rapidly. When the mall opens, business is expected to take off just as quickly. While the Ocean City Mall is not the only such establishment in Sarasota, it will be the first to open directly onto the boardwalk. The mall will feature boutiques, specialty stores, and various food vendors.

The mall management aims to attract business owners from outside of Sarasota. According to Stacy Weston, a rental manager, many of the businesses that have rented space are new to the area.

"This was by design," she explained. "The Sarasota City Council has offered a tax incentive to the mall owners as a way to encourage them to bring new businesses to Sarasota. We're still a little short of our goal of having 70% of our spaces rented to nonlocal businesses. We are currently providing discounted rental prices on new leases for out-of-town businesses."

Applications from business owners seeking to take out a lease on retail and dining spaces will be accepted until the June 15 deadline. Interested business owners are invited to contact Weston by e-mail at sweston@oceancitymall.com.

To: Michele Zampas <mzampas@tmail.com>
From: Stacy Weston <sweston@oceancitymall.com>
Date: April 29
Subject: Available space

Dear Ms. Weston,

I am a friend of Edgar Thompson, the owner of The Shoe Wonder. He recommended that I reach out to you regarding renting a space in the Ocean City Mall. He informed me about a valuable benefit that he had received, which is available to business owners such as myself. I possess Witchery Fashion, an establishment specializing in contemporary women's apparel. At the moment, I maintain two retail locations in the nearby city of Fruitville, and I am pondering the possibility of expanding to Sarasota. If possible, I would like to be located near my friend's store, but I prefer a space that is not adjacent to any restaurants or food services. A space on the boardwalk side that overlooks the beach would be ideal.

Would you be able to provide me with a map of the mall that shows any available spaces that might meet my needs? Could you also give me the dimensions of each space and the cost of the rentals?

Thank you in advance,

Michele Zampas

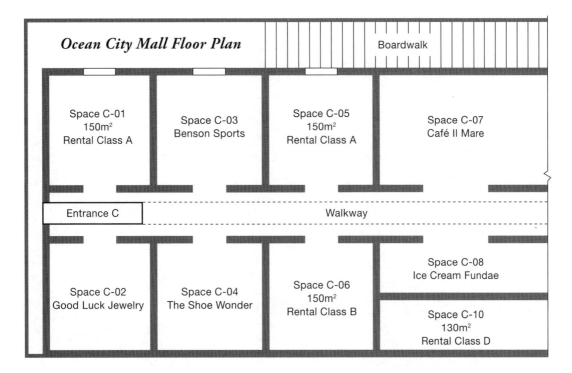

Ocean City Mall Floor Plan

Boardwalk

Space C-01 150m² Rental Class A	Space C-03 Benson Sports	Space C-05 150m² Rental Class A	Space C-07 Café Il Mare

Entrance C

Walkway

Space C-02 Good Luck Jewelry	Space C-04 The Shoe Wonder	Space C-06 150m² Rental Class B	Space C-08 Ice Cream Fundae
			Space C-10 130m² Rental Class D

142. What is the purpose of the article?

(A) To explain the cause of the delay in the opening of a new mall

(B) To announce plans to construct a new mall

(C) To review the stores and eateries in a new mall

(D) To encourage business owners to lease space in a new mall

143. In the article, the phrase "take off" in paragraph 1, line 5, is closest in meaning to

(A) remove

(B) discount

(C) increase quickly

(D) leave suddenly

144. What is stated about the Ocean City Mall?

(A) It will be the only mall in Sarasota.

(B) It will have direct access to the boardwalk.

(C) It will include 70 retail spaces to rent.

(D) It will open for business on June 15.

145. What is indicated about Mr. Thompson?

(A) He is a friend of Ms. Weston.

(B) His business was the first to open.

(C) He is paying a reduced rental rate.

(D) His store overlooks the beach.

146. What space will Ms. Zampas most likely be interested in renting?

(A) Space C-01

(B) Space C-05

(C) Space C-06

(D) Space C-10

정답 및 해설 p.126

Day

09

1. 도치 ★

주어와 동사가 도치되는 영어 문장 중 토익에 출제되는 것만 알아보자.

유형 1 **as, so, neither, nor (~와 같이, 마찬가지로)**

빈칸 뒤에 주어와 동사가 도치된 절이 있는 경우, 보기에서 as, so, neither 또는 nor 중 정답을 선택하자. 보기에 as 또는 so와 neither 또는 nor가 모두 있으면, 빈칸 앞의 절이 긍정문인지 부정문인지 확인해 보자.

Ms. Wanes spent quite many hours studying English, <u>as</u> **did several of her coworkers** .
Ms. Wanes는 영어를 공부하느라 매우 많은 시간을 보냈는데, 그녀의 몇몇 동료들도 마찬가지이다.

Manufacturing is a major industry of the country, and <u>so</u> **is sightseeing** .
제조업은 국가의 주요 산업이며, 관광업도 마찬가지이다.

She didn't attend the workshop on the surgical instruments and <u>neither</u> **did Dr. Johnson** .
그녀는 수술 기구에 관한 워크숍에 참석하지 않았고, Dr. Johnson도 마찬가지이다.

I can't go to the reception, <u>nor</u> **do I want to** .
나는 축하연에 갈 수 없고, 가고 싶지도 않다.

Ex 1. The survey results indicated that the majority of visitors believed the music festival was a great success, and ------- did most of the vendors.

(A) in fact
(B) so
(C) and
(D) also

빈칸 뒤에 주어(most of vendors)와 동사(did)가 도치된 절이 있으므로, (B) so가 정답이다.

어휘 survey 설문조사 result 결과 indicate 나타내다, 보여주다 majority 대다수 vendor 판매상

해석 설문조사 결과가 대다수 방문객이 음악 축제가 큰 성공이라고 생각한다는 것을 보여주었고, 대부분의 판매업자들도 마찬가지이다.

Ex 2. Mr. Kuiper will not be present at the time the work crew is scheduled to come in, and ------- will Ms. Ellerson.

(A) so
(B) also
(C) neither
(D) yet

빈칸 뒤에 주어와 동사가 도치된 문장(will Ms. Ellerson)이 있으므로 (A)와 (C) 중에서 정답을 선택해야 한다. 그런데 빈칸 앞의 절이 부정문이므로 (C)가 정답이다.

어휘 present 있는, 참석한 crew 팀, 반, 조 be scheduled to-V ~하기로 예정되어 있다
해석 Mr. Kuiper는 작업반이 들어올 예정된 시간에 자리에 없을 것이고, Ms. Ellerson도 마찬가지일 것이다.

유형 2 **little, seldom, hardly, rarely, scarcely, no sooner**

빈칸 뒤에 주어와 동사가 도치된 절이 있으면 보기에서 little, seldom, hardly, rarely, scarcely, no sooner와 같은 부정어를 정답으로 선택하자.

Little did I dream that I would meet her in the plane.
비행기에서 그녀를 만날 줄은 꿈에도 생각하지 못했다.

Seldom did experts predict that the exchange rate would increase so rapidly in a few months.
환율이 몇 개월 만에 그렇게 빨리 오르리라고는 전문가들도 거의 예상하지 못했다.

No sooner had I departed than I found my mobile phone left at home.
집을 나서자마자 휴대폰을 집에 놔두고 나온 것을 알았다.

Ex 3. ------- have market conditions been more conducive to purchasing a new house.

(A) Seldom
(B) Ever
(C) Appropriately
(D) Moreover

빈칸 뒤에 주어와 동사가 도치된 것(have market conditions)을 보고 (A)를 정답으로 선택하면 된다.

어휘 appropriately 적절히 moreover 게다가 be conducive to ~에 도움이 되다
해석 (지금처럼) 시장 상황이 새 집을 구입하는 데 더 도움이 되었던 적은 거의 없었다.

수동태 문장의 도치

수동태 문장에서 주어가 매우 길 경우 '과거분사 + be + 주어' 형태의 도치 문장을 만들 수 있다. 토익 시험에서는 과거분사 enclosed(동봉되어), attached(첨부되어), included(포함되어)가 이러한 도치 문장에 쓰인다. 따라서 빈칸 뒤에 'be + 긴 주어'가 나타나면 enclosed, attached, included 중 하나를 선택하자.

Enclosed is a reference letter from the renowned professor.
저명한 교수의 추천서가 동봉되어 있습니다.

Attached is a summary of the recent survey conducted among our local branches.
최근 저희 지사들을 대상으로 실시한 설문조사 요약본을 첨부합니다.

Ex 4. ------- in the packet is a guide to eateries in the vicinity of the conference center.

(A) Include
(B) Inclusion
(C) Including
(D) Included

전치사구 in the packet를 제외하면, 빈칸 뒤에 be동사(is)와 긴 주어(a guide to~)가 있어서 '과거분사 + be + 주어'의 도치 구문임을 알 수 있다. 그러므로 빈칸에는 과거분사 (D)가 알맞다.

어휘 packet 자료집 eatery 음식점, 식당 vicinity 부근, 인근
해석 자료집에는 회의장 인근의 음식점들에 대한 안내가 포함되어 있다.

유형 4 **Only + 부사구 / 부사절**

Only로 시작하는 부사구나 부사절 뒤에는 주어와 동사가 도치된 구문을 써야 한다.

Only by maintaining a precise flow of inventory **are we** able to minimize costs and ensure prompt shipments.
정확한 재고의 흐름을 유지해야만 비용을 최소화하고 신속한 수송을 보장할 수 있습니다.

Ex 5. Only on "Casual Fridays" can employees assigned to the reception area ------- jeans.

(A) wear
(B) wears
(C) wearing
(D) to wear

employees assigned to the reception area can -------이 일반적인 어순이지만, 부사구 Only on "Casual Fridays" 때문에 주어와 동사가 도치되었다. 따라서 빈칸은 동사 자리로, 조동사 can 뒤에 오는 동사원형 (A)가 알맞다.

어휘 assign 배치하다
해석 '캐주얼 금요일'에만 접수 구역에 배치된 직원들은 청바지를 입을 수 있다.

장소 전치사구

문장 맨 앞에 장소 전치사구가 나오면 주어와 동사가 도치된다.

Ex 6. Adjacent to the Treviso Hotel ------- an opulent recreational area, boasting a golf course and a swimming pool.

    (A) are
    (B) is
    (C) to be
    (D) being

문장 맨 앞의 장소 전치사구(Adjacent to the Treviso Hotel) 때문에 주어(an opulent recreational area)와 동사를 도치해야 한다. 그러므로 단수 명사인 주어의 수와 일치하는 동사 (B)가 빈칸에 알맞다.

어휘 adjacent ~에 인접한 opulent 호화로운 recreational area 휴양 단지 boast 뽐내다, 자랑하다

해석 Treviso 호텔에 인접하여 호화 휴양 단지가 있는데, 골프 코스와 수영장을 자랑하는 곳이다.

---

2. 여러 가지 어형 1 ★★

시험에는 알맞은 동사의 형태를 선택하는 문제로 15가지 유형이 출제된다. DAY 9에서는 다섯 가지, Day 10에서는 열 가지 유형을 공부해 보자.

조동사 + -------

조동사 뒤의 빈칸에는 동사원형이 들어가야 한다.

Ex 1. Because humidity can ------- wood, climate regulation in furniture storage units is a necessity.

    (A) damage
    (B) damaging
    (C) damaged
    (D) damages

빈칸 앞에 조동사 can이 있으므로 빈칸에는 동사원형 (A)가 들어가야 한다.

어휘 humidity 습도 damage 손상시키다 regulation 규제, 통제 necessity 필수, 불가피한 일

해석 습도가 목재를 손상시킬 수 있으므로 가구 보관 시설의 온도 조절은 필수이다.

유형 2 have[has/had] + -------

have[has/had] 뒤에 빈칸이 있으면 완료 시제의 동사가 들어가야 하므로 빈칸에는 과거분사가 들어가야 한다.

Ex 2. The new trade laws have ------- to stronger economies in many countries.

(A) contributed
(B) contributions
(C) contribute
(D) contributor

> have ------- 가 문장의 동사이므로 빈칸에는 과거분사 (A)가 들어가야 한다.

어휘 trade law 무역법 contribute to ~에 기여하다

해석 새로운 무역법은 많은 국가에서 경제를 더 강화하는데 기여해 왔다.

유형 3 병렬 구조

and, or, but, so, yet 같은 등위접속사는 앞뒤에 같은 품사의 단어, 같은 어형의 동사, 같은 구조의 구나 절이 있는 병렬 구조를 만든다. 토익에서는 and 앞이나 뒤에 빈칸이 있는 문제가 주로 출제된다.

Ex 3. Thanks to our engineers' hard work and -------, the new product development project has been successfully completed.

(A) dedicated
(B) dedication
(C) dedicating
(D) dedicates

> 빈칸 앞에 and가 있으면 '병렬 구조'를 만들어야 한다. and 앞에 명사(hard work)가 있으므로 and 뒤에도 명사 (B)가 들어가야 한다.

어휘 thanks to ~ 덕분에 dedication 헌신

해석 엔지니어들의 노고와 헌신 덕분에 신제품 개발 프로젝트는 성공적으로 완료되었다.

to부정사 목적어 VS 동명사 목적어

목적어로 to부정사나 동명사를 사용하는 동사를 구별하여 기억하는 것이 필요하다.

❶ 동명사를 목적어로 사용하는 동사

$$\left[\begin{array}{l} \text{suggest, recommend, consider, enjoy, appreciate, avoid, mind,} \\ \text{delay, postpone, include, keep, finish, quit, stop, discontinue, give up} \end{array}\right] + \text{V-ing}$$

❷ to부정사를 목적어로 사용하는 동사

$$\left[\begin{array}{l} \text{want, wish, hope, decide, plan, expect, intend, fail,} \\ \text{ask, afford, promise, pledge, refuse, decline, manage} \end{array}\right] + \text{to-V}$$

❸ 자동사로 명사를 목적어로 취하지는 않지만 to부정사와 함께 자주 사용하는 동사

$$\left[\text{aim, agree, aspire, chance, hesitate, strive, struggle, tend}\right] + \text{to-V}$$

Ex 4. For optimal performance, avoid ------- the food processing equipment on an uneven floor surface.

(A) to operate
(B) operation
(C) operating
(D) operates

빈칸 앞에 동사 avoid가 있으므로 동사인 (D)는 제외한다. the food processing equipment를 목적어로 취해야 하므로 명사 (B)도 제외한다. 동사 avoid는 동명사를 목적어로 사용하므로 (C)를 정답으로 선택하자.

어휘 optimal 최적의 performance 성능 processing equipment 가공 장비 uneven 평평하지 않은
해석 최고의 성능을 위해 식품 가공 장비를 평평하지 않은 바닥에서 작동하는 일은 피해 주세요.

Ex 5. Dr. Choi, the leader of the development team, plans ------- a detailed progress report to her supervisor every month.

(A) submit
(B) to submit
(C) submitting
(D) will submit

빈칸 앞에 동사 plans가 있으므로 동사인 (A)와 (D)는 제외한다. 동사 plan은 to부정사를 목적어로 사용하므로 (B)를 정답으로 선택하자.

어휘 detailed 자세한 progress report 경과보고 supervisor 상사
해석 개발팀장 Choi 박사는 매달 상사에게 자세한 중간 보고서를 제출할 계획이다.

주어 + 동사 + 목적어 + to부정사

5형식 동사 중 목적격 보어로 to부정사를 사용하는 동사를 암기해야 한다.

주어 + ⎡ enable, allow, permit   ⎤ + 목적어 + to-V
       ⎢ encourage, persuade, convince, advise, urge ⎢
       ⎢ ask, request, require, instruct, invite, want ⎢
       ⎣ expect, schedule, remind   ⎦

Ex 6. Consultants persuaded the management ------- whether to sell off the company or let it stand on its own feet.

(A) decide
(B) deciding
(C) to decide
(D) of deciding

빈칸 앞에 동사 persuaded는 목적격 보어로 to부정사를 사용한다. 빈칸은 목적격 보어 자리 이므로 (C)가 정답이다.

어휘 consultant 자문 위원, 고문 persuade 설득하다 management 경영진 decide whether A or B A나 B를 결정하다 sell off 매각하다 stand on one's own feet 자립하다

해석 자문 위원들은 경영진이 회사를 매각할 것인지 자립하게 할 것인지 결정하도록 설득했다.

101. Highly ------- is Carnegie Mellon College as a business school.

(A) regard
(B) regards
(C) regarded
(D) regarding

102. The newly introduced equipment for assembly lines allowed the manufacturer ------- its staff productivity substantially.

(A) improve
(B) to improve
(C) improved
(D) improving

103. Safe Job is a new software program which provides a ------- and secure environment for processing your employees' personal information.

(A) relied
(B) reliably
(C) reliable
(D) rely

104. The board of trustees has ------- to select the construction bid entered by Sullivan and Sons, Inc.

(A) picked
(B) settled
(C) decided
(D) established

105. An extensive research has indicated that television commercials do not necessarily ------- sales figures.

(A) boost
(B) to boost
(C) boosts
(D) boosting

106. Only after the city constructed a new stadium did the downtown area ------- popularity among out-of-town visitors.

(A) gain
(B) gained
(C) gaining
(D) had gained

107. Unfortunately, Hanabishi Electronics' M26 air-conditioning unit failed to meet the government's new energy-efficiency standards, and ------- did the company's M27 model.

(A) same
(B) either
(C) so
(D) rather

108. Filaret Inn does not refund deposits, ------- does it guarantee availability of all advertised amenities.

(A) and
(B) whether
(C) which
(D) nor

109. There was a slight decline in sales of this month, but in no way did that ------- the company's expansion plan.

(A) affect
(B) affected
(C) to affect
(D) affecting

110. Director Kassis has already ------- to boost Lingram Corporation's profits by 20 percent within a year.

(A) promised
(B) promise
(C) promising
(D) promises

111. ------- did industry analysts expect
that the government would lower the
interest rates so rapidly in a short
period of time.

(A) So
(B) Seldom
(C) As well
(D) As

112. Candidates for the position must
demonstrate their capacity to be
efficient and ------- under pressure.

(A) decisively
(B) decisive
(C) decider
(D) deciding

113. Wyn Automotive Design has recently
------- with Hydra Company.

(A) merge
(B) merger
(C) merged
(D) merging

114. Ms. Kovach will ------- the installation
of the new workstations in conjunction
with the supplier.

(A) coordinated
(B) to coordinate
(C) coordination
(D) be coordinating

115. ------- is the most up-to-date listing
of the distinguished companies and
institutions that employ our firm's
specialized consulting services.

(A) Enclosure
(B) Enclosing
(C) Enclose
(D) Enclosed

9. 2중/3중 지문

• 문제 풀이 전략

2중/3중 지문의 다섯 문제 중에서 두 개 또는 세 개가 '연계 추론 문제'이다. 두세 지문의 내용을 종합해서 풀어야 하며, 오답률이 높은 유형이다. 다수의 세부사항을 종합해서 정답을 추론해야 하므로, 정확하고 꼼꼼한 독해가 필요하다.

Examples 1-5 refer to the following résumé and e-mail.

Larisa Sharipova

157 Thanet Street, London WC1H 9QL

EXPERIENCE

Hong Kong Integration Systems, Hong Kong
Lead Programmer, 4 years
- Created financial accounting software at a large, multinational bank
- Managed a team of computer programmers on a systems integration project

Laurentian Bank of Canada, Quebec, Canada
Systems Analyst, Human Resources Department, 3 years
- Oversaw periodic upgrades of computer software
- Developed software to generate automatic reports of employee information
- Assisted management staff with training of new analysts

EDUCATION
M.A., Computer Science
Certificate in Business Administration
San Diego State University

B.A., Economics
University of Westminster, London, UK

SKILLS
Fluent Japanese and French, proficient Russian

From: Enzo Fernandez, Human Resources Director
To: Larisa Sharipova
Date: Tuesday, April 21 2:31 P.M.

Dear Ms. Sharipova:

Thank you for your interest in the principal consultant position at our firm. We were very impressed with your credentials and would like to extend an invitation to you for an interview at our office in Mexico City, on Thursday, April 30, at 9:00 A.M.

In reviewing your application, our team was particularly impressed with your background in human resources, especially since we recently undertook a project to overhaul a comparable system in our personnel department. It is highly recommended that you bring any other examples of your work related to this area to the interview. Additionally, your command of multiple languages may be beneficial, given that we have several clients overseas.

If the above date and time suit you, kindly respond to me by April 24, and my assistant will make all necessary arrangements concerning travel and accommodations. The Deloitte staff and I look forward to meeting you.

Sincerely,
Enzo Fernandez
Deloitte Management Services

Ex 1. Where did Larisa Sharipova train other analysts?

(A) At San Diego State University
(B) At Laurentian Bank of Canada
(C) At Hong Kong Integration Systems
(D) At Deloitte Management Services

Ex 2. What is NOT listed as one of Larisa Sharipova's qualifications?

(A) An accounting certificate
(B) Knowledge of multiple languages
(C) Experience with financial institutions
(D) A background in software development

Ex 3. What job is Larisa Sharipova applying for?

(A) Lead programmer
(B) Principal consultant
(C) Assistant to Mr. Fernandez
(D) Human resources director

Ex 4. Which part of Ms. Sharipova's experience is most interesting to Deloitte Management?

(A) She was a programmer at a bank in Russia.
(B) She has experience recruiting employees.
(C) She created a system for processing information about employees.
(D) She was the training manager of a personnel department.

Ex 5. In the e-mail, the word "accommodations" in paragraph 3, line 3, is closest in meaning to

(A) solutions
(B) adjustments
(C) fuel expenses
(D) hotel arrangements

Examples 1-5 refer to the following résumé and e-mail. 1–5번 예제는 다음 이력서와 이메일에 관한 것입니다.

Larisa Sharipova 157 Thanet Street, London WC1H 9QL	**Larisa Sharipova** 런던 WC1H 9QL Thanet 가(街) 157번지

EXPERIENCE

Hong Kong Integration Systems, Hong Kong
Lead Programmer, 4 years
- Ex2.(D)Created financial accounting software at a large, multinational bank
- Managed a team of computer programmers on a systems integration project

Ex1.Ex2.(C)**Laurentian Bank of Canada, Quebec, Canada**
Ex4.Systems Analyst, Human Resources Department, 3 years
- Oversaw periodic upgrades of computer software
- Ex2.(D)Ex4.Developed software to generate automatic reports of employee information
- Ex1.Assisted management staff with training of new analysts

EDUCATION
M.A., Computer Science
Certificate in Business Administration
San Diego State University

B.A., Economics
University of Westminster, London, UK

SKILLS
Ex2.(B)Fluent Japanese and French, proficient Russian

경력

홍콩 소재 Hong Kong Integration Systems
선임 프로그래머, 4년
- 대규모 다국적 은행의 재무 회계 소프트웨어 제작
- 시스템 통합 프로젝트에서 컴퓨터 프로그래머 팀 관리

캐나다 퀘벡 소재 Laurentian Bank of Canada
인사부 시스템 분석가, 3년
- 컴퓨터 소프트웨어 정기 업그레이드 감독
- 직원 정보에 관한 보고서 자동 생성 소프트웨어 개발
- 운영진의 신입 애널리스트 교육 지원

학력
샌디에이고 주립대학교
컴퓨터 공학 석사
경영학 과정 수료

영국 런던 Westminster 대학교
경제학 학사

보유 기술
일본어, 프랑스어 유창, 러시아어 능통

어휘 lead 수석의, 선임의 financial accounting 재무 회계 multinational 다국적의 integration 통합 analyst 분석가 human resources department 인사부서 oversee 감독하다 periodic 정기적인, 주기적인 generate 생성하다 assist A with B A를 〈일·업무 등의〉 B에서 지원하다 management 운영, 관리 M.A. 문학 석사(Master of Arts) certificate 수료 증명서 business administration 경영학 B.A. 문학 학사(Bachelor of Arts) fluent 유창한 proficient 능숙한, 능한

From: Enzo Fernandez, Human Resources Director
To: Larisa Sharipova
Date: Tuesday, April 21 2:31 P.M.

Dear Ms. Sharipova:

^{Ex3.}Thank you for your interest in the principal consultant position at our firm. We were very impressed with your credentials and would like to extend an invitation to you for an interview at our office in Mexico City, on Thursday, April 30, at 9:00 A.M.

^{Ex4.}In reviewing your application, our team was particularly impressed with your background in human resources, especially since we recently undertook a project to overhaul a comparable system in our personnel department. It is highly recommended that you bring any other examples of your work related to this area to the interview. Additionally, your command of multiple languages may be beneficial, given that we have several clients overseas.

  If the above date and time suit you, kindly respond to me by April 24, ^{Ex5.}and my assistant will make all necessary arrangements concerning travel and accommodations. The Deloitte staff and I look forward to meeting you.

Sincerely,
Enzo Fernandez
Deloitte Management Services

발신: 인사부장 Enzo Fernandez
수신: Larisa Sharipova
날짜: 4월 21일 화요일 오후 2:31

Ms. Sharipova께,

우리 회사 수석 컨설턴트 자리에 관심을 보여주셔서 감사합니다. 우리는 당신이 갖추고 있는 자격에 매우 깊은 인상을 받았으며, 4월 30일 목요일 오전 9시에 멕시코시티에 있는 우리 사무실에서 있을 면접에 초대하고 싶습니다.

지원서를 검토하면서 우리 팀은 특별히 당신의 인사부 경력에 깊은 인상을 받았는데, 특히 최근에 우리 회사 인사부에서 유사한 시스템을 점검하는 프로젝트에 착수했기 때문입니다. 이 분야에 관련된 당신의 작업 중 다른 어떤 사례든 면접에 가져오실 것을 적극 권장합니다. 아울러 우리가 해외에 몇몇 고객들이 있다는 점을 고려하면, 당신의 여러 언어 구사 능력이 유익할 것 같습니다.

위 날짜와 시간이 적합하다면 4월 24일까지 저에게 답장해 주시기를 바랍니다. 그러면 제 비서가 여행 및 숙박과 관련하여 필요한 모든 준비를 할 것입니다. Deloitte 직원들과 저는 당신을 만나기를 고대합니다.

진심을 담아,
Deloitte Management Services
Enzo Fernandez

어휘 principal 주요한, 수석의 firm 회사 impressed 깊은 인상을 받은 credentials 자격 extend an invitation to ~를 초대하다 review 검토하다 application 지원서 particularly 특히 background 배경, 경력 undertake ~에 착수하다, 나서다 overhaul 점검하다, 정비하다 comparable 비슷한, 비교할 만한 personnel 인사 (부서) highly recommend 적극 권장하다 related to ~와 관련된 area 분야, 부문 additionally 추가로 command (언어) 능력, 구사력 multiple 다수의, 여럿의 beneficial 유익한, 이로운 given that ~을 고려하면 suit ~에게 알맞다, 편하다 kindly 부디 arrangement 준비, 마련 concerning ~에 관한 accommodation 숙박 시설 look forward to ~를 고대하다

[문장 분석]

and my assistant will make all necessary arrangements concerning travel and accommodations

➡ 토익에서는 명사 arrangement의 용법을 반드시 알아야 한다.
  ① 기본적으로 동사 make와 함께 사용한다.
  ② make arrangements for sb to-V ~가 ~할 수 있도록 준비하다, 마련하다
    I will make arrangements for you to be met at the airport.
  ③ make + 명사 + arrangements ~를 준비하다
    make travel[transportation/hotel/lodging] arrangements

Ex 1. Where did Larisa Sharipova train other analysts?

(A) At San Diego State University
(B) At Laurentian Bank of Canada
(C) At Hong Kong Integration Systems
(D) At Deloitte Management Services

Larisa Sharipova는 어디에서 다른 애널리스트들을 교육했는가?

(A) 샌디에이고 주립대학교에서
(B) Laurentian Bank of Canada에서
(C) Hong Kong Integration Systems에서
(D) Deloitte Management Services에서

[해설] 이력서를 보면 캐나다 퀘벡의 Laurentian Bank of Canada에서 근무할 때 관리 직원을 도와 신입 애널리스트들을 교육하는 일에 참여했다고 나와 있으므로(Assisted management staff with training of new analysts) (B)가 정답이다.

Ex 2. What is NOT listed as one of Larisa Sharipova's qualifications?

(A) An accounting certificate
(B) Knowledge of multiple languages
(C) Experience with financial institutions
(D) A background in software development

Larisa Sharipova의 자격 중 하나로 언급되지 않은 것은 무엇인가?

(A) 회계사 자격증
(B) 여러 언어에 대한 지식
(C) 금융 기관에서의 경력
(D) 소프트웨어 개발 경력

[어휘] qualification 자격 list 기재하다, 목록에 올리다 accounting certificate 회계사 자격증 financial institution 금융 기관 background 배경, 경력

[해설] 일본어와 프랑스어, 러시아어를 할 수 있고(Fluent Japanese and French, proficient Russian), 소프트웨어 개발 경력은 두 건이 있는데(Created financial accounting software at a large, multinational bank / Developed software to generate automatic reports of employee information), 그중 하나는 은행에서 근무할 때 만들었다(Laurentian Bank of Canada, Quebec, Canada). 그러므로 언급되지 않은 자격은 (A) 회계사 자격증이다.

Ex 3. What job is Larisa Sharipova applying for?

(A) Lead programmer
(B) Principal consultant
(C) Assistant to Mr. Fernandez
(D) Human resources director

Larisa Sharipova는 어떤 직종에 지원하고 있는가?

(A) 선임 프로그래머
(B) 수석 컨설턴트
(C) Mr. Fernandez의 비서
(D) 인사부장

[어휘] apply for 지원하다 assistant 비서

[해설] 이메일 첫 문장에 수석 컨설턴트 자리에 지원했음이 나와 있으므로(Thank you for your interest in the principal consultant position at our firm) 정답은 (B)이다.

Ex 4. Which part of Ms. Sharipova's experience is most interesting to Deloitte Management?

(A) She was a programmer at a bank in Russia.
(B) She has experience recruiting employees.
(C) She created a system for processing information about employees.
(D) She was the training manager of a personnel department.

Deloitte Management에게 Ms. Sharipova의 경력 중 어느 부분이 가장 흥미로운가?

(A) 러시아의 어느 은행에서 프로그래머였다.
(B) 직원을 모집해 본 경험이 있다.
(C) 직원 정보를 처리하는 시스템을 만들었다.
(D) 인사부의 교육 담당자였다.

연계 추론 이메일에서 Mr. Fernandez는 회사 측에서 Ms. Sharipova의 인사부 경력에 특별히 흥미를 가지고 있다고 말하고 있는데(our team was particularly impressed with your background in human resources), 그 이유는 Ms. 가 인사부에서 만든 것과 비슷한 시스템을 Deloitte Management에서도 다루고 있기 때문이라고 했다(especially since we recently undertook a project to overhaul a comparable system in our personnel department). 이력서를 보면 Ms. Sharipova는 은행 인사부에서 근무할 때 직원 정보를 자동으로 생성하는 소프트웨어를 개발했음을 알 수 있다(Developed software to generate automatic reports of employee information). 두 지문의 내용을 종합해 보면 Deloitte Management는 Ms. Sharipova가 직원들에 대한 정보를 자동으로 처리하는 시스템을 만들었다는 사실에 깊은 인상을 받았음을 알 수 있다.

Ex 5. In the e-mail, the word "accommodations" in paragraph 3, line 3, is closest in meaning to

(A) solutions
(B) adjustments
(C) fuel expenses
(D) hotel arrangements

이메일 셋째 문단 셋째 줄의 단어 accommodations와 의미상 가장 가까운 것은

(A) 해법, 해결책
(B) 적응
(C) 연료비
(D) 호텔 예약

해설 accommodations가 '화해, 타협, 조정'이라는 뜻으로 사용되었다면 '문제에 대한 해결책'이라는 뜻인 (A)와 동의어가 되고, '적응, 순응, 조화'라는 뜻으로 사용했다면 '적응'이라는 뜻인 (B)와 동의어가 될 수 있다. 그러나 본문의 my assistant will make all necessary arrangements concerning travel and accommodations.는 여행과 숙박에 관련된 준비를 해 주겠다는 의미이므로, 바꿔 쓸 수 있는 표현은 (D)이다.

Today's
Vocabulary

▶Actual Test를 풀기 전에 이 단어들을 암기하자.

짝을 이루어 출제되는 단어

- · beginning
  starting
  effective
  + 시점 ~을 기하여

- · concentrate
  focus
  + on ~에 집중하다

- · increase. rise. expansion   + in 증가
  decrease. decline. reduction. fall. drop   감소
  change. fluctuation   변화
  experience   경험

as to ~에 관해
courtesy of (상이나 무료로) ~이 제공한
proficiency 숙달, 능숙, 능란
distinguished 유명한, 저명한
fellowship 연구비, 장학금
thorough 빈틈없는, 철두철미한
transit trade 중계 무역, 통과 무역
insightful 통찰력 있는
acquisition 쉬득, 획득
certification 증명(서)
be subject to ~의 대상이다
entitle 자격[권리]을 주다
accountable to ~에게 (해명할) 책임이 있는
transferable 이동[양도/전이] 가능한
negotiate 성사시키다, 타결하다
occasion 때, 경우
dispute 분쟁, 분규
superb 최고의, 최상의
if not ~까지는 아니라도
by means of ~을 이용하여
deliberate 고의의, 의도[계획]적인; 신중한
established 확립된, 기존의
publicize (일반인에게) 알리다, 홍보하다
intensify 심화시키다, 강화하다

shortly 얼마 안 되어, 곧
sparse (분포가) 드문, (밀도가) 희박한
pending 미결인, 계류 중인
attentive 배려하는, 신경을 쓰는
feed 먹이를 주다; 먹이
dominant 우세한, 지배적인
prestigious 명망 있는, 일류의
reliant 의존하는, 의지하는
initiative 솔선수범, 주도적임
engage (주의·관심을) 사로잡다, 끌다
feature 특별히 포함하다, 특징으로 삼다
footage (특정한 사건의) 장면, 화면
explore 탐구하다, 분석하다, 조사하다
manufacturing plant 제조 공장
along with ~에 덧붙여
post 올리다, 게시하다
ultrasonic 초음파의
apply 쓰다, 적용하다
debris 찌꺼기
release 방출하다
sound wave 음파
wave ‒파, 파동, 파장
generate 발생시키다, 만들어 내다
facilitate 용이하게 하다

detergent 세제(洗劑)

crack (좁은) 틈

crevice 갈라진 틈, 균열

access 접근하다

save on ~을 절약하다

every other week 격주로

trace 추적하다, 밝혀내다

chronicle 연대순으로 기록하다

evolution (점진적인) 발전, 진전

span (기간에) 걸치다, 걸쳐 이어지다

unconventional 색다른, 독특한

upbringing 양육, 훈육, 가정교육

prompt (일이 일어나도록) 하다, 촉발하다

offering 작품, 프로그램

regular 정기적인, 규칙적인

Actual Test

<table>
<tr><td>

PART 5

</td><td>

1. 빈칸 앞뒤를 보며 문제를 푼다.
2. 빈칸 앞뒤를 보고 정답을 알 수 없다면 문장을 해석한다.
3. 두 줄 분량의 어휘 문제는 문장 전체를 해석해서 푼다.
4. 접속사 어휘 문제는 빈칸 앞뒤만을 보고 풀 수 없다. 문장 전체를 해석해 보자.

</td></tr>
<tr><td>

PART 6

</td><td>

1. 문법 문제라면 Part 5와 같은 방식으로 빈칸 앞뒤를 보며 푼다.
2. 다른 유형의 문제는 문맥을 통해 정답을 파악한다.

</td></tr>
<tr><td>

PART 7

</td><td>

1. 문제와 보기 (A), (B), (C), (D)를 먼저 읽은 후에 지문을 읽는다.
2. 지문 위아래의 모든 부분을 자세히 읽어 본다.
3. 문제의 해설을 꼼꼼히 읽고, 문장 구조를 분석하며 복습한다.

</td></tr>
</table>

101. Trumont Clothier ------- each of its stores to prominently display the return policy near each cash register.

(A) covers
(B) spends
(C) records
(D) requires

102. As the number of local residents' visits to public swimming facilities grows, ------- the demand for lifeguards to monitor them.

(A) as long as
(B) whereas
(C) so does
(D) as to

103. The Canterville Museum will ------- on the development of new educational programs for patrons of varying ages this year.

(A) congratulate
(B) impose
(C) concentrate
(D) interpret

104. All images displayed in the brochure have been provided ------- of Ryke Photography Studio.

(A) courtesy
(B) courteous
(C) courteously
(D) courteousness

105. Dr. Giordano, among her many -------, has won a distinguished science award and a highly competitive fellowship.

(A) capabilities
(B) proficiencies
(C) performances
(D) accomplishments

106. ------- is a product catalog that also contains comprehensive information about our ordering procedure and our delivery policies.

(A) Enclosure
(B) Enclosed
(C) Enclosing
(D) Encloses

107. ------- developing the operating system, the technology team conducted a thorough study.

(A) In order to
(B) Assigned
(C) Before
(D) Since

108. ------- is an application to take part in the Air Traffic Controller Training Program.

(A) Attach
(B) Attaching
(C) Attached
(D) Attachment

109. The CFO cannot participate in the board meeting on Wednesday, and ------- can the CIO.

(A) so
(B) however
(C) neither
(D) also

110. Fishing is one of the major sources of income for the village, ------- is transit trade.

(A) too
(B) as
(C) also
(D) thus

111. Eabha Madigan's latest article is a ------- and insightful analysis of market timing.

(A) wise
(B) wisdom
(C) wisely
(D) wisest

112. Having five years of professional experience is considered ------- to the acquisition of certification for hiring purposes.

(A) reasonable
(B) appropriate
(C) equivalent
(D) significant

113. Any items of luggage exceeding Metzger Airline's weight and size restrictions will be ------- to additional charges.

(A) subject
(B) entitled
(C) accountable
(D) transferable

114. Wayfield Associates and Midtown Construction sought the assistance of a third party to negotiate the ------- to their contract dispute.

(A) occasion
(B) resolution
(C) impression
(D) situation

115. The Vietnamese-style fresh spring rolls at Madam Tran Restaurant is a superb selection for a tasty mid-day snack, ------- a full meal.

(A) whereas
(B) if not
(C) by means of
(D) whenever

116. Kaweiben Corporation's earnings have been steadily increasing despite significant fluctuations ------- the stock market.

(A) about
(B) in
(C) through
(D) onto

117. HBS Photo Studio is providing its ------- customers with an additional discount on the items currently on sale.

(A) deliberate
(B) established
(C) approximate
(D) concluded

118. Management cannot ------- the security of personal information sent while using the hotel's wireless Internet service.

(A) guarantee
(B) balance
(C) distinguish
(D) locate

119. We regret to inform you that your company credit card has -------, so we are currently unable to process your order.

(A) expiration
(B) expires
(C) expiring
(D) expired

120. Our technical expertise, accumulated over a long period of time, will enable your company ------- highly successful and reliable solutions.

(A) build
(B) building
(C) to build
(D) built

121. The automated fabric cutters work much faster than those ------- by hand.

(A) accepted
(B) operated
(C) publicized
(D) intensified

122. Mr. Mundine froze spending rates in view of a projected ------- in revenue.

(A) decline
(B) method
(C) rejection
(D) outlet

123. Dr. Hwang's research is published ------- in the Western Journal of Medicine.

(A) shortly
(B) deeply
(C) finely
(D) regularly

124. Industry analysts expect the ------- merger decision to be made soon by Sectorsys Ltd.

(A) sparse
(B) related
(C) pending
(D) attentive

125. ------- they have purchased preapproved animal feed from the park ranger station, visitors may feed the horses.

(A) Unless
(B) As long as
(C) In case
(D) Regardless

126. Mr. Heyer's responsibilities have ------- helping the company with its marketing efforts and taking over the company's North American operations.

(A) including
(B) include
(C) includes
(D) included

127. Since all the final corrections on the invitation have been provided, the print shop will now run it and then ------- the client when the job has been completed.

(A) notifying
(B) notified
(C) notification
(D) notify

128. Dr. Eun-Young Kwon will be awarded the ------- Schills Medal for her significant contributions in the field of immunology.

(A) successful
(B) dominant
(C) cooperative
(D) prestigious

129. Sales clerk Tim Davis demonstrated ------- by actively engaging customers as they entered the Musienko's Furniture showroom.

(A) amount
(B) objective
(C) reliant
(D) initiative

130. On the day of the show, tickets to the Max Theater can only ------- at the ticket office.

(A) purchasing
(B) were purchased
(C) to purchase
(D) be purchased

GO ON TO THE NEXT PAGE

PART 6

Questions 131-134 refer to the following article.

Women's History at the Seoul Museum of History

Now on display at the Seoul Museum of History is *She Makes History*. This

------- honors the female leaders who dedicated their lives to the Korean
131.

independence movement. It also focuses ------- significant figures in modern
132.

Korean history who earned acclaim in science, art, and sports. Valuable

documents, photographs, and paintings are being displayed. Museum visitors

------- a short film featuring actual footage of speeches and interviews from the
133.

early 20th century. -------. *She Makes History* runs through October 20.
134.

---

131. (A) article
(B) award
(C) exhibit
(D) documentary

132. (A) by
(B) on
(C) with
(D) after

133. (A) also enjoyed
(B) can also enjoy
(C) are also enjoying
(D) have also enjoyed

134. (A) The museum will be closed for maintenance on October 3.
(B) Unfortunately, the film is no longer obtainable.
(C) Join us to explore how these events changed history.
(D) To volunteer, please fill out an application at the museum Web site.

Questions 135-138 refer to the following memo.

MEMO

To: All Employees of Nautique Boats
From: Deepanjali Jaddoo, Vice President of Operations
Date: 10 September
Subject: Important updates

------- 1 January, we will expand our operations in Port Louis. We will also open
135.
a manufacturing plant for saltwater fishing boats in the coastal city of Saint-

Denis. The new ------- will enable Nautique Boats to better serve its customers
136.
in Madagascar and East Africa. ------- this expansion also comes the opportunity
137.
for Nautique Boats employees who are interested in doing so to relocate. -------.
138.
As always, we will provide a corporate package to cover relocation expenses.

Additional information will be available soon.

Please refer any questions you may have to your direct supervisor.

---

135. (A) Effective
(B) Effect
(C) To effect
(D) Effectively

136. (A) ship
(B) role
(C) process
(D) facility

137. (A) Compared with
(B) Along with
(C) Just as
(D) In contrast

138. (A) We have worked in Saint-Denis for decades.
(B) Job openings have already been posted on our Web site.
(C) There is a high demand for smaller recreational boats.
(D) There are many public transportation options in Port Louis.

GO ON TO THE NEXT PAGE

PART 7

Questions 139-142 refer to the following information from a Web site.

http://www.technologynews.com

TECHNOLOGY NEWS:

The new Ecotornado ultrasonic home dishwasher developed by the Supertech Company is an excellent way of cleaning dishes while benefiting the environment. The Ecotornado applies ultrasonic technology to remove debris from dishes in the same fashion as is used to clean jewelry. The dishwasher is equipped with a 100-liter tank with two metal converters that release high-frequency sound waves under water. The waves generate high-temperature, high-pressure bubbles which facilitate the cleaning of dishes with limited detergent usage. These micro-scrubbing bubbles can reach into the narrowest of cracks and crevices that sponges or brushes are unable to access.

A conventional machine consumes 200 to 300 liters of fresh water per cycle. The Ecotornado filters the water in its tank for reuse after each cycle. The water in its tank only needs to be replaced every other week. This way, the average household can conserve 250,000 to 500,000 liters of water annually. The shortened run time of the machine also saves on electricity. The Ecotornado cleaning cycle lasts only ten minutes where a conventional machine usually takes thirty minutes or longer.

The Ecotornado unit made its debut in India in March, and Supertech is aiming to introduce it around the world in the foreseeable future. Supertech is also able to customize dishwashers to meet the requirements of corporate clients such as those in the healthcare and hospitality industries. For additional details, go to www.supertech.com to watch demonstration videos, request a brochure, or find a local retailer.

139. What is the information mainly about?

(A) Selecting a dishwashing detergent
(B) Advances in jewelry cleaning technology
(C) Using sound waves to clean dishes
(D) A newly developed clothes washing machine

140. According to the information, what is an advantage of the Ecotornado?

(A) It eliminates the need for detergent.
(B) It adopts high-powered brushes.
(C) It takes only 30 minutes to complete a cycle.
(D) It consumes less energy than other machines.

141. How often should the water in the Ecotornado be replaced?

(A) Twice a week
(B) Once a week
(C) Once every two weeks
(D) Once a month

142. What is indicated about the Supertech Company?

(A) It will restrict the sale of Ecotornado to India only.
(B) It is a leader in the healthcare industry.
(C) It will start selling the Ecotornado in the upcoming year.
(D) It can adapt the Ecotornado for different uses.

Questions 143-147 refer to the following list, schedule, and e-mail.

Books by David Duchemin

Tracing the Origin of Jeans
Where did it all begin? Duchemin visually chronicles the evolution of jeans through the centuries, from their beginning as working wear to their current status as high fashion.

Glance Beyond the Runway
Duchemin captures the creative process of a selection of preeminent fashion designers from New York City to Paris. The book, filled with Duchemin's photographs, spans nearly two decades and reveals what goes on in fashion houses prior to garments being ready for the runway.

Walking into Clothes: My Story
An amusing memoir about childhood spent amid the fashion world. Duchemin describes his unconventional upbringing in New York City, where his parents began their careers as fashion models before launching their own design label.

Yards of Talent: A Decade of Vogue
Duchemin's compilation of images spanning a decade of fashion and displaying what was in style, what was out of style, and then what was back in style again.

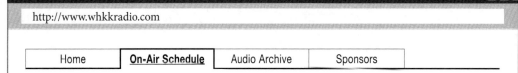

http://www.whkkradio.com

| Home | **On-Air Schedule** | Audio Archive | Sponsors |

WHKK Radio
Evening Programming, March 13

7:00 – *The Splendid Table*
Host Emily Johnson discusses the newest super foods; their characteristics, benefits, and ideal ways to cook them. Featured recipes will be available to view on our Web site after tonight's broadcast.

8:00 – *The Tech Guy*
Host Leo Laporte focuses on the latest electronics. He talks about products that are really innovative and practical and identifies those that are not.

9:00 - *Candid Tonight*
Host Stephanie Miller interviews photographer and author David Duchemin to find out what prompted him to write his newest book about his childhood. He shares stories about what it was like to grow up in the world of fashion.

To: listenercomments@whkkradio.com
From: ahankins@moonmail.net
Date: March 14
Subject: Radio Interview

I discovered WHKK Radio over 20 years ago and have been a regular listener of your evening shows for at least a decade. I just wanted to express my pleasure at your newest offering. I've been intrigued by a lot of the writers who have been featured on the show so far, but the guest last night was particularly enjoyable. I have a memory of David when he was a little boy. I had the chance to work with his parents when they lived in New York, and I recall seeing David in his parents' studio most days after school hours. I was surprised to learn that he has written about his childhood, and I eagerly await reading his new book.

Thank you for the excellent programming.

Arianna Hankins

143. What is one common feature in all of Mr. Duchemin's books?

(A) They contain fashion images.
(B) They focus on well-known models.
(C) They are set in New York City.
(D) They keep track of events over multiple years

144. What book did Mr. Duchemin discuss on WHKK Radio?

(A) *Tracing the Origin of Jeans*
(B) *Glance Beyond the Runway*
(C) *Walking into Clothes: My Story*
(D) *Yards of Talent: A Decade of Vogue*

145. What is indicated about *Candid Tonight*?

(A) It is broadcast every morning at 9:00.
(B) It was recently added to WHKK Radio.
(C) It is hosted by Emily Johnson.
(D) It was rescheduled to a different time.

146. In the e-mail, the word "regular" in paragraph 1, line 1, is closest in meaning to

(A) orderly
(B) typical
(C) frequent
(D) complete

147. What is probably true about Ms. Hankins?

(A) She has worked in the fashion industry.
(B) She has interviewed Mr. Duchemin.
(C) She was featured on *The Tech Guy*.
(D) She hosts a radio talk show.

Day 10

1. 여러 가지 어형 2 ★★

유형 6 **사역동사 + 목적어 + ————**

사역동사 make, have, let은 5형식 동사로서 목적격 보어로 동사원형과 과거분사를 사용할 수 있다. 목적격 보어 자리가 빈칸인 경우 목적어와 목적격 보어의 관계가 능동이면 동사원형, 수동이면 과거분사가 들어가야 한다.

능동 I **had the mechanic fix** my truck. 정비공이 수리한다

수동 I **had my car fixed** at the mechanic's garage. 자동차가 수리된다

Ex 7. Because of the mechanical problems with the truck that he rented, Mr. Olson would like to have his money ———.

(A) refund
(B) refunding
(C) refunded
(D) is refunded

> 빈칸 앞에 사역동사 have가 있으므로 목적격 보어 자리인 빈칸에는 동사원형 (A) 혹은 과거분사 (C)가 들어갈 수 있다. 목적어 his money는 환불'되는' 것이므로 수동의 의미인 과거분사 (C)가 정답이다.

어휘 mechanical 기계의 rent 빌리다, 대여하다 refund 환불하다
해석 빌린 트럭의 기계적 문제로 인해 Mr. Olson은 돈을 환불받고 싶어 한다.

유형 7 **지각동사 + 목적어 + ————**

지각동사 see, watch, observe, hear, feel, smell은 5형식 동사로서 목적격 보어로 동사원형과 현재분사, 과거분사를 모두 사용할 수 있다. 목적격 보어 자리가 빈칸인 문제에서, 목적어와 목적격 보어의 관계가 능동이면 동사원형이나 현재분사, 수동이면 과거분사가 정답이다.

능동 Kevin **saw the manager enter(ing)** the warehouse.
매니저가 들어가다

수동 The inspector **saw the walls** in the basement **cracked** due to the earthquake.
벽이 금이 가게 함을 당한다

Ex 8. The Ministry of Agriculture and Forestry announced that 2022 saw overall meat consumption among Koreans ------- for several consecutive years.

(A) to fall
(B) fallen
(C) fall
(D) falls

that절의 동사가 지각동사 saw이므로 목적격 보어 자리인 빈칸에는 동사원형 (C)나 과거분사 (B)가 들어갈 수 있다. fall은 1형식 자동사로 과거분사형으로 사용할 수 없다. 따라서 동사원형 (C)가 정답이다.

어휘 ministry (정부의) 부처 forestry 산림학 see (시대, 장소가) ~를 목격하다 overall 전반적인 consumption 소비 consecutive 연이은

해석 농림부는 2022년에 한국인들의 전반적인 육류 소비가 몇 해 연이어 감소했다고 발표했다.

유형 8 ability / effort / the right / enough 명사 + -------

'ability / effort / the right / enough + 명사(대부분 돈)'는 뒤에 to부정사를 추가하여 자연스러운 문장을 만들 수 있다. 이 명사들 뒤에 빈칸이 있으면 to부정사를, 반대로 to부정사 앞에 빈칸이 있으면 이 명사들을 정답으로 선택하자.

She has the **ability to communicate** with the animals.
He had just **enough money to buy** the ticket.
He made an **effort to finish** the race. but came in last place.
The company reserves **the right to change** its pricing structure at any time.

Ex 9. In an effort ------- accuracy, editors are encouraged to proofread the articles at least twice.

(A) ensured
(B) ensuring
(C) to ensure
(D) ensues

빈칸 앞의 명사 effort를 보고 바로 to부정사 (C)를 정답으로 선택해야 한다.

어휘 in an effort to-V ~를 위한 노력의 일환으로 ensure 보장하다 accuracy 정확성 editor 편집자 encourage 권장하다 proofread (책의) 교정을 보다

해석 정확성을 보장하기 위한 노력으로 편집자들은 적어도 두 번 기사를 교정하도록 권장된다.

'요구, 주장, 권고/추천, 제안' 동사 + that + 주어 + ━━━━━━

'요구, 주장, 권고/추천, 제안'을 나타내는 동사 뒤의 that절에서 'should + 동사원형'을 쓰던 것을 현대 영어에서는 should를 생략하고 있다. that절의 동사 자리가 빈칸이면 동사원형을 선택하자. 다음의 '요구, 주장, 권고/추천, 제안'의 동사를 암기하자. 특히 굵은 글씨로 된 동사들이 많이 출제된다.

요구/요청	**request**, require, ask, demand + that + 주어 + 동사원형
주장	**insist** + that + 주어 + 동사원형
권고/추천	**recommend**, advise, urge + that + 주어 + 동사원형
제안	**suggest**, propose + that + 주어 + 동사원형

Ex 10. The CEO will be returning from his business trip next Monday and has requested that the managers ------- him individually starting at 9:30 A.M.

(A) meet
(B) met
(C) have met
(D) will meet

that절 앞에서 동사 has requested를 보면 정답을 알 수 있다. '요구'를 나타내는 동사이므로 that절의 빈칸에는 동사원형 (A)가 들어가야 한다.

어휘 request 요청하다 individually 개별적으로, 각각 따로

해석 CEO는 다음 주 월요일에 출장에서 돌아올 예정이며 매니저들이 오전 9시 30분부터 자신과 개별적으로 만날 것을 요청했다.

It is + 당위성 형용사 + that + 주어 + ━━━━━━

당위성을 나타내는 형용사 important, critical, crucial, imperative, essential, necessary, natural을 기억하자. 종속 접속사 that 앞에 'It is +당위성 형용사'가 있을 때, that절의 동사는 동사원형을 사용한다.

Ex 11. In order to keep our company thriving, it is important that the management ------- to invest in the development of new technology.

(A) continues
(B) continue
(C) continuing
(D) continued

that절 앞의 it is important를 보자마자 정답을 알 수 있다. 당위성을 나타내는 형용사 important가 있으므로 that절의 동사 자리인 빈칸에 동사원형 (B)가 들어가야 한다.

어휘 thrive 번창하다. 잘 자라다 management 경영진. 운영진 invest in ~에 투자하다 development 개발

해석 우리 회사가 지속적으로 번창하기 위해서는 경영진이 신기술 개발에 계속 투자하는 것이 중요하다.

유형 11 in order to-V

in order to 뒤에 빈칸이 있으면 동사원형을, 반대로 동사원형 앞에 빈칸이 있으면 in order to를 정답으로 선택하면 된다.

Ex 12. The actors ran an extra rehearsal ------- perfect their performance in the final scene.

(A) considerably
(B) in order to
(C) nevertheless
(D) as a result of

perfect 뒤에 목적어 their performance가 있으므로 동사로 쓰였음을 알 수 있다. 빈칸 뒤에 동사원형이 있으므로 (B) in order to가 정답이다.

어휘 rehearsal 리허설. 예행연습 perfect 완벽하게 하다 performance 연기. 연주

해석 배우들은 마지막 장면의 연기를 완벽하게 하기 위해 추가로 예행연습을 했다.

유형 12 would like to-V

빈칸을 채워서 동사 구문 would like to-V를 완성하는 문제가 출제된다.

Ex 13. If you're satisfied with the service we provided to you, I would ------- you to write a positive review on our Web site.

(A) have liked asking
(B) have liked to ask
(C) like asking
(D) like to ask

보기에 모두 like가 있고, 빈칸 앞에 would가 있으므로 동사 구문 would like to-V를 완성하는 문제임을 알 수 있다. 그러므로 (D)를 정답으로 선택하자.

어휘 positive 긍정적인 review 논평. 비평

해석 저희가 제공해드린 서비스에 만족하셨다면 저희 홈페이지에 긍정적인 리뷰를 작성해 주세요.

Please ————————

Please 뒤에 빈칸이 있으면 동사원형이 정답이다.

Ex 14. Please ------- daily spending records, since online balance statements may not accurately reflect recent account activity.

    (A) kept
    (B) keep
    (C) keeps
    (D) keeping

> Please 뒤에 빈칸이 있으므로 동사원형 (B)가 들어가면 된다. since 이후부터는 부사절이고, 주절의 동사가 필요하다.

어휘 keep a record 기록하다 **spending** (정부, 조직의) 지출 **balance** (계좌의) 잔액 **statement** 명세서, 거래 내역서 **accurately** 정확하게 **reflect** 반영하다, 나타내다 **account** (은행 등과의) 거래, 신용 거래

해석 온라인 잔액 명세서에는 최근의 거래 활동이 정확히 반영되지 않을 수 있으므로 일일 지출을 기록해 두세요.

---

help + (목적어) + (to)-V

5형식 동사 help는 목적어를 생략할 수 있고, 목적격 보어로 to부정사나 동사원형을 사용할 수 있다.

Ex 15. In addition to exceptional print services, Kate Wei Communications has the expertise to help you ------- your online presence.

    (A) optimal
    (B) optimize
    (C) optimization
    (D) optimum

> 빈칸 앞에 5형식 동사 help와 목적어 you가 있으므로 빈칸에는 목적격 보어가 들어가야 한다. 보기에서 help의 목적격 보어가 될 수 있는 것은 동사원형 (B)이다.

어휘 in addition to ~ 외에 **exceptional** 탁월한, 예외적인 **expertise** 전문 지식 **optimal**(=optimum) 최고의, 최적의 **optimize** ~을 최적화하다 **presence** 존재(감), 입지

해석 Kate Wei Communications는 탁월한 인쇄 서비스 외에 온라인에서의 입지를 최적화하는데 도움이 될 전문 지식도 갖추고 있습니다.

유형 15 to부정사와 전치사 to의 구별

시험에서는 to ------가 to부정사를 나타내는 경우가 많다. 그러나 빈칸에 동사원형 대신 ~ing형을 사용하는 예외적인 경우도 있으므로 반드시 기억해야 한다.

- **look forward to + 목적어** ~을 고대하다
- **be used[accustomed] to + 목적어** ~에 익숙하다
- **object[be opposed] to + 목적어** ~에 반대하다
- **be subject to + 목적어** ~에 따라야 한다, ~의 영향을 받다, ~을 조건으로 하다
- **be committed[devoted/dedicated] to + 목적어** ~에 헌신하다, 전념하다
- **contribute to + 목적어** ~에 공헌하다
- **prior to + 목적어** ~하기 전에
- **when it comes to + 목적어** ~에 관해서는

시험에 자주 나오는 동사구들이지만 to ------를 to부정사로 착각하면 안 된다. 여기서 to는 전치사이므로 뒤에 목적어로 명사나 동명사가 와야 한다.

Ex 16. Zentiva Pharmaceuticals will be offering a variety of events this year to ------- its centennial anniversary.

(A) celebrate
(B) celebrates
(C) celebrating
(D) celebration

시험에서 to 뒤에 빈칸이 있으면 대부분 to부정사라고 생각하면 된다. to ------- its centennial anniversary가 '100주년을 기념하기 위하여'라는 뜻이 되도록 동사원형 (A)를 정답으로 선택하자.

어휘 pharmaceutical 제약(의) celebrate 기념하다 centennial 100주년(의) anniversary 기념일

해석 Zentiva 제약은 올해 100주년을 기념하여 다양한 행사를 제공할 것이다.

Ex 17. We are grateful to have you as our client and look forward to ------- you with outstanding customer service.

(A) provide
(B) providing
(C) provides
(D) provided

시험에서 to ------는 대부분 to부정사이지만, 여기서는 착각하면 안 된다. look forward to에서 to는 전치사로서 목적어가 필요하므로 동명사 (B)가 정답이다.

어휘 grateful 고마워하는, 감사하는 outstanding 뛰어난, 걸출한

해석 귀하를 고객으로 모시게 되어 감사드리며, 귀하에게 훌륭한 고객 서비스를 제공할 수 있기를 기대합니다.

101. Policy makers should not let the current rise in oil prices ------- the nation's long-term development plans and lead to a recession.

(A) affected
(B) to affect
(C) affect
(D) affecting

102. Dr. Wasem suggests that we ------- announcing the results of the analysis until we have accurate data.

(A) will delay
(B) have delayed
(C) delay
(D) would have delayed

103. It is imperative that the products ------- meticulously inspected before they are sent out to clients.

(A) be
(B) to be
(C) being
(D) are

104. The Connon XL4 Cooker has the ------- to cook rice, steam vegetables, and keep food warm for several hours.

(A) explanation
(B) ability
(C) talent
(D) preference

105. The company could not help but watch its competitors ------- the bigger chunk of the market share due to lack of advanced technologies.

(A) takes
(B) taking
(C) to take
(D) taken

106. The labor union requested that the management's decision to reduce corporate travel budget ------- immediately.

(A) is reconsidered
(B) are reconsidered
(C) reconsider
(D) be reconsidered

107. All advertisements at the National Fashion, Fabric & Garment Machinery Expo are subject to ------- by the board of directors.

(A) approve
(B) approvingly
(C) approving
(D) approval

108. By constantly developing state-of-the-art technologies, the Zanello Motor Company has shown its commitment to ------- the fuel consumption of all its automobile models.

(A) lowers
(B) lowering
(C) lowered
(D) lowest

109. The petroleum company didn't have enough money ------- a new waste oil processing plant.

(A) building
(B) of building
(C) to build
(D) in building

110. Fagan Law hired more paralegals ------- meet its commitment to clients.

(A) consequently
(B) in order to
(C) in any case
(D) additionally

111. Mr. Lee would like ------- a meeting about the Hinton account as soon as possible.

(A) to arrange
(B) arranging
(C) having arranged
(D) arrangement

112. ------- allow up to three hours for the preparation of meal orders over $300.

(A) Please
(B) Pleasing
(C) Pleasure
(D) Pleased

113. Patas Marketing is able to help any business ------- its products through multimedia advertising packages.

(A) promote
(B) promoted
(C) promotable
(D) promoter

114. Company Vice President Jo Gacutan had no ------- to being considered for the position of CEO.

(A) objected
(B) objecting
(C) objects
(D) objection

115. The increasing employment rate is one factor contributing to ------- in the housing construction trade.

(A) grow
(B) growth
(C) grew
(D) grown

정답 및 해설 p.157

10. 2중/3중 지문 문제의 함정

• 문제 풀이 전략

(1) 지문 모두 읽기

2중/3중 지문 문제는 읽어야 하는 내용이 많아서 시간을 아끼려고 일부분을 건너뛰고 싶을 수 있다. 그러나 절대 그러지 말자. 건너뛴 부분에 다음 문제의 정답에 대한 단서가 있는 경우가 많다. 2중/3중 지문 문제에서 시간을 절약하는 비결은 어느 부분도 건너뛰지 않고 꼼꼼하게 읽는 것이다.

(2) 표 안에 숨어 있는 정답

표의 한쪽 구석에 정답의 키워드가 숨어 있는 경우가 종종 있다. 표의 내용을 주의 깊게 살펴보는 습관을 들이자.

Examples 1-5 refer to the memo and report.

From: Megan Hill, Vice President – Accounting
To: Managers, Andovar, Inc.
Date: March 15

Attention all managers:

Thank you for your diligent efforts in keeping track of the travel expenses of the employees under your supervision. As you are aware, we only started this practice in the last year. The measure was taken as the company started to expand beyond a size where reimbursement could be handled informally.

We are implementing the following modifications and request that you communicate them to your department. First, it has come to our attention that a lot of employees do not consider the current daily amount allowed for food expenses to be adequate. This allowance will be increased to $60 per day effective April 1. Second, we aim to trim expenses by requiring that employees make advance copies here at the office of any documents they will need while traveling for business. When employees make use of commercial vendors for copying, it tends to cost the company more than is necessary. As of May 1, we request that you not approve any such expenses.

Thank you for your cooperation in this matter.

Megan Hill
Vice President, Accounting

Travel Expense Report

Employee Name: Jessica Agbayani   **Date Submitted**: April 25
Employee Number: 273835   **Department**: Human Resources – Recruiting

Please enter both the amount for each category and a description of what the expense was.

Date	April 15	April 16	April 20	April 21	April 22
Location	Atlanta	Atlanta	Nashville	Nashville	Nashville
Transport	$ 50 Car rental	$ 61 Car rental, Gas	$ 50 Taxi	$ 45 Car rental	$ 53 Car rental, Gas
Lodging	$ 185 Hotel–1 night	–	$ 300 Hotel–2 nights	–	–
Food	$ 45 2 meals	$ 50 3 meals	$ 42 2 meals	$ 48 2 meals	$ 46 2 meals
Supplies	$ 62 Brochure copies	–	–	$ 10 Pencils	$ 10 Pencils
Total	$ 342	$ 111	$ 347	$ 103	$ 109
Grand Total			$ 1027		

Employee Signature: *Jessica Agbayani*
Supervisor Signature: *Jenna Nguyen*

Ex 1. According to the memo, why did Andovar, Inc., begin requiring travel expense reports?

(A) Government regulations were revised.
(B) Some employees had not received reimbursement.
(C) The company was taken over by a new owner.
(D) The company grew in size.

Ex 2. What is stated about the food allowance?

(A) It is enough to cover employee expenses.
(B) It requires a separate form.
(C) It will be increased in April.
(D) It requires copies of receipts.

Ex 3. What is Ms. Agbayani's position?

(A) Accounting associate
(B) Employee recruiter
(C) Head of human resources
(D) Sales manager

Ex 4. What is indicated about Ms. Agbayani?

(A) She traveled to two cities in April.
(B) She traveled by air.
(C) She spent two nights in Atlanta.
(D) She submitted her expense report late.

Ex 5. Which of Ms. Agbayani's charges would not be approved after May 1?

(A) $50
(B) $61
(C) $62
(D) $185

Examples 1-5 refer to the following memo and report. 1–5번 예제는 다음 회람과 보고서에 관한 것입니다.

From: Megan Hill, Vice President – Accounting
To: Managers, Andovar, Inc.
Date: March 15

Attention all managers:

Ex1.Thank you for your diligent efforts in keeping track of the travel expenses of the employees under your supervision. As you are aware, we only started this practice in the last year. The measure was taken as the company started to expand beyond a size where reimbursement could be handled informally.

We are implementing the following modifications and request that you communicate them to your department. Ex2.First, it has come to our attention that a lot of employees do not consider the current daily amount allowed for food expenses to be adequate. This allowance will be increased to $60 per day effective April 1. Ex5.Second, we aim to trim expenses by requiring that employees make advance copies here at the office of any documents they will need while traveling for business. Ex5.When employees make use of commercial vendors for copying, it tends to cost the company more than is necessary. Ex5.As of May 1, we request that you not approve any such expenses.

Thank you for your cooperation in this matter.

Megan Hill
Vice President, Accounting

발신: Megan Hill, 부사장 – 회계
수신: 주식회사 Andovar 매니저들
날자: 3월 15일

모든 매니저들께 알립니다.

관리 하에 있는 직원들의 출장비를 파악하기 위해 성실하게 노력해 주셔서 고맙습니다. 아시다시피 우리는 이 관행을 작년에야 시작했습니다. 이 조치는 회사가 비공식적으로 환급이 처리될 수 있는 규모를 넘어 확장되기 시작했기 때문에 취해졌습니다.

다음 변경 사항을 시행하며 여러분의 부서에 전달해 주실 것을 요청하는 바입니다. 첫째, 우리는 많은 직원들이 현재 식비로 허용된 일일 금액이 충분하지 않다고 생각한다는 것을 알았습니다. 이 수당은 4월 1일을 기하여 하루 60달러로 증액될 것입니다. 둘째, 우리는 직원들이 출장 중에 필요한 어떤 문서든 이곳 사무실에서 미리 복사할 것을 요구함으로써 경비를 줄일 작정입니다. 직원들이 복사를 위해 상용 공급업체를 이용하면, 그것이 회사로 하여금 필요 이상의 비용을 쓰게 하는 경향이 있습니다. 5월 1일자로 우리는 여러분이 그러한 경비는 승인하지 않을 것을 요청하는 바입니다.

이 사안에 있어 여러분의 협조 고맙습니다.

Megan Hill
회계 부사장

어휘 accounting 회계 (업무) Inc.(Incorporated) 주식회사 diligent 근면한, 성실한 keep track of ~을 기록하다 travel expenses 출장비 supervision 감독, 관리 aware 알고 있는, 의식하는 practice 관행, 관례 take a measure 조치를 취하다 reimbursement 환급 handle 다루다, 처리하다 informally 비공식으로 implement 시행하다 modification 수정, 변경 communicate A to B A를 B에게 전달하다 come to one's attention ~을 알게 되다 adequate 충분한, 적절한 allowance 비용, 수당 effective ~를 기(期)하여 aim to-V ~할 작정이다, ~하려고 노력하다 trim 줄이다, 삭감하다 advance 사전(事前)의 make use of ~을 이용하다 commercial vendor 상용 공급업체 tend to-V ~하는 경향이 있다 as of ~일자로 approve 승인하다

Travel Expense Report

Ex3.**Employee Name**: Jessica Agbayani　　　　**Date Submitted**: April 25
Employee Number: 273835　　　　Ex3.**Department**: Human Resources – Recruiting

Please enter both the amount for each category and a description of what the expense was.

Date	April 15	April 16	April 20	April 21	April 22
Ex4.**Location**	Atlanta	Atlanta	Nashville	Nashville	Nashville
Transport	$ 50 Car rental	$ 61 Car rental, Gas	$ 50 Taxi	$ 45 Car rental	$ 53 Car rental, Gas
Lodging	$ 185 Hotel–1 night	—	$ 300 Hotel–2 nights	—	—
Food	$ 45 2 meals	$ 50 3 meals	$ 42 2 meals	$ 48 2 meals	$ 46 2 meals
Supplies	$ 62 Ex5.Brochure copies	—	—	$ 10 Pencils	$ 10 Pencils
Total	$ 342	$ 111	$ 347	$ 103	$ 109
Grand Total			$ 1027		

Employee Signature: Jessica Agbayani
Supervisor Signature: Jenna Nguyen

출장비 보고서

직원 이름: Jessica Agbayani　　　　제출 날짜: 4월 25일
직원 번호: 273835　　　　부서: 인사부 – 채용

각 범주의 금액과 경비에 대한 설명을 모두 입력해 주세요.

날짜	4월 15일	4월 16일	4월 20일	4월 21일	4월 22일
지역	Atlanta	Atlanta	Nashville	Nashville	Nashville
교통	50달러 자동차 렌트	61달러 자동차 렌트, 주유	50달러 택시	45달러 자동차 렌트	53달러 자동차 렌트, 주유
숙박	185달러 호텔 – 1박	—	300달러 호텔 – 2박	—	—
식사	45달러 2식	50달러 3식	42달러 2식	48달러 2식	46달러 2식
비품	62달러 안내 책자 복사	—	—	10달러 연필	10달러 연필
합계	342달러	111달러	347달러	103달러	109달러
총계			1027달러		

직원 서명: Jessica Agbayani
관리자 서명: Jenna Nguyen

어휘 recruiting 채용 활동 category 범주 description 설명 transport 차량, 이동 lodging 숙박 supplies 용품, 비품 grand total 총계 brochure 안내 책자 supervisor 관리자

Ex 1. According to the memo, why did Andovar, Inc., begin requiring travel expense reports?

(A) Government regulations were revised.
(B) Some employees had not received reimbursement.
(C) The company was taken over by a new owner.
(D) The company grew in size.

회람에 따르면 Andovar 사(社)는 왜 출장비 보고서를 요구하기 시작했는가?
(A) 정부 규정이 개정되었다.
(B) 일부 직원들이 환급을 받지 못했다.
(C) 회사가 새 소유주에 의해 인수되었다.
(D) 회사가 규모 면에서 성장했다.

어휘 memo 회람, 단체 메일 **regulation** 규정 **revise** 개정하다 **take over** (기업 등을) 인수하다

해설 첫 문단에서 직원들의 출장비를 파악하기 시작한(keeping track of the travel expenses of the employees) 것은 작년부터라고 말하면서(we only started this practice in the last year) 그 이유를 설명하고 있다. 일정한 공식 절차 없이 출장비 환급을 처리하기에는 회사가 너무 커졌기 때문이라고 했으므로(The measure was taken as the company started to expand beyond a size where reimbursement could be handled informally.) 정답은 (D)이다.

Ex 2. What is stated about the food allowance?

(A) It is enough to cover employee expenses.
(B) It requires a separate form.
(C) It will be increased in April.
(D) It requires copies of receipts.

식사 수당에 대해 무엇이 명시되어 있는가?
(A) 직원 경비를 충당하기에 충분하다.
(B) 별도 양식을 요구한다.
(C) 4월에 증액될 것이다.
(D) 영수증 사본을 요한다.

어휘 state 명시하다 **cover** ~의 비용을 치르다 **separate** 분리된, 별도의 **form** 서식 **receipt** 영수증

해설 둘째 문단에서 식비로 허용된 금액이 너무 적다는 직원들의 불만을 언급하면서(it has come to our attention that a lot of employees do not consider the current daily amount allowed for food expenses to be adequate), 4월 1일부터 이 수당을 증액하겠다고 발표하고 있으므로(This allowance will be increased to $60 per day effective April 1) 정답은 (C)이다.

Ex 3. What is Ms. Agbayani's position?

(A) Accounting associate
(B) Employee recruiter
(C) Head of human resources
(D) Sales manager

Ms. Agbayani의 직책은 무엇인가?
(A) 회계 담당 직원
(B) 직원 채용 담당자
(C) 인사부장
(D) 영업부장

어휘 position 직책 **associate** 직원 **recruiter** 채용 담당자

해설 출장비 보고서 윗부분에 Jessica Agbayani는 인사부 소속이며 채용 담당자라고 나와 있으므로(Human Resources – Recruiting) 정답은 (B)이다.

Ex 4. What is indicated about Ms. Agbayani?

(A) She traveled to two cities in April.
(B) She traveled by air.
(C) She spent two nights in Atlanta.
(D) She submitted her expense report late.

Ms. Agbayani에 대해 무엇이 나타나 있는가?
(A) 4월에 두 도시로 여행 갔다.
(B) 항공편으로 이동했다.
(C) Atlanta에서 이틀 밤을 보냈다.
(D) 경비 보고서를 늦게 제출했다.

어휘 by air 항공편으로 submit 제출하다

해설 출장비 보고서를 보면 Ms. Agbayani는 4월에 Atlanta와 Nashville에 다녀온 것을 알 수 있으므로 정답은 (A)이다.

Ex 5. Which of Ms. Agbayani's charges would not be approved after May 1?

(A) $50
(B) $61
(C) $62
(D) $185

5월 1일 이후에는 Ms. Agbayani의 청구 금액 중 어느 것이 승인되지 않겠는가?
(A) 50달러
(B) 61달러
(C) 62달러
(D) 185달러

연계 추론 회람을 중간까지 읽고 2번 문제를 푼 후 남아 있는 지문을 읽어 보는 것이 좋다. 두 번째 변경 사항을 언급하는 부분에서 앞으로는 출장에 필요한 서류를 사무실에서 미리 복사해서 출발해야 한다고 말하고 있다(we aim to trim expenses by requiring that employees make advance copies here at the office of any documents they will need while traveling for business). 그 이유는 복사업체를 이용하면 필요 이상으로 비용이 들기 때문이다(When employees make use of commercial vendors for copying, it tends to cost the company more than is necessary). 그리고 매니저들은 5월부터 출장비 보고서에서 복사비는 승인하지 않아야 한다는(As of May 1, we request that you not approve any such expenses) 내용이 이어지고 있다. Ms. Agbayani의 출장비 보고서를 보면 4월 15일에 안내 책자 복사비로 62달러를 썼다는($ 62 Brochure copies) 것을 알 수 있다. 4월에는 이 금액을 환급받을 수 있겠지만, 회사 정책에 따라 5월 1일 이후에는 승인되지 않을 것이므로 정답은 (C)이다.

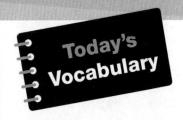

▶Actual Test를 풀기 전에 이 단어들을 암기하자.

짝을 이루어 출제되는 단어

- depend[rely] (up)on ~에 의지하다, ~에 달려 있다
- from + 시점 + on(ward) ~ 이후로

- ⎡noted⎤
  ⎢famous⎥ for ~로 유명한
  ⎣known⎦

- ⎡postpone⎤
  ⎢delay ⎥ – until 연기하다, 미루다
  ⎢put off⎥
  ⎣defer ⎦

escalate 증가하다, 악화되다
restructure 구조를 조정하다[개혁하다]
lead to ~로 이어지다
disrupt 방해하다, 지장을 주다
dismiss (모임·군대 등을) 해산시키다; 해고하다
strike 파업
pace (일의) 속도
establish 확립하다, 자리잡게 하다
emergent 신생의, 신흥의
field 분야
academic 학술적인, 학문의
source (뉴스의) 정보원, 소식통
ignite 불을 붙이다, 점화하다
flame 불길, 불꽃, 화염
tangible 만질 수 있는, 유형(有形)의
convert 전환시키다, 개조하다
exhausted 기진맥진한, 탈진한
combustible 불이 잘 붙는, 가연성인
within limits 어느 정도까지는, 한도 내에서는
captivating 매혹적인, 마음을 사로잡는
yet (최상급과 함께) 지금까지
warehousing 창고 저장[관리]
fall within ~의 범위에 들어가다, ~에 포함되다
supply chain 공급망
alternate between A and B A와 B를 번갈아 하다

information session 설명회
readable 읽기 쉬운, 재미있는
comparable 비슷한, 비교할 만한
make an attempt to-V ~하기를 시도하다
equip 장비를 갖추다
compile (자료를) 모으다, 하나로 종합하다
endorse (공개적으로) 지지하다
compose 구성하다
supplementary 보충의, 추가의
consequential ~의 결과로 일어나는, ~에 따른
persistent 끈질긴, 집요한
detect 감지하다, 탐지하다
corrosion 부식, 침식
contributor 요인, 원인 제공자
tremendous 엄청난, 굉장히 큰
fleet (비행기·버스·택시) 무리
corrode 부식시키다, 좀먹다
susceptible to ~에 영향 받기[감염되기] 쉬운
meanwhile 그 동안에
otherwise (만약) 그렇지 않으면[않았다면]
utilize 활용하다, 이용하다
scrutinize 면밀히 조사[검토]하다
faulty 결함이 있는, 불량의
conversion 전환, 변환, 변화
flaw (사물의) 결함

interfere with ~을 방해하다, ~에 지장을 주다

clarity (사진·소리·물질의) 선명도, 투명도

periodical 정기 간행물

resolution (컴퓨터 화면·프린터 등의) 해상도

sharpness 선명함, 명확성

issue (잡지·신문 같은 정기 간행물의) 호

expressly 분명히, 명확히; 특별히

summit (산의) 정상, 산꼭대기

bank 둑, 제방

ranger 산림 감시원, 공원 경비원

trailhead 등산로 입구

Actual Test

PART 5	1. 빈칸 앞뒤를 보며 문제를 푼다. 2. 빈칸 앞뒤를 보고 정답을 알 수 없다면 문장을 해석한다. 3. 두 줄 분량의 어휘 문제는 문장 전체를 해석해서 푼다. 4. 접속사 어휘 문제는 빈칸 앞뒤만을 보고 풀 수 없다. 문장 전체를 해석해 보자.
PART 6	1. 문법 문제라면 Part 5와 같은 방식으로 빈칸 앞뒤를 보며 푼다. 2. 다른 유형의 문제는 문맥을 통해 정답을 파악한다.
PART 7	1. 문제와 보기 (A), (B), (C), (D)를 먼저 읽은 후에 지문을 읽는다. 2. 지문 위아래의 모든 부분을 자세히 읽어 본다. 3. 문제의 해설을 꼼꼼히 읽고, 문장 구조를 분석하며 복습한다.

PART 5

101. The company is trying to make its employees ------- harder by offering them financial incentives.

    (A) work
    (B) to work
    (C) worked
    (D) working

102. The CFO will be more empowered beyond just making investment and accounting decisions ------- this day onward.

    (A) from
    (B) at
    (C) on
    (D) for

103. ------- escalating fuel prices, Pineford Trucking plans to restructure some of its divisions.

    (A) In that
    (B) Even if
    (C) Just as
    (D) Owing to

104. It is ------- that clients be made aware of inventory shortages immediately upon their occurrence.

    (A) sudden
    (B) critical
    (C) eventful
    (D) actual

105. Staff members of Three Rivers Medical Center are ------- to satisfying the needs of the community with a full range of medical services.

    (A) expressed
    (B) scheduled
    (C) designed
    (D) committed

106. City authorities insist that plans to install new digital parking meters will not ------- to an increase in parking charges.

    (A) experience
    (B) determine
    (C) lead
    (D) intend

107. Shipments of copper, the country's leading export, and fresh fruit just coming into season may be ------- by a long strike.

    (A) separated
    (B) disrupted
    (C) proposed
    (D) dismissed

108. The North Ridge Hospital mailed out a brochure to all member households to ------- them of the preventative medicine.

    (A) informing
    (B) information
    (C) inform
    (D) informed

109. Leekpai Consulting helps companies increase overall quality, not just quicken the ------- of production.

    (A) pace
    (B) dates
    (C) level
    (D) measure

110. Many DNB Bank's employees said that they could ------- read the last month's company newsletter because the print was so small.

    (A) barely
    (B) nearly
    (C) simply
    (D) almost

111. Due to the unexpected lack of funding for the project, the completion of the building has been postponed ------- there is another source of funds.

(A) while
(B) during
(C) upon
(D) until

112. Mertens Laboratories, Inc., is interested in exploring new technical partnerships as part of an ongoing ------- to expand its product line.

(A) effort
(B) growth
(C) strength
(D) rise

113. Innovative leading computer scientists have helped establish the emergent field of quantum computing ------- a new area of academic research.

(A) to
(B) as
(C) of
(D) at

114. Mr. Kadam has asked that we ------- the hazards more carefully before investing in new businesses.

(A) consider
(B) considered
(C) considering
(D) are considering

115. Ms. Egan will rely ------- department heads to develop employee incentive programs.

(A) onto
(B) into
(C) within
(D) upon

116. ------- business sources, the critically acclaimed Kinsley Restaurant on Gray Hills Avenue will be closing after 50 years of business.

(A) As soon as
(B) Rather than
(C) According to
(D) Whenever

117. It is imperative for all personnel to refrain from igniting flames around ------- materials.

(A) tangible
(B) converted
(C) exhausted
(D) combustible

118. Regional demands for new housing may increase exponentially within two years, within -------.

(A) limit
(B) limits
(C) limiting
(D) limited

119. Yuina Hashimoto's latest novel is his most captivating ------- and is sure to make Quality Books' best-seller list.

(A) just
(B) later
(C) yet
(D) very

120. Overseeing inventory control and warehousing strategies ------- within the responsibilities of the supply chain manager.

(A) has
(B) covers
(C) marks
(D) falls

121. Congress passed the bill granting the government the right ------- money transfers to hostile countries.

(A) ban
(B) to ban
(C) of banning
(D) banning

122. The implementation of a successful digital marketing campaign has helped Ainley Electronics ------- its profit margins.

(A) stabilized
(B) stability
(C) stabilizing
(D) stabilize

123. It is imperative that lawmakers ------- with local residents to find out about their views on current issues.

(A) communicate
(B) must communicate
(C) communicated
(D) communicating

124. Of all the vehicle models available today, it can be challenging to figure out ------- would best suit your company's needs.

(A) when
(B) why
(C) which
(D) where

125. At Barretto Securities, trainees alternate ------- participating in information sessions and working closely with assigned mentors.

(A) along
(B) against
(C) between
(D) near

126. Long-time admirers of Yoshiro Kasai who are ------- to the author's formal writing style will be astonished by her latest biography.

(A) fortunate
(B) readable
(C) comparable
(D) accustomed

127. The driver will make three ------- to deliver the package before it is brought back to our warehouse.

(A) attempts
(B) pursuits
(C) aims
(D) experiences

128. The staff has to ------- as much market-research data as possible prior to devising the advertising campaign.

(A) equip
(B) compile
(C) endorse
(D) compose

129. All Hershel Industries employees must have a valid ID card ------- enter the building.

(A) in order to
(B) as long as
(C) regarding
(D) always

130. ------- materials for the advanced Farsi course include audio files and an educational video series.

(A) Supplementary
(B) Consequential
(C) Persistent
(D) Cooperative

GO ON TO THE NEXT PAGE

PART 6

Questions 131-134 refer to the following article.

Eximion, Inc., Unveils Latest Development Initiative

SAN FRANCISCO (November 11) - Scientists from Eximion, Inc., a technology firm, are striving to develop a sensor capable of detecting corrosion caused by environmental exposure. Corrosion is a major contributor to the ------- losses
131.
the aircraft industry experiences each year. "This will be a tremendous ------- for
132.
commercial airline fleets," says Connie Hyun, Eximion's CEO. "The sensor will reduce both labor and maintenance costs without being too costly."

According to Ms. Hyun, the sensor is designed to identify corrosion in its initial stages, when the issue can be corrected simply by eliminating the corroded material. -------. In the structure of large aircraft, some critical joints can be
133.
particularly susceptible to corrosion. -------, the sensor can be utilized to
134.
scrutinize these areas and then target the most probable areas of concern.

---

131. (A) financially
(B) financed
(C) financial
(D) finances

132. (A) balance
(B) examination
(C) expectation
(D) asset

133. (A) This will minimize the need for making expensive structural repairs.
(B) The parts have all been replaced with higher quality materials.
(C) The project proceeds to scanning the affected areas.
(D) Its style and sleek design attracted the public.

134. (A) Meanwhile
(B) Similarly
(C) Otherwise
(D) Fortunately

Questions 135-138 refer to the following e-mail.

Date: 21 July
To: Hank Wilson <hwilson@everymail.co.za>
From: Myra Lewis <mlewis@zed.co.za>
Subject: Product recall

Dear Mr. Wilson,

Thank you for your recent ------- of the ZED Mini-X camera. We are notifying
135.
all those who have recently bought this product that certain models are

being recalled for repair. These models contain a faulty electronic chip that is

responsible for the digital conversion of light. -------. Please ------- whether your
136. **137.**
camera has this problem by taking a look at the serial number on the bottom

of the camera. If it ends with the letters ZLNT, a repair will be necessary. ZED

will cover all shipping costs for returning your Mini-X to us. Additionally, we will

repair ------- free of charge.
138.

Thank you.

Myra Lewis, Customer Service Manager

ZED Industries

---

135. (A) purchase
(B) review
(C) gift
(D) demonstration

136. (A) We are confident that you will savor
this product for many years to
come.
(B) It is outlined in the troubleshooting
section of the manual.
(C) This flaw will eventually interfere
with the clarity of your photographs.
(D) This special feature is not
compatible with some older
models.

137. (A) verification
(B) verified
(C) verify
(D) verifies

138. (A) mine
(B) it
(C) theirs
(D) these

GO ON TO THE NEXT PAGE

PART 7

Questions 139-142 refer to the following table.

Consumer Reports Monthly's Editor Report on 4 Selected Models of FISK digital cameras

	Fisk GQ540	Fisk GQ430	Fisk FZ300	Fisk FV340
Comments	Perfect for novice photographers with a straightforward and intuitive menu. Connected directly to the cloud storage.	Essentially a GQ540 with fewer features. Not suitable for outdoor photography; best used in interior settings. Tolerates higher levels of humidity.	Lightweight. Waterproof, designed for use at depths of up to 60 m.	Record-high resolution, outstanding sharpness and clarity. The most superior in the under-$500 price range.
Built-in		Built-in flash activates automatically in low light.	Features an Oceanears sound system audible in submersed environments.	
Negatives	Unusually heavy for a camera this size.	Picture quality compromised by lack of memory space.	Image quality inferior to FV340.	
Price	$350*	$250*	$750*	$480*

* Prices shown are valid at EG Stores. Since prices tend to vary from retailer to retailer, they may be different at InterTAN and NCIX, as well as online stores such as Croma Electronics. The product tables featured in every issue of Consumer Reports are impartial reviews by the magazine's editors, and are not part of the advertising supplements published bi-monthly.

139. Where would the table probably be found?

(A) In the catalog of a camera store
(B) In a guidebook for a camera
(C) In a photography textbook
(D) In a periodical that evaluates products

140. How is the FZ300 different from the GQ540?

(A) It is available via mail order.
(B) It is a newly released model.
(C) It is less expensive.
(D) It is relatively light.

141. What is suggested about the FV340?

(A) It is bigger than the other models reviewed.
(B) Its images are clearer than those of more expensive models.
(C) It does not perform optimally indoors.
(D) Its cloud storage space is insufficient.

142. How often do Consumer Reports' product tables appear?

(A) Every week
(B) Twice a month
(C) Every month
(D) Every two months

Redwood National Park Trails

Friendship Ridge Loop - *8.5 Kilometers*
Enjoy views of the Klamath River from the summit of Friendship Ridge. This path, of moderate difficulty, entails a steady incline to the summit of the ridge, followed by a well-defined trail that loops back and descends to the north parking lot.

Ossagon Slope - *6 Kilometers*
Trek up the side of Ossagon Ridge. This challenging trail features rocky terrain and intermittent steep climbs, providing scenic views of Orick Palisades Valley. The trailhead is located 100 meters to the south of the ranger station.

River's Edge - *6.7 Kilometers*
This trail stretches along the bank of the Klamath River. Starting at the north parking lot, the level trail leads to Orick Palisades Park.

Trillium Falls Trail - *3 Kilometers*
This leisurely trail commences at the rear of the main pavilion and extends through the Redwood Forest before culminating at Trillium Falls. Picnic and barbecue areas are scattered along the route.

To: Nature Explorers Club
From: Anne Zelnikova
Subject: Nature hike on Saturday
Date: September 12
Attachment: 📎 Map

Hi, everyone

The nature hike this month is set for Saturday at 6:00 A.M. Since a number of people during our last trip to Fern Canyon expressly mentioned their desire to view the Klamath River, we decided to meet up at Redwood National Park this month. Please arrive in the north parking lot by 5:45 A.M. I have attached a park map for your reference. Don't forget to pack a lunch and plenty of water. Our hike will last approximately 5–6 hours.

See you on Saturday!

Anne

NOTICE

Posted September 14

The River's Edge trail has been closed due to flooding caused by recent rain storms and will not reopen until further notice. Please refrain from traveling on this trail and locations adjacent to the Klamath River bank until the floodwaters recede. The north parking lot was also affected by the floodwaters, and is currently under construction. Kindly leave your automobile in the east parking lot and follow the Ranger Path to reach the trailheads.

143. How long is the trail that goes up Ossagon Ridge?

(A) 3 kilometers
(B) 6 kilometers
(C) 6.7 kilometers
(D) 8.5 kilometers

144. In the e-mail, the phrase "expressly" in paragraph 1, line 2, is closest in meaning to

(A) affectionately
(B) correctly
(C) specifically
(D) totally

145. Where will Nature Explorers Club members likely hike?

(A) On Friendship Ridge Loop
(B) On Ossagon Slope
(C) On River's Edge
(D) On Trillium Falls Trail

146. What is indicated about Redwood National Park?

(A) It offers guided nature walks.
(B) It has multiple parking areas.
(C) It provides food for purchase.
(D) It opens at 6:00 A.M.

147. What will Nature Explorers Club members likely do upon arriving at the park?

(A) See Trillium Falls
(B) Eat at the pavilion
(C) Purchase a trail map
(D) Walk along Ranger Path

저자 선생님과 함께 공부하기

- 우측 QR코드로 접속해서 저자 선생님이 올려 주신 부가학습 자료와 질문 코너를 이용해 보세요.
- 단어 시험지, 추가 어휘 문제 등을 다운받을 수 있습니다.
- 저자에게 질문하는 코너를 통해 교재에서 궁금했던 내용을 바로 질문하고 답변 받을 수 있습니다.

저자 질문 코너

단어 시험지

추가 어휘 문제

저자소개

이교희

2009년에 강남에서 강의를 시작하며 정기 토익에 응시해서 10회 만점을 달성했다. 가장 효율적인 문제 풀이 방식을 제시하는 깔끔한 강의로 수강생들의 호응을 얻었으며, 각종 인터넷 강의로도 수많은 수험생들과 만났다. 강사이자 저자로서 끊임없이 축적해 온 연구의 결실을 '토익 마법 – 2주의 기적 990'을 통해 맺게 되었다.

약력
● 학원
광주광역시 제제 외국어학원 대표 강사
파고다 외국어학원 토익 일타 강사(신촌, 종로)
현, 안산 이지어학원 토익 대표 강사

● 인터넷 강의
ujeje.com
Cracking TOEIC
파고다스타 '이교희의 탑토익 족보공개'

● 저서
토익 마법 2주의 기적 990 RC (2023)
토익 마법 2주의 기적 RC (2022)
토익 마법 2주의 기적 LC (2022)
시나공 토익 950 실전 모의고사 (2012)
파고다 외국어학원 월간 모의고사 해설

토익 마법 2주의 기적 990 RC

2024. 1. 3. 초 판 1쇄 인쇄
2024. 1. 10. 초 판 1쇄 발행

지은이 │ 이교희
펴낸이 │ 이종춘
펴낸곳 │ BM ㈜도서출판 **성안당**
주소 │ 04032 서울시 마포구 양화로 127 첨단빌딩 3층(출판기획 R&D 센터)
│ 10881 경기도 파주시 문발로 112 파주 출판 문화도시(제작 및 물류)
전화 │ 02) 3142-0036
│ 031) 950-6300
팩스 │ 031) 955-0510
등록 │ 1973. 2. 1. 제406-2005-000046호
출판사 홈페이지 │ www.cyber.co.kr
ISBN │ 978-89-315-5863-0 (13740)
정가 │ 18,900원

이 책을 만든 사람들
책임 │ 최옥현
진행 │ 김은주
편집 · 교정 │ 김은주, 이자영
영문 검수 │ Thomas Giammarco
본문 디자인 │ 나인플럭스
표지 디자인 │ 나인플럭스
홍보 │ 김계향, 유미나, 정단비, 김주승
국제부 │ 이선민, 조혜란
마케팅 │ 구본철, 차정욱, 오영일, 나진호, 강호묵
마케팅 지원 │ 장상범
제작 │ 김유석

■ **도서 A/S 안내**

성안당에서 발행하는 모든 도서는 저자와 출판사, 그리고 독자가 함께 만들어 나갑니다.
좋은 책을 펴내기 위해 많은 노력을 기울이고 있습니다. 혹시라도 내용상의 오류나 오탈자 등이
발견되면 "좋은 책은 나라의 보배"로서 우리 모두가 함께 만들어 간다는 마음으로 연락주시기
바랍니다. 수정 보완하여 더 나은 책이 되도록 최선을 다하겠습니다.
성안당은 늘 독자 여러분들의 소중한 의견을 기다리고 있습니다. 좋은 의견을 보내주시는 분께는
성안당 쇼핑몰의 포인트(3,000포인트)를 적립해 드립니다.

잘못 만들어진 책이나 부록 등이 파손된 경우에는 교환해 드립니다.

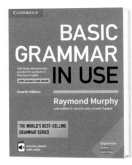

초급 Basic Grammar in use 4/e

전 세계 수백만 명의 학습자가 사용하는 영문법 교재입니다. 이 책의 구성은 스스로 공부하는 학생과 영어 수업의 필수 참고서로 적합한 교재입니다. 학습가이드를 통하여 영문법을 익히고 연습문제를 통하여 심화학습 할 수 있습니다. 쉽고 간결한 구성으로 Self-Study를 원하는 학습자와 강의용으로 사용하는 모두에게 알맞은 영어교재입니다.

▮ Book with answers and Interactive eBook 978-1-316-64673-1
▮ Book with answers 978-1-316-64674-8

초급 Basic Grammar in use 한국어판

한국의 학습자들을 위하여 간단 명료한 문법 해설과 2페이지 대면 구성으로 이루어져 있습니다. 미국식 영어를 학습하는 초급 단계의 영어 학습자들에게 꼭 필요한 문법을 가르치고 있습니다. 또한 쉽게 따라 할 수 있는 연습문제는 문법 학습을 용이하도록 도와줍니다. 본 교재는 Self-Study 또는 수업용 교재로 활용이 가능합니다.

▮ Book with answers 978-0-521-26959-9

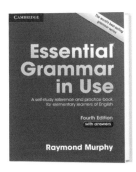

초급 Essential Grammar in use 4/e

영어 초급 학습자를 위한 필수 문법교재 입니다. 학습가이드와 연습문제를 제공하며 Self-Study가 가능하도록 구성되어 있습니다.

▮ Book with answers and Interactive eBook 978-1-107-48053-7
▮ Book with answers 978-1-107-48055-1

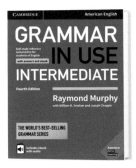

중급 Grammar in use Intermediate 4/e

미국식 영어학습을 위한 중급 문법교재입니다. 간단한 설명과 명확한 예시, 이해하기 쉬운 설명과 연습으로 구성되어 Self-Study와 강의용 교재 모두 사용 가능합니다.

▮ Book with answers and interactive eBook 978-1-108-61761-1
▮ Book with answers 978-1-108-44945-8

BM (주)도서출판 성안당　　🛡 **CAMBRIDGE**　│　도서문의 031-950-6394

중급 Grammar in use Intermediate 한국어판

이해하기 쉬운 문법 설명과 실제 생활에서 자주 쓰이는 예문이 특징인 \<Grammar in use Intermediate 한국어판\>은 미국 영어를 배우는 중급 수준의 학습자를 위한 문법 교재입니다. 총 142개의 Unit으로 구성되어 있는 이 교재는, Unit별로 주요 문법 사항을 다루고 있으며, 각 Unit은 간단명료한 문법 설명과 연습문제가 대면 방식의 두 페이지로 구성되어 있습니다. 문법과 전반적인 영어를 공부하고 하는 사람은 물론 TOEIC, TOEFL, IELTS 등과 같은 영어능력 시험을 준비하는 학습자에게도 꼭 필요한 교재입니다.

┃ Book with answers 978-0-521-14786-6

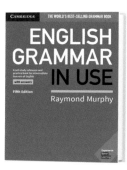

중급 English Grammar in use 5/e

최신판으로 중급 학습자를 위한 첫 번째 선택이며, 해당 레벨에서 필요한 모든 문법을 학습할 수 있는 교재입니다. \<IN USE\> 시리즈는 전 세계 누적 판매 1위의 영문법 교재로 사랑받고 있습니다. 145개의 Unit으로 이루어져 있으며, Study guide를 제공하여 Self-Study에 적합하며 강의용 교재로 활용할 수 있습니다.

┃ Book with answers and Interactive eBook 978-1-108-58662-7
┃ Book with answers 978-1-108-45765-1

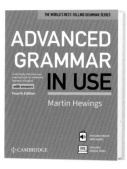

고급 Advanced Grammar in use 4/e

영어 심화 학습자를 위한 영문법 교재입니다. Study planner를 제공하여 자율학습을 용이하게 합니다. 포괄적인 문법 범위와 친숙한 구성으로 고급레벨 학습자에게 적합합니다. 이미 학습한 언어 영역을 다시 확인할 수 있는 Grammar reminder 섹션을 제공합니다. Cambridge IELTS를 준비하는 학생들에게 이상적인 교재입니다.

┃ Book with Online Tests and eBook 978-1-108-92021-6
┃ eBook with Audio and Online Tests 978-1-009-36801-8

BM (주)도서출판 **성안당** | ✠ **CAMBRIDGE** | 도서문의 031-950-6394

당신이 찾던 토익책!

READING

토익마법
2주의 기적
990
해설집

BM (주)도서출판 성안당

www.cambridge.org/unlock

비판적 사고력을 키워 주는 스킬북, Unlock 시리즈!

Unlock 시리즈는 학업에 필요한 스킬과 언어를 강화하는 코스입니다.
초기 언어 학습부터 학문적 맥락의 비판적 사고까지 기를 수 있도록 안내합니다.

- **Critical Thinking Skills** 목표 측정과 자기 평가를 통한 비판적 사고 기술 습득

- **Video Content** 학문, 시사 및 일반 상식 등 다양한 주제의 동영상 콘텐츠로 흥미 유발

- **Cambridge English Corpus** 수십억 개의 단어로 구성된 캠브리지 코퍼스로 실생활에
  쓰이는 언어를 제공하여 최신 언어 학습 가능

- **Cambridge One** 캠브리지 학습관리 플랫폼인 Cambridge One에서 추가 학습 가능
  - eBook, Class audio, Video, Digital Workbook with videos, Digital Classroom Material
  - 대체 읽기 및 듣기 자료, 통합 워크시트, 추가 읽기 및 대학 수업용 자료, 테스트

The digital resources

Powered by
Cambridge One

Presentation
Plus

eBook
with Audio
and Video

Video

Downloadable
Audio

Teacher Training
cambridge.org/training

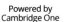

BM (주)도서출판 **성안당** | **CAMBRIDGE** | 도서문의 031-950-6394

READING

토익마법
2주의 기적
990

해설집

BM (주)도서출판 **성안당**

PART 5 & 6 Exercise

101 (A)	**102** (B)	**103** (D)	**104** (A)	**105** (A)
106 (D)	**107** (C)	**108** (B)	**109** (A)	**110** (D)
111 (A)	**112** (C)	**113** (D)	**114** (D)	**115** (A)

101. Mr. Kovách, Director of Marketing, will determine the ------- time to announce the launch date of Forari's new model of laptop computers.

(A) **optimal**
(B) optimize
(C) optimally
(D) optimist

어휘 director 이사 determine 결정하다 optimal 최적의 optimize 최적화하다 optimist 낙천주의자, 낙관론자 announce 발표하다 launch 출시

해석 마케팅 담당 이사 Mr. Kovách은 Forari의 노트북 컴퓨터 새 모델 출시 날짜를 발표할 최적의 시기를 결정할 것이다.

해설 빈칸 앞뒤 the ------- time만 보고 정답을 알아내자. 명사 앞에 빈칸이 있으므로 형용사가 정답이다.

102. Applicants for the position must be capable of typing at least 50 words per minute -------.

(A) accuracy
(B) **accurately**
(C) accurate
(D) accurateness

어휘 applicant 지원자 be capable of ~를 할 수 있다 at least 최소한 per ~당, ~ 마다 accuracy 정확도 accurateness 정확함, 틀림없음

해석 그 자리의 지원자는 최소 분당 50단어는 정확하게 타자할 수 있어야 한다.

해설 빈칸 앞의 typing at least 50 words per minute(최소 분당 50단어는 타자하기)을 보면서 정답을 알아내야 한다. '타동사 + 목적어 + -------' 구조이므로 부사가 정답이다.

103. All the issues addressed by members of the board of trustees remain ------- as a matter of organizational policy.

(A) confidence
(B) confidentially
(C) confidentiality
(D) **confidential**

어휘 address 다루다 board of trustees 이사회 confidence 신뢰; 자신(감) confidentially 비밀리에 confidentiality 비밀 유지 as a matter of policy 정책상 organizational 조직의

해석 이사회 임원들에 의해 다루어지는 모든 사안은 조직 정책상 기밀로 유지한다.

해설 빈칸 앞뒤 remain ------- as만 보면서 해결하자. 빈칸 앞에 remain이 있다면 be동사와 같다고 생각하면 된다. be동사 뒤에는 형용사가 와야 한다.

104. The latest novel by Byron Hayes is ------- based on the events that took place in Glasgow several decades ago.

(A) **loosely**
(B) loosened
(C) loose
(D) loosening

어휘 latest 최신의 be based on ~을 토대로 하다 loosely 막연히, 대략 loose 느슨한 loosen 느슨하게 하다, 완화하다 decade 십년

해석 Byron Hayes의 최신 소설은 대략적으로 수십 년 전 Glasgow에서 일어났던 사건들을 기반으로 하고 있다.

해설 빈칸 앞뒤 is ------- based에서 정답을 알 수 있다. 'be + ------- p.p.'가 있으면 부사가 정답이다.

105. Zat Industries wants to make the partnership between the Personnel and Planning teams -------.

(A) **stronger**
(B) strongly
(C) strength
(D) strengths

어휘 partnership 협력 personnel team 인사팀 planning team 기획팀

해석 Zat Industries는 인사팀과 기획팀 사이의 협력을 더 강화하기를 원한다.

해설 빈칸 앞에 있는 전치사구는 수식어구이므로 일단 지우고 생각하자. 빈칸 앞의 between the Personnel and Planning teams가 없다면 문장 구조가 더 분명하게 보인다. 5형식 동사 make가 있고 빈칸은 목적격 보어 자리이므로 형용사가 정답이다.

---

106. Regular mailing list updates have ------- supported TVS Company's efforts to find the right target markets.

    (A) succeed
    (B) succeeded
    (C) successful
    (D) successfully

어휘 regular 정기적인 mailing list 우편물 수신자 명단 target market 목표 시장

해석 우편물 수신자 명단의 정기적인 갱신은 알맞은 목표 시장을 찾으려는 TVS 사(社)의 노력을 성공적으로 뒷받침해 주었다.

해설 빈칸 앞뒤 have ------- supported가 정답을 알려준다. 'have + ------- p.p.' 구조이므로 부사가 정답이다.

---

107. Valery Lisov is the ------- choice for the position of board chairperson.

    (A) expects
    (B) expectantly
    (C) expected
    (D) expectation

어휘 expectantly 기대에 차서, 기대하며 expectation 기대, 예상 board 이사회 chairperson 의장

해석 Valery Lisov가 이사회 의장 자리에 예상되는 선택이다.

해설 빈칸 앞뒤 the ------- choice를 보며 정답을 알아내자. 명사 앞에 빈칸이 있으면 형용사가 정답이며, 보기 중 형용사가 없으면 분사가 정답이다.

---

108. Royalty payments will be divided ------- between the two writers of the coauthored book.

    (A) equals

    (B) equally
    (C) equal
    (D) equality

어휘 royalty 인세 payment 지급(금) equal ~와 같다, 동등하다; 동일한 equality 평등 coauthor 공동 집필하다

해석 인세 지급금은 공동 집필된 책의 두 저자들에게 동등하게 분배될 것이다.

해설 빈칸 앞의 will be divided를 보고 정답을 선택하면 된다. 수동태 동사 뒤에는 부사가 정답이다.

---

109. Although analysts deemed it -------, Kintetsu Corporation succeeded in generating large profits in their first fiscal year.

    (A) impossible
    (B) impossibility
    (C) impossibly
    (D) impossibleness

어휘 deem ~라고 여기다 generate 발생시키다 fiscal year 회계 연도

해석 분석가들은 그것을 불가능하다고 여겼지만, Kintetsu 사(社)는 첫 회계 연도에 큰 수익을 내는 데 성공했다.

해설 목적격 보어로 형용사를 사용하는 5형식 동사들을 기억해야 한다. 빈칸 앞의 deemed를 보면서 형용사를 정답으로 선택해야 한다.

---

110. Some of the members of the product development, marketing, and art departments worked ------- to design this year's packaging.

    (A) collaborate
    (B) collaborative
    (C) collaboration
    (D) collaboratively

어휘 development 개발 packaging 포장재

해석 제품개발부, 마케팅부, 미술부의 부서원 몇몇이 협업하여 올해의 포장재를 디자인했다.

해설 work는 1형식 자동사로 토익에서 가장 많이 출제되는 동사이다. 자동사 뒤에 빈칸이 있으면 고민 없이 부사를 정답으로 고르자.

111. Floor supervisors have complained that the unscheduled maintenance work has been ------- to their vehicle production.

(A) **disruptive**
(B) disruptions
(C) disrupt
(D) disrupted

어휘 floor supervisor 현장 관리자 complain that ~라고 항의하다 unscheduled 계획에 없던 maintenance 유지보수 disruptive 지장을 주는 disrupt ~에 지장을 주다 vehicle 차량

해석 현장 관리자들은 계획에 없던 유지보수 작업이 차량 생산에 지장을 준다고 항의했다.

해설 be동사 뒤 빈칸에는 형용사가 정답이다. 보기 중 형용사가 없으면 분사를 고르고, 둘 다 있으면 우선 형용사를 정답으로 선택하자.

112. Sales at Fairfield International's La Jolla office have been ------- lower than those at Hillcrest branch.

(A) notices
(B) noticing
(C) **noticeably**
(D) notice

어휘 sale 매출, 판매량 notice 알아채다; 통지 noticeably 현저히, 눈에 띄게

해석 Fairfield International의 La Jolla 사무소의 매출은 Hillcrest 지점의 매출보다 눈에 띄게 낮았다.

해설 빈칸 앞뒤 have been ------- lower만 보면 정답을 알 수 있다. 'be동사 + ------- + 형용사' 구조에서는 부사가 정답이다.

113. Mr. Sasaki's eloquent speech ------- convinced the members of the city council of the necessity for more public parks.

(A) easiest
(B) easy
(C) easier
(D) **easily**

어휘 eloquent 감동적인, 청중을 사로잡는 convince A of B A에게 B를 납득시키다, 확신시키다

해석 청중을 사로잡는 Sasaki 씨의 연설은 시의회 의원들에게 더 많은 공원의 필요성을 쉽게 납득시켰다.

해설 빈칸 앞뒤 Mr. Sasaki's eloquent speech ------- convinced를 보면서 정답을 알아내자. '주어 + ------- + 동사' 구조에서 빈칸은 부사가 들어가는 자리이고 가장 많이 출제되는 유형이다.

114. Keira Convention Center is ------- reopening after a year of renovation.

(A) final
(B) finality
(C) finals
(D) **finally**

어휘 final 최종의; 결승, 기말고사 finality 변경 불가능한 최후, 최종적임

해석 Keira 컨벤션 센터가 1년간의 보수 공사 후에 드디어 다시 문을 연다.

해설 빈칸 앞뒤 is ------- reopening이 정답을 알려 준다. 'be동사 + ------- + V-ing'에서 빈칸에는 부사가 알맞다.

115. President of Nichiro Industries is confident that the recent sluggish retail sales will not ------- affect its stock price.

(A) **adversely**
(B) adversarial
(C) adversary
(D) adversity

어휘 confident 확신하는 sluggish 부진한 retail 소매의 adversely 불리하게 adversarial 적대적인 adversary 상대방, 적수 adversity 역경 affect 영향을 미치다

해석 Nichiro Industries의 회장은 최근의 부진한 소매 판매고가 주가에 불리한 영향을 미치지 않을 것이라고 확신한다.

해설 빈칸 앞뒤 will not ------- affect에서 정답을 알 수 있다. '조동사 + ------- + 동사원형'에서 빈칸은 부사 자리이다.

Actual Test

101 (A)	**102** (C)	**103** (C)	**104** (D)	**105** (C)
106 (C)	**107** (C)	**108** (C)	**109** (C)	**110** (A)
111 (D)	**112** (A)	**113** (A)	**114** (C)	**115** (D)
116 (C)	**117** (D)	**118** (A)	**119** (B)	**120** (B)
121 (A)	**122** (A)	**123** (D)	**124** (C)	**125** (A)
126 (C)	**127** (C)	**128** (A)	**129** (D)	**130** (A)
131 (D)	**132** (A)	**133** (B)	**134** (A)	**135** (D)
136 (C)	**137** (A)	**138** (B)	**139** (B)	**140** (D)
141 (D)	**142** (C)	**143** (D)	**144** (B)	**145** (D)
146 (A)	**147** (C)			

Part 5

101. Speedflow Communications offers a ------- range of social media services as well as Web site development and maintenance.

(A) **wide**
(B) widen
(C) widely
(D) widest

어휘 offer 제공하다 range 다양성 a wide range of 매우 다양한 widen 넓어지다, 넓히다 development 개발 maintenance 유지관리

해석 Speedflow Communications는 웹사이트 개발과 유지관리뿐만 아니라 매우 다양한 소셜미디어 서비스도 제공한다.

해설 빈칸 앞뒤 a ------- range of만 보고 정답을 선택하자. 명사 앞 빈칸에는 형용사가 들어가야 한다. (A)와 (D)가 모두 형용사이지만 최상급 앞에는 관사 the를 사용해야 한다. 그런데 빈칸 앞에 관사 a가 있으므로 원급이 정답이다.

102. A ------- on the adverse effects of sitting for extended periods was recently published in the *New England Journal of Medicine*.

(A) research
(B) participant
(C) **study**
(D) request

어휘 adverse 반대의, 불리한 effect 효과 extended 장기간에 걸친 recently 최근에, 요즈음에 publish 게재하다, 싣다 journal 학술지

해석 장시간 앉아 있는 것의 부작용에 대한 연구가 최근에 New England Journal of Medicine에 게재되었다.

해설 (A)와 (C)가 모두 문장의 의미와 어울리지만 관사 a는 셀 수 있는 명사와 쓰므로 (C)가 정답이다. research는 관사 없이 단수형으로 주로 쓰인다.

103. In November, Premier Shoes will expand ------- by opening two additional stores.

(A) region
(B) regional
(C) **regionally**
(D) regionalize

어휘 regionally 지역 내에서 regionalize 지방 분권화하다[되다] expand 확장되다 additional 추가의

해석 11월에 Premier Shoes는 두 개의 매장을 추가로 오픈하여 지역적으로 확장할 예정이다.

해설 내용상 expand가 자동사로 사용됐기 때문에 빈칸에는 부사가 들어가야 한다.

104. The accounting figures from all the branch offices must be ------- verified for accuracy.

(A) regularity
(B) regular
(C) regularize
(D) **regularly**

어휘 accounting 회계(업무) figure 수치 verify 확인하다, 입증하다

해석 모든 지점의 회계 수치는 정확성을 위해 정기적으로 확인되어야 한다.

해설 빈칸 앞뒤 must be ------- verified에서 쉽게 정답을 알 수 있다. 'be + ------- + p.p.' 구조가 있다면 빈칸에는 부사가 들어가야 한다.

105. A limited ------- of time has been allotted for questions following Mr. Molinsky's speech.

(A) value
(B) record
(C) **amount**
(D) setting

어휘 allot 할당하다, 배당하다 following ~ 후에

해석 Molinsky 씨의 연설 후에 질문을 위해 제한된 시간이 배정되었다.

어휘 monitor (추적) 관찰하다 frequent 잦은, 빈번한; ~에 자주 다니다 frequency 빈도; 주파수 ensure 보장하다 humidity 습도 stability 안정성

해석 실험실 환경은 온도와 습도의 안정성을 보장하기 위해 자주 관찰되어야 한다.

해설 빈칸 앞 should be monitored만 보고 정답을 알아내자. 수동태 동사 뒤에 빈칸이 있으므로 부사가 정답이다.

해설 항상 짝을 이루어 출제되는 어휘 문제이다. considerable [substantial/significant/limited] ------- of effort[money/time]가 있으면 amount를 정답으로 선택하자.

106. Bano Cleaner removes mineral deposits from hard floors -------, so polishing is not required.

(A) chemical
(B) chemicals
(C) chemically
(D) chemist

어휘 deposit 침전물 chemical 화학적인; 화학 물질 polishing 광내기, 윤이 나게 닦기

해석 Bano 청소기는 단단한 바닥에서 미네랄 침전물을 화학적으로 제거하기 때문에 윤을 내는 것이 필요하지 않다.

해설 빈칸 앞의 전치사구 from hard floors는 수식어구이므로 지우고 removes mineral deposits만 보고 정답을 고르자. '타동사 + 목적어 + -------' 구조이므로 부사가 정답이다.

107. At the latest city council meeting, the subject of transportation was ------- by Ms. Pinter.

(A) shown up
(B) gotten up
(C) brought up
(D) used up

어휘 council 의회 subject 문제[사안] show up 나타내다, 드러내다 bring up (화제를) 꺼내다 use up ~를 다 쓰다

해석 최근 시의회 회의에서 교통 문제가 Pinter 씨에 의해 제기되었다.

해설 'be + ------- + by'는 수동태 구문이므로 빈칸에는 과거분사가 들어가야 한다. 문맥상 '회의에서 화두를 꺼내다'는 뜻이 자연스러우므로 (C)가 정답이다.

108. Laboratory conditions should be monitored ------- to ensure temperature and humidity stability.

(A) frequent
(B) frequents
(C) frequently
(D) frequency

109. Valdez City ------- reduced its electricity usage by replacing the old lampposts with the energy-efficient models.

(A) considerable
(B) consideration
(C) considerably
(D) considerate

어휘 considerate 사려 깊은, (남을) 배려하는 consideration 검토, 고려, 배려 replace A with B A를 B로 교체하다 lamppost 가로등 energy-efficient 에너지 효율이 좋은

해석 Valdez 시는 오래된 가로등을 에너지 효율이 좋은 모델로 교체함으로써 전기 사용량을 상당히 감소시켰다.

해설 빈칸 앞뒤 Valdez City ------- reduced를 보면 정답을 알 수 있다. '주어 + ------- + 동사' 구조에서 빈칸에는 부사가 들어가며, 이는 부사의 위치를 묻는 문제 중 가장 많이 출제되는 유형이다.

110. New recruits at Balally are ------- offered two weeks of vacation in a standard contract.

(A) initially
(B) shortly
(C) particularly
(D) completely

어휘 (new) recruit 신입 사원 initially 처음에 shortly 곧, 얼마 안 있어 particularly 특히, 특별히 completely 완전히

해석 Balally의 신입 사원은 표준 계약에 따라 처음에 2주의 휴가를 제공받는다.

해설 보기가 모두 부사인 경우 문장에서의 의미가 가장 자연스러운 것을 택한다. 신입 사원에게 주어지는 것이므로 "처음에는 2주의 휴가를 제공받는다."가 자연스럽다.

111. The online course focuses on how to expand and diversify your blog's -------.

(A) read
(B) reading
(C) reader
(D) readership

어휘 expand 확대하다 diversify 다양화하다 read 읽을거리, 독서 reading 읽기, 독서 readership 독자층

해석 온라인 코스는 블로그의 독자층을 확대하고 다양화하는 법에 초점을 맞춥니다.

해설 보기가 모두 명사인 어휘 문제이다. 'expand and diversify your blog's -------(블로그의 [(A) 독서 (B) 독서 (C) 독자 (D) 독자층]을 확대하고 다양화한다'를 자연스럽게 만들어 주는 것을 선택해야 한다.

---

112. Nairobi Move has a ------- team to accommodate all your travel requirements.

(A) dynamic
(B) surprised
(C) distracting
(D) succinct

어휘 dynamic 정력적인, 역동적인 distracting 산만하게 하는 succinct 간단명료한, 간결한 accommodate (요구 등을) 수용하다

해석 Nairobi Move에는 당신의 모든 여행 요구사항을 수용할 수 있는 역동적인 팀이 있습니다.

해설 Nairobi Move has a ------- team(Nairobi Move에는 [(A) 역동적인 (B) 놀란 (C) 정신을 산만하게 하는 (D) 간결한] 팀이 있습니다)의 의미를 자연스럽게 해 주는 (A)가 정답이다.

---

113. Using Dataretrieve software program, Mr. Wong recovered most files that he had ------- deleted from his computer's hard drive.

(A) accidentally
(B) accidental
(C) accidents
(D) accident

어휘 recover 되찾다, 회복하다 accidentally 우연히, 실수로 delete 삭제하다

해석 Wong 씨는 Dataretrieve 소프트웨어 프로그램을 이

용하여 컴퓨터 하드 드라이브에서 실수로 삭제한 파일 대부분을 복구했다.

해설 빈칸 앞뒤 had ------- deleted에서 정답을 알아내자. 'have + ------- + p.p.' 구조에서 빈칸에는 부사를 써야 한다.

---

114. The user guide provides a clear ------- of the features and capabilities of your device.

(A) agenda
(B) boundary
(C) overview
(D) formula

어휘 agenda 의제, 안건 boundary 경계(선), 한계 overview 개요, 개관 formula 공식, 방식 feature 특징, 특색 capability 성능; 능력

해석 사용 설명서는 장치의 특징과 성능에 대한 명확한 개요를 제공합니다.

해설 '사용 설명서는 장치의 특징과 성능에 대한 명확한 -------를 제공한다'는 의미를 자연스럽게 해 주는 것은 (C)이다.

---

115. Mr. Reynold's study shows that types of hay differ ------- in their nutritional content.

(A) significant
(B) signify
(C) significance
(D) significantly

어휘 study 연구 hay 건초 differ in ~에서 다르다 significant 중요한, 의미 있는 signify 의미하다; 중요하다 significance 중요성, 의의 significantly 상당히 nutritional 영양의 content 내용(물)

해석 Reynold 씨의 연구는 건초의 종류에 따라 영양 성분에서 상당히 다르다는 것을 보여준다.

해설 빈칸 앞에 있는 differ가 1형식 자동사이므로 정답으로 부사를 선택해야 한다.

---

116. The testimonials from satisfied customers show ------- how powerful and easy it is to use our product.

(A) near
(B) alike
(C) just
(D) along

어휘 testimonial 추천서, 추천 글 alike 둘 다, 똑같이 just 정말; 완전히

해석 만족한 고객들의 추천 글들이 우리 제품을 사용한다는 것이 정말이지 얼마나 강력하고 쉬운 일인지 보여줍니다.

해설 의미상 빈칸 뒤에 있는 how를 수식할 수 있는 부사는 (C) just이다.

---

117. Nervousness notwithstanding, Ms. Kim ------- presented her report to the Board of Directors.

(A) confide
(B) confidence
(C) confident
(D) confidently

어휘 nervousness 긴장, 초조 notwithstanding (명사 뒤에 쓸 수 있음) ~에도 불구하고 confide (비밀을) 털어놓다 confidence 신뢰; 자신(감); 확신 confident 자신감 있는; 확신하는 present 발표하다, 공개하다 board of directors 이사회

해석 긴장감에도 불구하고 Ms. Kim은 이사회에 자신 있게 보고서를 발표했다.

해설 빈칸 앞뒤 Ms. Kim ------- presented를 보고 쉽게 정답을 알 수 있다. '주어 + ------- + 동사' 구조는 부사 자리를 묻는 문제에서 가장 많이 출제되는 유형이다.

---

118. Articles should be submitted at least two weeks prior to the date of publication to leave ------- time for proofreading.

(A) adequate
(B) perpetual
(C) impulsive
(D) deficient

어휘 submit 제출하다 at least 최소한 prior to ~ 전에 publication 발행 adequate 충분한, 적절한 perpetual 끊임없이 계속되는 impulsive 충동적인 deficient in ~이 부족한, 결핍된 proofreading 교정, 교열

해석 기사는 최소 발행일 1주 전에 제출되어서 교정을 위한 충분한 시간을 남기도록 해야 한다.

해설 leave ------- time for proofreading(교정을 위한 [(A) 충분한 (B) 끊임없이 계속되는 (C) 충동적인 (D) 부족한] 시간을 남기다)의 의미를 자연스럽게 만들어 주는 형용사 (A)를 선택해야 한다. 참고로 adequate는 빈출 형용사로 보기에 나오면 정답일 확률이 매우 높다.

---

119. Mature perennial plants should be planted in your garden ------- six weeks before your first fall frost date.

(A) even if
(B) at least
(C) in case of
(D) away from

어휘 mature 다 자란 perennial 다년생의 in case of ~이 발생할 경우에 frost 서리

해석 다 자란 다년생 식물은 가을 첫서리 날짜로부터 최소 6주 전에 정원에 심어야 한다.

해설 ------- six weeks before가 '최소 6주 전에'라는 의미가 되는 것이 자연스럽다.

---

120. How ------- a company receives, documents, and reacts to complaints has an impact on customer satisfaction.

(A) efficient
(B) efficiently
(C) efficiency
(D) efficiencies

어휘 document 기록하다 react to ~에 대응하다 have an impact on ~에 영향을 주다 satisfaction 만족

해석 회사가 불만 사항을 얼마나 효율적으로 접수해서 기록하고 대응하느냐가 고객 만족도에 영향을 미친다.

해설 and가 receives, documents, reacts to 동사 세 개를 연결하고 있고 complaints는 세 동사의 목적어이다. 의문사 how 뒤에는 형용사와 부사를 모두 사용할 수 있는데, 빈칸 뒤에 '주어 + 타동사 + 목적어'로 완성된 3형식 문장이 있으므로 부사를 정답으로 선택해야 한다.

---

121. When members of the Hanoi ------- arrive on Thursday, Ms. Goldingay will give them a tour of the factory.

(A) delegation
(B) precision
(C) intention
(D) translation

어휘 delegation 대표단 precision 정확(성), 정밀(성) intention 의도; 목적 translation 번역 give sb a tour of ~에게 ~을 견학시켜 주다

해석 목요일에 Hanoi 대표단 구성원들이 도착하면 Ms. Goldingay가 공장을 안내할 것이다.

내용면에서 지명 Hanoi와 함께 복합명사를 이룰만한 것은 '대표단'밖에 없다.

---

122. Associates of LPN auto company are provided with ------ breakfast and lunch at Bain Hall cafeteria.

(A) complimentary
(B) accountable
(C) replaced
(D) secured

associate 직원 complimentary 무료의 accountable 책임이 있는 replaced 대체된 secure 안정된 cafeteria 구내식당

LPN 자동차 회사 직원들은 Bain 홀 구내식당에서 무료 아침 식사와 점심 식사를 제공받는다.

항상 짝을 이루어 출제되는 어휘 문제이다. 빈칸 뒤에 meal, breakfast, lunch, coupon 같은 명사가 있으면 complimentary가 정답이다. 참고로 accountable은 명사 앞에 사용하지 않는다.

---

123. Ms. Trinacria referred to the corporate travel policy to assert that her expenses are ------ reimbursable.

(A) definitive
(B) define
(C) definite
(D) definitely

refer to ~를 언급하다 corporate 기업[회사]의 policy 정책 assert 주장하다 expense 비용, 경비 definitive 최종적인, 확정적인 define 정의하다; 규정하다 definite 확실한; 분명한 reimbursable 환급할 수 있는

Ms. Trinacria는 회사 출장 정책을 언급하며 자기 경비가 확실히 환급 가능하다고 주장했다.

빈칸 앞뒤 are ------ reimbursable에서 정답을 알아내야 한다. 'be동사 + ------ + 형용사' 구조에서 빈칸은 부사 자리이다.

---

124. This ------ allows for the easy and convenient laundering of any garment without the use of harmful chemicals.

(A) management
(B) failure
(C) detergent
(D) satisfaction

management 운영 detergent 세제 satisfaction 만족 allow for ~을 가능하게 하다 laundering 세탁 garment 의복, 옷 harmful 해로운 chemical 화학 물질

이 세제는 해로운 화학 물질을 사용하지 않고 어떤 옷이든 쉽고 편리한 세탁을 가능하게 한다.

빈칸 앞뒤 This ------ allows for the easy and convenient laundering을 보면 '쉽고 편리한 세탁을 가능하게' 하는 것은 세제임을 알 수 있다.

---

125. Autroprime Inc., posted some quite ------ quarterly projections in its interim financial report.

(A) optimistic
(B) mutual
(C) inspired
(D) supportive

post (재정 관련) 발표하다 optimistic 낙관적인 mutual 상호간의 inspired 영감을 받은 supportive 지원하는, 도와주는 quarterly 분기별의 projection 예상, 추정 interim 중간의 financial 재무의

Autroprime 사(社)는 중간 재무 보고서에 매우 낙관적인 분기 전망을 내놓았다.

빈칸 앞뒤 some quite ------ quarterly projections(몇몇 매우 [(A) 낙관적인 (B) 상호간의 (C) 영감을 받은 (D) 도와주는] 분기별 예상)의 의미를 자연스럽게 만들어 주는 형용사를 정답으로 선택해야 한다.

---

126. Ms. Choi, ------ her co-presenter, will be asked to remain at the front of the conference room to speak with individual participants.

(A) as soon as
(B) in order to
(C) along with
(D) in case of

as soon as ~하자마자 in order to ~하기 위하여 along with ~와 함께 in case of ~인 경우에 co-presenter 공동 발표자 conference room 회의실

Ms. Choi는 공동 발표자와 함께 회의실 앞에 남아 개별 참가자들과 대화를 나누도록 요청받을 것이다.

as soon as는 부사절 접속사로 '주어 + 동사'로 이어져야 하고, in order to는 바로 뒤에 동사원형이 필요하므로 (A)와 (B)는 제외한다. 빈칸에 넣었을 때 '공동 발표자와 함께'라는 의미가 되는 (C)가 자연스럽다.

127. Shaloub Copies produces brochures on high-grade, glossy paper that was ------- chosen for its quality and sturdiness.

(A) caring
(B) careful
(C) carefully
(D) cares

brochure 소책자 high-grade 고급의 glossy paper 광택지 sturdiness 견고성

해석 Shaloub Copies는 품질과 견고성을 위해 신중하게 선택된 고급 광택지에 소책자를 제작한다.

해설 빈칸 앞뒤 was ------- chosen을 보면 정답을 알 수 있다. 'be + ------- + p.p.'가 있으면 부사를 정답으로 선택하자.

128. All users of this software program are required to ------- their e-mail addresses when security updates are performed.

(A) authenticate
(B) determine
(C) discover
(D) institute

어휘 be required to V ~하는 것이 요구되다 authenticate 증명하다, 인증하다 determine 결정하다 institute 제정하다 security 보안 perform 수행하다

해석 이 소프트웨어 프로그램의 모든 사용자는 보안 업데이트가 수행될 때 이메일 주소를 인증하는 것이 요구됩니다.

해설 '보안 업데이트가 있을 때 소프트웨어 사용자에게 요구하는 일은 이메일 계정이 본인 것임을 증명하는 것'이라는 의미가 자연스럽다.

129. ------- expanding its hours of operation at some locations, the restaurant began offering new menu items for patrons.

(A) Despite
(B) Likewise
(C) In comparison to
(D) In addition to

어휘 despite ~에도 불구하고 likewise 마찬가지로, 또한 in comparison to ~와 비교해서 hours of operation 영업 시간 location 지점 patron (특정 상점, 식당의) 단골손님, 고객

해석 그 식당은 일부 지점에서 영업 시간을 늘렸을 뿐만 아니라 고객들을 위한 새 메뉴 품목도 제공하기 시작했다.

해설 likewise를 문장 맨 앞에 놓으면 접속부사이다. 그러면 바로 뒤에 문장이 있어야 하므로 (B)는 제외하자. 고객들을 위한 조치로 '영업 시간 연장하기'와 '새 메뉴 품목 내놓기'라는 두 가지가 열거되었으므로 빈칸에는 In addition to가 알맞다.

130. Of the 645 executives questioned for the survey, 62 percent plan to check in with their offices ------- while on vacation.

(A) occasionally
(B) occasional
(C) occasion
(D) occasions

어휘 executive 간부, 중역 question 질문하다 check in with ~와 연락하다 occasional 가끔의 occasion 경우, 행사

해석 설문조사를 위해 질문받은 645명의 중역 중 62퍼센트는 휴가 중에 가끔 사무실과 연락할 계획이다.

해설 빈칸 앞의 check in with their offices를 보면서 정답을 알아내자. '타동사 + 목적어 + -------' 구조에서는 부사가 정답이다.

Part 6

Questions 131-134 refer to the following letter.

Mr. Anurag Khan
Bharat Heavy Electricals Ltd.
613 G.I.D.C. Industrial Estate
Gujarat 391350

Dear Mr. Khan:
We would like to extend an invitation to you to participate in the India Electrical Engineering Association (IEEA) trade fair this year. As always, this annual event will provide you with [131.]extensive opportunities for networking.
A number of vendors have already reserved their booth spaces. However, there are other ways to [132.]promote your

business. Those who close a sponsorship deal with us receive a special acknowledgment in the program. Enclosed please find the brochure for the trade fair. The information contains pricing ^{133.}details for reserving a booth space, posting advertisements, and sponsoring an event, as well as a list of past participants.

^{134.}We would be delighted if you decide to join us this year. If you have questions, feel free to contact me by e-mail at any time.

Sincerely,

Additi Gupta
IEEA Vendor Coordinator
agupta@elecengineer.org.in
Enclosure

131~134번 문제는 다음 편지에 관한 것입니다.

Mr. Khan께
올해 인도 전기 공학 협회(IEEA)의 무역 박람회에 참가하실 것을 제안하고 싶습니다. 늘 그렇듯 이 연례행사는 인적 네트워크 형성을 위한 폭넓은 기회를 제공해 드릴 것입니다.
이미 많은 판매 회사들이 전시 공간을 예약했습니다. 그러나 사업체를 홍보할 다른 방법도 있습니다. 저희와 후원 계약을 맺으시는 분들은 프로그램 책자에서 특별 감사 인사를 받으시게 됩니다.
무역 박람회 안내 책자를 동봉합니다. 정보에는 과거 참가 업체들의 명단뿐만 아니라 전시 공간 예약과 광고 게재, 행사 후원에 대한 가격 책정의 세부 사항이 포함되어 있습니다.
올해 저희와 함께하기로 해 주신다면 기쁘겠습니다. 문의 사항이 있으실 때는 언제든 저에게 이메일로 연락하시기 바랍니다.

IEEA 참가업체 조정관
Additi Gupta 올림
agupta@elecengineer.org.in
동봉 문서 있음

어휘 extend an invitation to *sb* to V ~를 초대하다, ~에게 ~를 제안하다 electrical engineering 전기 공학 association 협회 trade fair 무역 박람회 annual event 연례행사 networking 인적 네트워크 형성 vendor 판매 회사 close a deal with ~와 거래를 체결하

다 sponsorship 후원, 협찬 acknowledgment 감사의 말: 인정 program (공연, 경기의) 프로그램 책자 Enclosed please find ~를 동봉합니다 brochure (홍보용) 안내 책자 contain ~이 들어 있다 pricing 가격 책정 post 게시하다 sponsor 후원하다 participant 참가자 feel free to-V 마음 놓고 ~하다 coordinator (업무, 행사의) 조정자, 책임자 enclosure (편지에) 동봉된 것

---

131. (A) extend
  (B) extends
  (C) extensively
  (D) extensive

어휘 extend 확대하다, 연장하다 extensive 폭넓은, 포괄적인

해설 빈칸 앞뒤 with ------ opportunities에서 정답을 알아내자. 명사 앞 빈칸에는 형용사 (D)가 정답이다.

---

132. **(A) promote**
  (B) monitor
  (C) construct
  (D) negotiate

어휘 promote 홍보하다; 증진하다 monitor 감시하다 construct 건설하다; 구성하다 negotiate 협상하다

해설 앞 문장의 "이미 많은 판매 회사들이 전시 공간을 예약했다"라는 말은 회사 홍보를 위한 공간이 많이 남지 않았다는 의미이며, 뒤 문장의 "프로그램 책자에 특별 감사 인사가 실리는 것" 또한 회사가 홍보된다는 뜻이다. 그러므로 빈칸이 포함된 문장은 "사업체를 홍보할 (promote) 다른 방법도 있습니다"라는 의미가 알맞다.

---

133. (A) markets
  (B) details
  (C) labels
  (D) receipts

해설 빈칸 앞의 pricing(가격 책정)과 함께 사용하여 복합명사를 만들기에 알맞은 것은 (B) details 밖에 없다.

---

134. **(A) We would be delighted if you decide to join us this year.**
  (B) We will have placed your advertisement in the brochure by then.
  (C) Your participation in the event will be free of charge.
  (D) Your presentation on the novel material is scheduled for the second day.

해석 (A) 올해 저희와 함께하기로 해 주신다면 기쁘겠습니다.
(B) 그때까지는 광고를 안내 책자에 실어 놓겠습니다.
(C) 귀사는 행사 참가가 무료입니다.
(D) 신소재에 대한 당신의 강연은 둘째 날로 예정되어 있습니다.

해설 편지가 무역 박람회 참가를 제안하는 내용이며, 이를 마무리하기에 알맞은 문장을 선택해야 한다.

Questions 135-138 refer to the following e-mail.

To: Montserrat Caballé
From: Yeon-kyeong Kim
Date: June 2
Re: Yong-in Showcase Request

Dear Ms. Caballé,

Mr. Sunwoo, the owner of The Sunwoo Gallery of Seoul, was happy to display your work as part of the Contemporary Art Festival last month. He was [135.]particularly impressed with your beautiful collection of abstract paintings, and so was the audience. He now would like to ask for your permission to present these same pieces at his other gallery in Yong-in in September. Will they be available for [136.]exhibition and sale? [137.]Any piece that does not sell would be returned to you shortly thereafter.
Please let us know if you are interested and, [138.]if so, we can set up a meeting to discuss compensation and further details.

Sincerely yours,

Yeon-kyeong Kim
Administrative Assistant
The Sunwoo Gallery

135-138번 문제는 다음 이메일에 관한 것입니다.

수신: Montserrat Caballé
발신: Yeon-kyeong Kim
날짜: 6월 2일
제목: 용인 쇼케이스 요청

Ms. Caballé께

서울 선우 미술관 소유주인 Mr. Sunwoo는 지난달 현대 미술 축제의 일환으로 당 신의 작품을 전시하게 되어 기뻤습니다. 그는 특히 당신의 아름다운 추상화 컬렉션에 깊은 인상을 받았고 관람객들도 마찬가지였습니다. 이제 그는 9월에 용인에 있는 자신의 다른 미술관에서 같은 작품들을 전시할 수 있도록 당신의 허락을 구하고자 합니다. 전시와 판매가 가능할까요? 팔리지 않는 작품은 직후에 모두 반환될 것입니다.
관심이 있으신지 알려 주시고, 만약 그러시다면, 미팅을 잡아서 보상과 더 자세한 사항을 논의했으면 좋겠습니다.

선우 미술관
업무 총괄 비서
김연경 드림

---

135. (A) particular
(B) particularity
(C) particularize
(D) particularly

어휘 particularity 독특함 particularize 자세히 다루다

해설 빈칸 앞뒤 was ------- impressed를 보면 정답을 알 수 있다. 'be + ------- + + p.p'가 있으면 부사가 정답이다.

---

136. (A) repair
(B) analysis
(C) exhibition
(D) treatment

어휘 repair 수리 analysis 분석 treatment (주제·작품 등의) 해석

해설 앞 문장에서 작품을 다른 미술관에서도 전시할 수 있게 허락해 달라고 요구하고 있으므로 여기서 빈칸에 알맞은 명사를 알 수 있다.

---

137. **(A) Any piece that does not sell would be returned to you shortly thereafter.**
(B) We are committed to restoring the art to its original condition.
(C) The gallery's permanent collection includes sculptures of all kinds.
(D) You will receive a considerable discount on any piece you decide to buy.

어휘 be committed to ~에 전념하다 restore 복원[복구]하다 permanent 영구[영속]적인 collection 소장품

해석 (A) 팔리지 않는 작품은 직후에 모두 반환하겠습니다.
(B) 우리는 미술품을 원상태로 복구하는 일에 전념합니다.
(C) 미술관의 영구 소장품에는 모든 종류의 조각품들을 포함하고 있습니다.
(D) 구매하기로 결정한 어떤 작품에 대해서든 상당한 할인을 받으실 것입니다.

해설 바로 앞 문장에서 전시 및 판매 가능 여부를 묻고 있으므로, 이어지는 문장에서는 팔리지 않는 작품을 돌려주겠다고 말하는 것이 자연스럽다.

---

138. (A) even if
(B) if so
(C) so long as
(D) in case

어휘 even if 비록 ~일지라도 so long as ~하는 한 in case ~할 경우에 대비해서

해설 Day 02에서 설명할 예정으로, '-------, 주어 + 동사'가 있으면 부사가 정답이다. 보기 중 부사는 하나뿐이고 나머지는 모두 접속사이다.

Part 7

Questions 139-142 refer to the following article.

News from Kew Botanical Gardens

KEW (October 16)—[139.]Visitors to Royal Botanical Gardens, Kew are now greeted by a bright new logo displayed on the welcome sign at the entry gate. Most people say they are pleased with the new logo, which features a colorful bouquet of wildflowers.

The management of the botanical gardens decided to replace the old logo on the basis of public input. "We collected opinion cards deposited in boxes at the gardens and reviewed responses to an online questionnaire. We discovered that receptivity to the original logo had become negative," said Jacob Kunchai, the director of the gardens, when he was interviewed by the Kew Evening Courier. The old logo spelled out the name of the gardens above a drawing of an elaborate Tudor greenhouse.

[140.]New designs were submitted by Nonpareil Graphics. [142.]**Three of them were posted on the Botanical Gardens Web site.** Members were invited to choose which one would be the attractive logo. The board acknowledged that the members' decision was superb.

Jamie Lee, the manager of the Botanical Gardens on-site visitors' shop, is one of those happy with the new logo selected by members. The new logo now appears on clothing and other merchandise, and she is sure it will help increase sales. [141.]"Previously, I have often been disappointed. Even though a large number of visitors entered the store, many left without making any purchase. They weren't impressed by our imprinted items."

135-138번 문제는 다음 기사에 관한 것입니다.

Kew 식물원 소식

KEW (10월 16일) – Kew 왕립 식물원의 방문객들은 이제 입구에서 환영 표지판에 표시된 선명한 색채의 새 로고의 환영을 받는다. 대부분의 사람들이 이 새 로고에 만족한다고 말하는데, 이것은 형형색색의 야생화 꽃다발을 특징으로 하고 있다.

식물원 경영진은 대중의 의견에 근거하여 오래된 로고를 교체하기로 했다. "우리는 식물원에서 상자들에 들어 있는 의견 카드를 모으고 온라인 설문 조사에 대한 응답을 검토했습니다. 기존 로고에 대한 반응이 부정적이 되었다는 것을 알게 되었죠."라고 Kew Evening Courier와의 인터뷰에서 식물원 원장 Jacob Kunchai가 말했다. 옛 로고는 정교한 튜더 양식의 온실 그림 위에 식물원의 이름이 적혀 있었다.

새로운 디자인은 Nonpareil Graphics에서 제출되었다. **그중 세 개가 식물원 홈페이지에 게시되었다.** 회원들에게 청하여 어느 것이 가장 매력적인 로고가 될지 선정하도록 했다. 이사회는 회원들의 결정이 매우 훌륭하다고 인정했다. 식물원 현장 방문객 매장 운영자 Jamie Lee는 회원들이 선택한 새 로고에 만족하는 사람 중 한 명이다. 새 로고는 이제 의류와 기타 상품에 있고, 그녀는 그것이 판매량을 늘리는 데 도움을 줄 것이라고 확신한다. "이전에 저는 자주 실망했어요. 많은 수의 방문객이 매장에 들어왔는데도 상당수는 아무것도 구매하지 않고 나가버렸거든요. 로고가 새겨진 우리 제품들에 깊은 인상을 받지 않은 것이죠."

어휘 royal 왕립의 botanical garden 식물원 greet 맞다, 환영하다 bright (색채가) 선명한 display 진열하다, 표시하다 feature 특징으로 삼다 wildflower 야생화 management 경영진 on the basis of ~에 근거하여 input 의견; 입력 deposit 두다, 놓다 questionnaire 설문지 discover 알게 되다 receptivity 받아들임, 수용 director 책임자 courier 신문, 통신 spell out 철자를 옳게 말하다[쓰다] drawing 소묘, 데생 elaborate 정교한 Tudor 튜더 양식의 greenhouse 온실 submit 제출하다 invite sb to-V ~가 ~하도록 요청하다 board 이사회 acknowledge 인정하다 superb 대단히 훌륭한 on-site 현장의 merchandise (매장 판매용) 상품 previously 전에 make a purchase 구매하다 imprint (상표를) 찍다, 새기다

문장 분석

1. Visitors (to Royal Botanical Gardens, Kew) are now greeted / by a bright new logo (displayed on the welcome sign) / at the entry gate.

➡ ( )로 묶인 전치사구와 분사 구문은 각각 바로 앞에 있는 명사 Visitors와 logo를 수식한다. 동사 are now

greeted는 by와 at으로 시작하는 전치사구 두 개의 수식을 모두 받는다.

2. Jamie Lee, the manager of the Botanical Gardens on-site visitors' shop, is one of those (who are) happy with the new logo selected by members.

➡ those 뒤에 who are가 생략되어 있다. '주격 관계대명사 + be동사'는 생략할 수 있다. Part 5, 6 문법 문제로 one of ------- happy with the new logo가 출제될 수 있다. 빈칸 뒤에 who로 시작하는 구문이나, 분사 구문, 형용사구 등이 보이면 정답은 무조건 those이다.

3. Even though a large number of visitors entered the store, many (visitors) left without making any purchase.

➡ many는 부사절의 'visitors 중 상당수'를 가리킨다. many나 some은 앞에 등장하는 어떤 명사를 가리켜 그중 '그중 상당수'나 '일부'라는 의미로 사용된다.

---

139. What does the article discuss?

(A) A prospective business partnership
(B) A modification made to a graphic design
(C) Promotion of an upcoming exhibit
(D) New signs identifying plants in the gardens

어휘 prospective 예상되는, 장래의 modification 수정, 변경 promotion 홍보 upcoming 다가오는, 곧 있을 exhibit 전시 identify 식별하다, 알아보다

해석 기사는 무엇을 논하는가?
(A) 예상되는 업무 제휴
(B) 그래픽 디자인에 대한 변경
(C) 다가오는 전시회 홍보
(D) 식물원에서 식물을 식별하는 새 표지판

해설 주제를 물어보는 질문이므로 지문의 도입부를 잘 읽어야 한다. 첫 문단은 식물원 입구의 환영 표지판에 있는 로고가 변경되었고, 방문객들이 마음에 들어 한다는 내용이다.

---

140. Who made the final decision about the logo?

(A) Employees of Nonpareil Graphics
(B) The director of Kew Botanical Gardens
(C) The manager of the visitors' shop

(D) Members of Kew Botanical Gardens

어휘 make a final decision 최종 결정을 하다 employee 직원 director 책임자

해석 로고에 대한 최종 결정은 누가 내렸는가?
(A) Nonpareil Graphics의 직원들
(B) Kew 식물원 원장
(C) 방문객 매장 운영자
(D) Kew 식물원 회원들

해설 셋째 문단에 회원들에게 Nonpareil Graphics가 제출한 디자인 중 어느 것이 가장 매력적인지 선택하라고 요청했고, 식물원 이사회가 회원들의 선택이 탁월하다는 것을 인정했다는 내용이 있으므로 로고를 선택한 것은 식물원 회원들임을 추론할 수 있다.

---

141. What did Ms. Lee imply about the visitors' shop?

(A) It was not visited by enough people.
(B) Its aesthetics had to be improved.
(C) It was not easy to locate the spot.
(D) The business was not flourishing.

어휘 aesthetics 미학 locate ~의 위치를 찾아내다 spot 장소, 자리 flourish 번창하다

해석 Ms. Lee는 방문객 매장에 대해 무엇을 암시하는가?
(A) 충분한 수의 사람들이 방문하지 않았다.
(B) 미적인 요소들이 개선되어야 했다.
(C) 장소를 찾아내기가 쉽지 않았다.
(D) 사업이 번창하지 않았다.

해설 마지막 문단에 나오는 운영자의 인터뷰 내용으로 정답을 추론할 수 있다. 많은 사람이 매장에 들어왔지만, 상당수는 상품을 사지 않고 그냥 나가는 것을 보면서 실망한 날이 많았고, 로고가 새겨진 물건이 방문객들에게 깊은 인상을 주지 못했다고 생각하고 있으므로, 이전에는 이 사업이 잘되지 않았음을 암시하고 있다.

---

142. In which of the positions marked [1], [2], [3], and [4] does the following sentence best belong?

"Three of them were posted on the Botanical Gardens Web site."

(A) [1]
(B) [2]
(C) [3]
(D) [4]

어휘 post 게시하다 mark 표시하다 belong in ~에 맞다

해석 다음 문장은 [1], [2], [3], [4]로 표시된 자리 중 어느 곳에 가장 알맞은가?
"그중 세 개가 식물원 홈페이지에 게시되었다."
(A) [1]
(B) [2]
(C) [3]
(D) [4]

해설 주어진 문장 속에서 앞뒤 문장과 연결 고리가 되는 키워드를 찾아야 한다. 키워드인 them이 가리키는 복수 명사는 [3]의 앞 문장에 있는 New Designs이다. 주어진 문장을 [3]에 넣고 앞뒤 문장을 읽어 보면 문맥이 자연스럽다.

Questions 143-147 refer to the following article and letter.

TRANSFORMING THE LOOK OF RIVER STREET AREA

SAVANNAH CITY — 143.Following the announcement of the relocation of the city's art museum across town into a larger building on East Bay Street, the mayor's office has been soliciting proposals for a new use of the museum's existing space on River Street. Numerous proposals from both local and national developers have been presented. Two proposals in particular are emerging as strong contenders.

144.(D)Among the bids, the one submitted by Diwikar Corporation to put up a high-rise office building on the site was fairly promising. This project would attract a number of new businesses and generate jobs in the local area over the next five years. 146.Nevertheless, this is an ambitious plan that would require almost three years to realize. In addition, since business tenants normally require full-day parking privileges for their employees, 145.the parking situation in the district could become even more challenging than at present. 147.Diwikar, a ten-year-old firm headquartered in Portland, is currently completing similar construction projects in Vancouver and Seattle.

Another proposal has come from PXY Enterprises, a developer of commercial buildings in the city. 144.(C)The company has put forward an elaborate plan for a new shopping center, complete with department stores, restaurants, and a movie theater. This is an attractive option for the city because it would provide residents with a much sought-after shopping and entertainment area. PXY Enterprises is best known for its renovation of the city's Lake District.

In a recent poll, Savannah City residents were asked which plan they prefer. Results showed a somewhat higher level of support for the PXY Enterprises proposal, although the general feeling among residents is that both plans would be beneficial to the city's economy. 144.(A)One group of citizens, however, is strongly opposed to the development of the area for commercial interests and is petitioning the city to reserve the space for a community park.

— Dina Herrera

143-147번 문제는 다음 기사와 편지에 관한 것입니다.

RIVER 가(街) 지역 외관의 탈바꿈

SAVANNAH 시 – 시립 미술관을 도시 건너편 East Bay 가(街)에 있는 더 큰 건물로 이전한다는 발표 이후 시장실은 River 가(街)에 현재 미술관 자리의 새로운 용도를 위한 기획안을 받고 있다. 지역과 전국의 개발업체들로부터 수많은 기획안이 제출되었다. 특별히 두 개의 기획안이 강력한 경쟁 안(案)으로 대두되고 있다.

입찰 제안서 중에서 Diwikar 사(社)가 제출한 부지에 고층 사무실 건물을 짓겠다는 안이 상당히 유망하다. 이 프로젝트는 앞으로 5년에 걸쳐 해당 지역에 많은 신규 사업체를 끌어들이고 일자리를 창출할 것이다. 그렇지만, 이것은 실현하는 데 거의 3년을 요하는 원대한 계획이다. 게다가 사업을 하는 임차인들은 보통 자기 직원들을 위한 종일 주차 특전을 요구하기 때문에 이 지구(地區)의 주차 상황이

현재보다 훨씬 더 어려워질 수 있다. Portland에 본사를 두고 있는 10년 된 기업 Diwikar는 현재 Vancouver와 Seattle에서도 유사한 건설 프로젝트를 마무리 짓는 중이다.

다른 기획안은 시내의 상업용 건물 개발업체 PXY Enterprises에서 나왔다. 이 회사는 백화점, 식당, 영화관이 완비된 새 쇼핑센터를 위한 정교한 계획을 내놓았다. 이는 주민들에게 많은 사람들이 찾는 쇼핑 및 엔터테인먼트 공간을 제공하기 때문에 도시에 매력적인 옵션이다. PXY Enterprises는 시의 Lake 지구 보수 공사로 가장 잘 알려져 있다.

최근 한 여론 조사에서 Savannah 시 주민들은 어느 계획을 선호하는지 질문받았다. 결과는 PXY Enterprises의 기획안에 대한 약간 더 높은 지지도를 보여주었지만, 주민들 사이의 전반적인 의견은 양쪽 계획이 모두 시의 경제에는 유익하다는 것이다. 그러나 한 시민 단체는 상업적 이익을 위한 지역 개발에 강력히 반대하고 있으며 그 공간을 근린공원 자리로 남겨둘 것을 시에 탄원하고 있다.

— Dina Herrera

어휘 transform 완전히 바꿔 놓다, 탈바꿈시키다 look 모양, 외관 announcement 발표 relocation 이전, 재배치 mayor 시장 solicit 요청하다 proposal 제안서, 기획안 existing 현재 사용되는 numerous 매우 많은 national 전국의 present 제출하다 in particular 특히 emerge 부상하다 contender 경쟁자 bid 입찰 (제안서) put up 세우다, 짓다 high-rise 고층의 site 부지 fairly 상당히, 꽤 promising 유망한 attract 끌어들이다 nevertheless 그렇기는 하지만 ambitious 야심 찬, 원대한 in addition 게다가 tenant 세입자, 임차인 normally 보통 privilege 특전, 특혜 district 지구, 지역 challenging 힘든, 어려운 at present 현재는 firm 회사 headquartered ~에 본부[본사]가 있는 currently 현재 complete 마무리 짓다 enterprise 기업 commercial 상업의 put forward ~을 내놓다, 제안하다 elaborate 정교한 complete with ~이 완비된 resident 주민 sought-after 많은 사람이 찾는 renovation 개조, 보수 poll 여론 조사 somewhat 약간, 다소 general feeling 전반적인 의견 beneficial 유익한, 이로운 be opposed to ~에 반대하다 interest 이익 petition 탄원[청원]하다 reserve 따로 남겨두다 community park 근린공원

문장 분석

1. The company has put forward an elaborate plan for a new shopping center, (which is) complete with department stores, restaurants, and a

movie theater.

➡ '주격 관계대명사 + be동사'를 생략하고, complete with department stores, restaurants, and a movie theater가 앞에 있는 new shopping center를 수식하고 있다.

Dear Editor,

I would like to comment on Ms. Herrera's article in the Savannah Times (July 2) on the proposed construction plans for River Street. 146.There is one factual misstatement I feel must be corrected for the sake of your readers.

146.Under the present proposal, the commercial office building designed by Diwikar would be completed in about two years. Moreover, since the structure would be developed in phases, some of the offices would be available for use as quickly as eighteen months from the start of construction.

I agree with Ms. Herrera that the parking demands of a commercial building pose a potential problem. However, Asina Amorapanth, vice president of planning at Diwikar, has already met several times with council member Damien Cosme to explore possible solutions.

Sincerely,
147.Thaksin Panupong
President, Diwikar Corporation

편집자께

제안된 River 가(街) 건설 계획안에 관한 7월 2일자 Savannah Times에 실린 Ms. Herrera의 기사에 대해 의견을 말하고 싶습니다. 제가 생각하기에 독자들을 위해 바로잡아야 하는 사실 관계가 잘못 기재되어 있는 진술이 있습니다.

현재의 제안대로 하면 Diwikar에 의해 설계되는 상업용 사무실 건물은 약 2년 안에 완공될 것입니다. 더욱이 구조물이 단계적으로 개발될 것이기 때문에 일부 사무실들은 공사를 시작한 지 단 18개월 만에 이용할 수 있습니다.

상업용 건물의 주차 수요가 잠재적인 문제를 제기한다는 점에 대해서는 Ms. Herrera의 의견에 동의합니다. 그러나 Diwikar의 기획 담당 부회장 Asina Amorapanth가 이미 여러 번 의회 의원인 Damien Cosme와 만나 가능한 해결책을 모색했습니다.

Diwikar 사(社) 회장
Thaksin Panupong 올림

어휘 comment on ~에 대해 의견을 말하다 factual 사실에 관한 misstatement 잘못된 진술 correct 바로잡다, 고치다 for the sake of ~를 위해서 moreover 더욱이, 게다가 structure 구조물 in phases 단계적으로 available 이용 가능한 as quickly as 단 ~만에 demand 수요 pose (위협·문제 등을) 제기하다 potential 잠재적인 planning 기획 explore 모색하다

문장 분석

1. There is one factual misstatement (which) I feel must be corrected for the sake of your readers.

➡ 주로 관계대명사의 생략은 '주격 관계대명사 + be동사'와 목적격 관계대명사에서 일어난다. 이 문장과 같이 be동사가 I feel이라는 삽입 구문 다음에 오는 경우에도 주격 관계대명사를 생략할 수 있다. 주격 관계대명사의 생략은 '주어 + 동사' 삽입 구문(I feel)이 있을 경우 가능하다.

---

143. What is the purpose of the article?

(A) To announce upcoming cultural events
(B) To describe the new businesses on River Street
(C) To encourage local residents to share opinions about an issue
(D) To provide information about possible construction projects

어휘 encourage *sb* to-V ~에게 ~할 것을 권장하다

해석 기사의 목적은 무엇인가?
(A) 곧 있을 문화 행사를 발표하는 것
(B) River 가(街)의 신규 사업체들에 대해 설명하는 것
(C) 지역 주민들에게 어떤 사안에 대한 의견을 공유하도록 권장하는 것
(D) 가능한 공사 프로젝트에 대한 정보를 제공하는 것

해설 기사의 첫 번째 문단에서 정답을 알 수 있다. River 가(街)에 있던 미술관이 이전하면 비게 될 공간의 활용법에 대한 두 가지 제안을 논할 것이라는 내용이다.

144. What is NOT mentioned as a possible new use for the River Street area?

(A) A public park
(B) An art museum
(C) A shopping center
(D) An office building

해석 River 가(街) 지역의 가능한 새 용도로 언급되지 않는 것은 무엇인가?
(A) 공원
(B) 미술관
(C) 쇼핑센터
(D) 사무실 건물

해설 기사를 주의 깊게 읽으며 각 항목을 하나씩 대조하여 언급되지 않은 것을 찾아내 보자.

---

145. What is implied about Savannah City?

(A) Its Lake District is in need of renovation.
(B) The city has used Diwikar Corporation before.
(C) It is known for its downtown shopping district.
(D) Parking is considered a problem in the city.

어휘 in need of ~이 필요한 corporation 기업, 법인 downtown 중심부 shopping district 상점가

해석 Savannah 시에 대해 무엇이 암시되어 있는가?
(A) Lake 지구는 보수가 필요하다.
(B) 전에 Diwikar 사(社)를 이용한 적이 있다.
(C) 중심부의 상점가로 알려져 있다.
(D) 주차가 문제점으로 여겨지고 있다.

해설 기사의 두 번째 문단에서 "이 지구(地區)의 주차 상황이 현재보다 훨씬 더 어려워질 수 있다(the parking situation in the district could become even more challenging than at present)"는 내용이 이전부터 이 지역에서는 주차난이 있었음을 암시하고 있다.

---

146. What is Mr. Panupong's main complaint about the article?

(A) It provided an inaccurate timetable.
(B) It misquoted Asina Amorapanth.
(C) It did not report the results of a poll.
(D) It did not mention any benefits of his company's proposal.

어휘 inaccurate 부정확한, 오류가 있는 timetable 일정표 misquote (말·글을) 잘못 인용하다 benefit 이점

해석 기사에 대한 Mr. Panupong의 주요 불만 사항은 무엇인가?
(A) 오류가 있는 일정을 제시했다.
(B) Asina Amorapanth의 말을 잘못 인용했다.
(C) 여론 조사 결과를 보도하지 않았다.
(D) 자기 회사 제안의 이점을 전혀 언급하지 않았다.

연계 추론 Mr. Panupong은 편지 첫 번째 문단에서 기사에 사실에 대한 잘못된 진술(factual misstatement)이 있다고 지적하면서, 두 번째 문단에서 기획안이 채택된다면 Diwikar 가 설계하는 건물은 2년 정도면 완공될 것이며(Under the present proposal, the commercial office building designed by Diwikar would be completed in about two years.), 일부 사무실은 공사 18개월 만에 입주가 가능하다고(some of the offices would be available for use as quickly as eighteen months from the start of construction) 설명하고 있다. 그런데 기사에서는 건물 완공에 3년이 걸린다는 내용이 있다(this is an ambitious plan that would require almost three years to realize). 그러므로 Mr. Panupong의 불만 사항은 기사가 전달하는 일정에 오류가 있다는 점이다.

---

147. What is suggested about Mr. Panupong?

(A) He has an office in Savannah City.
(B) He recently built a shopping complex.
(C) He is involved with a project in Vancouver.
(D) He previously collaborated with Dina Herrera.

어휘 complex 복합 건물, (건물) 단지 be involved with[in] ~에 관여하다 previously 이전에 collaborate 협력하다

해석 Mr. Panupong에 대해 무엇이 암시되어 있는가?
(A) Savannah 시에 사무실이 있다.
(B) 최근에 쇼핑 단지를 지었다.
(C) Vancouver에서 하는 프로젝트에 관여하고 있다.
(D) 이전에 Dina Herrera와 협력했다.

연계 추론 편지 끝부분을 보면 Mr. Panupong이 Diwikar 사(社)의 회장임을 알 수 있고, 기사 둘째 문단에서 Diwikar 사(社)는 Vancouver에서 프로젝트를 진행하고 있다고 나와 있다(currently completing similar construction projects in Vancouver and Seattle). 따라서 Mr. Panupong은 이 프로젝트의 관계자라고 할 수 있다.

PART 5 & 6 Exercise

101 (D)	**102** (B)	**103** (C)	**104** (D)	**105** (D)
106 (D)	**107** (C)	**108** (A)	**109** (D)	**110** (D)
111 (D)	**112** (A)	**113** (D)	**114** (C)	**115** (A)

101. The designers have been asked to create a ------- new logo for the *Polymer Arts* Magazine.

(A) completion
(B) completes
(C) completing
(D) completely

어휘 be asked to-V ~하라고 요청받다 completion 완성 complete 완전한; 완료하다

해석 디자이너들은 Polymer Arts 잡지를 위해 완전히 새로운 로고를 만들어 달라는 요구를 받았다.

해설 빈칸 앞뒤 a ------- new logo를 보면 정답을 알 수 있다. '------- + 형용사 + 명사' 구조이면 부사 (D)가 정답이다.

102. The new layout of Voltas Electronics' Web site will make the company's product information more ------- accessible to consumers.

(A) ready
(B) readily
(C) readier
(D) readied

어휘 layout 배치, 레이아웃 readily 손쉽게 accessible to ~에 접근[입장/이용] 가능한

해석 Voltas 전자 웹사이트의 새 레이아웃은 회사의 제품 정보를 소비자들이 더 쉽게 이용할 수 있게 할 것이다.

해설 빈칸 앞뒤 more ------- accessible을 보고 정답을 알아내자. 빈칸은 형용사 accessible을 수식하는 자리이고 부사가 형용사를 수식하므로 부사 (B)가 정답이다.

103. Terms and conditions ------- agreed upon cannot be changed even when you order special goods or abnormal quantities.

(A) original
(B) origin
(C) originally
(D) originality

어휘 terms and conditions (계약, 지불의) 조건 original 원래의 origin 기원 originality 독창성 agree (up)on ~에 대해 의견이 일치되다, 합의를 보다 abnormal 비정상적인 quantity 수량

해석 최초에 합의된 계약 조건은 특별 상품이나 비정상적인 수량을 주문할 때에도 변경될 수 없습니다.

해설 빈칸 앞뒤 Terms and conditions ------- agreed upon을 잘 보자. agreed upon이 Terms and conditions를 수식하여 '합의된 계약 조건'이라는 뜻이다. 빈칸은 준동사인 과거분사를 수식하는 자리이므로 부사 (C)가 정답이다.

104. The ------- made by President Minako Ishikawa was well-received by the new employees of Eckero, Inc.

(A) addresses
(B) addressable
(C) addressed
(D) address

어휘 give[make/deliver] an address 연설하다 address 고심하다, 다루다 addressable 고심해 볼 만한, 다룰 수 있는 be well-received 호평받다

해석 Minako Ishikawa 회장이 한 연설은 Eckero 사(社) 신입 직원들로부터 호평을 받았다.

해설 빈칸 뒤에 있는 분사 구문 made by President Minako Ishikawa는 수식어구이므로 제외하고 빈칸 앞뒤 The ------- was well-received만 보면 정답을 알 수 있다. was well-received가 동사이고 빈칸은 주어 자리이므로 명사가 정답이다. 그런데 동사가 단수형이므로 단수 명사 (D)가 정답이다.

105. According to the survey results, Corchester residents were ------- in favor of adding bicycle paths along the riverbank.

(A) overwhelms
(B) overwhelm
(C) overwhelming
(D) overwhelmingly

어휘 overwhelm 압도하다 overwhelming 압도적인 in favor of ~를 찬성하여, 지지하여 bicycle path 자전거 전용 도로 riverbank 강둑, 강기슭

해석 설문 조사 결과에 따르면 Corchester 주민들은 강둑을 따라 자전거 도로를 추가하는 것에 압도적으로 찬성했다.

해설 빈칸 앞뒤 were ------- in favor of를 보면서 정답을 알아내자. 전치사구 in favor of를 수식하려면 부사가 필요하므로 (D)가 정답이다.

106. Please congratulate Rachel Hutchinson, ------- of the Leadership Award in Nursing at Winthrop Hospital.

(A) won
(B) wins
(C) winning
(D) winner

어휘 congratulate 축하하다 win 이기다; 승리 winning 우승한, 성공적인 winner 승리자, 수상자 nursing 간호직[업무]

해석 Winthrop 병원의 간호 부문 지도자상 수상자 Rachel Hutchinson을 축하해 주세요.

해설 Rachel Hutchinson과 ------- of the Leadership Award in Nursing이 동격이므로 의미상 사람이 되도록 (D)가 빈칸에 들어가야 한다.

107. -------, the engineering firm is going to invest more in ocean power technology by establishing another subsidiary in Denmark.

(A) Presumption
(B) Presumable
(C) Presumably
(D) Presumed

어휘 presumption 추정 presumable 추정할 수 있는, 있음직한 presumably 아마, 짐작건대 presume ~라고 추정하다[여기다/생각하다] firm 회사 subsidiary 자(子)회사

해석 짐작건대 그 엔지니어링 회사는 덴마크에 자회사를 하나 더 설립함으로써 해양 발전 기술에 더 많이 투자할 것이다.

해설 -------, the engineering firm is going to invest 까지 읽으면 정답을 알 수 있다. '-------, 주어 + 동사' 구조이므로, 빈칸에는 부사 (C)가 알맞다.

108. Since he assumed the ownership of JWT Express Transport five years ago, Astrid Barretto has earned the ------- of his staff.

(A) admiration
(B) admire
(C) admired
(D) admires

어휘 assume (책임, 역할을) 맡다, 획득하다 ownership 소유(권) express 속달의 transport 수송 earn 얻다[받다] admiration 감탄, 존경 admire 존경하다; 감탄하며 바라보다

해석 Astrid Barretto는 5년 전 JWT 특급 수송 회사의 소유주가 된 이후 직원들의 존경을 한 몸에 받아 왔다.

해설 빈칸 앞뒤 the ------- of만 보면 정답을 알 수 있다. '관사 + ------- + 전치사' 구조이므로 명사 (A)를 정답으로 고르자.

109. Yaris Ltd. welcomes your ------- regarding any aspect of our services.

(A) suggest
(B) suggests
(C) suggested
(D) suggestions

어휘 welcome 환영하다 regarding ~에 대하여 aspect 측면

해석 Yaris 사(社)는 서비스의 어떤 면에 대해서든 당신의 제안을 환영합니다.

해설 빈칸 앞뒤 your ------- regarding만 보면 정답을 알 수 있다. 소유격 대명사 뒤에 명사가 필요하므로 빈칸에는 (D)가 알맞다.

110. ------- fluctuating temperatures can cause various types of damage to specimens in the laboratory.

(A) Wide
(B) Widest
(C) Width
(D) Widely

어휘 wide 넓은; 완전히, 활짝 width 폭, 너비 widely 널리, 크게 fluctuate 변동[등락]을 거듭하다 specimen 표본

해석 크게 변동하는 온도는 실험실 표본에 여러 유형의 손상을 유발할 수 있다.

해설 ------- fluctuating temperatures를 보면서 정답을 알아내자. '------- + 형용사 + 명사'가 있으면 빈칸에는 형용사를 수식하는 부사를 써야 한다. (A)와 (D)가 모두 부사이지만, 의미상 '크게 변화하는 온도'가 자연스러우므로 (D)가 정답이다.

---

111. Judging from the ability to close deals he has shown in his previous job, Mr. Park is ------- a very skilled negotiator.

(A) clearest
(B) clear
(C) clarity
(D) clearly

어휘 judging from[by] ~로 판단하건대[미루어 보아] close a deal (with) 거래를 체결하다[성사시키다] previous 이전의 clear 분명한, 명확한 clarity 명확성, 선명도 skilled 숙련된, 노련한 negotiator 협상가, 교섭자

해석 이전 직장에서 보여준 거래를 성사시키는 능력으로 미루어 보아 Mr. Park은 분명히 매우 노련한 협상가이다.

해설 빈칸 앞뒤 is ------- a very skilled negotiator를 보면 정답을 알 수 있다. be동사와 명사 보어가 있는 완전한 2형식 문장으로 빈칸에는 부사 (D)가 알맞다.

---

112. Li Mines, Inc., a global ------- of copper, gold, and other metals, is trying to attract new clients in Europe.

(A) supplier
(B) supplying
(C) supplied
(D) supplies

어휘 mine 광산 global 세계적인 supplier 공급자, 공급 회사 supplies 용품, 비품; 공급품 copper 구리, 동 attract 유치(誘致)하다

해석 구리와 금 및 기타 금속의 세계적인 공급업체인 Li 광산 주식회사는 유럽에서 신규 고객을 유치하기 위해 노력하고 있다.

해설 빈칸 앞뒤 a global ------- of를 보면 형용사 뒤 빈칸에 명사가 들어가야 한다는 것을 알 수 있다. (A)와 (D)가 모두 명사이지만, 빈칸 앞에 관사 a가 있으므로 단수형 명사 (A)가 정답이다.

---

113. Alamitos West Health Care Center requests that all employees attending the international medical conference next month make travel ------- by the end of the week.

(A) arranged
(B) arranges
(C) arranging
(D) arrangements

어휘 health care center 보건 진료소 attend 참석하다 conference (대규모) 회의, 학술 대회 make travel arrangements 여행[출장]을 준비하다

해석 Alamitos 보건 진료소는 다음 달 국제 의료 학회에 참석하는 모든 직원들은 주말까지 출장을 준비할 것을 요청합니다.

해설 빈칸 앞뒤 make travel ------- by에서 정답을 알아내자. make는 동사이고, travel -------는 목적어이다. 명사 뒤 빈칸에는 명사가 들어가서 복합명사가 되어야 하므로 (D)가 정답이다.

---

114. President Yamada plans on ------- the company's expansion at the press conference, which will be held at Smith Convention Center tomorrow morning.

(A) outline
(B) outlined
(C) outlining
(D) outliner

어휘 plan on ~할 예정[계획]이다 outline 개요를 서술하다; 개요, 윤곽 outliner 문서 편집 프로그램 hold a press conference 기자 회견을 열다

해석 Yamada 회장은 기자 회견에서 회사의 확장에 대해 간단히 말할 계획이고, 이는 내일 아침 Smith 컨벤션 센터에서 열릴 것이다.

해설 빈칸에 전치사 on의 목적어가 들어가야 하므로 명사 (A)와 (D), 동명사 (C) 중 선택해야 한다. 빈칸 뒤에 목적어 the company's expansion이 있으므로 동명사 (C)가 정답이다.

---

115. The maintenance department has submitted an initial budget ------- for upgrading our security system.

(A) estimate
(B) estimates
(C) estimating

(D) estimations

어휘 maintenance department 시설관리부 initial 처음의, 초기의 estimate 견적서; 추산[추정]하다 estimation 판단, 평가; 평가치 security 보안

해석 시설관리부는 보안 시스템을 업그레이드하기 위한 초기 예산 견적서를 제출했다.

해설 빈칸 앞뒤 an initial budget ------- for를 보고 정답을 알아내자. 명사 budget 뒤에 빈칸이 있으므로 명사가 정답이다. (A)와 (B), (D)가 모두 명사인데, 앞에 관사 an이 있으므로 단수형 (A)가 정답이다.

Actual Test

101 (C)	**102** (B)	**103** (B)	**104** (C)	**105** (D)
106 (A)	**107** (D)	**108** (A)	**109** (B)	**110** (B)
111 (A)	**112** (A)	**113** (D)	**114** (A)	**115** (C)
116 (A)	**117** (A)	**118** (C)	**119** (D)	**120** (A)
121 (C)	**122** (A)	**123** (B)	**124** (D)	**125** (C)
126 (B)	**127** (B)	**128** (B)	**129** (B)	**130** (C)
131 (C)	**132** (D)	**133** (B)	**134** (A)	**135** (B)
136 (C)	**137** (B)	**138** (B)	**139** (C)	**140** (D)
141 (C)	**142** (A)	**143** (B)	**144** (D)	**145** (C)

Part 5

101. When applying a transparent screen protector to an Etin smartphone, affix the side with adhesive ------- to the display screen.

(A) direction
(B) directing
(C) directly
(D) directs

어휘 apply A to B A를 B에 바르다, 붙이다 transparent 투명한 protector 보호 장치 affix A to B A를 B에 붙이다, 부착하다 adhesive 접착제 direction 방향; 지시 directly (특정한 위치) 바로 ~에

해석 투명 스크린 보호 필름을 Etin 스마트폰에 붙일 때는 접착제가 있는 면을 바로 디스플레이 스크린에 부착하세요.

해설 빈칸 앞뒤 affix the side with adhesive ------- to the display screen을 보면서 정답을 알아내자. "접착제가 있는 면을 바로 디스플레이 스크린에 부착하세요."라는 의미가 되도록 빈칸에 부사 (C)를 넣어서 뒤에

있는 전치사구를 수식하게 한다.

102. Sales representatives are instructed to investigate the businesses of ------- customers before contacting them for the first time.

(A) total
(B) potential
(C) equal
(D) factual

어휘 sales representative 영업 사원 be instructed to-V ~하도록 지시받다, 교육받다 investigate 조사하다 factual 사실에 기반을 둔, 사실을 담은 for the first time 처음으로

해석 영업 사원들은 잠재 고객에게 처음 연락하기 전에 해당 고객이 하는 일을 조사하도록 교육받는다.

해설 항상 짝을 이루어 출제되는 어휘 문제를 암기하자. customers 앞에 빈칸이 있으면 언제나 형용사 potential이나 prospective가 정답이다.

103. The Mount Martha Briars Craft Market offers one-of-a-kind handcrafted ornaments that are not available -------.

(A) evidently
(B) elsewhere
(C) thoroughly
(D) beyond

어휘 craft 수공업, 공예 one-of-a-kind 특별한, 독특한 handcrafted 수공예품인 ornament 장식품 evidently 분명히, 눈에 띄게 elsewhere (어딘가) 다른 곳에서[으로] thoroughly 철저히, 꼼꼼하게 beyond 건너편에, 그 너머에

해석 Mount Martha Briars 공예품 시장은 다른 곳에서 구할 수 없는 독특한 수공예 장식품을 제공한다.

해설 빈칸 앞 단어만 보자. ornaments that are not available ------- ([(A) 분명히 (B) 다른 곳에서 (C) 철저히 (D) 그 너머에] 이용할 수 없는 장식품)의 의미를 자연스럽게 하는 부사 (B)를 선택해야 한다.

104. The Oceanic Preservation Society relies on generous donations from the local community for ------- its variety of research facilities.

(A) maintenance
(B) maintains

(C) maintaining

(D) maintain

어휘 oceanic 대양의, 바다의 preservation 보존, 보호 society 협회 generous 후한, 아낌없는 local community 지역 사회 maintenance 유지보수 maintain 유지하다 a variety of 다양한 facilities 시설

해석 해양 보존 협회는 다양한 연구 시설을 유지하기 위해 지역 사회의 아낌없는 기부에 의존하고 있다.

해설 빈칸 앞뒤 for ------- its variety of research facilities가 정답을 알려준다. 전치사 for의 목적어로 명사 (A)와 동명사 (C) 중 골라야 하는데, 빈칸 뒤에 목적어가 있으므로 동명사 (D)를 정답으로 선택해야 한다.

---

105. During exit interview surveys for employees leaving the company prematurely, you will be asked to reflect upon your ------- at this company.

(A) permission

(B) amount

(C) occasion

(D) experience

어휘 exit interview survey 퇴직자 면접 조사 prematurely 너무 이르게 reflect upon 되돌아보다, 반추하다 permission 허가 occasion 때, 경우

해석 너무 이르게 회사를 그만두는 직원들을 대상으로 하는 퇴사 면접 조사에서 당신은 이 회사에서의 경험을 되돌아보도록 요청받을 것입니다.

해설 빈칸 앞뒤 reflect upon your ------- at this company(이 회사에서의 [(A) 허가 (B) 금액/양 (C) 경우/때 (D) 경험]을 되돌아보다)의 의미를 자연스럽게 하는 (D)가 정답이다.

---

106. ------- Dr. Carreras, who will be in Barcelona, all the members of the surgical team will attend the appreciation gala dinner in Winnipeg.

(A) Except for

(B) Along with

(C) Whereas

(D) Likewise

어휘 along with ~와 마찬가지로 surgical 외과의, 수술의 appreciation 감사 gala 경축 행사

해석 Dr. Carreras를 제외하고, 그는 바르셀로나에 있을 것이고, 외과팀 전원은 Winnipeg에서 열리는 감사 경축

만찬에 참석할 예정이다.

해설 Dr. Carreras는 Barcelona에 있고, 나머지 팀원들은 모두 Winnipeg에 있을 것이다. 그러므로 'Dr. Carreras를 제외하고'라는 의미가 되도록 전치사 (D)를 정답으로 선택해야 한다.

---

107. The chapter on traveling in Southeast Asia was ------- the best part of the book.

(A) definite

(B) definitive

(C) defined

(D) definitely

어휘 definite 확실한, 확고한 definitive 최종적인, 확정적인 define 정의하다; 규정하다 definitely 분명히, 틀림없이, 절대로

해석 동남아시아 여행에 대한 장이 확실히 이 책에서 가장 좋은 부분이다.

해설 빈칸 앞뒤 was ------- the best part of the book을 보면서 정답을 알아내자. 'be + ------- + the(한정사)' 구조이면 빈칸에 부사 (D)가 들어가야 한다.

---

108. The investment manager will have extensive authority on asset selection and make a ------- assessment of the funds' profitability.

(A) regular

(B) contemporary

(C) frugal

(D) immature

어휘 extensive 광범위한, 폭넓은 authority 권한 asset 자산, 재산 contemporary 동시대의, 현대의 frugal 절약하는 immature 미숙한 make an assessment of ~를 평가하다 profitability 수익성

해석 투자 매니저는 자산 선택에 대한 광범위한 권한을 가질 것이며 펀드의 수익성을 정기적으로 평가할 것이다.

해설 빈칸 앞뒤 make a ------- assessment of(~를 [(A) 정기적으로 (B) 동시대에 (C) 절약하여 (D) 미숙하게] 평가하다)의 의미를 자연스럽게 하는 형용사 (D)를 정답으로 선택해야 한다.

---

109. The entire medical staff of CPC Hospital must take ------- while caring for patients to keep themselves safe and healthy.

(A) element
(B) precautions
(C) advantage
(D) conditions

어휘 entire 전체의 take precautions 예방 조치를 취하다 element 요소, 성분 care for ~를 돌보다

해석 CPC 병원의 전체 의료진은 환자를 돌보는 동안 자신을 안전하고 건강하게 지키기 위해 예방 조치를 취해야 한다.

해설 take precautions는 자주 사용되는 표현이므로 암기하고 있으면 쉽게 문제를 풀 수 있다.

---

110. ------- in the evening management classes has nearly tripled thanks to Professor Bradely's easy and efficient lecture.

(A) Enroll
(B) Enrollment
(C) Enrolls
(D) Enrolling

어휘 enroll in ~에 등록하다 enrollment 등록; 등록자 수 nearly 거의 triple 3배가 되다 thanks to ~ 덕분에 efficient 효율적인

해석 야간 경영학 수업의 등록자 수는 Bradely 교수의 쉽고 효율적인 강의 덕분에 거의 세 배가 되었다.

해설 빈칸 뒤의 전치사구 in the evening management classes를 제외하면 has nearly tripled는 동사(구)이고 빈칸은 주어 자리임을 알 수 있다. 그러므로 명사 (B)와 동명사 (D) 중에서 선택하면 된다. enroll은 enroll in으로 자주 사용되어 문법상 동명사가 빈칸에 들어갈 수 있지만, 동사 has nearly tripled(거의 세 배가 되었다)의 의미에 맞으려면 주어로는 '등록자 수'를 뜻하는 (B)가 정답으로 알맞다.

---

111. In spite of ------- pressure by other countries to open its automobiles market, the government refuses to discuss this sensitive issue.

(A) mounting
(B) approachable
(C) respective
(D) deceptive

어휘 mounting 증가하는, 고조되는 approachable 말을 붙이기 쉬운 respective 각자의, 각각의 deceptive 기만적인, 현혹하는

해석 다른 나라들로부터 자동차 시장을 개방하라는 압력이 증가함에도 불구하고 정부는 이 민감한 사안에 대해 논의하기를 거부하고 있다.

해설 항상 짝을 이루어 출제되는 어휘 문제를 암기해 두자. pressure 앞에 빈칸이 있으면 정답은 mounting이나 increasing이다.

---

112. ------- are the accounts that Sales Director asked Mike Thompson to update by the end of the day.

(A) These
(B) Something
(C) Another
(D) More

어휘 accounts (회계) 장부

해석 이것들은 영업 부장님이 Mike Thompson에게 퇴근 전까지 업데이트하라고 요청한 장부입니다.

해설 빈칸 뒤에 동사 are이 있으므로 단수 명사인 (B)와 (C)는 제외한다. (D)는 비교 대상과 함께 써야 하므로, (A)가 정답이다.

---

113. In an effort to improve -------, Moon Microprocessors is offering financial incentives for enhanced job performance.

(A) produces
(B) producer
(C) productive
(D) productivity

어휘 in an effort to-V ~하려는 노력의 일환으로 productivity 생산성 incentive 장려책, 우대책 job performance 업무 실적[성과]

해석 생산성을 높이기 위한 노력의 일환으로 Moon Microprocessors는 향상된 업무 실적에 대해 금전적 장려책을 제공하고 있다.

해설 타동사 improve의 목적어가 필요하므로 명사 (B)와 (D) 중 정답을 선택해야 한다. producer는 보통명사이고 productivity는 추상명사이다. 그런데 단수 명사인 producer를 빈칸에 넣으려면 앞에 관사가 있거나 복수형으로 써야 한다. 따라서 관사가 필요 없는 추상명사 (D)가 정답이다.

114. Entering the European market was the best decision we made over the ------- ten years.

(A) past
(B) next
(C) following
(D) ultimate

[어휘] following (시간상으로) 그 다음의 ultimate 궁극[최종]적인, 최후의

[해석] 유럽 시장에 진출한 것은 지난 10년 동안 우리가 내린 가장 좋은 결정이었다.

[해설] 'in[for/over] the past[last/next/following] + 기간'은 항상 짝을 이루어 출제되므로 반드시 기억하자. (A)와 (B), (C) 중 정답을 선택해야 하는데, 빈칸을 포함하는 절의 시제가 과거(we made)이므로 '지난 10년 동안'을 뜻하는 형용사 (B)가 정답이다.

---

115. Starting next month, ------- umbrella covers will no longer be available for visitors at the entrances of government buildings.

(A) driving
(B) thermal
(C) disposable
(D) gardening

[어휘] starting ~부터 (시작하여) driving 강력한, 영향력이 큰 thermal 보온성이 좋은 disposable 일회용의 gardening 원예

[해석] 다음 달부터 정부 청사 입구에서 일회용 우산 커버는 더 이상 방문객들에게 제공되지 않는다.

[해설] '------- umbrella covers([(A) 영향력이 큰 (B) 보온성이 좋은 (C) 일회용의 (D) 원예] 우산 커버)'의 의미를 자연스럽게 하는 형용사 (B)가 정답이다.

---

116. Leafman Capital has made successful ------- in two emerging data companies.

(A) investments
(B) invested
(C) invest
(D) investor

[어휘] make an investment in ~에 투자하다 emerging 최근 생겨난, 신흥의

[해석] Leafman Capital은 두 개의 신생 데이터 회사에 성공

적인 투자를 했다.

[해설] 빈칸 앞뒤 has made successful ------- in을 보고 정답을 알아내자. 동사 has made의 목적어가 되면서 형용사 successful의 수식을 받는 명사가 필요하다. (A)와 (D)가 명사이지만, 단수 보통명사 investor를 쓰려면 앞에 관사가 필요하므로 복수형인 (A)가 정답이다.

---

117. The steel maker said that its fast rise in overseas sales was attributable to its flexibility in meeting market changes and providing high quality material at ------- prices.

(A) affordable
(B) allowable
(C) accountable
(D) compatible

[어휘] steel maker 제강업자, 철강업체 rise in ~의 증가, 상승 attributable to ~가 원인인, ~에 기인하는 flexibility 유연성 meet changes 변화에 대응하다 high quality 고품질의, 고급의 affordable (가격 등이) 알맞은, 저렴한 allowable 허용되는 accountable (해명할) 책임이 있는 compatible 호환이 되는

[해석] 철강업체가 해외 판매의 빠른 증가는 시장 변화에 유연하게 대응하고 고품질의 자재를 저렴한 가격에 제공한 덕분이라고 말했다.

[해설] 짝을 이루어 출제되는 어휘 문제를 암기해 두자. price 앞에 빈칸이 있으면 언제나 affordable이나 reasonable이 정답이다.

---

118. Despite the ringing endorsement from the former chairperson, Mr. Ishihara has decided to ------- from consideration for the position.

(A) abandon
(B) classify
(C) withdraw
(D) absorb

[어휘] ringing 강력한, 호소력 있는 endorsement (공개적인) 지지 former 과거[이전]의 chairperson 의장, 회장 abandon 버리다; 포기하다 classify 분류하다, 구분하다 withdraw from ~을 그만두다, ~에서 탈퇴하다 absorb 흡수하다 consideration for ~대한 고려

[해석] 전 회장의 강력한 지지에도 불구하고 Mr. Ishihara는 그 자리에 대한 고려를 철회하기로 결정했다.

[해설] 빈칸 뒤에 전치사 from이 있는데, (A)와 (D)는 목적어가 필요한 타동사이므로 제외한다. (B)는 자동사이지만

from과 함께 사용하지 않는다. (C)가 '~을 그만두다'라는 뜻으로 from과 함께 사용하므로 정답이다.

---

119. The Texas Department of Public Safety has not yet given its ------- to Dhital Petroleum's request for building permits.

(A) approved
(B) approvingly
(C) approves
(D) approval

어휘 approvingly 시인하여, 만족스럽게 petroleum 석유 request 요청 building permit 건축 허가

해석 텍사스 공공안전부는 Dhital 석유회사의 건축 허가 요청에 아직 승인을 하지 않았다.

해설 빈칸 앞뒤 has not yet given its ------- to를 보고 정답을 알아내자. 소유격 대명사 뒤에는 명사가 필요하므로 빈칸에는 (D)가 알맞다.

---

120. Many ------- buyers have expressed intentions to take over the bankrupt company, but there has been no firm offer yet.

(A) prospective
(B) appreciable
(C) portable
(D) inevitable

어휘 prospective 유망한, 잠재의 appreciable 주목할 만한 portable 휴대가 쉬운, 휴대용의 intention 의사, 의도 take over 인수하다 bankrupt 파산한 firm 확고한, 변치 않을, 확실한

해석 많은 잠재 구매자가 파산한 회사를 인수하겠다는 의사를 표명했지만, 아직 확실한 제안은 없었다.

해설 client, customer, buyer 등의 명사 앞에 빈칸이 있으면 항상 potential이나 prospective가 정답이다.

---

121. The ------- of Saitama factory has had a significant impact on Lasner Technology's employee productivity.

(A) expanding
(B) expanded
(C) expansion
(D) expand

어휘 have an impact on ~에 영향을 주다 significant 중대

한, 의미 있는 employee productivity 직원 생산성

해석 Saitama 공장의 확장은 Lasner Technology의 직원 생산성에 큰 영향을 미쳤다.

해설 빈칸 앞뒤 The ------- of만 보고 정답을 알아내자. 빈칸은 관사와 전치사 사이로 명사가 들어가는 자리이다. 그러므로 정답은 (C)이다.

---

122. At Exraterram, all types of correspondence must be treated equally and responded to within three days ------- receipt.

(A) of
(B) throughout
(C) about
(D) by

어휘 correspondence 서신, 편지 respond to ~에 응답하다 receipt 받기, 수령, 인수, 접수

해석 Exraterram에서는 모든 유형의 서신이 동등하게 취급되어야 하며 수령 후 3일 이내에 응답하여야 한다.

해설 빈칸 앞뒤 within three days ------- receipt를 보고 '수령 후 3일 이내에'라는 의미가 되도록 전치사 (A)를 정답으로 선택해야 한다.

---

123. ------- Ms. Lee's blog dealing with workplace satisfaction is so popular, a major publishing house has offered her a book deal.

(A) In case
(B) Because
(C) Whenever
(D) Even if

어휘 deal with ~를 다루다 workplace 직장, 업무 현장 publishing house 출판사 book deal 출판 계약

해석 직장 만족도를 다루는 Ms. Lee의 블로그는 매우 인기 있었기 때문에 한 대형 출판사가 그녀에게 출판 계약을 제안했다.

해설 접속사 어휘 문제는 문장 전체를 읽고 두 절을 자연스럽게 연결하는 것을 선택하자. 첫 번째 절과 두 번째 절이 의미상 원인과 결과를 나타내므로 빈칸에는 (B)가 알맞다.

---

124. Mr. Bac's letter is in response to the fax and e-mail dated 20 and 23, March, -------.

(A) respects

(B) respecting
(C) respective
(D) respectively

어휘 in response to ~에 응하여[답하여] date 날짜를 적다[기입하다] respect 존경하다 respective 각자의, 각각의

해석 Mr. Bac의 편지는 각각 날짜가 3월 20일과 23일이라고 적혀 있는 팩스와 이메일에 대한 답장이다.

해설 명사를 제외한 모든 것은 부사가 수식한다. 빈칸은 20 and 23, March를 수식하는 자리이므로 부사 (D)가 정답이다.

---

125. The department is looking for a ------- candidate with experience in both the Singapore and Malaysia markets.

(A) retained
(B) numerous
(C) qualified
(D) definitive

어휘 retain 유지하다, 보유하다 definitive 최종적인, 확정적인

해석 부서에서는 싱가포르와 말레이시아 시장 모두에서 경험이 있는 자격을 갖춘 지원자를 찾고 있다.

해설 항상 짝을 이루어 출제되는 어휘 문제를 암기해 두자. candidate이나 applicant 앞에 빈칸이 있으면 언제나 qualified나 successful이 정답이다.

---

126. The newly hired logistics consultant's outstanding performance has resulted in faster ------- of goods to our stores.

(A) founding
(B) distribution
(C) treatment
(D) revision

어휘 logistics 물류 관리 logistics consultant 물류 관리사 outstanding 뛰어난, 걸출한 performance 수행, 실행 result in (그 결과) ~가 되다 founding 설립, 수립, 창립 distribution 배급, 유통 treatment 취급

해석 새로 고용된 물류 관리사의 뛰어난 업무 수행으로 상품이 우리 매장들에 더 빨리 유통되었다.

해설 빈칸 앞뒤 faster ------- of goods to our stores(상품이 우리 매장들에 더 빨리 [(A) 설립 (B) 유통 (C) 취급 (D) 수정])의 의미를 자연스럽게 하는 (B)가 정답이다.

---

127. -------, the college professor did not know that classes had been suspended in all levels because of an incoming typhoon.

(A) Apparent
(B) Apparently
(C) Appear
(D) Appearance

어휘 apparent ~인 것처럼 보이는 apparently 듣자[보아] 하니 (~인 것 같다) appearance 외모 suspend 중단하다, 유보하다 incoming 다가오는 typhoon 태풍

해석 보아하니 그 대학 교수는 다가오는 태풍으로 인해 모든 단계의 수업이 중단되었다는 것을 몰랐던 것 같다.

해설 '-------, 주어 + 동사' 구조이므로 빈칸에는 부사 (B)가 들어가야 한다.

---

128. The average precipitation in the contiguous U.S. ------- the past three years has been 26.57 inches.

(A) on
(B) for
(C) to
(D) under

어휘 average 평균의 precipitation 강수량 contiguous 인접한, 근접한

해석 지난 3년 동안 미국 인근의 평균 강수량은 26.57인치였다.

해설 'in[for/over] the past[last/next/following] + 기간'은 항상 짝을 이루어 출제되는 어휘이므로 문제를 보면 바로 정답을 고르자.

---

129. To provide quality feedback on the projects done by new employees, Ms. Vuong will be assigning individual mentors to ------- this year.

(A) recruited
(B) recruiter
(C) recruiting
(D) recruits

어휘 quality 양질의 assign 배치하다 recruit 모집하다; 신입 사원

해석 신입 직원들에 의해 진행된 프로젝트에 양질의 피드백을 제공하기 위해 Ms. Vuong은 올해 신입 사원들에게 개별 멘토를 배정할 것이다.

해설 빈칸 앞뒤 will be assigning individual mentors to ------- this year를 보면서 정답을 알아내자. 전치사 to의 목적어가 필요하므로 명사 (B)와 (D), 동명사 (C) 중에 정답을 고르면 된다. 빈칸 뒤에 목적어가 없으므로 (C)는 제외한다. 보통명사는 단수형으로 사용하려면 앞에 관사가 있어야 하므로 빈칸에는 (D)가 알맞다.

---

130. Although ------- planned for a warehouse, the facility was converted into another quality control laboratory by the management.

(A) original
(B) originality
(C) originally
(D) originate

어휘 warehouse 창고 originality 독창성 originate 비롯되다, 유래하다 be converted into ~로 전환되다, 개조되다 quality control 품질 관리 laboratory 실험실 management 경영진

해석 그 시설은 원래 창고로 계획되어 있었지만, 경영진에 의해 또 하나의 품질 관리 실험실로 전환되었다.

해설 빈칸 앞뒤 Although ------- planned for a warehouse에서 정답을 알아내자. 접속사 뒤에 분사 구문이 나와 있는데, 이를 수식할 수 있는 부사 (C)가 정답이다.

Part 6

Questions 131-134 refer to the following e-mail.

To: Tony Leung <tleung@mckinsey.com>
From: Megan Shetty
         <mshetty@mckinsey.com>
Subject: New Employee Forms
Date: September 1

Dear Mr. Leung,

Congratulations on your acceptance to our company. ^{131.}We are excited to have you join McKinsey & Associates. I have attached herewith some documents that will help you begin your successful career with us. They provide a brief ^{132.}orientation to McKinsey & Associates,

as well as an explanation of our company's various codes of conduct that you must adhere to. You will need to agree with these policies and rules, and some pages will require your signature to this effect. After ^{133.}signing those pages, please submit them to Thomas Lissner in the personnel department. He ^{134.}will file them for you.

Again, congratulations, and I look forward to working with you. Please feel free to contact me with any questions at extension 7532.

Best regards,
Megan Shetty

Enclosures

131-134번 문제는 다음 이메일에 관한 것입니다.

수신: Tony Leung ⟨tleung@mckinsey.com⟩
발신: Megan Shetty⟨mshetty@mckinsey.com⟩
제목: 신입 직원 서식
날짜: 9월 1일

Mr. Leung께,

회사에 채용되신 것을 축하합니다. McKinsey & Associates에 합류하시게 되어 기쁩니다. 여기 우리와 함께 성공적인 경력을 시작하도록 도와줄 몇 가지 문서를 첨부했습니다. 이 문서에서는 지켜야 할 McKinsey & Associates의 다양한 행동 강령에 대한 설명뿐 아니라 회사에 대한 간단한 오리엔테이션을 제공할 것입니다. 당신은 이 정책과 규칙에 동의해야 하며, 이런 취지로 몇몇 페이지는 서명을 요구합니다. 그 페이지에 서명하신 후에 인사부의 Thomas Lissner에게 제출하세요. 그가 당신을 위해 문서를 보관해 줄 것입니다.

다시 한 번 축하드리며, 함께 일하게 될 것을 기대하고 있습니다. 질문이 있을 때는 내선 번호 7532로 언제든지 문의해 주세요.

이만 줄입니다.
Megan Shetty

첨부 문서 있음

어휘 acceptance 채용 attach 첨부하다 herewith 여기(이

편지[책/서류]와 함께) **brief** 간단한 **orientation to** ~에 대한 오리엔테이션, 예비 교육 **as well as** ~뿐 아니라 **code of conduct** 행동 강령 **adhere to** ~을 준수하다 **signature** 서명 **to this effect** 이런 취지로 **file** (서류를) 보관하다 **feel free to-V** 마음 놓고 ~해도 괜찮다 **extension** 내선, 구내전화 **enclosure** (편지에) 동봉된 것

문장 분석
....

They provide ①[a brief orientation to McKinsey & Associates], as well as ②[an explanation of our company's various codes of conduct that you must adhere to].

➡ as well as가 ①과 ②를 연결하여 동사 provide의 목적어가 되게 한다.

---

131. (A) Mr. Lissner will assist you in completing the necessary paperwork.
 (B) Your application will be processed no later than the end of the month.
 (C) We are excited to have you join McKinsey & Associates.
 (D) Any assistance you can provide for our new coworker would be appreciated.

어휘 assist *sb* in ~ing ~가 ~하는 것을 지원하다 complete 기입하다, 작성하다 application 지원(서) process 처리하다 no later than 늦어도 ~까지는 assistance 도움, 지원

해석 (A) Mr. Lissner가 필요한 서류를 작성하도록 도와줄 것입니다.
(B) 지원서는 늦어도 월말까지는 처리될 것입니다.
(C) McKinsey & Associates에 합류하게 되어 기쁩니다.
(D) 새 동료에게 어떤 도움을 제공해 주시든 감사하겠습니다.

해설 회사에 채용된 것을 축하한다는 말이 빈칸 앞에 있으므로 인사말이 이어지는 것이 알맞다.

---

132. (A) orient
 (B) oriental
 (C) oriented
 (D) orientation

어휘 orient 지향하게 하다, 맞추다 oriental 동양의, 동양인의 oriented ~ 지향의, ~ 경향이 있는

해설 빈칸 앞뒤 a brief ------ to를 보면, 빈칸은 형용사

brief의 수식을 받는 명사 자리이므로 (D)가 정답이다.

---

133. (A) editing
 (B) signing
 (C) typing
 (D) e-mailing

해설 앞 문장 and some pages will require your signature to this effect.를 보면 정답을 알 수 있다. 몇몇 페이지는 서명이 필요하다고 했으므로 "서명한 후에 제출하라"는 내용이 이어지는 것이 자연스럽다. 그러므로 (B)가 정답이다.

---

134. **(A) will file**
 (B) had filed
 (C) file
 (D) filing

해설 빈칸에 동사가 들어가야 하므로 준동사인 (D)는 제외한다. 주어가 He이므로 복수 동사인 (C)도 들어갈 수 없다. 앞 문장이 "제출하라"는 명령문이므로 "제출하면 Mr. Lissner가 보관해줄 것"이라는 내용을 표현하는 미래 시제 (A)가 알맞다.

Questions 135-138 refer to the following article.

TORONTO (13 August) — Simonte unveiled its annual Plant Showcase today. According to Simonte spokesman Toru Okamoto, this [135.]yearly offering highlights the company's latest efforts in botanical research. Many of these efforts result from customer surveys that sought to comprehend the most typical difficulties. [136.]Afterward, the research and development team works to develop varietals that address these challenges. This year, the company's specialized nurseries have turned out drought-tolerant breeds, such as the Dovyalis Apple Tree. These varietals can withstand prolonged dry conditions without sustaining damage. "Gardeners in desert [137.]regions will be especially fond of the Dovyalis," noted Okamoto. "And [138.]they might be interested in our new R-7 rose bushes as well, which flourish in a similar climate."

135-138번 문제는 다음 기사에 관한 것입니다.

토론토 (8월 13일) – Simonte가 오늘 연례 식물 발표를 공개했다. Simonte의 대변인 Toru Okamoto의 말에 따르면 이 연례행사는 식물학 연구에 대한 회사의 최근 성과를 강조한다. 이러한 성과 중 상당수는 가장 대표적인 어려움을 파악하려고 시도한 고객 설문 조사의 결과로 나온 것이다. 그 후에 연구개발팀이 이러한 어려움을 해결해 주는 변종들을 개발하기 위해 노력한다. 올해는 회사의 전문 묘목장에서 Dovyalis 사과나무와 같은 가뭄에 잘 견디는 품종들을 생산해 냈다. 이 변종들은 손상을 입지 않고 장기간의 건조한 환경을 견뎌낼 수 있다. "사막 지역의 원예 애호가들이 특히 Dovyalis를 좋아할 겁니다."라고 Okamoto는 말한다. "그리고 새로 나온 R-7 장미 나무에도 관심이 있을 것 같은데, 그것은 비슷한 기후에서 잘 자랍니다."

어휘 unveil 처음 공개하다 showcase 공개 행사, 발표회 spokesman 대변인 yearly 연례의 offering 제공된 것, 프로그램 highlight 강조하다 latest 최근의, 최신의 effort (노력의) 성과 botanical 식물(학)의 result from (~의 결과로) 발생하다 seek to-V ~하려고 (시도)하다 comprehend 알다, 파악하다 typical 전형적인, 대표적인 afterward 그 후에, 나중에 varietal 변종, 품종 address 다루다, 해결하려 하다 specialized 전문화된 nursery 묘목장 turn out (대량으로) ~을 생산하다 drought-tolerant 가뭄을 잘 견디는, 내건성의 breed 품종 withstand 견뎌[이겨] 내다 prolonged 오래 계속되는, 장기적인 conditions 상황, 환경 sustain (피해·손상 등을) 입다, 받다 gardener (취미로) 정원을 가꾸는 사람 note 특별히 언급하다 bush 관목, 덤불 flourish 잘 자라다

135. (A) daily
(B) weekly
(C) monthly
(D) yearly

해설 this ------ offering은 앞 문장의 its annual Plant Showcase를 가리키는 것이므로 annual과 뜻이 같은 (D)가 정답이다.

136. (A) The company occupies one of the most profitable sectors in agriculture.
(B) The company recruits researchers from across the world.
(C) Afterward, the research and development team works to develop varietals that address these challenges.

(D) Their comprehensive research produces some of the most flavorful plants on the market.

어휘 occupy 차지하다 profitable 수익성이 있는 sector 분야 recruit 모집하다 development 개발 work to-V ~에 노력하다 challenge 어려움 comprehensive 포괄적인, 종합적인 flavorful 풍미 있는, 맛 좋은

해석 (A) 이 회사는 농업 분야에서 가장 수익성이 좋은 부문 중 하나를 차지하고 있다.
(B) 이 회사는 전 세계에서 연구원들을 모집한다.
(C) 그 후에는 연구개발팀이 이러한 어려움을 해결해 주는 변종들을 개발하기 위해 노력한다.
(D) 그들의 포괄적인 연구는 시장에서 가장 풍미 있는 식물 중 몇몇을 생산한다.

해설 앞 문장에서 고객이 겪는 가장 대표적인 어려움을 파악하기 위한 설문 조사(customer surveys that sought to comprehend the most typical difficulties)를 언급하고 있으므로 설문 조사 후에 연구개발팀이 이 어려움을 해결할 변종을 개발하기 위해 노력한다고 말하는 것이 문맥상 자연스럽다. 그러면 올해 Dovyalis 사과나무를 개발했다는 뒤 문장의 내용도 자연스럽게 이어질 수 있다.

137. (A) region
(B) regions
(C) regional
(D) regionally

해설 빈칸 앞뒤 in desert ------ will be에서 정답을 알 수 있다. 명사 뒤 빈칸에는 명사가 정답이므로 (A)와 (B) 중에서 고른다. region은 보통명사이므로 단수형을 사용하려면 앞에 관사가 있어야 하므로 (B)가 정답이다.

138. (A) he
(B) she
(C) we
(D) they

해설 빈칸에 들어갈 대명사는 R-7 장미 나무에도 관심을 가질 만한 사람들로, 앞 문장의 Dovyalis 사과나무를 좋아할 사막 지역의 원예 애호가들(Gardeners in desert regions)을 의미한다. 그러므로 복수명사 Gardeners를 대신하는 대명사 (B)가 정답이다.

Part 7

Questions 139-140 refer to the following press release.

139.New Database to Streamline Tracking of Archaeological Finds

Barr Associates is proud to announce that it will soon partner with museums and archaeological societies from all around the world to construct a broad database of artifacts excavated from archaeological sites. Says Christopher Barr, CEO of Barr Associates, "A significant portion of the information concerning treasures of the ancient world is not adequately documented and is not readily available. 139.140.Our goal is to establish an electronic database that will enable museums and professionals working in the field to obtain complete descriptions of artifacts." The initial database will store information on 500,000 objects, and will be updated periodically.

139-140번 문제는 다음 기사에 관한 것입니다.

고고학 발굴물 추적을 간소화하는 새로운 데이터베이스

Barr Associates는 곧 세계 각처의 박물관들과 고고학회들과 제휴하여 고고학 발굴 현장에서 출토된 유물들의 광범위한 데이터베이스를 구축할 것이라고 발표하게 되어 기쁩니다. Barr Associates의 CEO Christopher Barr는 말합니다. "고대 세계의 보물에 관한 정보의 상당 부분은 적절히 문서로 기록되어 있지 않아서 쉽게 이용할 수 없습니다. 우리의 목표는 박물관들과 현장에서 일하는 전문가들이 유물에 대한 완전한 설명을 얻을 수 있는 전자 데이터베이스를 확립하는 것입니다." 초기 데이터베이스는 500,000개의 물품에 대한 정보가 저장되며 주기적으로 갱신될 것입니다.

어휘 press release 보도 자료 streamline 간소화[능률화]하다 track 추적하다 archaeological finds 고고학 발굴물 partner with ~와 제휴하다 society 협회, 학회 construct 구축하다 artifact 인공 유물 excavate 발굴하다, 출토하다 a significant portion 상당 부분 concerning ~에 관한 adequately 충분히, 적절하게 document 기록하다 readily 쉽게, 손쉽게 establish 확립하다 field (실험실·연구실 등이 아닌) 현장 store 저장하다 object 물건 update (최신의 것으로) 갱신하다 periodically 주기적으로

문장 분석

Barr Associates is proud to announce / that it will soon partner with museums and archaeological societies (from all around the world) / to construct a broad database of artifacts (excavated from archaeological sites).

➡ 긴 문장의 구조를 빠르게 파악하는 훈련이 필요하다. /로 표시된 부분은 의미상 끊어서 해석하자. ( )로 표시된 부분은 앞에 있는 명사를 수식하는 부분이다.

---

139. What product will Barr Associates offer?

(A) Supplies for archaeological excavations
(B) Theft prevention systems for museums
(C) Software containing information about artifacts
(D) Devices for detecting fake artifacts

어휘 supplies 필수품, 물자 archaeological 고고학적인 excavation 발굴 theft 절도, 도난 contain 포함하다, 담다 artifact (인공) 유물 detect 감지하다, 탐지하다 fake 위조의, 모조의, 가짜의

해석 Barr Associates는 어떤 제품을 제공하는가?
(A) 고고학 발굴을 위한 필수품
(B) 박물관 도난 방지 시스템
(C) 유물 정보를 담은 소프트웨어
(D) 가짜 유물 감지 장치

해설 New Database to Streamline Tracking of Archaeological Finds(고고학 발굴물 추적을 간소화하는 새로운 데이터베이스)라는 제목만 봐도 정답을 짐작할 수 있다. 또한 첫 문장에서 고고학 발굴 현장에서 출토된 유물의 광범위한 데이터베이스를 구축할 것(to construct a broad database of artifacts excavated from archaeological sites)이라고 했고, 결정적으로 CEO가 한 말 중 an electronic database that will enable museums and professionals working in the field to obtain complete descriptions of artifacts(박물관들과 현장에서 일하는 전문가들이 유물에 대한 완전한 설명을 얻을 수 있는 전자 데이터베이스)에서도 정답을 확인할 수 있다.

---

140. According to the press release, who will use the product?

(A) Dealers who buy and sell antiques

(B) Security guards in museums
(C) Publishers that deal with books on archaeology
(D) Museum employees and archaeologists

dealer 중개인 antique 골동품 security guard 경비원, 보안 요원 publisher 출판인, 출판사 archaeology 고고학 archaeologist 고고학자

보도 자료에 따르면, 누가 그 제품을 사용할 것인가?
(A) 골동품을 사고파는 중개인
(B) 박물관 보안 요원
(C) 고고학에 관한 책을 취급하는 출판사
(D) 박물관 직원과 고고학자

CEO의 인터뷰 발췌문에 있는 an electronic database that will enable museums and professionals working in the field to obtain complete descriptions of artifacts(박물관들과 현장에서 일하는 전문가들이 유물에 대한 완전한 설명을 얻을 수 있는 전자 데이터베이스)를 통해 누가 이 소프트웨어를 사용하게 될지 알 수 있다.

Questions 141-145 refer to the following two letters.

Dear Ms. James,

I spoke with your assistant on the telephone last week, ¹⁴¹·and he suggested that I write directly to you to express my interest in an internship at your firm.

I will graduate soon and I am seeking hands-on experience in the field of market research. ¹⁴³·I am specifically interested in an internship where I will be trained as a focus group discussion moderator. I believe that my business degree and my interpersonal skills qualify me for an internship in this area.

As indicated in the enclosed résumé, ¹⁴²·I was employed in a part-time capacity as assistant to the moderator of focus groups at Mindspot Research for one academic year. Additionally, I have gained further experience through executing opinion polls for my university newspaper and monitoring focus groups

for an advertising class at the university. I am very eager to work at Unadilla Advertising Group and would appreciate an opportunity to have a conversation with you about the internships you have on offer.

Sincerely yours,
Lynnette Leathers

141-145번 문제는 다음 두 편지에 관한 것입니다.

Ms. James께,

지난주에 당신의 비서와 통화했는데, 그가 제안하기를 당신에게 직접 편지를 써서 회사의 인턴직에 관심이 있음을 전하라고 했습니다.

저는 곧 졸업할 예정이고 시장 조사 분야에서 실무 경험을 구하고 있습니다. 특별히 포커스 그룹 토론 사회자로 훈련받을 수 있는 인턴 자리에 관심이 있습니다. 제 경영학 학위와 대인 관계 능력이 이 영역에서 인턴을 할 만한 자격을 갖추게 했다고 생각합니다.

동봉된 이력서에 나와 있는 바와 같이, 저는 Mindspot Research에서 한 학년 동안 시간제로 포커스 그룹 사회자의 비서로 근무했습니다. 또한 대학교 신문사 소속으로 여론 조사를 시행하고 대학 광고 수업에서 포커스 그룹을 관찰하는 일을 통해 더 많은 경험을 쌓기도 했습니다. Unadilla Advertising Group에서 일하기를 매우 간절히 바라며 제공해 주실 수 있는 인턴직에 관해 대화 나눌 기회를 주신다면 감사하겠습니다.

진심을 담아
Lynnette Leathers

assistant 비서 directly 직접 firm 회사 hands-on 실무의, 실제의 field(=area) (활동) 분야, 영역 specifically 특별히 focus group 포커스 그룹(시장 조사나 여론 조사를 위해 각 계층을 대표하도록 뽑은 소수의 사람들로 이뤄진 그룹) moderator (토론회 등의) 사회자 business degree 경영학 학위 interpersonal skill 대인 관계 능력 qualify sb for ~에게 ~에 대한 자격을 주다 enclose 동봉하다 capacity 지위, 역할 academic year 학년도 additionally 또한 execute 실행하다, 수행하다 opinion poll 여론 조사 monitor (추적) 관찰하다 be eager to-V ~하기를 간절히 바라다 on offer 제공되는, 이용할[살] 수 있는

....

Additionally, I have gained further experience / through [executing opinion polls for my university newspaper] and [monitoring focus groups for an advertising class at the university].

➡ 등위접속사 and가 전치사 through의 목적어로 executing과 monitoring으로 시작하는 두 개의 동명사 구를 연결하고 있다.

Dear Ms. Leathers,

Thank you for your letter and the accompanying résumé. Our organization is always interested in extending opportunities to recent graduates whose credentials and background match yours. 143.Regrettably, we do not have any current internships that align with your particular area of focus. 145.On a more positive note, however, we are currently in search of an apprentice to assist in the process of market research opinion polls. This is a twelve-month internship program that may culminate in an offer for permanent employment. 144.If this line of work intrigues you, I advise that you reach out to Ayesha Chandran, the head of our human resources department, to explore the duties of the internship.

Yours truly,
Marissa James

Ms. Leathers께,

편지와 함께 보내주신 이력서 고맙습니다. 우리 조직은 당신과 같은 자격 요건 및 배경이 일치하는 최근 졸업생에게 기회를 주는 데 언제나 관심이 있습니다. 유감스럽게도 현재는 당신이 특별히 관심을 두고 있는 분야에 일치하는 인턴 자리가 없습니다. 그러나 좀 더 긍정적으로 말해보자면, 우리는 현재 시장 조사용 여론 조사의 진행을 도와줄 수습생을 찾고 있습니다. 마지막에 정규직 채용 제안을 받을 수도 있는 12개월짜리 인턴쉽 프로그램입니다. 이 유형의 일이 당신의 흥미를 끈다면 인사부장 Ayesha Chandran에게 연락해서 인턴 업무에 대해 알아보기를 권하는 바입니다.

진심을 담아
Marissa James

어휘 accompany 첨부하고 있다 extend an opportunity 기회를 주다, 베풀다 graduate 졸업생 credentials 자격

background 소양, 경력, 학력 match (~와) 일치하다 regrettably 유감스럽게도 align with ~와 나란히 하다 area 분야, 영역 on a positive note 긍정적으로 말하면 in search of ~를 찾고 있는 apprentice 수습생 opinion poll 여론 조사 culminate in ~으로 끝나다, 마지막에 (~이) 되다 permanent employment 정규직 채용 line (사업·활동·관심) 분야, 유형 intrigue ~의 호기심을 유발하다 advise 권하다 reach out to (정보, 기회, 요청을 위해) ~에게 연락해 보다 explore 탐구하다, 알아보다 duty 업무

---

141. What does Ms. Leathers hope to do?

(A) Launch an advertising campaign
(B) Contribute to a newspaper
(C) Obtain training from a company
(D) Supervise a human resources department

어휘 launch 시작하다, 착수하다 contribute to ~에 기고하다, 투고하다 supervise 감독[지휘/지도]하다

해석 Ms. Leathers는 무엇을 하고 싶어 하는가?
(A) 광고 캠페인을 시작한다
(B) 신문에 기고한다
(C) 회사에서 교육을 받는다.
(D) 인사부를 감독한다.

해설 첫 번째 편지의 첫 문장 and he suggested that I write directly to you to express my interest in an internship at your firm(그가 제안하기를 당신에게 직접 편지를 써서 회사의 인턴직에 관심이 있음을 전하라고 했습니다)에서 Ms. Leathers가 회사에서 인턴(교육 받으며 일하는 사람)으로 일하고 싶어 한다는 것을 알 수 있다.

---

142. What previous experience does Ms. Leathers mention?

(A) She served as an assistant at an advertising agency.
(B) She was the instructor of a marketing course.
(C) She sold newspaper advertisements.
(D) She worked as a telephone marketer.

어휘 serve 근무하다, 일하다 advertising agency 광고 대행사 instructor 강사

해석 Ms.·Leathers는 이전의 어떤 경력을 언급하는가?
(A) 광고 대행사에서 비서로 근무했다.
(B) 마케팅 강좌 강사였다.

(C) 신문 광고를 판매했다.
(D) 텔레마케터로 일했다.

해설 첫 번째 편지의 마지막 문단에서 광고 대행사에서 포커스 그룹 사회자의 비서로 일한 경력(I was employed in a part-time capacity as assistant to the moderator of focus groups at Mindspot Research for one academic year.)을 언급하고 있다.

---

143. What news does Ms. James give Ms. Leathers?

(A) Ms. Leathers lacks the requisite work experience.
(B) The organization has no open positions for work with focus groups.
(C) Ms. Leathers needs more education to become eligible for a job.
(D) The organization is not currently offering internships.

어휘 requisite 필요한 eligible for ~할[될/의] 자격이 있는 currently 현재

해설 Ms. James는 Ms. Leathers에게 어떤 소식을 전하는가?
(A) Ms. Leathers는 필요한 업무 경력이 부족하다.
(B) 그 조직에 포커스 그룹 업무를 위한 공석이 없다.
(C) Ms. Leathers가 채용 자격을 갖추기 위해서는 더 많은 교육이 필요하다.
(D) 그 조직이 현재 인턴직을 제공하지 않고 있다.

연계 추론 Ms. James의 답장을 보면 현재 회사에 Ms. Leathers의 특별한 관심 분야에 일치하는 인턴 자리가 없다는(we do not have any current internships that align with your particular area of focus) 소식을 전하고 있다. Ms. Leathers의 관심 분야는 첫 번째 편지의 둘째 문단 I am specifically interested in an internship where I will be trained as a focus group discussion moderator.(특별히 포커스 그룹 토론 사회자로 훈련받을 수 있는 인턴 자리에 관심이 있습니다.)에서 알 수 있다. 두 부분의 내용을 연계하여 추론하면 현재 Ms. James의 회사에는 포커스 그룹을 대상으로 일하는 인턴 자리가 없다는 것을 알 수 있다.

---

144. Why should Ms. Leathers contact Ayesha Chandran?

(A) To arrange for a training session
(B) To secure work documents
(C) To participate in an opinion poll
(D) To acquire further information about an opportunity

어휘 arrange for 준비하다, 마련하다 training session 교육(시간) secure 확보하다 opinion poll 여론 조사 acquire 획득하다

해설 Ms. Leathers는 왜 Ayesha Chandran에게 연락해야 하는가?
(A) 교육 시간을 마련하기 위해
(B) 업무 문서를 확보하기 위해
(C) 여론 조사에 참여하기 위해
(D) 기회에 대한 추가 정보를 얻기 위해

해설 Ms. James는 Leathers에게 관심 분야는 아니지만 공석인 인턴 자리에 대해 설명한 후 관심이 있다면 Ayesha Chandran에게 연락해서 알아보라고 조언하고 있다(If this line of work intrigues you, I advise that you reach out to Ayesha Chandran, the head of our human resources department, to explore the duties of the internship).

---

145. In the second letter, the word "positive" in line 4 is closest in meaning to

(A) convinced
(B) plausible
(C) optimistic
(D) absolute

어휘 positive 긍정적인; 확신하는 convinced 확신하는 plausible (변명·설명 등이) 그럴듯한, 타당한 것 같은 optimistic 낙관적인, 낙관하는

해설 두 번째 편지에서 넷째 줄의 단어 positive와 의미상 가장 가까운 것은
(A) 확신하는
(B) 그럴듯한
(C) 낙관적인
(D) 절대적인

해설 positive가 '긍정적인'이라는 뜻으로 사용되었다면 (C)와, '확신하는'이라는 뜻으로 사용되었다면 (A)와 동의어다. on a positive note가 '긍정적으로 말하면'이라는 뜻이므로 여기서 positive 대신 사용될 수 있는 형용사는 optimistic이다.

PART 5 & 6 Exercise

101 (B)	**102** (A)	**103** (B)	**104** (B)	**105** (C)
106 (C)	**107** (D)	**108** (C)	**109** (C)	**110** (C)
111 (C)	**112** (D)	**113** (A)	**114** (C)	**115** (C)

101. Successful candidates for this position should have at least three years of working experience in a related field ------- strong academic credentials.

(A) otherwise
(B) in addition to
(C) meanwhile
(D) even though

어휘 successful candidate 합격자 working experience 실무 경력 related field 관련 분야 otherwise 그렇지 않으면 meanwhile 그동안에 academic credentials 학력 자격

해석 이 직책의 합격자가 되려면 우수한 학력에 더하여 관련 분야에서 최소 3년의 실무 경력이 있어야 한다.

해설 (A) 부사 (B) 전치사 (C) 부사 (D) 접속사이다. 우선 부사는 오답이므로 제외하자. 빈칸 뒤에 명사구인 strong academic credentials가 있으므로 전치사 (B)가 정답이다.

102. Please notify Ms. Kobayashi that ------- visit to the Osaka office has been postponed until February 20.

(A) my
(B) me
(C) myself
(D) mine

어휘 notify 알리다, 통보하다 postpone 연기하다

해석 Ms. Kobayashi께 저의 Osaka 지사 방문이 2월 20일로 연기되었다고 알려주시기 바랍니다.

해설 that절에서 동사가 has been postponed이므로 ------- visit to the Osaka office가 주어임을 알 수 있다. 전치사구 to the Osaka office를 제외하면 visit은 동사가 아니라 명사임을 알 수 있다. 그러므로 명사 앞 빈칸에는 소유격 (A)가 정답이다.

103. The customers who are picking up the rental vehicle should be told that ------- is the white minivan.

(A) their
(B) theirs
(C) they
(D) themselves

어휘 pick up ~을 찾다, 찾아오다 rental vehicle 임대 차량

해석 임대 차량을 찾고 있는 고객들에게 그들의 것은 흰색 미니밴이라고 말해 주어야 한다.

해설 빈칸은 that절의 주어 자리이므로 주격 (C)와 소유대명사 (B)가 들어갈 수 있다. 그런데 they는 복수대명사이므로 동사 is와 수가 일치하지 않으므로 소유대명사 (B)가 정답이다.

104. Please e-mail Mr. Mori to let ------- know when he can expect you in Tokyo.

(A) he
(B) him
(C) himself
(D) his own

어휘 expect (오기로 한) ~를 기다리다

해석 Mr. Mori에게 언제 당신이 도쿄에 가는지 알 수 있도록 이메일을 보내세요.

해설 빈칸에는 동사 let의 목적어가 있어야 하므로 목적격 (B)와 재귀대명사 (C)가 들어갈 수 있다. e-mail이라는 행위의 주체는 명령문의 생략된 주어인 you이므로 빈칸에 들어갈 목적어와 일치하지 않는다. 따라서 목적격 대명사인 (B)가 정답이다.

105. As ------- in the lease agreement, one of the maintenance team members will respond to every service request submitted online or by phone within 2 hours.

(A) notes
(B) note
(C) noted
(D) notation

어휘 note 메모; 언급하다 notation 표기법, 기호 lease agreement 임대차 계약서 maintenance 유지보수 request 요청서 submit 내다, 제출하다

해석 임대차 계약서에 나와 있는 대로 시설관리 팀원 중 한 명이 온라인이나 전화로 들어오는 모든 서비스 요청에 2시간 이내에 응답할 것이다.

해설 as는 접속사와 전치사로 모두 사용할 수 있다. '~로써'라는 뜻의 전치사로 as를 사용했다면 뒤에 목적어가 필요하므로 빈칸에 명사인 (A)와 (B), (D)가 들어갈 수 있다. 그런데 '임대차 계약서의 필기[메모/표기법](으)로써'라는 의미는 어색하므로 이 문장에서 as는 전치사가 아니다. 접속사라면 as 뒤에 '주어 + 동사'가 있어야 하는데, 보기를 보면 주어를 생략한 분사 구문임을 알 수 있으므로 분사 (C)가 정답이다.

---

106. Ms. Yang has requested the use of a company car from the airport to the new manufacturing plant for ------- and two clients this Thursday.

(A) her
(B) she
(C) herself
(D) hers

어휘 manufacturing plant 제조 공장

해석 Ms. Yang이 이번 주 목요일 본인과 두 명의 고객을 위해 공항에서 새 제조 공장까지 회사 차의 사용을 신청했습니다.

해설 전치사 for의 목적어가 필요하므로 목적격 (A)와 소유대명사 (D), 재귀대명사 (C) 중 정답을 선택해야 한다. 그런데 소유대명사의 단서는 문장에서 찾을 수 없으므로 (D)는 제외하자. has requested라는 행위의 주체가 Ms. Yang이고 빈칸의 목적어와 같은 사람임을 알 수 있으므로 재귀대명사 (C)가 정답이다.

---

107. Moon Micro Systems has been a major client of ------- for over 15 years in the Asia-Pacific region.

(A) us
(B) our
(C) we
(D) ours

해석 Moon Micro Systems는 아시아 태평양 지역에서 15년이 넘는 기간 동안 우리의 주요 고객사 중 한 군데였다.

해설 빈칸 앞 a major client of -------를 보면 정답을 알 수 있다. 'a(n) + 명사 + of + -------'가 있으면 빈칸에는 소유대명사가 들어가므로 (D)가 정답이다.

108. Mr. Kowalski will meet us for the initial consultation this afternoon, ------- his flight is not delayed.

(A) according to
(B) as well as
(C) as long as
(D) apart from

어휘 initial 처음의 consultation 상담 delay 연기하다

해석 비행 편이 연착되지 않는 한 Mr. Kowalski는 오늘 오후에 첫 상담을 위해 우리를 만날 것이다.

해설 (A) 전치사 (B) 접속사 (C) 접속사 (D) 전치사이다. (B) as well as는 앞뒤로 병렬구조가 되어야 하고 그 뒤에 '주어 + 동사'가 올 수 없다. 이 문제에서는 빈칸 뒤에 '주어 + 동사(his flight is not delayed)'가 있으므로 접속사 (C)가 정답이다.

---

109. To meet the deadline for the presentation at Monday's executive meeting, Mr. Kim completed the market research report by ------- over the weekend.

(A) he
(B) him
(C) himself
(D) his own

어휘 meet the deadline 마감 기한에 맞추다 executive 중역의 complete 완성하다

해석 월요일 중역 회의에서 할 발표 기한을 맞추기 위해 Mr. Kim은 주말 동안 혼자 시장 조사 보고서를 완성했다.

해설 빈칸 앞에 by가 있으면 뒤에 재귀대명사를 쓰므로 (C)가 정답이다.

---

110. Mr. Sarrafan has enrolled in a business management program to pursue the goal of establishing a venture of ------- in the long run.

(A) him
(B) himself
(C) his own
(D) his

어휘 enroll in ~에 등록하다 business management 경영(학) pursue 추구하다 in the long run 결국에는

해석 Mr. Sarrafan은 결국에는 자기 소유의 사업을 차리겠다는 목표를 추구하기 위해 경영 프로그램에 등록했다.

해설 빈칸 앞 빈칸 앞 a venture of ------를 보고 정답을 알아내야 한다. 'a(n) + 명사 + of + ------' 구조이므로 (C)와 (D) 중에서 선택하면 된다. 그런데 '자기 사업 중 하나'보다 '자기 소유의 사업'을 차린다는 뜻이 자연스러우므로 (C)가 정답이다.

---

111. The soccer tournament was ------- a popular event in the region that the stadiums were always packed on match days.

(A) so
(B) huge
(C) such
(D) too

어휘 tournament 대회, 토너먼트 packed 사람으로 꽉 찬

해설 축구 대회는 지역에서 매우 인기 있는 행사라서 경기가 있는 날이면 경기장이 언제나 사람들로 꽉 들어찼다.

해설 빈칸 뒤 ------- a popular event in the region that을 보고 정답을 알 수 있다. 'such + (a/an) + (형용사) + 명사 + that절' 구조로 정답은 (C)이다.

---

112. Blue Heron Paper Company encourages its staff members to take responsibility for ------- training schedules.

(A) they
(B) them
(C) themselves
(D) their own

어휘 encourage 장려하다 take responsibility for ~을 책임지다

해설 Blue Heron 제지(製紙)는 직원들이 자신의 교육 일정에 대한 책임을 지도록 장려한다.

해설 빈칸 앞뒤 for ------- training schedules에서 정답을 알아내자. 명사 앞에 빈칸이 있으면 소유격이, 소유격이 없을 때는 one's own이 들어가므로 (D)가 정답이다.

---

113. Director Angela Lane will be interviewing the final candidates for the manager position -------.

(A) herself
(B) she
(C) hers
(D) her

어휘 director 임원, 이사, 중역 final candidate 최종 후보자

해설 Angela Lane 이사가 직접 매니저 자리의 최종 후보자를 면접 볼 것이다.

해설 완성된 3형식 문장에 빈칸이 있고(부사 자리) 보기가 인칭대명사로 구성되어 있다. 그러므로 재귀대명사 (A)가 정답이다.

---

114. The South America team has already submitted its sales projection report, but we haven't completed ------- yet.

(A) we
(B) us
(C) ours
(D) our

어휘 projection 예상, 예측

해설 남미팀은 이미 자신들의 매출 예상 보고서를 제출했는데, 우리는 아직 우리 것을 완료하지 못했다.

해설 동사 haven't completed의 목적어가 필요하므로 목적격 (B)와 소유대명사 (C) 중에 정답을 선택하면 된다. 빈칸 앞 절에 '소유격 + 명사(its sales projection report)'가 있으므로 소유대명사 (C)가 정답이다.

---

115. Mark Walker maintained that he possessed the necessary expertise to complete the translation of all the documents on -------.

(A) him
(B) himself
(C) his own
(D) his

어휘 maintain 주장하다 possess 소유하다 expertise 전문지식 translation 번역

해설 Mark Walker는 자신이 모든 문서의 번역을 혼자 완료하는데 필요한 전문지식을 갖추고 있다고 주장했다.

해설 빈칸 앞에 on이 있으면 바로 one's own을 선택하면 되므로 정답은 (C)이다

101 (A)	**102** (A)	**103** (A)	**104** (C)	**105** (C)
106 (B)	**107** (C)	**108** (A)	**109** (A)	**110** (D)
111 (D)	**112** (C)	**113** (B)	**114** (B)	**115** (B)
116 (B)	**117** (D)	**118** (B)	**119** (C)	**120** (D)
121 (A)	**122** (D)	**123** (D)	**124** (A)	**125** (B)
126 (A)	**127** (A)	**128** (D)	**129** (A)	**130** (D)
131 (D)	**132** (B)	**133** (A)	**134** (B)	**135** (B)
136 (C)	**137** (D)	**138** (D)	**139** (A)	**140** (C)
141 (B)	**142** (D)	**143** (B)	**144** (C)	**145** (B)
146 (A)	**147** (D)			

Part 5

101. Sandy Sawyer is so versatile a writer that his books are always among the best sellers ------- the subject matter.

(A) **regardless of**
(B) consequently
(C) in addition to
(D) likewise

어휘 versatile 다재다능한 regardless of ~에 상관없이 consequently 그 결과, 따라서 likewise 똑같이, 마찬가지로 subject matter 주제, 소재

해석 Sandy Sawyer는 매우 다재다능한 작가라서 그의 책은 주제와 상관없이 언제나 인기 도서 중에 있다.

해설 (B)는 접속부사로 두 문장을 연결해야 하므로 빈칸에 알맞지 않다. 그러므로 빈칸 앞뒤 among the best sellers ------- the subject matter에서 자연스럽게 의미가 연결되는 전치사를 정답으로 선택해야 한다. '주제에 [(A) 상관없이 (C) 뿐만 아니라 (D) 똑같이]' 중 가장 자연스러운 것은 (A)이다.

102. Beximco Pharmaceuticals Ltd. reported a consolidated net profit of 106 million rupees last quarter, ------- it to fund its planned expansion.

(A) **allowing**
(B) allows
(C) allowance
(D) allowably

어휘 consolidated (모기업과 자회사) 통합의 net profit 순(이)익 rupee 루피(인도 · 파키스탄 등의 화폐 단위) allowance 허용량 allowably 허용 범위 내에서 fund 자금을 대다

해석 Beximco 제약은 지난 분기에 1억 6백만 루피의 통합 순이익을 기록했는데, 이것이 회사가 계획되어 있는 확장에 자금을 댈 수 있게 해 줬다.

해설 빈칸 앞에 있는 완성된 문장(3형식)이 주절이고, 빈칸부터는 부사절이다. 부사절은 '접속사 + 주어 + 동사' 구조인데, 보기에는 접속사와 주어가 없다. 그러므로 분사구문이 될 수 있도록 (A)를 정답으로 선택해야 한다.

103. When he made his debut in the opera, Jose could hardly stand on his feet because of the anxiety ------- singing before the audience for the first time in his life.

(A) **about**
(B) at
(C) of
(D) with

어휘 make one's debut 데뷔하다, 첫 무대에 서다 stand on one's feet 서 있다

해석 Jose는 오페라 무대에 데뷔했을 때 생애 처음으로 청중 앞에서 노래하는 것에 대한 불안으로 거의 두 발로 서 있을 수조차 없었다.

해설 항상 짝을 이루어 출제되는 어휘 문제이다. 걱정(concerns, worries, anxiety) 뒤에 빈칸이 있으면 about이 들어가야 하므로 (A)가 정답이다.

104. Most computer engineering students at Saint Joseph College work as interns before getting ------- first professional job.

(A) them
(B) theirs
(C) **their**
(D) they

해석 Saint Joseph 대학교의 컴퓨터 공학 학생들 대부분은 첫 전문 직업을 갖기 전에 인턴으로 일한다.

해설 빈칸 앞뒤 getting ------- first professional job에서 정답을 알아내자. 명사 앞 빈칸에는 소유격 대명사가 들어가야 하므로 (C)가 정답이다.

105. Before the new hi-tech devices are installed in the museum, the security team would first like to make sure that they are ------- with the existing security system.

(A) competitive
(B) comparable
(C) compatible
(D) comfortable

어휘 hi-tech device 최첨단 장치 install 설치하다 security 보안 make sure that ~임을 확인하다 competitive 경쟁력 있는 comparable 비슷한, 비교할 만한 compatible 호환이 되는 comfortable 편안한 existing 기존의, 현재 사용되는

해석 박물관에 새로운 최첨단 장치가 설치되기 전에 보안팀은 우선 그것들이 기존 보안 시스템과 호환이 되는지 확인하고 싶어 한다.

해설 항상 짝을 이루어 출제되는 어휘 문제이다. '호환이 되는'이라는 뜻의 compatible은 with와 함께 쓰이므로 (C)가 정답이다.

---

106. Mr. Frazier cannot attend today's board meeting but indicated that ------- would ask a colleague to take his place.

(A) him
(B) he
(C) his
(D) himself

어휘 board meeting 이사회 indicate (의견을) 밝히다, 알리다 take one's place ~을 대신하여 일하다

해석 Mr. Frazier는 오늘 이사회에 참석할 수 없지만 동료에게 대신해달라는 부탁을 할 것이라고 알렸다.

해설 빈칸 앞뒤 that ------- would ask에서 정답을 알아내자. 빈칸은 주어 자리로 주격 대명사와 소유대명사가 들어갈 수 있다. 그러나 앞 절에서 소유대명사가 가리킬 수 있는 '소유격+명사'가 없으므로 주격 대명사인 (B)가 정답이다.

---

107. New protective clothing will soon be available for use by factory floor workers and visitors -------.

(A) nearly
(B) quite
(C) alike
(D) cautiously

어휘 protective clothing 방호복 factory floor (공장의) 작업 현장 alike 양쪽 모두, 둘 다 똑같이 cautiously 조심스럽게, 신중히

해석 새 방호복은 곧 공장 작업장 근로자들과 방문객들이 모

두 이용할 수 있을 것이다.

해설 available for use by factory floor workers and visitors -------의 의미를 자연스럽게 만들어 주는 부사를 정답으로 선택해야 한다. '공장 작업장 근로자들과 방문객들이 [(A) 거의 (B) 꽤 (C) 둘 다 (D) 조심스럽게] 사용할 수 있는'에서 의미가 가장 자연스러운 (C)가 정답이다.

---

108. Sandra Contreras has set ------- apart from other candidates in the mayoral race by suggesting an amended version of the tax law to solve the city's financial crisis.

(A) herself
(B) her
(C) she
(D) hers

어휘 set sb/sth apart from ~를 ~과 차별화하다 mayoral race 시장 선거(전) amend 개정하다, 수정하다 financial crisis 재정 위기

해석 Sandra Contreras는 시의 재정 위기를 해결하기 위해 세법 개정안을 제안함으로써 시장 선거에서 자신을 다른 후보자들과 차별화했다.

해설 동사 has set의 목적어가 필요하므로 목적격 (B)와 소유대명사 (D), 재귀대명사 (A) 중에서 정답을 고를 수 있다. has set 행위의 주체가 Sandra Contreras라는 여성으로 목적어와 같다. 행위의 주체와 목적어가 동일한 대상이므로 재귀대명사 (A)가 정답이다.

---

109. West Virginia ended the most recent fiscal year with an overall budget ------- of over 450 million dollars.

(A) surplus
(B) assembly
(C) launch
(D) committee

어휘 fiscal year 회계 연도 overall 총액의 budget surplus 예산 흑자 assembly 모임, 집회 launch 출시 committee 위원회

해석 West Virginia는 가장 최근의 회계 연도를 4억 5천만 달러가 넘는 총 예산 흑자로 끝마쳤다.

해설 budget과 함께 사용하는 복합명사는 budget surplus와 budget committee 등이 있다. 빈칸 뒤에 of over 450 million dollars가 있으므로 '4억 5천만 달러가 넘는 총 예산 흑자'라는 뜻이 자연스러우므로 (A)가 정답이다.

110. The newly released accounting software package will allow all our clients to perform regular payroll tasks by -------.

(A) they
(B) them
(C) theirs
(D) themselves

어휘 release 발매하다, 출시하다 accounting 회계 regular 일반적인 payroll task 급여 관리 업무

해석 새로 출시된 회계 소프트웨어 패키지는 우리 고객 모두가 정기적인 급여 관리 업무를 혼자 수행할 수 있게 할 것이다.

해설 by 뒤에 빈칸이 있으면 재귀대명사가 들어갈 수 있으므로 (D)가 정답이다.

---

111. Mr. Park advises that the employees wait for the heavy snow to ------- before returning to the work site.

(A) compress
(B) anticipate
(C) prioritize
(D) diminish

어휘 compress 압축하다[되다] prioritize 우선적으로 처리하다 diminish 줄어들다; 약화되다

해석 Mr. Park은 직원들이 작업장으로 복귀하기 전에 폭설이 잦아들기를 기다리라고 권고한다.

해설 빈칸 앞 wait for the heavy snow to -------에서 '폭설이 [(A) 압축되기를 (B) 예상하기를 (C) 우선으로 처리하기를 (D) 약화되기를] 기다린다'에서 의미가 가장 자연스러운 동사는 (D)이다.

---

112. Alice Steele was delighted to discover that a proposal of ------- was endorsed by the committee.

(A) she
(B) her
(C) hers
(D) herself

어휘 proposal 제안, 제의 endorse (공개적으로) 지지하다

해석 Alice Steele은 자신의 제안 중 하나가 위원회의 지지를 받았다는 것을 알고 매우 기뻤다.

해설 빈칸 앞 a proposal of -------을 보면 정답을 알 수 있다. 'a(n) + 명사 + of + -------'가 있으면 빈칸에 소유대명사가 들어가므로 (C)가 정답이다.

---

113. Kulula Airways advises passengers planning to travel during the peak tourist season to purchase tickets ------- in advance in order to ensure availability.

(A) very
(B) far
(C) so
(D) hardly

어휘 peak 최고의, 성수기의 tourist season 관광철 in advance 미리, 사전에 ensure 보장하다 availability 이용 가능성

해석 Kulula 항공은 관광 성수기에 여행할 계획인 승객들에게 이용 가능성을 확보하기 위해 한참 전에 항공권을 구입할 것을 권고한다.

해설 in advance를 수식하기에 알맞은 부사는 far이다. '------- + 비교급 / too / beyond' 구문이 출제될 때, 빈칸에는 far가 들어간다고 기억해 두자.

---

114. The marketing consultants have trained the service representatives of Kaltex Electronics, Inc., thoroughly to address any customer complaints -------.

(A) recently
(B) promptly
(C) convincingly
(D) steadily

어휘 service representative 서비스 안내 직원 thoroughly 철저히, 철두철미하게 address 다루다, 처리하다 complaint 불만 사항 promptly 바로, 즉시 convincingly 설득력 있게 steadily 꾸준히, 착실하게

해석 마케팅 자문 위원들은 Kaltex 전자의 서비스 안내 직원들이 고객의 어떤 불만 사항이든 바로 처리할 수 있도록 철저히 교육하고 있다.

해설 항상 짝을 이루어 출제되는 어휘 문제이다. handle, address, deliver, answer, report 동사 뒤의 빈칸에는 항상 promptly가 들어가므로 (B)가 정답이다.

---

115. Mr. Alvarado will return from vacation tomorrow, but the steering committee will not meet with ------- until next week.

(A) himself
(B) him
(C) his
(D) he

어휘 steering committee 운영 위원회 meet with (회의 등을 위해) ~와 만나다

해석 Mr. Alvarado는 내일 휴가에서 돌아오지만 운영 위원회는 다음 주에나 그를 만날 것이다.

해설 전치사 with의 목적어로 재귀대명사 (A), 목적격 대명사 (B), 소유대명사 (C) 중에서 정답을 고를 수 있다. 앞부분에 재귀대명사가 대신할 수 있는 '소유격 + 명사'가 없고 행위의 주체인 the steering committee가 목적어와 같은 대상이 아니므로, 목적격 (B)가 정답이다.

---

116. ------- all the entries for the Arcoda Times Photograph Contest have been received, they will be distributed among the judges for evaluation.

(A) Near
(B) Once
(C) How
(D) Yet

어휘 entry 출품작, 응모작 receive 접수하다 judge 심사위원 evaluation 평가, 감정

해석 Arcoda Times 사진 대회의 출품작들이 모두 접수되면 평가를 위해 심사위원들에게 배포될 것이다.

해설 [(A) 전치사 (B) 부사절 접속사 (C) 명사절 접속사 (D) 부사]에서 일단 부사인 (D)는 제외하자. 빈칸 뒤에 '주어 + 동사' 구조가 있으므로 접속사인 (B)와 (C) 중 정답을 선택해야 한다. 그런데 쉼표 앞은 부사절이므로 빈칸에 부사절 접속사 (B)가 정답으로 알맞다. (C)는 의문사가 아니라 명사절 접속사이다.

---

117. Mr. Vasquez developed the architectural plans for the Onishi Firm's office building ------- since the client required a complicated design.

(A) he
(B) his
(C) him
(D) himself

어휘 architectural plan 건축 설계 도면 complicated 복잡한

해석 고객이 복잡한 설계를 요구했기 때문에 Mr. Vasquez가 Onishi사 사무실의 설계 도면을 직접 만들었다.

해설 빈칸 앞에 있는 전치사구 for the Onishi Firm's office building은 수식어구이므로 제외하자. 그 앞에 '타동사 + 목적어(developed the architectural plans)'가 있으므로 빈칸은 부사 자리이다. 그러므로 빈칸에 대명사가 들어가야 한다면, 재귀대명사 (D)가 정답으로 알맞다.

---

118. Please have ------- three tubes of revised posters delivered to our booth in the convention center by 8 A.M.

(A) many
(B) these
(C) other
(D) such

어휘 tube (그림 보관용) 통 revise 수정하다 deliver 전달하다

해석 오전 8시까지 이 수정된 세 통의 포스터가 컨벤션 센터의 우리 부스에 전달되게 해주세요.

해설 문장의 의미를 자연스럽게 하기 위해 ------- three tubes of revised posters가 '이 수정된 세 통의 포스터'라는 뜻을 나타내도록 (B)를 정답으로 선택해야 한다.

---

119. The supervisor notified them that all employees are ------- for seven days of sick leave per year after one full year of employment.

(A) approachable
(B) considerable
(C) eligible
(D) creditable

어휘 supervisor 감독관, 관리자 notify 통지하다, 알리다 approachable 말을 붙이기 쉬운 considerable 상당한, 많은 eligible for ~할 자격이 있는 creditable 칭찬할 만한, 훌륭한 sick leave 병가

해석 관리자는 모든 직원이 만 1년의 근무 후에 매년 7일의 병가를 낼 자격이 생긴다고 알려줬다.

해설 항상 짝을 이루어 출제되는 어휘 문제이다. 빈칸 앞뒤 are ------- for를 보자마자 eligible이나 qualified를 정답으로 선택하자.

---

120. This gift token is valid at its full face value and can be ------- only by the recipient within domestic locations.

(A) evaluated
(B) convened
(C) nominated
(D) redeemed

어휘 gift token 상품권 valid 유효한, 효력 있는 face value 액면가 evaluate 평가하다 convene 소집하다 nominate 지명하다 redeem (상품권 등을) 현금[상품]으로 바꾸다 recipient 수령인, 수취인 domestic 국내의, 자국의

[해석] 이 상품권은 액면가 전액만큼 효력이 있으며, 국내 지역 내에서 수령인만 상품으로 교환할 수 있다.

[해설] and 뒤의 절에서 주어와 동사를 생각하며 찾아보자. 'This gift token … can be -------' 의 의미를 자연스럽게 만들어 주는 동사가 정답이다. '이 상품권은 [(A) 평가받을 수 있다. (B) 소집될 수 있다. (C) 후보로 추천될 수 있다. (D) 상품으로 교환할 수 있다.]'에서 의미가 가장 자연스러운 것은 (D)이다.

---

121. Any inquiries regarding order tracking should be ------- to the New York office.

(A) directed
(B) recovered
(C) ensured
(D) allowed

[어휘] regarding ~에 관하여 order tracking 주문 추적 direct an inquiry to ~에게 문의하다

[해석] 주문 추적에 관한 어떤 문의든 뉴욕 지사에 해야 한다.

[해설] direct a(n) inquiry[question] to(ward)(~에게 문의[질문]하다)를 기억하자. 이 문제에서는 목적어인 an inquiry가 주어 자리에 온 수동태 문장이므로 (A)가 정답이다.

---

122. The product release of Intrawest Company's new line of coats will ------- with the winter holidays.

(A) argue
(B) compare
(C) produce
(D) coincide

[어휘] release 출시 line (상품의) 종류 compare with ~와 비교되다 coincide with ~와 시기가 일치하다

[해석] Intrawest 사(社)의 새로운 종류의 코트 제품 출시는 겨울 휴가철에 맞춰질 것이다.

[해설] The product release … will ------- with the winter holidays.의 의미를 자연스럽게 만들어 주는 동사가 정답이다. '제품 출시는 겨울 휴가철과 [(A) 논쟁할 (B) 비교될 (C) 생산할 (D) 시기가 일치할] 것이다.'에서 가장 자연스러운 것은 (D)이다.

---

123. Technology experts predict that virtual currencies used for online commerce will continue to gain in -------.

(A) personality
(B) attitude
(C) balance
(D) popularity

[어휘] virtual currency 가상화폐 commerce 상거래 gain in popularity 인기가 많아지다 personality 개성 balance 잔고, 잔액

[해석] 기술 전문가들은 온라인 상거래에 사용되는 가상화폐가 계속해서 인기가 많아질 것이라고 예상한다.

[해설] virtual currencies … will continue to gain in -------의 의미를 자연스럽게 만들어 주는 명사가 정답이다. '가상화폐는 계속해서 [(A) 개성이 (B) 태도가 (C) 잔액이 (D) 인기가] 많아질 것이다.'에서 의미가 가장 자연스러운 것은 (D)이다.

---

124. Mr. Schmidt discovered that ------- plumbing was the cause of the clogged drain line.

(A) faulty
(B) patient
(C) sufficient
(D) uneasy

[어휘] faulty 결함 있는, 불완전한 sufficient 충분한 uneasy 불안한, 걱정되는 plumbing 배관 작업[공사] clog 막히게 하다 drain line 배수관

[해석] Mr. Schmidt는 불완전한 배관 공사가 배수관 막힘의 원인이었다는 사실을 발견했다.

[해설] ------- plumbing의 의미를 자연스럽게 만들어 주는 형용사가 정답이다. '[(A) 불완전한 (B) 참을성 있는 (C) 충분한 (D) 불안한] 배관 공사'에서 의미가 가장 자연스러운 것은 (A)이다.

---

125. Mr. Rodriguez thinks that the article in *Cuanza Sul Times* will bring welcome ------- to the farm's greenhouse smart application project.

(A) publicize
(B) publicity
(C) publicist
(D) publicized

[어휘] welcome 반가운; 기쁜, 고마운 publicize 홍보하다 publicity 홍보, 광고 publicist 홍보 담당자 greenhouse 온실

[해석] Mr. Rodriguez는 Cuanza Sul Times에 실린 기사가

농장의 온실 스마트 앱 프로젝트에 반가운 홍보 효과를 가져다줄 것이라고 생각한다.

해설 빈칸 앞뒤 will bring welcome ------- to를 보면 빈칸은 동사 will bring의 목적어 자리로, 형용사 welcome의 수식을 받는 명사가 필요하다. 그러므로 (B)와 (C) 중에 정답을 선택해야 한다. (C)는 보통명사로 welcome 앞에 관사가 있어야 하므로 관사가 필요 없는 추상명사인 (B)가 정답이다.

---

126. The panel discussion is set to begin ------- after the guest speaker wraps up his speech.

(A) promptly
(B) assertively
(C) especially
(D) cordially

어휘 panel discussion 공개 토론회 be set to-V ~하도록 예정되어 있다 assertively 단정적으로 cordially 다정하게, 진심으로 guest speaker 초청 연사 wrap up (회의, 계약 등을) 마무리 짓다

해석 공개 토론회는 초청 연사가 연설을 마친 후 곧바로 시작될 예정이다.

해설 항상 짝을 이루어 출제되는 어휘 문제이다. after (ward), thereafter, before 앞에 빈칸이 있으면 '재빨리'라는 의미의 promptly, shortly, immediately 등을 정답으로 선택하자.

---

127. Mira Lawson is a widely recognized ------- in the area of customer satisfaction and retention.

(A) authority
(B) authorized
(C) authorizing
(D) authorization

어휘 widely 널리, 폭넓게 recognized 인정된, 알려진 authority 권위자 authorize 권한을 주다, 인가하다, 재가하다 authorization (공적인) 허가, 인가 retention 보유, 유지

해석 Mira Lawson은 고객 만족 및 유지 부문에서 널리 인정받는 권위자이다.

해설 빈칸 앞뒤 a widely recognized ------- in을 보면 '관사 + 부사 + 형용사 + -------' 구조이므로 빈칸에 명사가 들어가야 한다. 그러므로 (A)와 (D) 중에 정답을 선택해야 하는데, '널리 인정받는(a widely recognized)' 뒤에는 의미상 '권위자(authority)'가 자연스러우므로 정답은 (A)이다.

---

128. Mr. Wallace has already surpassed his sales quota, whereas Ms. Ellis has yet to reach -------.

(A) her
(B) herself
(C) she
(D) hers

어휘 surpass 능가하다, 뛰어넘다 quota 몫, 할당량 whereas 반면 have yet to-V 아직 ~하지 못하다

해석 Mr. Wallace는 이미 자신의 판매 할당량을 넘어섰지만, Ms. Ellis는 아직 자신의 할당량에 이르지 못했다.

해설 빈칸은 동사 reach의 목적어 자리이므로 목적격 대명사 (A), 재귀대명사 (B), 소유대명사 (D) 중에서 정답을 선택해야 한다. whereas 앞 절에 '소유격 + 명사 (his sales quota)'가 있으므로 her sales quota를 대신할 수 있는 소유대명사 (D)가 정답이다.

---

129. Barner Corporation's record profits resulted from the recent ------- to identify operating efficiencies.

(A) initiative
(B) initiating
(C) initiation
(D) initiator

어휘 record 기록적인 result from ~의 결과다 initiative (특정 목적을 위한) 계획, 프로젝트 initiation 시작, 개시 initiator 개시인, 발기인 identify 밝히다, 규명하다 operating 운영의 efficiency 효율성

해석 Barner 사(社)의 기록적인 수익은 운영 효율성을 규명하기 위한 최근 프로젝트의 결과다.

해설 빈칸 앞뒤 the recent ------- to identify를 보면 '관사 + 형용사 + -------' 구조로 빈칸에 명사가 필요하므로 형용사 (B)는 먼저 제외하자. record profits resulted from the recent -------의 의미로 '기록적인 수익은 최근 [(A) 프로젝트 (C) 개시 (D) 개시인]의 결과이다.'에서 가장 자연스러운 것은 (A)이다.

---

130. ------- the additional costs of maintaining the new PRX 3 printing press, the Voxel Printing Company has seen an overall decrease in its operating expenses.

(A) While
(B) Such
(C) Furthermore
(D) Despite

어휘 additional 추가의 maintain (보수하며) 유지하다
printing press 인쇄기 see 알아차리다. 목격하다
overall 전반적인 decrease 감소

해석 새로운 PRX 3 인쇄기를 유지, 관리하기 위한 추가적인
비용에도 불구하고 Voxel Printing 사(社)는 전반적으
로 운영 비용이 감소했음을 알게 되었다.

해설 [(A) 접속사 (B) 부사 (C) 부사 (D) 전치사]에서 부사
(B), (C)는 제외하자. 빈칸 뒤에 명사구가 있으므로 전치
사인 (D)가 정답이다.

Part 6

Questions 131-134 refer to the following invitation.

The San Bernardino Association of Photographic Artists invites you to the 5th $^{131.}$annual retreat at Rio Zadorra Conference Center from August 21 to August 24. This event is an opportunity for professional photographers to meet and share $^{132.}$their work at a serene and beautiful location every year. This year's program has been expanded to include both morning and afternoon sessions. $^{133.}$Participants are asked to bring several prints or digital files of their work to present at each of the sessions. The registration fee is $700 and includes room, meals, and gratuities. $^{134.}$Nonmembers are charged an extra program fee of $30.

131-134번 문제는 다음 초대장에 관한 것입니다.

San Bernardino 사진 예술가 협회가 8월 21일부터 8월
24일까지 Rio Zadorra 콘퍼런스 센터에서 열리는 제5회
연례 수련회에 여러분을 초대합니다. 이 행사는 전문 사
진작가들이 매년 평화롭고 아름다운 장소에 모여 작품에
관해 이야기 나눌 기회입니다. 올해 프로그램은 확대되어
오전과 오후 시간이 모두 있습니다. 참가자는 자기 작품
의 인쇄물이나 디지털 파일을 가져와서 각 시간에 발표해
야 합니다. 등록비는 700달러이며 숙박과 식사, 팁이 포
함됩니다. 비회원에게는 추가 프로그램비 30달러가 부과
됩니다.

어휘 association 협회 retreat 수련회, 캠프 serene 고요한,
평화로운 expand 확대하다 present 발표하다
registration fee 등록비 gratuity 팁 nonmember

비회원 charge 부과하다

---

131. (A) initial
(B) monthly
(C) early
(D) annual

해설 뒤 문장에서 이 행사는 매년(every year) 열린다고 말
하고 있으므로 (D)가 정답이다.

---

132. (A) they
(B) their
(C) them
(D) themselves

해설 빈칸 앞뒤 share ------- work에서 정답을 알아내
자. 명사 앞 빈칸에는 소유격이 들어가야 하므로 (B)가
정답이다.

---

133. **(A) Participants**
(B) Organizers
(C) Candidates
(D) Supervisors

어휘 organizer 주최자 supervisor 감독관, 관리자
해설 작품을 가져와서 발표하는 일은 캠프 참가자들이 할 일
이므로 (A)가 정답이다.

---

134. (A) The conference center houses the Museum of Photography.
(B) Nonmembers are charged an extra program fee of $30.
(C) The association accepts photo submissions via e-mail only.
(D) Nowadays most photographers prefer to use lightweight digital cameras.

어휘 house 보관하다. 소장하다 submission 제출(물) via
~을 통하여 lightweight 가벼운, 경량의
해석 (A) 콘퍼런스 센터 안에는 사진 박물관이 있다.
(B) 비회원에게는 30달러의 추가 프로그램비가 부과
된다.
(C) 협회는 이메일로만 사진 제출을 받는다.
(D) 요즘 대부분의 사진작가들은 가벼운 디지털 카메라
를 사용하는 것을 선호한다.

해설 빈칸 앞 문장에서 등록비를 알려주고 있으므로 빈칸에
는 비용에 관한 부연 설명인 (B)가 들어가는 것이 알맞
다.

Questions 135-138 refer to the following press release.

FOR IMMEDIATE RELEASE
Contact: Jean Iau, 604-555-0273
Ulsan Gains Momentum

SINGAPORE (December 1) - Kim Heng Offshore & Marine(KHOM) **135.**has acquired a 30 percent interest in the Ulsan offshore wind farm project. This was a critical component in the financing of Ulsan, which will be the largest offshore wind farm in Korea. During the pilot period of the project, two turbines were erected. **136.**Fifty more units will be constructed in the subsequent phase of the project. The total number of turbines in the Ulsan project will be enough to power a small urban area.

"We are delighted to offer assistance to the key players in a project of such consequence," said Thomas Tan, the CEO of KHOM. "Not only is Ulsan on track to become a major wind farm in Asia, **137.**but the involvement of international sponsors will also set a new precedent for projects of this nature. We hope this will stimulate future **138.**investment in the region."

135-138번 문제는 다음 보도 자료에 관한 것입니다.

즉시 보도 바랍니다.
연락: Jean Iau, 604-555-0273
울산, 탄력을 받다

싱가포르 (12월 1일) – Kim Heng Offshore & Marine(KHOM)는 울산 해상 풍력 발전 단지 프로젝트에서 30퍼센트의 지분을 획득했다. 이는 울산의 자금 조달에 있어서 매우 중요한 요소였는데, 울산은 한국에서 가장 큰 해상 풍력 발전 지역이 될 것이다. 프로젝트 시험 기간 동안 두 개의 터빈이 세워졌다. 프로젝트 후속 단계에서는 50기가 더 건설될 것이다. 울산 프로젝트에서 터빈의 총수는 소규모 도시 지역에 동력을 공급하기에 충분할 것이다.

KHOM의 CEO Thomas Tan은 "우리는 이렇게 중대한 프로젝트의 주역들에게 도움을 제공하게 되어 기쁩니다."라고 말했다. "울산은 아시아의 주요 풍력 발전 단지가 되는 궤도에 올라 있을 뿐 아니라 국제적인 후원 업체들의 참여는 이러한 성격의 프로젝트에 대한 새로운 전례를 남기게 될 것입니다. 우리는 이것으로 이 지역에 대한 향후 투자가 활성화되기를 바랍니다."

어휘 press release 보도 자료 immediate 즉시의 release 발표, 공개 momentum 탄력, 가속도 interest (사업의) 지분, 투자분 offshore 앞바다의, 연안의 wind farm 풍력 발전 단지 critical 결정적인, 중대한 component (구성) 요소 financing 자금 조달 pilot 시험(판)의 erect 건립하다, 세우다 unit 단위, (완성품) 한 개 construct 건설하다, 짓다 subsequent 그 다음의, 차후의 phase 단계, 국면, 시기 power 동력을 공급하다 urban 도시의 assistance 도움 key player 주역 of consequence 중대한 be on track to-V 정상 궤도에 오르다, 잘 진행되고 있다 involvement 참여, 관여 sponsor 후원자 set a precedent 전례를 세우다 nature 성질, 성격 stimulate 촉진하다, 자극하다

135. (A) was acquired
(B) has acquired
(C) is acquiring
(D) will acquire

해설 빈칸 뒤에 목적어 a 30 percent interest가 있으므로 수동태 동사 (A)는 제외한다. 이어지는 문장에서 KHOM의 지분 인수가 울산 프로젝트 자금 지원의 중요한 요소였다는 과거 시제로 말하고 있으므로(This was a critical component in the financing of Ulsan), 빈칸에는 현재완료 시제 동사 (B)가 알맞다.

136. (A) KHOM funds turbines on wind farms in other countries, too.
(B) The wind farms will encounter some challenges in the foreseeable future.
(C) Fifty more units will be constructed in the subsequent phase of the project.
(D) Multiple companies chose not to finance supplemental turbines.

어휘 fund(=finance) 자금을 대다 encounter ~에 직면하다 in the foreseeable future 가까운 장래에 supplemental 보충의, 추가의

해석 (A) KHOM는 다른 국가에서도 풍력 발전 단지의 터빈에 자금을 제공한다.

(B) 풍력 발전 단지들은 가까운 장래에 몇 가지 도전에 직면할 것이다.

(C) 프로젝트 후속 단계에서는 50기가 더 건설될 것이다.

(D) 다수의 기업이 추가 터빈에 대해서는 자금을 대지 않기로 했다.

해설 빈칸 앞 문장에서 '시험 가동 기간'과 터빈의 '개수'를 언급하고 있다. 그러므로 빈칸에는 '다음 단계'와 추가로 건설되는 터빈의 '개수'를 언급한 (C)가 들어가는 것이 알맞다.

---

137. (A) as
(B) or
(C) so
(D) but

해설 상관접속사 문제는 함께 쓰는 단어를 찾아야 한다. not only는 but also와 함께 쓰이므로 (D)가 정답이다.

---

138. (A) travel
(B) events
(C) regulations
(D) investment

어휘 regulation 규정

해설 앞 문장에서 국제적인 후원 업체들의 참여(the involvement of international sponsors)가 자금 지원의 선례를 남길 것(will also set a new precedent for projects of this nature)이라고 했다. 그러므로 다음 문장에서는 이 선례로 앞으로의 자금 지원, 즉 '투자'가 활발해지기를 바란다고 말하는 것이 자연스러우므로 (D)가 정답이다.

Part 7

Questions 139-142 refer to the following letter.

140.**Department of International Business**
Hong Kong Business University
4578 Pok Fu Lam, Hong Kong

September 30

Ms. J. Bian
Aramco Oil and Gas Corporation
Hong Kong

Dear Ms. Bian,

139.I am writing to express my gratitude for you allowing Mr. Pingyang Gao of your staff to coordinate a highly effective visit by twelve graduate students and faculty from the Hong Kong Business University to the Aramco Oil and Gas Corporation. Mr. Gao planned a very interesting round-table discussion in the morning with several of your senior executives responsible for the implementation of strategies, focusing in particular upon consumer behavior, cost dynamics, and corporate social responsibility — some of my students' particular areas of interest.

141.(A)After having lunch with the group, 141.(C),(D)Mr. Gao provided a highly polished overview of career opportunities in corporate Hong Kong, especially at Aramco Corporation. As a former executive of Aramco, I was pleased that he did such an outstanding job representing the company. His professional demeanor and 142.the scrupulous attention he paid to numerous details of the visit made a profound impression on us.

Very truly yours,

Hongbin Cai

139-142번 문제는 다음 편지에 관한 것입니다.

홍콩 경영대학교
국제경영학과
4578 Pok Fu Lam, Hong Kong

9월 30일

Ms. J. Bian
Aramco 석유가스회사
홍콩

Ms. Bian께,

귀하의 직원 Mr. Pingyang Gao가 홍콩 경영대학교에서

온 12명의 대학원생과 교수진의 Aramco 석유가스회사 방문을 매우 효과적으로 조율할 수 있도록 해주신 것에 대해 감사를 표하고자 이 편지를 씁니다. Mr. Gao가 오전에 전략 실행을 담당하는 최고위 중역 몇몇과 함께하는 매우 흥미로운 원탁 토론을 계획했는데, 특히 소비자 행동과 비용 역학, 기업의 사회적 책임 등에 초점을 맞춘 것으로 이는 우리 학생들의 관심 분야 중 일부입니다.

그룹과 점심을 먹은 후 Mr. Gao는 홍콩 기업 환경에서의, 특히 Aramco 사(社)에서의 취업 전망에 대해 매우 세련된 개요를 제공했습니다. Aramco의 전 간부로서 저는 그가 회사를 대표하는 일을 그렇게 훌륭하게 해낸 것이 기뻤습니다. 그의 전문가다운 품행과 방문의 여러 세부 사항에 세심한 주의를 기울인 것은 우리에게 깊은 감명을 주었습니다.

당신의 진정한 벗
Hongbin Cai

어휘 gratitude for ~에 대한 감사 coordinate 조율하다 effective 효과적인 graduate student 대학원생 faculty 교수진 corporation 기업 round-table discussion 원탁 토론 senior executive 최고 중역 implementation 이행, 수행 strategy 전략, 계획 in particular 특히 dynamics 역학 responsibility 책임 polished 세련된, 우아한 overview 개관, 개요 career opportunity 취업 전망 corporate Hong Kong 홍콩의 기업 환경 executive 경영 간부, 중역 outstanding 뛰어난, 걸출한 represent 대표하다 demeanor 행실, 품행 scrupulous 세심한, 꼼꼼한 profound 깊은, 심오한

문장 분석

1. I am writing / to express my gratitude for (you) [allowing Mr. Pingyang Gao of your staff to coordinate a highly effective visit (by twelve graduate students and faculty from the Hong Kong Business University) (to the Aramco Oil and Gas Corporation)].

➡ [ ]로 묶여 있는 동명사구는 전치사 for의 목적어이다. 그 사이에 있는 you는 의미상의 주어이다. 동명사의 의미상의 주어는 바로 앞에 소유격이나 목적격 (대)명사를 써서 표시한다.

➡ 5형식 동사 allow는 목적격 보어로 to 부정사를 사용한다.

2. Mr. Gao planned a very interesting round-table discussion (in the morning) (with several of your senior executives) (responsible for the implementation of strategies), / focusing in particular upon [consumer behavior], [cost dynamics], and [corporate social responsibility] — some of my students' particular areas of interest.

➡ discussion 뒤에 있는 어구들은 모두 수식어구이다.

➡ 동사 focus는 항상 전치사 (up)on과 함께 사용한다. Part 5에서 전치사 어휘 문제로 출제될 수 있다.

➡ [ ]로 묶여 있는 세 개의 명사구는 모두 전치사 upon의 목적어이다.

3. [His professional demeanor] and [the scrupulous attention (he paid to numerous details of the visit)] made a profound impression on us.

➡ [ ]로 묶여 있는 두 개의 명사구가 문장의 주어이다.

➡ ( )로 묶여 있는 절은 앞에 목적격 관계대명사가 생략된 채 선행사 the scrupulous attention을 수식하고 있다.

---

139. What is the purpose of this letter?

(A) **To commend a company employee**
(B) To issue official permission for a tour
(C) To set up a seminar
(D) To explore potential partnerships

어휘 commend 칭찬하다 issue 발부하다 set up 준비하다 explore 탐구하다

해석 이 편지의 목적은 무엇인가?
(A) 회사 직원을 칭찬하는 것
(B) 공식 견학 허가를 내주는 것
(C) 세미나를 준비하는 것
(D) 제휴 가능성을 모색하는 것

해설 주제, 목적은 대부분 지문의 도입부에서 확인할 수 있다. 첫 번째 문장에서 매우 인상적인 견학을 준비해 준 Mr. Pingyang Gao를 칭찬하기 위해 쓴 편지라는 것을 알 수 있으므로 (A)가 정답이다.

---

140. Where does Hongbin Cai work?

(A) At an accounting office
(B) At a travel agency
(C) **At a university**
(D) At an engineering firm

해석 Hongbin Cai는 어디에서 근무하는가?
(A) 회계 사무소
(B) 여행사
(C) 대학교

(D) 전문 기술 회사

편지의 본문만 보지 말고, 위아래에 있는 내용도 확인하자. 발신자 Hongbin Cai가 홍콩 경영대학교에서 근무한다는 것을 알 수 있으므로 (C)가 정답이다.

---

141. Which of the following did the visitors NOT do in the afternoon?

(A) Eat lunch with Mr. Gao

(B) Take a tour of Aramco Corporation

(C) Learn about corporate Hong Kong

(D) Hear about career opportunities

어휘 corporate 기업의 take a tour 견학하다

해석 방문자들은 오후에 다음 중 어느 것을 하지 않았는가?
(A) Mr. Gao와 함께 점심을 먹는다
(B) Aramco 사(社)를 둘러본다
(C) 홍콩의 기업 환경에 대해 알아본다
(D) 취업 전망에 대해 듣는다

해설 둘째 문단의 첫 문장에 (A)와 (C), (D)가 모두 오후에 한 일로 나와 있다.

---

142. What does Hongbin Cai say about Mr. Gao?

(A) He is employed in the human resources department.

(B) He possesses an adept sense of humor.

(C) He is placed in a senior executive position.

(D) He is scrupulous in his attention to detail.

어휘 adept 뛰어난 scrupulous 세심한, 꼼꼼한

해석 Hongbin Cai는 Mr. Gao에 대해 무엇이라고 말하는가?
(A) 인사부에 고용되었다.
(B) 뛰어난 유머 감각을 지니고 있다.
(C) 최고위 중역 자리에 있다.
(D) 세부 사항에 세심한 주의를 기울인다.

해설 맨 마지막 문장에 '여러 세부 사항에 기울인 세심한 주의(the scrupulous attention he paid to numerous details)'라는 표현이 있으므로 (D)가 정답이다.

Questions 143-147 refer to the following notice, review, and article.

Dear Valued Customers,

143.On October 14, after three decades in operation, Taste de France will shut its doors for the last time. During the week of October 8-14, please join us to commemorate the store's history. All customers will receive a piece of our specialty croissant for free with the purchase of any fresh baked goods.

144.Please keep an eye out for Taste de France pastry chef Melissa Murphy. Within the next few months, she is going to launch her own bakery, where customers will be able to order custom pastries and cakes for parties and weddings.

It has been a privilege to cater to our fantastic Louisville City customers.

Sincerely,
143.Florian Bellanger, owner

143-147번 문제는 다음 안내문과 논평, 기사에 관한 것입니다.

소중한 고객 여러분

Taste de France는 30년간 영업해온 끝에 10월 14일을 마지막으로 문을 닫습니다. 10월 8일부터 14일까지 일주일 동안 저희와 함께 가게의 역사를 기념해 주시기를 바랍니다. 갓 만든 어떤 제과류이든 구매한 모든 고객들께서는 저희 특제 크루아상 한 개를 무료로 받으실 수 있습니다.

Taste de France의 파티시에 Melissa Murphy를 지켜봐 주세요. 앞으로 몇 달 이내에 자기 제과점을 시작할 예정이며, 고객 여러분은 그곳에서 파티나 결혼식을 위한 맞춤형 페이스트리와 케이크를 주문하실 수 있습니다.

멋진 Louisville 시 고객 여러분께 제공하게 되어 영광이었습니다.

진심을 담아,
사장 Florian Bellanger

어휘 valued 귀중한, 소중한 operation 경영, 운영 commemorate 기념하다 specialty 특제품, 특산물 for free 무료로 fresh 신선한, 갓 만든 baked goods 제과류 keep an eye out for 지켜보다, 살펴보다 pastry chef

파티시에 launch 시작[개시/착수]하다 custom 맞춤의. 주문 제작의 privilege 영광 cater to ~에게 맞춰 제공하다

I was sad that Taste de France closed — I had wanted them to make my wedding cake. 144.So, I was excited when their former pastry chef opened Sweet Melissa Patisserie in the Hollydell Shopping Center. She made our cake, and it was perfect! 145.Our guests kept commenting on how much they liked the cake. I would recommend Sweet Melissa Patisserie to anyone.

Taste de France가 문을 닫아서 슬펐습니다. 저희 웨딩 케이크를 만들어 주시기 바랐거든요. 그래서 그곳의 전 파티시에께서 Hollydell 쇼핑센터에 Sweet Melissa 케이크 가게를 열었을 때 신이 났죠. 그분이 저희 케이크를 만들어 주셨고 완벽했습니다! 하객들이 케이크가 얼마나 좋았는지 계속 이야기합니다. 누구에게든 Sweet Melissa 케이크 가게를 추천하겠습니다.

어휘 patisserie 빵집. 제과점 keep V-ing 계속해서 ~하다 comment on ~에 대해 견해를 밝히다

The Evolution of a City

144.146.When the Hollydell Shopping Center opened on Cherry Hill Road in January of last year, Mayor Alfredo Rojas of Louisville City anticipated that it would be beneficial to the city by attracting shoppers from neighboring towns. Judging by the 20 percent growth in the city's sales tax revenues over the last six months, Mr. Rojas appears to have been correct.

However, less frequently mentioned was the potential effect of such commercial development on the city's downtown business district, which includes a number of small, family-owned stores and restaurants. 143.In the past two months, three of these businesses — Wayland Books, Amy's Beauty Salon, and Taste de France — have either closed or announced plans to close, all citing a decline in customers since the Hollydell's opening.

147.Notwithstanding, the mayor is of the opinion that the overall effects of new developments such as the Hollydell outweigh any potential drawbacks. "It's certainly disappointing when a beloved business like Wayland Books closes," he said. "But new businesses bring new opportunities for all residents of Louisville City, including new jobs."

도시의 발전

작년 1월 Hollydell 쇼핑센터가 Cherry Hill 가(街)에 문을 열었을 때 Louisville 시의 Alfredo Rojas 시장은 그것이 인근 도시들로부터 쇼핑객들을 끌어들임으로써 시에 유익할 것으로 예상했다. 지난 6개월 동안 판매세 수입의 20퍼센트 성장으로 판단하건대 Rojas 시장이 옳았던 것처럼 보인다.

그러나 그러한 상업용 개발이 시의 중심 상업 지구에 미치는 잠재적인 영향은 자주 언급되지 않았는데, 그곳은 가족 소유의 소규모 상점과 식당을 다수 포함하고 있다. 지난 두 달 동안 이러한 사업체 중 세 군데(Wayland 서점과 Amy's 미용실, Taste de France)가 문을 닫거나 문 닫을 계획을 발표했는데, 모두 Hollydell 개점 이후 고객 수 감소를 이유로 들었다.

그럼에도 불구하고 시장은 Hollydell과 같은 새로운 개발물의 전반적인 효과가 어떠한 잠재적 문제점보다 더 중요하다는 의견이다. 그는 말한다. "Wayland 서점 같은 사랑받는 사업체가 문을 닫을 때는 확실히 실망스럽습니다. 그러나 새로운 사업체들은 Louisville 시의 모든 주민에게 새 일자리를 포함하여 새로운 기회를 가져다줍니다."

어휘 evolution 발전. 진전 mayor 시장 anticipate 기대하다 beneficial 유익한 neighboring 인근의 judging by ~으로 판단하건대 sales tax 판매세 appear to have + p.p. ~했던 것으로 보이다 revenue 수입 frequently 자주. 흔히 potential 잠재적인 effect on ~에 미치는 영향 commercial 상업의 development 개발 downtown 중심가의 business district 상업지구 family-owned 가족 운영의, 가족 사업의 cite 언급하다. 인용하다 decline 감소 notwithstanding 그럼에도 불구하고 be of the opinion that ~라는 의견이다 certainly 확실히 disappointing 실망스러운 outweigh ~을 능가하다. 더 중요하다 drawback 결점. 문제점 beloved 사랑받는 resident 주민 including ~을 포함하여

1. Mayor Alfredo Rojas of Louisville City anticipated / that it would be beneficial to the city by attracting shoppers from neighboring towns.

➡ Part 5에서 would 자리를 빈칸으로 하는 시제 문제가 출제될 수 있다. 주절의 시제가 과거(anticipated)이기 때문에 종속절에서도 주절에 맞게 will이 아닌 과거형 would를 써야 한다.

2. Mr. Rojas appears to have been correct.

➡ appear[seem] to-V는 '~인(하는) 것으로 보이다'라는 뜻인데, 여기서는 완료형 부정사 to have p.p.를 사용했다. 완료형 부정사는 본동사(appears)보다 한 시제 앞선 일을 나타낸다.

3. However, less frequently mentioned was [the potential effect (of such commercial development) (on the city's downtown business district), (which includes a number of small, family-owned stores and restaurants)].

➡ [ ]로 묶여 있는 부분이 주어이다. less frequently mentioned는 보어로 이를 강조하기 위해 문장 맨 앞에 놓고, 주어와 동사를 도치한다. 또한 the potential effect의 수식어구가 많아 주어가 길어졌는데, 영어에서는 긴 주어를 문장 첫머리에 놓지 않는 경향이 있어 이러한 도치문이 자연스러운 문장이기도 하다.

➡ effect, impact, influence 등의 명사는 전치사 on과 함께 사용하는 것을 기억하자. Part 5에서 전치사의 어휘 문제로 출제될 수 있다.

---

143. Why most likely is Mr. Bellanger closing his business?

(A) Because he wants to retire
(B) Because he lost business to a new shopping center
(C) Because he cannot afford to make necessary renovations
(D) Because he intends to launch a different type of business

어휘 retire 은퇴하다 close one's business 폐업하다 afford to-V ~할 여유가 있다 renovation 보수, 개조 intend to-V ~할 생각이다, 계획이다

해석 Mr. Bellanger는 왜 폐업하겠는가?
(A) 은퇴하고 싶어서
(B) 새 쇼핑센터에 사업을 잃어서

(C) 필요한 보수를 할 여유가 없어서
(D) 다른 유형의 사업을 시작할 생각이어서

연계 추론 앞의 두 지문에서는 Mr. Bellanger가 Taste de France의 소유주라는 사실과 곧 문을 닫을 예정이라는 것만 알 수 있고, 사업을 접는 이유는 알 수 없다. 마지막 기사 지문까지 읽어야 정답을 추론할 수 있다. 기사 둘째 문단에서 쇼핑센터의 개점이 골목 상권에 미치는 영향을 언급하면서, Taste de France를 비롯한 세 군데의 상점이 문을 닫는다고 예를 들어 말하고 있는데, 모두 쇼핑센터에 사업을 잃은 것을 이유로 들고 있다(In the past two months, three of these businesses — Wayland Books, Amy's Beauty Salon, and Taste de France — have either closed or announced plans to close, all citing a decline in customers since the Hollydell's opening).

---

144. What is indicated about Ms. Murphy's bakery?

(A) It opened on October 14.
(B) It was once owned by Mr. Bellanger.
(C) It is located on Cherry Hill Road.
(D) It is giving away free croissants.

어휘 indicate 나타내다 give away 나누어 주다

해석 Ms. Murphy의 제과점에 대해 무엇이 나타나 있는가?
(A) 10월 14일에 개업했다.
(B) 한때 Mr. Bellanger가 소유했다.
(C) Cherry Hill 가(街)에 위치한다.
(D) 크루아상을 무료로 나누어 주고 있다.

연계 추론 안내문 둘째 문단에서 Ms. Murphy는 Taste de France에서 일하던 파티시에라는 사실을, 논평에서는 이 사람이 Sweet Melissa Patisserie라는 제과점을 열었는데, Hollydell 쇼핑센터에 있다는 것을 알 수 있다. 그리고 기사 첫 문장에 쇼핑센터가 Cherry Hill 가(街)에 있다고 나와 있다. 따라서 Ms. Murphy의 제과점은 Cherry Hill 가(街)에 있음을 추론할 수 있다.

---

145. In the review, the word "kept" on line 4 is closest in meaning to

(A) held
(B) continued
(C) saved
(D) gave

해석 논평에서 넷째 줄의 단어 kept와 의미상 가장 가까운 것은?
(A) 유지했다
(B) 계속했다

(C) 모았다
(D) 주었다

해설 keep -ing는 '계속해서 ~하다'라는 뜻이므로 바꿔 쓸
수 있는 동사는 continued이다.

---

146. What is suggested about the
Hollydell Shopping Center?

**(A) It has generated a lot of income
for Louisville City.**
(B) It has brought in business for
local family-owned stores.
(C) It was financed by Mayor Rojas.
(D) It was constructed in downtown
Louisville City.

어휘 generate 발생시키다, 만들어 내다 bring in 끌어오다
business 거래 finance 자금을 대다

해석 Hollydell 쇼핑센터에 대해 무엇이 암시되어 있는가?
(A) Louisville 시에 많은 수입을 발생시키고 있다.
(B) 지역의 가족 사업인 상점들에 거래를 가져왔다.
(C) Rojas 시장이 재원을 마련했다.
(D) Louisville 시 중심가에 건설되었다.

연계 추론 기사의 첫 문장을 읽어 보자. Hollydell 쇼핑센터가
문을 열었을 때 시장이 그것으로 인한 이익이 있을 것이라고
예상했다(When the Hollydell Shopping Center opened
on Cherry Hill Road in January of last year, Mayor
Alfredo Rojas of Louisville City anticipated that it would
be beneficial to the city by ...). 이어지는 문장에서 시장의
예상에 걸맞게 시의 판매세 수입이 20퍼센트 증가했다고 나
와 있으므로(Judging by the 20 percent growth in the
city's sales tax revenues over the last six months),
Hollydell 쇼핑센터는 시에 많은 수입을 발생시킨 것을 알 수
있다.

---

147. According to his statement, why
does Mr. Rojas have a positive view
of the Hollydell Shopping Center?

(A) Because it has a good beauty
salon
(B) Because it was completed on
schedule
(C) Because it offers discounts on
expensive products
**(D) Because it provides city
residents with jobs**

어휘 view 견해 on schedule 일정대로

해석 Mr. Rojas의 진술에 따르면, 그는 왜 Hollydell 쇼핑센

터에 대해 긍정적인 견해를 가지고 있는가?
(A) 좋은 미용실이 있어서
(B) 일정대로 완공되었기 때문에
(C) 값비싼 상품에 대해 할인을 제공하기 때문에
(D) 시 주민들에게 일자리를 제공하기 때문에

연계 추론 기사 마지막 문단에 시장의 견해가 나오는데, 우선
그는 쇼핑센터의 전반적인 효과가 단점보다 더 중요하다고 생
각한다(Notwithstanding, the mayor is of the opinion that
the overall effects of new developments such as the
Hollydell outweigh any potential drawbacks). 이어지는
인용문에서 견해의 근거를 알 수 있는데, 쇼핑센터의 새 사업
체들이 주민들에게 새 일자리를 마련해 준다는 점이다(But
new businesses bring new opportunities for all
residents of Louisville City, including new jobs).

Day 04

PART 5 & 6 Exercise

101 (D)	102 (C)	103 (C)	104 (D)	105 (B)
106 (A)	107 (D)	108 (A)	109 (A)	110 (C)
111 (B)	112 (A)	113 (A)	114 (C)	115 (A)

101. Those who register in advance for the seminar will be ------- the privilege to interact with Dr. Suarez in person.

(A) offers
(B) offering
(C) offer
(D) offered

어휘 register 등록하다 in advance 미리, 사전에 privilege 특전, 혜택 interact with 교류하다 in person 직접, 몸소

해석 세미나에 미리 등록하시는 분들은 Dr. Suarez와 직접 교류하는 특전을 제공받을 것이다.

해설 be동사 뒤에는 분사 (B)와 (D)가 올 수 있다. 빈칸에 (B)가 들어가면 능동태가 되고, (D)가 들어가면 수동태가 된다. 빈칸 뒤에 목적어 the privilege가 있지만, offer는 4형식 동사로써 빈칸 뒤에 목적어가 두 개 있을 때 능동태, 이 문장처럼 하나만 있으면 수동태가 되므로 정답은 (D)이다. 정답을 선택한 후에는 4형식 동사는 3형식으로도 사용할 수 있다는 사실을 기억하여 빈칸 앞뒤 구문 해석을 통해 수동태로 해석하는 것이 자연스러운지 확인하고 넘어가자.

102. Ms. Gwok will prepare a marketing budget and present ------- during the client meeting.

(A) those
(B) its
(C) it
(D) her

어휘 budget 예산 present 발표하다

해석 Ms. Gwok는 마케팅 예산안을 준비해서 고객과의 회의에서 발표할 것이다.

해설 동사 present의 목적어가 필요하다. (B)를 제외하면 모두 목적어로 사용할 수 있으므로, 대명사의 수와 성에

알맞은 것을 정답으로 선택해야 한다. 빈칸이 가리키는 명사는 a marketing budget이므로 (C)가 정답이다.

103. ------- who have faith in the expansion of the solar power industry will likely put money into solar-panel-manufacturing business this year.

(A) Ours
(B) Them
(C) Those
(D) Their

어휘 have faith in ~을 믿다, 신뢰하다 expansion 확대 solar power 태양열 발전 likely 아마도 solar panel 태양 전지판 manufacturing 제조(업)

해석 태양열 발전 산업의 확대를 믿는 사람들은 아마 올해 태양 전지판 제조 사업에 돈을 투입할 것이다.

해설 빈칸 뒤에 who로 시작하는 구문이나 분사 구문이 있으면 언제나 those가 정답이다. ------- who have faith in the expansion of the solar power industry가 문장의 주어로 '태양열 발전 산업의 확대를 믿는 사람들'이라는 의미가 되도록 (C)를 정답으로 선택하자.

104. Our company's shoes can be distinguished from ------- of other companies by the spiral pattern imprinted on the vamps.

(A) this
(B) them
(C) that
(D) those

어휘 distinguish A from B A를 B와 구별하다 spiral 나선형의 imprint 새기다; 인쇄하다 vamp (구두의) 등가죽

해석 우리 회사의 신발은 등가죽에 인쇄된 나선형 패턴으로 다른 회사들의 신발과 구별될 수 있다.

해설 전치사구 of other companies가 빈칸을 수식하고 있으므로 빈칸에는 that이나 those가 들어가야 한다. 빈칸이 가리키는 것은 복수 명사 shoes이므로 (D) those를 정답으로 선택하자.

105. Since online coding courses are increasingly popular, -------

interested in programming can easily enhance their skills at home.

(A) they

(B) those

(C) he

(C) who

> 해설 온라인 코딩 코스가 점점 인기를 얻고 있기 때문에 프로그래밍에 관심이 있는 사람들은 집에서 쉽게 실력을 향상시킬 수 있다.

> 해설 ------- interested in programming이 주절의 주어로 '프로그래밍에 관심 있는 사람들'이라는 의미가 되도록 (B)를 정답으로 선택해야 한다. who로 시작하는 구문이나 분사 구문, 특히 interested로 시작하는 구문 앞에 빈칸이 있으면 정답은 언제나 those이다.

---

106. After the levels of fine dust reached a record high, ------- with respiratory problems are being warned to stay indoors.

(A) those

(B) them

(C) whose

(D) which

> 어휘 fine dust 미세 먼지 record high 최고 기록 respiratory 호흡의, 호흡 기관의 be warned to-V ~하라고 주의를 받다

> 해설 미세 먼지 수치가 최고 기록에 도달한 이후 호흡기 질환이 있는 사람들은 실내에 머무르도록 주의를 받고 있다.

> 해설 ------- with respiratory problems가 주절의 주어로 '호흡기 질환이 있는 사람들'이라는 의미가 되도록 (A)를 정답으로 선택해야 한다. 관계대명사 who로 시작하는 구문이나 분사 구문, 형용사구, 전치사구 앞에 빈칸이 있을 때는 언제나 those가 정답이다.

---

107. When you buy a chicken, make sure to place it in a plastic bag to keep ------- juices from leaking onto other foods.

(A) they

(B) it

(C) their

(D) its

> 어휘 make sure to-V 반드시 ~하다 plastic bag 비닐봉지 keep ~ from -ing ~하는 것을 막다 juice 육즙 leak 새다, 새어 나오다

> 해설 닭고기를 살 때 육즙이 다른 음식에 새지 않도록 반드시 그것을 비닐봉지에 넣으세요.

> 해설 빈칸 앞뒤 to keep ------- juices를 보자. 명사 앞에 빈칸이 있으므로 소유격 (C)와 (D) 중에 정답을 선택해야 한다. 빈칸은 단수 명사 a chicken을 가리키고 있으므로 (D) its가 정답이다.

---

108. Orlingo Data International ------- a shuttle van service for all employees attending the digital marketing conference in Manchester next week.

(A) has arranged

(B) was arranged

(C) arranging

(D) arrangement

> 어휘 arrange 준비하다, 마련하다 employee 직원 conference 회의, 학회

> 해설 Orlingo Data International은 다음 주에 Manchester에서 디지털 마케팅 학회에 참석하는 모든 직원을 위해 셔틀 밴 서비스를 마련했다.

> 해설 문장에 동사가 없으므로 능동태 동사 (A)와 수동태 동사 (B) 중 정답을 선택해야 한다. 빈칸 뒤에 목적어 a shuttle van service가 있으므로 능동태 (A)가 정답이다.

---

109. Any requests to obtain a leave of absence must be ------- to a department manager at least two weeks in advance.

(A) submitted

(B) submit

(C) submitting

(D) submission

> 어휘 leave of absence 휴가 submit 제출하다 department manager 부서장

> 해설 어떤 휴가 신청서이든 최소 2주 전에 부서장에게 제출되어야 한다.

> 해설 be동사 뒤에 사용할 수 있는 분사 (A)와 (C) 중 정답을 선택해야 한다. 빈칸 뒤에 목적어가 없으므로 수동태 문장이 되어야 하므로 과거분사 (A)가 정답이다.

---

110. As a former chief financial officer of Beneful Foods, Ms. Collins recently ------- chairperson of the International Chamber of Commerce.

(A) named
(B) is named
(C) was named
(D) has named

former 전의 chief financial officer 최고 재무 책임자 name 지명하다, 임명하다 chairperson 의장, 회장 the International Chamber of Commerce 국제 상공 회의소

해석 Beneful 식품의 전 최고 재무 책임자로서 Ms. Collins 는 최근에 국제 상공 회의소 의장으로 지명되었다.

해설 빈칸 뒤에 있는 명사 chairperson을 목적어로 착각하지 말자. name은 5형식 동사이기 때문에 빈칸 뒤에 명사가 하나만 있으면 목적어가 아니라 목적격 보어이다. 주어진 문장에서 목적어가 없으므로 수동태 동사 (B)와 (C) 중 정답을 선택해야 한다. 빈칸 앞에 부사 recently 가 있으므로 과거 시제 (C)가 정답으로 알맞다.

---

111. Since the information on performance appraisals is highly confidential, only the senior managers are ------- to access it.

(A) allowing
(B) allowed
(C) allowance
(D) allow

어휘 performance appraisal 인사 고과 confidential 비밀의, 기밀의 allowance 허용량 access 접근하다, 이용하다

해석 인사 고과에 관한 정보는 극비이므로 오직 고위 간부들만 접근하도록 허용된다.

해설 be동사 뒤에 올 수 있는 분사 (A)와 (B) 중 정답을 선택해야 한다. allow는 to부정사를 목적격 보어로 사용하는 5형식 동사이다. 빈칸 뒤의 to access가 목적격 보어이고 목적어가 없으므로 동사는 수동태가 되어야 한다. 따라서 과거분사 (B)가 정답이다.

---

112. ------- eager to become part of the task force team may see Mr. North or send him an e-mail before July 25.

(A) Those
(B) They
(C) Them
(D) These

어휘 task force team 특별대책반

해석 특별 대책반의 일원이 되기를 바라는 사람들은 7월 25

일 전에 Mr. North를 만나거나 그에게 이메일을 보내면 된다.

해설 ------- eager to become part of the task force team이 주어로 '특별 대책반의 일원이 되기를 바라는 사람들'이라는 의미가 되도록 빈칸에 (A)가 들어가야 한다. 관계대명사 who로 시작하는 구문이나 분사 구문, 형용사구, 전치사구 앞에 빈칸이 있을 때는 those 가 정답이다.

---

113. Kothari Gowns returned three boxes of lace to the supplier because the actual color differed from ------- in the catalog description.

(A) that
(B) including
(C) those
(D) only

어휘 supplier 공급업체, 납품업체 differ from ~와 다르다 description 설명

해석 Kothari Gowns는 실제 색상이 카탈로그 설명서에 있는 것과 달라서 레이스 세 상자를 납품업체에 반품했다.

해설 전치사구 in the catalog description이 빈칸을 수식하고 있다. 이때 빈칸에는 that이나 those가 들어가야 하는데, 단수 명사 color를 가리키므로 (A) that이 정답이다.

---

114. Mr. Campbell ------- that only the senior loan officers should participate in the conference on recent trends in lending.

(A) specify
(B) to specify
(C) has specified
(D) is specified

어휘 specify 명시하다, 분명히 말하다 loan officer 대출 담당자 trend 동향, 추세 lending 대출, 대부

해석 Mr. Campbell은 오직 고위 대출 담당자들만 최신 대출 동향에 대한 학회에 참가한다고 분명히 말했다.

해설 that절은 종속절이고 앞부분이 주절이다. 빈칸은 주절의 동사 자리이므로, 준동사인 (B)는 제외하자. that절은 목적어인 명사절로 주절의 동사는 능동태여야 하므로 수동태인 (D)도 제외하자. 마지막으로 (A)와 (C) 중 단수 명사인 주어 Mr. Campbell과 동사의 수가 일치하도록 (C)를 정답으로 선택해야 한다.

115. Mr. Martinez was ------- a medal in recognition of his performance in the contest last weekend.

(A) given
(B) won
(C) received
(D) acquired

어휘 acquire 획득하다 in recognition of ~를 인정하여 performance 성과, 성적

해석 Mr. Martinez는 지난 주말 대회의 성적을 인정받아 메달을 받았다.

해설 문장의 동사가 수동태인데 목적어 a medal이 있으므로 4형식 문장의 수동태임을 알 수 있다. 따라서 4형식 동사인 (A)가 정답이다.

Actual Test

101 (A)	**102** (A)	**103** (C)	**104** (D)	**105** (B)
106 (B)	**107** (B)	**108** (A)	**109** (B)	**110** (A)
111 (C)	**112** (C)	**113** (D)	**114** (B)	**115** (D)
116 (B)	**117** (B)	**118** (D)	**119** (A)	**120** (C)
121 (A)	**122** (B)	**123** (C)	**124** (C)	**125** (C)
126 (A)	**127** (D)	**128** (D)	**129** (A)	**130** (D)
131 (B)	**132** (B)	**133** (A)	**134** (D)	**135** (A)
136 (C)	**137** (B)	**138** (B)	**139** (D)	**140** (C)
141 (B)	**142** (A)	**143** (A)	**144** (C)	**145** (D)
146 (B)	**147** (A)			

Part 5

101. To boost morale, employees who report best sales in their teams ------- a special bonus for their hard work.

(A) are offered
(B) was offered
(C) offering
(D) offers

어휘 boost 진작시키다, 북돋우다 morale 사기, 의욕

해석 사기를 진작시키기 위해 팀 내 최고 판매량을 기록하는 직원은 노고에 대한 특별 상여금을 받는다.

해설 빈칸 앞 who report best sales in their teams는 주어인 employess를 수식하는 어구이고 빈칸은 동사 자리이므로 준동사 (C)는 제외하자. 빈칸 뒤에 목적어 a

special bonus가 있다고 능동태 (D)가 정답은 아니다. offer는 4형식 동사이므로 목적어가 두 개일 때 능동태, 하나이면 수동태가 되므로 복수 명사 employees의 수에 맞는 수동태 복수 동사 (A)가 정답이다. 4형식 동사는 3형식 문장에도 사용될 수 있으므로 빈칸 앞뒤를 해석해서 수동태 문장의 의미가 자연스러운지 확인하자.

102. Researchers at the University of Cambridge have developed a type of smart glass that transforms ------- transparent to opaque in less than a minute.

(A) from
(B) against
(C) between
(D) throughout

어휘 transform (완전히) 바뀌다, 변형되다 transparent 투명한 opaque 불투명한

해석 Cambridge 대학교 연구원들은 1분도 안 되어 투명에서 불투명으로 바뀌는 일종의 스마트 유리를 개발했다.

해설 빈칸 앞뒤 transforms ------- transparent to opaque만 보고 정답을 알아내자. '투명에서 불투명으로 바뀌는'이라는 뜻이므로 빈칸에는 (A) from이 알맞다.

103. Greer Agency's travel insurance can be purchased over the phone, though most of ------- plans are bought online.

(A) whose
(B) his
(C) its
(D) this

어휘 agency 대리점 plan (보험) 상품, 정책

해석 Greer Agency의 여행자 보험은 대부분 온라인으로 가입되기는 하지만, 전화로도 가입할 수 있다.

해설 most of와 같은 '수량대명사 + of' 뒤에 목적격 관계대명사는 들어갈 수 있지만 소유격 관계대명사는 사용할 수 없으므로 (A)는 제외하자. 명사 plans 앞에 소유격 대명사 his, its와 지시형용사 this를 모두 사용할 수 있다. 그런데 빈칸은 Greer Agency를 가리키므로 정답은 (C) its이다.

104. The restaurant is ------- located in the middle of the entertainment district, so that diners can comfortably attend a movie or concert either before or after a meal.

(A) superficially
(B) unanimously
(C) prudently
(D) perfectly

어휘 superficially 표면적으로, 겉보기에는 unanimously 만장일치로 prudently 신중하게, 분별력 있게 entertainment district 유흥가 diner 식사하는 사람[손님] comfortably 편안하게 attend a movie 영화를 보러 가다

해석 그 식당은 정확하게 유흥가에 있어서 손님들이 식사 전이나 후에 편안하게 영화나 콘서트를 보러 갈 수 있다.

해설 짝으로 출제되는 어휘를 암기해 두면 시간을 절약할 수 있다. located나 situated 앞의 빈칸에는 언제나 conveniently, perfectly, ideally가 정답이다.

---

105. ------- who would like to view the statistics featured in the presentation to the board of directors should contact Mr. Dominguez.

(A) Whichever
(B) Anyone
(C) Other
(D) Themselves

어휘 view (특정 관점으로) 보다 statistics 통계 (자료) feature 특별히 포함하다 board of directors 이사회

해석 이사회에서 한 발표에 포함된 통계 자료를 보고자 하는 사람은 누구든지 Mr. Dominguez에게 연락해야 한다.

해설 ------- who would like to view the statistics가 '통계 자료를 보고자 하는 사람은 누구든지'라는 의미가 되도록 anyone을 선택하자. 관계대명사 who로 시작하는 구문이나 분사 구문, 형용사구, 전치사구 앞에 빈칸에는 언제나 those나 anyone이 들어간다. 그러므로 정답은 (B) anyone이다.

---

106. Each full-time permanent employee's travel expenses can be ------- from taxable income by a certain percentage.

(A) deduct
(B) deducted
(C) deductive
(D) deducting

어휘 full-time employee 상근 직원 permanent

employee 정규 직원 travel expenses 여행 경비, 출장비 deduct 공제하다, 차감하다 deductive 연역의 taxable income 과세 소득

해석 각 상근 정규직 사원의 출장비는 일정 비율만큼 과세 소득에서 공제될 수 있다.

해설 be동사 뒤의 빈칸에는 형용사나 분사가 들어갈 수 있다. 그런데 deductive는 '연역적인'이라는 뜻으로 주어 travel expenses와 의미상 어울리지 않아 정답이 아니다. 따라서 분사 (B)와 (D) 중에서 선택해야 한다면, 빈칸 뒤에 목적어가 없어 수동태가 되어야 하므로 (B)가 정답이다.

---

107. Food prices rose nearly 15 percent overall, with the price of meat going up by 10 percent, and ------- of vegetables by 20 percent.

(A) this
(B) that
(C) these
(D) those

어휘 with + 명사 + 형용사[분사/전치사구/to-V] [명사]가 ~인 채로

해석 식품 가격은 전반적으로 거의 15% 상승하였으며, 고기 가격은 10% 오르고 채소 가격은 20% 올랐다.

해설 전치사구 of vegetables가 앞에 있는 빈칸을 수식하고 있다. 이때 빈칸에는 that이나 those가 들어갈 수 있다. 빈칸이 단수 명사 the price를 가리키고 있으므로 (B) that이 정답이다. 참고로 and와 빈칸 사이에는 with가, vegetables와 by 사이에는 going up이 생략되어 있다.

---

108. Eli Fry is ------- the most competent person working in the R&D Department.

(A) considered
(B) appeared
(C) regarded
(D) agreed

어휘 regard A as B A를 B로 여기다 competent 유능한 R&D 연구 개발(research and development)

해석 Eli Fry는 R&D 부서에서 근무하는 가장 유능한 사람으로 여겨진다.

해설 consider와 같은 5형식 동사를 수동태로 사용할 때 그 뒤에 목적격 보어인 명사(구)를 쓸 수 있다. 따라서 the most competent person을 목적격 보어로 사용하는 (A)가 정답이다. appear는 자동사라서 수동태로 만들

수 없고, regard는 consider와 같은 뜻이지만 빈칸 뒤
에 as가 있어야 하므로 정답이 아니다.

---

109. The delivery charge for your
purchase ------- on the shipping
method you choose at the checkout
step on our Web site.

(A) have depended
(B) will depend
(C) depending
(D) are depended

어휘 shipping 운송. 배송 checkout 계산. 결제
해석 구매품의 배송 요금은 저희 웹사이트의 결제 단계에서
선택하신 운송 방식에 따라 결정됩니다.
해설 빈칸은 문장의 동사 자리이고, depend는 자동사로 수
동태를 만들 수 없으므로 (C)와 (D)는 제외하자. 빈칸
앞 전치사구 for your purchase를 지우면 The
delivery charge가 문장의 주어임을 알 수 있다. 그런
데 동사 (A)는 단수 명사인 주어의 수와 일치하지 않으
므로 (B)가 정답으로 알맞다.

---

110. The various means used to determine
appropriate annual pay increases
------- to as the merit criteria.

(A) are referred
(B) referring
(C) have referred
(D) to refer

어휘 means 수단. 방법 appropriate 적절한 pay increase
임금 인상 refer to A as B A를 B라고 부르다 merit 성과
criterion(pl. criteria) 기준
해석 적절한 연간 임금 인상액을 결정하는 데 사용되는 다양
한 수단을 성과 기준이라고 부른다.
해설 빈칸은 문장의 동사 자리이므로, 보기를 보면 수동태
(A)나 능동태 (C)가 들어가야 하는 것을 알 수 있다. 그
런데 빈칸 뒤 to as를 보면 동사구 refer to의 목적어가
빠져 있음을 알 수 있으므로 수동태 (A)가 정답이다.

---

111. Each manager is required to evaluate
their employees' job ------- at the
end of every quarter and submit the
results to the personnel department.

(A) confirmation
(B) medication
(C) performance

(D) emission

어휘 be required to-V ~해야 한다 evaluate 평가하다
confirmation 확인 medication 약물 performance
성과. 실적 emission 배출; 배기가스 personnel
department 인사부
해석 각 매니저는 매 분기 말에 담당 직원들의 업무 실적을
평가해서 인사부에 결과를 제출해야 한다.
해설 evaluate their employees' job -------(담당 직원
들의 업무 [(A) 확인을 (B) 약물을 (C) 실적을 (D) 배출
을] 평가한다)의 의미를 자연스럽게 해 주는 명사 (C)를
정답으로 선택해야 한다. 토익에 매우 자주 등장하는
복합명사 job performance(업무 성과[실적])를 기억하
자.

---

112. The annual profit of the Singapore
branch ------- for one-third of
the total annual profit of CNTC
Enterprise.

(A) calculates
(B) takes
(C) accounts
(D) features

어휘 account for (부분 · 비율을) 차지하다 feature in (~의) 특
징을 이루다 one-third 3분의 1
해석 싱가포르 지사의 연간 수익이 CNTC Enterprise의 총
연간 수익의 3분의 1을 차지한다.
해설 시험에 매우 자주 등장하는 account for의 의미를 알
고 있으면 쉽게 문제를 풀 수 있다.

---

113. ------- wishing to join the task force
team should notify Cynthia Holt by
e-mail no later than April 24.

(A) Fewer
(B) Another
(C) Whoever
(D) Anyone

어휘 task force team 특별 대책반 notify 알리다 no later
than 늦어도 ~까지는
해석 특별 대책반에 합류하기를 바라는 사람은 누구나 늦어
도 4월 24일까지 이메일로 Cynthia Holt에게 알려야
한다.
해설 ------- wishing to join the task force team이 '특
별 대책반에 합류하기를 바라는 사람은 누구나'라는 의
미가 되도록 Anyone (D)를 정답으로 선택해야 한다.
관계대명사 who로 시작하는 구문이나 분사 구문, 형용

사구, 전치사구 앞의 빈칸에는 those나 anyone이 정답이다.

---

114. The building has been left ------- for almost three years, prompting the city to tear it down.

(A) revealed
(B) unoccupied
(C) unopposed
(D) disappointed

어휘 reveal 밝히다, 드러내다 unoccupied (좌석, 집이) 비어 있는 unopposed 반대가 없는 prompt ~ to-V ~하도록 촉구하다 tear down 허물다, 철거하다

해석 그 건물은 거의 3년 동안 빈 채 방치되어 있어서 시가 철거를 결정하게 되었다.

해설 The building has been left -------(그 건물은 [(A) 밝혀진 (B) 비어 있는 (C) 반대가 없는 (D) 실망한] 채로 있었다.)의 의미를 자연스럽게 해 주는 형용사 (B)가 정답이다.

---

115. Mr. Nettles understands what needs to be done better than ------- originally in charge of the project.

(A) who
(B) them
(C) those who
(D) those

어휘 originally 원래, 본래 in charge of ~을 담당하는

해석 Mr. Nettles는 해야 할 일을 원래 프로젝트를 담당하던 사람들보다 더 잘 이해하고 있다.

해설 ------- originally in charge of the project가 '원래 프로젝트를 담당하던 사람들'이라는 의미가 되도록 (D)를 정답으로 선택하자. 관계대명사 who로 시작하는 구문이나 분사 구문, 형용사구, 전치사구 앞에 빈칸이 있을 때는 언제나 those가 정답이다.

---

116. PX-001 printer model has been -------, but the contents of the instruction manual for PX-005 are almost the same.

(A) deferred
(B) discontinued
(C) upheld
(D) sustained

어휘 defer 미루다, 연기하다 discontinue 중단하다, 단종하다 uphold 들어 올리다, 떠받치다 sustain 지속하다 content 내용 instruction manual 사용 설명서

해석 PX-001 프린터 모델은 단종되었지만, PX-005의 사용 설명서 내용이 거의 똑같다.

해설 PX-001이 단종되어서 사용 설명서를 구할 수 없어도, 내용이 거의 같은 PX-005의 설명서를 보면 된다는 의미가 자연스러우므로 (B)가 빈칸에 알맞다.

---

117. Any ------- product can be returned to our offices for an exchange, provided the customer brings the merchandise to our customer care center with a valid receipt.

(A) relieved
(B) defective
(C) perplexed
(D) confused

어휘 relieved 안도하는, 다행으로 여기는 defective 결함이 있는 perplexed 당혹한 confused 혼란스러워 하는 provided (만약) ~라면 valid 유효한

해석 고객께서 상품을 저희 고객 서비스 센터로 유효한 영수증과 함께 가져오시면, 결함이 있는 어떤 제품이든 저희 지점으로 반품하시고 교환하실 수 있습니다.

해설 Any ------- product([(A) 안도하는 (B) 결함이 있는 (C) 당혹한 (D) 혼란스러운] 어떤 제품이든)의 의미를 자연스럽게 해 주는 형용사 (B)가 정답이다.

---

118. Ms. Anderson was appointed ------- for the outreach program.

(A) facilitate
(B) facilitated
(C) facilitating
(D) facilitator

어휘 appoint A (as) B A를 B로 임명하다 facilitate 용이하게 하다 facilitator 진행자, 조정자 outreach 봉사 활동

해석 Ms. Anderson이 봉사 활동 진행자로 임명되었다.

해설 5형식 동사 appoint는 능동태일 때는 뒤에 목적어와 목적격 보어인 명사 두 개가, 수동태일 때는 목적격 보어인 명사 한 개가 있다. was appointed는 수동태 동사로 빈칸에 목적격 보어인 명사가 들어가야 하므로 (D)가 정답이다.

---

119. Advanced ------- skills both in Spanish and English are required for

---

the qualified applicants along with a strong business and accounting background.

(A) communication
(B) communicates
(C) communicate
(D) communicative

> 어휘 advanced 고급의, 상급의 communication skill 의사소통 능력 background 배경 지식

> 해석 자격을 갖춘 지원자가 되려면 강력한 경영 및 회계 배경 지식과 더불어 스페인어와 영어 모두에서 고급 의사소통 능력이 요구된다.

> 해설 품사 문제를 가장한 어휘 문제이다. 빈칸 앞뒤 Advanced ------ skills를 보고 명사 앞의 빈칸이라고 형용사를 정답으로 선택하면 안 된다. communication skill(의사소통 능력)이라는 복합명사를 알고 있어야 한다.

---

120. ------ donors substantially increase their pledges will Doctors Without Borders be able to meet its goals.

(A) In case
(B) Even
(C) Only if
(D) Except

> 어휘 donor 기부자 substantially 상당히, 많이 pledge 서약, 기부금 border 국경

> 해석 국경없는 의사회는 기부자들이 기부금을 상당히 늘려주는 경우에만 목표를 달성할 수 있을 것이다.

> 해설 빈칸 뒤는 '주어 + 동사(donors substantially increase)' 구조로 접속사가 필요하므로 부사 (B)와 전치사 (D)는 제외하자. 접속사는 문장 전체를 해석해서, 두 절을 자연스럽게 연결해 주는 것을 선택해야 한다. '기부자들이 기부금을 상당히 늘린다'와 '국경없는 의사회는 목표를 달성할 수 있을 것이다.'를 자연스럽게 연결하는 (C)가 정답이다. 참고로 only로 시작하는 부사(구/절) 뒤에 나오는 주절은 주어와 동사가 도치된다는 규칙을 기억하자.

---

121. The official spokesperson of the Orion Technologies announced at a press ------ held at the Hilton Hotel today that a merger negotiation with their rival H&D Electronics is in progress.

(A) conference

(B) committee
(C) maintenance
(D) participation

> 어휘 spokesperson 대변인 press conference 기자 회견 maintenance 유지보수 participation 참여 merger 합병 negotiation 협상, 교섭 in progress 진행 중인

> 해석 Orion Technologies의 공식 대변인은 오늘 Hilton 호텔에서 열린 기자 회견에서 경쟁사 H&D 전자와의 합병 협상이 진행 중이라고 발표했다.

> 해설 at a press ------ held at the Hilton Hotel today가 '오늘 Hilton 호텔에서 열린 기자 회견에서'라는 의미가 되도록 (A)를 정답으로 선택해야 한다.

---

122. A diverse range of employee comments and suggestions are regularly ------ to the multifunctional review team.

(A) filled in
(B) passed on
(C) broken in
(D) counted on

> 어휘 a diverse range of 다양한 fill in (서식을) 작성하다 pass on 넘겨주다, 전달하다 break in 끼어들다, 방해하다 count on ~을 믿다, 기대하다 multifunctional 다기능의, 다목적의

> 해석 직원들의 다양한 의견과 제안이 정기적으로 다목적 평가단에게 전달된다.

> 해설 are regularly ------ to the multifunctional review team(정기적으로 다목적 평가단에게 [(A) 작성된다 (B) 전달된다 (C) 방해된다 (D) 기대된다])의 의미를 자연스럽게 해 주는 동사 (B)가 정답이다.

---

123. Thanks to the newly installed equipment, we are currently well ahead of our initial ------ schedule for most of the important items.

(A) producing
(B) productive
(C) production
(D) produce

> 어휘 thanks to ~ 덕분에 install 설치하다 currently 현재 well ahead of schedule 예정보다 훨씬 앞선 initial 초기의 production schedule 생산 일정

> 해석 새로 설치된 장비 덕분에 현재 우리는 대부분의 중요한 품목들에 대한 초기 생산 일정보다 훨씬 앞서 있다.

해설 품사 문제를 가장한 어휘 문제이다. 빈칸 앞뒤 our initial ------- schedule을 보고 명사 앞의 빈칸이라고 형용사를 정답으로 선택하면 안 된다. production schedule[time/cost/facility/complex](생산 일정[시간/비용/시설/복합단지])와 같은 복합명사를 알고 있어야 하며 (C)가 정답이다.

---

124. Mr. Mangal ------- obtained estimates from several companies before hiring a caterer.

(A) sharply
(B) shortly
(C) wisely
(D) purely

어휘 sharply 급격히 shortly 얼마 안 되어 wisely 현명하게 purely 순전히, 전적으로, 오직 estimate 견적(서) caterer 출장 뷔페 업체

해석 Mr. Mangal은 현명하게 출장 뷔페 업체를 고용하기 전에 몇몇 회사들로부터 견적을 받았다.

해설 sharply나 purely는 의미상 동사 obtained를 수식하기에 알맞지 않다. shortly는 주어와 동사 사이에 사용하는 대신, shortly after[before](직후에[직전에])의 형태로 사용한다. 그러므로 '현명하게 고용할 업체를 결정하기 전에 몇 군데에서 견적을 받았다'라는 뜻의 (C)가 정답으로 알맞다.

---

125. A major ------- of the convention center's design was the lack of adequate parking space.

(A) category
(B) portion
(C) shortcoming
(D) responsibility

어휘 category 범주 portion 부분; 몫 shortcoming 결점, 단점 responsibility 책임 adequate 적절한, 적당한

해석 컨벤션 센터 설계의 중대한 결점은 적절한 주차 공간의 부족이다.

해설 내용상 주차 공간 부족은 '단점'이므로 (C)가 정답으로 알맞다.

---

126. Ms. Wagner is planning to conduct a training session on the new time tracking software since ------- people know how to use it.

(A) few

(B) more
(C) other
(D) all

어휘 conduct 실시하다 training session 교육 (과정)

해석 Ms. Wagner는 새 시간 추적 소프트웨어의 사용법을 아는 사람이 거의 없어서 그것에 대한 교육을 시행할 계획이다.

해설 교육을 시행하는 이유로 사용법을 아는 사람이 거의 없다는 내용이 자연스러우므로 (A)가 정답이다.

---

127. In an effort to increase employee -------, the company has introduced an automated assembly line in their new processing plant.

(A) necessity
(B) possibility
(C) complexity
(D) productivity

어휘 in an effort to-V ~하려는 노력의 일환으로 employee productivity 직원 생산성 complexity 복잡성, 복잡함 automated 자동화된 assembly line 조립 라인 processing plant 가공처리 공장

해석 직원 생산성을 높이기 위한 노력의 일환으로 회사는 새 가공처리 공장에 자동화된 조립 라인을 도입했다.

해설 employee와 함께 사용할 수 있는 명사는 productivity이다. improve[enhance/increase] employee productivity(직원 생산성을 향상시키다)는 시험에 자주 나오는 표현이므로 기억해 두자.

---

128. The performance ratings of the veteran salesman were overshadowed by ------- of a newcomer who joined the sales department only a year ago.

(A) they
(B) that
(C) them
(D) those

어휘 performance 실적, 성과 rating 평점 overshadow 빛을 잃게[무색하게] 만들다

해석 그 베테랑 영업 사원의 실적 평점이 겨우 1년 전에 영업부에 합류한 신입 사원의 실적 평점에 가려져 있었습니다.

해설 전치사구 of a newcomer가 앞의 빈칸을 수식하고 있으므로 빈칸에는 that이나 those가 들어가야 한다. 빈칸이 복수 명사 performance ratings를 가리키고 있

으므로 정답은 (D)이다.

---

129. The Aargenso Telecommunication's new TV, Internet, and phone bundle plan is a ------- move to attract more customers.

(A) **strategic**
(B) preventable
(C) distant
(D) previous

bundle plan 패키지 상품 strategic 전략적인 preventable 예방할 수 있는 distant 먼 previous 이전의 move 조치, 행동 attract 끌어들이다, 유치하다

Aargenso Telecommunication의 새로운 TV, 인터넷, 전화 패키지 상품은 더 많은 고객을 유치하기 위한 전략적인 조치이다.

bundle plan is a ------- move to attract more customers(패키지 상품은 더 많은 고객을 유치하기 위한 [(A) 전략적인 (B) 예방할 수 있는 (C) 멀리 떨어진 (D) 이전의] 조치이다)의 의미를 자연스럽게 만들어 주는 형용사 (A)가 정답이다.

---

130. Ms. Aguilar and Mr. Liu are in ------- about the agenda for the next board meeting.

(A) submission
(B) fulfillment
(C) force
(D) **agreement**

submission 제출 fulfillment 이행, 수행 in force 시행 중인 in agreement 동의하는, 일치하는 agenda 의제, 안건 board meeting 이사회 회의

Ms. Aguilar와 Mr. Liu는 다음 이사회 회의의 안건에 대해 서로 동의한다.

전치사 in과 함께 사용하는 주요 표현은 in force와 in agreement이다. Ms. Aguilar and Mr. Liu are in ------- about the agenda가 "안건에 대해 서로 동의한다."라는 의미가 되는 것이 자연스러우므로 빈칸에 (D) agreement가 들어가는 것이 알맞다.

Part 6

Questions 131-134 refer to the following e-mail.

Dear Ms. Johnson,

We are pleased that you have accepted our invitation to join Aflac Financial. We would like you to fill out three documents and [131.]either e-mail them to us or bring them with you for your first day of work next Monday. You must complete the Personnel Information Form, the Confidentiality Agreement Form, and the Method of Payment Form, which are [132.]attached to this e-mail. [133.]Please fill them out completely and correctly so that your file can be processed. If you have any trouble accessing the forms, please let me know immediately. We look forward to the commencement of your [134.]employment at Aflac Financial.

Sincerely,

Akari Ito

131-134번 문제는 다음 이메일에 관한 것입니다.

Ms. Johnson께,

Aflac Financial에 합류해달라는 제안을 수락해 주셔서 기쁩니다. 세 개의 문서를 작성하셔서 이메일로 보내주시거나 다음 주 월요일 첫 출근 하시는 날 가져오시기를 바랍니다. '인사 정보 서식'과 '기밀 유지 서약서', '지급 방식 서식'을 작성하셔야 하는데, 이 이메일에 첨부되어 있습니다. 당신의 파일이 처리될 수 있도록 빠짐없이 정확히 작성하시기를 바랍니다. 서식을 이용하시는 데 어려움이 있으면 즉시 저에게 알려주시기를 바랍니다. Aflac Financial에서 근무를 시작하게 되기를 기대합니다.

Akari Ito 올림

invitation 요청, 제안 fill out 작성하다 complete (빠짐없이) 작성하다 confidentiality 비밀성, 기밀 유지 correctly 올바르게, 정확하게 process 처리하다 access 접근하다; 이용하다 immediately 즉시 look

forward to ~를 기대하다 commencement 시작, 개시
employment 고용, 근무

---

131. (A) if
(B) either
(C) as
(D) both

해설 상관접속사 문제이다. 빈칸 뒤에 있는 or를 보고 짝이
되는 (B) either를 선택하자.

---

132. (A) attach
(B) attached
(C) attaching
(D) attachment

해설 빈칸은 관계대명사(which) 절의 동사 자리이다. 빈칸
뒤에 목적어가 없으므로 수동태 (B)가 정답이다.

---

133. **(A) Please fill them out completely
and correctly so that your file
can be processed.**
(B) Your Personnel Information Form
has been omitted from your
personal file.
(C) Please submit all these forms
six weeks before you leave the
company.
(D) You can find the latest version of
this employee handbook in your
office.

어휘 omit 빠뜨리다, 누락하다 employee handbook 직원 편
람

해석 (A) 당신의 파일이 처리될 수 있도록 빠짐없이 정확히
작성하시기를 바랍니다.
(B) 당신의 개인 파일에서 인사 정보 서식이 누락되었
습니다.
(C) 이 모든 서식을 퇴사하기 6주 전에 제출하시기 바
랍니다.
(D) 이 직원 안내서의 최신 버전은 사무실에 있습니다.

해설 바로 앞 문장에서 신규 입사자로서 세 가지 서류를 작
성해야 한다고 했으므로(You must complete the
Personnel Information Form, the Confidentiality
Agreement Form, and the Method of Payment
Form), 이에 대한 부연 설명인 (A)가 이어지는 것이 자
연스럽다.

134. (A) event
(B) presentation
(C) visit
(D) employment

해설 빈칸에 employment가 들어가야 회사에 새로 합류하
는 사람에게 건네는 인사말로 편지를 마무리하게 되어
문맥상 자연스럽다.

Questions 135-138 refer to the following
e-mail.

To: Kaylee Keane, Staff Writer
From: Lizanne Schwartz, Editor in Chief
Date: February 3
Re: Cover Story Assignment

Thank you for agreeing to work on
the feature article about Valia Zulli's
135.double role in her recent film as
actress and director. By the end of
next week, please submit a general
overview explaining what your plans are
in regard to the focus of the interview
with her. Once your 136.proposal has
been met with approval by our editors,
make sure to confirm the date and time
of the interview with one of our staff
photographers. It would be ideal if the
article 137.compared the two roles Ms.
Zulli assumed in the production of the
film. 138.Furthermore, it should discuss
the distinct skills she exerted in each
aspect. If you have any questions, I will
be available throughout the week before
going on vacation next week.

135-138번 문제는 다음 이메일에 관한 것입니다.

수신: Kaylee Keane, 전속 작가
발신: Lizanne Schwartz, 편집장
날짜: 2월 3일
제목: 표지 기사 업무

최근 Valia Zulli의 영화에서 그가 맡은 배우와 감독으
로서의 두 가지 역할에 대한 특집 기사 작업에 동의
해 주셔서 감사합니다. 다음 주말까지 그녀와의 인터
뷰 초점과 관련하여 계획이 무엇인지 설명하는 대략

적인 개요를 제출해 주시기를 바랍니다. 일단 기획안이 편집 직원들의 동의를 얻으면 반드시 당사의 사진작가 중 한 명과 인터뷰 날짜와 시간을 확정해 주세요. 기사가 Ms. Zulli가 영화 제작에서 맡은 두 가지 역할을 비교한다면 이상적일 것입니다. 그뿐만 아니라 각각의 측면에 그녀가 발휘한 개별 기법들도 논해야 합니다. 질문이 있으시면, 저는 다음 주에 휴가 가기 전 주중 내내 시간을 낼 수 있습니다.

어휘 staff 전속의, 직원 editor in chief 편집장 Re: (이메일의) 제목(regarding ~ 에 관하여); 회신 cover story 표지 기사 wok on ~에 대해 작업하다 assignment 할당된 일 feature 특집 (기사, 방송) general 개괄적인, 대략적인 overview 개관, 개요 in regard to ~와 관련하여 proposal 기획안 be met with approval 동의를 얻다 make sure to-V 반드시 ~하다 confirm 확정하다 assume 맡다 furthermore 뿐만 아니라 distinct 뚜렷이 다른, 구별되는 exert 쓰다, 발휘하다 aspect 측면 available 시간이 있는

문장 분석

1. By the end of next week, please submit a general overview (explaining what your plans are in regard to the focus of the interview with her).

➡ explaining ~ with her 부분이 앞에 있는 명사구 a general overview를 수식하고 있다.

2. It would be ideal / if the article compared the two roles (which) Ms. Zulli assumed in the production of the film.

➡ 선행사 the two roles와 Ms. Zulli 사이에 목적격 관계대명사 which가 생략되어 있다.

3. Furthermore, it should discuss the distinct skills (which) she exerted in each aspect.

➡ 선행사 the distinct skills와 she 사이에 목적격 관계대명사 which가 생략되어 있다.

135. (A) double
(B) doubles
(C) doubling
(D) to double

해설 빈칸 앞뒤 Valia Zulli's ------ role만 보면 정답을 알아낼 수 있다. 명사 앞에 빈칸이 있으므로 형용사 (A)가 정답이다.

136. (A) drawing
(B) hiring
(C) proposal
(D) edition

해설 바로 앞 문장에서 인터뷰 계획을 설명하는 개요를 제출하라고 지시했으므로(please submit a general overview explaining what your plans are in regard to the focus of the interview with her), 빈칸을 포함한 절의 의미는 이 개요(a general overview)가 편집자들의 동의를 얻어야 한다는 것이다. 그러므로 대신 사용할 수 있는 명사는 (C) proposal(기획안)이다.

137. (A) comparing
(B) compared
(C) to compare
(D) were compared

해설 빈칸은 if절의 동사 자리이므로 능동태 (B)와 수동태 (D) 중 정답을 선택해야 한다. 빈칸 뒤에 목적어 the two roles가 있으므로 능동태 (B)가 정답이다.

138. (A) For instance, you might ask her about the upcoming project on her schedule.
(B) Furthermore, it should discuss the distinct skills she exerted in each aspect.
(C) In other words, your work should be completed in three weeks.
(D) In addition, the article will be published in the May issue.

어휘 for instance 예를 들어 upcoming 다가오는, 곧 있을 in other words 다시 말해서 in addition 게다가 publish 게재하다, 싣다 issue (간행물의) 호

해석 (A) 예를 들어 그녀의 일정 중 다가오는 프로젝트에 관해 물어볼 수 있을 것입니다.
(B) 그뿐만 아니라 각각의 측면에 그녀가 발휘한 개별 기법들도 논해야 합니다.
(C) 다시 말해서 당신의 작업은 3주 내로 완료되어야 합니다.
(D) 게다가 기사는 5월호에 실릴 것입니다.

해설 바로 앞 문장에서 기사가 Ms. Zulli가 맡았던 두 가지 역할을 비교해야 한다는 내용상의 요구 사항을 알려줬다(It would be ideal if the article compared the two roles Ms. Zulli assumed in the production of the film). 그러므로 두 가지 역할에 대해 기사에서 추가로 다루어야 할 점을 언급하는 (B)가 정답으로 알맞다.

Part 7

Questions 139-142 refer to the following e-mail.

To: Linas Pilypas <lpilypas@moto.net>
From: Jennifer Goodies <jgoodies@pdn_mag.com>
Date: 4 July
Subject: Your submission

We've got some great news for you. [139.]Your photograph *Volcanic Eruption in Reykjanes* has been selected as the third-place winner in the third Natural Landscape Photography Awards sponsored by *Photo District News Magazine*. Our judges felt that your scene of the orange lava cascading down the steep slope, with the ambient blue light on the background layers, conveys a feeling of radiating heat and that the impressionistic image you captured shows your skill as an artist.

[140.]Your photograph will be featured in the September issue of *Photo District News Magazine*, alongside the other winning photographs. In addition, your work will be featured in a special nature landscape photography exhibit in Milan at Luciana Matalon Art Museum from 18 November to 30 November.

You will receive a prize of €2,000 as well as a two-year subscription to *Photo District News Magazine*. A cheque for the amount of the prize will be sent to you in August, and [140.]your subscription will be activated with the issue featuring your photograph.

[141.]When you submitted your photograph, you stated that you used a Pillai DSLR 240 camera and a Summilux M ASPH lens. Kindly confirm if this is accurate by responding to this e-mail. This information will accompany your photograph in the magazine and in the museum exhibit.

Congratulations on your success! [142.]We are excited to be able to share your work with our international readership and look forward to seeing more of your work in the future.

Sincerely,

Jennifer Goodies
Editor

139–142번 문제는 다음 이메일에 관한 것입니다.

수신: Linas Pilypas 〈lpilypas@moto.net〉
발신: Jennifer Goodies 〈jgoodies@pdn_mag.com〉
날짜: 7월 4일
제목: 제출물

정말 좋은 소식 전해드립니다. 당신의 사진 'Reykjanes 화산 폭발'이 Photo District News Magazine이 후원하는 제3회 자연 풍경 사진 대회에서 3위 입상작으로 선정되었습니다. 심사위원들은 은은한 푸른빛이 배경에 깔린 채 오렌지색 용암이 가파른 산비탈을 따라 폭포수처럼 흘러내리는 장면이 뿜어져 나오는 열기를 전달하고 있고, 당신이 담아낸 인상주의적 이미지가 예술가로서 역량을 보여준다고 느꼈습니다.

당신의 사진은 Photo District News Magazine 9월호에 다른 입상 사진들과 함께 특집으로 실립니다. 그뿐만 아니라 당신의 작품은 11월 18일부터 11월 30일까지 밀라노에 있는 Luciana Matalon 미술관에서 열리는 자연 풍경 사진 특별 전시회에도 포함됩니다.

당신은 Photo District News Magazine 2년 구독권뿐만 아니라 2,000유로의 상금도 받게 됩니다. 상금 금액에 해당하는 수표가 8월에 발송될 것이며 구독은 당신의 사진이 실리는 호와 함께 시작됩니다.

사진을 제출하실 때 Pillai DSLR 240 카메라와 Summilux M ASPH 렌즈를 사용하셨다고 밝히셨습니다. 이것이 정확한지 이 이메일에 답장하셔서 확인해 주시기를 바랍니다. 이 정보는 잡지와 미술관 전시회에서 당신의 사진과 함께 제시될 것입니다.

성공을 축하드립니다! 우리는 당신의 작품을 전 세계의 저희 독자들과 공유할 수 있게 된 것에 기쁘게 생각하며 앞으로 당신의 작품을 더 많이 보게 될 것을 기대합니다. 진심을 담아

어휘 submission 제출 volcanic 화산의 eruption (화산의) 폭발, 분화 sponsor 후원하다 judge 심사위원 lava 용암 cascade 폭포처럼 흐르다 steep 가파른 slope 경사면. (산비탈) ambient 잔잔한, 은은한 convey 전달하다 radiate 뿜어져 나오다 impressionistic 인상주의적인 capture 포착하다 feature 특집으로 다루다 alongside ~와 함께 exhibit 전시회 as well as ~뿐만 아니라 cheque 수표 subscription 구독 activate 활성화시키다 state 말하다. 밝히다 kindly(=please) 부디 accurate 정확한 accompany ~와 함께 제공되다 readership 독자층

문장 분석
....

Our judges felt ①[that your scene of the orange lava (cascading down the steep slope), (with the ambient blue light on the background layers), conveys a feeling of radiating heat] and ②[that the impressionistic image (you captured) shows your skill as an artist].

➡ [ ]로 묶여 있는 두 개의 that 절이 and로 연결되어 있으며 모두 동사 felt의 목적어이다.
➡ ①의 주어, 동사는 your scene of the orange lava와 conveys이며, ②의 주어, 동사는 the impressionistic image와 shows이다. ( )로 묶여 있는 부분은 모두 수식 어구이다.
➡ with the ambient blue light on the background layers 은은한 푸른빛이 배경에 깔린 채 '[명사]가 ~인 채로'라는 뜻의 'with + 명사 + 형용사[분사/전치사구/to-V]' 구문은 자주 사용되므로 꼭 알아두어야 한다.

139. What is implied about Mr. Pilypas' photograph?

(A) It is in black and white.
(B) It has previously been published.
(C) It has been purchased by a collector.
(D) It depicts a nature landscape scene.

어휘 previously 이전에 collector 수집가 depict 묘사하다
해석 Mr. Pilypas의 사진에 대해 무엇이 암시되어 있는가?
(A) 흑백이다.
(B) 전에 출판되었던 적이 있다.
(C) 수집가에 의해 구매되었다.
(D) 자연 풍경을 묘사한다.
해설 사진 제목이 'Reykjanes 화산 폭발(Volcanic Eruption in Reykjanes)'이고 입상한 대회 이름도 '제3회 자연 풍경 사진 대회(the third Natural Landscape Photography Awards)'이므로 Mr. Pilypas의 사진은 당연히 자연 풍경을 묘사한 것이라고 추론할 수 있다.

140. When will Mr. Pilypas' subscription begin?

(A) In July
(B) In August
(C) In September
(D) In November

해석 Pilypas의 구독은 언제 시작되는가?
(A) 7월
(B) 8월
(C) 9월
(D) 11월
해설 세 번째 문단에서 구독은 Mr. Pilypas의 사진이 실리는 호와 함께 시작된다고 했는데(your subscription will be activated with the issue featuring your photograph), 두 번째 문단을 보면 사진이 잡지에 실리는 것은 9월인 것을(Your photograph will be featured in the September issue of *Photo District News Magazine*, alongside the other winning photographs) 알 수 있으므로, (C)가 정답이다.

141. What is Mr. Pilypas asked to do?

(A) Provide some additional photographs
(B) Verify that some information is correct
(C) Sign a release form
(D) Confirm a mailing address

어휘 additional 추가의 verify 입증하다. 확인해 주다 correct 정확한 release form 양도 계약서
해석 Mr. Pilypas는 무엇을 하라고 요구받는가?
(A) 추가로 몇 장의 사진을 제출한다.
(B) 어떤 정보가 맞는지 확인해 준다.
(C) 양도 계약서에 서명한다.
(D) 우편 주소를 확인해 준다.
해설 네 번째 문단에서 Mr. Pilypas가 제출한 장비에 대한 정보를 언급하면서(you stated that you used a Pillai DSLR 240 camera and a Summilux M ASPH lens) 이 정보가 맞는지 확인해 달라고 요구하고 있으므로(Kindly confirm if this is accurate) (B)가 정답이다.

142. What is mentioned about Photo District News Magazine?

(A) It is read in many places around the world.

(B) It sponsors multiple competitions annually.

(C) It is a newly released publication.

(D) It is published quarterly.

어휘 competition 대회 annually 매년, 해마다 release 발매하다 publication 출판물 quarterly 분기별로

해석 Photo District News Magazine에 대해 무엇이 언급되는가?
(A) 전 세계 여러 곳에서 읽힌다.
(B) 매년 다수의 대회를 후원한다.
(C) 새로 발매된 출판물이다.
(D) 분기마다 발간된다.

해설 마지막 문단에 등장하는 our international readership이라는 키워드를 보면 이 잡지가 여러 나라에서 판매되고 있다는 것을 알 수 있다. 그러므로 정답은 (A)이다.

Questions 143-147 refer to the following notice and e-mails.

The Museum of Contemporary Art Barcelona presents...

Time Travel

By Teresa Gancedo
11-25 October
Ms. Gancedo is a painter and sculptor who lives in Barcelona.

143. 147.Teresa Gancedo's artwork will occupy our entire museum, with each museum hall dedicated to a different time period in Spanish history, particularly highlighting the city of Barcelona. 143. 147.Ms. Gancedo commemorates moments from Barcelona's history that are not widely known, sourced from literature and film.

144.Upon entering the museum, visitors will experience Barcelona as it was 2,200 years ago, at the beginning of Roman occupation. Each succeeding

gallery that visitors encounter will portray younger versions of the city up to present-day Barcelona. Ms. Gancedo's creative output makes use of a broad range of media, including paint, video, and even recycled material. All pieces in this exhibition are Ms. Gancedo's original creations.

Tickets:
Museum entrance: €12 per person

145.Teresa Gancedo will discuss her exhibition at Meier Hall on Friday, 19 October, at 7:00 P.M. Tickets are €15 and half of all proceeds will be donated to the Institute of Historic Building Conservation. Please call (093) 481 3368 for further information.

143-147번 질문은 다음 안내문과 이메일에 관한 것입니다.

바르셀로나 현대 미술관이 선보입니다.
시간 여행
Teresa Gancedo 작
10월 11-25일
Ms. Gancedo는 바르셀로나에 사는 화가이자 조각가입니다.

Teresa Gancedo의 작품이 미술관 전체를 차지하는 가운데 각 전시관이 스페인 역사의 각기 다른 시대를 전담하며 특별히 바르셀로나를 두드러지게 보여줍니다. Ms. Gancedo는 문학 작품과 영화를 출처로 한 널리 알려지지 않은 바르셀로나 역사의 순간들을 기념합니다.

미술관에 들어서자마자 방문객은 로마 점령기가 시작된 2,200년 전 모습의 바르셀로나를 경험하게 됩니다. 방문객이 접하게 될 이어지는 각각의 전시관은 도시의 더 젊은 버전들을 오늘날의 바르셀로나에 이르기까지 묘사합니다. Ms. Gancedo의 창작품은 페인트, 동영상, 심지어 재활용 재료까지 아우르는 폭넓은 표현 수단을 활용합니다. 이번 전시회의 모든 작품은 Ms. Gancedo의 창작품 원본입니다.

티켓:
미술관 입장: 인당 12유로

Teresa Gancedo가 10월 19일 금요일 저녁 7시에

Meier 홀에서 자신의 전시회에 관해 논합니다. 입장권은 15유로이며 모든 수익금의 절반은 역사적 건물 보존 협회에 기부됩니다. 더 자세한 정보는 전화 (093) 481 3368로 문의하세요.

어휘 contemporary art 현대 미술 present 선보이다 sculptor 조각가 occupy 차지하다 entire 전체의 museum hall 전시관 dedicated to ~를 전담하는 commemorate 기념하다 source ~을 출처로 하다 (up)on + 명사[V-ing] ~하자마자 occupation 점령 (기간) succeeding 다음의, 계속되는 encounter 접하다, 마주치다 portray 묘사하다, 그리다 present-day 현대의, 오늘날의 creative output 창작품 make use of ~을 이용하다, 활용하다 a broad range of 폭넓은, 다양한 medium(pl. media) (예술가의) 표현 수단 piece 작품, (작품) 한 점 proceeds 수익금 institute 기관, 협회 conservation 보존

문장 분석

with each museum hall dedicated to a different time period in Spanish history,

➡ 각 전시관이 스페인 역사의 각기 다른 시대를 전담하는 가운데
*'with + 명사 + 형용사[분사/전치사구/to-V]'는 '~가 ~인 채로'라는 뜻으로 모든 파트에서 매우 자주 사용되는 구문이므로 절대 잊어버리면 안 된다.

From: aragallj@libris.co.es
To: tgancedo@likmail.com
Date: 30 October
Subject: Book project

Dear Ms. Gancedo,

145.I was present at the recent event where you talked about your work, and I had the joy of visiting your exhibition afterwards.

147.I'm in the process of writing a novel set in 15th century Spain, mainly Barcelona, and I am seeking an illustrator for this work. My publisher, Moleiro and Co., is prepared to provide generous compensation and has granted me the discretion to select a collaborator. I am certain that you would make an ideal creative companion.

Are you interested in partnering with me on this endeavor? 146.Your agent informed me that you are currently in Marseille. I will be there myself next week. Should you be available for a meeting, please feel free to reach out to me at aragallj@libris.co.es.

Jaume Aragall

수신: aragallj@libris.co.es
발신: tgancedo@likmail.com
날짜: 10월 30일
제목: 도서 프로젝트

Ms. Gancedo께,

저는 당신이 당신의 작품에 관해 이야기 나눠주신 최근 행사에 참석했고, 전시회를 방문하는 즐거움은 그 후에 누렸습니다.

저는 15세기 스페인, 주로 바르셀로나를 배경으로 하는 소설을 쓰는 중이며, 이 작품을 위해 삽화가를 찾고 있습니다. 제가 계약한 출판사 Moleiro and Co.는 후한 보수를 제공할 준비가 되어 있으며, 저에게 협력 작가를 선택할 수 있는 재량권을 주었습니다. 저는 당신이 이상적인 창작 동지가 될 것이라고 확신합니다.

저와 협력하여 이 일을 해보실 생각이 있으신가요? 당신의 대리인이 당신이 현재 Marseille에 계신다고 알려줬습니다. 저도 다음 주에 그곳에 갑니다. 미팅에 참석하실 수 있다면 부담 없이 언제든 저에게 aragallj@libris.co.es로 연락해 주세요.

Jaume Aragall

어휘 present 참석[출석]한 afterwards 그 뒤에 set in ~을 배경으로 하는 illustrator 삽화가 publisher 출판사 generous 후한, 아낌없는 compensation 보수 grant 주다 discretion 재량(권) collaborator 협력자 companion 동지, 동반자 partner with ~와 협력하다 endeavor 노력, 시도 agent 대리인 inform 알리다 reach out to ~에게 연락하다, ~와 접촉하다

From: tgancedo@likmail.com
To: aragallj@libris.co.es
Date: 1 November
Re: Book project

Dear Jaume,

I am greatly intrigued by your invitation and would be absolutely thrilled to discuss the project you have outlined. 146.I am arranging to travel to Rome next Friday, so please let me know where you will be lodging and when, so that we will find the time to explore your proposal further.

Best wishes,
Teresa Gancedo

발신: tgancedo@likmail.com
수신: aragallj@libris.co.es
날짜: 11월 1일
회신: 도서 프로젝트

Jaume께,

당신의 제안에 매우 흥미 있으며 대략 말씀하신 그 프로젝트에 대해 논의하게 된다면 정말 좋겠습니다.

저는 다음 주 금요일에 로마로 이동하려고 계획 중입니다. 그래서 언제 어디서 묵으실 건지 말씀해 주시면, 당신의 기획안에 대해 더 깊이 알아볼 시간을 찾을 수 있을 것 같습니다.

이만 줄입니다.
Teresa Gancedo

어휘 intrigued 아주 흥미로워 하는 absolutely 정말, 진짜로 thrilled 매우 기쁜, 아주 흥분된 outline 개요를 서술하다 arrange to-V ~을 계획하다, 준비하다 lodge 묵다, 숙박하다 explore 탐구하다 further 더 깊이

---

143. What does the notice suggest about the exhibition?

(A) It portrays a city from a unique perspective.
(B) It is made entirely of recycled materials.
(C) It contains historical artifacts.
(D) It is inspired by a well-known

novel.

어휘 portray 묘사하다, 그리다 perspective 관점, 시각 entirely 전부 contain 포함하다, 담다 artifact 유물 inspire 영감을 주다

해석 안내문은 전시회에 관하여 무엇을 시사하는가?
(A) 도시를 독특한 관점에서 묘사한다.
(B) 전부 재활용 재료로 만들어졌다.
(C) 역사적인 유물들을 포함한다.
(D) 유명 소설에서 영감을 받았다.

해설 첫 문단에 이 전시회는 바르셀로나 역사에서 잘 알려지지 않은 순간들을 기념한다는(Ms. Gancedo commemorates moments from Barcelona's history that are not widely known, sourced from literature and film.) 설명이 나오는데, 이것은 작가가 도시의 역사를 독특한 관점에서 바라보았다는 것을 의미한다. 그러므로 (A)가 정답이다.

---

144. What is implied in the notice?

(A) The museum exhibition will commence with a lecture.
(B) Self-guided audio tours of the exhibition are available for an extra fee.
(C) Viewers of the exhibition are urged to experience it in a particular order.
(D) Ms. Gancedo is overseeing a building restoration project.

어휘 commence 시작되다 extra fee 추가 요금 urge 강권하다 order 순서 oversee 감독하다 restoration 복원, 복구

해석 안내문에 무엇이 암시되어 있는가?
(A) 미술관 전시회는 강연으로 시작될 것이다.
(B) 추가 요금으로 전시회의 셀프가이드 오디오 투어를 이용할 수 있다.
(C) 관람객은 전시회를 특정 순서로 경험할 것이 권장된다.
(D) Ms. Gancedo가 건물 복원 프로젝트를 감독하고 있다.

해설 첫 문단에 각 전시관이 스페인 역사의 한 시대씩을 담당하고 있다고 진술되어 있다(with each museum hall dedicated to a different time period in Spanish history). 이어서 두 번째 문단에는 첫 전시관이 바르셀로나 역사의 태동기를, 마지막 전시관이 현대 바르셀로나의 모습을 묘사한다는 설명이 나온다(Upon entering the museum, visitors will experience Barcelona as it was 2,200 years ago, at the beginning of Roman occupation. Each succeeding gallery that visitors encounter will portray younger versions of the city up to present-day Barcelona). 내용을 종합해서 추론해 보면 스페인 역사의 흐름을 보여주는 이 전시회는 중간부터 관람하면 이해도가 떨어질 수 있어 순서대로 경험하는 것이 좋을 것이다. 그러므로 (C)가 정답이다.

---

145. Where most likely did Mr. Aragall hear Ms. Gancedo speak?

(A) At a meeting of the Institute of Historic Building Conservation
(B) At the Museum of Contemporary Art
(C) At Moleiro and Co. headquarters
(D) At an event at Meier Hall

어휘 institute 기관, 협회 headquarters 본사, 본부

해석 Mr. Aragall은 어디에서 Ms. Gancedo가 이야기하는 것을 들었겠는가?
(A) 역사적 건물 보존 협회 회의에서
(B) 현대 미술관에서
(C) Moleiro and Co. 본사에서
(D) Meier 홀의 한 행사에서

연계 추론 안내문 마지막 문단에서 Ms. Gancedo가 Meier 홀에서 자신의 전시회에 대해 논하는 행사를 홍보하고 있는데(Teresa Gancedo will discuss her exhibition at Meier Hall on Friday, 19 October, at 7:00 P.M.), Mr. Aragall이 보낸 이메일 첫 문장에서 자신이 참석했다고 말한 행사가 바로 이 행사이다(I was present at the recent event where you talked about your work). 그러므로 Mr. Aragall이 Ms. Gancedo의 담화를 들은 곳은 Meier 홀이다.

---

146. What is suggested about Ms. Gancedo?

(A) She has agreed to a contract with Mr. Aragall.
(B) She will meet with Mr. Aragall in Marseille.
(C) She is returning from Rome next week.
(D) She is selling some of her paintings.

해석 Ms. Gancedo에 대해 무엇이 암시되어 있는가?
(A) Mr. Aragall과의 계약에 합의했다.
(B) Mr. Aragall과 Marseille에서 만날 것이다.
(C) 다음 주에 로마에서 돌아온다.
(D) 자기 그림 몇 점을 팔 것이다.

연계 추론 첫 이메일 마지막 문단을 보면 Ms. Gancedo는 현재 Marseille에 있고(you are currently in Marseille), Mr. Aragall은 다음 주에 그곳으로 가서 Ms. Gancedo를 만나고 싶다고(I will be there myself next week. Should you be available for a meeting, please feel free to reach out to me at aragallj@libris.co.es) 나와 있다. 답장에서 Ms. Gancedo는 다음 주 금요일에 로마로 이동해야 하지만(I am arranging to travel to Rome next Friday), 그도 역시 Mr. Aragall을 만나고 싶어 한다(so please let me know where you will be lodging and when, so that we will find the time to explore your proposal further) 것을 알 수 있다. 두 서신의 내용을 종합하면 두 사람은 다음 주 금요일이 되기 전에 Marseille에서 만날 것으로 추론할 수 있다.

---

147. In what field do Mr. Aragall and Ms. Gancedo share some expertise?

(A) Spanish history
(B) Fictional writing
(C) Contemporary art
(D) Museum administration

어휘 field 분야, 영역 expertise 전문 지식

해석 Mr. Aragall과 Ms. Gancedo는 어느 분야에서 전문지식을 공유하는가?
(A) 스페인 역사
(B) 소설 집필
(C) 현대 미술
(D) 미술관 운영

연계 추론 안내문을 보면 Ms. Gancedo의 전시회는 스페인 역사를 소재로 하는 것이다. Mr. Aragall이 보낸 이메일을 보면 그는 15세기 스페인을 배경으로 하는 소설을 쓰고 있다(I'm in the process of writing a novel set in 15th century Spain, mainly Barcelona). 그러므로 두 사람이 공통으로 스페인 역사에 대한 전문 지식을 가지고 있다고 추론할 수 있다.

PART 5 & 6 Exercise

101 (B)	102 (A)	103 (C)	104 (D)	105 (D)
106 (D)	107 (A)	108 (A)	109 (B)	110 (B)
111 (B)	112 (A)	113 (C)	114 (C)	115 (A)

101. Ms. Perez, as chief information officer for Dayton Enterprises, ------- responsibilities for all technology training workshops.

(A) assume
(B) will assume
(C) to assume
(D) assuming

어휘 chief information officer(CIO) 최고 정보 책임자 assume responsibility for ~에 대한 책임을 맡다, ~을 담당하게 되다

해석 Ms. Perez는, Dayton Enterprises의 최고 정보 책임자로서, 모든 기술 교육 워크숍을 담당하게 될 것이다.

해설 [(A) 동사 (B) 동사 (C) 준동사 (D) 준동사]이다. 문장에 동사가 없으므로 빈칸에는 동사가 들어가야 한다. 주어 Ms. Perez가 단수 명사이므로 (B)가 정답으로 알맞다.

102. The discount coupon ------- customers receive with their initial order is redeemable within six months.

(A) that
(B) whom
(C) whose
(D) who

어휘 initial 처음의, 초기의 redeemable 현금으로 사용 가능한

해석 고객이 첫 주문으로 받는 할인 쿠폰은 6개월 이내에 사용할 수 있다.

해설 선행사 The discount coupon은 사람이 아니므로 (B)와 (D)는 제외하자. 빈칸 뒤에 있는 타동사 receive의 목적어가 없으므로, 목적격 관계대명사 (A)가 정답이다.

103. The school is seeking teachers ------- job will involve regularly caring for or being in charge of disabled children under 12.

(A) whom
(B) what
(C) whose
(D) when

어휘 seek 찾다 involve 포함하다 regularly 정기적으로 in charge of ~을 담당하는 disabled 장애를 가진

해석 학교는 업무에 12세 미만의 장애 아동을 정기적으로 돌보거나 전담하는 일을 포함하는 교사를 구하고 있다.

해설 teachers가 선행사이므로 선행사가 필요 없는 (B) what과 관계부사 (D)는 제외하자. 빈칸 뒤에는 involves의 목적어로 동명사구인 regularly caring for or being in charge of disabled children under 12를 포함한 3형식 문장이 완성되어 있다. 그러므로 ------- job이 관계사절의 주어가 되는 소유격 관계대명사 (C)가 정답이다.

104. Dr. Montaine is offering a four-hour workshop during ------- she will share some perspectives on effective time management.

(A) whose
(B) while
(C) whatever
(D) which

어휘 perspective 관점, 시각 effective 효과적인 management 관리, 운영

해석 Dr. Montaine은 4시간짜리 워크숍을 진행하며 효과적인 시간 관리에 대한 몇 가지 관점을 나눌 것이다.

해설 관계사가 아닌 (B)는 먼저 제외하자. 빈칸 앞 a four-hour workshop during -------을 보고 정답을 선택하자. '선행사 + 전치사 + -------'이므로 목적격 관계대명사 (D)가 정답이다.

105. Four diamonds, two of ------- were over a carat in size, were unexpectedly discovered on the site.

(A) them
(B) what

(C) who
(D) which

carat 캐럿(보석의 무게 단위: 약 200mg) unexpectedly 뜻밖에, 예상외로 site 현장, 장소

네 개의 다이아몬드가 현장에서 예기치 않게 발견되었는데, 그중 두 개는 크기가 1캐럿이 넘는다.

관계사가 아닌 (A)는 제외하고, 선행사 Four diamonds가 있으므로 (B)도 빈칸에 올 수 없다. two of ------를 보고 정답을 알아내자. '수량 표현 + of' 뒤에 빈칸이 있으면 목적격 관계대명사 (D)가 정답이다. 빈칸 뒤에 있는 동사만을 보고 주격 관계대명사를 선택하지 않도록 주의하자.

---

106. All shipments are brought to the receiving dock, ------ a warehouse worker verifies their tracking labels.

(A) who
(B) which
(C) when
(D) where

shipment 수송품, 적하물 receiving dock 하역장 warehouse 창고 verify 확인하다

모든 수송품은 하역장으로 가져오는데, 거기서 창고 작업자가 추적 라벨을 확인한다.

선행사 the receiving dock이 사람이 아니므로 (A)를 제외하자. (C)도 선행사가 시간 표현이 아니므로 정답이 될 수 없다. 빈칸 뒤에 완성된 3형식 문장이 있으므로 관계부사 (D)가 정답으로 알맞다.

---

107. The director has decided to hire a systems engineer ------ he thought would solve the software interface problems.

(A) who
(B) whose
(C) which
(D) what

부장은 소프트웨어 인터페이스 문제를 해결해 줄 것으로 생각한 그 시스템 엔지니어를 채용하기로 결정했다.

선행사 the systems engineer가 사람이므로 (C)는 사용할 수 없고, 선행사가 필요 없는 (D)도 정답이 아니다. 빈칸 뒤의 he thought는 삽입 구문이므로 이를 지우면, would solve가 관계대명사 절에서 동사임을 알 수 있다. 그러므로 빈칸에는 주격 관계대명사인 (A)가 알맞다.

---

108. The toaster ovens we compared ------ in terms of price, size, and durability.

(A) vary
(B) varying
(C) variety
(D) variously

vary 다양하다, 다르다 in terms of ~ 면에서 durability 내구성

우리가 비교한 토스터 오븐들은 가격과 크기, 내구성 면에서 다양하다.

목적격 관계대명사가 생략되어 we compared가 주어인 the toaster ovens를 수식하고 있다. 전체 문장에 동사가 없으므로 빈칸에는 동사 (A)가 들어가는 것이 알맞다.

---

109. Peake Ltd. is a company ------ for its comprehensive employee training and skill development programs.

(A) knowledge
(B) known
(C) knowing
(D) knows

comprehensive 포괄적인, 종합적인 development 개발

Peake Ltd.는 광범위한 직원 교육 및 기술 개발 프로그램으로 알려진 회사이다.

is가 문장의 동사이므로 빈칸에 동사 (D)는 들어갈 수 없다. 명사 (A)가 빈칸에 들어가면 "Peake Ltd.는 회사 지식이다."라는 어색한 문장이 되므로 제외한다. 빈칸을 포함한 뒷부분이 앞의 명사(a company)를 수식하는 which is(주격 관계대명사 + be동사)가 생략된 구문임을 알아야 한다. 그러므로 a company ------ for가 '~으로 알려진 회사'라는 의미가 되도록 (B)를 정답으로 선택한다.

---

110. Derek Levin from our shipping department will contact you on Friday ------ transportation and installation of your furniture at your office.

(A) will discuss
(B) to discuss
(C) discussion
(D) discusses

shipping department 배송 부서 transportation

운송, 수송 installation 설치 furniture 가구

해석 저희 발송부의 Derek Levin이 금요일에 연락해서 사무실로 가구를 운반해서 설치하는 일에 대해 논의할 겁니다.

해설 [(A) 동사 (B) 준동사 (C) 명사 (D) 동사]이다. will contact가 문장의 동사이므로 동사인 (A)와 (D)는 제외한다. 빈칸 뒤의 transportation and installation of your furniture는 명사구이므로 명사인 (C)와 함께 올 수 없다. 따라서 명사를 목적어로 취하는 준동사 (B)가 정답이다.

---

111. ------- interests many visitors about the city's downtown area is its rich array of historical buildings and varied architectural styles.

(A) This
(B) What
(C) While
(D) Besides

어휘 interest ~의 흥미를 끌다 downtown area 도심 지역 rich 다채로운 array 집합체[모음/무리] varied 다양한 architectural 건축의

해석 그 도시의 도심 지역에 대해 많은 방문객의 흥미를 끄는 것은 다채롭게 모여 있는 역사적 건물들과 다양한 건축 양식이다.

해설 빈칸 뒤에 '동사 + 목적어(interests many visitors about the city's downtown area)'가 있고, 동사 is가 이어서 나온다. 즉 전체 문장에서 is가 동사이고 그 앞의 절은 주어이다. 그러므로 빈칸에는 명사절 접속사인 의문사 (B)가 들어가는 것이 알맞다.

---

112. The city has decided to grant the land ------- which the company wants to construct its production facilities.

(A) on
(B) for
(C) from
(D) to

어휘 grant 부여하다. 허가하다 production facilities 생산 시설

해석 시는 회사가 생산 시설을 건설하고 싶어 하는 토지를 부여하기로 결정했다.

해설 빈칸 뒤에 목적격 관계대명사가 있으므로, 빈칸에 들어갈 전치사를 골라야 한다. 선행사 the land를 수식하는 절은 ------- which the company wants to construct its production facilities이다. 빈칸을 원래 있던 자리인 관계대명사절 끝으로 옮기고 선행사 the land를 그 뒤에 적어 보자. the company wants to construct its production facilities ------- the land가 된다. 여기서 '땅 위에 생산 시설을 짓는다'는 의미가 자연스러우므로 (A) on이 정답이다.

---

113. Whenever customers need some technical assistance, they may contact us by telephone or through our Web site, ------- they prefer.

(A) whoever
(B) however
(C) whichever
(D) where

어휘 assistance 지원 prefer 선호하다

해석 고객께서는 기술 지원이 필요할 때마다 전화 또는 웹사이트를 통해, 어느 쪽이든 선호하는 방식으로 저희에게 연락하시면 됩니다.

해설 빈칸 뒤에 목적어가 없는 불완전한 문장이 있으므로, 복합관계대명사인 (A)와 (C) 중 정답을 선택해야 한다. '누가 ~하든(whoever)'보다 '어느 쪽이든(Whichever)'이 의미가 자연스러우므로 (C)가 정답이다.

---

114. Tourists are encouraged to participate in the tour of the Libbey–Owens Glassware factory to see ------- various glass products are made.

(A) during
(B) what
(C) how
(D) whom

어휘 be encouraged to-V ~하도록 권장되다, 장려되다 glassware 유리 제품[그릇]

해석 관광객들에게 Libbey–Owens Glassware 공장 견학에 참여해서 다양한 유리 제품이 어떻게 만들어지는지 보는 것이 권장된다.

해설 관계사가 아닌 (A)는 제외하고 빈칸 앞에 선행사가 없으므로 (D)도 정답이 될 수 없다. 그러므로 관계대명사 (B)와 관계부사 (C) 중에서 정답을 선택해야 한다. 빈칸 뒤에 수동태로 완성된 문장이 있으므로 관계부사인 (C)가 정답이다.

---

115. The survey showed ------- almost all members of the focus group found Eucalyptus soap's floral scent appealing.

(A) that
(B) what
(C) these
(D) whose

어휘 focus group 포커스 그룹(시장 조사나 여론 조사의 대상으로 뽑힌 소수 집단) floral 꽃의, 꽃으로 된 scent 향기, 냄새 appealing 매력적인

해석 설문조사는 포커스 그룹의 거의 모든 참가자가 유칼립 투스 비누의 꽃향기가 매력적이라고 생각했다는 점을 보여 주었다.

해설 동사 showed 다음에 빈칸이 있고 바로 뒤에 절이 있어서 선행사가 필요 없는 관계대명사 what이 들어가야 할 것 같지만 빈칸 뒤의 절은 완성된 5형식이므로 what은 빈칸에 맞지 않다. 이 문제에서는 빈칸 이후의 절이 동사 showed의 목적어가 되는 명사절 접속사를 선택해야 한다. (A), (B), (D)가 모두 명사절 접속사이지만, 자연스러운 해석이 되는 (A)가 정답이다. 해석이 어렵다면 명사절 접속사의 90%는 that이라는 점을 기억하자.

Actual Test

101 (D)	**102** (A)	**103** (C)	**104** (C)	**105** (B)
106 (A)	**107** (C)	**108** (A)	**109** (A)	**110** (B)
111 (A)	**112** (B)	**113** (D)	**114** (C)	**115** (C)
116 (A)	**117** (D)	**118** (C)	**119** (B)	**120** (D)
121 (D)	**122** (D)	**123** (C)	**124** (B)	**125** (A)
126 (B)	**127** (C)	**128** (B)	**129** (A)	**130** (D)
131 (C)	**132** (B)	**133** (D)	**134** (A)	**135** (A)
136 (C)	**137** (D)	**138** (B)	**139** (B)	**140** (A)
141 (B)	**142** (B)	**143** (B)	**144** (A)	**145** (A)
146 (B)	**147** (D)			

Part 5

101. All the fragile items should be ------- wrapped in foam plastic before being boxed for shipping.

(A) unilaterally
(B) steadily
(C) perilously
(D) adequately

어휘 fragile 깨지기 쉬운 unilaterally 일방적으로 steadily 꾸준히 perilously 위험하게 adequately 충분하게, 적절하게 foam plastic 발포 플라스틱 box ~을 상자에 넣다 shipping 운송, 수송

해석 모든 깨지기 쉬운 제품은 배송을 위해 상자에 넣기 전에 발포 플라스틱으로 적절히 포장되어야 한다.

해설 [(A) 일반적으로 (B) 꾸준히 (C) 위험하게 (D) 적절히]이다. 빈칸 앞뒤 should be ------- wrapped를 보면, '------- 포장되어야 한다'의 의미를 자연스럽게 만들어 주는 부사는 (D)이다.

102. The software has been ------- entirely designed in India, proving that Indian programmers are capable of original and creative work.

(A) almost
(B) most
(C) most of
(D) partly

어휘 entirely 완전히, 전부 prove 증명하다 be capable of ~할 수 있다

해석 그 소프트웨어는 거의 전부 인도에서 설계되어 인도 프로그래머들이 고유의 창의적인 작업을 할 능력이 있다

는 것을 증명한다.

해설 항상 짝을 이루어 출제되는 어휘를 익혀야 한다. 빈칸 뒤에 entire(ly)가 있으면, 빈칸에는 항상 nearly나 almost가 들어가야 하므로 (A)가 정답이다.

---

103. The magazine article presents a list of precautions ------- delicate fabric such as silk usually requires.

(A) who
(B) whose
(C) which
(D) of which

어휘 present 제시하다 precaution 예방책, 주의 사항 delicate 섬세한, 연약한 fabric 직물

해석 잡지 기사에서는 실크와 같은 섬세한 직물이 보통 필요로 하는 주의 사항 목록을 제시한다.

해설 빈칸 앞에 있는 선행사 precautions가 사람이 아니므로 (A)는 제외하자. 빈칸 뒤에 동사 requires의 목적어가 없는 불완전한 문장이 있기 때문에 목적격 관계대명사 (C)가 정답이다. of which를 사용하면 앞에 있는 선행사와 함께 '선행사 + 전치사 + 목적격 관계대명사'의 구조를 이루는데, 이때 뒤에는 완성된 문장이 와야 하므로 (D)는 정답으로 알맞지 않다.

---

104. The new radio talk show, ------- which listeners can phone in with their questions, will start broadcasting at 2 P.M. next Thursday.

(A) even
(B) while
(C) during
(D) between

어휘 phone in (방송국에) 전화하다 broadcast 방송하다

해석 새 라디오 토크쇼는 청취자가 질문을 가지고 전화로 참여할 수 있는데, 다음 주 목요일 오후 2시에 방송을 시작한다.

해설 목적격 관계대명사 앞에는 전치사가 있어야 하므로 부사인 (A)와 접속사인 (B)는 먼저 제외하자. ------- which listeners can phone in with their questions가 선행사 The new radio talk show를 수식하고 있는 구조이다. 빈칸을 관계사절 내 마지막으로 옮긴 후, 선행사를 그 뒤로 옮기면 Listeners can phone in with their questions ------- the new radio talk show.가 된다. 토크쇼가 진행되는 '동안' 전화를 거는 것이므로 정답은 (C)이다.

---

105. At the upcoming Building Your Business workshop, attendees will gain insight into ------- small businesses can create a unique brand image.

(A) which
(B) how
(C) what
(D) who

어휘 upcoming 다가오는, 곧 있을 attendee 참가자 gain insight into ~에 대한 식견을 얻다 unique 독특한, 고유한

해석 다가오는 '사업체 설립하기' 워크숍에서 참가자는 소규모 사업체가 고유한 브랜드 이미지를 어떻게 구축하는지에 대한 식견을 얻을 것이다.

해설 빈칸 앞에 선행사가 없으므로 빈칸에는 관계부사 (B)나 관계대명사 (C)가 들어가야 한다. 빈칸 뒤가 완전한 3형식 문장이므로(small businesses can create a unique brand image.) 관계부사 (B)가 정답이다.

---

106. The project manager cannot continue the work until she receives an explicit answer about the changes ------- proposed.

(A) she
(B) that
(C) were
(D) until

어휘 explicit 분명한, 명쾌한

해석 프로젝트 관리자는 자신이 제안한 변경 사항에 대한 명쾌한 답변을 받을 때까지는 작업을 계속할 수 없다.

해설 빈칸에 보기를 하나씩 넣어보자. (A) she를 넣으면 she proposed가 목적격 관계대명사가 생략된 채 the changes를 수식하는 구조이므로 정답이다. (B) 관계대명사 that을 넣으면 주어와 목적어가 모두 없는 절이 되므로 정답이 아니다. (C) were를 넣으면 were proposed라는 수동태 동사가 생기는데 부사절에 이미 동사 receives가 있으므로 알맞지 않다. (D) until은 부사절이 이미 until로 시작하기 때문에 적절하지 않다.

---

107. We have to choose a ------- who can lead our sessions during the seminar in order to create a positive work environment.

(A) preside
(B) presidential
(C) president

(D) presidency

어휘 preside 주재하다 presidential 대통령의, 주재하는 president 주재자, 사회자 presidency 회장직, 회장 임기 session 기간, 시간 positive 긍정적인

해석 우리는 긍정적인 업무 환경 형성을 위한 세미나 동안 우리 시간을 이끌 수 있는 사회자를 뽑아야 한다.

해설 관사 a 뒤에 명사가 있어야 하므로, (C)와 (D) 중 정답을 선택해야 한다. 빈칸 뒤 관계대명사 who는 선행사가 사람일 때 사용하므로 (C)가 정답이다.

---

108. New Heritage, an antique store ------- in unique home furnishings and garden decorations, opened in Belk Department Store yesterday.

(A) specializing
(B) will be specializing
(C) is to be specializing
(D) is specializing

어휘 antique 골동품 furnishings 가구, 세간, 비품 decoration 장식품

해석 New Heritage는 독특한 가정용 가구와 정원 장식품을 전문으로 하는 골동품 가게로, 어제 Belk 백화점에 문을 열었다.

해설 opened가 문장의 동사이므로 빈칸에는 준동사인 (A)가 알맞다.

---

109. Security personnel must ensure that all employees ------ the office building promptly after the fire alarm goes off.

(A) have vacated
(B) to vacate
(C) vacating
(D) vacancy

어휘 security personnel 보안 요원 ensure 확실하게 하다 vacate 비우다 vacancy 결원, 공석; (호텔 등의) 빈 방 promptly after ~ 직후에 go off (경보기 등이) 울리다

해석 보안 요원은 화재경보기가 울린 직후에 모든 직원이 사무실 건물에서 나가도록 확실하게 해야 한다.

해설 [(A) 동사 (B) 준동사 (C) 준동사 (D) 명사]이다. that절에서 all employees는 주어이고, the office building은 목적어이므로 그 사이의 빈칸에는 동사를 넣는 것이 알맞다. 그러므로 (A)가 정답이다.

---

110. The board of directors has decided to acquire Arbus Autos, ------- will make Bikkel Motors the largest vehicle manufacturer in Asia.

(A) there
(B) which
(C) whose
(D) that

어휘 board of directors 이사회 acquire 인수하다 vehicle manufacturer 자동차 제조업체

해석 이사회는 Arbus Autos를 인수하기로 결정했는데, 이것은 Bikkel Motors를 아시아 최대의 자동차 제조업체로 만들어 줄 것이다.

해설 관계사가 아닌 (A)는 제외하고, 빈칸 앞에 쉼표가 있으므로 that도 사용할 수 없다. 빈칸 뒤 will make는 관계사절의 동사이므로 주격 관계대명사 (B)가 정답이다.

---

111. Cars from Tarnall Motors come with a warranty lasting 36 months or 60,000 kilometers, ------- is reached first.

(A) whichever
(B) whoever
(C) whenever
(D) however

어휘 come with ~이 딸려 있다 warranty 품질 보증서 last 지속되다

해석 Tarnall Motors의 자동차에는, 어느 쪽에 먼저 도달하든, 36개월 혹은 60,000킬로미터까지 지속되는 보증서가 딸려 있다.

해설 보기가 모두 복합관계사이므로 빈칸 앞은 볼 필요가 없다. 빈칸 뒤에 주어가 없는 불완전한 문장이 있으므로 복합관계대명사가 들어가야 한다. (A)와 (B) 중 '누가 ~ 하든(whoever)'보다 '어느 쪽이 ~하든(whichever)'이라는 의미가 자연스러우므로 (A)가 정답이다.

---

112. Pacific Cargo was able to expand profits ------- by attracting new customers in China and Thailand.

(A) tightly
(B) substantially
(C) warmly
(D) subjectively

어휘 cargo 화물 expand 확대하다 tightly 꽉, 단단히 substantially 꽤, 상당히 subjectively 주관적으로 attract customers 고객을 유치하다

해석 Pacific 화물은 중국과 태국에서 신규 고객을 유치함으로써 이윤을 크게 확대할 수 있었다.

해설 항상 짝을 이루어 출제되는 어휘 문제이다. '증가/감소'를 의미하는 동사는 substantially, significantly, considerably, dramatically, markedly, sharply와 같은 '많음'을 나타내는 부사와 함께 쓴다. 동사 expand를 보고 바로 정답을 고르자.

---

113. The repair shop is well known for its expertise in repairing old watches, some of ------- have been discontinued.

(A) their
(B) whose
(C) whom
(D) which

어휘 be well know for ~로 유명하다 expertise 전문지식 discontinue (생산을) 중단하다

해석 그 수리점은 오래된 손목시계를 고치는 기술로 유명하며, 그중 일부는 생산이 중단되었다.

해설 일단 관계사가 아닌 (A)는 제외하자. 빈칸 앞 '수량 표현(some) + of' 구문이므로 빈칸에는 목적격 관계대명사가 알맞다. (C)와 (D) 중에서, 선행사 old watches는 사람이 아니므로 (D)가 정답이다.

---

114. This year's Harbortown Poetry Prize will be awarded to Miranda Blethyn, ------- poem "Atlas" was selected from over 300 entries.

(A) which
(B) whom
(C) whose
(D) what

어휘 award 수여하다 entry 응모작, 출품작

해석 올해의 Harbortown 시상(詩賞)은 Miranda Blethyn에게 수여될 것이며, 그녀의 시 Atlas는 300개 이상의 출품작 중에서 선정되었다.

해설 빈칸 앞의 선행사 Miranda Blethyn가 사람이므로 (A)는 제외하자. 선행사가 있는 경우 (D)도 사용할 수 없으므로 (B)와 (C) 중 정답을 선택해야 한다. 빈칸 뒤의 "Atlas" was selected from over 300 entries가 완성된 수동태 문장이므로 소유격 관계대명사 (C)가 정답이다.

---

115. We're looking forward to our colleague's return from Canada, ------- he gave a presentation to the potential clients.

(A) while
(B) which
(C) where
(D) why

어휘 look forward to ~를 기대하다 colleague 동료 give a presentation 발표하다, 프레젠테이션하다 potential client 잠재 고객

해석 우리는 우리 동료가 캐나다에서 돌아오는 것을 기대하고 있는데, 그곳에서 그는 잠재 고객들에게 프레젠테이션을 했다.

해설 관계사가 아닌 (A)는 제외하자. 빈칸 뒤에 he gave a presentation to the potential clients라는 완성된 3형식 문장이 있으므로 관계부사 (C)나 (D) 중 정답을 골라야 한다. 선행사가 지명 Canada이므로 (C)가 정답이다.

---

116. When you are to change a ------- reservation, there will be at least a 10 percent extra charge.

(A) confirmed
(B) determined
(C) decided
(D) suspended

어휘 be to-V ~해야 한다 confirm 확인하다, 확정하다 determine 결정하다 suspend 중지하다, 정지시키다

해석 확정된 예약을 변경해야 할 때는 최소 10 퍼센트의 추가 요금이 있습니다.

해설 '예약하다'는 make a reservation, '예약을 확인하다'는 confirm a reservation이다. 그러므로 (A)가 정답이다. reservation과 함께 사용하는 동사를 기억하자.

---

117. ------- uncomfortable they may be, safety gear such as helmets, goggles, and gloves absolutely must be worn by anyone entering the construction site.

(A) Almost
(B) Nevertheless
(C) Seldom
(D) However

어휘 uncomfortable 불편한 safety gear 안전 장비

absolutely 빠짐없이 누구라도 construction site 공사
현장

해석 헬멧이나 고글, 장갑 같은 안전 장비가 아무리 불편하더
라도 공사 현장에 들어가는 사람이라면 누구나 빠짐없
이 착용해야 한다.

해설 보기가 모두 부사이며 (D)는 복합관계부사이다. 복합관
계부사는 부사절을 이끌며, 특히 however는 바로 뒤
에 형용사나 부사가 올 수 있다는 사실을 기억하자.
------- uncomfortable they may be이 부사절이
므로 (D)가 정답이다.

---

118. The Prodeliax Pro-6 software
program captures ------- is visible on
your computer screen and stores it in
its archive.

(A) wherever
(B) everything
(C) whatever
(D) anyway

어휘 capture 캡처하다 visible 보이는 store 저장하다
archive 파일 저장고

해석 Prodeliax Pro-6 소프트웨어 프로그램은 컴퓨터 화면
에 보이는 것은 무엇이든 캡처해서 저장 장치에 저장한
다.

해설 ------- is visible on your computer screen이 동
사 captures의 목적어이므로 명사절이어야 한다. 따라
서 명사절을 이끄는 복합관계대명사 (C)가 정답이다.

---

119. Promotions should not automatically
be granted to ------- has the most
seniority.

(A) nobody
(B) whoever
(C) anyone
(D) oneself

어휘 promotion 승진 automatically 자동으로 grant 부여
하다, 승인하다 seniority 연공서열, 근속 연수

해석 승진은 연공서열이 가장 높다고 해서 누구에게나 자동
으로 부여되어서는 안 된다.

해설 ------- has the most seniority가 전치사 to의 목적
어이므로 명사절이여야 한다. 따라서 명사절을 이끄는
복합관계대명사 (B)가 알맞다.

---

120. Ventralcom recently announced
------- Pamela Wang has been named
senior vice president of mergers and
acquisitions at the company.

(A) what
(B) because
(C) while
(D) that

어휘 announce 발표하다 name 지명하다, 임명하다 senior
vice president 수석 부사장 mergers and
acquisitions (M&A) 기업 인수 합병

해석 Ventralcom은 최근 Pamela Wang이 회사의 M&A
담당 수석 부사장으로 지명되었다고 발표했다.

해설 ------- Pamela Wang has been named senior
vice president of mergers and acquisitions at
the company가 동사 announced의 목적어이므로
명사절이 되어야 한다. 보기 중 (A)와 (D)가 명사절을
이끌 수 있는데, 빈칸 뒤에 완전한 문장이 있으므로 (D)
가 정답이다.

---

121. The CEO has an ------- commitment
to enhancing market value of the
company in any manner possible.

(A) immune
(B) undisciplined
(C) according
(D) unwavering

어휘 immune 면역성이 있는 undisciplined 규율이 안 잡힌,
버릇없는 according 부합되는 unwavering 변함없는, 확
고한 commitment to ~하겠다는 약속, 의지 enhance
높이다 manner 방식

해석 CEO는 가능한 어떤 방식으로든 회사의 시장 가치를
높이겠다고 확약했다.

해설 빈칸 앞뒤 has an ------- commitment([(A) 면역성
이 있는 (B) 규율이 안 잡힌 (C) 부합되는 (D) 확고한]
약속을 했다)의 의미를 자연스럽게 만들어주는 형용사
(D)가 정답이다.

---

122. Management ------- recommends
that all employees familiarize
themselves with the new software
that will be installed in the office next
week.

(A) intermittently
(B) superbly
(C) collaboratively

(D) strongly

어휘 management 운영진, 경영진 intermittently 간헐적으로 superbly 매우 훌륭하게 collaboratively 공동으로 strongly 강력히, 적극 familiarize oneself with ~을 익히다

해석 경영진은 모든 직원이 다음 주 사무실에 설치될 새 소프트웨어를 익힐 것을 적극 권장합니다.

해설 항상 짝을 이루어 출제되는 어휘를 익히도록 하자. recommend 앞에 빈칸이 있으면 highly나 strongly를 써야 한다. 그러므로 정답은 (D)이다.

---

123. The merger negotiation of Dexia International and Devon Ltd. is expected to be finalized ------- next month.

(A) amid
(B) already
(C) within
(D) until

어휘 merger 합병 negotiation 협상, 교섭 be expected to-V ~할 것으로 예상되다 finalize 완료하다 amid ~하는 가운데, ~의 와중에

해석 Dexia International과 Devon Ltd.의 합병 협상은 다음 달 안에 마무리될 것으로 예상된다.

해설 빈칸 앞뒤에 있는 is expected to be finalized ------- next month가 "다음 달 안에 마무리될 것으로 예상된다."라는 뜻이 되도록 전치사 (C)를 정답으로 선택해야 한다. (D)는 until이 '~까지 ~을 지속한다'라는 뜻으로 by처럼 '~까지 ~을 완료한다'의 의미로는 사용할 수 없기 때문에 정답이 아니다.

---

124. ------- events showed that the company's decision to acquire the property adjacent to their main office had been a great one.

(A) Suspended
(B) Subsequent
(C) Subjective
(D) Sustaining

어휘 subsequent 그 다음의, 이후의 subjective 주관적인 sustain 유지하다, 지속하다 acquire 획득하다, 인수하다 property 부동산, 건물 adjacent to ~에 인접한

해석 이후의 사건들이 본사에 인접한 부동산을 인수하기로 한 회사의 결정이 아주 좋은 것이었음을 보여 주었다.

해설 부동산을 매입하기로 한 결정이 사건들보다 먼저 일어

난 일이므로 '이후의 사건들'이라는 의미가 자연스럽다. 그러므로 (B)가 정답이다.

---

125. The managing director, Allen Schmidt, remains ------- to any changes to the company logo and motto.

(A) opposed
(B) anxious
(C) eager
(D) interfered

어휘 managing director 상무, 전무 be opposed to ~에 반대하다 interfere 참견하다, 간섭하다 motto 모토, 좌우명

해석 Allen Schmidt 전무는 여전히 회사 로고와 모토의 어떠한 변경에도 반대한다.

해설 anxious는 전치사 about, eager는 to부정사나 전치사 for와 함께 사용한다. interfere는 자동사여서 수동태로 사용할 수 없다. 그러므로 '~에 반대하다(be opposed to)'라는 뜻의 (A)가 정답으로 가장 알맞다.

---

126. The company was lagging ------- its competitors in a number of important technological fields, which caused a continual reduction in market share.

(A) away
(B) behind
(C) ongoing
(D) afterwards

어휘 lag behind ~에 뒤처지다 ongoing 진행 중인, 지속적인 afterwards 나중에, 그 뒤에 competitor 경쟁자 a number of 여럿의 field 분야, 영역 continual 지속적인 reduction 감소 market share 시장 점유율

해석 회사는 여러 중요한 기술 분야에서 경쟁사보다 뒤처져 있었고, 이것이 시장 점유율에서 지속적인 감소를 초래했다.

해설 lag behind(~보다 뒤떨어지다) 표현을 기억하고, (B)를 정답으로 선택하자.

---

127. According to the most ------- inventory figures, Kakua brand denim jackets need to be reordered immediately.

(A) close
(B) near
(C) recent

(D) present

어휘 close 근접한 recent 최근의 present 현재의 inventory 재고 figure 수치 reorder 재주문하다, 추가 주문하다 immediately 즉시

해석 가장 최근의 재고 수치에 따르면 Kakua 브랜드의 데님 재킷을 즉시 추가 주문해야 한다.

해설 빈칸 앞에 있는 the most는 최상급에 사용되는 표현이다. (A)와 (B)의 최상급은 closest와 nearest이고, (D)는 의미상 최상급이 존재할 수 없으므로 (C)가 정답이다.

---

128. The Woodward City Council is requesting all households to collect ------- containers, which will be forwarded to a designated recycling center.

(A) derived
(B) discarded
(C) precious
(D) priceless

어휘 council 의회 household 가구, 세대 container 용기 derive ~을 얻다, 끌어내다 discard 버리다, 폐기하다 precious 대단히 귀중한 priceless 값을 매길 수 없는 forward 보내다, 전송하다 designate 지정하다

해석 Woodward 시의회는 모든 가구에 버려진 용기를 모아 달라고 요청하고 있는데, 그것은 지정된 재활용센터로 전송될 것이다.

해설 재활용센터로 보내기 위해 '버려진 용기'를 모은다는 의미가 자연스러우므로 (B)가 정답이다.

---

129. Please make sure you check the ------- date on the bottom of the milk carton before you purchase it.

(A) expiration
(B) expire
(C) expiring
(D) expired

어휘 make sure 반드시 ~하다 expiration date 유통 기한 expire (기한이) 만료되다 carton 종이 팩, 판지 상자

해석 구매하기 전에 우유팩 바닥에 있는 유통기한을 반드시 확인하세요.

해설 명사 date 앞에 빈칸이 있다고 해서 형용사나 분사를 고르는 문제가 아니다. 복합명사 expiration date를 기억하자.

---

130. We regret to inform you that we don't have any refrigerated trucks available right now, so we cannot transport these ------- items until tomorrow afternoon.

(A) durable
(B) fragile
(C) spoiled
(D) perishable

어휘 regret to-V ~하게 되어 유감이다 inform 알리다 refrigerate 냉장하다, 냉장고에 보관하다 transport 수송하다 durable 오래 지속되는 fragile 깨지기 쉬운, 부서지기 쉬운 spoiled (음식이) 상한 perishable 상하기 쉬운

해석 당장은 이용할 수 있는 냉장 트럭이 없어서 내일 오후까지 이 상하기 쉬운 제품을 운송할 수 없음을 알려드리게 되어 유감입니다.

해설 "냉장 트럭이 없으면 '상하기 쉬운' 제품을 수송할 수 없다."는 뜻이 자연스러우므로 (D)가 정답이다.

Part 6

Questions 131-134 refer to the following letter.

February 18

Dear Mr. Welsh:

This letter serves to confirm that Natsume Sugahara [131.]is employed with Tommykaira Motors. Ms. Sugahara has held the title of business Technology Analyst for five years and earns a salary at the top of the pay grade range for that post. [132.]Additionally, she is paid an annual bonus that is higher than average. I will also attest to [133.]her high level of performance. [134.]While working with Tommykaira Motors, Ms. Sugahara has demonstrated an unparalleled work ethic and a profound insight into our business affairs.
Should you have any further inquiries, please do not hesitate to contact me at 04-2103-9485.

Sincerely,

Jasmine Keller
Director, Engineering Program
Management
Tommykaira Motors

131-134번 문제는 다음 편지에 관한 것입니다.

2월 18일

Mr. Welsh께,

이 편지는 Natsume Sugahara가 Tommykaira Motors에 고용되어 있음을 확인시켜 드립니다. Ms. Sugahara는 5년 동안 비즈니스 기술 분석가라는 직책을 맡아왔으며 해당 직책의 급여 등급 범위에서 가장 높은 급여를 받고 있습니다. 추가로 평균보다 높은 연간 상여금도 받습니다. 또한 그녀의 높은 수준의 성과도 증명할 수 있습니다. Tommykaira Motors에서 근무하는 동안, Ms. Sugahara는 비길 데 없는 직업 윤리와 비즈니스 업무에 대한 깊은 통찰력을 보여 주었습니다.

추가적인 문의 사항이 있으시다면 주저 말고 저에게 04-2103-9485로 연락하시기를 바랍니다.

성심성의껏 도와드리겠습니다.

Tommykaira Motors
엔지니어링 프로그램 운영 책임자
Jasmine Keller 드림

어휘 serve to-V ~하는 역할을 하다 be employed with ~에 고용되어 있다 hold 맡다 title 직책 pay grade 급여 등급 post 직책, 자리 attest to ~을 입증하다, ~의 증거가 되다 additionally 추가로 annual 연간의 performance 성과, 실적 demonstrate 보여주다 unparalleled 비길 데 없는, 유례없는 work ethic 직업 윤리 profound 깊은, 심대한 business affairs 비즈니스 업무 inquiry 질문, 문의 hesitate to-V ~할 것을 주저하다

131. (A) had been employed
(B) will be employed
(C) is employed
(D) has employed

해설 시제를 파악하기 위해 뒤에 이어지는 문장을 읽어 봐야 한다. 5년 동안 기술 분석가라는 직책을 맡아왔다는 내용이 현재완료 시제로, 급여를 받고 있다는 내용이 현재 시제이므로(Ms. Sugahara has held the title of Business Technology Analyst for five years and earns a salary at ~), Ms. Sugahara는 현재 이 회사에 고용된 상태임을 알 수 있으므로 (C)가 정답이다.

132. (A) Our new entry-level vehicle is also scheduled to be released.
(B) Additionally, she is paid an annual bonus that is higher than average.
(C) Likewise, she is doing well despite the mounting pressure.
(D) I will be happy to offer her a position in the upper management of our company.

어휘 entry-level 초보자용의 be scheduled to-V ~할 예정이다 release 출시하다 likewise 마찬가지로 despite ~에도 불구하고 mounting 증가하는, 커져 가는 upper management 고위 경영진

해석 (A) 우리의 새 경차도 출시될 예정이다.
(B) 추가로 그녀는 평균보다 높은 연간 상여금도 받는다.
(C) 마찬가지로 그녀는 증가하는 압박에도 불구하고 잘 지내고 있다.
(D) 기꺼이 나는 그녀에게 우리 회사 고위 경영진 자리를 제안하겠다.

해설 앞 문장에서 "높은 급여를 받는다(earns a salary at the top of the pay grade range for that post)."고 했으므로, 이어지는 문장으로 "높은 상여금을 받는다"는 의미인 (B)가 알맞다.

133. (A) our
(B) its
(C) your
(D) her

해설 내용상 빈칸에 들어갈 말이 가리키는 대상은 Natsume Sugahara이므로 정답은 (D)이다.

134. **(A) While**
(B) Whether
(C) Prior to
(D) As long as

해설 Natsume Sugahara가 Tommykaira Motors에서 근무하는 '동안' 보여준 모습을 입증하는 내용이므로 (A)가 알맞다.

To: Baey Yam Keng
From: Meiplus Dental Care
Date: 23 July
Subject: Your teeth

Dear Mr. Pon,

Your smile is ¹³⁵·important to us. It is time for you to schedule a checkup and cleaning appointment. It has been over fifteen months since your last ¹³⁶·visit with us. Meiplus Dental Care advises ¹³⁷·that you schedule a routine cleaning every six months and an examination each year.

We look forward to hearing from you and are prepared to take care of your dental needs. ¹³⁸·Feel free to contact us if you have any queries or apprehensions.

Sincerely,
Jeanette Aw, Hygienist

135-138번 문제는 다음 이메일에 관한 것입니다.

수신: Baey Yam Keng
발신: Meiplus Dental Care
날짜: 7월 23일
제목: 당신의 치아

Mr. Pon께,

당신의 미소는 우리에게 중요합니다. 검진과 세정 예약을 잡으실 때가 되었습니다. 마지막으로 저희를 방문하신지 15개월이 넘었습니다. Meiplus Dental Care에서는 정기 치아 세정은 6개월마다, 검진은 매년 일정을 잡으실 것을 권고합니다.

저희는 당신의 연락을 기다리며 치과에서 치아에 필요한 것들을 처리할 준비가 되어 있습니다. 문의나 우려되는 사항이 있으실 때는 언제든 저희에게 연락해 주세요.

진심을 담아,
치위생사 Jeanette Aw 드림

어휘 checkup (건강) 검진 appointment (진찰) 예약 advise

권고하다 routine 정기적인 examination 검사 hear from ~로부터 연락을 받다 look forward to ~를 고대하다 query 문의 apprehension 우려, 불안 hygienist 치위생사

---

135. **(A) important**
(B) polite
(C) available
(D) similar

해설 "당신의 미소는 우리에게 ------ 합니다."에서 문장의 의미를 자연스럽게 해 주는 것은 '중요한'이라는 뜻의 (A)이다.

---

136. (A) course
(B) reunion
(C) visit
(D) stay

해설 환자가 치과 병원을 '방문'하는 것이 의미상 자연스러우므로 (C)가 정답이다.

---

137. (A) what
(B) each
(C) most
(D) that

해설 ------ you schedule a routine cleaning every six months and an examination each year가 앞에 있는 동사 advises의 목적어이므로 명사절이 되어야 한다. 명사절 접속사로 (A)와 (D)가 있는데, 문장의 의미를 자연스럽게 해주는 (D)가 정답이다.

---

138. (A) It has been a privilege doing business with your firm.
(B) Feel free to contact us if you have any queries or apprehensions.
(C) This is your last opportunity to alter your decision.
(D) We look forward to welcoming new patients to our practice.

어휘 it is a privilege ~한 것이 영광이다 do business with ~와 거래하다 firm 회사 query 문의 apprehension 우려, 불안 opportunity 기회 alter 바꾸다, 고치다 practice (의사·변호사 등의) 영업 (장소)

해석 (A) 당신의 회사와 거래하게 되어 영광이었습니다.
(B) 문의나 우려되는 사항이 있으실 때는 언제든 저희에게 연락해 주세요.

(C) 이번이 결정을 바꿀 수 있는 마지막 기회입니다.
(D) 우리 병원에 새 환자를 맞이하기를 기대합니다.

해설 고객에게 병원 방문을 권장하는 내용의 편지이므로 마무리 짓는 문장으로 알맞은 것은 (B)이다.

Part 7

Questions 139-142 refer to the following document.

Fabrication - Sales - Installation - Repairs
Residential - Commercial - Industrial
Privacy - Security - Ornamental - Guard Rail
Aluminum - Vinyl - Metal - Wood

139.Proposal submitted to *Ganesha Mahajan*	
Street *25 Anthony Wayne Trail*	
City and State *Toledo, OH*	
Home Phone *607-555-1327*	
Job Location *East on Stitt Road to River Road. Right after two miles to Dutch Road. Left onto Anthony Wayne Trail.*	

We hereby tender specifications and estimates for the furnishing and installation of the following:

140.*Dismantle and dispose of 18 sections of 4-rail fence with attached wire mesh. Erect approximately 210 feet of 4.5-foot-tall fence with standard posts. 25 fence sections, two 4.5-foot gates. Strive to make the top of the fence level.*

141.(C)Customer accountable for defining property lines and location of fence, clearing space for fence, and obtaining relevant permits.

141.(D)We hereby propose to furnish labor and materials in accordance with the above specifications for the sum of *Four Thousand Three Hundred and Ninety dollars ($4,390)*. 141.(B)50 percent deposit required. Outstanding balance due upon completion.

141.(A)Toledo Fence and Supply, Inc., reserves the right to withdraw this proposal if not accepted within 30 days.

139-142번 문제는 다음 문서에 관한 것입니다.

제작 – 판매 – 설치 – 수리
주거용 – 상업용 – 산업용
사생활 보호 – 보안 – 장식 – 가드레일
알루미늄 – 비닐 – 금속 – 목재

제안서 제출처 Ganesha Mahajan	
도로명 25 Anthony Wayne Trail	
시, 주 Toledo, OH	
집 전화 607-555-1327	
작업 위치 Stitt 가(街)를 따라 동쪽으로 River 가(街)까지. Dutch 가(街)까지 2마일 직진 후 우회전. 좌회전하여 Anthony Wayne 길 진입.	

이에 의하여 다음 사항의 제공과 설치를 위한 명세서와 견적을 제출합니다:

철망이 붙어 있는 가로대 4개짜리 펜스 18칸을 해체 및 처분한다. 4.5피트 높이의 펜스 약 210피트를 표준 규격 기둥으로 세운다. 펜스 25칸, 4.5피트 높이의 출입문 2개. 펜스 윗부분은 평평하게 하도록 노력한다.

고객은 대지 경계선 및 펜스 위치 규정하기와 펜스 자리 정리하기, 관련 허가를 취득할 책임이 있습니다.

이에 의하여 위의 사양에 따라 총합 사천삼백구십 달러($4,390)에 해당하는 노동과 자재를 제공할 것을 제안합니다. 50퍼센트의 착수금이 요구됩니다. 미지급 잔액은 완공 즉시 지급되어야 합니다.

Toledo Fence and Supply 사(社)는 이 제안이 30일 이내에 수락되지 않을 경우 철회할 권리를 보유합니다.

어휘 fabrication 제작, 제조 repair 수리 residential 주거의 commercial 상업의 industrial 산업의 ornamental

장식의 **proposal** 제안(서) **hereby** 이에 의하여, 이로써 **tender** 제출하다 **specification** 설계 명세서 **estimate** 견적 **furnishing** 제공 **dismantle** 철거하다, 분해하다 **dispose of** ~을 처리하다, 처분하다 **rail** 가로대 **attached** 붙어 있는 **wire mesh** 철망 **erect** 세우다 **approximately** 약 **post** 기둥 **strive to-V** ~하려고 노력하다 **level** 평평한, 수평의 **accountable for** ~에 대해 책임이 있는 **define** 정의하다, 규정하다 **property line** 대지 경계선 **location** 위치 **relevant** 관련이 있는 **permit** 허가(증) **propose** 제안하다 **furnish** 제공하다 **labor** 노동 **material** 자재 **in accordance with** ~에 따라, ~에 의거하여 **sum** 합계, 총계 **deposit** 착수금 **outstanding** 미지불된 **balance** 잔금, 나머지 금액 **due** 지불 기일이 되는 **upon completion** 완성하는 대로 **reserve the right to-V** ~할 권리를 보유하다 **withdraw** 철회하다

---

139. What type of document is this?

(A) An advertisement
(B) A proposal
(C) A work schedule
(D) An order form

[해석] 이것은 어떤 유형의 문서인가?
(A) 광고
(B) 제안서
(C) 업무 일정표
(D) 주문 양식

[해설] 표 안에 제안서(proposal)라고 쓰여 있으므로 (B)가 정답이다.

---

140. What kind of work is being discussed?

(A) Replacement of a fence
(B) Construction of a patio
(C) Lawn maintenance
(D) Furniture restoration

[해석] 어떤 유형의 작업을 논하고 있는가?
(A) 펜스 교체
(B) 테라스 공사
(C) 잔디 유지보수
(D) 가구 복원

[해설] 제공되는 서비스는 원래 있던 펜스를 헐고 새로 세우는 것이므로(Dismantle and dispose of 18 sections of 4-rail fence with attached wire mesh. Erect approximately 210 feet of 4.5-foot-tall fence with standard posts) (A)가 정답이다.

---

141. What is NOT stated in the document?

(A) The terms will become void after 30 days.
(B) The total amount must be paid up front.
(C) The customer must secure permits for the work.
(D) The materials are included in the cost.

[어휘] **terms** 조건, 조항 **void** 무효의, 법적 효력이 없는 **up front** 선불로 **secure** 획득[확보]하다

[해석] 무엇이 문서에서 진술되지 않는가?
(A) 계약 조건은 30일 후에 무효가 된다.
(B) 총금액이 선불로 지급되어야 한다.
(C) 고객이 작업을 위한 허가를 확보해야 한다.
(D) 자재가 비용에 포함된다.

[해설] 지문을 읽으며 보기 하나하나 대조해 보자. 우선 관련 허가를 취득하는 것은 고객의 책임이라는 내용(Customer accountable for ... obtaining relevant permits.)이 있으므로 (C)는 지운다. 총비용 4,390달러에 노동과 자재를 모두 제공한다는 내용도(We hereby propose to furnish labor and materials in accordance with the above specifications for the sum of Four Thousand Three Hundred and Ninety dollars ($4,390).) 있으므로 (D)도 지우자. 지문 마지막에는 Toledo Fence and Supply 사(社)가 30일 동안 수락되지 않는 제안은 철회할 수 있다는 말이(Toledo Fence and Supply, Inc., reserves the right to withdraw this proposal if not accepted within 30 days.) 있으므로 (A)도 지워야 한다. 그런데 착수금으로는 50퍼센트만 요구한다는(50 percent deposit required.) 내용이 있으므로 (B)가 언급되지 않은 것이다.

---

142. The word "balance" in paragraph 4, line 3 is closest in meaning to

(A) deficit
(B) remainder
(C) resource
(D) supply

[해석] 넷째 문단 셋째 줄의 단어 "balance"와 의미상 가장 가까운 것은
(A) 적자; 부족액, 결손
(B) 나머지
(C) 자원, 재원
(D) 공급량

[해설] 착수금을 제외한 나머지 금액이라는 뜻이므로 (B)가 정답이다. balance는 시험에서 대부분 '잔고, 잔액'이라

는 뜻으로 사용된다. 참고로 the balance due(차감 부족액)는 (A)와 동의어이다.

Questions 143-147 refer to the following article, review, and letter.

Care Delivered to Your Doorstep

143.147.In our current hectic lifestyles, it is not uncommon to prioritize a work commitment or a social gathering over seeing a medical professional. Even with proper exercise and diet, though, periodic medical examinations are integral to maintaining optimal health. One medical practitioner in Melbourne devised a strategy to aid time-pressed people in obtaining the necessary attention. "If people don't have the time to come to me, I'll go to them instead," said Bradley Martin, M.D. Mondays and Thursdays are the days when Dr. Martin closes his clinic to carry out home visits to clients. "Making home visits to clients can now eliminate the need for clients to come to the clinic in the future," said Dr. Martin. "For this reason, preventive health care is the foundation of my approach to medicine. 143.I believe this will play a part in making Melbourne a healthier environment."

— Greta Harrison for *Health Today*

143-147번 문제는 다음 기사와 평론, 편지에 관한 것입니다.

문 앞까지 배달되는 진료

현재 우리의 정신없이 바쁜 생활 방식 안에서는 직장 업무나 사교 모임을 의료 전문가를 만나는 것보다 우선시하는 게 드문 일이 아니다. 하지만 적절한 운동과 식습관이 있다 하더라도 최상의 건강을 유지하는 데는 주기적인 건강 검진이 필수적이다. Melbourne의 한 개업의가 시간에 쫓기는 사람들이 필요한 진료를 받도록 돕기 위한 전략을 고안했다. "사람들이 저에게 올 시간이 없다면 대신 제가 가면 되죠." 라고 의학 박사 Bradley Martin은 말했다. 월요일과 목요일은 Martin 박사가 병원 문을 닫고 고객 가정 방문을 하는 날이다. Martin 박사는 "고객의 집을 찾아

가는 것은 이제 고객이 나중에 병원에 와야 할 필요를 없앨 수 있습니다."라고 박사 Bradley Martin은 말했다. "이러한 이유로 예방적 건강 관리는 제 의료 접근법의 토대가 됩니다. 저는 이것이 Melbourne을 더 건강한 환경으로 만드는 데 일익을 담당할 것이라고 믿습니다."
— 헬스 투데이, Greta Harrison

어휘 care 치료, 진료 doorstep 현관 계단 hectic 정신없이 바쁜 uncommon 흔하지 않은 prioritize A over B B보다 A를 우선시하다 commitment 약속, 책무 gathering 모임 medical professional 의료 전문가 proper 적절한 though (문장 끝에서) 그렇지만 periodic 정기적인 medical examination 건강검진 integral 필수적인 maintain 유지하다 optimal 최적의 medical practitioner 개업의 devise 고안하다 strategy 전략 aid 돕다 time-pressed 시간에 쫓기는 attention 돌봄, 치료 M.D.(Doctor of Medicine) 의학 박사 carry out ~을 수행하다 make a visit to ~를 방문하다, 찾아가다 eliminate 제거하다, 없애다 preventive 예방의 foundation 토대, 기반 approach 접근법 play a part in ~에 일익을 담당하다

Irish Author's Stellar Performance Continues

Mayanti Langer's newest Book, *Ireland's Changing Waves*, is an exceptional chronicle of the evolution of the fishing industry in Ireland, from self-sustaining fishing villages to present-day fish farming. A Howth native, Ms. Langer was taught the trade by her fisherman father, so her book contains vivid firsthand accounts of the Irish fishing lifestyle as well as top-notch research. 145.She makes her preference for traditional fishing practices over modernized seafood harvesting very clear. Along with that, 144.she makes a good case for the ecological value of a less complicated way of life in rural communities. All in all, *Ireland's Changing Waves* is a worthy companion volume to Ms. Langer's preceding book on the history of agriculture, *Proliferating Prosperity*. 146.Ms. Langer has already made known her plan to create a new book dealing with medical care, entitled Mending the Crowd.

Ireland's Changing Waves and other titles written by Ms. Langer can be located on her publisher's Web site, www.mercierpress.ie.

아일랜드 작가의 눈부신 성과가 계속되다

Mayanti Langer의 신간 '아일랜드 변화의 물결'은 아일랜드 어업 발전사의 특출한 연대기로, 자급자족하는 어촌에서부터 현대의 양식업까지 이어진다. Howth 출신의 Ms. Langer는 어부인 아버지에게 어업을 배웠기 때문에 그녀의 책에는 아주 뛰어난 연구뿐만 아니라 아일랜드의 어촌 생활 방식에 대해 직접 체험한 생생한 이야기를 포함하고 있다. 그녀는 현대화된 해산물 채취보다 전통적인 어업 관행을 선호한다는 점을 매우 분명히 하고 있다. 그와 더불어 그녀는 지방 공동체에서 보이는 덜 복잡한 생활 방식의 생태학적 가치에 대해 옹호론을 훌륭히 펼치고 있다. 전체적으로 '아일랜드 변화의 물결'은 농업의 역사에 관한 Ms. Langer의 전작 '확산하는 번영'의 자매편이 될 만한 가치가 있다. Ms. Langer는 이미 의료 서비스를 다루는 '군중 치료하기'라는 제목의 새 책을 집필할 계획을 발표했다. '아일랜드 변화의 물결'과 Ms. Langer가 쓴 다른 작품들은 출판사 홈페이지 www.mercierpress.ie 에서 찾을 수 있다.

어휘 Irish 아일랜드의 author 작가, 저자 stellar 뛰어난, 눈부신 exceptional 탁월한, 특출한 chronicle 연대기 evolution 진화, 발전 self-sustaining 자급자족하는 fish farming 양식업 native ~ 출신자, 현지인 trade 업계 contain 담고 있다 vivid 생생한 firsthand 직접 겪은 account 설명, 진술 top-notch 최고급의, 일류의 preference for ~에 대한 선호 practice 관행, 관례 modernize 현대화하다 harvesting 수확, 채취 along with ~에 덧붙여 make a case for ~에 대한 정당성을 밝히다, 옹호론을 펴다 ecological 생태학적인 complicated 복잡한 rural 시골의, 지방의 all in all 대체로 worthy 훌륭한 companion volume 자매편 preceding 선행하는, 지난 proliferate 급증하다, 확산하다 prosperity 번영, 번창 make ~ known ~을 알리다, 발표하다 deal with ~를 다루다 entitled ~라는 제목의 mend 치료하다, 고치다 title 서적, 출판물 be located on ~에 위치해 있다 publisher 출판사

문장 분석

She makes her preference (for traditional fishing practices) (over modernized seafood harvesting) very clear.

➡ ( )로 묶여 있는 두 구문이 수식어구라는 것을 파악하면 5형식 문장임을 알 수 있다.

➡ preference for A over B 구문을 사용했는데, 동사

prefer의 용법에도 적용할 수 있다. prefer A over B 뿐 아니라 prefer A to B로도 쓸 수 있다. Part 5에서 over를 빈칸으로 하는 문제가 출제된 적이 있다.

1 September

Bradley Martin, M.D.
Healthjoy Distributors Clinic
537 George St.
Fitzroy North Victoria 3068
Australia

Dear Dr. Martin,

I recently came across an article in Health Today that highlighted your unique medical practice. 146.I am currently writing a book that explores the history of medical care, and I think your story would be beneficial to my research. 146.I'd very much like to interview you for the book when I visit Melbourne this winter. If this is possible, please contact my office at +353 (020) 918-2148.

147.On a personal note, I'd like to applaud your efforts to make your city healthier. I think your approach is brilliant, and I'm sending you my best wishes.

Most sincerely,
Mayanti Langere.

9월 1일

의학 박사 Bradley Martin
Healthjoy Distributors 병원
537 George St.
Fitzroy North Victoria 3068
Australia

Martin 박사님께,
최근에 '헬스 투데이'에 실린 당신의 독특한 의료 행위를 조명한 기사를 우연히 접했습니다. 저는 현재 의료 서비스의 역사를 탐구하는 책을 쓰고 있는데, 제 생각에는 당신의 이야기가 제 연구에 도움이 될 것 같습니다. 올겨울에 Melbourne을 방문했을 때 책을 위해 당신과 인터뷰를 정말 하고 싶습니다. 이것이 가능하다면 전화번호 +353 (020) 918-2148로 제 사무실에 연락 주시기 바랍니다.

개인적으로 도시를 더 건강하게 만들기 위한 당신의 노력에 박수를 보내고 싶습니다. 제 생각에 당신의 접근법은 탁월하며, 성공하기를 기원합니다.

진심을 담아,
Mayanti Langer

어휘 come across ~을 우연히 발견하다 practice (전문직의) 업무, 일 highlight 강조하다, 조명하다 explore 탐구하다 medical care 의료 서비스 beneficial 유익한, 이로운 on a personal note 개인적 의견으로 applaud ~에게 박수를 보내다 brilliant 탁월한, 눈부신

---

143. What is the article mainly about?

(A) A clinic adjusting its hours
(B) A new type of patient visits
(C) Guidance for selecting a physician
(D) Health benefits of exercise

어휘 adjust 조정하다 guidance 안내, 지도 health benefit 건강상의 이익[이점]

해설 기사는 주로 무엇에 관한 것인가?
(A) 영업시간을 조정하는 병원
(B) 새로운 유형의 환자 방문
(C) 의사 선택에 대한 안내
(D) 운동의 건강상 이점

해설 최상의 건강을 유지하기 위해 정기 검진이 필수이지만, 바쁜 현대인들은 시간을 내기 어려운 실정이다. 이러한 어려움을 해결하기 위해 병원에 오기 힘든 사람들을 의사가 직접 찾아가는 새로운 유형의 의료 서비스가 등장했다는 내용이다.

---

144. In the review, the word "case" in paragraph 1, line 7, is closest in meaning to

(A) argument
(B) container
(C) situation
(D) encounter

해설 평론에서 첫 문단 일곱째 줄의 단어 "case"와 의미상 가장 가까운 것은
(A) 주장
(B) 용기
(C) 상황
(D) 만남

해설 case는 여러 의미가 있어서, (D)를 제외한 나머지 보기가 모두 동의어가 될 수 있다. 지문에 등장하는 make

a case for는 '~에 대한 옹호론을 펴다'라는 의미이므로 여기에 사용된 case는 '주장, 논거'라는 뜻인 (A)가 정답이다.

---

145. What does the review suggest about Ms. Langer?

(A) She is in favor of traditional fishing methods.
(B) She is currently authoring a book about farming.
(C) She spent her childhood in Australia.
(D) She recently set up her own Web site.

어휘 in favor of ~을 찬성하는 author 저술하다 set up ~을 세우다, 설립하다

해설 평론은 Ms. Langer에 관하여 무엇을 시사하는가?
(A) 전통적인 어업 방식을 찬성한다.
(B) 현재 농업에 관한 책을 저술하고 있다.
(C) 유년기를 호주에서 보냈다.
(D) 최근에 자신의 홈페이지를 만들었다.

해설 현대화된 해산물 채취보다는 전통적인 어업 관행을 선호한다고 진술하고(She makes her preference for traditional fishing practices over modernized seafood harvesting very clear) 있으므로 (A)가 정답이다.

---

146. For what book does Ms. Langer want to interview Dr. Martin?

(A) *Ireland's Changing Waves*
(B) *Mending the Crowd*
(C) *Proliferating Prosperity*
(D) *Health Today*

해설 Ms. Langer는 어느 책을 위해 Martin 박사를 인터뷰하고 싶어 하는가?
(A) 아일랜드 변화의 물결
(B) 군중 치료하기
(C) 확산하는 번영
(D) 헬스 투데이

연계 추론 평론에 소개된 바에 따르면 Ms. Langer는 현재 의료 서비스 분야를 다루는 책을 집필하고 있는데, 이 책의 제목이 '군중 치료하기'이다(Ms. Langer has already made known her plan to create a new book dealing with medical care, entitled *Mending the Crowd*). 한편 편지에서 Ms. Langer는 자기가 현재 의료 서비스의 역사를 탐구하는 책을 쓰는 중이며(I am currently writing a book that explores the history of medical care), 이 책을 위해 인터

뷰를 진행하고 싶다고(I'd very much like to interview you for the book) 말했다. 두 지문의 내용을 종합하면 Ms. Langer가 '군중 치료하기'를 위해 Martin 박사를 인터뷰하고 싶어 한다는 내용을 추론할 수 있다.

---

147. What does Ms. Langer imply in her letter?

    (A) She is convinced that eating fish is part of a healthy diet.

    (B) She desires to present Dr. Martin with a copy of her book.

    (C) She is eager to suggest a medical strategy to Dr. Martin.

    (D) She believes that doctors visiting homes is a good idea.

`어휘` convinced 확신하는 desire to-V ~를 간절히 바라다 present 증정하다 copy (책 의) 한 부 be eager to-V ~하기를 열망하다 strategy 전략, 계획

`해석` Ms. Langer는 편지에서 무엇을 암시하는가?
    (A) 생선을 먹는 것은 건강한 식습관의 일부라고 확신한다.
    (B) Martin 박사에게 자신의 책을 한 권 선물하고 싶다.
    (C) Martin 박사에게 의료 전략을 제안하기를 간절히 바란다.
    (D) 의사들이 가정을 방문하는 것은 좋은 생각이라고 믿는다.

`연계 추론` 기사의 주요 내용이 의사가 환자의 가정을 방문하는 새로운 유형의 의료 행위를 소개하는 것인데, 마지막 문장에서 Martin 박사는 자신의 이러한 시도가 도시를 더 건강한 곳으로 만들어 줄 것이라고 말한다(I believe this will play a part in making Melbourne a healthier environment). 편지에서는 Ms. Langer가 도시를 더 건강하게 만들기 위한 노력에 박수갈채를 보내고 싶고(I'd like to applaud your efforts to make your city healthier.), 이러한 접근법은 훌륭하다고(I think your approach is brilliant) 평가하고 있다. 여기서 말하는 접근법이란 기사에서 소개한 의사의 환자 가정 방문을 가리키는 것이다. 따라서 Ms. Langer는 의사들이 환자를 방문하는 것이 좋은 아이디어라고 말하고 있음을 추론할 수 있다.

PART 5 & 6 Exercise

101 (A)	**102** (A)	**103** (C)	**104** (B)	**105** (D)
106 (B)	**107** (B)	**108** (A)	**109** (A)	**110** (B)
111 (C)	**112** (A)	**113** (A)	**114** (B)	**115** (D)

101. Taking advantage of online banking, bills can be settled ------- it fits your schedule.

(A) **whenever**
(B) simply
(C) accordingly
(D) quite

어휘 take advantage of ~을 이용하다 settle a bill 청구서를 지불하다 fit ~에 맞추다

해석 온라인 뱅킹을 이용하면 일정에 맞춰 언제든 청구된 금액을 낼 수 있다.

해설 빈칸 앞에 수동태로 완성된 문장이 있고, 빈칸 뒤에 다시 '주어 + 동사'가 있다. 여기서 빈칸 앞은 주절, 빈칸 뒤는 부사절이므로 빈칸에는 부사절 접속사 (A)가 들어가야 알맞다.

102. ------- Mr. Villalobos has been employed at Atzeret Communications for ten years, he is still eager to learn new skills and take on additional responsibilities.

(A) **Although**
(B) But
(C) Neither
(D) Yet

어휘 be employed (at) ~에 고용되다, 근무하다 be eager to-V ~에 열심이다 take on (일 등을) 맡다, (책임을) 지다 additional 추가의 responsibility 책임, 책무

해석 Mr. Villalobos는 Atzeret Communications에서 10년 동안 근무해 왔지만, 여전히 새로운 기술을 익히고 더 많은 일을 맡아 하는 데 열심이다.

해설 '------- + 주어 + 동사 ~, 주어 + 동사 ~'의 구조가 있으면 쉼표 앞은 부사절, 쉼표 뒤는 주절이다. 그러므로 빈칸에는 부사절 접속사 (A)가 들어가야 한다.

103. A thorough review of staff recruitment procedures ------- in the annual report to First Commonwealth Bank's board of directors.

(A) includes
(B) including
(C) **was included**
(D) were included

어휘 thorough 빈틈없는, 철두철미한 recruitment 신규 모집, 채용 board of directors 이사회

해석 First Commonwealth 은행의 이사회에 제출한 연례 보고서에는 직원 채용 절차에 대한 철저한 검토가 포함되었다.

해설 [(A) 능동태 동사 (B) 준동사 (C) 수동태 동사 (D) 수동태 동사] 문장에 동사가 필요하므로 빈칸에 준동사 (B)는 들어갈 수 없다. 빈칸 뒤에 목적어가 없으므로 수동태 동사 (C)와 (D) 중 정답을 선택해야 한다. 빈칸 앞 전치사구(of staff recruitment procedures)를 제외하면 주어가 단수 명사(A thorough review)임을 알 수 있다. 그러므로 수가 일치하는 (C)가 정답이다.

104. Matt Yoon, president of Anyang Industries, ------- to disclose substantial profits at the end of the year.

(A) expect
(B) **is expected**
(C) expecting
(D) were expecting

어휘 disclose 발표하다, 공개하다 substantial 상당한

해석 Anyang Industries의 회장 Matt Yoon은 연말에 상당한 이익을 공개할 것으로 예상된다.

해설 문장에 동사가 필요하므로 빈칸에 준동사 (C)는 들어갈 수 없다. 주어 Matt Yoon이 단수 명사이므로 수가 일치하는 (B)가 정답이다.

105. At Romulus Ltd., there are ------- opportunities for career advancement.

(A) plenty
(B) each

(C) every
(D) many

어휘 plenty 많음, 대량, 다량 career advancement 승진

해석 Romulus 사(社)에서는 승진 기회가 많다.

해설 명사 opportunities 앞에 빈칸이 있으므로 형용사 중에서 복수 명사 앞에 사용할 수 있는 (D)가 정답이다.

---

106. Roughly a third of the employees at Bryer Accounting ------- to work by bus.

(A) commutes
(B) commute
(C) is commuting
(D) has commuted

어휘 roughly 대략, 거의 a third 1/3 accounting 회계 commute 통근하다

해석 Bryer Accounting의 약 3분의 1의 직원들은 버스로 통근한다.

해설 빈칸 앞의 전치사구 at Bryer Accounting은 제외하자. '분수 of' 뒤에 복수형 the employees가 있으므로 동사는 복수 명사의 수와 일치하는 (B)가 정답이다.

---

107. We were surprised and pleased that our job posting for an assistant manager generated so much -------.

(A) interested
(B) interest
(C) interests
(D) interesting

어휘 job posting 채용 공고 assistant 부(副), 보좌의 generate 발생시키다, 일으키다

해석 우리는 차장 채용 공고가 그렇게 많은 관심을 불러일으킨 것에 놀랍고도 기뻤다.

해설 타동사 generated의 목적어가 필요하므로 명사 (B)와 (C) 중 정답을 선택해야 한다. 빈칸 바로 앞에 much가 있으므로 셀 수 없는 명사인 (B)가 들어가야 한다.

---

108. Mr. and Mrs. Rodriguez ------- in charge of the development of the medicine since the company was merged with Miracle Pharmaceuticals.

(A) have been

(B) were
(C) to be
(D) has been

어휘 in charge of ~을 맡고 있는, 담당하는 development 개발 merge 합병하다 pharmaceuticals 의약품, 제약회사

해석 Rodriguez 부부는 회사가 Miracle 제약과 합병한 이후 그 의약품의 개발을 담당해 왔다.

해설 since 이후는 부사절, 앞부분은 주절이다. 주절의 빈칸에 동사가 필요하므로 준동사 (C)는 들어갈 수 없다. 주어 Mr. and Mrs. Rodriguez는 복수 명사이므로 단수 동사 (D)를 제외하고 (A)와 (B) 중 알맞은 시제의 동사를 정답으로 선택해야 한다. 문장에 since가 있으면 현재완료 시제이므로 (A)가 정답이다. 참고로 시제 문제는 Day 08에서 다룬다.

---

109. A price reduction in public transportation fares ------- people to drive less and decrease fuel usage.

(A) would encourage
(B) is encouraged
(C) encouraging
(D) encourage

어휘 reduction 인하 public transportation 대중교통 fare 요금 decrease 줄이다 fuel usage 연료 사용량

해석 대중교통 요금 인하는 사람들이 운전을 덜 하고 연료 사용량을 줄이도록 유도할 것이다.

해설 [(A) 능동태 동사 (B) 수동태 동사 (C) 준동사 (D) 능동태 동사] 문장의 빈칸에 동사가 필요하므로 준동사 (C)는 들어갈 수 없다. 빈칸 뒤에 목적어 people이 있으므로 수동태 동사 (B)도 정답이 될 수 없다. 빈칸 앞의 전치사구 in public transportation fares를 제외하면, 주어(A price reduction)가 단수 명사임을 알 수 있으므로 (D)도 빈칸에 들어갈 수 없다. 그러므로 (A)가 정답이다. 수의 일치 문제는 다양한 문법 요소를 고려해야 하는 경우가 많다.

---

110. Invitations to the annual charity reception were sent to all board members, but ------- will be able to attend.

(A) little
(B) few
(C) whoever
(D) so

어휘 invitation 초대(장) charity 자선 reception 축하연

board (of directors) 이사회

해석 연례 자선 축하연 초대장이 모든 이사회 임원에게 발송 되었지만, 참석할 수 있는 사람은 거의 없을 것이다.

해설 빈칸 뒤에 동사(구) will be able to attend가 있으므로 빈칸은 주어 자리이다. 그러므로 주어가 될 수 없는 (D) 는 제외하자. 빈칸 앞에 있는 등위접속사 but은 병렬 구조로 문장을 연결하기 때문에 종속절(명사절, 부사절)을 연결하는 복합관계대명사 (C)도 정답이 될 수 없다. 또한 빈칸은 셀 수 있는 명사 board members를 가리키므로 (B)가 정답이다.

---

111. Tassel Tower, one of the premium office ------- in Bogotá, has lowered its monthly rents by 10 percent, but many of its offices still remain unoccupied.

(A) location
(B) located
(C) locations
(D) locating

어휘 premium 고급의, 고가의 lower 내리다, 낮추다 monthly rent 월세 unoccupied 비어 있는

해석 Bogotá의 고급 사무실 자리 중 하나인 Tassel Tower 는 월세를 10퍼센트 낮췄지만, 많은 사무실이 여전히 비어 있는 상태이다.

해설 one of the premium office -------를 보면 빈칸에 명사가 들어가야 하므로 (A)와 (C) 중 정답을 선택하자. one of 뒤에는 복수 명사와 단수 동사가 있어야 하므로, 복수 명사 (C)가 정답이다. 과거분사 (B)가 빈칸에 들어가면 one of 뒤에 셀 수 있는 명사의 단수형만 남기 때문에 알맞지 않다.

---

112. The Incheon Airport has an underground train system that ------- the international and domestic flight terminals.

(A) connects
(B) connecting
(C) connection
(D) connect

어휘 underground 지하의 domestic 국내의

해석 인천 공항에는 국제선과 국내선 터미널을 연결하는 지하철 시스템이 있다.

해설 빈칸 앞뒤 an underground train system that ------- the international and domestic flight terminals를 살펴보면 빈칸은 주격 관계대명사 that 뒤

에 있는 동사 자리임을 알 수 있다. 그러므로 (A)와 (D) 중 정답을 선택해야 한다. 선행사(an underground train system)가 단수 명사이므로 수가 일치하는 (A)가 정답이다.

---

113. Employees who consistently finish their assignments ------- they are due may receive bonuses in accordance with the compensation guidelines.

(A) before
(B) how
(C) why
(D) either

어휘 consistently 일관되게, 항상 assignment 업무 due 기한이 ~까지인 in accordance with ~에 따라 compensation 보상

해석 항상 기한이 되기 전에 업무를 끝마치는 직원은 보상 지침에 따라 상여금을 받을 수 있다.

해설 주격관계대명사 who가 이끄는 절 who consistently finish their assignments ------- they are due에서, 빈칸 앞에 3형식으로 완성된 문장이 있으므로(who 를 주어로 보기) 빈칸 이후로는 부사절이 된다. 따라서 빈칸에는 부사절 접속사 (A)가 들어가야 한다.

---

114. ------- Vice President Jepsen's schedule alters, we will reschedule the strategy session for a different date.

(A) Ever
(B) If
(C) In order that
(D) So

어휘 in order that ~하기 위해 vice president 부사장 alter 변하다, 달라지다 reschedule ~의 일정을 변경하다 session (특정 활동) 시간, 기간

해석 Jepsen 부사장의 일정이 달라지면, 우리는 전략 회의의 일정을 다른 날짜로 변경할 것이다.

해설 in order that[so that] 뒤에는 '주어 + can[may/will] + 동사' 형태의 절이 오므로 일단 제외하자. '------- + 주어 + 동사 ~, 주어 + 동사 ~'의 구조가 있으므로 쉼표 앞은 부사절, 쉼표 이후는 주절이다. 따라서 빈칸에는 부사절 접속사 (B)가 들어가야 한다.

---

115. One of the ------- of the researchers at Rangel-Moreno Laboratories is to keep materials in their work areas labeled accurately at all times.

(A) responsible
(B) responsibly
(C) responsibility
(D) responsibilities

어휘 at all times 항상, 언제나 accurately 정확하게

해석 Rangel-Moreno 연구소 연구원들의 업무 중 하나는 작업 구역 내의 재료들에 항상 정확하게 라벨이 붙어 있도록 하는 것이다.

해설 관사와 전치사 사이에는 명사가 들어가야 하므로 (C)와 (D) 중 정답을 선택해야 한다. 'one[each/either/neither] of + 복수 명사 + 단수 동사' 구조이므로 빈칸에 복수 명사 (D)가 알맞다.

Actual Test

101 (C)	102 (C)	103 (C)	104 (A)	105 (B)
106 (A)	107 (B)	108 (A)	109 (A)	110 (C)
111 (D)	112 (A)	113 (D)	114 (A)	115 (D)
116 (C)	117 (D)	118 (C)	119 (A)	120 (B)
121 (A)	122 (C)	123 (A)	124 (A)	125 (C)
126 (A)	127 (C)	128 (C)	129 (A)	130 (D)
131 (C)	132 (D)	133 (A)	134 (B)	135 (A)
136 (D)	137 (A)	138 (C)	139 (C)	140 (D)
141 (A)	142 (D)	143 (B)	144 (C)	145 (B)
146 (A)	147 (D)			

Part 5

101. Through his vibrant oil paintings, Kyung-Ho Park, a Korean artist, presents innovative ways of ------- color and light.

(A) appreciate
(B) appreciative
(C) appreciating
(D) appreciation

어휘 vibrant (색채가) 강렬한, 선명한 present 제시하다 innovative 혁신적인 appreciate 인식하다 appreciative 안목이 있는

해석 한국의 미술가 Kyung-Ho Park은 선명한 유화를 통해 색깔과 빛을 인식하는 혁신적인 방식을 제시한다.

해설 of ------- color and light를 보면서 명사 앞에 빈칸이 있다고 해서 형용사 (B)를 정답으로 선택하면 안 된다. 뒤에 있는 명사와 의미상 어울리지 않기 때문이다. 빈칸에는 전치사 of의 목적어가 들어가야 하는데, 빈칸 뒤에 있는 목적어를 취할 수 있는 동명사 (C)가 정답이다.

102. The contractor ------- it would take five hours to replace the cracked tiles in the lobby.

(A) designed
(B) managed
(C) estimated
(D) installed

어휘 contractor 도급업자 estimate 추산[추정]하다 install 설치하다 replace 교체하다 cracked 금이 간, 갈라진

해석 도급업자는 로비의 금 간 타일들을 교체하는 데 5시간이 걸릴 것이라고 추산했다.

해설 빈칸에 들어갈 동사의 목적어로 that이 생략된 명사절을 사용하고 있다. 구문이나 형태상 that절을 쓸 수 있는 (C)가 정답이다.

---

103. Ms. Yakut appears ------- to undertake more demanding administrative tasks.

    (A) friendly
    (B) likable
    (C) determined
    (D) separate

어휘 appear ~한 것 같다 likable 호감이 가는, 마음에 드는 determined 단단히 결심한 separate 분리된, 별도의 undertake 맡다, ~에 착수하다 demanding 부담이 큰, 힘든 administrative 관리의, 행정의

해석 Ms. Yakut는 더 힘든 행정 업무를 맡기로 결심한 것 같다.

해설 '~하기로 단단히 결심하다'라는 뜻의 be determined to-V를 알면 (C)를 정답으로 쉽게 고를 수 있다.

---

104. When sending ------- to customers, it is imperative to utilize the organization's revised letterhead.

    (A) correspondence
    (B) corresponded
    (C) corresponding
    (D) correspondent

어휘 correspondence 서신, 편지 correspond (to/with) 일치하다, 부합하다; (~에) 해당하다 (to); (~와) 편지를 주고받다 (with) correspondent 통신원, 특파원 imperative 반드시 해야 하는, 긴요한 utilize 활용하다, 이용하다 revise 개정하다, 수정하다 letterhead 레터헤드(편지지 위쪽의 인쇄 문구, 회사명·소재지·전화 번호 등); (레터헤드가 적힌) 업무용 편지지

해석 고객에게 편지를 보낼 때는 반드시 조직의 수정된 레터헤드를 사용해야 한다.

해설 빈칸에 현재분사 sending의 목적어가 될 명사가 들어가야 하므로 (A)와 (D) 중에서 정답을 선택해야 한다. (D)는 셀 수 있는 명사로서 앞에 관사가 있어야 하므로, 관사가 필요 없는 추상명사 (A)가 정답이다.

---

105. Ms. Chen stated that the vacation policy will be ------- once the employee handbook has been updated.

    (A) connected
    (B) clarified
    (C) familiarized
    (D) participated

어휘 clarify 명확하게 하다 familiarize 익숙하게 하다 participate 참가하다 employee handbook 직원 편람 update 갱신하다, 개정하다

해석 Ms. Chen은 직원 편람이 개정되면 휴가 정책이 명확히 설명될 것이라고 말했다.

해설 the vacation policy will be ------- once the employee handbook has been updated(일단 직원 편람이 개정되면 휴가 정책이 [(A) 연결될 (B) 명확히 설명될 (C) 보급될 (D) 참가될] 것이다)의 의미를 자연스럽게 만들어 주는 동사 (B)가 정답이다.

---

106. Anyone who ------- an oil change at Frank's Auto Care will be offered a complimentary car wash.

    (A) purchases
    (B) purchasing
    (C) purchasable
    (D) purchase

어휘 purchasable 살 수 있는 oil change 윤활유 complimentary 무료의 car wash 세차

해석 Frank 자동차 정비소에서 윤활유를 구매하시는 분은 누구나 무료 세차를 제공받습니다.

해설 주격 관계대명사 뒤에 동사가 있어야 하므로 (A)와 (D) 중 정답을 선택해야 한다. 선행사가 단수 명사 Anyone이므로 수가 일치하는 (A)가 정답이다.

---

107. For safety reasons, warehouse employees who work at sites of construction projects must wear protective gear at ------- times.

    (A) every
    (B) all
    (C) full
    (D) each

어휘 warehouse 창고 site 현장, 장소 construction 공사, 건설 protective gear 보호 장비 at all times 항상

해석 안전상의 이유로 공사 현장에서 근무하는 창고 직원들은 항상 보호 장비를 착용해야 한다.

해설 일단 (C)는 의미상 알맞지 않다. 나머지 보기 중 복수 명사 times 앞에 사용할 수 있는 (B)가 정답이다. (A)와 (D)는 셀 수 있는 단수 명사 앞에만 사용할 수 있다.

108. Zarb Shoes will cease operations in all of its remaining retail outlets and shift ------- to online sales.

(A) entirely
(B) commonly
(C) famously
(D) equally

어휘 cease 그만두다, 끝내다 operation 사업, 영업 remaining 남아 있는 retail 소매의 outlet 직판장, 할인점 shift to ~로 옮기다, 전환하다 entirely 전적으로, 완전히 equally 똑같이, 공평하게

해석 Zarb 제화는 남아 있는 모든 소매점에서 영업을 중단하고 완전히 온라인 판매로 전환할 것이다.

해설 남아 있는 소매점을 '모두' 정리하고 온라인 판매로 '완전히' 전환한다는 의미가 자연스러우므로 (A)가 정답이다.

109. Employees must affix the mandatory warning labels ------- transferring products to the quality control department.

(A) prior to
(B) and
(C) last
(D) otherwise

어휘 affix 부착하다, 붙이다 mandatory 법에 정해진, 의무적인 warning 경고 prior to ~ 전에 otherwise 그렇지 않으면 transfer A to B A를 B로 옮기다, 나르다 quality control 품질 관리

해석 직원은 제품을 품질 관리 부서로 옮기기 전에 법으로 정해진 경고 라벨을 부착해야 한다.

해설 제품을 옮기기(transferring products) '전에(prior to)' 라벨을 부착해야(must affix the mandatory warning labels) 한다는 의미가 자연스러우므로 (A)가 정답이다.

110. We monitored the temperature at fifteen-minute ------- throughout the experiment.

(A) divisions
(B) priorities
(C) intervals
(D) intersections

어휘 monitor 추적 관찰하다 division 분할, 분배 priority 우선순위 interval 간격 intersection 교차로

해석 우리는 실험 내내 15분 간격으로 온도를 관찰했다.

해설 at fifteen minute -------의 의미를 자연스럽게 해주는 명사 (C)가 정답이다.

111. Foreign financial firms have a number of ------- about regulations governing their business activities.

(A) complain
(B) complaint
(C) complaining
(D) complaints

어휘 financial firm 금융회사 complaint 불평, 불만 regulation 규정 govern 통제하다, 통치하다

해석 외국계 금융사들은 사업 활동을 규제하는 규정에 대해 불만이 많다.

해설 a number of 뒤에는 복수 명사를 써야 하므로 (D)가 정답이다.

112. Production of the second shift machine operators ------- significantly lower than that of the third shift workers.

(A) is
(B) to be
(C) are
(D) being

어휘 shift 교대조 operator (기계의) 기사, 조작자 significantly 상당히, 크게

해석 2조 기계 기사들의 생산량은 3조 근로자들의 생산량보다 훨씬 더 낮다.

해설 문장에 동사가 없으므로 빈칸에는 동사 (A)나 (C)가 들어가야 한다. 빈칸 앞 전치사구 of the second shift machine operators를 제외하면 주어(Production)가 단수 명사임을 알 수 있으므로 수가 일치하는 (A)가 정답이다.

113. The goal of the customer service department ------- all customer complaints that they have in both a friendly and timely manner.

(A) resolve
(B) is resolved
(C) had resolved
(D) is to resolve

어휘 resolve 해결하다 complaint 불평, 불만 timely 시기적절한, 때맞춘 in a ~ manner ~하게, ~한 방식으로

해석 고객 서비스 부서의 목표는 접수되는 모든 고객의 불만 사항을 친절하면서 시기적절하게 해결하는 것이다.

해설 [(A) 능동태 (B) 수동태 (C) 능동태 (D) 능동태] 빈칸 뒤에 목적어가 있으므로 수동태인 (B)는 제외한다. 빈칸 앞 전치사구 of the customer service department를 제외하면 주어 The goal이 단수 명사임을 알 수 있으므로 복수 동사인 (A)도 제외한다. 과거완료 시제는 과거의 어떤 사건보다 더 과거에 있었던 일을 나타내므로, (C)가 정답이 되려면 과거 사건이 언급되어야 한다. 그런데 문장에서 과거 사건이 나타나 있지 않으므로 (D)가 정답이다.

---

114. Employees who want to file for client entertainment reimbursement must submit a written ------- detailing their expenditure with valid receipts to the company.

(A) **notification**
(B) approach
(C) information
(D) introduction

어휘 file for ~을 신청하다 entertainment 접대 reimbursement 환급 submit 제출하다 written notification 서면 통지 detail (상세히) 열거하다 expenditure 지출, 경비 valid 유효한 receipt 영수증

해석 고객 접대비 환급을 신청하고자 하는 직원은 유효한 영수증과 함께 지출 내역을 상세히 기재한 서면 통지서를 회사에 제출해야 한다.

해설 항상 짝을 이루어 출제되는 어휘 문제이다. written 뒤에 빈칸이 있으면 notice, notification, consent가 들어갈 수 있으므로 (A)가 정답이다.

---

115. All guests who ------- our services to book hotel rooms in Bangkok will be provided a free tour of the city and its temples.

(A) to use
(B) uses
(C) using
(D) **use**

어휘 book 예약하다 temple 사원

해석 저희 서비스를 이용하여 방콕의 호텔을 예약하시는 모든 투숙객은 도시와 사원의 무료 투어를 제공받습니다.

해설 주격 관계대명사 who 뒤에 동사가 있어야 하므로 (B)

와 (D) 중 정답을 선택해야 한다. 선행사의 수와 일치해야 하므로 복수 명사 guests에 알맞은 (D)가 정답이다.

---

116. Greenwood Printing has ------- from a local supplier to a widely recognized regional distributor.

(A) determined
(B) focused
(C) **evolved**
(D) permitted

어휘 determine 알아내다, 밝히다 evolve from ~에서 발전하다, 진전하다 supplier 공급자 local 특정 지역의 widely 널리 recognized 인정된, 알려진 regional 지역(전체)의 distributor 배급사, 유통사

해석 Greenwood Printing은 특정 지역의 공급업체에서 널리 인정받는 지역 유통업체로 발전했다.

해설 빈칸은 동사 자리이다. from 뒤에는 '특정 지역에만 공급하는 사업체', to 뒤에는 '지역 전체에서 널리 인정받는 유통업체'라고 나와 있다. 작은 사업체에서 큰 사업체로 '발전했다'는 의미가 자연스러우므로 (C)가 정답이다.

---

117. Front Force Ltd. offers customized digital and print design ------- that meet the individual client's needs.

(A) to service
(B) service
(C) serviced
(D) **services**

어휘 customized 맞춤형의 meet needs 요구를 충족시키다

해석 Front Force 사(社)는 각 고객의 요구에 맞는 맞춤형 디지털 및 인쇄 디자인 서비스를 제공한다.

해설 빈칸 앞 digital and print design -------을 보면 명사 뒤 빈칸에는 명사가 들어가야 한다는 것을 알 수 있다. 주격 관계대명사(that)의 선행사인 복합 명사이고 동사 meet와 수가 일치되어야 하므로 복수 명사 (D)가 정답이다.

---

118. Nature Hills Nursery utilizes the ------- latest agricultural techniques.

(A) so
(B) more
(C) **very**
(D) much

어휘 nursery 묘목장 the very (최상급을 강조하여) 그야말로, 실로, 단연 agricultural 농업의

해석 Nature Hills 묘목장은 가장 최신의 농업 기술을 활용한다.

해설 최상급 형용사 latest를 강조하는 표현을 고르는 문제로, 정답은 (C)이다. 최상급을 강조하는 표현으로 the very, easily, by far 등이 있다.

---

119. Computer science, especially High Performance Computing, has become a key ------- in the development of many research fields, establishing a new paradigm called computational science.

(A) factor
(B) position
(C) instructor
(D) composition

어휘 factor 요인, 요소 instructor 강사 composition 구성 field 분야 establish 확립하다 paradigm 인식 체계, 패러다임 computational science 계산과학

해석 컴퓨터 과학, 특히 고성능 컴퓨팅은 계산과학이라는 새 패러다임을 확립하면서 많은 연구 분야의 발전에 있어 핵심 요소가 되었다.

해설 Computer science has become a key ------- in the development of many research fields(컴퓨터 과학은 많은 연구 분야의 발전에 있어 핵심 [(A) 요소 (B) 지위 (C) 강사 (D) 구성]가(이) 되었다)를 자연스럽게 만들어 주는 명사 (A)가 정답이다.

---

120. The burnt-out museum will be closed to the public until further -------.

(A) mark
(B) notice
(C) consent
(D) bill

어휘 burnt-out 다 타버린 mark 자국, 표시 until further notice 추후 공지가 있을 때까지 consent 동의, 허락

해석 다 타버린 미술관은 추후 공지가 있을 때까지 일반에 개방되지 않을 것이다.

해설 항상 짝을 이루어 출제되는 어휘 문제이다. prior notice, until further notice, unless otherwise noted를 반드시 통째로 기억하자.

---

121. ------- the Golden One Credit Union parking area is now available to the public, a portion of it has been designated for credit union personnel.

(A) While
(B) When
(C) For
(D) But

어휘 credit union 신용 조합 available to ~가 이용 가능한 portion 부분, 일부 designate 지정하다 personnel 직원

해석 Golden One 신용 조합 주차장은 이제 일반 대중이 이용할 수 있지만, 일부는 신용 조합 직원용으로 지정되어 있다.

해설 빈칸이 부사절 접속사 자리이므로 (A)와 (B) 중 정답을 선택해야 한다. 접속사 어휘 문제는 문장 전체의 의미를 생각해야 풀 수 있다. '주차장을 일반에 개방하지만, 한 구역만큼은 직원 전용으로 지정해 놓았다'는 내용이므로 접속사 (A)가 빈칸에 알맞다.

---

122. Please take note of the attached flowchart, which illustrates the ------- of responsibilities among the various leadership positions.

(A) support
(B) attention
(C) division
(D) statement

어휘 take note of ~에 주목하다 attach 붙이다, 첨부하다 flowchart 플로 차트, 업무 흐름도 illustrate (실례 · 도해 등으로) 분명히 보여주다 attention 주목 division 분할, 분배 statement 진술 responsibility 책무, 업무

해석 첨부된 업무 흐름도에 주목하세요. 그것은 여러 간부직 사이의 업무 분담을 보여줍니다.

해설 the ------- of responsibilities among the various leadership positions(여러 간부직 사이의 업무 [(A) 지지 (B) 주목 (C) 분담 (D) 진술])의 의미를 자연스럽게 만들어 주는 명사 (C)가 정답이다.

---

123. Mr. Tang is ------- with instituting a few modifications that have led to an increase in Bentler Stationery's business.

(A) credited

(B) scored
(C) agreed
(D) relied

어휘 be credited with ~한 공로를 인정받다 institute 제정하다, 시행하다 modification 수정, 변경 lead to ~로 이어지다

해석 Mr. Tang은 Bentler 문구의 영업 실적 증가로 이어진 몇몇 변경 사항을 시행한 공로를 인정받았다.

해설 '~한 공로를 인정받다'는 의미가 자연스러우므로 (A)가 정답이다. be credited with를 통째로 암기하고 있으면 정답을 쉽게 찾을 수 있다.

---

124. The hospital regulations stipulates that the patient should be asked to sign a written ------- before an operation.

(A) consent
(B) condition
(C) contraction
(D) convergence

어휘 stipulate 규정하다, 명시하다 written consent 서면 동의 contraction 수축, 축소 convergence 수렴, 집중 operation 수술

해석 병원 규정에는 수술 전 환자에게 서면 동의서에 서명하도록 요구해야 한다고 명시되어 있다.

해설 항상 짝을 이루어 출제되는 어휘 문제이다. written 뒤에 빈칸이 있으면 notice, notification, consent가 정답이다.

---

125. In the photograph, President Vieira is shown standing ------- Dr. Stanton.

(A) from
(B) reverse
(C) opposite
(D) distant

어휘 reverse 거꾸로의, (정)반대의 opposite 맞은편에 distant 먼, 떨어져 있는

해석 사진에 Vieira 회장이 Stanton 박사 맞은편에 서 있는 것이 보인다.

해설 빈칸 앞뒤 standing ------- Dr. Stanton을 보면 빈칸에 위치를 나타내는 전치사가 들어가야 하는 것을 알 수 있다. 따라서 형용사인 (B)와 (D)는 정답이 될 수 없다. 문맥상 'Stanton 박사 맞은편에 서 있는'이라는 뜻이 자연스러우므로 (C)가 정답이다.

---

126. Municipal authorities have ------ McLeod Avenue businesses that street improvements will be completed within 48 hours.

(A) assured
(B) arranged
(C) disclosed
(D) committed

어휘 municipal 지방 자치의, 시[읍/군]의 authorities 당국, 관계자 assure sb that ~를 장담하다, 확언하다 arrange 마련하다, 처리하다 disclose 발표하다, 공개하다 commit 전념하다, 약속하다

해석 시 당국은 McLeod 가(街) 사업체들에게 도로 개선 작업이 48시간 이내에 완료될 것이라고 확언했다.

해설 '동사 + 목적어 + that절' 구문을 사용하는 동사가 와야 하므로 (A)가 정답이다.

---

127. Friday is the deadline for nominations to the ------ seat on the Heirs Holdings Board of Trustees.

(A) approaching
(B) adjustable
(C) vacant
(D) united

어휘 nomination (후보) 지명, 추천 approaching 다가가는 adjustable 조절 가능한 vacant 비어 있는, 결원의 united 연합된, 단결된 board of trustees 이사회

해석 금요일이 Heirs Holdings 이사회의 공석에 대한 후보 추천의 마감 기한이다.

해설 nominations to the ------- seat([(A) 다가오는 (B) 조절 가능한 (C) 비어 있는 (D) 연합된] 자리에 대한 후보 추천)의 의미를 자연스럽게 만들어 주는 형용사 (C)가 정답이다.

---

128. ------ poorly the high-speed printer may be operating, it is still capable of making copies that are sufficient for our purposes.

(A) Rather
(B) Seldom
(C) However
(D) Thoroughly

어휘 thoroughly 철저히 poorly 형편없이 operate 작동하다 be capable of ~할 수 있다 make a copy 사본을 만들다, 복사하다 sufficient 충분한 purpose 목적

해석 고속 인쇄기가 아무리 형편없이 작동하더라도 여전히 우리 목적에 맞는 복사본을 만들 수 있다.

해설 '------- + 주어 + 동사 ~, 주어 + 동사 ~.' 구조이므로 쉼표 앞이 부사절, 쉼표 뒤가 주절이다. 빈칸에 부사절 접속사가 들어가야 한다. 따라서 복합관계부사이면서 부사절 접속사인 (C)가 정답이다. However 바로 뒤에 형용사나 부사가 올 수 있다는 규칙도 기억하자.

---

129. By means of our vast national network, Supertech can send a technician to help ------- assistance is needed.

(A) wherever
(B) quickly
(C) each other
(D) out

어휘 by means of ~을 이용하여[통해] vast 방대한, 막대한 technician 기술자 assistance 도움

해석 Supertech는 방대한 네트워크를 사용하여 도움이 필요한 곳이라면 어디든지 기술자를 보내 도와드릴 수 있습니다.

해설 빈칸 앞의 문장이 3형식으로 완성된 문장이고, 빈칸 이후로는 부사절이다. 따라서 부사절을 이끌 수 있는 복합관계부사 (A)가 정답이다.

---

130. ------- of Ardashir Ali's international performances was captured on camera for a documentary.

(A) All
(B) Others
(C) Their own
(D) Each one

어휘 capture A on B A를 B에 담다, 포착하다

해석 Ardashir Ali의 해외 공연 하나하나가 다큐멘터리를 위해 카메라에 담겼다.

해설 'one of + 복수 명사 + 단수 동사'를 기억하고 정답을 선택하자. of 뒤에 복수 명사 Ardashir Ali's international performances가 있고, 그 뒤에 단수 동사 was captured가 있다. 그러므로 단수 대명사인 (D)가 정답이다.

Part 6

Questions 131-134 refer to the following memo.

To: All staff
From: Vitale Renato, Vice President of Product Development
Date: February 17
Subject: Elegante game (Product #ET9103)

Considering the results from our trial customer testing, we have opted to postpone the release of the Elegante video game. Results from customer surveys suggested that the game was less [131.]appealing than anticipated. For the next few months, the game development team will implement several [132.]modifications to make the product more attractive. [133.]At that point, additional tests will be conducted. If the changes prove to be successful, our hope is to release the game by July [134.]or August.

131-134번 문제는 다음 메모에 관한 것입니다.

수신: 전 직원
발신: 제품 개발 부사장 Vitale Renato
날짜: 2월 17일
제목: Elegante 게임(제품 번호 ET9103)

우리는 시험 사용 고객 테스트 결과를 참작하여 Elegante 비디오 게임의 출시를 연기하기로 했습니다. 고객 설문 조사 결과가 게임이 예상보다 덜 흥미롭다는 것을 보여줍니다. 앞으로 몇 달 동안 게임 개발팀이 몇 가지 수정을 시행하여 제품을 더 매력적으로 만들 것입니다. 그 시점에 추가 테스트가 시행될 것입니다. 만약 변경 사항이 성공적인 것으로 드러난다면 우리의 바람은 7월이나 8월까지 게임을 출시하는 것입니다.

어휘 vice president 부사장 considering ~을 고려하여 result 결과 trial 무료 체험 opt to-V ~하는 쪽을 택하다 postpone 연기하다 release 출시(하다) survey 설문 조사 suggest (that) ~임을 보여주다 appealing 매력적인, 흥미로운 anticipate 기대하다 implement 시행하다 modification 수정, 변경 attractive 매력적인 conduct

시행하다 prove to-V ~임이 드러나다, 확실하다

131. (A) expensive
(B) repetitive
(C) appealing
(D) surprising

어휘 expensive 비싼 repetitive 반복적인 appealing 매력적인, 흥미로운

해설 빈칸 앞 문장은 시험 사용 고객들의 테스트 결과 제품 출시를 연기한다는 내용이고(we have opted to postpone the release of the Elegante video game), 빈칸 뒤 문장은 제품을 더 매력적으로 만들기 위한(to make the product more attractive) 수정을 한다는 내용이다. 그러므로 설문 조사 결과 제품이 예상보다 매력적이지 않다는 점이 드러났다고 하는 것이 자연스러우므로 (C)가 정답이다.

132. (A) modification
(B) modifies
(C) modifying
(D) modifications

어휘 modify 수정하다, 바꾸다

해설 several ------는 동사 will implement의 목적어이고 several 뒤에는 셀 수 있는 복수 명사만 가능하므로 (D)가 정답이다

133. **(A) At that point, additional tests will be conducted.**
(B) The release will be our biggest of the year.
(C) Nevertheless, the surveys are not reliable.
(D) Each team member must sign the form.

어휘 nevertheless 그런데도 reliable 신뢰할 만한

해설 (A) 그 시점에 추가 테스트가 시행될 것입니다.
(B) 이 출시는 올해 가장 큰 규모가 될 것입니다.
(C) 그런데도 설문조사가 신뢰할 만하지는 않습니다.
(D) 각 팀원은 서식에 서명해야 합니다.

해설 빈칸 앞 문장에서 제품의 수정이 시행될 것이라고 했고(the game development team will implement several modifications), 빈칸 뒤에서는 "만약 변경 사항이 성공적인 것으로 드러난다면(If the changes prove to be successful)"이라는 가정이 나와 있다. 제품 수정의 성공 여부가 드러나야 함을 알 수 있으므로 빈칸에 추가 테스트가 시행될 것이라는 (A)가 내용상 가장 알맞다.

134. (A) since
(B) or
(C) if
(D) later

해설 달 이름 July와 August를 연결해 주는 것은 등위접속사 or이다.

Questions 135-138 refer to the following e-mail.

From: cyoo@pomarius.com
To: erikjohansson@skansennursery.se
Subject: Sparreholm Yellow
Date: October 12

Dear Mr. Johansson,

I am writing on behalf of the Pomarius Garden Stores chain, which is currently in the process of [135.]expanding its range of products to include newly developed types of trees. We would like to carry Sparreholm Yellow apple saplings in our stores. Given that this [136.]variety originated in Sweden, we consulted the Association of Swedish Fruit Exporters, which referred us to your apple nursery. It appears from your Web site that you do [137.]indeed have the product in stock. Initially, we would be interested in procuring a small sample of saplings. [138.]However, we plan to place a larger order in the foreseeable future. Do you offer discounts for bulk purchases? I look forward to hearing from you.

Sincerely,

Carol Yoo
Pomarius Garden Stores

135-138번 문제는 다음 이메일에 관한 것입니다.

발신: cyoo@pomarius.com
수신: erikjohansson@skansennursery.se
제목: Sparreholm 노랑
날짜: 10월 12일

Mr. Johansson께,

Pomarius 정원용품 체인을 대표하여 연락드립니다. 우리는 현재 제품 범위를 확대하여 새로 개발된 종류의 나무들을 포함하는 과정 중에 있습니다. 우리는 매장에서 Sparreholm 노란 사과 묘목을 취급하고 싶습니다. 이 품종이 스웨덴에서 시작되었다는 점을 고려하여 스웨덴 과일 수출 협회에 조언을 구했고, 그곳에서 귀하의 묘목장을 소개해 줬습니다. 웹사이트를 보니 확실히 제품을 재고로 보유하고 계신 것 같습니다. 처음에는 견본으로 소량의 묘목을 구하고자 합니다. 하지만 가까운 장래에 더 많은 주문을 할 계획입니다. 대량 구매에 할인을 제공하시나요?

소식 듣기를 기대합니다.

진심을 담아,

Carol Yoo
Pomarius Garden Stores

어휘 on behalf of ~을 대표하여 currently 현재 expand 확장하다 range 범위, 폭 carry (품목을) 취급하다 sapling 묘목, 어린나무 given that ~을 고려하여 variety 품종, 종류 originate 비롯되다, 유래하다 consult ~에게 조언을 구하다 association 협회 exporter 수출업자 refer A to B A에게 B를 안내하다 nursery 묘목장 it appears that ~인 것 같다 indeed 정말, 확실히 stock 재고(품) initially 처음에 procure 구하다, 입수하다 place an order 주문하다 in the foreseeable future 가까운 장래에 bulk 대량의, 대량으로 매매되는

---

135. (A) **expanding**
(B) expanded
(C) expands
(D) expand

해설 전치사 of의 목적어가 되면서 빈칸 뒤의 its range of products를 목적어로 취할 수 있는 동명사 (A)가 정답이다.

---

136. (A) response
(B) method
(C) ability
(D) **variety**

해설 this -------가 앞 문장에 있는 Sparreholm Yellow apple를 가리키므로 이를 대신하는 명사 (D)가 정답이다.

137. (A) **indeed**
(B) alone
(C) quite
(D) ever

해설 앞 문장이 "해당 품종을 구하기 위해 스웨덴 과일 수출 협회에 문의했고(Given that this variety originated in Sweden, we consulted the Association of Swedish Fruit Exporters), 협회가 수신자의 묘목장을 소개했다(which referred us to your apple nursery)"는 내용이다. 즉 수신자의 묘목장에 해당 품종이 있을 것이라고 알려줬다는 말이므로, 이어지는 문장은 "웹사이트를 보니 '정말로' 그 제품이 있는 것 같다(It appears from your Web site that you do 'indeed' have the product in stock)."가 알맞다.

---

138. (A) Our nursery has been family-owned for more than a century.
(B) I'm sorry to say that they are not in stock at the moment.
(C) **However, we plan to place a larger order in the foreseeable future.**
(D) Please visit our Web site to learn more about our offer.

어휘 nursery 묘목장 family-owned 가족 운영의, 가족 사업의 in stock 재고가 있는, 입고된 at the moment (지금) 당장은

해석 (A) 우리 묘목장은 백 년 이상 가족에 의해 운영되어 왔습니다.
(B) 그것들이 지금 당장은 재고가 없다는 말씀을 드리게 되어 미안합니다.
(C) 하지만 가까운 장래에 더 많은 주문을 할 계획입니다.
(D) 우리 웹사이트를 방문하여 제안에 대해 더 알아보시기를 바랍니다.

해설 앞 문장에서는 우선 소량만 원한다고 했는데(Initially, we would be interested in procuring a small sample of saplings.), 빈칸 뒤로 이어지는 문장에서는 대량 주문 할인에 대해 묻고 묻고 있다(Do you offer discounts for bulk purchases?). 그러므로 중간에 들어갈 문장은 "앞으로는 주문량이 늘어날 수 있다."는 내용의 (C)가 오는 것이 자연스럽다.

Part 7

Questions 139-142 refer to the following online chat discussion.

Venkatraju Blunt (1:30 P.M.)
Hello, Saira and Kristiono. Welcome to Venkat Spices! Thank you for joining me for this online meeting on a short notice. ^{139.}You are two of the many overseas farmers we collaborate with. ^{142.}Do you have any products ready to ship?

Saira Gupta (1:31 P.M.)
^{139.140.}I have 150 kilos of fresh Tellicherry black peppercorns that were just picked yesterday here in India. ^{142.}They'll be ready for shipment within a few days.

Venkatraju Blunt (1:32 P.M.)
That's great to hear! I can't wait to try them. Kristiono, you will be our first supplier from Indonesia.

Kristiono Agus (1:33 P.M.)
I'm pleased to join the team. ^{140.142.}I have 200 kilos of beautiful, freshly picked black Lampong peppercorns that are ready to ship.

Venkatraju Blunt (1:34 P.M.)
Super! ^{141.}Have you both made shipping arrangements with Atlantic-Pacific Express?

Saira Gupta (1:35 P.M.)
^{141.}Yes, I've already got in touch with them.

Kristiono Agus (1:35 P.M.)
^{141.}Me too.

Venkatraju Blunt (1:36 P.M.)
^{142.}I'll let our warehouse staff in Amsterdam know about your peppercorns. Upon arrival, I will transfer your payments. I look forward to having a long and productive relationship with both of you. Thank you very much!

139-142번 문제는 다음 온라인 채팅에 관한 것입니다.

Venkatraju Blunt (오후 1:30)
안녕하세요, Saira and Kristiono, Venkat Spices에 오신 걸 환영합니다! 갑작스러운데도 저와 함께 이 온라인 회의에 참여해 주셔서 고맙습니다. 당신들은 우리와 협력하는 많은 해외 농장주 중 두 분이세요. 배송할 수 있게 준비된 제품이 있으신가요?

Saira Gupta (오후 1:31)
이곳 인도에서 바로 어제 수확한 신선한 Tellicherry 검정 후추 150킬로그램이 있습니다. 며칠 내로 배송 준비가 될 거예요.

Venkatraju Blunt (오후 1:32)
잘됐네요! 빨리 한 번 써 보고 싶어요. Kristiono, 당신은 우리의 첫 인도네시아 공급업체예요.

Kristiono Agus (오후 1:33)
팀에 합류하게 되어 기쁩니다. 갓 수확한 아름다운 검은 람퐁 후추 200킬로그램을 배송할 준비가 되어 있습니다.

Venkatraju Blunt (오후 1:34)
좋습니다! 두 분 모두 Atlantic-Pacific Express와 배송 준비는 하셨나요?

Saira Gupta (오후 1:35)
네, 이미 그쪽과 연락했습니다.

Kristiono Agus (오후 1:35)
저도요.

Venkatraju Blunt (오후 1:36)
Amsterdam에 있는 저희 창고 직원들에게 여러분의 후추에 관해 얘기해 놓을게요. 도착하자마자 대금도 보내 드리겠습니다. 두 분 모두와 장기적이고 생산적인 관계 맺기를 고대합니다. 정말 고맙습니다!

어휘 spice 양념, 향신료 join ~와 같이 하다 on a short notice 충분한 예고 없이, 갑자기 collaborate with ~와 협력하다 ship 운송하다 peppercorn 후추 열매 pick (과일 등을) 따다 freshly 갓 ~한 shipment 수송(품) can't wait to-V 빨리 ~하고 싶다 supplier 공급자, 공급 회사 super 엄청 좋은, 매우 멋진 make arrangements 준비하다, 마련하다 get in touch with ~와 연락하다 warehouse 창고 (up)on + 명사[V-ing] ~하자마자 transfer 송금하다 payment 지불금 productive 생산적인

---

139. Who most likely Is Ms. Blunt?

(A) A farmer
(B) An event promoter
(C) A business owner
(D) A grocery store manager

해석 Ms. Blunt는 누구이겠는가?
(A) 농장주

(B) 행사 기획자
(C) 사업 소유주
(D) 식료품점 운영자

해설 1시 30분과 31분의 대화를 읽어 보면 Ms. Blunt는 해외 농장들로부터 농산물을 대량으로 납품받아 판매하는 유통업체의 경영자라는 것을 추론할 수 있다. 그러므로 (C)가 정답이다.

---

140. What is indicated about Ms. Gupta's and Mr. Agus's peppercorns?

(A) They will be delivered within three business days.
(B) They all belong to the same variety.
(C) They were all grown in Indonesia.
(D) They were harvested recently.

어휘 deliver 배달하다 business day 영업일 variety 품종. 종류 harvest 수확하다 recently 최근에

해석 Ms. Gupta와 Mr. Agus의 후추에 대해 무엇이 나타나 있는가?
(A) 영업일 기준 3일 이내에 배송될 것이다.
(B) 같은 품종에 속한다.
(C) 모두 인도네시아에서 재배되었다.
(D) 최근에 수확되었다.

해설 1시 31분에 Ms. Gupta는 자기 농장의 후추가 어제 딴 것이라고 말했고(I have 150 kilos of fresh Tellicherry black peppercorns that were just picked yesterday here in India.), 1시 33분에 Mr. Agus도 갓 수확한 후추를 가지고 있다고 말했다(I have 200 kilos of beautiful, freshly picked black Lampong peppercorns that are ready to ship). 그러므로 (D)가 정답이다.

---

141. At 1:35 P.M., what does Mr. Agus most likely mean when he writes, "Me too"?

(A) He has arranged for shipping.
(B) He is excited about his new business.
(C) He wants to try Ms. Gupta's peppercorns.
(D) He is pleased to adopt new crop varieties.

어휘 arrange for ~을 준비하다, 계획하다 shipping 운송, 수송 adopt 채택하다 crop (농)작물

해석 1시 35분에 Mr. Agus는 "저도요."라고 쓸 때 무엇을

의미할 가능성이 가장 높은가?
(A) 운송을 준비했다.
(B) 새 사업으로 인해 신이 났다.
(C) Ms. Gupta의 후추를 써 보고 싶다.
(D) 새 작물 품종을 채택하게 되어 기쁘다.

해설 바로 앞 대사를 읽으면 정답을 알 수 있다. 1시 34분에 Ms. Blunt가 운송 업체와 협의를 마쳤는지 묻자(Have you both made shipping arrangements with Atlantic-Pacific Express?) 1시 35분에 Ms. Gupta가 연락해서 운송 준비를 마쳤다는 뜻의 대답을 했고(Yes, I've already got in touch with them.), Mr. Agus도 "저도요(Me too)."라고 말했으므로, 운송을 위한 준비가 되었다는 뜻이다. 그러므로 (A)가 정답이다.

---

142. What will Ms. Blunt most likely do next?

(A) Request recommendations of other vendors
(B) Sign an agreement with Atlantic-Pacific Express
(C) Inspect the items sent by Ms. Gupta and Mr. Agus
(D) Tell the warehouse staff to expect two shipments

어휘 recommendation 추천(서) vendor 판매 회사 agreement 협정, 협약 inspect 검사하다 warehouse 창고 expect 기다리다

해석 Ms. Blunt는 이후에 무엇을 할 가능성이 가장 높은가?
(A) 다른 판매업체의 추천서 요구하기
(B) Atlantic-Pacific Express와 계약 체결하기
(C) Ms. Gupta와 Mr. Agus가 보낸 제품 검사하기
(D) 창고 직원들에게 두 건의 수송을 기다리라고 말하기

해설 1시 30분에 Ms. Blunt가 보내 줄 수 있는 제품이 있는지 물었을 때(Do you have any products ready to ship?), Ms. Gupta와 Mr. Agus가 각각 1시 31분과 33분에 "며칠 내로 준비될 것이다(They'll be ready for shipment within a few days.)", "지금 준비되어 있다(peppercorns that are ready to ship)"라고 대답하고 있다. 그러므로 1시 36분에 Ms. Blunt가 창고 직원들에게 후추에 관해 얘기해 놓겠다고 말한 것은(I'll let our warehouse staff in Amsterdam know about your peppercorns.) 대화가 끝난 후에 창고 직원들에게 며칠 내로 두 군데에서 보낸 제품을 받을 준비를 하라고 말하겠다는 뜻이다. 그러므로 (D)가 정답이다.

Questions 143-147 refer to the following e-mail, letter, and calendar.

To: dsoto@abengineer.com
From: jcarroway@abengineer.com
Date: March 27
Subject: Corporate credit card

Dear Ms. Soto,

I have received your application for a corporate credit card. In order to issue a card to you, I require verification of one of the following.
- 143.Anticipated business-related expenses of $400 or more
- Two or more scheduled international business trips for this year
- Signed documentation from a manager confirming your responsibility to entertain corporate patrons

As you await your card, kindly take time to look over our expense and travel policies in pages 46-62 of the employee handbook. Here are some highlights from those policies.
- All transportation (airline, train, etc.) and lodging arrangements must be made through the corporate travel department.
- 147.Your supervisor's permission must be obtained before initiating a request for a car rental through the corporate travel department.
- Meals are covered by the company provided they do not exceed daily allowances (refer to section 10, page 51).

Thank you,
Jeff Carroway
Corporate Travel Department, Aucoin-Braud Engineering

143-147번 문제는 다음 이메일과 편지, 일정표에 관한 것입니다.

수신: dsoto@abengineer.com
발신: jcarroway@abengineer.com
날짜: 3월 27일
제목: 법인 카드

Ms. Soto께,

당신의 법인 카드 신청서를 접수했습니다. 카드를 발급해 드리기 위해 다음 사항 중 하나에 대한 입증을 요구합니다.
– 400달러 이상 예상되는 비즈니스 관련 경비
– 올 한 해 동안 2회 이상 예정된 해외 출장
– 기업 고객을 접대할 책임이 있음을 확인해 주는 관리자가 서명한 증빙 서류

카드를 기다리시면서 시간을 내서 직원 편람 46-62페이지에 있는 경비 및 출장에 관한 방침들을 살펴보시기를 바랍니다. 다음은 그 방침 중 중요한 몇 가지입니다.
– 모든 교통편(항공, 열차 등)과 숙박 준비는 출장관리부를 통해 이루어져야 한다.
– 출장관리부를 통해 렌터카 신청을 시작하기 전에 관리자의 허가를 받아야 한다.
– 식사는 1일 허용치를 초과하지 않는 한 회사가 비용을 부담한다(51페이지, 10항 참조).

고맙습니다.
Aucoin-Braud Engineering 출장관리부
Jeff Carroway

어휘 corporate 기업의, 법인의 issue 발행하다, 발급하다 application 신청(서) verification 증명, 입증 anticipate 예상하다 expense 경비 scheduled 예정된 documentation 증빙 서류 confirm 확인해 주다 responsibility 책임, 의무 entertain 접대하다 patron 고객 await 기다리다 kindly 부디, 죄송하지만 take time to-V 시간을 내서 ~하다 look over ~을 살펴보다 policy 정책 employee handbook 직원 편람 make + 명사 + arrangements ~을 준비하다 lodging 숙박 supervisor 관리자, 감독 permission 허가 initiate 시작하다 cover (비용을) 대다 provided (that) (만약) ~라면 allowance 허용량 refer to ~을 참조하다

The Institute of Science and Technology (IST)

Dear Denise Soto,

143.144.You have successfully registered for the IST Conference in Rio de Janeiro, Brazil, and your payment of $450 has been processed. Thank you.

IST advises that you make travel and hotel arrangements as early as possible to ensure availability. [145.]We have secured discounted rates for conference participants at Hotel Miramar, which is the conference venue, and also at Hotel Prodigy; [146.]rooms at Hotel Miramar are exclusively available for booking by the IST members, however. Complimentary breakfast will be available from 6 to 10 A.M. and coffee and tea from 1 to 4 P.M. daily, both in the hotel lobby. Participants are responsible for all other meals.

For inquiries or recommendations, feel free to contact us at info@istconference.org.

Sincerely,

IST Conference Committee

과학기술연구소(IST)

Denise Soto께,

브라질 Rio de Janeiro에서 열리는 IST 학회에 성공적으로 등록하셨으며 450달러의 결제가 처리되었습니다. 고맙습니다.

IST는 이용 가능성을 보장하기 위해 여행과 호텔 준비를 되도록 일찍 하실 것을 권고합니다. 학회 장소인 Miramar 호텔과 Prodigy 호텔에서도 학회 참가자들을 위한 할인 요금을 확보했습니다. 그러나 Miramar 호텔의 방은 오직 IST 회원만 예약하실 수 있습니다. 매일 오전 6시부터 10시까지는 무료 아침 식사와 오후 1시부터 4시까지는 커피와 차를 모두 호텔 로비에서 이용하실 수 있습니다. 기타 모든 식사는 참가자가 부담해야 합니다.

문의나 건의가 있으실 때는 info@istconference.org로 부담 없이 저희에게 연락하시기를 바랍니다.

진심을 담아,

IST 학회 위원회

어휘 register for ~에 등록하다 institute 협회, 연구소 conference 회의, 학회 payment 결제 process 처리하다 advise (that) ~하기를 권고하다 ensue 보장하다 availability 이용 가능성 secure 확보하다 rate 요금

---

participant 참가자 venue 장소 exclusively 독점적으로; 오로지 (~만) booking 예약 complimentary 무료의 inquiry 문의

Calendar for Denise Soto: Week of June 26

June 26
Depart 9:30 A.M., New York, NY (flight BW288)
Arrive 8:25 P.M., Rio de Janeiro, Brazil
[146.147.]Travel via Taxi Minuto to Hotel Miramar (late check-in confirmed by hotel manager)

June 27
9:30 A.M.- 4:00 P.M. conference sessions
5:00 P.M. Alexa Alves job interview, hotel lobby

June 28
9:30 A.M.- 3:30 P.M. conference sessions
3:40 P.M. Alexa Alves presentation

June 29
9:30 A.M.- 4:00 P.M. conference sessions
5:30 P.M. closing ceremony and reception, Salon C

June 30
7:45 A.M. [147.]Travel to airport via hotel courtesy bus
Depart 10:00 A.M., Rio de Janeiro, Brazil (flight BW424)
Arrive 7:00 P.M., New York, NY

Denise Soto의 일정표: 6월 26일 주간

6월 26일
오전 9:30 출발, 뉴욕, NY (BW288 항공편)
오후 8:25 도착, 브라질 Rio de Janeiro
Minuto 택시로 Miramar 호텔까지 이동 (호텔 매니저가 늦은 체크인 확인)

6월 27일
오전 9:30 – 오후 4:00 학회 모임
오후 5:00 Alexa Alves 입사 면접, 호텔 로비

6월 28일
오전 9:30 – 오후 3:30 학회 모임
오후 3:40 Alexa Alves 발표

6월 29일
오전 9:30 – 오후 4:00 학회 모임
오후 5:30 폐회식 및 리셉션, 살롱 C

6월 30일
오전 7:45 호텔 무료 버스로 공항까지 이동
오전 10시 출발, 브라질 Rio de Janeiro (BW424 항공편)
오후 7:00 도착, 뉴욕, NY

> **어휘** calendar 일정표 via ~을 통해서, ~에 의해서 session (활동) 시간, 기간 salon 큰 홀 presentation 발표 courtesy 무료의

---

143. What qualifies Ms. Soto to receive a corporate credit card?

(A) Her upcoming business trip is international.
(B) Her registration fee is over $400.
(C) She will be traveling for more than two days.
(D) She will be entertaining corporate clients.

> **어휘** qualify 자격을 주다 upcoming 다가오는, 곧 있을 entertain 접대하다
>
> **해석** 무엇이 Ms. Soto에게 법인 카드를 받을 수 있도록 자격을 주는가?
> (A) 다가오는 출장이 해외로 가는 것이다.
> (B) 등록비가 400달러가 넘는다.
> (C) 이틀 이상 여행할 것이다.
> (D) 회사 고객을 접대할 것이다.
>
> **연계 추론** 이메일에 법인 카드를 발급받을 수 있는 경우 중 한 가지로 '예상되는 비즈니스 관련 경비가 400달러 이상일 때 (Anticipated business-related expenses of $400 or more)'가 나와 있다. 또한 편지 첫 문장에서 Ms. Soto의 학회 등록비가 450달러임을 알 수 있으므로(You have successfully registered for the IST Conference in Rio de Janeiro, Brazil, and your payment of $450 has been processed.), 두 군데의 내용을 종합하여 추론하면 정답을 알 수 있다.

---

144. What is a purpose of the letter?

(A) To share opinions about a hotel

(B) To advertise a dining establishment
(C) To confirm a successful registration
(D) To encourage participation in a conference

> **어휘** dining establishment 음식점 registration 등록 encourage 독려하다 participation 참여
>
> **해석** 편지의 목적은 무엇인가?
> (A) 호텔에 대한 의견을 공유하는 것
> (B) 음식점을 광고하는 것
> (C) 성공적인 등록을 확인해 주는 것
> (D) 학회 참가를 독려하는 것
>
> **해설** 편지 첫 문장(you have successfully registered for the IST Conference in Rio de Janeiro, Brazil)에서 정답을 알 수 있다.

---

145. In the letter, the word "secured" in paragraph 2, line 2, is closest in meaning to

(A) guarded
(B) established
(C) paid
(D) enclosed

> **해석** 편지에서 둘째 문단 둘째 줄의 "secured"와 의미상 가장 가까운 것은
> (A) 지키다, 보호하다
> (B) (제도 등을) 확립하다, 마련하다
> (C) 지불하다
> (D) 둘러싸다
>
> **해설** secure는 '지키다, 보호하다'라는 뜻이 있어서 (A)와 동의어가 될 수 있다. (D)는 '둘러싸다, 에워싸다'라는 뜻인데, 담이나 울타리 등으로 둘러싸면 토지, 장비 등을 보호할 수 있으므로 역시 동의어가 될 수 있다. 이 편지에서는 have secured discounted rates는 "할인 요금을 확보했다"는 뜻이므로, "할인 요금을(요금 제도를) 마련했다"로 바꿔 쓸 수 있는 (B)가 정답이다.

---

146. What is suggested about Ms. Soto?

(A) She is a member of the IST.
(B) She will give a presentation at the conference.
(C) She is leaving the conference before its conclusion.
(D) She works with Ms. Alves at Aucoin-Braud Engineering.

어휘 conference 회의, 학회

해석 Ms. Soto에 대해 무엇이 시사되고 있는가?
(A) IST 회원이다.
(B) 학회에서 발표를 할 것이다.
(C) 학회가 끝나기 전에 떠날 것이다.
(D) Aucoin-Braud Engineering에서 Ms. Alves와 함께 근무한다.

연계 추론 편지에 Miramar 호텔의 방은 오직 IST 회원만 예약할 수 있다는 규정이 나와 있는데(rooms at Hotel Miramar are exclusively available for booking by the IST members, however), 일정표에서 Ms. Soto의 6월 26일 일정을 살펴보면 Miramar 호텔에 투숙할 예정임을 알 수 있다(Travel via Taxi Minuto to Hotel Miramar). 이를 종합해 보면 Ms. Soto는 IST 회원임을 알 수 있다.

---

147. What expense policy does NOT apply to Ms. Soto's trip?

(A) The policy about food costs
(B) The policy about lodging arrangements
(C) The policy about flight bookings
(D) The policy about car rentals

어휘 apply to ~에 적용되다, 해당되다 lodging 숙박 arrangement 준비, 마련 booking 예약 car rental 렌터카

해석 어느 경비 방침이 Ms. Soto의 여행에 적용되지 않는가?
(A) 식비에 관한 방침
(B) 숙박 준비에 관한 방침
(C) 비행편 예약에 관한 방침
(D) 렌터카에 관한 방침

연계 추론 (A) 식사, (B) 호텔 숙박, (C) 비행기 여행은 출장에 모두 필요하므로 비용에 해당된다. 이메일에서 렌터카 신청에 관한 방침을 언급하고 있고(Your supervisor's permission must be obtained before initiating a request for a car rental through the corporate travel department.), 일정표를 살펴보면 Ms. Soto는 첫날 공항에서 호텔까지 택시를 타고 이동하며(Travel via Taxi Minuto to Hotel Miramar), 마지막 날 호텔에서 공항까지는 호텔에 제공하는 무료 버스를 이용하는 것을 알 수 있다(Travel to airport via hotel courtesy bus). Ms. Soto는 이번 출장에서 렌터카를 이용하지 않으므로 이와 관련된 정책은 적용할 수 없다.

Day 07

PART 5 & 6 Exercise

101 (D)	**102** (B)	**103** (B)	**104** (C)	**105** (B)
106 (D)	**107** (D)	**108** (C)	**109** (D)	**110** (A)
111 (B)	**112** (A)	**113** (A)	**114** (C)	**115** (C)

101. Online retailers are not as ------- as they used to be as prices remain generally the same across all stores.

(A) competitively
(B) competition
(C) more competitive
(D) competitive

어휘 retailer 소매업자 competitive 경쟁력 있는 as ~ used to be ~가 예전만큼 generally 일반적으로

해석 가격이 모든 상점 간에 일반적으로 똑같이 유지되기 때문에 온라인 소매상들이 예전만큼 경쟁력 있지는 않다.

해설 빈칸 앞뒤 are not as ------- as they used to be를 보면 빈칸에 형용사 원급이 들어가야 하므로 정답은 (D)이다.

102. Ericsson laptop computers are ------- than those of its competitors and features more powerful processors for faster computing.

(A) slim
(B) slimmer
(C) slimness
(D) sliming

어휘 competitor 경쟁자, 경쟁 상대 feature 특별히 포함하다 computing 컴퓨터 사용[조작]

해석 Ericsson 노트북 컴퓨터는 경쟁업체들의 것보다 더 얇고 더 빠른 컴퓨팅을 위해 더 강력한 프로세서를 포함하고 있다.

해설 빈칸 앞뒤 are ------- than을 보고 정답을 선택하자. than이 있으면 비교급이 들어가야 하므로 (B)가 정답이다.

103. The ratings received by Nancy Meyer's television news program were the ------- of all local news shows.

(A) high
(B) highest
(C) highly
(D) heightened

어휘 ratings 시청률, 청취률

해석 Nancy Meyer가 진행하는 텔레비전 뉴스 프로그램의 시청률은 지역의 모든 뉴스 프로그램 중 가장 높았다.

해설 빈칸 앞뒤 were the ------- of all만 보면 정답을 알 수 있다. 관사 the와 of all은 모두 빈칸이 최상급임을 알려주는 키워드이므로 정답은 (B)이다.

104. Most customers think that the new registration system is excessively -------.

(A) complicate
(B) complicating
(C) complicated
(D) complicatedly

어휘 registration 등록 excessively 지나치게

해석 대부분 고객은 새 등록 시스템이 지나치게 복잡하다고 생각한다.

해설 빈칸 앞 수식어 excessively를 제외하면 is 뒤의 빈칸은 형용사 자리이므로 현재분사 (B)와 과거분사 (C) 중 정답을 선택해야 한다. 그런데 complicate는 분사로 만들 때 항상 과거분사로만 사용하므로 정답은 (C)이다.

105. The company has decided to liquidate some of its subsidiaries and increase investment in some areas of information technology that are obviously more -------.

(A) to promise
(B) promising
(C) promised
(D) promises

어휘 liquidate (사업체를) 청산하다, 정리하다 subsidiary 자(子)

회사 obviously 확실히, 분명히

해석 회사는 자회사 몇 개를 청산하고 확실히 더 유망한 몇 몇 정보기술 분야에 대한 투자를 늘리기로 결정했다.

해설 빈칸 앞 are obviously more ------를 보고 정답을 알아내자. be동사 뒤의 빈칸은 형용사 자리이므로 보기에서 현재분사 (B)와 과거분사 (C) 중 정답을 선택해야 한다. 그런데 promise는 명사를 수식할 때 항상 현재분사만 사용하므로 (B)가 정답이다.

---

106. E-mail is the ------ means of communication for the transaction of business among colleagues.

(A) preferring
(B) preference
(C) preferably
(D) preferred

어휘 preferably 되도록 means 수단, 방법 transaction 거래, 처리

해석 이메일은 동료들 사이의 업무 처리를 위해 선호되는 통신 수단이다.

해설 명사(구) means of communication 앞의 빈칸은 형용사 자리이므로, 보기에서 현재분사 (A)와 과거분사 (D) 중 정답을 선택해야 한다. means of communication (통신 수단)이 '선호'되는 것이므로 수동의 의미인 과거분사 (D)가 정답이다.

---

107. All employees are asked to turn off the lights when ------ their offices to reduce electricity costs.

(A) exit
(B) exits
(C) exited
(D) exiting

어휘 be asked to-V ~를 요청받다 exit 나가다 reduce 줄이다 electricity cost 전기 비용

해석 모든 직원은 사무실을 나갈 때 전기 요금을 절감하기 위해 불을 끄라는 요청을 받습니다.

해설 부사절 접속사 when 뒤에는 '주어 + 동사'가 있어야 하는데, 보기에는 주어가 없다. 주어 없는 부사절은 분사 구문이므로 과거분사 (C)와 현재분사 (D) 중 정답을 선택해야 한다. 이 유형에서는 주절의 주어를 봐야 한다. 모든 직원(All employees)이 '나가는' 것이므로 능동의 의미인 현재분사 (D)가 정답이다.

---

108. Accountants and other finance professionals are busy ------ to the filing due date for tax returns.

(A) suited
(B) conducive
(C) prior
(D) forward

어휘 accountant 회계사 suited 어울리는, 적당한 conducive 도움이 되는 file 제출하다 due date 마감일 tax return 소득세 신고서

해석 회계사와 기타 재무 전문가들은 소득세 신고서 제출 마감일 전에는 바쁘다.

해설 빈칸 앞뒤 are busy ------ to the filing due date for tax returns는 "소득세 신고서 제출 마감일 전에는 바쁘다"라는 의미가 자연스러우므로 빈칸에는 (C)가 알맞다.

---

109. Coffee is a good gift idea for almost everyone whether you want to show your appreciation to a client or keep your employees ------ every morning.

(A) energizing
(B) has energized
(C) energize
(D) energized

어휘 appreciation 감사 energize 활력을 주다

해석 고객에게 감사를 표하고 싶든, 매일 아침 담당 직원들에게 활력을 주고 싶든, 커피는 거의 모든 사람에게 좋은 선물 아이디어다.

해설 빈칸 앞에 5형식 동사 keep이 있고 빈칸은 목적격 보어 자리이므로 형용사가 정답이다. 보기에 형용사가 없으므로 현재분사 (A)와 과거분사 (D) 중 정답을 선택해야 한다. 목적어 '당신의 직원들(your employees)'이 '격려받는' 것이므로, 수동의 의미인 과거분사 (D)가 정답이다.

---

110. The National Organization for Rare Disorders, also ------ as NORD, publishes a quarterly medical journal.

(A) known
(B) knowing
(C) knew
(D) knows

어휘 organization 조직, 기구 rare 희귀한 disorder 장애, 질

환 quarterly 분기의

해석 NORD라고도 알려진 국립 희소 질병 연구소는 분기마다 의학 학술지를 발간한다.

해설 문장에 동사 publishes가 있으므로 동사인 (C)와 (D)는 빈칸에 들어갈 수 없다. 빈칸 뒤에 목적어가 없기 때문에 과거분사 (A)가 정답이다.

---

111. When you step into the aisles of the supermarket, you may encounter a ------- array of products, making it difficult to decide what to buy.

(A) bewildered
(B) bewildering
(C) bewilderment
(D) bewilders

어휘 aisle 통로 encounter 부딪히다, 마주치다 bewilder 어리둥절하게 만들다, 당황하게 하다 array 배열, 진열

해석 그 슈퍼마켓의 통로에 들어서면 당황스러울 정도의 많은 제품 배열을 마주하게 되어 무엇을 살지 결정하기가 어려워질 수 있다.

해설 명사 array 앞의 빈칸에는 형용사가 들어가므로 현재분사 (B)와 과거분사 (A) 중 정답을 선택해야 한다. 제품 배열(array of products)이 '당황하게 하는' 것이므로 능동의 의미인 현재분사 (B)가 정답이다.

---

112. Since the regulations governing importation became too ------- to accommodate, the Importers Association asked them to be revised.

(A) frustrating
(B) frustrated
(C) frustrate
(D) frustration

어휘 regulation 규정 govern 지배하다, 통제하다 importation 수입 accommodate 수용하다 frustrate 불만스럽게 하다, 좌절시키다 importer 수입업자 association 협회 revise 개정하다

해석 수입을 규제하는 규정이 수용하기에는 너무 불만스러워져서 수입업자 협회는 그것을 수정해달라고 요구했다.

해설 빈칸 앞에 be동사와 같은 2형식 동사인 became이 있다. 그러므로 빈칸에는 형용사가 필요하고 현재분사 (A)와 과거분사 (B) 중 정답을 선택해야 한다. 이 유형에서는 주어와 보어의 의미 관계를 생각해야 한다. 수식어구인 governing importation을 제외하면 주어는

the regulations임을 알 수 있다. 규정이 '좌절감을 주는' 것이므로 능동의 의미인 현재분사 (A)가 정답이다.

---

113. Please visit our office in San Jose by noon on that day so that we can complete any ------- paperwork before you begin your tour.

(A) remaining
(B) remained
(C) remains
(D) remain

어휘 so that ~하기 위해, ~할 수 있도록 complete 기입하다 paperwork 서류 작업, 문서 업무

해석 투어를 시작하시기 전에 저희가 남은 서류 작업을 완료할 수 있도록 그날 정오까지 San Jose에 있는 저희 사무실을 방문해 주세요.

해설 명사 앞에 빈칸이 있으므로 형용사가 필요하고 현재분사 (A)와 과거분사 (B) 중 정답을 선택해야 한다. remain은 자동사이므로 항상 현재분사만 정답이 될 수 있다.

---

114. The latest software from Stripo Tek makes it much ------- for companies to create newsletters.

(A) easy
(B) easily
(C) easier
(D) ease

어휘 latest 최신의 newsletter 소식지, 회보

해석 Stripo Tek의 최신 소프트웨어는 기업들의 회보 제작을 훨씬 더 쉽게 만들어 준다.

해설 빈칸 앞에 5형식 동사 makes가 있으므로 목적격 보어 자리인 빈칸에는 형용사가 들어가야 한다. 보기에 원급 형용사 (A)와 비교급 형용사 (C)가 있는데, 빈칸 앞의 much는 비교급을 강조하는 부사이므로 (C)가 정답이다.

---

115. The analysis of the spreadsheet ------- data on retail sales during the last quarter will provide valuable insights for our marketing strategy.

(A) contains
(B) contained
(C) containing
(D) containable

어휘 **analysis** 분석 **quarter** 분기 **containable** 억제할 수 있는 **contain** 포함하다, 들어 있다 **retail** 소매의 **insight** 통찰, 식견 **marketing strategy** 마케팅 전략

해석 지난 분기 소매 판매량 데이터를 포함하고 있는 스프레드시트의 분석이 우리 마케팅 전략을 위한 귀중한 통찰을 제공해 줄 것이다.

해설 문장에 동사 will provide가 있으므로 빈칸에 동사 (A)가 들어갈 수 없고, 의미상 (D)도 맞지 않다. 그러므로 빈칸에는 분사 (B)나 (C)를 넣어서 ------- data on retail sales during the last quarter가 앞의 명사 the spreadsheet를 수식하게 해야 한다. 이 유형에서는 빈칸 뒤에 목적어가 있는지 없는지 보면 된다. 목적어 data가 있으므로 현재분사 (C)가 정답이다.

Actual Test

101 (A)	**102** (B)	**103** (D)	**104** (B)	**105** (B)
106 (A)	**107** (B)	**108** (A)	**109** (D)	**110** (A)
111 (A)	**112** (A)	**113** (B)	**114** (C)	**115** (B)
116 (A)	**117** (B)	**118** (C)	**119** (D)	**120** (D)
121 (C)	**122** (C)	**123** (B)	**124** (B)	**125** (C)
126 (C)	**127** (A)	**128** (C)	**129** (C)	**130** (B)
131 (A)	**132** (B)	**133** (B)	**134** (C)	**135** (B)
136 (A)	**137** (D)	**138** (B)	**139** (D)	**140** (B)
141 (C)	**142** (C)	**143** (D)	**144** (C)	**145** (B)
146 (B)	**147** (A)			

Part 5

101. New recruits should attend their ------- training workshops at 9 A.M. with all necessary materials.

(A) assigned
(B) assign
(C) assigns
(D) assigning

어휘 **(new) recruit** 신입 사원 **assign** 할당하다, 배정하다 **material** 자료

해석 신입 사원들은 오전 9시에 모든 필요한 자료를 가지고 배정된 교육 워크숍에 참석해야 합니다.

해설 빈칸 앞뒤 their ------- training workshops를 보면, 명사 앞에 빈칸이 있으므로 형용사가 들어가야 한다. 그러므로 보기에 현재분사 (D)와 과거분사 (A) 중 정답을 선택해야 하는데, 수식받는 명사 training workshops이 '배정되는' 것이므로 과거분사 (A)가 정답이다.

102. ------- the effectiveness of Dominic Campion's leadership on the city council, he will likely win next month's mayoral election.

(A) Since
(B) Given
(C) Among
(D) Upon

어휘 **given** ~을 고려해 볼 때 **effectiveness** 효과, 유효성 **mayoral** 시장(직)의 **election** 선거

해석 Dominic Campion의 지도력이 시 의회에서 미치는 효과성을 고려해 볼 때 다음 달 시장 선거에서는 아마 그

가 이길 것이다.

해설 ------- the effectiveness에서 빈칸에 (A) Since가 들어가면 '효과성 이후에'라는 뜻으로 어색하고, 전치사 among 뒤에는 복수 명사가 와야 하므로 (C)도 제외하자. 빈칸에 Upon이 들어가면 'Dominic Campion의 지도력이 시 의회에서 갖는 유효성에 관하여'라는 의미가 되어서 주절과 어울리지 않는다. 그러므로 문장 전체의 의미를 자연스럽게 해 주는 (B)가 정답이다.

---

103. Customers are still accustomed to placing concise notices in the classified section ------- there is no longer a mandated word limit.

(A) as if
(B) so that
(C) in case
(D) even though

어휘 be accustomed to ~에 익숙하다 place notice 공고문을 내다 concise 간결한 classified section 광고면 as if 마치 ~인 것처럼 so that ~하기 위해, ~할 수 있도록 in case ~할 경우에 대비해서 mandated 법에 규정된

해석 더 이상 정해진 단어 수 제한이 없지만, 고객들은 여전히 광고면에 간결한 공지를 게재하는 데 익숙하다.

해설 접속사 어휘 문제는 문장 전체를 해석해야 정답을 알 수 있다. 고객들이 '여전히' '간결한' 공고를 내고 있다고 했으므로, 부사절의 내용은 '전에는 있었던 단어 수 제한이 이제는 없음에도 불구하고'가 알맞다. 참고로 접속사 어휘 문제에서 정답으로 가장 많이 출제되는 것이 '양보 접속사'이다. 문장 해석이 어렵다면 정답일 확률이 가장 높은 것을 찍자.

---

104. Studies have ------- that positive interactions with coworkers are associated with high job satisfaction levels.

(A) prepared
(B) shown
(C) outgrown
(D) funded

어휘 outgrow ~보다 더 커지다[많아지다] fund 자금을 대다 interaction 소통, 상호작용 be associated with ~와 관련되다

해석 동료들과의 긍정적인 상호작용이 높은 직업 만족도와 관련이 있다고 여러 연구가 보여주었다.

해설 Today's Vocabulary에서 알려주는 '항상 짝으로 출제되는 어휘'를 암기해서 빠르고 정확하게 문제를 풀어

보자. 빈칸 앞뒤 Studies have ------- that를 보고 (B)가 정답임을 알 수 있다. 명사 research [survey/study/test]가 주어라면 동사 suggest [reveal/indicate/show]가 정답이다.

---

105. The Busan Visitor Centre offers boat rides ------- the city's renowned waterfront every day.

(A) between
(B) along
(C) below
(D) apart

어휘 visitor centre(center) 관광 안내소 renowned 유명한, 명성 있는 waterfront (도시의) 해안가

해석 부산 관광 안내소는 매일 도시의 유명한 해안가를 따라가는 보트 탑승을 제공한다.

해설 배를 타는 관광은 해안가를 '따라서' 하는 것이 알맞으므로 (B)가 정답이다.

---

106. Milngavie's Farmers Market sells the ------- fruit and vegetables in all of Glasgow.

(A) freshest
(B) fresh
(C) freshly
(D) fresher

어휘 farmers market 농산물 직판장

해석 Milngavie 농산물 직판장은 Glasgow 전역에서 가장 신선한 과일과 채소를 판매한다.

해설 [(A) 최상급 (B) 원급 (C) 원급 (D) 비교급]이므로 비교 문제이다. 빈칸 앞뒤에 관사 the나 'in + 기준명사(in all of Glasgow)'가 있으므로 최상급 (A)가 정답이다.

---

107. Industry experts predicted that Brent crude oil price would rise to as ------- as 90.65 dollars per barrel this year, up more than 5 dollars from the previous year.

(A) more
(B) much
(C) most
(D) many

어휘 predict 전망하다 crude oil 원유

해설 업계 전문가들은 올해 브렌트유 가격이 전년도보다 5달

러 이상 높은 배럴당 90.65달러 정도까지 오를 것으로 전망했다.

해설 [(A) 비교급 (B) 원급 (C) 최상급 (D) 원급]이므로 비교 문제이다. as ------ as에서 빈칸에 원급이 들어가야 하므로 (B)와 (D) 중 정답을 선택해야 한다. 빈칸 뒤의 90.65 dollars와 함께 '90.65달러만큼 많이'라는 뜻이 자연스럽고 금액을 나타내는 90.65 dollars는 셀 수 없는 명사이므로(dollars가 복수 명사라고 해서 셀 수 있는 명사로 생각하지 말자), (B)가 정답이다.

---

108. Fissel School has business mentors who are retired executives with a ------ of expertise across a wide range of industries.

(A) wealth
(B) height
(C) labor
(D) fame

어휘 retired 은퇴한, 퇴직한 executive 경영 간부, 이사, 중역 a wealth of 풍부한 a wide range of 광범위한, 다양한

해석 Fissel School에는 다양한 업계에 걸쳐 풍부한 전문지식을 갖춘 은퇴한 중역들인 비즈니스 멘토들이 있다.

해설 a ------ of의 형태로 사용할 수 있는 것은 '풍부한'이라는 뜻의 a wealth of 밖에 없으므로 (A)가 정답이다.

---

109. Techmania Science Museum offers the ------ collection of facts and information ever to be made available.

(A) wide
(B) widely
(C) more widely
(D) widest

어휘 collection 소장품, 수집품

해석 Techmania 과학 박물관은 지금까지 사용할 수 있었던 가장 광범위한 지식과 정보를 소장하여 제공한다.

해설 보기가 [(A) 원급 (B) 원급 (C) 비교급 (D) 최상급]이므로 비교 문제이다. 관사 the나 부사 ever가 있으면 최상급이 쓰이므로 (D)가 정답이다.

---

110. Last quarter Eximion Technology did not sell ------ as many downloads as it had hoped to.

(A) nearly

(B) nearest
(C) nearer
(D) nearing

어휘 not nearly as + 형용사[부사] + as ~만큼 ~하지 못한[못하게] download 다운로드 (프로그램)

해석 지난 분기에 Eximion Technology는 기대했던 것만큼 다운로드 상품을 판매하지 못했다.

해설 not nearly as ------ as는 '~만큼 ~하지 못한[못하게]'이라는 뜻으로 원급 비교 부정문을 강조하는 표현이다. 따라서 (A)가 정답이다.

---

111. In a press release ------ yesterday, Raleigh Convention Center announced plans to improve its facilities.

(A) issued
(B) issuing
(C) to issue
(D) was issued

어휘 press release 언론 보도 자료 issue 발표하다, 발행하다 announce 발표하다 facilities 시설

해석 어제 발표된 언론 보도 자료에서 Raleigh 컨벤션센터는 시설을 개선하는 계획을 발표했다.

해설 In a press release ------ yesterday는 전치사구로 빈칸에 동사가 들어갈 수는 없으므로 (D)는 제외하자. 분사 (A)나 (B), 또는 to부정사 (C)가 빈칸에 들어가면 a press release를 수식하는 구조가 된다. 빈칸 뒤에 목적어가 없으므로 과거분사 (A)가 정답이다.

---

112. The Chairman of the Board of Governors of the Federal Reserve System is one of the ------ influential figures in the world.

(A) most
(B) many
(C) more
(D) much

어휘 chairman 의장 the Board of Governors of the Federal Reserve System 연방 준비 제도 이사회 figure 인물 influential 영향력 있는

해석 연방 준비 제도 이사회 의장은 세계에서 가장 영향력 있는 인물 중 한 명이다.

해설 [(A) 최상급 (B) 원급 (C) 비교급 (D) 원급]이므로 비교 문제이다. 빈칸 앞에 관사 the와 one of가 있고 빈칸 뒤에 'in + 기준명사(in the world)'가 있으므로 최상급

(A)가 정답이다.

---

113. We are continually upgrading our surveillance systems, ------- you the highest level of security services available in the industry today.

(A) ensured
(B) ensuring
(C) be ensured
(D) will ensure

어휘 continually 끊임없이 surveillance 감시 ensure 보장하다

해석 우리는 끊임없이 감시 시스템을 업그레이드하며 오늘날 업계에서 이용할 수 있는 가장 높은 수준의 보안 서비스를 보장합니다.

해설 빈칸 앞에 3형식으로 완성된 문장이 주절이므로 빈칸 이후로는 부사절이 되어야 한다. 부사절은 '접속사 + 주어 + 동사 ~'의 구조인데, 보기에 접속사와 주어가 없으므로 분사 구문임을 알 수 있다. 주절의 주어 We가 '보장하는' 것이고, 빈칸 뒤에 목적어 you가 있으므로 현재분사 (B)가 정답이다.

---

114. Pomodoro Bistro has requested that we ------- the number of banquet guests by Tuesday.

(A) personify
(B) magnify
(C) specify
(D) testify

어휘 bistro (작은) 식당 personify 의인화하다 magnify 확대하다 specify 명시하다, 지정하다 testify 증명하다, ~의 증거가 되다 banquet 연회, 만찬

해석 Pomodoro 식당은 연회의 손님 수를 화요일까지 명시해 달라고 요청했다.

해설 we ------- the number of banquet guests by Tuesday(우리는 화요일까지 연회의 손님 수를 [(A) 의인화한다 (B) 확대한다 (C) 명시한다 (D) 증명한다])의 의미를 자연스럽게 하는 (C)가 정답이다.

---

115. Popovich Textiles, Inc., is well-known ------- the fashion industry as being a trendsetter for young men's clothing.

(A) toward
(B) throughout
(C) regarding

(D) aboard

어휘 textile 직물, 옷감 Inc. 주식회사(Incorporated) aboard ~을 타고 trendsetter 유행의 선도자

해석 Popovich 직물 주식회사는 젊은 남성 의류의 유행 선도자로서 패션업계 전체에 걸쳐 잘 알려져 있다.

해설 well-known ------- the fashion industry(패션업계[(A)를 향하여 (B) 전체에 걸쳐 (C)에 관하여 (D)를 타고] 잘 알려져 있다)의 의미를 자연스럽게 해주는 전치사 (B)가 정답이다.

---

116. After twenty years in business, Arai and Ramos Home Health Services remains dedicated to customer -------.

(A) satisfaction
(B) production
(C) energy
(D) opportunity

어휘 dedicated to ~에 전념하는

해석 Arai and Ramos 가정 요양 서비스는 사업을 20년 한 후에도 고객 만족에 전념하고 있습니다.

해설 Today's Vocabulary에서 알려주는 '항상 짝으로 출제되는 어휘'를 암기해서 빠르고 정확하게 문제를 풀어보자. customer와 함께 쓰는 어휘는 satisfaction이나 service representative[desk]와 같은 명사이다. 그러므로 (A)가 정답이다.

---

117. Please submit the ------- sales report by the end of the week for senior accountant Sugata Mitra's review.

(A) revise
(B) revised
(C) revising
(D) revision

어휘 submit 제출하다 revise 수정하다 sales report 영업 보고서 senior accountant 선임 회계사

해석 선임 회계사 Sugata Mitra의 검토를 위해 주말까지 수정된 영업 보고서를 제출하시기 바랍니다.

해설 명사 sales report 앞에 빈칸이 있으므로 형용사 역할을 하는 현재분사 (C)와 과거분사 (B) 중 정답을 선택해야 한다. 수식받는 명사 sales report(영업 보고서)가 '수정되는' 것이므로 과거분사 (B)가 정답이다.

118. Analysts were ------ by the increasing number of consumers who are planning to buy property this year.

(A) startle
(B) startling
(C) startled
(D) startles

어휘 startle 깜짝 놀라게 하다 increasing 늘어나는 property 부동산

해석 분석가들은 올해 부동산 구매를 계획하고 있는 소비자 수의 증가에 놀랐다.

해설 be동사 뒤 빈칸에 형용사가 필요하므로 현재분사 (B) 와 과거분사 (C) 중 정답을 선택하자. 주어인 Analysts (분석가들)가 늘어나고 있는 소비자들의 수에(by the increasing number of consumers) '놀라는' 것이므로 과거분사 (C)가 정답이다.

119. For additional information regarding international flight fares, please consult the list ------ in the envelope.

(A) provide
(B) providing
(C) was provided
(D) provided

어휘 regarding ~에 관한 fare 요금 consult 참고하다

해석 국제 항공 요금에 관한 추가 정보를 보시려면 봉투에 제공된 목록을 참고하시기 바랍니다.

해설 빈칸 앞에 동사 consult가 있으므로 동사 (A)와 (C)는 정답이 될 수 없다. 빈칸에 분사 (B)나 (D)가 들어가면 ------ in the envelope가 앞에 있는 명사 the list 를 수식하는 구조이다. 빈칸 뒤에 목적어가 없으므로 과거분사 (D)가 정답이다.

120. The software for tracking orders has been ------ successful as it has substantially reduced the amount of time spent on the task.

(A) haltingly
(B) intimately
(C) permissibly
(D) markedly

어휘 track 추적하다 haltingly 주저하며 intimately 친밀하게

permissibly 허용되어, 무방하게 markedly 현저하게, 눈에 띄게 substantially 상당히, 많이

해석 주문 추적 소프트웨어는 업무에 드는 시간을 상당히 줄여 주었으므로 눈에 띄게 성공적이었다.

해설 has been ------ successful([(A) 주저하며 (B) 친밀하게 (C) 허용되어 (D) 눈에 띄게) 성공적이었다)의 의미를 자연스럽게 만들어 주는 부사 (D)가 정답이다.

121. The next generation Airbus is expected to offer 20 percent more cabin space and twice ------ cargo capacity as the previous model.

(A) much more
(B) more than
(C) as much
(D) too much

어휘 cabin (항공기의) 선실 cargo 화물 capacity 용량

해석 차세대 에어버스는 이전 모델보다 20퍼센트 더 많은 선실 공간과 두 배 더 많은 화물 용량을 제공할 것으로 예상된다.

해설 빈칸 앞 twice(두 배)와 빈칸 뒤 as는 빈칸에 원급이 들어간다는 단서가 된다. twice ------ cargo as가 원급 비교 문장의 구조가 되려면 (C)가 알맞다

122. Please use the attached questionnaire to inform us of how ------ your recent stay at the Sandy Shores Inn was.

(A) knowledgeable
(B) considerable
(C) enjoyable
(D) available

어휘 attach 붙이다, 첨부하다 questionnaire 설문지 knowledgeable 해박한, 많이 아는 considerable 상당한 enjoyable 즐거운 inn 호텔

해석 첨부된 설문지를 이용하셔서 저희에게 Sandy Shores 호텔에서의 최근 투숙이 얼마나 즐거우셨는지 알려주시기를 바랍니다.

해설 how ------ your recent stay at the Sandy Shores Inn was(Sandy Shores 호텔에서의 최근 투숙이 얼마나 [(A) 해박했는지 (B) 상당했는지 (C) 즐거웠는지 (D) 이용할 수 있었는지])의 의미를 자연스럽게 해주는 형용사 (C)가 정답이다.

123. Although Ms. Eisner is absent today, she ------- attends all school board meetings.

(A) previously
(B) typically
(C) almost
(D) well

어휘 absent 결석한 typically 보통, 일반적으로 board meeting 이사회 (회의)

해석 Ms. Eisner가 오늘은 불참했지만, 보통은 모든 학교 이사회 회의에 참석한다.

해설 부사절이 '비록 오늘은 결석했지만'이라는 뜻이므로 주절은 '보통은 참석한다'는 의미가 되어야 자연스럽다. 그러므로 (B)가 정답이다.

124. Present this postcard to a sales ------- at any of our stores to receive a £3.00 gift card.

(A) accessory
(B) associate
(C) faculty
(D) formula

어휘 present 제시하다 sales associate 판매 직원 faculty 교수진 formula 공식; 제조법 gift card 상품권

해석 저희 매장 아무 곳에서나 판매 직원에게 이 엽서를 제시하고 3파운드짜리 상품권을 받으세요.

해설 항상 짝으로 출제되는 어휘 문제이다. 빈칸 앞에 sales가 있으므로 representative나 associate가 정답이다.

125. Last night, Channel Fifteen News aired an exclusive interview with the ------- actress Paula Olivera.

(A) accomplish
(B) accomplishment
(C) accomplished
(D) accomplishing

어휘 air 방송하다 exclusive 독점의 accomplished (실력이) 뛰어난

해석 어제 저녁에 Channel Fifteen 뉴스는 뛰어난 여배우 Paula Olivera와의 독점 인터뷰를 방송으로 내보냈다.

해설 명사 actress 앞 빈칸에는 형용사가 들어가야 하므로 현재분사 (D)와 과거분사 (C) 중 정답을 선택해야 한다. accomplish는 과거분사로만 쓰이기 때문에 (C)가 정답이다.

126. The songs on Young Ho Woo's latest album are ------- the most innovative musical arrangements of his artistic journey.

(A) beside
(B) over
(C) among
(D) upon

어휘 innovative 혁신적인 arrangement 편곡

해석 Young Ho Woo의 최신 앨범에 있는 노래들은 그의 예술 여정 중 가장 혁신적인 편곡에 속한다.

해설 가장 혁신적으로 편집된 곡들 '사이에' 이번 앨범의 노래들이 들어 있다는 의미이므로 빈칸에 (C)가 알맞다.

127. Processes such as automated cutting and stitching will enable factory workers to complete their tasks much -------.

(A) more efficiently
(B) efficiently
(C) efficient
(D) most efficiently

어휘 stitching 꿰매기 enable 가능하게 하다 efficiently 효율적으로

해석 자동화된 자르기와 꿰매기 같은 과정들은 공장 근로자들이 업무를 훨씬 더 효율적으로 완수할 수 있게 해준다.

해설 [(A) 비교급 (B) 원급 (C) 원급 (D) 최상급]이므로 비교 문제이다. 빈칸 앞에 much는 비교급을 수식하는 부사이므로 (A)가 정답이다. much, still, even, far, a lot 등은 비교급을 강조 수식하는 부사들이다.

128. Skystream Air, an airline ------- in Kuala Lumpur, is offering budget flights to Manila and Hong Kong.

(A) stored
(B) stayed
(C) based
(D) moved

어휘 based (~에) 본사를 둔 budget 저가의, 저렴한

해석 Kuala Lumpur에 본사를 둔 항공사 Skystream 항공은 Manila와 Hong Kong으로 가는 저가 항공편을 제공한다.

해설 자동사 stay는 과거분사로 명사를 수식할 수 없으므로 (B)는 제외하자. an airline ------- in Kuala

Lumpur(Kuala Lumpur에 [(A) 보관된 (C) 본사를 둔 (D) 옮겨진] 항공사)의 의미를 자연스럽게 해 주는 분사 (C)가 정답이다.

---

129. Once quality control inspectors ------- that all specifications have been met, the product is able to be shipped.

(A) affect
(B) replace
(C) certify
(D) associate

어휘 quality control 품질관리 inspector 조사관, 검사관 affect 영향을 미치다 replace 대신하다 certify 인증하다 associate 연관 짓다 specification 사양(서), 명세서 meet 충족시키다 ship 출하하다

해석 일단 품질 관리 검사관들이 모든 사양이 충족되었다고 인증하면 제품을 출하할 수 있다.

해설 빈칸에 that절을 목적어로 취하는 동사가 들어가야 하므로 (C)가 정답이다.

---

130. The ------- meadowlands in the vicinity of the museum are designated as wildlife habitat.

(A) ethical
(B) vast
(C) absolute
(D) economic

어휘 ethical 윤리적인 vast 방대한, 광활한 absolute 절대적인 meadowland 목초지 vicinity 인근 designate 지정하다 wildlife habitat 야생 생물 서식지

해석 박물관 인근의 광활한 목초지들은 야생 생물 서식지로 지정되어 있다.

해설 The ------- meadowlands([(A) 윤리적인 (B) 광활한 (C) 절대적인 (D) 경제적인] 목초지)의 의미를 자연스럽게 해 주는 형용사 (B)가 정답이다.

Part 6

Questions 131-134 refer to the following customer review.

I have been recently extended a last-minute invitation to a formal dinner. I purchased a suit and had to have it tailored as [131.]quickly as possible. A friend recommended that I use Riccardo Tailoring in downtown Wellington. When I met Riccardo, he gave me his entire attention [132.]even though his shop was crowded. He listened to me patiently and diligently wrote down all my measurements. He then outlined all the tailoring charges up front and assured me that he would have my suit done in three days, but it was ready within two! [133.]The suit fits me perfectly as well. Riccardo has been running his shop for more than two decades, and his experience really shows. He is a [134.]superb tailor. I highly recommend him.

131-134번 문제는 다음 고객 평가에 관한 것입니다.

최근에 공식 만찬에 막바지에 초대받았습니다. 정장을 구매했고 되도록 빨리 몸에 맞게 맞춰야 했습니다. 친구가 Wellington 시내에 있는 Riccardo 양복점을 이용해 보라고 권하더군요. Riccardo를 만났을 때 그는 가게가 북적이고 있었는데도 저에게 온전한 관심을 기울여 주었습니다. 제가 하는 말을 끝까지 듣고 모든 치수를 잘 적어 두었습니다. 그리고 나서 모든 재단 요금을 미리 설명해 주고 양복은 3일 후에 완성될 것이라고 약속했는데, 이틀도 안 되어 준비되었습니다! 양복은 저에게 딱 맞기도 합니다. Riccardo는 20년 이상 가게를 운영해 왔는데, 그의 경험이 정말 잘 드러납니다. 그는 최고의 재단사입니다. 적극 추천합니다.

어휘 review 비평, 평가 extend an invitation to ~에 초대하다 last-minute 마지막 순간의, 막바지의 suit 정장 tailor 맞춰 만들다 tailoring 재단; 양복점업 downtown 번화가 [중심가]의 give sb attention ~에게 관심을 보이다 patiently 참을성 있게, 차분히 diligently 부지런히, 성실하게 measurement 치수 outline 개요를 설명하다 up front 미리, 사전에 assure 장담하다, 확언하다 done 완료

된 as well 또한 show 잘 보이다. 눈에 띄다 superb 최고의, 대단히 훌륭한 highly recommend 강력히 추천하다

131.
(A) quickly
(B) quicken
(C) quickest
(D) quickness

해설 as ------ as가 있으면 원급 형용사나 부사가 들어가야 하므로 (A)가 정답이다.

132.
(A) as far as
(B) even though
(C) such as
(D) whether

해설 가게가 손님으로 북적이고 있었는데도(his shop was crowded) 온전히 관심을 기울여 줬다는(he gave me his entire attention) 내용이 자연스러우므로 빈칸에는 even though가 알맞다.

133.
(A) Saturday is always the busiest day for the shop.
(B) The suit fits me perfectly as well.
(C) I made an additional purchase.
(D) He used to sell shirts.

어휘 make a purchase 구매하다 additional 추가의

해석 (A) 토요일은 언제나 가게가 가장 바쁜 날입니다.
(B) 양복은 저에게 딱 맞기까지 합니다.
(C) 하나 더 샀습니다.
(D) 그는 예전에는 셔츠를 팔았습니다.

해설 빈칸 앞 문장들이 모두 Riccardo를 칭찬하는 내용이다. '바쁜 와중에도(even though his shop was crowded) 새로 온 손님에게 온전히 관심을 기울여 줬고(he gave me his entire attention), 말을 끝까지 듣고 모든 치수를 잘 적어 두고(He listened to me patiently and diligently wrote down all my measurements.), 재단 요금을 미리 설명한 후(He then outlined all the tailoring charges up front) 약속한 것보다 하루 앞서 양복을 완성해 주었다(assured me that he would have my suit done in three days, but it was ready within two!)'고 했다. 그러므로 칭찬하는 내용의 문장인 (B)가 부연 설명으로 이어지는 것이 자연스럽다.

134.
(A) former
(B) temporary

(C) superb
(D) best

어휘 former 이전의 temporary 일시적인, 임시의

해설 지문 전체가 재단사를 칭찬하는 내용이므로 (C)가 알맞다. 최상급인 (D)는 앞에 관사 the가 있어야 하므로 정답이 아니다.

Questions 135-138 refer to the following information.

EBR Industries guarantees that its products will work as 135.advertised for a minimum of one year from date of purchase. 136.This period may be extended for certain products. This 137.warranty is valid only for products purchased from EBR Industries stores and other licensed distributors. Products that are found to be defective can be sent to our address for either repair or replacement. When feasible, please make sure that products being returned due to damage are shipped back to us in their 138.original packaging.

135-138번 문제는 다음 안내문에 관한 것입니다.

EBR 산업은 상품이 구매 날짜로부터 최소 1년 동안 광고에 나온 대로 작동할 것임을 보장합니다. 어떤 제품에 대해서는 이 기간이 연장될 수 있습니다. 이 품질 보증은 오직 EBR 산업 매장과 기타 공인 대리점에서 구매하신 제품에 대해서만 유효합니다. 결함이 있는 것으로 발견되는 제품은 저희 주소로 보내셔서 수리나 교체를 받으실 수 있습니다. 가능하다면, 손상 때문에 반품하시는 제품은 반드시 원래의 포장재에 넣어서 저희에게 반송되게 해주시기를 바랍니다.

어휘 guarantee 보장하다 a minimum of 최소 ~ extend 연장하다 warranty 품질 보증(서) valid 유효한 licensed 공인의, 허가받은 distributor 판매 대리점 defective 결함이 있는 repair 수리 replacement 교체 feasible 실현 가능한 make sure that 반드시 (~하도록) 하다 damage 손상 ship back 반송하다 original 원래의 packaging 포장재

135.
(A) advertising
(B) advertised

(C) advertisement
(D) advertises

해설 as ------는 'as + 과거분사'의 형태로 사용하는 관용 표현이므로 정답은 (B)이다.

---

136. **(A) This period may be extended for certain products.**
(B) EBR Industries stores are located in four countries.
(C) At that moment, an electronic receipt was generated.
(D) Product samples are available in stores.

어휘 be located in ~에 위치하다 generate 발생시키다
electronic receipt 전자 영수증

해설 (A) 어떤 제품에 대해서는 이 기간이 연장될 수 있습니다.
(B) EBR 산업 매장은 4개국에 있습니다.
(C) 그때 전자 영수증이 생성되었습니다.
(D) 매장에서 제품 견본을 이용하실 수 있습니다.

해설 앞 문장에서 품질 보증 기간을 알려주고 있으므로(EBR Industries guarantees that its products will work as advertised for a minimum of one year from date of purchase.) 관련 내용인 (A)가 부연 설명으로 이어지는 것이 자연스럽다.

---

137. (A) agenda
(B) sale
(C) requirement
(D) warranty

어휘 agenda 의제, 안건 requirement 요건

해설 1년 이상 제품의 정상 작동을 보장하고 있다(guarantees that its products will work as advertised for a minimum of one year .... This period may be extended ....). 이 내용을 나타내기에 알맞은 명사는 warranty(품질보증)이다.

---

138. (A) originally
(B) original
(C) origin
(D) originality

어휘 origin 기원 originality 독창성

해설 명사 packaging 앞의 빈칸에는 형용사가 들어가야 하므로 (B)가 정답이다.

Part 7

Questions 139-142 refer to the following article.

Positive Change for Charleroi

139.140.Lagerwey Wind, the leading developer of wind turbines and wind energy technology across Europe, has announced plans to open a manufacturing plant in Charleroi, Belgium. —[1]—. 140.The Dutch firm is allocating in excess of €20 million to acquire, refurbish, and equip the abandoned C-Tech Telephone factory. 142.It is anticipated that the venture will generate approximately two hundred manufacturing positions and fifty administrative positions over the following two years. This is a welcome announcement for Charleroi, an industrial area that has been adversely affected by the closure of numerous factories and the subsequent diminishment of employment opportunities in recent years. —[2]—. 142.Caddell Builders has already been contracted to undertake the plant's transformations. —[3]—.

The facility will primarily be utilized for the assembly and testing of gear drives to be incorporated in the company's wind turbines. —[4]—. 141.Lagerwey Wind, in partnership with the Charleroi Business Development Association (CBDA), will furnish development grants to train its incoming workforce in green technology. 141.Jomarie Fredericks, CBDA president, says "the city is proud to be part of an effort that is beneficial to energy conservation and to the economic prosperity of our region."

139–142번 문제는 다음 기사에 관한 것입니다.

Charleroi의 긍정적인 변화

유럽 전역의 풍력 발전용 터빈과 풍력 에너지 기술의 선도 개발업체인 Lagerwey Wind가 벨기에 Charleroi

에 제조 공장을 열겠다는 계획을 발표했다. 이 네덜란드 회사는 2천만 유로 이상을 할당하여 버려진 C-Tech 전화 공장을 인수해서 재단장하고 장비를 들여놓을 것이다. 이 벤처 사업은 향후 2년에 걸쳐 대략 200개의 생산직 일자리와 50개의 관리직 일자리를 창출해낼 것으로 예상된다. 이것은 최근 몇 년 동안 많은 공장의 폐쇄와 이어진 구직 기회의 감소에 악영향을 받아 온 산업 지역인 Charleroi에 반가운 소식이다. Caddell 건축이 이미 계약이 되어 있어 공장을 탈바꿈시키는 일에 착수했다.

시설은 주로 회사의 풍력 발전용 터빈에 포함될 기어 구동장치의 조립과 테스트에 활용될 것이다. Lagerwey Wind는 Charleroi 사업 개발 협회(CBDA)와 협력하여 개발 보조금을 제공함으로써, 신규 인력에게 친환경 기술을 교육할 것이다. CBDA 회장 Jomarie Fredericks은 "시는 에너지 보존과 우리 지역의 경제적 번영에 유익한 활동의 일원이 된 것을 자랑스럽게 여깁니다."라고 말한다.

어휘 leading 주요한, 선도하는 wind turbine 풍력 발전용 터빈 manufacturing plant 제조 공장 Dutch 네덜란드의 firm 회사 allocate 할당하다 in excess of ~이상의 acquire 인수하다 refurbish 개장하다, 재단장하다 equip 장비를 갖추다 abandoned 버려진 anticipate 기대하다 generate 창출하다 approximately 약 manufacturing position 생산직 administrative 관리의, 행정의 announcement 발표 adversely 불리하게 closure 폐쇄 subsequent 그 다음의, 이후의 diminishment 축소 be contracted to-V ~하기로 계약을 맺다 undertake 떠맡다, 착수하다 transformation 변화, 탈바꿈 facility 시설 mainly 주로 utilize 활용하다 assembly 조립 drive 구동장치 incorporate (일부로) 포함하다 in partnership with ~와 제휴하여, 협력하여 association 협회 furnish 제공하다 grant (정부나 단체의) 보조금 train A in B A에게 B를 교육하다 incoming 들어오는, 신입의 workforce 인력 effort (집단의) 활동 beneficial 유익한, 이로운 conservation 보존, 절약 prosperity 번영, 번창

---

139. What does the article mainly discuss?

(A) The appointment of a new company president
(B) The consolidation of two firms
(C) The process of manufacturing wind turbines
(D) The opening of a facility

어휘 appointment 임명 consolidation 합병, 통합 firm 회사 manufacture 제조하다, 생산하다 wind turbine 풍력 발전용 터빈

해설 기사는 주로 무엇을 논하는가?

(A) 새 회사 회장의 임명
(B) 두 회사의 합병
(C) 풍력 발전용 터빈을 생산하는 과정
(D) 어떤 시설의 개업

해설 주제는 대부분 지문 도입부에서 알 수 있다. 첫 문장에서 제조 공장을 열 계획(plans to open a manufacturing plant)을 알리고 있으므로 (D)가 정답이다.

---

140. What will happen to the C-Tech Telephone factory?

(A) It will be preserved as a historic site.
(B) It will be employed by a different industry.
(C) It will be relocated to another location.
(D) It will be demolished to form an unoccupied space.

어휘 preserve 보존하다 historic site 유적지 employ 이용하다 relocate 이전하다 demolish 철거하다 unoccupied 비어 있는

해설 C-Tech 전화 공장에 무슨 일이 있을 것인가?
(A) 유적지로 보존될 것이다.
(B) 다른 업계에서 이용될 것이다.
(C) 다른 장소로 이전될 것이다.
(D) 공간을 만들기 위해 철거될 것이다.

해설 첫 문장에서 Lagerwey Wind는 풍력 발전용 터빈 개발업체로 소개하고(Lagerwey Wind, the leading developer of wind turbines and wind energy technology across Europe), 이어지는 문장에서는 이 회사가 많은 돈을 들여 사용되지 않는 전화기 공장을 인수할 것이라는 계획을 알리고 있다(The Dutch firm is allocating in excess of €20 million to acquire, refurbish, and equip the abandoned C-Tech Telephone factory). 그러므로 C-Tech 전화 공장은 이제 개조되어 업종이 바뀌게 될 것임을 알 수 있다.

---

141. Who is Ms. Fredericks?

(A) A Lagerwey Wind executive
(B) A media correspondent
(C) The head of an organization
(D) The mayor of a city in Belgium

어휘 executive 중역, 이사 correspondent 특파원 head (조직의) 장 mayor 시장

해설 Ms. Fredericks는 누구인가?
(A) Lagerwey Wind의 중역

(B) 대중 매체 특파원
(C) 어떤 기관의 장(長)
(D) 벨기에 어느 도시의 시장

해설 지문 마지막 문장에서 Jomarie Fredericks를 CBDA 회장(president)으로 소개하고, 바로 앞 문장에서 CBDA는 the Charleroi Business Development Association(Charleroi 사업 개발 협회)의 약자라고 말하고 있다. 그러므로 Ms. Fredericks이 협회 회장임을 알 수 있어 정답은 (C)이다.

---

142. In which of the positions marked [1], [2], [3], and [4] does the following sentence best belong?

"It also anticipates hiring supplementary personnel to complete the construction project."

(A) [1]
(B) [2]
(C) [3]
(D) [4]

어휘 supplementary 보충의, 추가의 personnel 인력 construction 공사

해석 다음 문장은 [1], [2], [3], [4]로 표시된 자리 중 어느 곳에 가장 적당한가?

"그 회사도 공사 프로젝트를 완료하기 위해 보충 인원을 채용할 예정이다."

해설 앞뒤 문장과의 연결고리가 되어 줄 키워드를 생각해 보자. 주어진 문장의 It도 또한(also) 채용(hiring)을 준비하고 있으므로, 앞부분에는 다른 기관이 직원을 채용한다는 내용이 나와야 한다. 또한 the construction project가 어떤 공사를 가리키는지도 앞부분에 언급되어 있어야 한다. 첫 문단 세 번째 문장에 Lagerwey Wind가 새 공장 가동을 위해 생산직 직원과 관리직 직원을 많이 채용할 것이라는 내용이 나온다(It is anticipated that the venture will generate approximately two hundred manufacturing positions and fifty administrative positions over the following two years.). 그리고 지문에 Lagerwey Wind 외에 채용의 주체가 될 만한 기업은 [3] 바로 앞 문장에 등장하는 Caddell Builders밖에 없으므로, 주어진 문장의 It이 가리키는 것은 이 회사이다. 그러므로 주어진 문장의 the construction project는 Caddell Builders가 착수했다는 공장 개조 공사일 수밖에 없고(Caddell Builders has already been contracted to undertake the plant's transformations.), Caddell Builders는 이 공사의 완수를 위해 추가로 직원을 채용할 예정인 것이다. 그러므로 정답은 (C)이다.

Questions 143-147 refer to the following notice, e-mail, and comment form.

Waikiki Monarch Hotel	

Scheduled activities for guests in August
Start time for all activities is 10:00 A.M. at the Guest Services desk in the lobby.

Activity and instructor/guide	Description
Every Tuesday 147.Surfing lesson Conducted by Kalani Kealoha	Master the art of surfing in Waikiki. Should be an adept swimmer. $60 per person. All participants must be 12 years or older.
Every Wednesday 146.Hawaiian flower crafts Conducted by Elina Aquino	Your instructor will provide you with guidance in creating a lei: an ornamental Hawaiian flower garland or necklace. All supplies included. $12 per person.
Every Thursday History tour Conducted by Leilani Ogawa	This 2-hour walking tour will provide participants with an insight into Waikiki's history. No charge.
143.*Every Friday* Hawaiian cookery class Conducted by head chef Jessica Chen	Learn how to prepare authentic Hawaiian cuisine. (143.Lessons can be tailored to focus solely on vegetarian recipes.) All participants must be 12 years or older. $25 per person.
Visit the Guest Services desk for more information and to sign up.	

143-147번 문제는 다음 안내문과 이메일, 의견 서식에 관한 것입니다.

Waikiki Monarch 호텔

예정된 8월 투숙객 활동
모든 활동의 시작 시각은 오전 10시, 장소는 로비의 고객 서비스 데스크

활동 및 강사/가이드	설명
매주 화요일 서핑 교습 진행 Kalani Kealoha	와이키키에서 파도 타는 기술을 익혀보세요. 수영에 능숙해야 합니다. 일인당 60달러. 모든 참가자는 12세 이상이어야 합니다.
매주 수요일 하와이식 꽃 공예 진행 Elina Aquino	강사가 레이(하와이식 장식용 화관 혹은 꽃목걸이) 만들기를 지도해 드립니다. 모든 용품 포함. 일인당 12달러.
매주 목요일 역사 탐방 진행 Leilani Ogawa	이 2시간짜리 도보 투어는 참가자에게 와이키키의 역사에 대한 통찰을 제공합니다. 무료.
매주 금요일 하와이식 요리 강습 진행 수석 셰프 Jessica Chen	정통 하와이식 요리 만드는 법을 배우세요. (강습은 채식주의자 조리법에만 초점을 맞춰 준비되어 있습니다) 모든 참가자는 12세 이상이어야 합니다. 일인당 25달러.

추가 정보나 등록을 위해 고객 서비스 데스크를 방문해 주세요.

어휘 instructor 강사 conduct 진행하다 art 기술 adept 능숙한 participant 참가자 craft (수)공예 guidance 지도 ornamental 장식용의 garland 화환, 화관 supplies 용품 insight 통찰 cookery 요리(법) authentic 정통인 cuisine 요리 tailor 맞춰 준비하다 solely 오로지, 단지 vegetarian 채식주의자의 sign up 등록하다

To: Guest Services Staff
<gsstaff@waikikimonarchhotel.com>
146. From: Soo-Min Lee
<smlee@waikikimonarchhotel.com>
Date: August 17
Subject: Update

Hi all,

144. This month's program of guest activities needs to be revised. 146. Elina Aquino and Jessica Chen will be away August 20-26. I will lead Elina's activities and Astrid Geensen will lead Jessica's. Everything will return to normal on August 27, when Elina and Jessica both return.

Sincerely,

Soo-Min Lee
Guest Services Director,
Waikiki Monarch Hotel

수신: 고객 서비스 직원들
<gsstaff@waikikimonarchhotel.com>
발신: Soo-Min Lee
<smlee@waikikimonarchhotel.com>
날짜: 8월 17일
제목: 업데이트

모두 안녕하세요.

이번 달 투숙객 활동 프로그램에 수정이 필요합니다. Elina Aquino와 Jessica Chen이 8월 20일부터 26일까지 자리를 비우게 됩니다. 제가 Elina의 활동을 맡고 Astrid Geensen이 Jessica의 활동을 맡습니다. 모든 것은 Elina와 Jessica가 모두 복귀하는 8월 27일에 정상으로 돌아옵니다.

그럼 이만 줄입니다.

Waikiki Monarch 호텔 고객 서비스 책임자
Soo-Min Lee

어휘 revise 수정하다 away 자리에 없는, 결석한 return to normal 정상으로 돌아오다

Comments:

My family and I thoroughly enjoyed our stay at your hotel. We really appreciated the activities that were planned and I would like to give all the instructors my compliments. ¹⁴⁵·I had to skip the activity guided by Ms. Ogawa, but my family told me they learned a lot from her. ¹⁴⁶·My daughter and I found it very entertaining to learn how to make flower garlands, and my husband has already cooked some of the dishes he was taught in Ms. Geensen's class. ¹⁴⁷·Finally, my son and daughter both had a wonderful time with Mr. Kealoha. They are looking forward to putting his lessons to use when we travel on holiday to Costa Rica next year.

Name: Sarah Virtanen
Today's date: 13 September
Number of guests: 4
¹⁴⁶·Date of stay: 20-26 August

의견:

우리 가족과 저는 귀 호텔에서의 투숙이 정말 즐거웠습니다. 계획된 활동에 정말 감사하고 모든 강사분을 칭찬해드리고 싶습니다. 저는 Ms. Ogawa가 지도한 활동에는 참가하지 못했는데, 우리 가족이 그분으로부터 많이 배웠다고 말하더군요. 제 딸과 저는 화관 만들기를 배우는 게 참 재미있었고, 제 남편은 Ms. Geensen의 수업에서 배운 요리 몇 가지를 벌써 만들어 봤답니다. 끝으로 저희 아들, 딸은 모두 Mr. Kealoha와 멋진 시간을 보냈습니다. 아이들은 내년에 Costa Rica로 휴가 여행을 가면 배운 것을 써먹어 보기를 기대하고 있습니다.

이름: Sarah Virtanen
작성 날짜: 9월 13일
투숙객 수: 4
투숙 날짜: 8월 20-26일

어휘 comment 논평, 의견 thoroughly 대단히; 완전히 appreciate ~에 대해 감사하다 give *sb* a compliment ~를 칭찬하다 skip 거르다, 빼먹다, 건너뛰고 읽다 entertaining 재미있는, 즐거움을 주는 garland 화환, 화관 look forward to ~를 기대하다 put *sth* to use ~을 활용하다

143. What activity can be customized?

(A) Tuesday's activity
(B) Wednesday's activity
(C) Thursday's activity
(D) Friday's activity

해석 어느 활동을 원하는 대로 바꿀 수 있는가?
(A) 화요일 활동
(B) 수요일 활동
(C) 목요일 활동
(D) 금요일 활동

해설 안내문에서 금요일 활동인 요리 강습이 채식주의자를 위한 조리법에만 초점을 맞춰 준비할 수 있다고 설명하고 있다(Lessons can be tailored to focus solely on vegetarian recipes.).

144. What is the purpose of the e-mail?

(A) To welcome two new employees
(B) To address a guest inquiry
(C) To make changes to a schedule
(D) To arrange training sessions for staff

어휘 employee 직원 address 다루다, 대처하다 inquiry 질문, 문의 make a change to ~를 변경하다 arrange 마련하다

해석 이메일의 목적은 무엇인가?
(A) 두 명의 신입 직원을 환영하는 것
(B) 투숙객의 문의를 다루는 것
(C) 일정을 변경하는 것
(D) 직원들을 위한 교육을 마련하는 것

해설 8월 20일부터 26일까지 자리를 비우는 직원들이 있어서(Elina Aquino and Jessica Chen will be away August 20-26.), 원래 그들이 맡던 강습을 다른 사람들이 대신 진행한다(I will lead Elina's activities and Astrid Geensen will lead Jessica's.) 내용이다. 그러므로 이메일의 목적은 투숙객들을 위한 활동 일정의 변경을 알리는 것이다.

145. In the comment form, the word "skip" in paragraph 1, line 3, is closest in meaning to

(A) jump
(B) miss
(C) pay for
(D) look over

해석 의견 서식에서 첫 문단 셋째 줄의 단어 "skip"과 의미상 가장 가까운 것은

(A) 뛰어 넘다
(B) 거르다, ~을 하지 않다
(C) 지불하다
(D) 대충 훑어보다

> **해설** skip을 '뛰어 넘다'라는 뜻으로 사용하면 (A)와, '어떤 일을 거르다'라는 뜻으로 사용하면 (B)와, '~을 건너뛰고 읽다'라는 뜻으로 사용하면 (D)와 동의어가 된다. 본문에서는 Ms. Ogawa가 진행한 활동에 참여하지 않았다고 했으므로(I had to skip the activity guided by Ms. Ogawa), (B)로 바꿔 쓸 수 있다.

---

146. Who taught the course enjoyed by Ms. Virtanen and her daughter?

(A) Ms. Aquino
(B) Ms. Lee
(C) Ms. Ogawa
(D) Ms. Chen

> **해석** Ms. Virtanen과 그녀의 딸이 즐긴 코스는 누가 지도했는가?
> (A) Ms. Aquino
> (B) Ms. Lee
> (C) Ms. Ogawa
> (D) Ms. Chen

> **연계 추론** 의견 서식을 보면 8월 20일부터 26일까지 이 호텔에 묵은(Date of stay: 20–26 August) Ms. Virtanen이 딸과 참여한 활동은 화관 만들기 강습이었다(My daughter and I found it very entertaining to learn how to make flower garlands). 안내문을 보면 이 수업의 강사는 Elina Aquino인데(Hawaiian flower crafts Conducted by Elina Aquino), 이메일에서 이 가족이 투숙한 기간에 Elina Aquino가 자리를 비우기 때문에(Elina Aquino and Jessica Chen will be away August 20–26.), Ms. Aquino가 맡고 있던 활동은 Ms. Lee가 대신 진행한다고 말하고 있다(I will lead Elina's activities).

---

147. What are Ms. Virtanen's children planning to do in Costa Rica?

(A) Go surfing
(B) Learn traditional crafts
(C) Take a walking tour
(D) Try local food

> **어휘** craft (수)공예
> **해석** Ms. Virtanen의 자녀들은 Costa Rica에서 무엇을 하려고 계획하고 있는가?
> (A) 서핑하러 간다
> (B) 전통 공예를 배운다
> (C) 도보 관광을 한다

(D) 지역의 음식을 먹어 본다

> **연계 추론** 의견 서식을 보면 Ms. Virtanen의 자녀들은 Mr. Kealoha의 강습을 재미있어 했으며(my son and daughter both had a wonderful time with Mr. Kealoha.), 내년에 Costa Rica로 휴가를 가면 Mr. Kealoha에게서 배운 것을 활용해 보려고 기대하고 있다(They are looking forward to putting his lessons to use when we travel on holiday to Costa Rica next year). 안내문을 보면 Mr. Kealoha가 진행한 활동은 서핑 강습이므로(Surfing lesson Conducted by Kalani Kealoha), Ms. Virtanen의 자녀들은 Costa Rica에서 서핑을 할 것이라고 추론할 수 있다.

Day 08

PART 5 & 6 Exercise

101 (D)	**102** (B)	**103** (D)	**104** (B)	**105** (C)
106 (A)	**107** (A)	**108** (D)	**109** (A)	**110** (A)
111 (A)	**112** (C)	**113** (C)	**114** (A)	**115** (C)

101. ------- Mr. Wilkinson not out of town on a business trip, he would be the one to lead today's training session for the new interns.

(A) In fact
(B) Whereas
(C) Only
(D) Were

어휘 out of town 외부로 나간 on a business trip 출장 간

해석 Mr. Wilkinson이 출장으로 자리를 비우지 않았다면 그가 새 인턴 직원들을 위한 오늘의 교육을 이끈 사람이 었을 것이다.

해설 쉼표 뒤가 주절이고 쉼표 앞이 부사절이므로 빈칸은 부사절의 동사 자리이다. 주절의 동사가 would be이므로 가정법 과거 시제 문장인 것을 알 수 있다. 부사절에서 if를 생략한 주어와 동사를 도치한 형태이므로 (D)가 정답이다.

102. Management was notified yesterday that the arrival of the shipment sent to the London office ------- due to a customs issue.

(A) being delayed
(B) would be delayed
(C) has been delayed
(D) have delayed

어휘 notified 통보하다, 알리다 management 경영진, 운영진 shipment 수송품, 적하물 be delayed 지연되다 customs 세관; 관세

해석 경영진은 런던 지사로 보낸 수송품의 도착이 세관 문제로 인해 지연될 것이라고 어제 통보받았다.

해설 that절의 빈칸에는 동사가 들어가야 하므로 준동사인 (A)는 제외하자. 전치사구 of the shipment와 수식어구인 sent to the London office를 제외하면 the

arrival이 that절의 주어임을 알 수 있다. 주어가 단수 명사이므로 복수 동사 (D)도 제외한다. "도착이 지연되었다고 통보받았다"는 의미라면 that절이 주절(was notified)보다 먼저 일어난 일이므로 빈칸에 과거완료 시제 동사가 들어가야 하는데 보기에 없다. "도착이 지연될 것이라고 통보받았다"는 의미라면 주절이 과거 시제이므로 종속절에 will의 과거형 would를 써야 한다. 따라서 (B)가 정답으로 알맞다.

103. Golota Remodeling may charge more than the initial estimate ------- additional time be required to install the shelves and cabinets.

(A) in fact
(B) when
(C) through
(D) should

어휘 charge 요금을 청구하다 initial 초기의 estimate 견적 install 설치하다 shelf 선반

해석 선반과 캐비닛을 설치하는 데 추가적인 시간이 요구되는 경우 Golota 리모델링은 초기 견적보다 많은 요금을 청구할 수도 있다.

해설 보기가 [(A) 부사 (B) 접속사 (C) 전치사 (D) 조동사]로 구성되어 있으므로 '접속사 vs 전치사' 유형의 문제로 보인다. 따라서 부사 (A)는 제외하자. 빈칸 뒤에 '주어 + 동사(additional time be required)'가 있으므로 전치사 (C)도 정답이 아니다. 그렇다고 접속사 (B)를 정답으로 선택하지 말고, 동사원형(be required)에 주목하자. 보기에 조동사 should가 있으므로 가정법 미래 시제 문장으로 if를 생략한 주어와 should를 도치한 부사절임을 알 수 있다. 그러므로 (D)가 정답이다.

104. If we had not received approval for the additional funding so quickly, we ------- in establishing our presence in Asia in only 12 months.

(A) have to succeed
(B) would not have succeeded
(C) had not succeeded
(D) have not succeeded

어휘 approval 승인 funding 자금 establish 확립하다, 구축하다 presence 입지

해석 우리가 추가 자금 지원에 대한 승인을 그렇게 빨리 받지 못했다면 아시아에서 겨우 12개월 만에 입지를 확립하는데 성공하지 못했을 것이다.

해설 if절에 과거완료 시제 동사(had not received)를 사용한 가정법 문장이므로, 정해진 규칙에 맞는 어형의 동사를 선택해야 한다. 가정법 과거완료 시제 문장에서는 주절에 would have + p.p. 형태의 동사가 있어야 하므로 (D)가 정답이다.

---

105. Ms. Han ------- employed by the same company in many different positions over the last 20 years.

(A) is
(B) has
(C) has been
(D) could be

어휘 be employed 취직하다, 근무하다　position 직책

해석 Ms. Han은 지난 20년 넘게 같은 회사에서 여러 다양한 직책으로 근무해 왔다.

해설 동사 ------- employed 뒤에 목적어가 없어서 수동태가 되어야 하므로 능동태 동사형를 만드는 (B)는 제외하자. 문장 마지막의 over the last 20 years를 보면 현재완료 시제 (C)가 정답인 것을 알 수 있다.

---

106. ------- receiving notice that the conductor of the Cape Philharmonic Orchestra will retire, the operations committee has been searching for a replacement.

(A) Since
(B) While
(C) Once
(D) For

어휘 notice 통보　conductor 지휘자　retire 은퇴하다
operation 운영, 경영　committee 위원회
replacement 대신할 사람, 후임자

해석 Cape 교향악단의 지휘자가 은퇴할 것이라는 통보를 받은 이후 운영 위원회는 후임자를 물색해 오고 있다.

해설 보기가 접속사와 전치사로 구성되어 있고 since나 for가 있으면 주절의 시제를 확인하자. 주절의 시제가 현재완료진행(has been searching)이고, 빈칸 뒤 receiving notice(통보 받음)는 과거 '시점'을 나타내므로 (A)가 정답으로 알맞다.

---

107. ------- the region's tallest skyscraper was completed, Pace and Brown Architects had already begun designing a taller one.

(A) By the time
(B) Whenever
(C) Unless
(D) Due to

어휘 skyscraper 고층 건물　complete 완성하다　architect 건축가

해석 지역에서 가장 높은 건물이 완공되었을 때쯤에 Pace and Brown 건축은 이미 더 높은 건물을 설계하기 시작했다.

해설 'by the time + 주어 + 과거 시제 동사'를 과거완료 시제의 키워드로 기억해 두자. '더 높은 건물을 설계하기 시작'한 일이 '지역에서 가장 높은 건물을 완공'한 것보다 먼저 일어난 일이다. 부사절의 동사(was completed)가 과거 시제이고, 주절의 동사(had begun)가 과거완료 시제이므로 (A)가 정답으로 알맞다.

---

108. Starting next Monday, Lehman's Hardware ------- its hours of operation until 9:00 P.M. daily.

(A) had extended
(B) was extending
(C) will be extended
(D) will be extending

어휘 hardware 철물　extend 연장하다　hours of operation 영업시간

해석 다음 주 월요일을 기하여 Lehman 철물점은 영업시간을 매일 오후 9시로 연장하게 될 것이다.

해설 빈칸 뒤에 목적어 its hours of operation이 있으므로 수동태 동사인 (C)는 제외하자. 문장 앞부분에 next Monday가 있으므로 미래진행 시제 동사인 (D)가 정답이다.

---

109. Amanda Lee ------- the suit designs by the time she meets the president of Klim Clothing next week.

(A) will have completed
(B) is completing
(C) completed
(D) completes

해석 Amanda Lee는 다음 주에 Klim Clothing 회장을 만날 때쯤이면 양복 디자인을 끝내놓았을 것이다.

---

110. ------- the recruiting team received a greater number of responses to the online job posting, the candidate selection process would have taken more time.

(A) Had
(B) Instead of
(C) Except
(D) Whether

어휘 recruiting 채용 (활동) job posting 채용 공고 candidate 지원자 selection 선발

해석 채용팀이 온라인 채용 공고에 대한 응답을 더 많이 받았으면 지원자 선발 절차에 더 많은 시간이 걸릴 뻔했다.

해설 보기가 [(A) 동사/조동사 (B) 전치사 (C) 전치사 (D) 접속사]로 이루어져 있으므로 '접속사 vs 전치사' 문제로 파악해야 한다. 빈칸 뒤에 '주어 + 동사(the recruiting team received)'가 있으므로 전치사 (B)와 (C)는 오답이지만 바로 (D)를 선택하지는 말자. whether를 부사절 접속사로 사용하려면 or (not)가 필요하지만 이 문장에는 whether의 짝이 되는 표현이 없다. 주절의 동사(would have taken)를 보면, 가정법 과거완료 문장으로 부사절이 if를 생략한 주어와 동사를 도치한 형태임을 알아야 한다. 그러므로 (A)가 정답이다.

---

111. I eagerly anticipate hearing from you as soon as you ------- from your vacation.

(A) return
(B) will return
(C) would return
(D) had returned

어휘 eagerly anticipate 간절히 기다리다 hear from ~에게서 연락을 받다, 소식을 듣다

해석 휴가에서 돌아오시자마자 소식을 들을 수 있기를 간절히 기대합니다.

해설 '당신이 휴가에서 돌아오는 것'은 미래의 일이지만 미래 시제 동사 (B)를 선택하면 안 된다. as soon as로 시작하는 시간 부사절이므로 미래 시제 대신 현재(완료) 시제 동사를 사용해야 한다. 그러므로 (A)가 정답이다.

---

112. Bank employees will forward the loan application to the appropriate department as soon as the form ------- submitted.

(A) was
(B) will be
(C) has been
(D) to be

어휘 employee 직원 forward 전달하다 loan application 대출 신청서 appropriate 적절한, 해당의 submit 제출하다

해석 대출 신청서가 제출되자마자 은행 직원들이 해당 부서로 전달할 것입니다.

해설 '대출 신청서가 제출되는 것'은 미래의 일이지만 as soon as로 시작하는 시간 부사절에서는 미래 시제 대신 현재(완료) 시제 동사를 사용해야 한다. 그러므로 (C)가 정답이다.

---

113. Mr. Lehrman ------- at this school three years ago and may return this fall.

(A) teaches
(B) is teaching
(C) taught
(D) has taught

해석 Mr. Lehrman은 3년 전에 이 학교에서 가르쳤으며 올 가을에 돌아올지도 모른다.

해설 ago는 과거 시제를 나타내므로 (C)가 정답이다.

---

114. On Saturday, the train service from Kingston Station to Waterloo Station ------- from 8:00 P.M. to midnight while the railroad is closed for maintenance.

(A) will be suspended
(B) was suspended
(C) is suspended
(D) to suspend

어휘 suspend (일시적으로) 중단하다 maintenance 유지 보수

해석 토요일에는 보수 작업을 위해 철도가 폐쇄되는 동안 오후 8시부터 자정까지 Kingston 역부터 Waterloo 역까지 열차 서비스가 중단될 예정입니다.

해설 빈칸은 주절의 동사 자리이므로 준동사인 (D)는 제외하자. while로 시작하는 부사절에 쓰인 현재 시제 동사(is closed)는 미래의 일을 나타내므로 빈칸에는 미래 시제 동사 (A)가 정답이다. 현재 시제 동사 (C)는 지속적인 상태나 반복되는 행위에서 사용하므로 일시적인 중

단을 뜻하는 이 문장에는 알맞지 않다.

---

115. We plan to visit Rosie's Cantina after work because it ------- authentic Mexican cuisine.

(A) offered
(B) offer
(C) offers
(D) offering

어휘 authentic 정통인 cuisine 요리

해석 우리는 근무 후에 Rosie's Cantina를 방문할 계획인데, 그곳이 정통 멕시코 요리를 제공하기 때문이다.

해설 빈칸에 부사절의 동사가 들어가야 하므로 준동사인 (D)는 제외하고, 주어 it과 수가 일치하지 않는 (B)도 제외하자. 문맥상 Rosie's Cantina가 정통 멕시코 요리를 제공하는 것은 식당에서 늘 하는 일이므로, 지속적인 상태나 반복되는 행위를 나타내는 현재 시제 동사 (C)가 정답이다.

Actual Test

101 (B)	102 (D)	103 (D)	104 (A)	105 (B)
106 (C)	107 (B)	108 (B)	109 (C)	110 (C)
111 (C)	112 (C)	113 (D)	114 (C)	115 (C)
116 (D)	117 (D)	118 (A)	119 (A)	120 (D)
121 (D)	122 (C)	123 (D)	124 (D)	125 (D)
126 (D)	127 (A)	128 (B)	129 (B)	130 (B)
131 (D)	132 (A)	133 (C)	134 (B)	135 (B)
136 (A)	137 (A)	138 (C)	139 (B)	140 (D)
141 (B)	142 (D)	143 (C)	144 (B)	145 (C)
146 (A)				

Part 5

101. Based on recent data, Mesmio Trucking's plan to expand its business into Eastern Europe would be only ------- successful.

(A) conspicuously
(B) marginally
(C) regrettably
(D) intriguingly

어휘 expand 확장하다 conspicuously 눈에 잘 띄게

---

marginally 아주 조금, 미미하게 regrettably 유감스럽게 (도), 애석하게(도) intriguingly 흥미를 자아내어, 호기심을 자극하여

해석 최근 데이터를 근거로 보면 사업을 동유럽으로 확장하려는 Mesmio Trucking의 계획은 약간만 성공할 것이다.

해설 빈칸 앞뒤 would be only ------- successful(오직 [(A) 눈에 잘 띄게만 (B) 미미하게만 (C) 유감스럽게만 (D) 흥미를 자아내기만] 성공할 것이다.)의 의미를 자연스럽게 해주는 (B)가 정답이다.

---

102. Had Blue Veil Production not signed the contract with the young film director, another production company ------- so.

(A) should do
(B) will be doing
(C) has done
(D) would have done

어휘 sign a contract with ~와 계약을 체결하다 film director 영화감독

해석 만약 Blue Veil Production이 그 젊은 영화감독과 계약을 체결하지 않았다면 다른 제작사가 계약을 체결했을 것이다.

해설 Had Blue Veil Production not signed를 보면 가정법 과거완료 시제 문장의 부사절로 if를 생략하고 주어와 동사가 도치되었음을 알 수 있다. 그러므로 주절의 동사 자리인 빈칸에는 would have p.p.의 형태인 (D)가 정답으로 알맞다.

---

103. Neatly Apparel has seen an increase in sales ------- the introduction of their new outerwear line last quarter.

(A) over
(B) for
(C) besides
(D) since

어휘 apparel 의류 introduction 도입, 출시 outerwear 겉옷, 외투 line 제품군 last quarter 지난 분기

해석 Neatly Apparel은 지난 분기에 새 외투 제품군을 출시한 이후 판매량 증가를 경험했다.

해설 보기가 전치사로만 구성되어 있고 주절의 시제가 현재완료이면(has seen) since나 for가 정답이다. 빈칸 뒤의 '신제품 출시(the introduction of their new outerwear line)'는 과거 '시점'을 나타내므로 정답은 (D)이다.

104. Mr. Dixon could successfully complete the project by the end of the week ------- the necessary materials arrived today.

(A) if
(B) or
(C) even
(D) both

해석 필요한 재료가 오늘 도착한다면 Mr. Dixon이 주말까지 성공적으로 프로젝트를 마무리할 수 있을 것이다.

해설 주절의 동사(구)가 could successfully complete이고 빈칸 뒤의 동사가 arrived(과거)이므로 가정법 과거 시제 문장을 알 수 있다. 따라서 정답은 (A)이다.

---

105. It is essential that all components of the production line ------- with every quality standard listed on the form.

(A) associate
(B) comply
(C) compare
(D) bring

어휘 it is essential that ~가 필수다 component 부품, 구성 요소 associate 교제하다; 제휴하다 comply 준수하다, 따르다 compare 비교하다 list (목록에) 올리다, 기재하다

해석 생산 설비의 모든 부품은 양식에 기재된 모든 품질 기준을 준수하는 것이 필수이다.

해설 항상 짝으로 출제되는 어휘를 암기해 두자. 빈칸 뒤에 with가 있고 보기에 comply가 있으면 바로 정답으로 선택하자. associate with는 '~와 교제하다[어울리다]'라는 뜻이므로 뒤에 사람이 와야 하며, compare with(~와 비교되다)는 대부분 부정문이나 의문문에 사용한다.

---

106. If the board of directors ------- about the situation prior to the takeover, some measures could have been taken.

(A) have known
(B) has known
(C) had known
(D) knew

어휘 board of directors 이사회 prior to ~ 전에 takeover 기업[경영권] 인수 take a measure 조치를 취하다

해석 이사회가 인수 전에 상황을 알았더라면 어떤 조치가 있었을지도 모른다.

해설 if절에 빈칸이 있고, 주절의 동사가 could have been taken이므로 가정법 과거완료 시제 문장임을 알 수 있다. 그러므로 빈칸에는 had p.p. 형태인 (C)가 정답으로 알맞다.

---

107. Some 120 engineers and 10 organizations ------- collaboratively to develop a new superconductor since 2019 with an investment of 3.5 billion dollars.

(A) worked
(B) have worked
(C) work
(D) has worked

어휘 some 약, ~ 정도 organization 기관 collaboratively 협력하여, 합작으로 superconductor 초전도체

해석 120명 정도의 엔지니어들과 10개의 기관이 2019년부터 35억 달러를 투자하여 새로운 초전도체를 개발하기 위해 협력해서 일해 왔다.

해설 시제 문제에서 키워드 since가 있으면 정답은 현재완료이다. 복수 명사인 주어의 수와 일치하는 (B)가 정답이다.

---

108. Income tax returns should be ------- with relevant receipts and documents by the end of May.

(A) brought
(B) filed
(C) done
(D) declared

어휘 income tax return 소득세 신고 file (기관에) 제출하다 relevant 관련 있는, 적절한

해석 소득세 신고서는 5월 말까지 관련 영수증 및 문서와 함께 제출되어야 한다.

해설 동사 file의 용법을 알아두자. file a(n) (income) tax return(소득을 신고하다, 소득세 신고서를 제출하다), file a complaint[lawsuit](항의서를 제출하다, 소송을 제기하다) 등을 함께 암기하면 좋다.

---

109. Nowadays, electronic manufacturers are ------- with high precision instruments to build complex electronic and industrial components.

(A) taking

(B) evacuating
(C) dealing
(D) describing

어휘 nowadays 요즘 electronic 전자의 manufacturer 제조업자 deal with ~를 다루다 precision 정밀 evacuate 대피시키다 describe 묘사하다 instrument 기구, 기기

해석 요즘에는 전자제품 제조업체들이 복잡한 전자 및 산업용 부품을 만들기 위해 고정밀 기기를 다루고 있다.

해설 항상 짝으로 출제되는 어휘를 암기해 두자. 빈칸 뒤에 with가 있고 보기에 deal이 있으면 바로 정답으로 선택하자.

---

110. A professor from Worley University will ------- a speech on the future of the global biotech sector.

(A) talk
(B) open
(C) deliver
(D) take

어휘 give[make/deliver] a speech 연설하다 biotech 생명 공학 sector 분야

해석 Worley 대학교의 한 교수가 세계 생명 공학 분야의 미래에 대해 연설했다.

해설 'presentation(발표), speech(연설), address(연설), lecture(강연) 등을 하다'라는 의미의 표현에서 동사는 give, make, deliver를 사용한다. 그러므로 정답은 (C)이다.

---

111. I am sending this e-mail to ------- receipt of your formal letter of complaint to our customer service center.

(A) suggest
(B) connect
(C) acknowledge
(D) pronounce

어휘 acknowledge receipt of ~수신[수령] 사실을 알리다 complaint 항의

해석 저희 고객 서비스 센터에 보내신 공식 항의 서한을 수령했음을 알려 드리고자 이 이메일을 보냅니다.

해설 '~를 받았음을 알리다'라는 뜻의 acknowledge receipt of를 암기해 두면 문제 풀이가 쉬워진다.

---

112. The spokesperson of Sparrow International Airlines ------- a press conference once a decision has been made regarding a potential merger with Malmo Aviations.

(A) is held
(B) holds
(C) will hold
(D) has been held

어휘 spokesperson 대변인 press conference 기자 회견 make a decision 결정을 내리다 regarding ~에 관하여 potential 가능성이 있는, 잠재적인 merger 합병 aviation 항공(술)

해석 Sparrow International 항공사의 대변인은 Malmo 항공과의 잠재적 합병에 대한 결정이 내려지면 기자 회견을 열 것이다.

해설 빈칸 뒤에 목적어 a press conference가 있으므로 수동태 동사인 (A)와 (D)는 제외하자. once로 시작하는 시간 부사절의 시제가 현재완료(has been made)이므로 '미래'의 사건을 의미한다. 그러므로 주절의 동사 자리인 빈칸에는 미래형인 (C)가 정답으로 알맞다.

---

113. The new hotel built near the beach is expected to ------- more tourists to St. Corbino's Island, because of the fantastic view of the water that it provides.

(A) compel
(B) appeal
(C) detect
(D) attract

어휘 compel 강요하다, ~하게 만들다 appeal to ~에게 매력적이다, 마음을 끌다 detect 감지하다, 알아채다 attract 끌어들이다

해석 해변 근처에 지어지는 새 호텔은 그것이 제공하는 환상적인 바다 경관으로 인해 더 많은 관광객을 St. Corbino 섬에 끌어들일 것으로 예상된다.

해설 customers, shoppers, tourists, visitors, investors 등과 주로 함께 사용하는 동사는 (D) attract이다. compel은 to부정사를 목적격 보어로 사용하는 5형식 동사이며, appeal은 주로 전치사 to와 함께 사용한다.

114. The annual profit of the Singapore branch ------- for one-third of the total annual profit of CNTC Enterprise.

(A) calculates
(B) takes
(C) accounts
(D) features

어휘 account for (부분 · 비율을) 차지하다 feature 특별히 포함하다, 특징으로 삼다 one-third 3분의 1 enterprise 기업, 회사

해석 싱가포르 지점의 연수익이 CNTC 사(社)의 총 연수익의 3분의 1을 차지한다.

해설 '(부분 · 비율을) 차지하다'라는 뜻의 account for를 알아야 문제를 해결할 수 있다. 분수 읽는 법도 기억하자. ⅓은 one(a) third, ⅔는 two thirds이다.

---

115. The impending construction of several new office buildings in Berkshire has necessitated a ------- demand for highly skilled workers.

(A) lengthy
(B) plenty
(C) sizable
(D) durable

어휘 impending 곧 닥칠, 임박한 necessitate 필요로 하다 lengthy 너무 긴, 장황한 plenty 많음, 다량 sizable 꽤 큰, 상당한 durable 내구성이 있는, 오래가는 skilled 숙련된

해석 Berkshire에서 곧 있을 몇몇 새 사무실 건물 공사는 고도로 숙련된 노동자에 대한 상당한 수요를 필요로 하고 있다.

해설 명사 demand 앞 빈칸에는 형용사가 들어가야 하므로 명사인 (B)는 제외하자. a ------- demand([(A) 너무 긴 (C) 상당한 (D) 내구성 있는] 수요)의 의미를 자연스럽게 해주는 형용사 (C)가 정답이다.

---

116. It is the ------- of the marketing assistant to coordinate focus groups and write detailed reports.

(A) promotion
(B) offering
(C) production
(D) responsibility

어휘 promotion 홍보, 승진 offering 제공된 것, 내놓은 것 assistant 보좌역 coordinate 조직화[편성]하다 focus group 포커스 그룹(시장 조사나 여론 조사를 위해 각 계층을 대표하도록 뽑은 소수의 사람들로 이뤄진 그룹)

해석 포커스 그룹을 편성하고 자세한 보고서를 쓰는 것은 마케팅 보좌역의 책무이다.

해설 포커스 그룹을 편성하고 보고서를 쓰는 것처럼 특정한 업무나 책임을 나타내는 명사로 (D) responsibility가 알맞다.

---

117. Our team ------- in the policy meeting last Tuesday, but we had a scheduling conflict.

(A) can participate
(B) must have participated
(C) should participate
(D) would have participated

어휘 policy 정책 conflict 갈등, 충돌

해석 우리 팀은 지난주 화요일 정책 회의에 참석할 예정이었지만, 일정이 겹쳤습니다.

해설 이 문장은 "지난주 화요일에 우리 팀의 일정이 겹치지 않았다면 우리는 정책 회의에 참석했을 것이다(Our team would have participated in the policy meeting last Tuesday if we had not had a scheduling conflict)."라는 뜻으로 뒷절은 if절 대신 직설법을 사용한 것임을 알 수 있다. 따라서 앞절은 가정법 과거완료 시제 문장 내 주절의 동사 형태인 would have p.p.를 사용해야 한다. 그러므로 (D)가 정답이다.

---

118. ------- the proliferation of small, individual furnaces, glassblowing has become a more accessible and sought-after art medium.

(A) Because of
(B) Instead of
(C) Rather than
(D) Such as

어휘 proliferation 급증, 확산 individual 개인의, 1인용의 furnace 용광로 glassblowing 유리 불기(녹인 유리를 파이프 끝에서 불어서 형태를 만드는 것) accessible 접근 가능한, 쉽게 이용할 수 있는 sought-after 많은 사람들이 찾는, 인기가 높은 medium 표현 매체

해석 소형 1인용 용광로의 확산으로 유리 불기는 더 쉽게 이용할 수 있고 인기 있는 미술 매체가 되었다.

해설 소규모 1인용 용광로의 확산은 유리 불기가 인기를 얻게 된 원인이다. 그러므로 빈칸에는 이유를 나타내는 전치사 (A)가 알맞다.

119. Renewable energies are regarded as a key ------- in tackling global climate changes and energy shortage crisis.

(A) factor
(B) role
(C) basis
(D) agency

renewable 재생 가능한 be regarded as ~로 여겨지다 factor 요인, 요소 basis 기초 tackle 대처하다 shortage 부족 crisis 위기

해설 재생 에너지는 세계 기후 변화와 에너지 부족 위기에 대처하는 핵심 요소로 여겨진다.

해설 'Renewable energies are regarded as a key -------(재생 에너지는 핵심적인 [(A) 요소 (B) 역할 (C) 기초 (D) 대행사]로 여겨진다.)'의 의미를 자연스럽게 해주는 명사 (A)가 정답이다.

---

120. The Chief of Staff of Dalytown Hospital meets with the staff on a regular basis to ensure that procedures ------- correctly.

(A) to be performed
(B) would have performed
(C) had been performed
(D) are being performed

어휘 chief of staff 병원장 on a regular basis 정기적으로 ensure 확실하게 하다 correctly 바르게, 적절하게

해설 Dalytown 병원 원장은 정기적으로 직원들을 만나 절차들이 바르게 수행되고 있는지 확인한다.

해설 that절의 빈칸에 동사가 들어가야 하므로 준동사인 (A)는 제외하자. 빈칸 뒤에 목적어가 없으므로 능동태 동사인 (B)도 오답이다. 과거완료 시제인 (C)는 과거의 사건보다 먼저 일어난 일을 나타내는데 문장 속에 해당 사건이 없으므로 정답은 (D)이다.

---

121. ------- the city implemented parking restrictions in the downtown area, the number of people using public transportation has risen.

(A) If
(B) Why
(C) Yet
(D) Since

어휘 implement 시행하다 restriction 제한, 규제

해설 시에서 도심 지역에 주차 제한을 시행한 이후 대중교통

을 이용하는 사람들의 수가 증가했다.

해설 주절의 시제가 현재완료(has risen)이므로 과거의 시점을 나타내는 말과 함께 오는 (D)가 정답이다.

---

122. The attorneys have reported that the merger was successfully concluded ------- last-minute negotiations.

(A) as well as
(B) overall
(C) thanks to
(D) even if

어휘 attorney 변호사 merger 합병 conclude 끝내다, 마치다 last-minute 마지막 순간의, 막바지의 overall 전반적으로 thanks to ~ 덕분에 negotiation 협상

해설 변호사들은 막판 협상 덕분에 합병이 성공적으로 마무리되었다고 보고했다.

해설 합병이 성공적으로 완료된 것은 막판 협상 '덕분'이라고 해야 자연스러우므로 (C)가 정답이다.

---

123. In 2023, Pack-Pro Company ------- an internship program for trade school students, providing valuable experience in the field of electrical engineering.

(A) expressed
(B) specialized
(C) signaled
(D) established

어휘 specialize in ~를 전공하다 signal 신호를 보내다 establish 설립하다, 신설하다 trade school 직업 학교 field 분야 valuable 소중한, 유용한 electrical 전기의

해설 2023년에 Pack-Pro 사(社)는 직업 학교 학생들을 위한 인턴 프로그램을 신설하여 전기공학 분야에서의 소중한 경험을 제공했다.

해설 specialize는 '~를 전공하다'라는 의미로 in과 함께 사용하므로 제외하자. 빈칸 앞뒤 Pack-Pro Company ------- an internship program(Pack-Pro 사(社)는 인턴 프로그램을 [(A) 표현했다 (B) 신호로 나타냈다 (D) 신설했다])의 의미를 자연스럽게 해주는 동사 (D)가 정답이다.

---

124. ------- in the news, the Honorable Evelyn Chu is now garnering headlines with her proposal to drastically lower local taxes.

(A) Less
(B) Enough
(C) Apart
(D) Seldom

어휘 Honorable 고위 관직자에게 붙이는 경칭 garner
headlines 헤드라인을 장식하다 proposal 법안, 계획
drastically 급격하게, 대폭

해석 뉴스에 거의 등장하지 않는 Evelyn Chu 의원은 요즘 지
방세를 대폭 낮추는 법안으로 머리기사를 장식하고 있다.

해설 원래는 거의 뉴스에 등장하지 않는 정치가가 요즘 들어
파격적인 법안으로 신문 지면을 장식하고 있다는 내용
이 자연스러우므로 (D)가 정답으로 알맞다. 쉼표 앞은
부사절(Although she is seldom in the news)을 접
속사(Although)와 분사(being)를 생략한 분사 구문
(Seldom in the news)으로 바꾼 것이다.

---

125. After assessing the G-P Meridian
payroll management system, we
concluded that it was the only one
------- for our needs.

(A) cooperative
(B) deliberate
(C) extensive
(D) adequate

어휘 assess 평가하다 payroll 급여 업무 conclude 결론을
내리다 cooperative 협력하는 deliberate 고의의, 의도
적인 extensive 광범위한 adequate 적합한

해석 G-P Meridian 급여 관리 시스템을 평가해 본 후 우리
는 그것이 우리의 요구에 적합한 유일한 것이라는 결론
을 내렸다.

해설 빈칸 앞뒤 the only one ------- for our needs(우
리의 필요에 [(A) 협력하는 (B) 의도적인 (C) 광범위한
(C) 적합한] 유일한 것)의 의미를 자연스럽게 해주는 형
용사 (D)가 정답이다.

---

126. Ms. Hong has correctly forecast that
sales would increase ------- as the
company's radio commercial keeps
being aired.

(A) arguably
(B) reportedly
(C) productively
(D) incrementally

어휘 arguably 이론의 여지는 있지만; (최상급 앞에서) 거의 틀림없
이 reportedly 전하는 바에 따르면, 소문에 의하면

incrementally 점진적으로 commercial 광고 (방송)
keep V-ing ~을 계속하다 air 방송하다

해석 Ms. Hong은 회사의 라디오 광고가 계속 방송됨에 따
라 판매량이 점진적으로 증가할 것이라고 정확하게 예
측했다.

해설 '점차 증가할 것이다'라는 의미가 자연스러우므로 (D)가
정답이다. (A) arguably와 (B) reportedly는 문장 전체
를 수식하는 부사로, arguably는 최상급 형용사나 부
사를 수식하기도 한다. 그러므로 동사(구) would
increase를 수식하기에 두 부사는 적합하지 않다.

---

127. We will have already begun work on
a new building in Surabaya ------- we
end the construction in Abu Dhabi.

(A) by the time
(B) as soon as
(C) except when
(D) in the same way

어휘 end 끝내다 construction 공사

해석 Abu Dhabi에서 공사를 끝냈을 때쯤이면 우리는 이미
Surabaya에서 새 건물 작업을 시작했을 것이다.

해설 미래완료 시제 동사 will have already begun과
'------- we end'를 보고 정답을 알아내야 한다. 미
래의 특정 시간을 나타내는 'by the time + 주어 + 현
재 시제 동사'가 미래완료 시제인 주절에 어울리므로
(A)가 정답이다.

---

128. Ms. Xu's responsibilities as Mr. Al-
Omani's assistant includes -------
him on the latest financial news.

(A) discussing
(B) briefing
(C) resuming
(D) narrating

어휘 brief 요약하다 resume 재개하다 narrate 이야기를 들려
주다

해석 Mr. Al-Omani의 비서로서 Ms. Xu의 업무에는 그에게
최신 금융 뉴스에 대해 요약해 주는 일이 포함된다.

해설 빈칸 뒤에 'sb on sth(him on the latest financial
news)'을 보면 알맞은 동사를 알 수 있다. brief sb on
sth과 notify[inform/advise/remind] sb of sth 구문
을 기억하자. 그러므로 (B)가 정답이다.

---

129. By this time next year, Komplet
Industries ------- two new plants in

East Java.

(A) launches
(B) will have launched
(C) is launching
(D) had launched

어휘 launch 착수하다, 시작하다 plant 공장

해석 내년 이맘때쯤이면 Komplet Industries는 East Java 에서 두 개의 새로운 공장을 시작할 것이다.

해설 'by + 미래 시점'이 있으면 미래완료 시제 문장이므로 (B)가 정답으로 알맞다.

---

130. C.F. Martin & Co. ------- high-quality acoustic guitars for almost two centuries.

(A) to be designed
(B) has been designing
(C) was designed
(D) is designing

어휘 acoustic 전자 장치를 쓰지 않는

해석 C.F. Martin & Co.는 거의 두 세기 동안 고품질의 어쿠스틱 기타를 디자인해 왔다.

해설 문장의 빈칸에 동사가 들어가야 하므로 준동사인 (A)는 제외하자. 빈칸 뒤에 목적어 high-quality acoustic guitars가 있으므로 수동태 동사인 (C)도 오답이다. '거의 두 세기 동안(for almost two centuries)'이라는 표현은 현재완료 시제 문장에 자연스러우므로 (B)가 정답이다.

Part 6

Questions 131-134 refer to the following customer notice.

> **The Stadni Inn: Reservations**
>
> We suggest making reservations because hotel accommodations in Stadni are very ¹³¹·limited. Accommodations will be secured upon receipt of a one-night deposit or 50 percent of total room charges for stays exceeding one night. Reservations canceled seven days or more before the planned arrival date ¹³²·will be reimbursed in their entirety. Should a reservation need to be cancelled within

seven days of your scheduled arrival date, you will be charged for the entire ¹³³·length of your stay. ¹³⁴·This policy applies to those who depart earlier than expected as well.

131-134번 문제는 다음 안내문에 관한 것입니다.

> **Stadni 호텔: 예약**
>
> Stadni 호텔은 숙박 시설이 매우 제한되어 있으므로 예약을 권장합니다. 숙박 시설은 1박 요금에 해당하는 보증금이나 1박을 초과하는 투숙을 위해서는 총 요금의 50퍼센트가 접수되는 대로 확보됩니다. 예정된 입실 날짜에서 7일 이상 남겨두고 취소된 예약은 전액 환불됩니다. 예약이 예정된 입실 날짜로부터 7일 이내에 취소해야 한다면 전체 투숙 기간에 대한 요금이 청구됩니다. 이 정책은 예정보다 일찍 퇴실하는 분들께도 적용됩니다.

어휘 inn 호텔 accommodations 숙박 시설 secure 확보하다 (up)on + 명사[V-ing] ~하자마자 receipt 받기, 수령 deposit 착수금, 보증금 charge 요금; 부과하다 exceed 초과하다 reimburse 환불하다 in its[their] entirety 통째로, 전부 length 길이, 기간 policy 정책 apply to ~에 적용되다, 해당되다 depart 출발하다, 떠나다 than expected 예정보다 as well 또한

---

131. (A) limitation
(B) limit
(C) limits
(D) limited

어휘 limitation 한계, 규제 limit 제한하다

해설 빈칸 앞의 부사 very를 제외하면 그 앞에 be동사가 있는 것을 알 수 있다. be동사 뒤 빈칸에는 형용사가 정답이다. 그런데 보기 중 형용사가 없을 때는 분사를 선택하면 되므로 (D)가 정답이다.

---

132. **(A) will be reimbursed**
(B) were reimbursed
(C) are reimbursing
(D) had been reimbursing

해설 빈칸 뒤에 목적어가 없으므로 수동태 동사 (A)와 (B) 중 알맞은 시제를 선택해야 한다. 예약을 취소하는 경우 숙박비 환급에 관한 규정을 설명하고 있으므로 미래 시제가 알맞다. 그러므로 (A)가 정답이다.

133.
(A) area
(B) degree
(C) length
(D) week

해설 빈칸이 있는 문장이 "예약이 예정된 입실 날짜로부터 7일 이내에 취소되어야 한다면 전체 투숙 기간에 대한 요금이 청구됩니다."라는 의미가 자연스러우므로 '기간'이라는 뜻의 (C) length를 정답으로 선택해야 한다.

134.
(A) Hotel guests are granted access to our fitness center.
(B) This policy applies to those who depart earlier than expected as well.
(C) Furthermore, we are soon to launch another hotel in the region.
(D) We hope that your experience with us has been satisfactory.

어휘 grant 허가하다 access 입장, 접근 furthermore 더욱이 be to-V ~할 예정이다 launch 착수하다, 시작하다 satisfactory 만족스러운

해석 (A) 호텔 고객께는 헬스클럽 입장이 허용됩니다.
(B) 이 정책은 예정보다 일찍 퇴실하는 분들께도 적용됩니다.
(C) 더욱이 우리는 곧 지역에서 또 다른 호텔을 시작할 예정입니다.
(D) 저희와 함께 하신 경험이 만족스러우셨기를 바랍니다.

해설 앞 문장이 예정된 입실 날짜로부터 7일이 남지 않은 때에 예약을 취소하면 전체 투숙 기간에 대한 요금이 청구된다는 내용이므로 "이 정책은 예정보다 일찍 퇴실하는 분들께도 적용됩니다."가 이어지는 것이 부연 설명으로 자연스럽다.

Questions 135-138 refer to the following article.

December 8 — Today the Hagersville City Council approved an agreement with Eurosan Enterprises. In accordance with the agreement, Eurosan [135.]will develop the 22-acre lot on State Street. The proposal calls for the construction of both offices and retail stores on the site. Hagersville's Mayor, Eun Sung Han, expresses his welcome for the [136.]economic opportunities this project will afford the area. "We expect the project to create 500 permanent full-time jobs," he said. "I'm delighted that it was finally approved after so many postponements." [137.]While the city is anxious for work to get underway, delays are typical for major commercial endeavors such as this. Aishah Noor, a Eurosan spokesperson, has said that it is expected to take five years to complete the project, yet cautions that setbacks may still occur. "We've given the council our best [138.]estimate, but it's not possible to foresee all complications that may arise," Noor said.

135-138번 문제는 다음 기사에 관한 것입니다.

12월 8일 – Hagersville 시의회는 오늘 Eurosan Enterprises와의 협약을 승인했다. 협약에 따라 Eurosan은 State 가(街)에 있는 22에이커의 부지를 개발할 것이다. 이 제안은 부지에 사무실과 소매상점을 모두 건설할 것을 요구한다. Hagersville 시장 Eun Sung Han은 이 프로젝트가 지역에 제공할 경제적 기회에 환영을 표한다. 그는 말했다. "우리는 이 프로젝트가 500개의 정규직 일자리를 창출할 것으로 예상합니다. 많은 연기 끝에 마침내 승인되어서 기쁩니다." 시에서는 일이 시작되기를 간절히 바라지만, 이번과 같이 중요한 상업적 시도에서 지연은 일반적이다. Eurosan 대변인 Aishah Noor는 프로젝트를 완료하는 데 5년이 걸릴 것으로 예상된다고 말했지만, 차질은 여전히 생길 수 있다고 주의를 준다. Noor는 "저희가 의회에 최선의 추정치를 제시했지만, 발생할 수 있는 모든 복잡한 문제를 예견하는 것은 가능하지 않습니다."라고 말했다.

어휘 approve 승인하다 agreement 협정, 협약 in accordance with ~에 따라 acre 에이커(토지 면적 단위; 1 acre = 4046.8㎡) lot 지역, 부지 call for ~을 요구하다 retail 소매의 site 부지, 터, 현장 afford 제공하다 permanent 영구적인 postponement 연기, 뒤로 미루기 be anxious for sb to-V ~가 ~하기를 몹시 바라다 get underway 시작하다 delay 지연, 연기 typical 전형적인, 일반적인 endeavor 노력, 시도 spokesperson 대변인 caution 주의를 주다, 경고하다 setback 차질 estimate 추정(치), 추산 foresee 예견하다 complication 복잡한 문제 arise 생기다, 발생하다

135.
(A) to develop
(B) will develop
(C) has developed
(D) could have developed

해설 문장의 빈칸에는 동사가 들어가야 하므로 준동사인 (A)는 제외하자. 앞 문장에서 '오늘 협약을 승인했다'고 했으므로(Today the Hagersville City Council approved an agreement with Eurosan Enterprises.), 부지 개발은 앞으로 일어날 일임을 알 수 있다. 그러므로 미래 시제인 (B)가 정답이다.

136.
(A) economic
(B) unforeseen
(C) volunteer
(D) frequent

어휘 unforeseen 예측하지 못한, 뜻밖의 frequent 잦은, 빈번한

해설 이어지는 문장에서 500개의 일자리가 생길 것을 예상한다고 했으므로(We expect the project to create 500 permanent full-time jobs,) 이 프로젝트가 제공하는 것은(this project will afford the area) '경제적' 기회이다. 그러므로 (A)가 정답이다.

137.
(A) While the city is anxious for work to get underway, delays are typical for major commercial endeavors such as this.
(B) Nearby tenants, however, have raised some valid worries about the construction noise.
(C) In spite of the assurance of city officials to grant the company a long-term agreement, they now may have to reconsider.
(D) Council members will vote on four different proposals submitted by the architects.

어휘 nearby 인근의 tenant 세입자 raise 제기하다, 언급하다 valid 타당한 in spite of ~에도 불구하고 assurance 확약 official (고위) 공무원 long-term 장기적인 reconsider 재고하다 proposal 기획안 architect 건축가

해석 (A) 시에서는 일이 시작되기를 간절히 바랐지만, 이번과 같이 중요한 상업적 시도에서 지연은 일반적이다.
(B) 그러나 인근 세입자들은 공사 소음에 대해 몇 가지 타당한 우려를 제기했다.

(C) 시 공무원들이 회사에 장기 협약을 내주겠다고 확약했음에도 불구하고 이제 그들은 재고해야 할지도 모른다.
(D) 의회 의원들은 건축가들이 제출한 다른 네 개의 기획안에 투표할 것이다.

해설 "이번과 같이 중요한 상업적 시도에서 지연은 일반적이다"가 프로젝트가 여러 번 연기되었다고 말하는(I'm delighted that it was finally approved after so many postponements.) 앞 문장에 대한 부연 설명으로 자연스럽다.

138.
(A) argument
(B) background
(C) estimate
(D) combination

어휘 argument 말다툼, 논쟁 estimate 추정(치), 추산 combination 조합

해설 We've given the council our best -------라고 말했으므로 의회에 무엇을 주었는지 알아야 한다. 앞 문장에서 프로젝트를 완료하는 데 5년이 걸릴 것으로 예상된다고(it is expected to take five years to complete the project) 했으므로 회사가 의회에 준 것은 소요 기간에 대한 '추산치'이다. 그러므로 (C)가 정답이다.

Part 7

Questions 139-141 refer to the following article.

Engineering Company to Expand

August 25 — [139.]Rosette, a well-known French engineering company recognized for its energy-efficient power generators, unveiled today its plans for expansion.

[139.]Speaking at a press conference in Nantes, Christian Frémont, the President of Rosette, announced plans to build a new global headquarters in the city.

[139.140.]Construction projects are also slated for the company's foreign subsidiaries, Astaldi, in Rome, Italy, and Belgatech, Inc., in Brussels, Belgium. Construction of extra production plants and expansion of personnel will occur at both companies.

In order to prioritize ocean power and other alternative energy sources, Rosette will establish an additional subsidiary in another international market. When pressed by reporters to provide more details, Frémont chose not to disclose the specific location, but instead mentioned that "Northern Europe has great potential in this regard and is crucial for our long-term objectives."

141.For industry analyst Marc Fiero, this comes as no surprise. "Rosette has invested heavily in ocean power technology, making Northern European nations like Denmark or Norway ideal venues for the company's expansion."

Frémont's final comment at the press conference is certain to fuel speculation on this point. When asked what his short-term goals were, he replied that he is "currently planning a vacation by the seaside in Denmark."

139-141번 문제는 다음 기사에 관한 것입니다.

엔지니어링 회사 확장 예정

8월 25일 – 에너지 효율이 높은 발전기로 인정받는 프랑스의 유명 엔지니어링 회사 Rosette가 오늘 확장 계획을 밝혔다.

Nantes에서 열린 기자 회견에서 Rosette 회장 Christian Frémont는 그 도시에 새 글로벌 본사를 건설할 계획을 발표했다.

공사 프로젝트가 이 회사의 해외 자회사들인 Astaldi(이탈리아 로마)와 Belgatech Inc.(벨기에 브뤼셀)에서도 예정되어 있다. 두 회사 모두에서 추가 생산 공장의 건설과 인원 확충이 있을 것이다.

Rosette는 해양 발전과 기타 대체 에너지원에 우선순위를 두기 위해 다른 국제 시장에 추가로 자회사를 설립할 것이다. 더 자세한 사항을 알려달라는 기자들의 요청에 Frémont는 구체적인 지역은 밝히지 않기로 하면서, 대신 "북유럽은 이 분야에서 큰 잠재력을 가지고 있으며 우리의 장기적인 목표에 매우 중요하다."라고 언급했다.

업계 분석가 Marc Fiero에게 이것은 전혀 놀라운 일이 아니다. "Rosette는 해양 발전 기술에 많이 투자해 왔고 이것은 덴마크나 노르웨이 같은 북유럽 국가들을 회사의 확장을 위한 이상적인 장소가 되게 합니다."

기자 회견에서 Frémont의 마지막 발언은 분명히 이 점에 대한 억측을 부채질할 것이다. 단기적인 목표는 무언인지 질문받았을 때 그는 "현재 덴마크 해변에서의 휴가를 계획하고 있다."라고 대답했다.

어휘 expand 확장하다 recognized for ~로 인정받은 energy-efficient 에너지 효율이 높은 power generator 발전기 unveil 공개하다. 발표하다 expansion 확장 press conference 기자 회견 headquarters 본사 be slated for ~할 예정이다 subsidiary 자(子)회사 plant 공장 personnel 인원, 직원들 prioritize 우선적으로 처리하다 alternative energy source 대체 에너지원 establish 설립하다 press sb to-V ~에게 ~하라고 재촉하다 reporter 기자 disclose 발표하다, 공개하다 specific 구체적인 location 장소 mention 언급하다 potential 잠재적인 in this regard 이 점에 관하여 crucial 매우 중요한, 결정적인 long-term 장기적인 objective 목적, 목표 analyst 분석가 come as no surprise 놀라운 일이 아니다 heavily 심하게, 많이 venue 장소 be certain to-V 분명히 ~하다 fuel 부채질하다 speculation 추측, (어림)짐작 short-term 단기적인

[문장 분석]
. . . .

Engineering Company to Expand

➡ 영자 신문은 통상적으로 제목에서 be동사와 관사를 생략한다. 원래 문장은 An engineering company is to expand.이다.

➡ 원래 문장에 들어 있는 be to-V를 해석할 줄 알아야 한다. 문맥에 따라 '① 예정 ② 의무 ③ 의도 ④ 가능 ⑤ 운명'의 의미로 해석할 수 있다. '예정'이나 '의무'의 의미로 대부분 사용된다.

---

139. How does Rosette plan to expand?

(A) By increasing funding for research and development

(B) By enlarging its international presence

(C) By generating greater sales in regions beyond Northern Europe

(D) By consolidating with another company

어휘 funding 자금 지원 research and development (R&D) 연구 개발 presence 입지 generate 일으키다, 창출하다 consolidate 통합하다, 합병하다

해석 Rosette는 어떻게 확장할 계획인가?
(A) 연구 개발의 자금을 늘림으로써
(B) 해외에서의 입지를 확대함으로써

(C) 북유럽 이외의 지역에서 더 많은 매출을 창출함으로써

(D) 다른 회사와 합병함으로써

해설 첫 문장에서 Rosette는 확장 계획이 있다고(unveiled today its plans for expansion) 말하고, 이어지는 문장에서 확장 방식을 설명하고 있다. 글로벌 본사를 수립하고(plans to build a new global headquarters) 이탈리아와 벨기에에 있는 해외 자회사에서 추가로 생산 공장을 짓고 인원을 확충하겠다고(Construction projects are also slated for the company's foreign subsidiaries, Astaldi, in Rome, Italy, and Belgatech, Inc., in Brussels, Belgium. Construction of extra production plants and expansion of personnel will occur at both companies.) 했으므로, Rosette의 확장 방식은 해외에서의 입지 확대이다.

---

140. What is stated as one of Rosette's goals?

(A) To recruit additional staff in Norway

(B) To develop a new line of generators

(C) To focus exclusively on ocean power

(D) To add to its facilities in Rome

어휘 recruit 모집하다, 채용하다　line 제품군　generator 발전기　exclusively 오로지 (~만)　add to ~을 늘리다

해석 Rosette의 목표 중 하나로 무엇이 언급되는가?

(A) 노르웨이에서 직원을 추가로 모집하는 것

(B) 새 발전기 제품군을 개발하는 것

(C) 해양 발전에만 집중하는 것

(D) 로마에서 시설을 확충하는 것

해설 셋째 문단에 로마에 있는 자회사에 새 생산 공장이 지어질 것이라고 나와 있다(Construction projects are also slated for the company's foreign subsidiaries, Astaldi, in Rome, Italy, and Belgatech, Inc., in Brussels, Belgium. Construction of extra production plants and expansion of personnel will occur at both companies).

---

141. What does Mr. Fiero suggest about Denmark?

(A) It is gaining in popularity among tourists.

(B) It possesses resources for alternative energy.

(C) Fuel costs are lower there than elsewhere.

(D) Rosette might relocate its headquarters there.

어휘 gain in popularity 인기를 얻다　possess 소유하다　fuel cost 연료비　elsewhere (어딘가) 다른 곳에서[으로]　relocate 이전하다

해석 Mr. Fiero는 덴마크에 대해 무엇을 암시하는가?

(A) 관광객들 사이에 인기를 얻고 있다.

(B) 대체 에너지 자원을 보유하고 있다.

(C) 연료비가 다른 곳보다 낮다.

(D) Rosette가 그곳으로 본사를 이전할지 모른다.

해설 다섯 번째 문단에 Mr. Fiero의 말이 실려 있다. Rosette가 해양 발전 기술에 많이 투자해 왔기 때문에 덴마크나 노르웨이와 같은 북유럽 국가들이 회사 확장에 이상적인 장소라고(Rosette has invested heavily in ocean power technology, making Northern European nations like Denmark or Norway ideal venues for the company's expansion.) 한 말은 덴마크에 해양에너지 자원, 즉 대체 에너지원이 풍부하게 있음을 암시하고 있다.

Questions 142-146 refer to the following article, e-mail, and floor plan.

[143.]The grand opening of the Ocean City Mall in Sarasota is scheduled for October, and the available spaces are filling up rapidly. When the mall opens, business is expected to take off just as quickly. [144.]While the Ocean City Mall is not the only such establishment in Sarasota, it will be the first to open directly onto the boardwalk. The mall will feature boutiques, specialty stores, and various food vendors.

The mall management aims to attract business owners from outside of Sarasota. According to Stacy Weston, a rental manager, many of the businesses that have rented space are new to the area. "This was by design," she explained. "The Sarasota City Council has offered a tax incentive to the mall owners as a way to encourage them to bring new businesses to Sarasota.

We're still a little short of our goal of having 70% of our spaces rented to nonlocal businesses. [145.]We are currently providing discounted rental prices on new leases for out-of-town businesses."

[142.]Applications from business owners seeking to take out a lease on retail and dining spaces will be accepted until the June 15 deadline. Interested business owners are invited to contact Weston by e-mail at sweston@oceancitymall.com.

142-146번 문제는 다음 기사와 이메일, 평면도에 관한 것입니다.

Sarasota의 Ocean City 쇼핑몰 그랜드 오픈이 10월로 예정되어 있으며 사용할 수 있는 공간이 빠르게 채워지고 있다. 쇼핑몰이 문을 열면 비즈니스도 그만큼 빠르게 성장할 것으로 예상된다. Ocean City가 Sarasota에서 유일한 쇼핑몰은 아니지만, 해변 판자 산책로 쪽으로 바로 통하는 최초의 몰이 될 것이다. 쇼핑몰에는 양품점과 특산품점, 다양한 음식점들을 포함할 것이다.

쇼핑몰 경영진은 Sarasota 외부에서 사업주들을 유치하는 것을 목표로 하고 있다. 임대 담당자 Stacy Weston에 따르면 공간을 임차한 사업체 중 상당수가 이 지역에 새로 들어왔다. 그녀는 "이것은 계획된 것입니다."라고 설명했다. "Sarasota 시의회가 쇼핑몰 소유주들이 Sarasota로 신규 사업체들을 유치하도록 독려하는 방편으로 세금 우대를 제안했습니다. 우리는 전체 공간의 70퍼센트를 이 지역 출신이 아닌 사업체들에 임대한다는 목표에 아직 약간 못 미쳤습니다. 현재 외지에서 온 사업체들과의 신규 임대차 계약에 대해 할인된 임대료를 제공하고 있습니다."

소매업과 식당 공간을 임차하려는 사업주들의 신청은 6월 15일 마감일까지 접수될 것이다. 관심 있는 사업주는 이메일 sweston@oceancitymall.com로 Weston에게 연락하면 된다.

어휘 floor plan (건물의) 평면도 be scheduled for ~로 예정되어 있다 fill up 가득 차다 rapidly 신속하게, 빠르게 take off 급격히 인기를 얻다. 성공하다 establishment 기관, 시설 open into/onto 통하다. 이어지다 boardwalk (해변가의) 판자길, 판자 산책로 specialty store 특산품점 vendor 판매상 aim to-V ~하는 것을 목표로 하다 rental 임차, 대여 by design 고의로, 계획적으로 incentive 장려책, 우대책 encourage 독려하다 be short of ~에 이르지 못하다. 못 미치다 lease 임대차 계약 out-of-town 외지의 application 신청 seek to-V ~하려고 (시도)하다 take out a lease on 세를 주고 빌리다

dining 식사 be invited to-V ~하도록 요청받다

From: Michele Zampas <mzampas@tmail.com>
To: Stacy Weston <sweston@oceancitymall.com>
Date: April 29
Subject: Available space

Dear Ms. Weston,

[145.146.]I am a friend of Edgar Thompson, the owner of The Shoe Wonder. He recommended that I reach out to you regarding renting a space in the Ocean City Mall. [145.]He informed me about a valuable benefit that he had received, which is available to business owners such as myself. I possess Witchery Fashion, an establishment specializing in contemporary women's apparel. [145.]At the moment, I maintain two retail locations in the nearby city of Fruitville, and I am pondering the possibility of expanding to Sarasota. [146.]If possible, I would like to be located near my friend's store, but I prefer a space that is not adjacent to any restaurants or food services. A space on the boardwalk side that overlooks the beach would be ideal.

Would you be able to provide me with a map of the mall that shows any available spaces that might meet my needs? Could you also give me the dimensions of each space and the cost of the rentals?

Thank you in advance.

Michele Zampas

발신: Michele Zampas <mzampas@tmail.com>
수신: Stacy Weston <sweston@oceancitymall.com>
날짜: 4월 29일
제목: 이용할 수 있는 공간

Ms. Weston께,

저는 The Shoe Wonder의 소유주인 Edgar Thompson

의 친구입니다. 그가 Ocean City 쇼핑몰의 공간을 임차하는 것에 관하여 당신께 연락해 보라고 추천했습니다. 자기가 받은 유용한 혜택에 대해 알려 주었는데, 저와 같은 사업주가 이용할 수 있다고 했습니다. 저는 Witchery Fashion을 소유하고 있으며 현대 여성복을 전문으로 하는 가게입니다. 현재는 가까운 Fruitville 시에서 두 개의 소매점을 운영하는데, Sarasota로 확장할 가능성을 고려하고 있습니다. 가능하다면 제 친구의 가게 가까이에 위치하길 원하지만, 식당이나 식품 서비스업과 인접하지 않은 공간을 선호합니다. 해변이 내려다보이는 판자길 쪽에 있는 공간이라면 이상적이겠습니다.

제 요구 사항을 충족시킬 수 있는 사용 가능한 공간을 보여주는 쇼핑몰 지도를 제공해 주실 수 있을까요? 또한 각 공간의 면적과 임차 비용도 알려 주실 수 있나요?

미리 감사드립니다.

Michele Zampas

어휘 reach out to 연락을 취하다 regarding ~에 관하여 rent 임차하다, 빌리다 inform A about B A에게 B에 대해 알리다 specialize in ~을 전문으로 다루다 contemporary 현대의 at the moment 지금, 현재 maintain 유지하다 retail location 소매점 nearby 인근의 ponder 숙고하다 be located ~에 위치하다 adjacent to ~에 인접한 boardwalk (해변가) 판자 길, 판자 산책로 overlook 내려다보이다 meet 충족시키다 dimension 면적 rental 임대, 임차 in advance 미리, 사전에

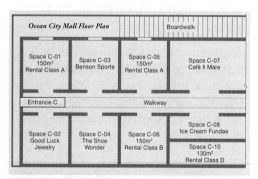

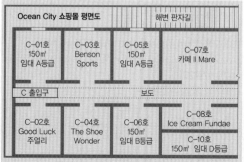

어휘 floor plan (건물의) 평면도 class 등급

---

142. What is the purpose of the article?

(A) To explain the cause of the delay in the opening of a new mall

(B) To announce plans to construct a new mall

(C) To review the stores and eateries in a new mall

(D) To encourage business owners to lease space in a new mall

어휘 cause 원인 eatery 음식점, 식당 review 평가하다 lease 임대하다

해석 기사의 목적은 무엇인가?
(A) 새 쇼핑몰 개장이 지연되는 원인을 설명하는 것
(B) 새 쇼핑몰 건설 계획을 발표하는 것
(C) 새 쇼핑몰의 상점과 음식점을 평가하는 것
(D) 사업주에게 새 쇼핑몰의 공간을 임대하도록 독려하는 것

해설 기사 문제에서는 주제나 목적이 도입부에 드러나지 않는 경우가 종종 있다. 첫 문단에서는 새로 문을 열 예정인 쇼핑몰이 고객을 끌어들일 만한 요소로 해변 판자길을 언급하고 있으며, 둘째 문단은 외부에서 들어오는 사업주에게 주어지는 임차료 할인 혜택을 소개하고 있다. 또한 마지막 문단에서 임차 신청의 마감 기한과 문의처를 알려주고 있다(Applications from business owners seeking to take out a lease on retail and dining spaces will be accepted until the June 15 deadline. Interested business owners are invited to contact Weston by e-mail at sweston@oceancitymall.com). 전체 내용을 종합하면 기사의 목적은 사업주들에게 쇼핑몰 입점을 권장하는 것이다.

---

143. In the article, the phrase "take off" in paragraph 1, line 5, is closest in meaning to

(A) remove

(B) discount

(C) increase quickly

(D) leave suddenly

해석 기사에서 첫 문단 다섯째 줄의 어휘 take off와 의미상 가장 가까운 것은?
(A) (옷 등을) 벗다
(B) 할인하다
(C) 빠르게 증가하다
(D) 갑자기 떠나다

해설 보기의 동사 네 개가 모두 take off의 동의어가 될 수 있지만, 앞의 문장과 함께 읽어 보면 개업 예정인 쇼핑몰의 비어 있는 공간이 빠르게 채워지는 것처럼, 개업 후에는 입점 업체들의 사업도 빠르게 성장할 것이라는 내용임을 알 수 있다. 그러므로 본문의 take off를 increase quickly로 바꾸면 business is expected to increase quickly가 되고, 영업 실적이 금방 증가할 것이라는 뜻이므로 (C)가 정답이다.

---

144. What is stated about the Ocean City Mall?

(A) It will be the only mall in Sarasota.
(B) It will have direct access to the boardwalk.
(C) It will include 70 retail spaces to rent.
(D) It will open for business on June 15.

어휘 have access to ~에 접근할 수 있다 direct 직접적인

해석 Ocean City 쇼핑몰에 대해 무엇이 진술되어 있는가?
(A) Sarasota에서 유일한 쇼핑몰이다.
(B) 해변 판자길에 직접 출입할 수 있다.
(C) 임대할 수 있는 70개의 소매업 공간이 있다.
(D) 6월 15일에 영업을 시작한다.

해설 기사 첫 문단에서 Ocean City는 해변 판자길로 바로 통하는 최초의 쇼핑몰이 될 것이라고(it will be the first to open directly onto the boardwalk.) 말하고 있다.

---

145. What is indicated about Mr. Thompson?

(A) He is a friend of Ms. Weston.
(B) His business was the first to open.
(C) He is paying a reduced rental rate.
(D) His store overlooks the beach.

어휘 reduced 할인된 rental rate 임대료, 임차료

해석 Mr. Thompson에 관하여 무엇이 나타나 있는가?
(A) Ms. Weston의 친구이다.
(B) 그의 사업체가 처음으로 문을 연 곳이다.
(C) 할인된 임차료를 내고 있다.
(D) 그의 상점은 해변을 내려다보고 있다.

연계 추론 기사 둘째 문단 마지막 문장을 보면 Sarasota 외부에서 들어오는 사업체들은 Ocean City 쇼핑몰에서 임차료 할인 혜택을 받을 수 있음을 알 수 있다(We are currently providing discounted rental prices on new leases for out-of-town businesses). 그리고 이메일을 읽어 보면 Ms. Zampas는 인근 도시에서 Sarasota로 사업을 확장하려는 사업주이므로(At the moment, I maintain two retail locations in the nearby city of Fruitville, and I am pondering the possibility of expanding to Sarasota.), 이 임차료 할인 혜택을 받을 수 있음을 알 수 있다. 그런데 이 메일 앞부분을 보면, Ms. Zampas와 같은 사업주가 받을 수 있는 혜택을 그의 친구인 Mr. Thompson도 받고 있다고 나와 있으므로(He informed me about a valuable benefit that he had received, which is available to business owners such as myself), 즉 Mr. Thompson도 현재 할인된 임차료를 내며 사업을 하고 있다는 사실을 추론할 수 있다.

---

146. What space will Ms. Zampas most likely be interested in renting?

(A) Space C-01
(B) Space C-05
(C) Space C-06
(D) Space C-10

해석 Ms. Zampas는 어느 공간을 임차하는 데 가장 관심이 있겠는가?
(A) C-01호
(B) C-05호
(C) C-06호
(D) C-10호

연계 추론 이메일에 따르면 Ms. Zampas의 친구 Mr. Thompson은 The Shoe Wonder를 운영하고 있다. 친구의 가게 가까운 곳에 자리를 얻고 싶다고 했으므로(I would like to be located near my friend's store), 평면도에서 C-01호와 C-05호, C-06호를 고를 수 있다. 그중 해변이 내려다보이는 판자길 쪽 자리(A space on the boardwalk side that overlooks the beach would be ideal.)라는 조건에도 부합되는 C-01호가 Ms. Zampas가 가장 관심을 가질 만한 자리이다. 그리고 식품 판매점 인근은 싫다고 했으므로(but I prefer a space that is not adjacent to any restaurants or food services.), 카페 옆의 C-05호와 아이스크림 가게 옆의 C-06호는 Ms. Zampas가 원하지 않는 곳이다.

PART 5 & 6 Exercise

101 (C)	**102** (B)	**103** (C)	**104** (C)	**105** (A)
106 (A)	**107** (C)	**108** (D)	**109** (A)	**110** (A)
111 (B)	**112** (B)	**113** (C)	**114** (D)	**115** (D)

101. Highly ------- is Carnegie Mellon College as a business school.

(A) regard
(B) regards
(C) regarded
(D) regarding

어휘 highly 높이, 크게 regard A as B A를 B로 여기다, 평가하다 business school 경영 대학원

해석 Carnegie Mellon 대학은 경영 대학원으로 높은 평가를 받고 있다.

해설 주어진 문장은 "Carnegie Mellon College is highly regarded as a business school."에서 과거분사가 문장 맨 앞으로 와서 주어와 동사를 도치한 구조이다. 그러므로 빈칸에는 과거분사 (C)가 알맞다.

102. The newly introduced equipment for assembly lines allowed the manufacturer ------- its staff productivity substantially.

(A) improve
(B) to improve
(C) improved
(D) improving

어휘 introduce 내놓다, 도입하다 assembly line 조립 라인 manufacturer 제조사, 생산 회사 productivity 생산성 substantially 상당히, 많이

해석 조립 라인에 새로 도입된 장비는 제조업체가 직원 생산성을 상당히 향상할 수 있게 해 주었다.

해설 5형식 동사 allow는 목적격 보어로 to부정사를 사용한다. 빈칸은 목적격 보어 자리이므로 (C)가 정답이다.

103. Safe Job is a new software program which provides a ------- and secure environment for processing your employees' personal information.

(A) relied
(B) reliably
(C) reliable
(D) rely

어휘 reliable 신뢰할 수 있는 secure 안전한 process 처리하다

해석 Safe Job은 직원들의 개인정보를 처리할 수 있는 신뢰할 수 있고 안전한 환경을 제공하는 새 소프트웨어 프로그램이다.

해설 빈칸 뒤의 등위접속사 and는 '병렬 구조'를 만든다. and 뒤에 형용사(secure)가 있으므로 빈칸에는 형용사가 들어가야 한다. 그러므로 (C)가 정답이다.

104. The board of trustees has ------- to select the construction bid entered by Sullivan and Sons, Inc.

(A) picked
(B) settled
(C) decided
(D) established

어휘 board of trustees 이사회 enter a bid 입찰에 참가하다

해석 이사회는 Sullivan and Sons 사(社)가 제출한 공사 입찰을 선정하기로 결정했다.

해설 빈칸 뒤의 to부정사(to select)를 목적어로 취하는 동사를 선택해야 하므로 정답은 (C)이다.

105. An extensive research has indicated that television commercials do not necessarily ------- sales figures.

(A) boost
(B) to boost
(C) boosts
(D) boosting

어휘 extensive 광범위한 indicate 나타내다 commercial 광고 (방송) boost 끌어올리다, 증가시키다 not necessarily 반드시 ~하는 것은 아닌 sales figures 매출액

해석 광범위한 조사로 텔레비전 광고가 반드시 매출액을 증가시키지는 않는다고 나타났다.

해설 빈칸 앞의 부사 necessarily는 수식어이므로 제외하면, 빈칸 앞에 do not이 있는 것을 알 수 있다. do not 뒤에는 동사원형을 써야 하므로 (A)가 정답이다.

---

106. Only after the city constructed a new stadium did the downtown area ------- popularity among out-of-town visitors.

(A) gain
(B) gained
(C) gaining
(D) had gained

어휘 gain popularity 인기를 얻다 out-of-town 외지에서의

해석 시에서 새 경기장을 건설한 후에야 도심 지역이 외지 방문객들 사이에 인기를 얻었다.

해설 Only로 시작하는 부사구나 부사절 뒤에서 주어와 동사를 도치한다. the downtown area gained를 도치하면 did the downtown area gain이 된다. 그러므로 정답은 (A)이다.

---

107. Unfortunately, Hanabishi Electronics' M26 air-conditioning unit failed to meet the government's new energy-efficiency standards, and ------- did the company's M27 model.

(A) same
(B) either
(C) so
(D) rather

어휘 unfortunately 유감스럽게도 air-conditioning unit 에어컨 장치 meet ~를 충족시키다. ~에 부합하다 energy-efficiency 에너지 효율

해석 유감스럽게도 Hanabishi 전자의 M26 에어컨 장치는 정부의 새 에너지 효율성 기준에 부합하는 데 실패했으며, 같은 회사의 M27 모델도 마찬가지이다.

해설 빈칸 뒤에 주어와 동사가 도치된 구문 did the company's M27 model을 보고 빈칸에 '마찬가지로'라는 뜻의 (C) so를 넣어야 한다.

---

108. Filaret Inn does not refund deposits, ------- does it guarantee availability of all advertised amenities.

(A) and
(B) whether
(C) which

(D) nor

어휘 inn 호텔 deposit 착금금, 보증금 amenity 편의 시설

해석 Filaret 호텔은 보증금을 환급하지 않으며, 광고된 모든 편의 시설의 이용 가능 여부를 보장하지도 않는다.

해설 빈칸 뒤에 주어와 동사가 도치된 구문 does it guarantee를 보고 빈칸에 '마찬가지로'라는 뜻으로 (D) nor를 넣어야 한다.

---

109. There was a slight decline in sales of this month, but in no way did that ------- the company's expansion plan.

(A) affect
(B) affected
(C) to affect
(D) affecting

어휘 slight 약간의 decline 감소 in no way 결코[조금도] ~ 않은 affect 영향을 미치다 expansion 확장

해석 이번 달 판매량에 약간의 감소가 있기는 했지만 그것은 회사의 확장 계획에 전혀 영향을 미치지 못했다.

해설 주어진 문장은 in no way를 강조하기 위해 도치된 형태이다. 도치할 때 일반동사는 '시제 조동사(did) + 주어 + 동사원형' 구조가 되므로 빈칸에는 동사원형 (A)가 알맞다.

---

110. Director Kassis has already ------- to boost Lingram Corporation's profits by 20 percent within a year.

(A) promised
(B) promise
(C) promising
(D) promises

어휘 director 임원, 중역, 이사 profit 이윤

해석 Kassis 이사는 Lingram 사(社)의 이윤을 1년 이내에 20퍼센트 신장시키겠다고 이미 약속했다.

해설 has already -------가 문장의 동사(구)이다. 현재완료형이므로 빈칸에는 과거분사 (A)가 들어가야 한다.

---

111. ------- did industry analysts expect that the government would lower the interest rates so rapidly in a short period of time.

(A) So
(B) Seldom

(C) As well

(D) As

어휘 analyst 분석가 lower 내리다, 낮추다 interest rate 금리, 이율

해석 업계 분석가들은 정부가 단시일에 그렇게 빨리 금리를 낮출 것이라고 거의 예상하지 못했다.

해설 빈칸 뒤에 주어와 동사가 도치된 구문인 did industry analysts expect가 있기 때문에, (A), (B), (D) 중에서 정답을 선택해야 한다. (A) so와 (B) as는 '마찬가지로'라는 의미로 가리키는 내용을 포함한 다른 절이 필요하다. 그러므로 빈칸에는 '드물게', '거의 ~않다'는 의미인 (D) seldom이 정답으로 알맞다.

---

112. Candidates for the position must demonstrate their capacity to be efficient and ------- under pressure.

(A) decisively

(B) decisive

(C) decider

(D) deciding

어휘 candidate 지원자 demonstrate 입증하다, 실증하다 capacity 능력 efficient 효율적인 decisive 결단력 있는 under pressure 압박감을 느끼는

해석 이 직책의 지원자는 압박감 속에서 효율적이고 결단력 있는 능력을 입증해야 한다.

해설 빈칸 앞 등위접속사 and는 '병렬 구조'를 만든다. and 앞에 형용사 efficient가 있으므로 빈칸에는 형용사 (B)가 들어가야 한다.

---

113. Wyn Automotive Design has recently ------- with Hydra Company.

(A) merge

(B) merger

(C) merged

(D) merging

어휘 automotive 자동차의 merge with ~와 합병하다

해석 Wyn Automotive Design은 최근 Hydra 사(社)와 합병했다.

해설 현재완료형 has recently -------가 문장의 동사이므로 빈칸에는 과거분사가 (C)가 들어가야 한다.

---

114. Ms. Kovach will ------- the installation of the new workstations in conjunction with the supplier.

(A) coordinated

(B) to coordinate

(C) coordination

(D) be coordinating

어휘 coordinate 조정하다, 조율하다 installation 설치 workstation 사무실에서 작업자 한 사람용 공간 in conjunction with ~와 함께

해석 Ms. Kovach가 공급업체와 함께 새 워크스테이션 설치 작업을 조율할 것이다.

해설 빈칸 앞에 조동사 will이 있으므로 빈칸에는 동사원형 (D)가 정답으로 알맞다.

---

115. ------- is the most up-to-date listing of the distinguished companies and institutions that employ our firm's specialized consulting services.

(A) Enclosure

(B) Enclosing

(C) Enclose

(D) Enclosed

어휘 up-to-date 최근의, 최신의 distinguished 유명한, 성공한 institution 기관, 협회 employ 쓰다, 이용하다 firm 회사 specialized 전문적인, 전문화된

해석 우리 회사의 전문 컨설팅 서비스를 이용하는 유명 기업들과 기관들의 최신 명단이 동봉되어 있습니다.

해설 be enclosed[attached/included](동봉[첨부/포함]되어 있다)가 동사인 수동태 문장은 과거분사를 문장 맨 앞으로 보내고 주어와 동사를 도치시키는 경우가 있다. 빈칸 뒤의 도치 구문을 보고 과거분사 (D)를 정답으로 선택해야 한다.

101 (D)	**102** (C)	**103** (C)	**104** (A)	**105** (D)
106 (B)	**107** (C)	**108** (C)	**109** (C)	**110** (B)
111 (A)	**112** (C)	**113** (A)	**114** (B)	**115** (B)
116 (B)	**117** (B)	**118** (A)	**119** (D)	**120** (C)
121 (B)	**122** (A)	**123** (D)	**124** (C)	**125** (B)
126 (D)	**127** (D)	**128** (D)	**129** (D)	**130** (D)
131 (C)	**132** (B)	**133** (B)	**134** (C)	**135** (A)
136 (D)	**137** (B)	**138** (B)	**139** (C)	**140** (D)
141 (C)	**142** (D)	**143** (D)	**144** (C)	**145** (B)
146 (C)	**147** (A)			

Part 5

101. Trumont Clothier ------- each of its stores to prominently display the return policy near each cash register.

(A) covers
(B) spends
(C) records
(D) requires

> **어휘** clothier 의류 회사 prominently 눈에 잘 띄게 display 표시하다, 게시하다 return policy 반품 정책 cash register 금전 등록기

> **해석** Trumont Clothier는 매장마다 각 금전 등록기 가까운 곳에 반품 정책을 눈에 잘 띄게 게시하도록 요구한다.

> **해설** 빈칸 뒤에 목적어 each of its stores와 목적격 보어 to prominently display가 있으므로 to부정사를 목적격 보어로 취하는 5형식 동사 (D)를 정답으로 선택해야 한다.

102. As the number of local residents' visits to public swimming facilities grows, ------- the demand for lifeguards to monitor them.

(A) as long as
(B) whereas
(C) so does
(D) as to

> **어휘** resident 주민 as to ~에 관해 facilities 시설 lifeguard 인명 구조원, 안전 요원 monitor 감시하다, 관리하다

> **해석** 지역 주민들의 공공 수영 시설 방문이 늘어남에 따라 이들을 감시할 안전 요원에 대한 수요도 함께 증가한다.

> **해설** 부사절 접속사 (A)와 (B) 뒤에는 '주어 + 동사'가 있어야 하므로 제외하자. 수영장 방문이 늘어남에 따라 안전 요원에 대한 수요도 마찬가지로 증가한다는 내용의 문장이므로, '마찬가지로'라는 뜻의 부사 so 뒤에 주어와 동사를 도치하는 문장 구조가 알맞다. 그러므로 정답은 (C)이다.

103. The Canterville Museum will ------- on the development of new educational programs for patrons of varying ages this year.

(A) congratulate
(B) impose
(C) concentrate
(D) interpret

> **어휘** impose 부과하다, 지우다 interpret 설명하다, 해석하다 patron (특정 식당, 기관의) 고객 varying 다양한

> **해석** Canterville 미술관은 올해 다양한 연령대의 고객들을 위한 새 교육 프로그램 개발에 집중할 것이다.

> **해설** 항상 짝으로 출제되는 어휘 문제이다. 동사 바로 뒤에 전치사 on과 함께 쓸 수 있는 것은 '~에 집중하다'라는 뜻의 (C) concentrate이다.

104. All images displayed in the brochure have been provided ------- of Ryke Photography Studio.

(A) courtesy
(B) courteous
(C) courteously
(D) courteousness

> **어휘** brochure 안내 책자 courtesy of (상이나 무료로) ~이 제공한 courteous 공손한, 정중한

> **해석** 안내 책자에 나와 있는 모든 이미지는 Ryke 사진 스튜디오에서 무상으로 제공되었다.

> **해설** have been provided ------- of Ryke Photography Studio가 'Ryke 사진 스튜디오에서 무상으로 제공되었다'라는 뜻이 자연스러우므로 (A)가 정답이다.

105. Dr. Giordano, among her many -------, has won a distinguished science award and a highly competitive fellowship.

(A) capabilities
(B) proficiencies
(C) performances
(D) accomplishments

어휘 capability 능력, 역량 proficiency 숙달, 능숙, 능란 performance 실적, 성과 accomplishment 업적, 공적 distinguished 유명한, 저명한 competitive 경쟁이 치열한 fellowship 연구 장학금

해석 Giordano는 많은 업적 가운데 저명한 과학상과 매우 경쟁이 치열한 연구 장학금을 받은 적이 있다.

해설 과학계의 유명한 상과 매우 경쟁이 치열한 연구비를 탄 것을 나타내므로 업적을 뜻하는 (D)가 정답으로 알맞다.

---

106. ------- is a product catalog that also contains comprehensive information about our ordering procedure and our delivery policies.

(A) Enclosure
(B) Enclosed
(C) Enclosing
(D) Encloses

어휘 enclosure (편지에) 동봉된 것 contain ~이 들어 있다 comprehensive 포괄적인, 종합적인 procedure 절차 delivery policy 배송 정책

해석 우리의 주문 절차와 배송 정책에 대한 포괄적인 정보도 담고 있는 제품 카탈로그를 동봉했습니다.

해설 be enclosed[attached/included](동봉[첨부/포함]되어 있다)가 동사인 수동태 문장은 과거분사를 문장 맨 앞으로 보내고 주어와 동사를 도치시키는 경우가 있다. 빈칸 뒤의 도치 구문을 보고 과거분사 (B)를 정답으로 선택해야 한다.

---

107. ------- developing the operating system, the technology team conducted a thorough study.

(A) In order to
(B) Assigned
(C) Before
(D) Since

어휘 assigned 할당된 operating system 운영 체제 conduct 수행하다 thorough 빈틈없는, 철두철미한

해석 기술팀은 운영 체제를 개발하기 전에 철저한 연구를 했다.

해설 문맥상 철저한 연구는 본격적인 시스템 개발 '전에' 실시하는 것이 자연스러우므로 (C)가 빈칸에 알맞다.

---

108. ------- is an application to take part in the Air Traffic Controller Training Program.

(A) Attach

(B) Attaching
(C) Attached
(D) Attachment

어휘 take part in 참여하다 air traffic controller 항공 교통 관제사

해석 항공 교통 관제사 교육 프로그램에 참여하기 위한 지원서를 첨부했습니다.

해설 빈칸 뒤에 be동사(is)와 긴 주어(an application to~)가 있어서 '과거분사 + be + 주어' 형태의 수동태 문장 도치 구문임을 알 수 있다. 그러므로 빈칸에는 과거분사인 (C)가 알맞다.

---

109. The CFO cannot participate in the board meeting on Wednesday, and ------- can the CIO.

(A) so
(B) however
(C) neither
(D) also

어휘 CFO 최고 재무 책임자(Chief Financial Officer) participate in ~에 참여하다 board meeting 이사회 (회의) CIO 최고 정보 책임자(Chief Information Officer)

해석 CFO는 수요일에 열리는 이사회에 참석할 수 없으며 CIO도 마찬가지이다.

해설 빈칸 뒤에 주어(the CIO)와 동사(can)가 도치된 구문이 있으므로 빈칸에는 '마찬가지로'라는 뜻의 (A)나 (C)가 들어가야 한다. 그런데 빈칸 앞의 절이 부정문이므로 (C)를 정답으로 선택해야 한다.

---

110. Fishing is one of the major sources of income for the village, ------- is transit trade.

(A) too
(B) as
(C) also
(D) thus

어휘 sources of income 수입원 transit trade 중계 무역, 통과 무역

해석 어업은 마을의 주요 수입원 중 하나이며, 중계 무역도 마찬가지이다.

해설 빈칸 앞의 절이 '어업이 마을의 주요 수입원'이라는 내용이므로 빈칸 뒤는 '중계 무역도 마찬가지'라는 의미가 되는 것이 자연스럽다. 또한 빈칸 뒤에 주어와 동사가 도치되어 있으므로 '마찬가지로'라는 뜻의 (B) as를 정답으로 선택해야 한다.

111. Eabha Madigan's latest article is a ------- and insightful analysis of market timing.

(A) wise
(A) wise
(B) wisdom
(C) wisely
(D) wisest

어휘 latest 최신의 wisdom 지혜, 현명함 insightful 통찰력 있는 analysis 분석 market timing 시장 적시성(주식 시 장의 상승과 하락을 예측하여 높은 수익률을 얻으려는 투자 행위)

해석 Eabha Madigan의 최신 기사는 마켓 타이밍에 대한 현명하고 통찰력 있는 분석이다.

해설 빈칸 뒤에 있는 등위접속사 and 다음에 형용사 (insightful)가 있으므로 빈칸에는 형용사 (A)가 와야 한 다. (D)도 형용사이지만 최상급으로 관사 the가 필요하 므로 정답이 아니다.

---

112. Having five years of professional experience is considered ------- to the acquisition of certification for hiring purposes.

(A) reasonable
(B) appropriate
(C) equivalent
(D) significant

어휘 reasonable 합리적인 appropriate 적절한 equivalent 동등한, 상응한 significant 중대한 acquisition 취득, 획득 certification 증명(서) for ~ purposes ~의 용도로

해석 채용 시 5년의 전문 경력이 있는 것은 자격증 취득에 상응하는 것으로 간주한다.

해설 5년의 경력이 자격증 취득에 상응한다는 의미가 자연스 러우므로 전치사 to와 짝을 이루는 (C) equivalent가 정답으로 알맞다.

---

113. Any items of luggage exceeding Metzger Airline's weight and size restrictions will be ------- to additional charges.

(A) subject
(B) entitled
(C) accountable
(D) transferable

어휘 luggage 수하물 exceed 초과하다 restriction 제한 be subject to ~의 대상이다 entitle 자격[권리]을 주다 accountable to ~에게 (해명할) 책임이 있는 transferable 양도 가능한 charge 요금

해석 Metzger 항공의 중량 및 크기 제한을 초과하는 수하물 은 어느 것이든 추가 요금 징수 대상이다.

해설 중량이나 크기 제한을 초과하는 수하물은 추가 요금 징 수의 '대상'이라는 뜻이 적합하므로 (A)가 정답이다.

---

114. Wayfield Associates and Midtown Construction sought the assistance of a third party to negotiate the ------- to their contract dispute.

(A) occasion
(B) resolution
(C) impression
(D) situation

어휘 seek(sought-sought) 청하다, 구하다 third party 제삼 자 negotiate 협상하다, 이끌어내다 occasion 때, 경우 dispute 분쟁, 분규

해석 Wayfield Associates와 Midtown 건설은 계약 분쟁 의 해결을 이끌어내기 위해 제삼자의 도움을 구했다.

해설 빈칸 앞뒤 to negotiate the ------- to their contract dispute(계약 분쟁의 [(A) 때를 (B) 해결을 (C) 인상을 (D) 상황을] 성사시키기 위해)의 의미를 자 연스럽게 해 주는 명사 (B)가 정답이다.

---

115. The Vietnamese-style fresh spring rolls at Madam Tran Restaurant is a superb selection for a tasty mid-day snack, ------- a full meal.

(A) whereas
(B) if not
(C) by means of
(D) whenever

어휘 superb 최고의, 최상의 mid-day 한낮의 if not ~까지는 아니라도 by means of ~을 이용하여

해석 Madam Tran 식당의 베트남 스타일의 신선한 스프링 롤은 정식 식사는 아니라도 맛있는 한낮의 간식으로는 최고의 선택이다.

해설 부사절 접속사 (A)와 (D)는 뒤에 '주어 + 동사'가 있어 야 하므로 제외하자. 빈칸 앞뒤 an superb selection for a tasty mid-day snack, ------- a full meal이 '제대로 차려진 식사는 아니더라도 한낮의 간식으로는 최고의 선택'이라는 의미가 되도록 (B)를 정답으로 선택 해야 한다.

116. Kaweiben Corporation's earnings have been steadily increasing despite significant fluctuations ------- the stock market.

(A) about
(B) in
(C) through
(D) onto

어휘 earnings 수익 steadily 꾸준히 fluctuation 변동

해석 Kaweiben 사(社)의 수익은 주식 시장의 큰 변동에도 불구하고 꾸준히 증가해 왔다.

해설 항상 짝으로 출제되는 어휘 문제이다. '증가(increase, rise, expansion), 감소(decrease, decline, reduction, fall, drop), 변화(change, fluctuation), 경험(experience)' 뒤에 빈칸이 있다면 정답은 전치사 in이다.

---

117. HBS Photo Studio is providing its ------- customers with an additional discount on the items currently on sale.

(A) deliberate
(B) established
(C) approximate
(D) concluded

어휘 deliberate 고의의, 의도적인; 신중한 established 확립된, 기존의

해석 HBS 사진 스튜디오는 기존 고객들에게 현재 할인 중인 제품들에 대한 추가 할인을 제공하고 있다.

해설 빈칸 앞뒤 its ------- customers([(A) 고의적인 (B) 기존의 (C) 근사치인 (D) 결론이 난] 고객)의 의미를 자연스럽게 해 주는 형용사 (B)가 정답이다. 같은 뜻의 existing customer(기존 고객)도 자주 출제된다.

---

118. Management cannot ------- the security of personal information sent while using the hotel's wireless Internet service.

(A) guarantee
(B) balance
(C) distinguish
(D) locate

어휘 management 경영진, 운영진 security 보안 wireless 무선의

해석 운영진은 호텔 무선 인터넷 서비스를 사용하는 동안 발송된 개인 정보의 보안은 보장할 수 없습니다.

해설 빈칸 앞뒤 cannot ------- the security of personal information(개인 정보의 보안은 [(A) 보장할 (B) 균형을 잡을 (C) 구별할 (D) 위치를 찾아낼] 수 없다)의 의미를 자연스럽게 해 주는 동사 (A)가 정답이다.

---

119. We regret to inform you that your company credit card has -------, so we are currently unable to process your order.

(A) expiration
(B) expires
(C) expiring
(D) expired

어휘 regret to-V ~하게 되어 유감이다 inform 알리다 company credit card 법인 카드 be unable to-V ~할 수 없다 process 처리하다

해석 법인 카드가 만료되어 현재 주문을 처리할 수 없음을 알려드리게 되어 유감입니다.

해설 has -------가 that절의 동사로 완료형이므로 빈칸에 과거분사 (D)가 들어가야 한다.

---

120. Our technical expertise, accumulated over a long period of time, will enable your company ------- highly successful and reliable solutions.

(A) build
(B) building
(C) to build
(D) built

어휘 expertise 전문 지식 accumulate 축적하다 build 구축하다 enable sb to-V ~하는 것을 가능하게 하다 reliable 신뢰할 만한 solution 솔루션(소프트웨어)

해석 오랫동안 축적된 우리의 기술적 전문 지식은 귀하의 회사가 매우 성공적이고 신뢰할 만한 솔루션을 구축할 수 있게 해드릴 것입니다.

해설 5형식 동사 enable은 목적격 보어로 to부정사를 사용하므로 (C)가 정답이다.

---

121. The automated fabric cutters work much faster than those ------- by hand.

(A) accepted
(B) operated
(C) publicized
(D) intensified

어휘 automate 자동화하다 publicize 알리다. 홍보하다 intensify 강화하다 fabric 직물 by hand 사람 손으로

해석 자동화된 직물 절단기가 수동으로 가동되는 것보다 훨씬 더 빨리 움직인다.

해설 those는 앞에 있는 명사 fabric cutters를 가리킨다. 빈칸 앞뒤 those ------ by hand(수동으로 [(A) 수락되는 (B) 가동되는 (C) 홍보되는 (D) 강화되는] 직물 절단기)의 의미를 자연스럽게 해 주는 동사 (B)가 정답이다.

---

122. Mr. Mundine froze spending rates in view of a projected ------ in revenue.

(A) decline
(B) method
(C) rejection
(D) outlet

어휘 freeze 동결하다 spending rate 지출 비율 in view of ~을 고려하여 project 예상하다. 추정하다 rejection 거절. 거부 outlet 할인점. 아울렛; 배출구; 콘센트 revenue 수입

해석 Mr. Mundine은 예상되는 수입 감소를 고려하여 지출 비율을 동결했다.

해설 항상 짝으로 출제되는 어휘 문제이다. '증가(increase, rise, expansion), 감소(decrease, decline, reduction, fall, drop), 변화(change, fluctuation), 경험(experience)'은 언제나 전치사 in과 함께 사용한다. a projected ------ in revenue가 '예상되는 수입 감소'라는 의미가 자연스러우므로 (A)가 정답이다.

---

123. Dr. Hwang's research is published ------ in the Western Journal of Medicine.

(A) shortly
(B) deeply
(C) finely
(D) regularly

어휘 publish 게재하다. 싣다 shortly 얼마 안 되어. 곧

해석 Hwang 박사의 연구는 Western 의학 저널에 정기적으로 게재된다.

해설 (B) deeply(깊이)와 (C) finely(멋있게, 아름답게)는 의미상 is published(게재된다)를 수식하기에 알맞지 않으므로 제외하자. 반복되는 동작이나 지속되는 상태를 나타내는 현재 시제에 맞는 부사 (D)가 정답이다.

---

124. Industry analysts expect the ------ merger decision to be made soon by Sectorsys Ltd.

(A) sparse
(B) related
(C) pending
(D) attentive

어휘 sparse (분포가) 드문, (밀도가) 희박한 pending 미결의. 보류 중인 attentive 배려하는, 신경을 쓰는 merger 합병

해석 업계 분석가들은 보류 중인 합병 결정이 곧 Sectorsys 사(社)에 의해 내려질 것으로 예상한다.

해설 빈칸 앞뒤 expect the ------ merger decision to be made soon([(A) 희박한 (B) 관련된 (C) 보류 중인 (D) 배려하는] 합병 결정이 곧 내려질 것으로 예상하다)의 의미를 자연스럽게 해 주는 형용사 (C)가 정답이다.

---

125. ------ they have purchased preapproved animal feed from the park ranger station, visitors may feed the horses.

(A) Unless
(B) As long as
(C) In case
(D) Regardless

어휘 preapproved 사전에 승인된 feed 사료; 먹이를 주다 ranger station (공원, 산림의) 관리소

해석 방문객은 공원 관리 사무소에서 사전에 승인된 동물 사료를 구매하기만 하면 말에게 먹이를 줄 수 있다.

해설 접속사 어휘 문제는 빈칸 앞뒤를 봐서는 정답을 알 수 없고, 문장 전체의 의미를 생각해야 한다. 빈칸이 있는 부사절과 뒤의 주절을 자연스럽게 연결하는 접속사는 '~하는 한, ~한다면'을 뜻하는 (B) As long as이다.

---

126. Mr. Heyer's responsibilities have ------ helping the company with its marketing efforts and taking over the company's North American operations.

(A) including
(B) include
(C) includes
(D) included

어휘 responsibility 책무 effort (조직적인) 활동 take over 인수하다 operation 운영

해석 Mr. Heyer의 업무는 회사의 마케팅 활동을 돕고 북미 운영을 인수하는 것을 포함했다.

해설 현재완료형인 have ------가 동사이므로 빈칸에 과거분사 (D)가 들어가야 한다.

127. Since all the final corrections on the invitation have been provided, the print shop will now run it and then ------- the client when the job has been completed.

(A) notifying
(B) notified
(C) notification
(D) notify

어휘 correction 수정 (사항) run 실행하다 notify 통보하다

해석 초대장의 모든 최종 수정 사항이 제공되었으므로 이제 인쇄소가 그것을 실행한 후 작업이 완료되면 고객에게 통보할 것이다.

해설 빈칸 앞의 수식어인 부사 then은 제외하면 그 앞에 병렬 구조를 만드는 등위접속사 and가 있다. and 앞에 '동사원형 + 목적어(run it)'가 있고, 빈칸 뒤에 목적어 the client가 있으므로 빈칸에는 동사원형 (D)가 들어가야 한다.

---

128. Dr. Eun-Young Kwon will be awarded the ------- Schills Medal for her significant contributions in the field of immunology.

(A) successful
(B) dominant
(C) cooperative
(D) prestigious

어휘 dominant 우세한, 지배적인 prestigious 명망 있는, 일류의 significant 중대한 contribution 공헌 field 분야 immunology 면역학

해석 Eun-Young Kwon 박사는 면역학 분야에서의 중대한 공헌으로 권위 있는 Schills 메달을 수여받을 것이다.

해설 빈칸 앞뒤 will be awarded ------- Schills Medal([(A) 성공적인 (B) 지배적인 (C) 협조적인 (D) 권위 있는] Schills Medal을 수여받을 것이다)의 의미를 자연스럽게 해 주는 형용사 (D)가 정답이다.

---

129. Sales clerk Tim Davis demonstrated ------- by actively engaging customers as they entered the Musienko's Furniture showroom.

(A) amount
(B) objective
(C) reliant
(D) initiative

어휘 sales clerk 판매사원 demonstrate 보여주다, 발휘하다 actively 적극적으로 reliant 의존하는 initiative 솔선수범, 주도적임 engage (주의·관심을) 사로잡다, 끌다 showroom 전시장

해석 판매 사원 Tim Davis는 고객이 Musienko 가구의 전시장에 들어왔을 때 적극적으로 관심을 끌면서 솔선수범을 보였다.

해설 동사 demonstrated의 목적어로 명사가 필요하므로 형용사인 (C)는 제외하자. 빈칸 앞뒤 demonstrated ------- by actively engaging customers(적극적으로 고객의 관심을 끌면서 [(A) 양을 (B) 목적을 (D) 솔선수범을] 보였다)의 의미를 자연스럽게 해 주는 명사 (D)가 정답이다.

---

130. On the day of the show, tickets to the Max Theater can only ------- at the ticket office.

(A) purchasing
(B) were purchased
(C) to purchase
(D) be purchased

어휘 purchase 구매하다 ticket office 매표소

해석 공연 당일에 Max 극장의 표는 매표소에서만 구매할 수 있다.

해설 빈칸 앞의 수식어인 부사 only를 제외하면 그 앞에 조동사 can이 있다. 조동사 뒤에 동사원형이 와야 하므로 (D)가 정답이다.

Part 6

Questions 131-134 refer to the following article.

Women's History at the Seoul Museum of History

Now on display at the Seoul Museum of History is *She Makes History*. This [131.]exhibit honors the female leaders who dedicated their lives to the Korean independence movement. It also focuses [132.]on significant figures in modern Korean history who earned acclaim in science, art, and sports. Valuable documents, photographs, and paintings are being displayed. Museum

---

visitors [133.]can also enjoy a short film featuring actual footage of speeches and interviews from the early 20th century. [134.]Join us to explore how these events changed history. *She Makes History* runs through October 20.

131-134번 문제는 다음 기사에 관한 것입니다.

> ### 서울 역사 박물관에서 보는 여성의 역사
>
> 현재 서울 역사 박물관에서는 '그녀, 역사를 만들다'가 전시 중입니다. 이 전시회는 대한민국 독립운동에 일생을 바친 여성 지도자들을 기립니다. 또한 과학 및 예술, 스포츠 분야에서 찬사를 받은 현대 한국사의 중요한 인물들에 초점을 맞추고도 있습니다. 귀중한 문서, 사진, 그림이 전시되어 있습니다. 관람객 여러분은 또한 20세기 초의 연설과 인터뷰의 실제 영상을 담은 단편 영화도 감상하실 수 있습니다. 이러한 사건들이 어떻게 역사를 변화시켰는지 저희와 함께 탐구해 보시기를 바랍니다. '그녀, 역사를 만들다'는 10월 20일까지 진행됩니다.

어휘 on display 전시 중인 exhibit 전시회 honor 기리다 dedicate A to B A를 B에 바치다, 헌신하다 independence 독립 significant 중요한, 중대한 figure 인물 earn 얻다, 받다 acclaim 찬사, 호평 valuable 귀중한 feature 특별히 포함하다, 특징으로 삼다 actual 실제의 footage (특별한 사건의) 장면, 영상 explore 탐구하다 run (강좌, 전시회 등이) 진행되다 through (~을 포함하여) ~까지

---

131. (A) article
(B) award
(C) exhibit
(D) documentary

해설 This ------는 앞 문장에서 소개하고 있는 She Makes History라는 전시회를 가리키고 있으므로 (C)가 정답이다.

---

132. (A) by
(B) on
(C) with
(D) after

해설 항상 짝으로 출제되는 어휘 문제이다. focus나 concentrate 뒤에 빈칸이 있는 문제의 정답은 (B) on 이다.

---

133. (A) also enjoyed
(B) can also enjoy
(C) are also enjoying
(D) have also enjoyed

해설 앞 문장에서 문서, 사진, 그림이 전시되어 있다고 했는데(Valuable documents, photographs, and paintings are being displayed.), 빈칸이 있는 문장에서 영화를 추가로 소개하고 있으므로 '관람객들이 ~도 즐길 수 있다'는 의미인 (B)가 정답으로 알맞다.

---

134. (A) The museum will be closed for maintenance on October 3.
(B) Unfortunately, the film is no longer obtainable.
(C) Join us to explore how these events changed history.
(D) To volunteer, please fill out an application at the museum Web site.

어휘 maintenance 유지 보수 obtainable 얻을[구할] 수 있는 volunteer 지원하다 fill out (서식을) 작성하다

해석 (A) 박물관은 10월 3일에 보수 작업을 위해 폐관합니다.
(B) 안타깝지만, 그 영화는 더 이상 구할 수 없습니다.
(C) 이러한 사건들이 어떻게 역사를 변화시켰는지 저희와 함께 탐구해 보시기를 바랍니다.
(D) 자원하시려면 박물관 웹사이트에서 지원서를 작성하시기를 바랍니다.

해설 앞 문장에서 20세기 초의 연설과 인터뷰를 보여주는 영화에 대해 언급하고 있으므로(Museum visitors can also enjoy a short film featuring actual footage of speeches and interviews from the early 20th century.), 영화의 관람을 권장하는 내용인 (C)가 이어지는 문장으로 알맞다. (C)에서 these events는 speeches and interviews를 가리킨다.

Questions 135-138 refer to the following memo.

> **MEMO**
>
> To: All Employees of Nautique Boats
> From: Deepanjali Jaddoo, Vice President of Operations
> Date: 10 September
> Subject: Important updates

135. Effective 1 January, we will expand our operations in Port Louis. We will also open a manufacturing plant for saltwater fishing boats in the coastal city of Saint-Denis. The new **136.**facility will enable Nautique Boats to better serve its customers in Madagascar and East Africa. **137.**Along with this expansion also comes the opportunity for Nautique Boats employees who are interested in doing so to relocate. **138.**Job openings have already been posted on our Web site. As always, we will provide a corporate package to cover relocation expenses. Additional information will be available soon.

Please refer any questions you may have to your direct supervisor.

135-138번 문제는 다음 회람에 관한 것입니다.

회람

수신: Nautique Boats 전 직원
발신: 운영 부사장 Deepanjali Jaddoo
날짜: 9월 10일
제목: 중요 최신 정보

1월 1일을 기하여 우리는 Port Louis에서의 운영을 확대할 것입니다. 해안 도시인 Saint-Denis에 바다낚시용 보트 제조 공장도 열 것입니다. 새 시설은 Nautique Boats가 Madagascar와 동아프리카에서 고객들에게 더 좋은 서비스를 제공할 수 있게 해줄 것입니다. 이번 확장과 함께 업무 재배치에 관심 있는 Nautique Boats 직원에게는 그렇게 할 기회도 생깁니다. 채용 공고가 이미 우리 홈페이지에 게시되어 있습니다. 항상 그렇듯이 복리 후생을 제공하여 이전 경비를 치르도록 하겠습니다. 추가 정보를 곧 이용하실 수 있을 겁니다.

질문이 있으시다면 직속 상사에게 하시기를 바랍니다.

> **어휘** memo (memorandum) 회람, 단체 메일 **effective** ~을 기하여 **expand** 확장하다 **operation** 운영 **manufacturing plant** 제조 공장 **saltwater** 바닷물의, 바다의 **coastal** 해안의, 연안의 **along with** ~에 덧붙여 **relocate** 재배치되다, 이전하다 **job opening** 채용 공고 **post** 올리다, 게시하다 **corporate package** 복리 후생 **cover** ~의 (비용을) 치르다, 대다 **refer A to B** A를 B에게 문의하다 **direct supervisor** 직속 상사

문장 분석

Along with this expansion also comes the opportunity for Nautique Boats employees who are interested in doing so to relocate.

➡ the opportunity가 문장의 주어로 to relocate의 수식을 받고 있다. for Nautique Boats employees who are interested in doing so는 의미상의 주어로 relocate하는 주체이다. 주어가 길면 의미를 전달하기 어렵기 때문에, 영어 문장에서는 긴 주어를 꺼리는 경향이 있다. 그래서 Along with this expansion이 문장 맨 앞에 오고 주어와 동사를 도치시켰다.

135. **(A) Effective**
(B) Effect
(C) To effect
(D) Effectively

> **해설** 품사 문제가 아니라 어휘 문제이다. 빈칸 뒤에 시점을 나타내는 표현(1, January)이 있으면 정답은 언제나 effective나 beginning, starting이다.

136. (A) ship
(B) role
(C) process
(D) facility

> **해설** 바로 앞 문장에서 제조 공장을 열 것이라고 했으므로(We will also open a manufacturing plant), 빈칸은 앞의 a manufacturing plant를 대신할 수 있는 명사 (D)가 정답이다.

137. (A) Compared with
(B) Along with
(C) Just as
(D) In contrast

> **어휘** compared with ~와 비교해서 in contrast 그에 반해서, 그와 대조적으로

> **해설** this expansion(이번 확장)은 Port Louis에서의 운영 확대와(we will expand our operations in Port Louis.) 새 제조 공장 개설을(We will also open a manufacturing plant for saltwater fishing boats in the coastal city of Saint-Denis.) 의미한다. 그러므로 '회사 확장'과 함께' 근무지 이전의 기회가 오는 것이므로, 빈칸에는 (B)가 알맞다.

138. (A) We have worked in Saint-Denis for decades.

(B) Job openings have already been posted on our Web site.

(C) There is a high demand for smaller recreational boats.

(D) There are many public transportation options in Port Louis.

> **어휘** decade 10년 job opening 채용 공고, 공석 recreational 여가의

> **해석** (A) 우리는 수십 년 동안 Saint-Denis에서 일해 왔습니다.
> (B) 채용 공고는 홈페이지에 이미 게시되어 있습니다.
> (C) 소형 여가용 보트에 대한 수요가 높습니다.
> (D) Port Louis에는 대중교통 옵션이 많습니다.

> **해설** 새 제조 공장을 열면서(We will also open a manufacturing plant) 근무지 이전의 기회가 생겼다고 했으므로(Along with this expansion also comes the opportunity for Nautique Boats employees who are interested in doing so to relocate.), '채용 공고가 이미 게시되었다'는 (B)가 이어지는 것이 문맥상 자연스럽다.

Part 7

Questions 139-142 refer to the following information from a Web site.

TECHNOLOGY NEWS:

139.The new Ecotornado ultrasonic home dishwasher developed by the Supertech Company is an excellent way of cleaning dishes while benefiting the environment. The Ecotornado applies ultrasonic technology to remove debris from dishes in the same fashion as is used to clean jewelry. The dishwasher is equipped with a 100-liter tank with two metal converters that release high-frequency sound waves under water. The waves generate high-temperature, high-pressure bubbles which facilitate the cleaning of dishes with limited detergent usage. These micro-scrubbing bubbles can reach into the narrowest of cracks and crevices that sponges or brushes are unable to access.

A conventional machine consumes 200 to 300 liters of fresh water per cycle. The Ecotornado filters the water in its tank for reuse after each cycle. 141.The water in its tank only needs to be replaced every other week. This way, the average household can conserve 250,000 to 500,000 liters of water annually. 140.The shortened run time of the machine also saves on electricity. The Ecotornado cleaning cycle lasts only ten minutes where a conventional machine usually takes thirty minutes or longer.

The Ecotornado unit made its debut in India in March, and Supertech is aiming to introduce it around the world in the foreseeable future. 142.Supertech is also able to customize dishwashers to meet the requirements of corporate clients such as those in the healthcare and hospitality industries. For additional details, go to www.supertech.com to watch demonstration videos, request a brochure, or find a local retailer.

139-142번 문제는 다음 웹사이트 정보에 관한 것입니다.

기술 뉴스:

Supertech 사(社)가 개발한 새 Ecotornado 가정용 초음파 식기 세척기는 환경에 도움이 되면서 접시를 닦을 수 있는 탁월한 방식이다. Ecotornado는 보석을 세척할 때 사용하는 것과 같은 방식으로 초음파 기술을 적용하여 접시에서 찌꺼기를 제거한다. 식기세척기에는 물속에서 고주파 음파를 방출하는 두 개의 금속 변환기가 있는 100리터 탱크가 갖춰져 있다. 음파는 제한된 세제 사용만으로 접시 세척을 용이하게 해 주는 고온 고압의 기포를 발생시킨다. 이 미세 세척 기포는 스펀지나 솔은 닿을 수 없는 가장 좁은 틈새에도 도달할 수 있다.

기존 기계는 주기당 200~300리터의 맑은 물을 소비한다. Ecotornado는 각 주기 후에 재사용을 위해 탱크 안에서 물을 여과한다. 탱크 안의 물은 2주에 한 번씩만 교체하면 됩니다. 이런 식으로 일반 가정이 매년 250,000~500,000 리터의 물을 아낄 수 있다. 기계의 단축된 가동 시간은 전기도 절약해 준다. 기존 기계의 세척 주기가 보통 30분 이상 지속되는 데 반해 Ecotornado는 10분밖에 걸리지 않는다.

Ecotornado는 3월에 인도에서 첫선을 보였는데, Supertech는 가까운 장래에 제품을 전 세계에 내놓는 것을 목표로 하고 있다. Supertech는 또한 건강 관리나 서비스 산업과 같은 기업 고객들의 요구에 맞도록 식기 세척기를 주문 제작할 수도 있다. 추가적인 세부 사항을 원한다면 www.supertech.com에 들어가서 시연 동영상을 시청하거나 안내 책자를 신청하거나 지역의 소매상을 찾아보면 된다.

ultrasonic 초음파의 **dishwasher** 식기 세척기 **benefit** ~에 유익하다 **apply** 쓰다, 적용하다 **remove** 제거하다 **debris** 찌꺼기 **fashion** 방법, 방식 **be equipped with** ~을 갖추고 있다 **converter** 변환기, 컨버터 **release** 방출하다 **high-frequency** 고주파의 **sound wave** 음파 **generate** 발생시키다 **facilitate** 용이하게 하다 **detergent** 세제 **micro-** 미세한 **scrubbing** 문지르기, 세척 **crack** (좁은) 틈 **crevice** 갈라진 틈, 균열 **access** 접근하다 **conventional** 종래의, 기존의 **consume** 소비하다 **filter** 여과하다, 거르다 **every other week** 격주로 **replace** 교체하다 **average** 보통의, 일반적인 **household** 가정, 가구 **conserve** 보존하다, 아끼다 **annually** 매년 **shortened** 단축된 **run time** 가동 시간 **save on** ~을 절약하다 **electricity** 전기 **where** ~하는 데 반하여 **last** 지속되다 **make one's debut** 처음 등장하다 **aim to-V** ~하는 것을 목표로 하다 **introduce** 내놓다, 도입하다 **in the foreseeable future** 가까운 장래에 **customize** 주문 제작하다 **requirement** 요건 **corporate** 기업의, 회사의 **healthcare** 건강 관리 **hospitality industry** 서비스업(호텔, 식당업 등) **demonstration** 실연, 시연 **retailer** 소매업자

문장 분석

1. The Ecotornado applies ultrasonic technology to remove debris from dishes in the same fashion as is used to clean jewelry.

➡ LC 문제에도 debris가 자주 등장하기 때문에, 발음을 알고 있어야 한다. 프랑스어처럼 [dəbriː](드브리, 뒤 음절에 강세, s 묵음)라고 읽어야 한다.

➡ as는 관계대명사로 상관접속사처럼 the same, such 등과 짝을 이루어 'the same[such] + 명사 + as + 불완전한 문장' 형태로 사용한다.

2. The Ecotornado cleaning cycle lasts only ten minutes where a conventional machine usually takes thirty minutes or longer.

➡ where는 대조를 나타내는 부사절 접속사로 사용할 수 있다.

---

139. What is the information mainly about?

(A) Selecting a dishwashing detergent
(B) Advances in jewelry cleaning technology
(C) Using sound waves to clean dishes
(D) A newly developed clothes washing machine

advance 진전, 발전
이 정보는 주로 무엇에 관한 것인가
(A) 식기 세척 세제 선택하기
(B) 보석 세척 기술의 발전
(C) 음파를 이용해 그릇 닦기
(D) 새로 개발된 의류 세탁기
첫 번째 문단에서 새로 나온 Ecotornado를 초음파 가정용 식기 세척기(ultrasonic home dishwasher)로 소개하고 있다. 초음파 기술을 적용하여 찌꺼기를 제거한다든가(applies ultrasonic technology to remove debris from dishes) 고온, 고압의 기포가 세제 사용을 최소화하여 식기를 세척해 주는(The waves generate high-temperature, high-pressure bubbles which facilitate the cleaning of dishes with limited detergent usage.) 등의 내용이 이어지고 있으므로, 이를 통해 (C)가 정답임을 알 수 있다.

---

140. According to the information, what is an advantage of the Ecotornado?

(A) It eliminates the need for detergent.
(B) It adopts high-powered brushes.
(C) It takes only 30 minutes to complete a cycle.
(D) It consumes less energy than other machines.

eliminate 없애다, 제거하다 **adopt** 채택하다 **high-powered** 고성능의
정보에 따르면 Ecotornado의 장점은 무엇인가?
(A) 세제가 필요 없다.
(B) 고성능 솔을 채택한다.
(C) 한 주기를 완료하는 데 30분밖에 걸리지 않는다.
(D) 다른 기계보다 더 적은 에너지를 소비한다.
둘째 문단에 가동 시간이 짧아서 전기가 절약된다고 (The shortened run time of the machine also saves on electricity.) 했으므로 (D)가 정답이다.

141. How often should the water in the Ecotornado be replaced?

(A) Twice a week
(B) Once a week
(C) Once every two weeks
(D) Once a month

해석 Ecotornado의 물을 얼마나 자주 교체해야 하는가?
(A) 일주일에 두 번
(B) 일주일에 한 번
(C) 2주마다 한 번
(D) 한 달에 한 번

해설 둘째 문단에서 격주마다 갈면 된다고(The water in its tank only needs to be replaced every other week.) 했으므로 (C)가 정답이다.

142. What is indicated about the Supertech Company?

(A) It will restrict the sale of Ecotornado to India only.
(B) It is a leader in the healthcare industry.
(C) It will start selling the Ecotornado in the upcoming year.
(D) It can adapt the Ecotornado for different uses.

어휘 restrict 제한하다, 한정하다 upcoming 다가오는, 곧 있을 adapt 맞추다, 조정하다

해석 Supertech 사(社)에 대해 무엇이 나타나 있는가?
(A) Ecotornado의 판매를 인도로만 제한할 것이다.
(B) 건강 관리 업계의 선두 주자이다.
(C) 다가오는 해에 Ecotornado를 판매하기 시작할 것이다.
(D) Ecotornado를 다양한 용도에 맞게 조정할 수 있다.

해설 마지막 문단에 여러 기업 고객의 필요에 맞게 기계를 맞춤 제작해 줄 수 있다는 내용이 있으므로(Supertech is also able to customize dishwashers to meet the requirements of corporate clients such as those in the healthcare and hospitality industries.) (D)가 정답이다.

Questions 143-147 refer to the following list, schedule, and e-mail.

Books by David Duchemin

Tracing the Origin of Jeans
Where did it all begin? [143.]Duchemin visually chronicles the evolution of jeans through the centuries, from their beginning as working wear to their current status as high fashion.

Glance Beyond the Runway
Duchemin captures the creative process of a selection of preeminent fashion designers from New York City to Paris. [143.]The book, filled with Duchemin's photographs, spans nearly two decades and reveals what goes on in fashion houses prior to garments being ready for the runway.

[144.]*Walking into Clothes: My Story*
An amusing memoir about childhood spent amid the fashion world. [143.147.]Duchemin describes his unconventional upbringing in New York City, where his parents began their careers as fashion models before launching their own design label.

Yards of Talent: A Decade of Vogue
[143.]Duchemin's compilation of images spanning a decade of fashion and displaying what was in style, what was out of style, and then what was back in style again.

143~147번 문제는 다음 목록과 일정표, 이메일에 관한 것입니다.

David Duchem의 책

청바지의 기원을 추적하다
이 모든 것이 어디에서 시작되었는가? Duchemin이 작업복으로서의 시작부터 하이패션으로의 현재의 지위에 이르기까지 수세기에 걸친 청바지의 발전 과정을 시각 자료를 사용하여 연대순으로 보여준다.

런웨이 너머를 보다
Duchemin이 뉴욕부터 파리에 이르기까지 몇몇 걸출한

패션 디자이너들의 창작 과정을 잘 보여준다. Duchemin의 사진들로 가득한 이 책은 거의 20년에 걸쳐 의상이 런웨이에 나가기 전에 패션 하우스에서는 어떤 일이 벌어지는지 보여준다.

옷 안으로 걸어 들어가기: 나의 이야기
패션계 한복판에서 보낸 어린 시절에 대한 재미있는 회고록. Duchemin이 뉴욕에서 보낸 자신의 색다른 성장기를 묘사하는데, 그곳에서 그의 부모가 패션 모델로 경력을 시작하고 후에 자기들의 디자인 브랜드를 출시했다.

수 야드 길이의 재능: 10년간의 유행
10년에 걸쳐 무엇이 유행했고, 무엇이 유행이 지났고, 무엇이 다시 유행했는지 보여주는 Duchemin의 이미지 모음집

어휘 trace 추적하다, 조명하다 **visually** 시각 자료를 써서 **chronicle** 연대순으로 기록하다 **evolution** 발전, 진전 **working wear** 작업복 **status** (사회적) 지위 **high fashion** 최신 유행 스타일 **glance** 흘낏 봄 **runway** (패션 쇼장의) 무대 **capture** 정확히 포착하다, 담아내다 **preeminent** 걸출한, 뛰어난 **span** (기간에) 걸치다 **reveal** (드러내) 보여주다 **fashion house** 유명 디자이너의 의상실 **prior to** ~ 전에 **garment** 의상 **amusing** 재미있는 **memoir** 회고록 **amid** ~의 한복판에 **describe** 묘사하다 **unconventional** 색다른, 독특한 **upbringing** 양육 **launch** 출시하다, 출간하다 **label** 상표, 브랜드 **vogue** 유행 **compilation** 모음집, 편집본 **in style** 유행되는 **out of style** 유행이 지난

문장 분석

1. The book, filled with Duchemin's photographs, [spans nearly two decades] and [reveals what goes on in fashion houses prior to garments being ready for the runway].

➡ 등위접속사 and가 앞뒤에 있는 동사 spans와 reveals를 연결해 주고 있다.

➡ 동명사 being은 전치사 prior to의 목적어이다. 그 사이에 있는 garments는 동명사 being의 의미상 주어이다. 동명사의 의미상 주어는 바로 앞에 소유격이나 목적격 (대)명사로 쓰고 동명사의 행위의 주체가 된다.

Home	On-Air Schedule	Audio Archive	Sponsors

WHKK Radio
145.Evening Programming, March 13

7:00 – *The Splendid Table*
Host Emily Johnson discusses the newest super foods; their characteristics, benefits, and ideal ways to cook them. Featured recipes will be available to view on our Web site after tonight's broadcast.

8:00 – *The Tech Guy*
Host Leo Laporte focuses on the latest electronics. He talks about products that are really innovative and practical and identifies those that are not.

145.**9:00 - *Candid Tonight***
144.145.Host Stephanie Miller interviews photographer and author David Duchemin to find out what prompted him to write his newest book about his childhood. He shares stories about what it was like to grow up in the world of fashion.

홈	방송 일정	오디오 자료실	후원 업체

WHKK 라디오
3월 13일 저녁 방송 편성

7:00 - *멋진 식탁*
진행자 Emily Johnson이 최신 슈퍼 푸드의 특징과 이점, 이상적인 조리법 등을 논합니다. 특별 조리법은 오늘밤 방송 후 홈페이지에서 보실 수 있습니다.

8:00 - *The Tech Guy*
진행자 Leo Laporte가 최신 전자 제품들을 집중 조명합니다. 정말 혁신적이고 실용적인 제품들에 관해 이야기하고 그렇지 못한 것들도 알아봅니다.

9:00 - *투나잇 솔직 토크*
진행자 Stephanie Miller가 사진작가 겸 저자 David Duchemin과 인터뷰하여 어떤 계기로 어린 시절에 관한 새 책을 쓰게 되었는지 알아봅니다. Duchemin이 패션계에서 성장하는 것이 어떠했는지에 대해 이야기를 나눕니다.

어휘 on-air 방송 중의 archive 기록 보관소 programming 방송 편성 splendid 훌륭한, 멋진 host 진행자 super food 슈퍼 푸드(활성산소, 콜레스테롤 등을 제거하고 체내에서 필요로 하는 영양소를 많이 함유하는 웰빙 식품) characteristic 특징 electronics 전자제품 innovative 혁신적인 practical 실용적인 identify 알아

보다, 밝혀내다 **candid** 솔직한 **author** 저자 **prompt** (계기가 되어) 촉구하다

To: listenercomments@whkkradio.com
From: ahankins@moonmail.net
145. Date: March 14
Subject: Radio Interview

146.I discovered WHKK Radio over 20 years ago and have been a regular listener of your evening shows for at least a decade. **145.**I just wanted to express my pleasure at your newest offering. I've been intrigued by a lot of the writers who have been featured on the show so far, but the guest last night was particularly enjoyable. I have a memory of David when he was a little boy. **147.**I had the chance to work with his parents when they lived in New York, and I recall seeing David in his parents' studio most days after school hours. I was surprised to learn that he has written about his childhood, and I eagerly await reading his new book.

Thank you for the excellent programming.

Arianna Hankins

수신: listenercomments@whkkradio.com
발신: ahankins@moonmail.net
날짜: 3월 14일
제목: 라디오 인터뷰

20여 년 전에 WHKK 라디오를 알게 되었고 최소 10년 동안 이브닝쇼의 애청자였습니다. 새로운 프로그램에 대한 기쁨을 표현하고 싶네요. 지금까지 쇼에 출연했던 많은 작가들이 흥미로웠지만, 어젯밤 출연자는 특별히 즐거웠습니다. 저는 어린 소년이었을 때의 David에 대한 기억이 있습니다. 그의 부모님이 뉴욕에 살았을 때 함께 일할 기회가 있었는데요, 방과 후에 거의 매일 부모의 스튜디오에서 David를 봤던 기억이 납니다. 그가 어린 시절에 대한 책을 썼다는 것을 알고 놀랐고, 그의 새 책을 읽게 될 날을 간절히 기다립니다.

훌륭한 방송 편성 고맙습니다.

Arianna Hankins

어휘 **discover** 알게 되다, 발견하다 **regular** 잦은, 정기적인 **offering** 작품, 프로그램 **intrigued** 아주 흥미로워 하는 **feature** 출연시키다 **so far** 지금까지 **enjoyable** 즐거운 **recall** 기억해 내다 **eagerly** 간절히 **await** 기다리다

---

143. What is one common feature in all of Mr. Duchemin's books?

(A) They contain fashion images.
(B) They focus on well-known models.
(C) They are set in New York City.
(D) They keep track of events over multiple years.

어휘 **feature** 특징 **be set in** ~을 배경으로 하다 **reliant** 의존하는, 의지하는 **keep track of** ~를 추적하다

해석 Mr. Duchemin의 모든 책에서 한 가지 공통된 특징은 무엇인가?
(A) 패션 이미지가 포함되어 있다.
(B) 잘 알려진 모델들에 초점을 맞춘다.
(C) 뉴욕을 배경으로 한다.
(D) 여러 해에 걸쳐 일어난 일들을 추적한다.

해설 Tracing the Origin of Jeans는 여러 세기에 걸친 청바지의 발전 과정이며(Duchemin visually chronicles the evolution of jeans through the centuries), Glance Beyond the Runway는 거의 20년 동안 촬영한 사진으로 채워져 있고(The book, filled with Duchemin's photographs, spans nearly two decades), *Walking into Clothes: My Story*는 Duchemin의 어린 시절 성장 과정(Duchemin describes his unconventional upbringing in New York City), Yards of Talent: A Decade of Vogue는 10년 동안 촬영한 사진들의 모음집이다(Duchemin's compilation of images spanning a decade of fashion). 모든 책이 여러 해에 걸친 일들임을 기록하고 있으므로 (D)가 정답이다.

---

144. What book did Mr. Duchemin discuss on WHKK Radio?

(A) *Tracing the Origin of Jeans*
(B) *Glance Beyond the Runway*
(C) *Walking into Clothes: My Story*
(D) *Yards of Talent: A Decade of Vogue*

해석 Mr. Duchemin은 WHKK 라디오에서 어느 책을 논할 것인가?
(A) 청바지의 기원을 추적하다
(B) 런웨이 너머를 보다
(C) 옷 안으로 걸어 들어가기: 나의 이야기

(D) 수 야드 길이의 재능: 10년간의 유행

[연계 추론] Mr. Duchemin이 라디오에 출연해서 어린 시절에 대한 새 책을 쓰게 된 계기를 알려준다고 일정표에 나와 있는데(Host Stephanie Miller interviews photographer and author David Duchemin to find out what prompted him to write his newest book about his childhood.), 목록을 보면 Mr. Duchemin의 어린 시절에 대한 책은(An amusing memoir about childhood spent amid the fashion world) *Walking into Clothes: My Story*임을 알 수 있다. 그러므로 (C)가 정답이다.

---

145. What is indicated about *Candid Tonight*?

(A) It is broadcast every morning at 9:00.
(B) It was recently added to WHKK Radio.
(C) It is hosted by Emily Johnson.
(D) It was rescheduled to a different time.

[어휘] broadcast 방송하다 host 진행하다 reschedule 일정을 변경하다

[해석] 투나잇 솔직 토크에 대해 무엇이 나타나 있는가?
(A) 매일 오전 9시에 방송된다.
(B) 최근에 WHKK 라디오에 추가되었다.
(C) Emily Johnson이 진행한다.
(D) 다른 시간으로 일정이 변경되었다.

[연계 추론] 이메일을 보면 Ms. Hankins는 David Duchemin을 어린아이였을 때 본 기억이 있으며(I have a memory of David when he was a little boy.), Mr. Duchemin이 어제 저녁(3월 13일) 라디오에 출연했고(the guest last night was particularly enjoyable). 이 라디오 프로그램이 최근에 시작된 프로그램이라고 했다(I just wanted to express my pleasure at your newest offering). 일정표를 보면 3월 13일에 David Duchemin이 출연한 프로그램은 Candid Tonight이므로, 두 지문의 내용을 종합하면 Candid Tonight은 최근에 추가 편성된 프로그램임을 추론할 수 있다.

---

146. In the e-mail, the word "regular" in paragraph 1, line 1, is closest in meaning to

(A) orderly
(B) typical
(C) frequent
(D) complete

[해석] 이메일 첫 문단 첫째 줄의 단어 regular와 의미상 가장 가까운 것은

(A) 정돈된, 정연한
(B) 전형적인
(C) 잦은, 빈번한
(D) 완전한

[해설] regular는 '보통의, 일반적인(B)'이라는 뜻도 있고, '정연한, 질서 있는(A)'이라는 의미로도 사용할 수 있다. 구어체 문장에서는 '완전한(D)'이라는 뜻으로도 사용한다. 본문에서는 저녁 쇼를 자주 듣는 사람이라고 말하고 있으므로(a regular listener of your evening shows), regular를 (C) frequent로 바꿔 쓸 수 있다.

---

147. What is probably true about Ms. Hankins?

(A) She has worked in the fashion industry.
(B) She has interviewed Mr. Duchemin.
(C) She was featured on *The Tech Guy*.
(D) She hosts a radio talk show.

[해석] Ms. Hankins에 대해 무엇이 진실이겠는가?
(A) 패션업계에서 일한 적이 있다.
(B) Mr. Duchemin을 인터뷰했다.
(C) The Tech Guy에 출연했다.
(D) 라디오 토크쇼를 진행한다.

[연계 추론] 이메일에서 Ms. Hankins는 뉴욕에서 Mr. Duchemin의 부모와 함께 일한 적이 있다고 했는데(I had the chance to work with his parents when they lived in New York), 목록을 보면 Mr. Duchemin의 부모는 뉴욕에서 패션 디자이너와 의류 사업가로 일했던 것을 알 수 있다(New York City, where his parents began their career as fashion models before launching their own design label). 그러므로 두 지문의 내용을 종합하면 Ms. Hankins는 패션업계 종사자였다는 사실을 추론할 수 있다.

Day 10

PART 5 & 6 Exercise

101 (C)	**102** (C)	**103** (A)	**104** (B)	**105** (B)
106 (D)	**107** (D)	**108** (B)	**109** (C)	**110** (B)
111 (A)	**112** (A)	**113** (A)	**114** (D)	**115** (B)

101. Policy makers should not let the current rise in oil prices ------- the nation's long-term development plans and lead to a recession.

(A) affected
(B) to affect
(C) affect
(D) affecting

[어휘] policy maker 정책 입안자 current 현재의 long-term 장기적인 lead to ~로 이어지다 recession 경기 후퇴, 불황

[해석] 정책 입안자들은 현재의 유가 상승이 국가의 장기적 개발 계획에 영향을 미쳐 불황으로 이어지지 않도록 해야 한다.

[해설] 빈칸 앞에 사역동사 let이 있으므로 목적격 보어 자리인 빈칸에는 동사원형 (C)와 과거분사 (A)가 들어갈 수 있다. 목적어 '현재의 유가 상승(the current rise in oil prices)'이 '국가의 장기적 개발 계획(the nation's long-term development plans)'에 영향을 '미치는' 것이므로 능동형인 동사원형 (C)가 정답으로 알맞다.

102. Dr. Wasem suggests that we ------- announcing the results of the analysis until we have accurate data.

(A) will delay
(B) have delayed
(C) delay
(D) would have delayed

[어휘] analysis 분석 연구 accurate 정확한

[해석] Wasem 박사는 정확한 데이터를 가지게 될 때까지 분석 연구 결과의 발표를 미루자고 제안한다.

[해설] that절 앞의 동사 suggests를 보고 정답을 알 수 있다. '제안'을 나타내는 동사이므로 that절에서 동사원형을 사용해야 한다. 그러므로 (C)가 정답이다.

103. It is imperative that the products ------- meticulously inspected before they are sent out to clients.

(A) be
(B) to be
(C) being
(D) are

[어휘] imperative 반드시 해야 하는, 긴요한 meticulously 꼼꼼하게, 세심하게 inspect 검사하다 send out ~을 보내다, 발송하다

[해석] 제품은 고객에게 발송되기 전에 반드시 꼼꼼하게 검사되어야 한다.

[해설] that절 앞의 it is imperative를 보고 정답을 알 수 있다. 당위성을 나타내는 형용사 imperative가 있으므로 that절의 동사 자리인 빈칸에는 동사원형 (A)가 알맞다.

104. The Connon XL4 Cooker has the ------- to cook rice, steam vegetables, and keep food warm for several hours.

(A) explanation
(B) ability
(C) talent
(D) preference

[어휘] cooker (냄비, 솥 등) 조리 기구 explanation 설명 talent 재능 preference 선호 steam (음식을) 찌다

[해석] The Connon XL4 밥솥은 밥을 짓고, 채소를 찌고, 몇 시간 동안 음식을 따뜻하게 유지하는 기능이 있다.

[해설] 빈칸 뒤에 to부정사가 있으면 명사 'ability / effort / the right / enough + 명사'를 떠올리자. 빈칸에 (B)가 들어가면 된다.

105. The company could not help but watch its competitors ------- the bigger chunk of the market share due to lack of advanced technologies.

(A) takes
(B) taking
(C) to take
(D) taken

해석 그 회사는 첨단 기술의 부족으로 경쟁업체들이 시장 점
유율을 더 많이 차지하는 것을 지켜볼 수밖에 없었다.

해설 빈칸 앞에 지각동사 watch가 있으므로 목적격 보어인
빈칸에는 현재분사 (B)와 과거분사 (D)가 들어갈 수 있
다. 목적어 '경쟁업체들(its competitors)'이 '시장 점유
율에서 더 많은 부분(the bigger chunk of the
market share)을 차지하는' 것이므로 능동형인 현재분
사 (B)가 정답으로 알맞다.

---

106. The labor union requested that the
management's decision to reduce
corporate travel budget -------
immediately.

(A) is reconsidered
(B) are reconsidered
(C) reconsider
(D) be reconsidered

어휘 labor union 노동조합, 노조 management 경영진, 운영
진 corporate 기업의, 회사의 budget 예산 reconsider
재고하다 immediately 즉시

해석 노조는 출장 예산을 삭감하기로 한 경영진의 결정이 즉
시 재고되어야 한다고 요구했다.

해설 requested가 '요구'를 나타내는 동사이므로 that절에
는 동사원형을 사용해야 한다. 빈칸 뒤에 목적어가 없
으므로 수동태 동사 (D)가 정답이다.

---

107. All advertisements at the National
Fashion, Fabric & Garment Machinery
Expo are subject to ------- by the
board of directors.

(A) approve
(B) approvingly
(C) approving
(D) approval

어휘 subject to ~을 받아야 하는 approve 승인하다
approvingly 찬성하여 board of directors 이사회

해석 전국 패션 및 직물, 의류 기계 박람회의 모든 광고는 이
사회의 승인을 받아야 한다.

해설 시험에서 to -------는 대부분 to부정사이지만, 이 문
제의 are subject to에서 to는 전치사이다. 빈칸에는
전치사의 목적어가 될 수 있는 명사 (D)나 동명사 (C)가
들어갈 수 있다. 그런데 빈칸 뒤에 목적어가 없으므로
명사 (D)가 정답으로 알맞다.

---

108. By constantly developing state-of-
the-art technologies, the Zanello
Motor Company has shown its
commitment to ------- the fuel
consumption of all its automobile
models.

(A) lowers
(B) lowering
(C) lowered
(D) lowest

어휘 constantly 끊임없이, 거듭 state-of-the-art 최첨단의
commitment to ~에 대한 전념, 헌신 lower 내리다, 낮추
다 automobile 자동차

해석 Zanello 자동차 회사는 지속적으로 최첨단 기술을 개
발함으로써 모든 자동차 모델의 연료 소비량을 낮추는
일에 전념하고 있음을 보여주었다.

해설 commitment to -------에서 to는 전치사이다. 그러
므로 빈칸에는 목적어로 (동)명사가 들어가야 하므로
(B)가 정답이다.

---

109. The petroleum company didn't have
enough money ------- a new waste
oil processing plant.

(A) building
(B) of building
(C) to build
(D) in building

어휘 petroleum 석유 waste oil 폐유 processing plant
가공처리 공장

해석 그 석유 회사는 새 폐유 처리 공장을 지을 돈이 충분하
지 않았다.

해설 빈칸 앞의 enough money(enough + 명사)를 보고
to부정사 (C)를 정답으로 선택해야 한다.

---

110. Fagan Law hired more paralegals
------- meet its commitment to
clients.

(A) consequently
(B) in order to
(C) in any case
(D) additionally

어휘 paralegal 변호사 보조원 consequently 그 결과
in any case 어쨌든 additionally 추가로 meet one's
commitment 약속한 일을 하다, 의무를 다하다

해석 Fagan Law는 고객에 대한 의무를 다하기 위해 변호사 보조원을 추가로 채용했다.

해설 빈칸 앞에 완성된 3형식 문장이 있고 빈칸 뒤에 동사원형이 있으므로 정답은 (B) in order to이다.

---

111. Mr. Lee would like ------- a meeting about the Hinton account as soon as possible.

(A) to arrange
(B) arranging
(C) having arranged
(D) arrangement

어휘 arrange 마련하다. 주선하다 account 거래 관계
해석 Mr. Lee는 되도록 빨리 Hinton 사(社)와의 거래에 대한 회의를 마련하고 싶어 한다.

해설 빈칸 앞에 would like가 있으므로 would like to-V 구문을 완성하는 문제임을 알 수 있다. 그러므로 to부정사 (A)가 정답이다.

---

112. ------- allow up to three hours for the preparation of meal orders over $300.

(A) Please
(B) Pleasing
(C) Pleasure
(D) Pleased

어휘 allow (시간·돈 등을) 할당하다. 잡다 up to 최대 ~까지
해석 300달러 이상의 식사 주문 준비에는 최대 3시간이 소요될 수 있습니다.

해설 빈칸 뒤에 동사원형으로 시작하는 명령문이 있으므로 빈칸에는 (A) Please가 들어가야 한다.

---

113. Patas Marketing is able to help any business ------- its products through multimedia advertising packages.

(A) promote
(B) promoted
(C) promotable
(D) promoter

어휘 promote 홍보하다 package 종합 서비스, 패키지
해석 Patas Marketing은 어떤 사업체든 멀티미디어 광고 패키지를 통해 상품을 홍보하도록 도울 수 있습니다.

해설 빈칸 앞에 5형식 동사 help와 목적어 any business가

있으므로 빈칸에는 목적격 보어가 들어가야 한다. 따라서 동사원형 (A)가 정답이다.

---

114. Company Vice President Jo Gacutan had no ------- to being considered for the position of CEO.

(A) objected
(B) objecting
(C) objects
(D) objection

어휘 object 물건: 반대하다 objection 이의, 반대
해석 회사 부사장 Jo Gacutan이 CEO 자리에 거론되는데 이의가 없다.

해설 빈칸 앞에 had no가 있으므로 동사 had의 목적어가 되도록 명사 (C)와 (D) 중에서 정답을 선택해야 한다. had no ------- to being considered가 '거론되는데 이의가 없다'라는 뜻으로 해석하는 것이 자연스러우므로 (D)가 정답이다. 명사 objection은 동사 object처럼 전치사 to와 함께 사용한다.

---

115. The increasing employment rate is one factor contributing to ------- in the housing construction trade.

(A) grow
(B) growth
(C) grew
(D) grown

어휘 employment rate 취업률 factor 요인, 요소 contribute to ~에 기여하다 housing construction 주택건설 trade 사업[-업]

해석 증가하는 취업률은 주택 건설업의 성장에 기여하는 한 가지 요인이다.

해설 시험에서 to -------는 대부분 to부정사이지만, contributing to에서 to는 전치사이다. 빈칸은 전치사의 목적어 자리이므로 명사 (B)가 정답이다.

101 (A)	**102** (A)	**103** (D)	**104** (B)	**105** (D)
106 (C)	**107** (B)	**108** (C)	**109** (A)	**110** (A)
111 (D)	**112** (A)	**113** (B)	**114** (A)	**115** (D)
116 (C)	**117** (D)	**118** (B)	**119** (C)	**120** (D)
121 (B)	**122** (D)	**123** (A)	**124** (C)	**125** (C)
126 (D)	**127** (A)	**128** (B)	**129** (A)	**130** (A)
131 (C)	**132** (D)	**133** (A)	**134** (D)	**135** (A)
136 (C)	**137** (C)	**138** (B)	**139** (D)	**140** (D)
141 (B)	**142** (C)	**143** (B)	**144** (C)	**145** (A)
146 (B)	**147** (D)			

Part 5

101. The company is trying to make its employees ------- harder by offering them financial incentives.

(A) **work**
(B) to work
(C) worked
(D) working

어휘 incentives 장려책, 우대책

해석 그 회사는 재정적 장려책을 제공함으로써 직원들이 더 열심히 일할 수 있도록 노력하고 있다.

해설 사역동사 make가 있으므로 목적격 보어인 빈칸에는 동사원형 (A)와 과거분사 (C)가 들어갈 수 있다. work는 1형식 자동사로 과거분사로 사용될 수 없으므로 정답은 동사원형 (A)이다.

102. The CFO will be more empowered beyond just making investment and accounting decisions ------- this day onward.

(A) **from**
(B) at
(C) on
(D) for

어휘 CFO(chief financial officer) 재무 담당 최고 책임자 empower 권한을 주다 investment 투자 accounting 회계 from this day onward 오늘 이후

해석 CFO는 오늘 이후 단지 투자와 회계에 관한 결정을 내리는 것을 넘어서 더 많은 권한을 갖게 될 것이다.

해설 짝으로 출제되는 어휘들을 암기해 두자. 빈칸 뒤에 '시점 + on(ward)'가 있으면 정답은 (A) from이다.

103. ------- escalating fuel prices, Pineford Trucking plans to restructure some of its divisions.

(A) In that
(B) Even if
(C) Just as
(D) **Owing to**

어휘 in that ~라는 점에서] escalate 증가하다, 악화되다 trucking 트럭 수송(업) restructure 구조 조정하다 division 부서

해석 Pineford Trucking은 증가하는 연료 가격 때문에 일부 사업부를 구조 조정할 계획이다.

해설 빈칸 뒤에 '주어 + 동사'가 없으므로 접속사인 (A)와 (B)는 제외한다. 연료 가격 상승은 구조 조정의 원인이므로 '~ 때문에'라는 뜻의 (D) owing to가 정답으로 알맞다.

104. It is ------- that clients be made aware of inventory shortages immediately upon their occurrence.

(A) sudden
(B) **critical**
(C) eventful
(D) actual

어휘 sudden 갑작스러운 critical 중대한, 결정적인 eventful 다사다난한, 파란만장한 actual 사실의 aware of ~을 알고 있는, 의식하는 inventory 재고(품) shortage 부족 (up)on + 명사[V-ing] ~하자마자 occurrence 발생, 사건

해석 고객이 재고 부족 발생 즉시 알도록 하는 것이 중요하다.

해설 that절의 동사가 be made인 것을 보면 정답을 알 수 있다. 주절에 당위성을 나타내는 형용사가 있을 때 that절에 동사원형을 사용하므로 정답은 (B)이다.

105. Staff members of Three Rivers Medical Center are ------- to satisfying the needs of the community with a full range of medical services.

(A) expressed
(B) scheduled
(C) designed
(D) **committed**

어휘 a full range of 다양한, 폭넓은

해석 **해석** Three Rivers 의료 센터의 직원들은 다양한 의료 서비스로 지역 사회의 요구를 충족시키는 데 전념하고 있다.

해설 빈칸 앞뒤 are ------- to satisfying을 보고 'be + p.p. + 전치사 to' 구문으로 사용할 수 있는 동사를 선택해야 한다. 그러므로 (D)가 정답이다.

---

106. City authorities insist that plans to install new digital parking meters will not ------- to an increase in parking charges.

(A) experience
(B) determine
(C) lead
(D) intend

어휘 authorities 당국 install 설치하다

해석 시 당국은 새 디지털 주차 미터기를 설치하려는 계획이 주차 요금 인상으로 이어지지는 않을 것이라고 주장한다.

해설 타동사 experience는 목적어가 필요하므로 (A)는 제외하자. determine과 intend는 뒤에 to부정사를 사용해야 하므로 정답은 (C)이다. '~로 이어지다'라는 뜻의 lead to는 시험에 자주 등장하는 표현이므로 암기해 두자.

---

107. Shipments of copper, the country's leading export, and fresh fruit just coming into season may be ------- by a long strike.

(A) separated
(B) disrupted
(C) proposed
(D) dismissed

어휘 shipment 수송 copper 구리. 동 leading 주요한, 선두의 export 수출품 come into season 제철이 되다 separate 분리하다 disrupt 방해하다, 지장을 주다 dismiss 해산하다; 해고하다 strike 파업

해석 오랜 파업으로 그 나라의 주요 수출품인 구리와 막 제철을 맞은 신선 과일의 수송에 지장이 있을 수 있다.

해설 Shipments가 문장의 주어이다. Shipments ~ may be ------- by a long strike(오랜 파업으로 인해 수송이 [(A) 분리될 (B) 방해받을 (C) 제안될 (D) 해산될] 수 있다.)의 의미를 자연스럽게 해 주는 (B)가 정답이다.

---

108. The North Ridge Hospital mailed out a brochure to all member households to ------- them of the preventative medicine.

(A) informing
(B) information
(C) inform
(D) informed

어휘 mail out ~을 일괄 발송하다 brochure 안내 책자 household 가정, 가구, 세대 inform A of B A에게 B를 알리다 preventative 예방의, 방지의

해석 North Ridge 병원은 예방약을 알리기 위해 모든 회원 가정에 안내 책자를 일괄 발송했다.

해설 to 뒤에 빈칸이 있으면 대부분 to부정사라고 생각하면 된다. to ------- them of the preventative medicine이 '예방약에 대해 알리기 위해'라는 뜻이 되도록 동사원형 (C)를 정답으로 선택하자.

---

109. Leekpai Consulting helps companies increase overall quality, not just quicken the ------- of production.

(A) pace
(B) dates
(C) level
(D) measure

어휘 quality 품질 not just ~뿐만 아니라 quicken 빠르게 하다 pace (일의) 속도 measure 조치, 정책

해석 Leekpai 컨설팅은 기업들이 생산 속도를 빠르게 하는 것뿐만 아니라 전반적인 품질을 높일 수 있도록 돕는다.

해설 빈칸 앞뒤 quicken the ------- of production(생산의 [(A) 속도를 (B) 날짜를 (C) 수준을 (D) 조치를] 빠르게 한다)의 의미를 자연스럽게 하는 명사 (A)가 정답이다.

---

110. Many DNB Bank's employees said that they could ------- read the last month's company newsletter because the print was so small.

(A) barely
(B) nearly
(C) simply
(D) almost

어휘 barely 거의 ~아니게[없이] print 인쇄 활자

해설 DNB 은행의 많은 직원들은 활자가 너무 작아서 지난

달 회사 소식지를 거의 읽을 수 없었다고 말했다.

해설 "활자가 너무 작아서 거의 읽을 수 없었다."라는 뜻이 자연스러우므로 (A) barely가 정답으로 알맞다.

---

111. Due to the unexpected lack of funding for the project, the completion of the building has been postponed ------- there is another source of funds.

(A) while
(B) during
(C) upon
(D) until

어휘 unexpected 예상치 못한 funding 기금, 자금 completion 완성 postpone 연기하다

해석 예상치 못한 프로젝트 자금 부족 때문에 건물 완공은 다른 자금원이 마련될 때까지 연기되었다.

해설 짝으로 출제되는 어휘들을 암기해 두자. '연기하다'라는 뜻의 동사 postpone, delay, put off, defer가 있으면 정답은 (D) until이다.

---

112. Mertens Laboratories, Inc., is interested in exploring new technical partnerships as part of an ongoing ------- to expand its product line.

(A) effort
(B) growth
(C) strength
(D) rise

어휘 explore 탐구하다, 조사하다 partnership 협력; 제휴 ongoing 진행 중인, 지속적인 line 제품군

해석 Mertens Laboratories 사(社)는 제품군을 확대하기 위한 지속적인 노력의 일환으로 새로운 기술 제휴를 알아보는 데 관심이 있다.

해설 'ability / effort / the right / enough + 명사' 뒤에 빈칸이 있으면 to부정사를 떠올리자. '~하려는 노력의 일환으로'라는 뜻이 자연스러우므로 (A)가 정답이다.

---

113. Innovative leading computer scientists have helped establish the emergent field of quantum computing ------- a new area of academic research.

(A) to
(B) as

(C) of
(D) at

어휘 innovative 혁신적인 establish 확립하다 emergent 신생의, 신흥의 field 분야 quantum computing 양자 컴퓨팅 academic 학문의

해석 혁신적인 선도 컴퓨터 과학자들이 양자 컴퓨팅이라는 신생 분야를 학술 연구의 새 분야로 확립하는데 도움을 주었다.

해설 establish the emergent field of quantum computing ------- a new area of academic research는 "퀀텀 컴퓨팅 분야를 학술 연구의 새 분야로 확립하다."라는 뜻이 자연스러우므로 (B) as가 정답으로 알맞다.

---

114. Mr. Kadam has asked that we ------- the hazards more carefully before investing in new businesses.

(A) consider
(B) considered
(C) considering
(D) are considering

어휘 hazard 위험 (요소)

해석 Mr. Kadam은 우리가 신규 사업에 투자하기 전에 위험 요소들을 더 신중하게 고려해 달라고 요청했다.

해설 that절 앞의 동사 has asked가 '요청하다'라는 뜻이므로 빈칸에는 동사원형 (A)가 알맞다.

---

115. Ms. Egan will rely ------- department heads to develop employee incentive programs.

(A) onto
(B) into
(C) within
(D) upon

어휘 rely upon 의존하다 department head 부서장 incentive 장려책, 우대책

해석 Ms. Egan은 부서장에게 의존하여 직원 인센티브 프로그램을 개발할 것이다.

해설 짝으로 출제되는 어휘들을 암기해 두자. '~에 의존하다'라는 뜻으로 rely, depend 뒤에는 전치사 (up)on이 있어야 한다. 그러므로 빈칸에 (D)가 들어가야 한다.

---

116. ------- business sources, the critically acclaimed Kinsley Restaurant on

Gray Hills Avenue will be closing after 50 years of business.

(A) As soon as
(B) Rather than
(C) According to
(D) Whenever

어휘 source 정보원, 소식통 critically acclaimed 비평가들의 찬사를 받는

해석 업계 소식통에 따르면 Gray Hills 가(街)에 있는 비평가들의 찬사를 받은 Kinsley 식당이 50년간의 영업을 마무리하고 문을 닫을 것이다.

해설 빈칸 뒤에 '주어+동사'가 없으므로 접속사인 (A)와 (D)는 제외하자. 문맥상 '------- business sources'는 '업계 소식통에 따르면'이라는 뜻이 자연스러우므로 (C)가 정답으로 알맞다.

---

117. It is imperative for all personnel to refrain from igniting flames around ------- materials.

(A) tangible
(B) converted
(C) exhausted
(D) combustible

어휘 imperative 반드시 해야 하는 personnel 직원 refrain from ~을 삼가다, 자제하다 ignite 불을 붙이다, 점화하다 flame 불길, 불꽃, 화염 tangible 만질 수 있는, 유형(有形)의 convert 전환시키다, 개조하다 exhausted 기진맥진한, 탈진한 combustible 불이 잘 붙는, 가연성인

해석 모든 직원은 가연성 물질 주변에서 점화하는 것을 삼가야 한다.

해설 refrain from igniting flames around ------- materials([(A) 유형의 (B) 전환된 (C) 기진맥진한 (D) 가연성인] 물질 주변에서 점화하는 것을 삼가다)의 의미를 자연스럽게 해 주는 형용사 (D)가 정답이다.

---

118. Regional demands for new housing may increase exponentially within two years, within -------.

(A) limit
(B) limits
(C) limiting
(D) limited

어휘 housing 주택 (공급) exponentially 기하급수적으로 within limits 어느 정도까지, 한도 내에서

해석 신규 주택에 대한 지역의 수요가 2년 이내에 한도 내에

서 기하급수적으로 증가할 수 있다.

해설 within limits는 '한도 내에서, 적당한 선에서'라는 뜻의 관용 표현이므로 정답은 (B)이다.

---

119. Yuina Hashimoto's latest novel is his most captivating ------- and is sure to make Quality Books' best-seller list.

(A) just
(B) later
(C) yet
(D) very

어휘 latest 최신의 captivating 매혹적인, 마음을 사로잡는 yet (최상급과 함께) 지금까지 be sure to-V 확실히 ~하다 make one's list ~의 목록에 오르다

해석 Yuina Hashimoto의 최신 소설은 지금까지 나온 것 중 가장 매혹적이며 Quality 출판사의 베스트셀러 목록에 들 것이 확실하다.

해설 부사 yet은 최상급 형용사 뒤에서 의미를 강조할 때 사용한다. his most captivating -------은 '이제껏 가장 마음을 사로잡는'이라는 뜻이 자연스러우므로 (C)가 정답이다.

---

120. Overseeing inventory control and warehousing strategies ------- within the responsibilities of the supply chain manager.

(A) has
(B) covers
(C) marks
(D) falls

어휘 oversee 감독하다 inventory control 재고 관리 warehousing 창고 보관 strategy 전략, 계획 fall within ~의 범위에 있다, ~에 포함되다 supply chain 공급망

해석 재고 관리와 창고 보관 계획을 감독하는 일은 공급망 관리자의 책임에 속한다.

해설 재고 관리나 창고 보관 계획을 감독하는 것은 공급망 매니저의 책임에 '포함된다'가 어울리므로 '~의 범위에 있다, ~에 포함되다'라는 뜻의 (D)가 정답이다.

---

121. Congress passed the bill granting the government the right ------- money transfers to hostile countries.

(A) ban

(B) to ban
(C) of banning
(D) banning

> **어휘** congress (미국 등의) 의회 bill 법안 right 권리, 권한 ban 금지하다 money transfer 송금 hostile 적대적인

> **해석** 의회는 정부에게 적대국으로의 송금을 금지할 권한을 부여하는 법안을 통과시켰다.

> **해설** 'ability / effort / the right / enough + 명사(대부분 돈)' 다음에는 to부정사가 오므로 (B)가 정답이다.

---

122. The implementation of a successful digital marketing campaign has helped Ainley Electronics ------- its profit margins.

(A) stabilized
(B) stability
(C) stabilizing
(D) stabilize

> **어휘** implementation 실행 stabilize 안정시키다 profit margin 이윤 폭

> **해석** 성공적인 디지털 마케팅 캠페인의 실행이 Ainley 전자가 이윤 폭을 안정화하는데 도움을 주었다.

> **해설** 빈칸 앞에 5형식 동사 help와 목적어 Ainley Electronics가 있으므로 빈칸에는 목적격 보어로 동사원형 (D)가 들어가야 한다.

---

123. It is imperative that lawmakers ------- with local residents to find out about their views on current issues.

(A) communicate
(B) must communicate
(C) communicated
(D) communicating

> **어휘** lawmaker 입법자 resident 주민 find out about ~에 대해 알아보다 view 견해 current issue 현안, 현재의 쟁점

> **해석** 의원들은 지역 주민들과 소통하여 현안에 대한 그들의 견해를 알아보는 것이 필수적이다.

> **해설** that절 앞에 당위성을 나타내는 형용사 imperative가 있으므로 빈칸에는 동사원형 (A)가 들어가야 한다.

---

124. Of all the vehicle models available today, it can be challenging to figure out ------- would best suit your company's needs.

(A) when
(B) why
(C) which
(D) where

> **어휘** challenging 힘든, 어려운 figure out ~을 이해하다, 알아내다 suit ~에 알맞다, 괜찮다

> **해석** 오늘 이용하실 수 있는 모든 차량 모델 중에서 어느 것이 당신 회사의 필요에 가장 맞을지 알아내는 것은 어려울 수 있습니다.

> **해설** 보기를 살펴보면 관계사 문제인 것 같지만, 빈칸 앞에 선행사가 없어서 관계대명사도 정답이 될 수 없고, 빈칸 뒤에는 불완전한 문장이 있어서 관계부사도 정답이 아니다. 여러 차량 모델 중 '어느 것'이 당신 회사의 필요에 알맞을지 모르겠다는 내용이므로, 빈칸에 의문사 (C)가 알맞다.

---

125. At Barretto Securities, trainees alternate ------- participating in information sessions and working closely with assigned mentors.

(A) along
(B) against
(C) between
(D) near

> **어휘** securities 유가 증권 trainee 교육생, 수습 직원 alternate between A and B A와 B를 번갈아 하다 information session 설명회 closely 긴밀하게 assigned 배정된

> **해석** Barretto 증권에서는 수습 직원들이 설명회 참석하기와 배정된 멘토와 긴밀하게 작업하기를 번갈아 한다.

> **해설** 설명회 참석(participating in information sessions)과 멘토와 함께 하는 작업(working closely with assigned mentors), 즉 '수업'과 '실습'을 and로 연결하고 있다. 그러므로 and와 짝을 이루어 사용할 수 있는 (C) between이 정답이다. alternate between A and B는 'A와 B를 번갈아 하다'라는 뜻이다.

---

126. Long-time admirers of Yoshiro Kasai who are ------- to the author's formal writing style will be astonished by her latest biography.

(A) fortunate
(B) readable
(C) comparable
(D) accustomed

해석 저자의 격식 있는 문체에 익숙한 Yoshiro Kasai의 오랜 팬들은 그녀의 최신 전기를 읽으면 깜짝 놀랄 것이다.

해설 Long-time admirers of Yoshiro Kasai who are ------- to the author's formal writing style(저자의 격식 있는 문체에 [(A) 운 좋은 (B) 읽기 쉬운 (C) 비교할 만한 (D) 익숙한] Yoshiro Kasai의 오랜 팬들)의 의미를 자연스럽게 해 주는 (D)가 정답이다.

---

127. The driver will make three ------- to deliver the package before it is brought back to our warehouse.

(A) attempts
(B) pursuits
(C) aims
(D) experiences

어휘 make an attempt to-V ~하기를 시도하다 warehouse 창고

해석 기사가 소포 배달하기를 3회 시도한 후에는 소포가 저희 창고로 회수될 것입니다.

해설 소포를 창고로 가지고 돌아가기 전에 배송을 세 번 '시도'해 본다는 뜻이 자연스러우므로 (A)가 정답이다.

---

128. The staff has to ------- as much market-research data as possible prior to devising the advertising campaign.

(A) equip
(B) compile
(C) endorse
(D) compose

어휘 equip 장비를 갖추다 compile (자료를) 모으다 endorse (공개적으로) 지지하다 compose 구성하다 prior to ~하기 전에

해석 직원들은 광고 캠페인을 고안하기 전에 되도록 많은 시장 조사 데이터를 모아야 한다.

해설 has to ------- as much market-research data as possible(되도록 많은 시장 조사 데이터를 [(A) 장비를 갖춰야 (B) 모아야 (C) 지지해야 (D) 구성해야] 한다.)의 의미를 자연스럽게 해 주는 (B)가 정답이다.

---

129. All Hershel Industries employees must have a valid ID card ------- enter the building.

(A) in order to
(B) as long as
(C) regarding
(D) always

어휘 valid 유효한 as long as ~하는 한 regarding ~에 대해

해석 모든 Hershel Industries 직원들은 건물에 들어가기 위해 유효한 사원증이 있어야 한다.

해설 빈칸 앞에 완성된 3형식 문장이 있고 빈칸 뒤에 동사원형이 있으므로 빈칸에 (A) in order to가 들어가야 한다.

---

130. ------- materials for the advanced Farsi course include audio files and an educational video series.

(A) Supplementary
(B) Consequential
(C) Persistent
(D) Cooperative

어휘 supplementary 보충의, 추가의 consequential ~의 결과로 일어나는, ~에 따른 persistent 끈질긴, 집요한 advanced 고급의, 상급의 Farsi 페르시아어

해석 고급 페르시아어 과정의 보충 자료에는 오디오 파일과 교육용 동영상 시리즈를 포함한다.

해설 Consequential은 단어의 의미상 원인을 나타내는 내용이 앞에 있어야 하므로 (B)는 제외하자. ------- materials([(A) 보충 (C) 끈질긴 (D) 협동하는] 자료)의 의미를 자연스럽게 하는 (A)가 정답이다.

Part 6

Questions 131-134 refer to the following article.

Eximion, Inc., Unveils Latest Development Initiative

SAN FRANCISCO (November 11) - Scientists from Eximion, Inc., a technology firm, are striving to develop a sensor capable of detecting corrosion caused by environmental exposure. Corrosion is a major contributor to the ^131.financial losses the aircraft industry experiences each year. "This will be a tremendous ^132.asset for commercial airline fleets," says Connie Hyun, Eximion's CEO. "The sensor will reduce both labor and maintenance costs without being too costly."

According to Ms. Hyun, the sensor is designed to identify corrosion in its initial stages, when the issue can be corrected simply by eliminating the corroded material. ^133.This will minimize the need for making expensive structural repairs. In the structure of large aircraft, some critical joints can be particularly susceptible to corrosion. ^134.Fortunately, the sensor can be utilized to scrutinize these areas and then target the most probable areas of concern.

131-134번 문제는 다음 기사에 관한 것입니다.

Eximion 사(社), 최신 개발 계획을 공개하다

샌프란시스코(11월 11일) – 기술 주식회사 Eximion의 과학자들이 환경 노출로 인한 부식을 탐지할 수 있는 센서를 개발하려고 애쓰고 있다. 부식은 매년 항공기 업계가 겪는 재정적 손실의 주요 요인이다. Eximion 의 CEO Connie Hyun은 "이것은 상업 항공사들의 항공기에 엄청난 자산이 될 것입니다."라고 말한다. "큰 비용이 들지도 않는 이 센서는 인건비와 유지보수비를 모두 줄여줄 것입니다."

Ms. Hyun에 따르면 이 센서는 부식을 초기 단계에 찾아내도록 설계되었는데, 이때는 단순히 부식된 부분을 없애기만 하면 문제가 해결된다. 이것은 값비싼 구조적 수리를 해야 할 필요를 최소화할 것이다. 대형 항공기의 구조에서는 일부 중요한 연결 부위가 특히 부식에 영향을 받기 쉽다. 다행히 이 센서를 활용하면 이러한 부위를 정밀 검사한 후 우려되는 가장 가능성 있는 부분을 겨냥할 수 있다.

어휘 unveil (계획, 상품을) 공개하다, 발표하다 initiative 계획, 프로젝트 strive to-V ~하려고 노력하다, 애쓰다 detect 감지하다, 탐지하다 corrosion 부식, 침식 exposure 노출 contributor 요인; 기부자 aircraft 항공기 experience 겪다, 경험하다 tremendous 엄청난, 굉장히 큰 asset 자

산 fleet (비행기·버스·택시 등의) 무리 maintenance 유지 보수 costly 많은 비용이 드는 be designed to-V ~하도록 설계되다 identify 찾다, 발견하다 initial 처음의, 초기의 correct 바로잡다 eliminate 없애다, 제거[삭제]하다 corrode 부식시키다, 좀먹다 minimize 최소화하다, 되도록 적게 하다 structural 구조상의 critical 대단히 중요한 joint 연결 부위 particularly 특히 susceptible to ~에 영향 받기 쉬운 fortunately 다행히 utilize 활용하다, 이용하다 scrutinize 면밀히 조사하다

---

131. (A) financially
(B) financed
(C) financial
(D) finances

해설 빈칸 앞뒤 a major contributor to ------ losses를 보고 정답을 선택하자. 명사 앞에 빈칸이 있으므로 형용사 (C)가 정답이다.

---

132. (A) balance
(B) examination
(C) expectation
(D) asset

어휘 examination 검사 expectation 기대

해설 빈칸 앞의 This가 가리키는 것은 지문 첫 문장에 나오는 a sensor capable of detecting corrosion이다. 둘째 문장에서 항공기 업계가 매년 부식으로 인해 겪는 재정적 손실에 대해 언급하고 있으므로(Corrosion is a major contributor to financial losses the aircraft industry experiences each year.), 부식을 탐지하는 기능이 있는 이 센서는 항공사에게 엄청난 '자산'이라고 하는 것이 자연스러우므로 (D)가 정답이다.

---

133. **(A) This will minimize the need for making expensive structural repairs.**
(B) The parts have all been replaced with higher quality materials.
(C) The project proceeds to scanning the affected areas.
(D) Its style and sleek design attracted the public.

어휘 part 부품, 부분 be replaced with ~로 대체되다 proceed to ~로 넘어가다, 진행되다 scan 검사하다, 탐색하다 affect ~에 영향을 미치다, ~에 작용하다 area 부위, 부분 sleek 매끈한, 날렵한 attract ~의 관심을 끌다

해석 (A) 이것은 값비싼 구조적 수리를 해야 할 필요를 최소

화할 것이다.

(B) 부품은 모두 더 좋은 품질의 자재로 대체되었다.

(C) 프로젝트는 영향받은 부위를 살펴보는 작업으로 진행된다.

(D) 그것의 스타일과 매끈한 디자인이 대중의 관심을 끌었다.

앞 문장에서 이 센서를 사용하면 부식을 초기 단계에 탐지할 수 있으므로, 부식된 부분만 제거하면 문제가 해결된다(According to Ms. Hyun, the sensor is designed to identify corrosion in its initial stages, when the issue can be corrected simply by eliminating the corroded material)고 했다. 일부분만 수리해서 초기에 문제를 해결하면, 이후에 비용이 많이 드는 대규모 수리를 하게 될 확률이 낮아진다. 이러한 추론을 통해 (A)가 빈칸에 들어가는 것이 알맞다.

---

134. (A) Meanwhile
(B) Similarly
(C) Otherwise
(D) Fortunately

meanwhile 그 동안에 similarly 마찬가지로 otherwise 그렇지 않으면

앞 문장이 항공기의 중요한 연결 부위가 부식에 취약하다는 내용이므로(In the structure of large aircraft, some critical joints can be particularly susceptible to corrosion.), 센서를 이용하여 이러한 부위를 정밀 조사하여 처리할 수 있다는 내용의 문장이 이어지려면(the sensor can be utilized to scrutinize these areas and then target the most probable areas of concern.), 빈칸에 '다행히도'라는 뜻의 (D)가 들어가는 것이 알맞다.

Questions 135-138 refer to the following e-mail.

Date: 21 July
To: Hank Wilson
    <hwilson@everymail.co.za>
From: Myra Lewis <mlewis@zed.co.za>
Subject: Product recall

Dear Mr. Wilson,

Thank you for your recent [135.]purchase of the ZED Mini-X camera. We are notifying all those who have recently bought this product that certain models are being recalled for repair. These models contain a faulty electronic chip that is responsible for the digital conversion of light. [136.]This flaw will eventually interfere with the clarity of your photographs. Please [137.]verify whether your camera has this problem by taking a look at the serial number on the bottom of the camera. If it ends with the letters ZLNT, a repair will be necessary. ZED will cover all shipping costs for returning your Mini-X to us. Additionally, we will repair [138.]it free of charge.

Thank you.

Myra Lewis, Customer Service Manager
ZED Industries

135-138번 문제는 다음 이메일에 관한 것입니다.

날짜: 7월 21일
수신: Hank Wilson 〈hwilson@everymail.co.za〉
발신: Myra Lewis 〈mlewis@zed.co.za〉
제목: 제품 리콜

Mr. Wilson께,

최근에 ZED Mini-X 카메라를 구매해 주셔서 감사합니다. 최근이 이 제품을 구매하신 모든 분께 특정 모델이 수리를 위해 리콜되고 있다고 알려드리고 있습니다. 이 모델들에는 빛의 디지털 전환을 담당하는 전자 칩이 하자가 있는 채 들어 있습니다. 이 결함은 결국 사진의 선명도를 떨어뜨릴 것입니다. 고객님의 카메라에 이러한 문제가 있는지 카메라 바닥에 있는 일련번호를 봄으로써 확인해 보시기 바랍니다. 일련번호가 문자 ZLNT로 끝난다면 수리가 필요합니다. ZED가 고객님의 Mini-X를 반품하는 데 드는 모든 운송 요금을 부담하겠습니다. 아울러 수리도 무료로 해드리겠습니다.

고맙습니다.

ZED Industries
고객 서비스 매니저 Myra Lewis

recall 리콜(하다), 회수(하다) purchase 구매 notify 알리다, 통보하다 repair 수리 contain ~이 들어 있다 faulty 결함이 있는, 불량의 electronic 전자의 be responsible for ~를 담당하다 **conversion** 전환, 변환, 변화 **flaw** (사물의) 결함 **eventually** 결국 **interfere with** ~을 방해하다, ~에 지장을 주다 **clarity** 선명도, 투명도 **verify** 확인하다 **take a look at** ~을 살펴보다 **serial number** 일련번호 **cover** (돈을) 대다 **shipping cost** 운송비 **additionally** 아울러, 추가로 **free of charge** 무료로

---

135. **(A) purchase**
    (B) review
    (C) gift
    (D) demonstration

> **어휘** review 후기, 비평 demonstration 시연, 입증

> **해설** 이어지는 문장에서 발신자는 최근에 제품을 구매한 사람들에게 알리고 있다(We are notifying all those who have recently bought this product). 따라서 앞 문장으로 "최근에 구매해 주셔서 감사합니다."라는 뜻의 (A)가 알맞다.

---

136. (A) We are confident that you will savor this product for many years to come.
    (B) It is outlined in the troubleshooting section of the manual.
    (C) This flaw will eventually interfere with the clarity of your photographs.
    (D) This special feature is not compatible with some older models.

> **어휘** confident 확신하는 savor 마음껏 즐기다, 만끽하다 outline ~의 개요를 서술하다, 요점을 말하다 troubleshooting 고장의 수리 feature 특징, 기능 compatible with ~와 호환이 되는

> **해석** (A) 우리는 당신이 앞으로 여러 해 동안 이 제품을 즐기실 것이라고 확신합니다.
> (B) 그것은 설명서의 문제해결 섹션에 요약되어 있습니다.
> (C) 이 결함은 결국 사진의 선명도를 떨어뜨릴 것입니다.
> (D) 이 특별 기능은 일부 구형 모델과 호환되지 않습니다.

> **해설** 앞 문장에서 리콜되는 제품에 어떤 문제가 있는지 설명하고 있으므로(These models contain a faulty electronic chip that is responsible for the digital conversion of light.), 이어지는 문장에서는 그 문제로 인해 생기는 결과를 알려주는 것이 자연스럽다. 그러므로 빈칸에는 (C)가 알맞다.

---

137. (A) verification
    (B) verified
    (C) verify
    (D) verifies

> **해설** 빈칸은 whether로 시작하는 명사절을 목적어로 취하는 동사 자리이고, Please 뒤에 있으므로 동사원형 (C)가 정답이다.

---

138. (A) mine
    (B) it
    (C) theirs
    (D) these

> **해설** 빈칸이 가리키는 명사가 앞 문장의 your Mini-X이므로, (B) it이 알맞다.

Part 7

Questions 139-142 refer to the following table.

139.142.Consumer Reports Monthly's Editor Report on 4 Selected Models of FISK digital cameras		
	Fisk GQ540	**Fisk GQ430**
Comments	Perfect for novice photographers with a straightforward and intuitive menu. Connected directly to the cloud storage.	Essentially a GQ540 with fewer features. Not suitable for outdoor photography; best used in interior settings. Tolerates higher levels of humidity.
Built-in		Built-in flash activates automatically in low light.
Negatives	140.Unusually heavy for a camera this size.	Picture quality compromised by lack of memory space.
Price	$350*	$250*

	Fisk FZ300	Fisk FV340
Comments	140.Lightweight. Waterproof, designed for use at depths of up to 60 m.	141.Record-high resolution, outstanding sharpness and clarity. The most superior in the under-$500 price range.
Built-in	Features an Oceanears sound system audible in submersed environments.	
Negatives	141.Image quality inferior to FV340.	
Price	141.$750*	141.$480*

*Prices shown are valid at EG Stores. Since prices tend to vary from retailer to retailer, they may be different at InterTAN and NCIX, as well as online stores such as Croma Electronics. 142.The product tables featured in every issue of Consumer Reports are impartial reviews by the magazine's editors, and are not part of the advertising supplements published bi-monthly.

135–138번 문제는 다음 표에 관한 것입니다.

월간 Consumer Reports가 엄선한 FISK 디지털 카메라 4개 모델에 대한 편집자 보고서

	Fisk GQ540	Fisk GQ430
단평	간단하고 직관적인 메뉴로 초보 사진작가에게 안성맞춤. 클라우드 저장 공간에 직접 연결	기본적으로 GQ540에 기능만 더 적은 제품. 야외 촬영에 알맞지 않음; 실내 환경에서 사용했을 때 가장 좋음. 높은 습도 견딤.
내장기능		낮은 조명에서 때 내장 플래시가 자동으로 작동.
단점	이 크기의 카메라 치고는 유별나게 무거움	메모리 공간의 부족으로 인한 사진 품질 저하.
가격	$350*	$250*

	Fisk FZ300	Fisk FV340
단평	가벼움. 방수, 최대 60미터 깊이에서 사용하도록 설계	사상 최고의 해상도, 탁월한 선명도와 투명도. 500달러 미만 가격대에서 가장 우수함.
내장기능	수중 환경에서 들을 수 있는 Oceanears 사운드 시스템 포함.	
단점	이미지 품질이 FV340보다 떨어짐.	
가격	$750*	$480*

*표시된 가격은 EG Store에서 유효합니다. 가격은 소매업체마다 달라지는 경향이 있으므로 Croma 전자와 같은 온라인 매장뿐만 아니라 InterTAN과 NCIX에서도 다를 수 있습니다. Consumer Reports 매 호마다 실린 제품표는 잡지 편집자들의 공정한 평가이며, 격월로 게재되는 광고용 부록의 일부가 아닙니다.

어휘 table 표, 목록 comment 논평, 의견 built-in 내장된 negative 결함, 단점 consumer 소비자 novice 초보자 straightforward 간단한, 쉬운 intuitive 직관적인 storage 저장 essentially 본질적으로, 기본적으로 suitable 알맞은, 적합한 setting 환경, 배경 tolerate 견디다 humidity 습도 activate 작동하다, 활성화되다 automatically 자동으로 compromise (품질을) 저하시키다 lightweight 가벼운, 경량의 waterproof 방수(防水)의 depth 깊이 feature 특별히 포함하다, 특징으로 삼다 audible 잘 들리는 submersed 물속에 잠긴 inferior to ~보다 못한, 질 낮은 record-high 사상 최고의 resolution 해상도 outstanding 뛰어난, 걸출한 sharpness 선명함 superior 우수한, 고급의 valid 유효한 tend to-V ~하는 경향이 있다 vary from ~ to ~마다 다르다 retailer 소매업자 as well as ~뿐 아니라 issue (간행물의) 호 impartial 공정한 supplement (책의) 부록, 보충판 publish 게재하다, 싣다 bi-monthly 2개월 마다, 격월로

---

139. Where would the table probably be found?

(A) In the catalog of a camera store
(B) In a guidebook for a camera
(C) In a photography textbook
(D) In a periodical that evaluates products

어휘 guidebook 안내서 목록 textbook 교과서 periodical 정기 간행물 evaluate 평가하다

표가 어디에서 발견될 수 있겠는가?

(A) 카메라 매장 카탈로그

(B) 카메라 안내서

(C) 사진 교과서

(D) 제품을 평가하는 정기 간행물

표가 실린 잡지 이름이 Consumer Reports Monthly 이다. 월간지에 실려 있으며, 특정 상품을 평가하는 내용이므로(Editor Report on 4 Selected Models of FISK digital cameras), 이 표는 상품을 평가하는 정기 간행물에 들어 있는 것을 알 수 있다. 그러므로 (D)가 정답이다.

---

140. How is the FZ300 different from the GQ540?

(A) It is available via mail order.

(B) It is a newly released model.

(C) It is less expensive.

(D) It is relatively light.

via ~을 통하여 release 공개하다, 발표하다 relatively 비교적으로

FZ300은 GQ540과 어떻게 다른가?

(A) 우편 주문을 통하여 이용할 수 있다.

(B) 새로 출시된 모델이다.

(C) 덜 비싸다.

(D) 비교적 가볍다.

GQ540은 크기에 비해 무겁다는 단점이 있는 반면 (Unusually heavy for a camera this size) FZ300 은 가볍다는(Lightweight) 평가가 있으므로 (D)가 정답이다.

---

141. What is suggested about the FV340?

(A) It is bigger than the other models reviewed.

(B) Its images are clearer than those of more expensive models.

(C) It does not perform optimally indoors.

(D) Its cloud storage space is insufficient.

review 논평하다, 비평하다 perform 작동하다 optimally 최적으로 insufficient 불충분한

FV340에 대해 무엇이 암시되어 있는가?

(A) 평가된 다른 모델들보다 더 크다.

(B) 이미지가 더 비싼 모델들보다 더 선명하다.

(C) 실내에서는 최적으로 작동하지 않는다.

(D) 클라우드 저장 공간이 충분하지 않다.

FZ300의 단점을 설명할 때 FV340을 언급하고 있다 (Image quality inferior to FV340). 가격은 FZ300($750)이 FV340($480)보다 훨씬 비싼데, 이미지 품질은 FV340이 더 좋다. 게다가 FV340은 사상 최고의 해상도(Record-high resolution, outstanding sharpness and clarity)를 가지고 있으므로 (B)가 정답이다.

---

142. How often do Consumer Reports' product tables appear?

(A) Every week

(B) Twice a month

(C) Every month

(D) Every two months

appear 나오다, 실리다

Consumer Reports의 제품 표는 얼마마다 한 번씩 나오는가?

(A) 매주

(B) 한 달에 두 번

(C) 매달

(D) 두 달에 한 번

Part 7에서 *가 붙은 문장에는 반드시 정답이 있으므로 해석해야 한다. 이 제품 표는 잡지의 매 호마다 실린다고 했고(The product tables featured in every issue of Consumer Reports), 표 윗부분의 잡지 이름 Consumer Reports Monthly는 월간지이므로, 표는 매달 게재되는 것을 알 수 있다. 따라서 정답은 (C)이다.

Questions 143-147 refer to the following brochure, e-mail, and notice.

Redwood National Park Trails

[145.]**Friendship Ridge Loop** - *8.5 Kilometers*
[145.]Enjoy views of the Klamath River from the summit of Friendship Ridge. This path, of moderate difficulty, entails a steady incline to the summit of the ridge, followed by a well-defined trail that loops back and descends to the north parking lot.

[143.]**Ossagon Slope** - *6 Kilometers*
[143.]Trek up the side of Ossagon Ridge. This challenging trail features rocky terrain and intermittent steep climbs,

providing scenic views of Orick Palisades Valley. The trailhead is located 100 meters to the south of the ranger station.

[145.]River's Edge - *6.7 Kilometers*
[145.]This trail stretches along the bank of the Klamath River. Starting at the north parking lot, the level trail leads to Orick Palisades Park.

Trillium Falls Trail - *3 Kilometers*
This leisurely trail commences at the rear of the main pavilion and extends through the Redwood Forest before culminating at Trillium Falls. Picnic and barbecue areas are scattered along the route.

143–147번 문제는 다음 안내 책자와 이메일, 안내문에 관한 것입니다.

Redwood 국립 공원 등산로

Friendship 산등성이 순환로 – 8.5 킬로미터
Friendship 산등성이 정상에서 Klamath 강의 경치를 즐기세요. 중간 난이도의 이 길은 산등성이 정상까지 이어지는 꾸준한 경사로이며, 돌아 나와 북쪽 주차장까지 내려오는 윤곽이 뚜렷한 등산로가 이어집니다.

Ossagon 경사로 – 6 킬로미터
Ossagon 산등성이 측면을 올라가 보세요. 이 어려운 등산로는 바위가 많은 지형과 간헐적으로 나타나는 가파른 오르막이 특징이지만, Orick Palisades 계곡의 훌륭한 경치를 제공합니다. 등산로 입구는 관리 사무소 남쪽으로 100미터 지점에 있습니다.

강변로 – 6.7 킬로미터
이 등산로는 Klamath 강둑을 따라 뻗어 있습니다. 이 평탄한 등산로는 북쪽 주차장에서 시작하여 Orick Palisades 공원으로 이어집니다.

Trillium 폭포 등산로 – 3 킬로미터
이 여유로운 등산로는 메인 파빌리온 뒤편에서 시작하여 Redwood 숲을 통과하여 이어지다가 Trillium 폭포에서 절정을 이룹니다. 경로를 따라 피크닉 및 바비큐 장소가 간간이 있습니다.

어휘 brochure 안내 책자 trail 등산로 ridge 산등성이, 산마루
loop 순환로; 고리 모양으로 이동하다 view 경관, 경치

---

summit 정상, 산꼭대기 moderate 보통의, 중간의 entail 수반하다 steady 꾸준한 incline 경사(면) well-defined 윤곽이 뚜렷한 descend 내려오다, 내려가다 trek (오랫동안 힘겹게) 등반하다 challenging 힘든, 어려운 terrain 지형, 지역 intermittent 간헐적인 steep 가파른, 비탈진 climb 등반 코스 scenic 경치가 좋은 palisades (강가, 해안의) 절벽 trailhead 등산로 입구 be located ~에 위치해 있다 ranger station (공원) 관리 사무소 stretch 뻗어 있다 bank 둑, 제방 level 평평한 falls 폭포 leisurely 여유로운 commence 시작하다 at the rear of ~ 뒤편에서 pavilion 파빌리온(공원 안의 쉼터 · 공연장 등으로 쓰이는 건물) extend 펼쳐지다 culminate ~에서 절정을 이루다 scattered 간간이 있는, 산재한

To: Nature Explorers Club
From: Anne Zelnikova
Subject: Nature hike on Saturday
Date: September 12
Attachment: Map

Hi, everyone

The nature hike this month is set for Saturday at 6:00 A.M. [144.][145.]Since a number of people during our last trip to Fern Canyon expressly mentioned their desire to view the Klamath River, we decided to meet up at Redwood National Park this month. [147.]Please arrive in the north parking lot by 5:45 A.M. I have attached a park map for your reference. Don't forget to pack a lunch and plenty of water. Our hike will last approximately 5–6 hours.

See you on Saturday!

Anne

발신: 자연 탐사 클럽
수신: Anne Zelnikova
제목: 토요일 자연 탐사 하이킹
날짜: 9월 12일
첨부 파일: 지도

모두 안녕하세요.

이번 달 자연 탐사 하이킹이 토요일 오전 6시로 정해졌습니다. 지난번 Fern Canyon 여행 때 많은 사람이 특별히 Klamath 강을 보고 싶다는 바람을 말씀하셨기 때문에 이

번 달에는 Redwood 국립 공원에서 만나기로 했습니다. 북쪽 주차장으로 오전 5시 45분까지 와주세요. 참고로 공원 지도를 첨부했습니다. 잊지 말고 점심과 충분한 물을 챙기시기 바랍니다. 하이킹은 대략 5~6시간 동안 계속될 것입니다.

토요일에 만납시다!

Anne

어휘 hike 하이킹, (장거리) 도보 여행 attachment 첨부 파일 set 정해진 expressly 특별히, 명확히 mention 언급하다 meet up (~하려고) 만나다 for one's reference 참고할 수 있게 attach 첨부하다 plenty of 많은 last 계속되다 approximately 약

NOTICE

Posted September 14

145.The River's Edge trail has been closed due to flooding caused by recent rain storms and will not reopen until further notice. Please refrain from traveling on this trail and locations adjacent to the Klamath River bank until the floodwaters recede. 146,147.The north parking lot was also affected by the floodwaters, and is currently under construction. Kindly leave your automobile in the east parking lot and follow the Ranger Path to reach the trailheads.

안내문

9월 14일 게시

최근의 호우로 유발된 범람으로 강변 등산로가 폐쇄되었으며 추후 공지가 있을 때까지 재개방하지 않습니다. 범람한 물이 빠질 때까지 이 등산로와 Klamath 강둑에 인접한 장소에서는 통행을 삼가시기 바랍니다. 북쪽 주차장 또한 범람한 물의 영향을 받아 현재 공사 중입니다. 자동차를 동쪽 주차장에 세워 놓으시고 공원 관리 직원용 통행로를 따라 등산로 입구로 가시기 바랍니다.

어휘 post 게시하다, 공고하다 trail 등산로 flooding 범람, 홍수 rain storm 폭풍우, 호우 until further notice 추후 공지가 있을 때까지 refrain from ~을 삼가다, 자제하다 location 장소 adjacent to ~에 인접한 floodwaters

홍수로 불어난 물 recede (서서히) 물러나다 affect 영향을 미치다 under construction 공사 중인 kindly 부디 automobile 자동차 ranger 공원 관리원[경비 대원]

143. How long is the trail that goes up Ossagon Ridge?

(A) 3 kilometers
(B) 6 kilometers
(C) 6.7 kilometers
(D) 8.5 kilometers

해석 Ossagon 산등성이를 따라 올라가는 등산로는 길이가 얼마나 되는가?
(A) 3킬로미터
(B) 6킬로미터
(C) 6.7킬로미터
(D) 8.5킬로미터

해설 Ossagon 산등성이를 따라 올라가는 등산로는(Trek up the side of Ossagon Ridge.) Ossagon 경사로이고, 길이는 6킬로미터(Ossagon Slope – 6 Kilometers)라고 쓰여 있으므로 정답은 (B)이다.

144. In the e-mail, the phrase "expressly" in paragraph 1, line 2, is closest in meaning to

(A) affectionately
(B) correctly
(C) specifically
(D) totally

해석 이메일에서 첫 문단 둘째 줄의 어구 expressly와 의미상 가장 가까운 것은
(A) 애정을 담아, 다정하게
(B) 올바르게, 정확히
(C) 특히, 특정해서
(D) 완전히, 전적으로

해설 expressly를 '분명히, 명확히'라는 뜻으로 사용하면 (B)가, '특별히'라는 뜻으로 쓰면 (C)가 동의어이다. 본문에서는 Klamath 강을 보고 싶은 바람을 '특별히' 언급한 회원들을 언급하고 있으므로(Since a number of people during our last trip to Fern Canyon expressly mentioned their desire to view the Klamath River), 바꿔 쓸 수 있는 부사는 (C) specifically이다.

145. Where will Nature Explorers Club members likely hike?

(A) On Friendship Ridge Loop
(B) On Ossagon Slope